STATE POLITICS IN INDIA

STATE POLITICS IN INDIA

EDITED BY MYRON WEINER

CONTRIBUTORS

Paul R. Brass
Marcus F. Franda
Hugh Gray
Ram Joshi
Baldev Raj Nayar
Balraj Puri
Lawrence L. Shrader
Wayne Wilcox

PRINCETON UNIVERSITY PRESS
PRINCETON, NEW JERSEY
1968

Library of Congress Catalog Card No. 67-16954

Printed in the United States of America
by Princeton University Press
Princeton, New Jersey

Preface

THIS volume is the result of the work of the Committee on State Politics in India, an informal group organized by the editor under the auspices of the Committee on South Asia of the Association for Asian Studies to further our understanding of political development in the states of India.

This symposium represents a first effort to deal systematically with politics in the Indian states, and we are painfully aware of its limitations. It was not possible to include studies of all seventeen states, and we very much regret the omission of nine of them. We are hopeful, however, that this volume will both direct the attention of scholars to the vacuum that now exists and stimulate the research already under way on state politics in India. We believe that the eight studies in this volume shed light on the changing patterns of political participation in India, the problems of integration within the states, the variety of state party systems which have developed, and the performance of the state governments. These studies were completed before the 1967 elections but all the authors have made some modifications and additions to take these elections into account.

Although each author takes full responsibility for his chapter contribution, I believe I speak for all the contributors when I say that we have all profited from a frank exchange of ideas at two seminars, one at the University of Chicago in April 1961, and another at the Massachusetts Institute of Technology in late 1964. The introductory chapter represents the editor's attempt to bring together some of the insights provided by the authors in the several chapters. Complete responsibility for such interpretation, however, rests with the editor.

We acknowledge with appreciation support from the Committee on South Asia of the Association for Asian Studies, the Committee on South Asian Studies of the University of Chicago, and the Center for International Studies of the Massachusetts Institute of Technology.

I wish to extend my personal appreciation to several people who read and commented on my introductory chapter or who provided critical guidance on the manuscript as a whole: Bernard S. Cohn, Carolvn Elliott, Gilbert Etienne, Selig Harrison, and Richard Lambert; to Vineeta Singh who aided in the editorial work and prepared the tables for chapter 1; and to Mrs. Eleanor Mamber, Nancy Weber, and Helaine Levi, who provided splendid secretarial assistance.

MYRON WEINER

Paris
May 1967

Table of Contents

List of Illustrations

MAPS

FIGURES

List of Tables

I. POLITICAL DEVELOPMENT IN THE INDIAN STATES

II. UTTAR PRADESH

III. MADHYA PRADESH

IV. MAHARASHTRA

POLITICAL DEVELOPMENT IN THE INDIAN STATES

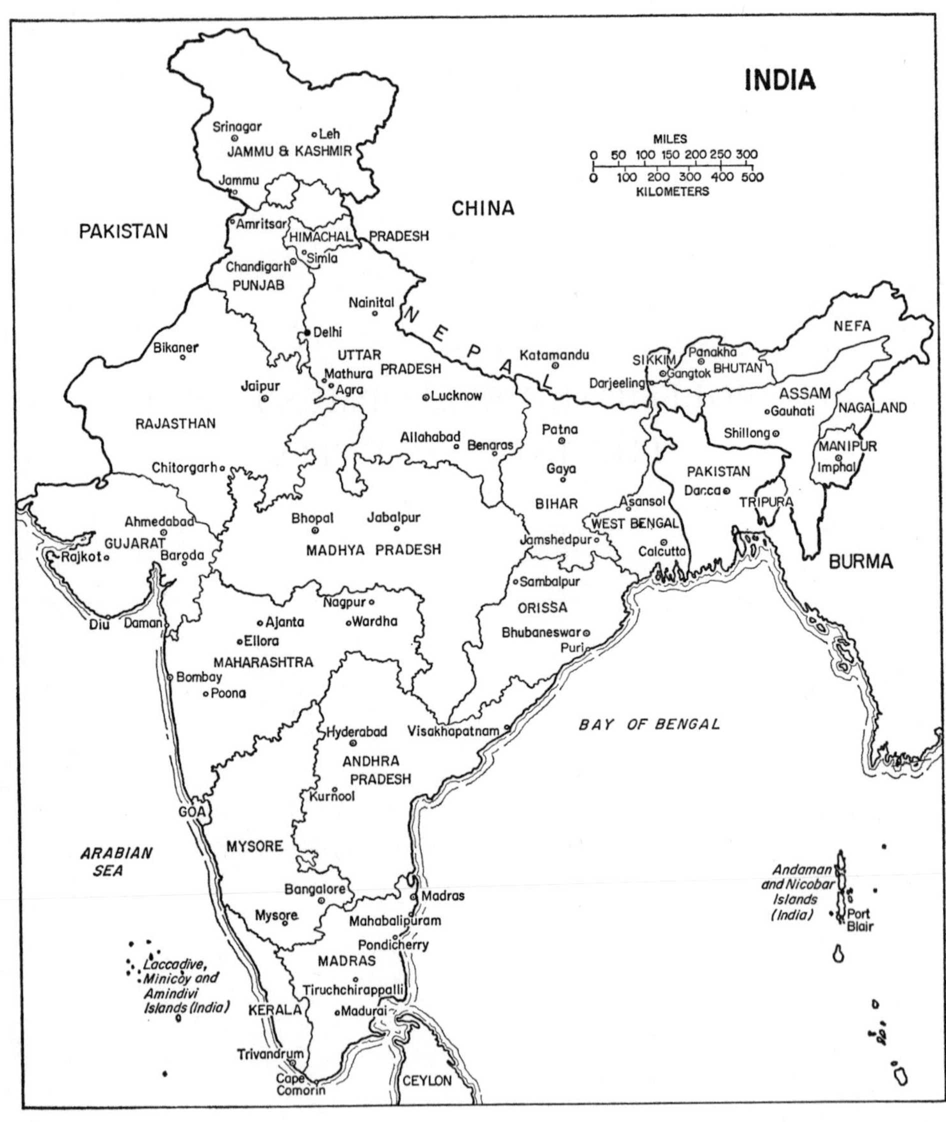

INDIA
MILES
0 50 100 150 200 250 300
0 100 200 300 400 500
KILOMETERS
PAKISTAN
CHINA
Srinagar
Leh
JAMMU & KASHMIR
Jammu
Amritsar
HIMACHAL PRADESH
Simla
Chandigarh
PUNJAB
Nainital
Delhi
NEPAL
Bikaner
UTTAR PRADESH
Mathura
Agra
Jaipur
Lucknow
RAJASTHAN
Allahabad
Benaras
Katamandu
SIKKIM
Panakha
Gangtok
BHUTAN
Darjeeling
NEFA
ASSAM
Gauhati
NAGALAND
Shillong
MANIPUR
Imphal
PAKISTAN
Dacca
TRIPURA
BURMA
Patna
Gaya
BIHAR
Asansol
WEST BENGAL
Jamshedpur
Calcutta
Chitorgarh
Ahmedabad
GUJARAT
Rajkot
Baroda
Bhopal
Jabalpur
MADHYA PRADESH
Sambalpur
ORISSA
Bhubaneswar
Puri
Nagpur
Wardha
Ajanta
Ellora
MAHARASHTRA
Diu
Daman
Bombay
Poona
Hyderabad
Visakhapatnam
BAY OF BENGAL
ANDHRA PRADESH
Kurnool
GOA
ARABIAN SEA
MYSORE
Bangalore
Madras
Mysore
Mahabalipuram
Pondicherry
MADRAS
Laccadive, Minicoy and Amindivi Islands (India)
Tiruchchirappalli
KERALA
Madurai
Trivandrum
Cape Comorin
CEYLON
Andaman and Nicobar Islands (India)
Port Blair

I

Political Development in the Indian States

MYRON WEINER

THE ESSAYS in this volume analyze and compare the political processes of selected states within the Indian Union. In recent years comparative studies in political science have been expanded to include the developing areas and in particular to focus on the political aspects of modernization. This volume seeks to extend this approach by applying comparative methods to the analysis of political units within a single system.

An examination of politics in the Indian states is long overdue. In a world in which sovereignty bespeaks international recognition, the Indian states have gone, in the main, unrecognized and unstudied. Though there have been many studies on each of the new states of Asia and Africa, little has appeared on the Indian states even though each of them is in area and population alone larger than most of the members of the United Nations. (See Table 1.1.) Uttar Pradesh, for example, a state sprawling across northern India, numbers 75 million, and Andhra Pradesh, Madhya Pradesh, West Bengal, Maharashtra, Rajasthan, and the Punjab all have populations ranging from 15 to 35 million—more than most of the new nations of Africa and Southeast Asia.

To fill a gap in knowledge concerning such large political units is but one, though by no means the least important, justification for a volume on the Indian states. It can be argued that our very understanding of the Indian political system depends upon our assessment of patterns of development within the constituent states. India is, after all, a federal system containing seventeen states.[1] As we shall see later, the states have important powers over agricultural development, education, and rural taxation, and the effectiveness of national planning is conditioned by the performance of the state governments. Moreover, the instabilities and shocks associated with the economic development process are felt first at the state level, and only thereafter move into national politics. Thus, state governments affect and are affected by patterns of economic development.

The states are also training grounds for national politicians. While before independence political leaders in Calcutta, Madras, Bombay,

[1] The seventeenth state was created by the division of the Punjab into two states, one called the Punjab, the other Haryana.

TABLE 1.1

AREA AND POPULATION OF THE INDIAN STATES

	Population	*% of Union population*	*Area (sq. miles)*	*% of Union area*	*Density per sq. mi.*
Andhra Pradesh	35,983,447	8.20	106,052	9.03	339
Assam	11,872,772	2.71	84,899	4.00	252
Bihar	46,455,610	10.59	67,198	5.71	691
Gujarat	20,633,350	4.70	72,138	6.14	286
Kashmir[a]	3,560,976	0.81	53,665	4.25	66
Kerala	16,903,715	3.85	15,003	1.27	1,127
Madhya Pradesh	32,372,408	7.38	171,210	14.54	189
Madras	33,686,953	7.68	50,132	4.27	669
Maharashtra	39,553,718	9.02	118,530	10.08	333
Mysore	23,586,772	5.38	74,122	6.30	318
Nagaland	369,200	.08	6,366	.50	58
Orissa	17,548,846	4.00	60,162	5.11	292
Punjab	20,306,812	4.63	47,084	4.01	430
Rajasthan	20,155,602	4.60	132,150	11.22	153
Uttar Pradesh	73,746,401	16.81	113,454	9.65	649
West Bengal	34,926,279	7.96	33,928	2.87	1,032
India	439,235,082		1,259,797		370[b]

[a] These figures are only for censused (1961) areas and not for the whole of Jammu and Kashmir.

[b] Excludes Jammu and Kashmir.

SOURCE: *Census of India, Paper No. 1 of 1962* (1961 census).

Allahabad, Ahmedabad, and Poona often moved directly into national politics, today politicians first carve their careers in state politics. Prime Minister Lal Bahadur Shastri, for example, was a minister in the state government in Uttar Pradesh before moving to the central cabinet, and K. Kamaraj, the President of the Congress party, was for a decade the chief minister of the state of Madras.

Finally, and this is a theme we shall develop at some length later, each of the Indian states provides us with an unusual microcosm and macrocosm for studying processes of development: a microcosm since the states are constituent units of a larger system, and a macrocosm because the units are themselves so large that they can be studied as total systems. We have, therefore, a rare opportunity to compare patterns of political development in large political systems functioning within a single framework. Thus, the states share a common legal system, a common constitutional framework, a common administrative structure, and a common international environment, but their internal political patterns vary considerably. Why is it, for example, that West Bengal, Andhra Pradesh, and Kerala have active Communist movements, while the other states do not? Why is it that the political system of Madhya Pradesh has been so weak that the central government was able to impose a chief minister there but has not influenced the selection of chief ministers in West Bengal or Madras? Why is political participation—as measured by voting, number of voluntary associations, degree of party organization, and the like—so high in Kerala, Madras, and the Punjab (where over 65 per cent of the population vote in state-wide elections) and so low in Orissa (23 per cent), Madhya Pradesh (44 per cent), and Bihar (47 per cent)? Why is factionalism within the governing party and fragmentation among opposition parties greater in some states than in others? Why do some states have more tensions and violence among caste, linguistic, and religious groups than others? And finally, to what extent does the operation of the political system and the policies pursued by state governments and implemented by state administrations account for the enormous differentials in economic growth rates to be found among the Indian states, from the Punjab, where agricultural production has doubled in a decade, to Uttar Pradesh, where per capita income has declined? In short, many of the questions which perplex students of development can be illuminated, if not answered, by an analysis of politics within each of the Indian states and a systematic comparison of the states.

In view of their importance, it is interesting to reflect briefly on why there has been so little political research on the Indian states. One reason, as has been noted, is that international scholarly attention has been directed to the national systems of new states; insofar as subordinate units within a nation have received notice, it has often been because of the breakdown of the national framework. A second consideration is that social scientists have only gradually broken out of their self-imposed constraints. Thus, anthropologists have been primarily concerned with studying the smallest units—the tribe, the village, and the lineage. Only in recent years has there been a massive shift from the study of social statics to a study of the relationship between these units and their larger environment. Political scientists have been prone to focus almost exclusively on national politics in the developing areas or, more recently, on patterns of urban politics. Both political scientists and anthropologists have increasingly come to recognize that in modern and in modernizing societies individuals belong to many levels in a political system and that the states in a federal system are important links connecting village, town, and city politics to the national political system.

Surprisingly, few Indian scholars have concentrated on developments within their own states. There is, first of all, a feeling among many Indian scholars that too much attention to state affairs is a mark of parochial attachments. Another inhibiting consideration is the lack of pride in the political life of the states. Although Indian intellectuals have become increasingly critical of their national government, there has at least been some pride in India's role in world affairs, in her attention to economic planning, and, before 1964, in Nehru's leadership. But there has been little indeed at the state level to command respect. It is at this level that the struggle for office has been most intense, and that the conflicts among castes, religious groups, tribes, and linguistic groups and factions are played out. It is here that economic development programs often appear to falter and traditional sentiments, loyalties, and behavior intrude most into efforts to modernize.

There is, however, one important exception to these remarks. Political behavior within the states has commanded attention insofar as it has appeared to affect India's national unity. In the early 1950s, mass agitations erupted throughout the country, especially in the south, prompted by the demand that the states be reorganized along linguistic lines. Previously, the southern and western states of India each contained two or three major linguistic groups. Thus, Bombay state consisted of the Gujarati-speaking people in the north, the Marathi-speaking people in the middle, and the Kannada-speaking people in the south. Madras state also consisted of three major linguistic groups each demanding its own state. As the linguistic movement swept the country, there was increasing concern about the powerful sense of regional attachment and what then appeared to be a low level of national identification. Scholarly and journalistic attention was then given to development within the states, but the focus was on the relationship of one linguistic group to another, the attitudes that existed in each multilingual state toward linguistic reorganization, and the relationship between the states and the central government. With the reorganization of the Indian states in 1956 along linguistic lines there was considerable apprehension that the states would be concerned primarily with their own development, that national authority would be eroded, and that only a slender thread—Nehru's leadership—would bind the Union.

THE FRAMEWORK OF ANALYSIS

The concern not only proved to be ill-founded—after Nehru's death the Indian Union did not disintegrate, although it is true that national authority over the states has dwindled—but it also obscured the dynamics of development within the states. Each state has in fact been undergoing its own pattern of political development and its own internal political crises. It was to these developments that several contributors to this volume turned when they first assembled for a seminar in the spring of 1961. As a result of this seminar,* the editor agreed to prepare a framework which would permit each of the authors to analyze the political processes within his state and would make it possible simultaneously for the editor to explore a set of themes comparatively. Each of the contributions to this volume is concerned with the description and analysis of the political process in a single state and with relating that process to (a) the social and economic environment in which politics occurs and (b) the performance of government. Each study, therefore, treats the state as a constituent unit within a larger system, but nonetheless also as a separate political system.

In exploring the social and economic environment of the political process, each contributor has selected from a list of variables those which seemed to him most relevant to his state. Typically, attention has been given to the social configurations in each state on the grounds that the system of social stratification is an important determinant of patterns of political organization. Each of the contributors has made use of sociological and anthropological studies, census reports, and his own field investigations in describing the socio-economic environment of the stratification system, particularly patterns of land tenure, urban-rural distribution, and occupational and educational patterns. Where information has been available, the authors describe some of the changes taking place in the system of social stratification, and the tensions and conflicts associated with these changes. They have also been concerned with the kinds of social linkages which exist in the state as these affect the state's political integration. To what extent, for example, is each state a single cultural region or a number of cultural regions manifest by political blocs in political parties and in the state assemblies? Is there widespread economic disparity among the regions within the state which results in political conflicts? Are there widespread differentials in educational opportunities which are reflected in conflicts among social groups as each tries to increase its access to education?

The authors then turn to a description of the political process itself. Attention is given to the configuration of political parties in the state. Though Congress easily dominates the national parliament, there is a far more competitive party situation in some of the states. In Kerala, for example, Congress has lost office to the Socialist and Communist parties, and in Madhya Pradesh and Rajasthan, Congress has won state elections

* A report on this seminar was published in the June 1961 issue of *Asian Survey*.

with a bare majority. In states in which Congress has won easily over the opposition, intense competition for power often takes place within the Congress party. For this reason, considerable attention is given to the analysis of internal conflict within Congress in an effort to understand what divides and what unites this party. Some of the authors also had enough data to explore the relationship between parties and interest groups, to trace the changes in leadership patterns in state politics, and to describe and analyze some of the significant political conflicts within the state, both those which involve conflicts over public policy (land reform, tax policy, and so on) and those which involve diffuse struggles of castes and factions for political control. Finally, some of the contributors describe the techniques and strategies employed by political parties and other political groups in attempting to assess the extent to which there are agreed-upon rules for political action. In short, are the techniques used to influence governmental policy and administration generally considered to be legitimate?

In the conclusions to their papers, the contributors were asked to examine the performance of the state govenment. Here we had in mind—among some of the burdens faced by the new governments—the pressures for greater distribution of goods and services by an increasingly participant population, pressures by the central government for land reform legislation, new local government legislation, and increased agricultural taxes. What are the limits and capabilities of the state apparatus, both the administrative and political framework? How much politicalization, for example, has taken place within the bureaucracy and how has this affected bureaucratic performance? How has factionalism within the governing Congress party affected the distribution of responsibilities within and among state ministries? How has the composition of the Congress party, particularly its dependence in some areas upon the rural gentry, limited the capacity of the state government to pass and to administer land legislation affecting the interests of their supporters? Finally, what are the directions in which the various states are moving? Is Congress rule at the state level likely to continue but become increasingly ineffectual and immobile, or is there likely to be greater cohesion within the government and greater clarity of purpose among the state's governmental leadership? Are the promodernizing elements growing in power within the states, or is the effort to achieve stability resulting in increasing concessions to traditionalist elements? Will political participation and political demands for social justice and equity increase? Will the state governments be able to cope with these demands, or will there be increasing violence, disorder, and central intervention?

It would be presumptuous to say that the essays in this volume have answered all these questions, or, indeed, to say they are answerable. As pioneers in their research, the contributors have had few studies to fall back on and have often had to base their generalizations on woefully inadequate data. Readers with a penchant for comparability and order may be dismayed at the wide and differing range of problems dealt with, but it seemed to both editor and authors that it would be inappropriate at this stage of research, and probably impossible among colleagues scattered in four countries (India, the United States, Canada, and England), rigidly to impose a common framework. The result is that certain dimensions called for by the outline are discussed in greater detail by some contributors than by others. Moreover, problems not even raised by the outline are dealt with by a few of the contributors. For example, though they were not asked to examine state-center relations, several contributors dealt with this theme—Puri, because Kashmir has so successfully resisted federal intervention while extracting substantial financial aid from Delhi, and Wilcox, because the center has played an important role in the political and economic development of Madhya Pradesh. It was also agreed that the contributors would deal exclusively with politics at the state level, omitting an examination of local politics, but since the state governments of Rajasthan and Andhra Pradesh had adopted new local government legislation which has already had effects on the state party organization, both Shrader and Gray give attention to this development in some detail.

Fortunately, in spite of these variations, the studies provide us with such a richness of detail and analysis that it is possible to suggest some significant common patterns of development. In the remainder of this introductory chapter I shall try to suggest some of the major themes emerging out of each state analysis, and then examine comparatively some of these major patterns of development.

STATE CONFIGURATIONS

Punjab

The focus of Nayar's essay is on the integrating of diverse social, linguistic, religious, and regional groups into a single state. The Punjab is divided not only by regions, but also between Sikhs and Hindus, religious reformists and the orthodox, higher-caste Hindus and ex-untouchables, and natives and refugees from Pakistan. Moreover, the Punjab remained one of the few states in which the issue of states reorganization persisted as sections of the Sikhs (a religious community) and some of the people who dwell in the hills each demanded a state of their own. (In early 1966 the central government agreed to carve out of the Punjab a Punjabi-speaking state.) In the early years of government in the Punjab, violence was rampant, ministries were unstable, and the central government was forced to intervene in the factional conflicts within the party. It was in this environment of extraordinary conflict that there arose a chief minister dedicated to the use of massive patronage, skilled in assigning loyal men to strategic political and administrative positions, and prepared to politicize the administrative system in an effort to consolidate his own power and that of the Congress organization. Nayar suggests that machine politics, considerably developed in most of the Indian states, has been more ruthless in the Punjab than elsewhere because the threats to the survival of the state have been greater.

Contrary to what one might expect, the level of governmental stability seems to have had little bearing upon the performance of the economy in the Punjab. From 1952-53 to 1958-59, the growth rate seems to have averaged 10 per cent a year, and the production of foodgrain doubled in the decade of the fifties. Nayar suggests that where the people of a state have a drive toward entrepreneurship and economic innovation, the performance of the government may be of less importance than in a state where the drive for modernization is not prevalent and development depends upon initiative from the state government. (See Table 1.2.)

Uttar Pradesh

In the neighboring state of Uttar Pradesh, there appear to be fewer pressures for modernization than in the Punjab. There are proportionately fewer innovators, and the state ministers, according to Brass, are concerned more with patronage and political support than with policy. The result is that in the decade 1950-51 to 1960-61 the income of the state rose by only 20.6 per cent compared to 41.6 per cent for India as a whole, and foodgrains production increased by only 22 per cent as against a national figure of 52 per cent. Brass spells out some of the inhibitions of the state government: a reluctance to increase land taxes because of a fear of loss of political support, and a factionalism within the governing Congress party so intense that governmental policy is uncoordinated. To explain this paralysis, Brass explores the nature of factionalism within the Congress party, the low degree of

TABLE 1.2

PER CAPITA INCOME BY STATE

	Per capita income (in rupees)	*Index (India = 100)*
West Bengal	319	138
Bombay[a]	288	125
Punjab	283	122
Rajasthan	243	105
Mysore	234	101
Assam	233	101
Madras	233	101
Madhya Pradesh	228	98
Andhra Pradesh	218	94
Kerala	213	92
Uttar Pradesh	210	91
Kashmir	190	82
Orissa	157	68
Bihar	144	62
India	232	100

[a] According to the report of the Central Statistical Organization, *National Income Statistics: Proposal for a Revised Series of National Income Estimates for 1955-56 to 1959-60* (Delhi, 1961), the per capita income of Gujarat is rupees 275 and of Maharashtra rupees 292.

SOURCE: Mahinder D. Chaudhry, *Regional Income Accounting in an Underdeveloped Economy: A Case Study of India* (State University of New York at Buffalo, 1964), pp. 95-96. Chaudhry's estimates are based upon the above-cited report of the Central Statistical Organization. Similar estimates have also been made by K. N. Raj, "Some Features of the Economic Growth of the Last Decade in India," *Economic Weekly*, XIII (February 4, 1961), 253-71.

party loyalty among both voters and party members, and the absence of a sense of state-wide identification which might serve to bind men together. Party bosses have sought to build the kind of machine one finds in the Punjab and in some other Indian states (notably West Bengal and Madras), but Uttar Pradesh is so large in size and population and linkages so few that no one has thus far succeeded.

Brass also deals at some length with the character of identifications in Uttar Pradesh and suggests that many Hindus in the state tend to think of it as the center of Hindu India rather than as simply one regional culture among many in a heterogeneous social and cultural system. Others are more oriented toward the portion of the state in which they live or the community to which they belong. Brass concludes that identifications are typically parochial and sub-regional, or supra-regional (another form of parochialism), embracing the Hindi-speaking region of India. One consequence of this pattern of loyalty, especially the supra-regional pattern, is that greater tension exists between Uttar Pradesh and other regions of India than is typical among states. It takes the form of conflict over India's national language policy, with many of the political parties of Uttar Pradesh pressing for the rapid adoption of Hindi and the rejection of English, while politicians in West Bengal and particularly in the southern states press for the maintenance of English, and, in effect, parity among the dozen regional languages, with Hindi, if used at all, as a secondary link language.

Andhra Pradesh

A central theme of Gray's analysis of Andhra Pradesh politics is the rise of the Kammas, the Reddis, and other rural gentry castes to displace the predominantly urban Brahmans. Gray is concerned with some of the struggles for power within and between the Kammas and the Reddis, but he also suggests that the growth of rural power has had important consequences for the performance of the state government. He suggests, for example, that the agrarian portions of the economy are undertaxed and that Congress leaders are torn between their desire to raise more revenue for the state government and their hesitation to increase taxes upon their supporters. Another consequence of rising rural power is the emergence of conflict between the bureaucracy and politicians at the rural level. With the establishment of the system of local government known as *panchayati raj*, under which elected rural leaders have control over rural development funds, the district collectors and their staff are no longer all-powerful district figures. Indeed, Gray suggests that in some districts the local administration is virtually controlled by the local Congress organization and Congressmen now categorize local bureaucrats by how pliable or inflexible they are.

Accompanying the entrance of the Kammas and the Reddis into statewide politics has been a proliferation of factional disputes not only within the Congress party but within the Communist and other parties as well. The most important skill of a successful state politician therefore is his capacity to forge effective factional alliances within Congress and to balance the political groups in the major regions which make up Andhra Pradesh.

Kashmir

Although Kashmir has had a special relationship to the Indian government since independence, Puri's description of internal political developments suggests that in certain respects the patterns of Kashmiri development conform to developments elsewhere in India. He describes, for example, the rise of regionalism within the state, the awareness of cultural heritage and historical traditions, and a sense of political individuality. But while the Kashmiris have a sense of belonging to a common unit, Kashmir, like many other states, also has its internal divisions. The state is divided into three regions—Ladakh, Jammu, and Kashmir—each characterized by a distinctive culture, language, and religion.

One important difference between Kashmir and the other states is that Kashmir has been able to extract more financial support from the central government and has been subject to less political control. The central government, eager to maintain the loyalty of the Kashmiris, has provided grants totaling 36.7 per cent of the state budget, compared to an average of 15.5 per cent for other states. (See Table 1.3.) With central aid, the state government has expanded the schools, improved public services, and increased developmental expenditures—all on the lowest per capita taxation in India. Puri suggests as one of his major themes that the state's economic development has facilitated political regimentation by the government. The government of Prime Minister Bakshi virtually created a one-party state; the freedom allowed opposition parties throughout the country was denied to opponents of the regime. The Bakshi government established rigid bureaucratic controls, and the prime minister was able to use the state administration to solidify his power without fear of central intervention.

Maharashtra

In contrast to Kashmir, the Congress party in Maharashtra has been able to establish a dominant one-party system in which opposition parties freely criticize the government. This has been a difficult task for the Congress leadership since Maharashtra is divided into regions with their own political interests—Western Maharashtra, Marathwada, and Vidarbha. But Joshi suggests that, in spite of their differences, these three regions were a single political community before they became a single political unit. Before 1956 these three regions, though they shared a common language and common memories of having belonged to an historic empire in western India, were divided among three different Indian states. Joshi describes the negotiations among the leaders of these regions to agree upon the terms of integration, and the attention paid by the present government to providing regional representation in the government and to balancing state expenditures among the three regions.

TABLE 1.3

REVENUE RESOURCES OF THE STATES, 1960–61
(by percentage of total revenue)

	% of Tax revenue	*% of Non-tax revenue*	*% of Devolution of central taxes*	*% of Grants-in-aid*
Andhra Pradesh[a]	49.6	11.2	20.6	18.6
Assam	34.5	15.0	15.4	35.1
Bihar	39.0	19.2	20.8	21.0
Gujarat	42.8	18.1	30.8	8.3
Kashmir	11.7	37.0	14.6	36.7
Kerala	44.6	23.7	15.4	16.3
Madhya Pradesh	37.7	26.6	18.8	16.9
Madras	44.9	21.2	21.5	12.4
Maharashtra	54.8	24.8	13.4	7.0
Mysore	29.0	41.0	13.3	16.7
Orissa	23.4	27.7	19.6	29.3
Punjab	41.4	31.5	15.9	11.2
Rajasthan	41.1	21.1	19.4	18.4
Uttar Pradesh	38.8	24.3	23.8	13.1
West Bengal[a]	50.5	15.0	22.6	11.9
India	41.8	23.2	19.5	15.5

[a] 1960-61 was selected as a relatively typical year illustrating the sources of income for each of the state governments. However, it was an atypical year for the states of Andhra Pradesh and West Bengal. For Andhra the non-tax revenue is generally higher and the remaining sources proportionately lower. More typical percentages of non-tax income are as follows: 19.3% (1959-60), 16.6% (1958-59), and 20% (1957-58). For West Bengal, grants-in-aid from the central government have generally been higher. More typical percentages are as follows: 22.8% (1959-60), 17.3% (1958-59), and 15.9% (1957-58).

SOURCE: *Report of the Finance Commission, 1961* (New Delhi: Government of India Press, 1962).

In assessing the extraordinary success of the Congress party in establishing a stable and reasonably progressive government in the state in spite of regional differences, Joshi suggests three factors. He notes, first, the historic social reform, anti-caste movement in the state which served to improve the position of the large Maratha caste in relation to the Chitpavan Brahmans. The Marathas are a numerically large caste holding most of the remunerative agricultural positions in the state and, increasingly, professional jobs in the cities. Once the Maratha caste took over the Congress party, displacing the Brahmans, Congress was virtually assured of commanding mass support. Secondly, Joshi describes another familiar theme—the close relationship between the party and the state and local administration—and he suggests that villages voting against the government are less likely to receive a favorable hearing than those supporting the government. Finally, though this is a point on which there is considerable disagreement, Joshi suggests that the rural politicians of Maharashtra are very much influenced by ideas from the urban centers, particularly since Maharashtra is the most urbanized state in India (27 per cent).

Rajasthan

The political contrasts between Maharashtra and the state of Rajasthan are enormous. While Maharashtra has a well-developed administrative system established by the British, Rajasthan lacks experienced administrative personnel. Rajasthan is made up of twenty-one former princely states only indirectly ruled by the British. The area lacks adequate communication and transportation, suffers from food deficits, and has next to the lowest literacy rate of the states (15.2 per cent). Shrader notes that in a single decade some 4,000 dacoits—highway robbers—were killed by the police. This gives us some sense of the turbulence in the state.

Not only did Rajasthan lack a modern administration before independence, but also it lacked a strong nationalist movement. The Rajput princes and their Rajput supporters first sought to prevent Congress from gaining control of the state, then, at the invitation of many Congress leaders, decided to join Congress so as to influence the conduct of government. One result, according to Shrader, is that the Congress party is torn between the established Rajput rural-based elite, the rising Jat peasant elite, and the Brahman-Mahajan urban elite; another consequence is that the state has moved gingerly into the area of land reform legislation. Rural political participation continues to be low, and though the state is predominantly rural, political leadership remains predominantly urban. Nonetheless, Shrader concludes that the present cabinet is more representative of the state's social structure than the cabinet was in the early fifties.

Rajasthan is thus faced with a fundamental problem of institution building—of building both a bureaucracy and a political party simultaneously. As Shrader puts it, "Congress is faced with the problem of balancing social mobilization and political institutionalization."

Madhya Pradesh

Neighboring Madhya Pradesh shares with Rajasthan some of the problems of political integration and administrative development.

Geographically, Madhya Pradesh is the largest state in India but it is, as Wilcox notes, not the result of a political movement by culturally conscious groups for a state of their own—the pattern of Maharashtra, Andhra Pradesh, Mysore, and many other states. It exists because there was nothing else to do with its constituent parts. Although Hindi is the state's lingua franca, there is in fact little communication from one part of the state to another and from one social group to another. Roads and railways are underdeveloped. There are few interest associations linking regions of the state along functional lines. Rather, the four major regions making up the state are in intense competition for state assistance and patronage. Factional conflict within the Congress party has been so intense that the central government brought in a chief minister from outside the state. In short, as Wilcox points out, Madhya Pradesh is characterized by the absence of a political community. It is this absence of a coherent state political system that has made it possible for the central government to play a more active role in the internal affairs of Madhya Pradesh than in other states.

The problems of integration have beset the state administration also in Madhya Pradesh. Being a congeries of former princely states and scattered units of former British India, the new state was faced with the initial problem of amalgamating disparate administrative systems. Moreover, in a state marked by unusually underdeveloped regions, by large tracts with predominantly tribal populations, and, especially in the ex-princely states, by an inadequate administrative cadre, the new state services have been confronted with formidable tasks extending their domain. Here, then, is a state in which there is neither a political community nor a well-established administrative framework for government at a time when parties and administration are developing simultaneously.

West Bengal

West Bengal belongs to that category of coastal states in India in which British rule was established relatively early and Westernization and modernization has moved most rapidly. Along with Maharashtra, Gujarat, and Madras, West Bengal has a well-developed administrative system, a substantial urban population, and a comparatively high literacy rate (29.3 per cent). But the dislocations associated with unbalanced modernization are somewhat greater than in these other states. The number of educated unemployed is extraordinarily high, urban violence is particularly great, and opposition parties tend to be more ideologically oriented than parties elsewhere in India and therefore less inclined to bargain and compromise. To these problems one must add the special dislocations associated with independence, since Bengal, along with the Punjab, was partitioned in 1947. The economies and administrative services of both states were disrupted and both encountered severe refugee problems. In the Punjab, however, a nearly equal number of Muslims flocked into Pakistan leaving land available to Hindu refugees for cultivation; moreover, the Punjabi peasantry turned more readily to small-scale industrial occupations and to entrepreneurship than did the Bengali refugees. While the problems of urban areas have increased, the representation of rural areas in the state legislature and within the Congress party has gradually increased with the result that the Congress government has deliberately turned its attention to the development of the rural sector from which the party receives the bulk of its support. Rural taxation is low and developmental expenditures in rural areas high. The strategy of wooing the numerous rural voters has succeeded, for though the opposition remains strong in Calcutta and left-wing militancy is more virulent in the city than in other urban areas, Congress has deftly retained and even increased its support in the rural areas, and until the 1967 elections increased its seats in the state legislature. A split in the Congress party led to its defeat in 1967.

THE CONTEXT OF POLITICAL DEVELOPMENT

Many of the developmental processes and problems experienced by nations throughout the developing areas can be observed within the Indian states. Moreover, since the Indian states function within a common political system and operate within the same constitutional structures and national constraints, we have a rare opportunity to observe developmental changes in a system controlled for governmental structures. Thus, if there are variations among the states as to the type of party systems, we know that these cannot be the result of different legislation involving election procedures since these procedures are set by national legislation. If there are differences in the way state governments respond to new efforts at mass participation, we know that it is not the result of differences in legal powers among the states. And if there are variations in the effectiveness of chief ministers in controlling their state legislatures, we know that these differences cannot be the consequence of differing distributions of power provided by the state constitutions. From a methodological point of view it would be much more satisfactory if we could hold all variables constant but one. But short of experimental situations, it is rare that a social scientist can order his data in such a way. In this situation, however, we are at least able to eliminate one major category of explanations for observed differences.

There are few problems in political development in other countries not found in some form within the Indian states, and no problems of development within the Indian states not found outside of India. The national government does, however, impose limits on the way in which the states resolve their problems, so that before turning to an examination of these problems, it is necessary that we take a brief look at the Indian federal system and suggest how that system has affected two important features of India's institutional development—the Congress party and the administrative system.

Indian Federalism

India's present federal system went into effect with the adoption of the Indian constitution by an independent India in 1950. But the pattern of relationship between the states and the center, and indeed the legal basis of that relationship, has its origin in Mughal India. Moreover, the regional cultures associated with many of the states have their origins in the pre-Mughal period when no single power ruled the subcontinent, and independent kingdoms reigned. Thus, many of the Indian states—like a few of the African nations—can claim to be the cultural inheritors of historic kingdoms: Mysore, of the ancient kingdoms of the Rashtrakuta and Chalukya dynasties; Bengal of the Pala, and Madras of the Chola dynasties; Andhra of the kingdom of the Satavahanas, and so on. During the Mughal period when much of the subcontinent was consolidated under a single ruler, some of the regional kingdoms persisted. Moreover, Mughal rule itself was based upon an areal distribution of authority. The domain of the Mughal emperors was divided into provinces governed by appointed (and in practice, hereditary) governors, and the Mughals established what was later known as a relationship of paramountcy to the quasi-independent kingdoms which paid tribute and respected the superior power in Agra and Delhi.

When the East India Company expanded its control in the latter part of the eighteenth century, it followed many of the Mughal patterns. A relationship of paramountcy was established with the princes (some of whom were former Mughal governors who had established their independence from the Mughal emperor), and the system of provinces was maintained. In theory the British governors appointed to govern the provinces were responsible to the viceroy, but in practice (especially in an age of limited communication) there was considerable autonomy. The main point, however, is that under the British, India was divided into two kinds of political units: the Indian princely, or "native," states under hereditary rulers who owed fealty to the British, and the provinces under direct British rule.

The growth of the nationalist movement in the latter part of the nineteenth century was accompanied by British reforms directed at providing Indians with a share of governmental power. Since the British were unwilling to surrender any power at the national level and since they viewed local government as a device for preparing Indians for greater governmental responsibility, concessions were made first in the sphere of local—then provincial—government. A succession of acts granted Indians representative institutions: the Morley-Minto reforms of 1909, the Montague-Chelmsford reforms of 1919, the Government of India Act of 1935, and finally the Indian Independence Act of 1947.

The pre-independence acts were directed less at changing the relationship between the provincial governments and the center than at changing the relationship between the Indians and their British rulers. However, beginning with the Montague-Chelmsford reforms of 1919, greater powers were allocated to the provinces. Certain powers in the areas of education, agriculture, and public health were transferred to partially elected legislative councils while the more important functions of controlling law and order, land revenue, canals, and finance remained under the control of the governor. The 1935 act greatly extended the powers of the provincial legislatures and expanded the suffrage. Though the powers of the provincial governments remained limited and though the governments elected in 1937 remained in office for little more than two years, the experience of running provincial governments had important consequences for subsequent Indian political developments. It provided Indian politicians with experience in running governments before they took power in 1947—experience in some of the less glamorous but essential functions of government. Countless Indians who took office in 1947 in the state and central governments had their initial governmental experience in the 1937 provincial governments. Moreover, the federal provisions of the 1935 act were the basis for the constitution of India in 1950.

The provisions of the 1950 constitution affect the internal political developments of the states in at least three significant ways. First, the constitution specifies that all the states shall have similar governmental structures. The state governments, therefore, do not have state constitutions of their own (as in the United States), but are governed by the provisions of the constitution of India. The constitution provides for the establishment of bicameral or unicameral legislatures popularly elected and a chief minister responsible to the assemblies. A governor is appointed by the central government with the power to dissent from a bill and refer it to the President of India and the power to appoint, with the approval of the legislature, the state's chief minister.

Second, under an emergency provision of the constitution, the President of India may declare a proclamation of emergency in order to place a state under the direct control of the central government. He may do so if there is a threat to the "security of India," if there has been a breakdown in law and order, or if political parties in the state have failed to form a stable government. When the emergency provisions are applied to a state, the Union parliament legislates for the state, and the state is administered by officers appointed by the central government. In the Punjab, Andhra Pradesh, and Kerala, these powers have been exercised. The knowledge that the central government can intervene and has intervened provides an important constraint on the internal politics of the states.

Finally, it is important to note that though the central government has the ultimate authority to take over a state, in day-to-day matters the state governments have considerable powers. They have exclusive taxation rights over agricultural income and control the important areas of agriculture and education. The development of the country's rural sector thus depends in large measure upon the actions of the state governments. Moreover, in the development of industry, in the conduct of industrial relations policies, and in the enforcement of economic controls, the central government depends upon the cooperation of the states.

In two fundamental respects the federal system affects the political structures within the states: in its impact on the dominant Congress party and in its impact on the system of administration.

The Congress Party

Since independence, the central government and almost all of the states governments (until the 1967 elections when Congress won control of only half of the state assemblies) have been under the control of the Congress party. In theory, Congress is a centralized party similar to the British Labour party, but it must function within a federal system, and its own structure has been influenced by that system. The party constitution provides for a relatively centralized structure, and party policy is made by a national council consisting of representatives from the states. This council (known as the All-India Congress Committee or AICC) elects a president who in turn selects his executive committee (the Working Committee). The Working Committee and the President (known collectively as the High Command) are the spokesmen for the party. They select the Parliamentary Board, which is given the power to select candidates not only for the national parliamentary elections but for the state legislative assembly elections as well.

There are structural incompatibilities in having a centralized party structure function in a federal system with the result that over the years the state party units have become increasingly autonomous and the central units have been increasingly unable to control subordinate bodies. The chief ministers and their ministers control the distribution of patronage within the states and are thus better able to elicit the loyalty of party members than is the central party organization. Moreover, the state Congress party units have generally become financially independent of the central party secretariat. Increasingly, therefore, the recommendations of the state Congress party for parliamentary and assembly seats are accepted by the national party except when the state party is severely divided in its nominations. Furthermore, the national party is reluctant to award nominations to dissidents within the state units, for to do so is to express a lack of confidence in the chief minister.

In each of the states, party leaders have sought to establish themselves as powerful chief ministers. In at least half of the states such leaders have emerged, and they are among the most powerful men in India. Since the demise of Nehru, the influence of the chief ministers has increased, though the pattern was already well established during the Nehru era. Some of the influence is formally exercised through the National Development Council, consisting of all the state chief ministers meeting with members of the Planning Commission several times a year to discuss (in closed session) development problems for the country as a whole. It is not uncommon for the Council, which was formed in 1956, to modify, or even reject, proposals of the Planning Commission. Chief ministers have been especially effective in making claims on the central government for their states—for larger grants-in-aid, and, above all, for the establishment of public sector enterprises—and in providing licenses for expansion to the private sector.

The influence of the chief ministers on national politics was dramatically demonstrated in the procedure by which Nehru's successor was chosen. K. Kamaraj, ex-chief minister of Madras and, at the time of Nehru's death, Congress President, met with the chief ministers and Congress presidents of the major states, and it was their choice that was ultimately ratified by the Congress Parliamentary Board and by Parliament itself. In short, it was the state leadership rather than the parliamentary leadership which, in practice, played a decisive role in the selection process.

It would be quite wrong to conclude from this example that the states are all-powerful and the center weak, and that the Congress party has become a congeries of state parties similar to the Republican and Democratic parties in the United States. Where the state Congress party is internally divided as it is in many states, there the central party organization still retains effective power. Some people have concluded that strong viable state governments would result in a disintegration of central authority in India, and that it may be in the interest of maintaining central authority in India for the states to remain (or become) unstable. This would hardly constitute a satisfactory resolution of the dilemma, however, since unstable state governments often become a barrier to development and further tax the resources of the central government.

The Administrative System

This conflict between the centralizing features of a national institution and the decentralizing features of the federal system also affects the functioning of the administrative system. In the middle of the nineteenth century, the British established a system of competitive examinations for recruitment into the Indian Civil Service (ICS), a national cadre of senior officers who provided the framework for ruling the subcontinent. In time, state administrative systems were also established, but ICS officers continued to be appointed to senior administrative positions in the states, from the secretariat in the capital to the posts of collectors in the districts. Even today, members of the national service (now, the Indian Administrative Service, the IAS) continue to be appointed to the states, and in some states it is not unusual for half of the senior officials to be from outside the state. This pattern facilitates not only the maintenance of an all-India tone in some state services, but also the continuance of central standards and influence in the states. It makes it possible for a high degree of professionalism to be maintained and for administrative officers to resist pressures for politicalization. But the very triumph of professionalism over politicalization and of national over states' concerns among the state administrative offices creates severe tensions within the state administration since the local cadre often resents the continued presence of outsiders. It also results in heightened tension between the centrally appointed officers and the state politicians who often resent the very effort of these officers to resist their pressures. These tensions are particularly great in states like Orissa and Madhya

Pradesh which have substantial numbers of centrally appointed officers from other states in prominent positions, and pose less of a problem in states like Madras and Maharashtra where there are fewer "outsiders" in influential posts.

It should be noted, however, that in most states only a small proportion of the senior civil service belong to the IAS or the ICS. The state public services are by far the largest of the administrative services. Moreover, members of the Union service, once assigned to a state, are posted, transferred, promoted, and disciplined by the state government, and are therefore affected by state politics no matter how strong their national identification nor how acute their sense of professionalism. District officers, for example, may be members of the Indian Administrative Service but they are responsible to and therefore, in terms of their career, dependent upon the state rather than the Union government. In short, the relationship between the state and Union administrative systems, particularly as they intertwine with the constitutional and party structure, is too complicated to apply such simple descriptive labels as "centralized" or "decentralized."

But insofar as state political development is concerned, perhaps the most significant feature of the Indian administrative system is that it does penetrate all portions of the country. Although there are many problems India shares with the new nations of Asia and Africa, it would be fair to say that few of the Indian states are confronted with comparable problems of establishing effective governmental authority—that is, of creating an administrative structure, a judicial organization, and a police system with the power to exercise control over the territory and the people within it. The British erected a governmental system and proceeded to recruit and train Indians to manage that structure with greater success than has been characteristic of other colonial areas. Early in the century, Indians entered the Indian Civil Service, and by 1947 the withdrawal of the British left only a modest administrative vacuum. The lower and intermediate administrative positions were predominantly Indian, and at the highest administrative level, nearly half of the officers in what is now India and Pakistan (more in India than in Pakistan) were Indian. Nonetheless, the withdrawal of the British and the expanding functions of administration as government took on massive responsibility for economic planning meant a phenomenal increase in the senior civil service. It is estimated that in India the elite cadre expanded by nearly 350 per cent from 1947 to 1964.

By 1947, there were few areas of India which could be described as unadministered. The exceptions were portions of the Northeast Frontier

Agency (NEFA), the Naga Hill areas nearby, and some of the hill areas of northern India stretching from Assam across to the Aksai Chin region of Ladakh (now occupied by Communist China). Some of the remoter jungle areas of Madhya Pradesh and Orissa, in which dwell many of India's tribesmen, were infrequently visited by government officers and simply paid taxes through a village or tribal headman—if at all. Some of the native states had poorly developed administrative systems, but even the smallest states received regular visits from British government officers. With a few local exceptions, therefore, independent India did not have a serious problem of penetrating the countryside with a governmental administrative system. The problems, in the main, were those of establishing new relationships between administrators and politicians, and between administrators and citizens, taking on new and expanded functions, and amalgamating administrative systems as state boundaries changed.

Thus far we have discussed two of the constants in state development—the ubiquitous character of the Congress party and of the administrative system and the way in which both of these institutions have been affected by Indian federalism. Now we shall turn to the heart of our concern, the varied patterns of development experienced by the states and the reasons for these variations. We shall examine the varied problems of integration within the states, the changing patterns of political participation, the variety of state party systems, and finally, the performance of the state governments.

POLITICAL INTEGRATION IN THE STATES

The problems of integration, that is, the process of bringing culturally and socially discrete groups together into a single territorial unit, and the establishment of a sense of loyalty to that unit, exist in India not only at the national level but at the state level as well. The development of regional movements identifying with regional languages and traditions obscures the fact that within most of the states there are serious divisions.

There has been, first of all, the problem of forming the present states themselves out of separate administrative units. Between 1947 and 1950, the smaller princely states were merged with one another to form larger units or were merged with the states of British India. In 1956, the states were again redrawn to coincide, more or less, with linguistic regions, and units were carved out of some states and added to others. Each of these reorganizations was accompanied by adjustment problems as the new units had to establish new relationships with one another. Bureaucrats had to be shifted from one state to another, and there was considerable tension as men found themselves in new administrative posts and the internal bureaucratic rules of one state were imposed upon another. Since the laws of states often differed (on land revenue matters, for example), there was some strain as uniformity was imposed. Both within the structures of authority (the administration) and within the structures of consent and participation (the political parties) there had to be some adjustment. Political leaders in different regions of the newly established states quickly fought over where the capital should be located and even over the name of the new state. The groups of each region fought for control over the Congress party and ultimately for the government itself. Within the state governments, disputes arose over the share of each region in the state's economic development programs. The states with structural integration problems include Madhya Pradesh, Orissa, Mysore, and Rajasthan—all containing former princely states—and Andhra Pradesh and Maharashtra, both pieced together out of regions which had previously been parts of adjoining states.

A second integration problem involves the relationship of minority groups to the states. There are at least two special types of minorities: (a) linguistic minorities belonging to linguistic groups which are majorities elsewhere, and (b) minorities which are not majorities anywhere. The first group is often found in a state bordering on its own linguistic region. Thus, Marathi-speaking people are found on the borders of neighboring Mysore, and Kannada-speaking people (the language of Mysore) are found in neighboring Andhra Pradesh. Typically, the "minority" group presses for the preservation of its language in the schools, may demand that local administrative ordinances be published in its own language, and, in a few instances, may press for the reorganization of state boundaries so that it will be transformed from minority to majority status by a redrawing of state boundaries. (See Table 1.4.)

The second type of minority is typically a tribe, a religious group, or a cultural-linguistic group confined (though not necessarily or entirely) to the boundaries of a single state. Thus, there is a large Sikh minority (33.3 per cent) in the Punjab, a large number of tribes (more than 10 per cent of the population) in Orissa, Madhya Pradesh, Rajasthan, Bihar, Andhra Pradesh, and Gujarat, and substantial linguistic minorities in virtually every state. It should be recalled that there are 844 languages spoken in India of which 47 are spoken by 100,000 persons or more. Many of these languages are dialectical variants of one of the

TABLE 1.4

LINGUISTIC MAJORITIES AND MINORITIES

Ranked according to highest % of linguistic minorities[a]	*Majority language*	*% of Majority language*	*Largest minority language*	*% of Largest linguistic minority*	*% of All linguistic minorities*
Assam	Assamese	55.0	Bengali	19.0	45.0
Rajasthan	Rajasthani	70.1	Hindi	21.4	29.9
Mysore	Kannada	71.1	Telugu	10.9	28.9
Madhya Pradesh	Hindi	76.7	Rajasthani	3.4	23.3
Bihar	Hindi	81.5	Urdu	7.0	19.1
Madras	Tamil	82.4	Telugu	11.0	17.6
Orissa	Oriya	82.4	Telugu	2.3	17.6
West Bengal	Bengali	84.6	Hindi	6.3	15.4
Andhra Pradesh	Telugu	84.8	Urdu	5.4	15.2
Uttar Pradesh	Hindi[b]	89.1	Urdu	7.0	10.9
Kerala	Malayalam	94.3	Tamil	3.7	5.7

[a] Data not available for Punjab, Maharashtra, Gujarat, or Kashmir.
[b] Includes Hindustani.

SOURCE: *Report of the Commissioner for Linguistic Minorities*, Ministry of Home Affairs, Government of India, 1960 (based on 1951 census).

regional languages, but many are distinct tongues. In any event, 9 per cent of the population (in 1951) did not speak any of the 14 official languages specified in the constitution. And among religious minorities, there are more than 46 million Muslims in India (10.6 per cent of the population), another 10 million Christians (2.4 per cent) and nearly 8 million Sikhs (1.7 per cent). (See Tables 1.5 and 1.6.)

Whether the minority group is a tribe or a religious or linguistic group, it is often concerned with preserving its cultural identity and resisting assimilation into a larger regional culture. Regionalism, like its earlier counterpart, nationalism, has become a powerful loyalty within most of the states and has resulted in a degree of assimilation of related social groups, but minorities are often even more protective of their status in the midst of growing regional sentiments. This protectiveness takes many forms: there is often a fight over representation in the governing Congress party and in the state assembly, insistence upon a share of appointments in the state administration or a proportion of admissions and scholarships to colleges, technical schools and universities, and, where the minority group has its own language, pressure for the use of the mother tongue as the medium of instruction in local schools and in the publication of state laws and administrative regu-

TABLE 1.5

RELIGIOUS MAJORITIES AND MINORITIES

Ranked according to highest % of religious minorities	*Majority religion*	*% of Majority religion*	*Largest minority religion*	*% of Largest religious minority*	*% of All religious minorities*
Kerala	Hindu	60.8	Christian	21.2	39.2
Punjab	Hindu	63.7	Sikh	33.3	36.3
Kashmir	Muslim	68.3	Hindu	28.5	31.7
West Bengal	Hindu	78.7	Muslim	20.0	21.3
Maharashtra	Hindu	82.2	Muslim	7.7	17.8
Uttar Pradesh	Hindu	84.7	Muslim	14.6	15.3
Bihar	Hindu	84.7	Muslim	12.5	15.3
Mysore	Hindu	87.3	Muslim	9.9	12.7
Andhra Pradesh	Hindu	88.4	Muslim	7.5	11.6
Gujarat	Hindu	89.0	Muslim	8.5	11.0
Madras	Hindu	89.9	Christian	5.2	10.1
Rajasthan	Hindu	90.0	Muslim	6.5	10.0
Madhya Pradesh	Hindu	94.0	Muslim	4.1	6.0
Orissa	Hindu	97.6	Muslim	1.2	2.4

SOURCE: Computed from figures available in *India 1964*, Publications Division, Ministry of Information and Broadcasting, Government of India, 1964, p. 19 (based on 1961 census).

TABLE 1.6

RELIGION: ALL INDIA FIGURES (per cent)

Hindu[a]	83.5
Muslim	10.7
Christian	2.4
Sikh	1.8
Buddhist	0.7
Others	.4

[a] It should be noted that tribes which do not identify themselves as belonging to a religious minority are generally classified as Hindu.

SOURCE: *India 1964*, Publications Division, Ministry of Information and Broadcasting, Government of India, 1964 (based on 1961 census).

lations. Muslims, for example, have played an active role as a minority pressure group in Uttar Pradesh, Bihar, Andhra Pradesh, and Kerala; the Sikhs have been an active political force in the Punjab; and the tribes have their own political parties in Bihar and in Assam. We might also include here India's largest minority, members of the Scheduled Castes who constitute approximately one-seventh of the Indian population. Although scattered throughout the country, they are a particularly substantial minority in Uttar Pradesh (13.1 million in 1951), Madras (5.4 million), Bihar (4.9 million), Andhra Pradesh (4.4 million), Maharashtra (4.0 million), Madhya Pradesh (3.9 million), and the Punjab (3.5 million). (See Table 1.7.) The untouchables are perhaps the

TABLE 1.7

SCHEDULED CASTES AND TRIBES

Ranked according to highest % of scheduled castes and tribes	*% Scheduled castes*	*% Scheduled tribes*	*Total %*
Orissa	15.8	24.1	39.9
Madhya Pradesh	13.1	20.6	33.7
Rajasthan	16.7	11.5	28.2
West Bengal	19.9	5.9	25.8
Assam	6.2	17.4	23.6
Bihar	14.1	9.1	23.2
Uttar Pradesh	20.9	—	20.9
Punjab	20.4	0.1	20.5
Gujarat	6.6	13.4	20.0
Madras	18.0	0.8	18.8
Andhra Pradesh	13.8	3.7	17.5
Mysore	13.2	0.8	14.0
Maharashtra	5.6	6.1	11.7
Kerala	8.4	1.2	9.6
Kashmir	7.5	—	7.5
India	14.2	6.8	21.0

SOURCE: *Census of India, Paper No. 1 of 1962* (1961 census).

least organized of the major minorities in India, but where they are organized they actively press for many of the same claims in administration, in the colleges and universities, and in the legislative assemblies as other minority groups.

In only a few states have minority groups succeeded in having one of their leaders selected as the state chief minister, the highest ranking state political office. In the Punjab, the Sikhs have had a chief minister from their community; in Andhra Pradesh, a Harijan was selected chief minister in 1961; and in Kerala, a Christian has become chief minister. In each instance, the selection of a minority leader as the chief minister by the Congress party was an important element in the integration of the minority groups into the Congress party and also into the framework of state politics itself. In the Punjab, for example, the selection of a Sikh as chief minister played for a long time an important role in minimizing the strength of a separatist Sikh party which had pressed for the establishment of a Sikh-majority state.

A third and final dimension of the integration problem in the states is the type and extent of regional loyalties. The extent or spread of loyalties is a function partly of the structural relationships we have already discussed and partly of the extent to which there are minorities within the state. There are some states in which a shared language and shared cultural and political traditions exist and in which no significant parties represent the interests of sub-regions within the state. The states which approximate this model include West Bengal, Madras, and Uttar Pradesh. The political differences which exist within these states and within the Congress party involve factions, personalities, religion, castes, and ideologies, but rarely sub-regions, and insofar as sub-regional factions and parties exist, they do not cluster around distinct cultural traditions associated with the territory in which the political group resides.

A second, quite similar pattern exists in those states in which cultural and regional loyalties predate the formation of the present state boundaries, as in Maharashtra and Andhra Pradesh. It should be noted, however, that though each state is now composed of elements which, even before the state was formed, advocated the bringing together of Marathi- and Telugu-speaking peoples, respectively, each state continues to be made up of distinct sub-regions which play an active role in contemporary political struggles. In this category we might also include the Punjab, Kerala, and Mysore, all composite states with strong antecedent cultural traditions.

A third pattern is one in which identifications are local and fragmented and where the formation of the state preceded the establishment of regional loyalties. Among the fragmented states, Rajasthan is an excellent example, as it is a state made up of a large number of small princely states, feudal (and martial) in character and organized in the main by Rajput clans according to ties of blood and marriage. Similarly, the neighboring state of Madhya Pradesh and, farther to the east, Orissa are both composed of ex-princely states which have been merged with portions of British India to form new states. Thus in contrast to Maharashtra, Andhra Pradesh, and Mysore, in these states no strong movement existed for the establishment of linguistic states.

The three types are well represented in this volume. In West Bengal we see a state in which regional loyalties are coterminous with state boundaries and in which identity problems play no significant role in the state's internal disputes. In Andhra Pradesh we see a state historically united but fragmented during the British period and in which regionalism predates the existence of the present state. But regionalism is not so great that it has eliminated sub-regional loyalties manifested in struggles between parties and within Congress, and involving allocation disputes. And in our third case, Rajasthan, we have a state in which no region-wide loyalties appeared to exist before the state in its present form was created so that even today, a politician from Rajasthan may identify himself as a Jaipuri, Udaipuri or Jodhpuri (the names of regions) rather than as a Rajasthani. If the labels men go by are a good indication of the extent of regional identification among the Indian states, then clearly Bengal and Madras are among the most integrated states in India, and Rajasthan and Madhya Pradesh among the least integrated.

In the absence of survey research data, it remains difficult to assess with precision how widespread and intense is the sense of regional identification in each of the states, but on the basis of public pronouncements by state politicians we can have some appreciation of the different forms taken by regional identifications. On this dimension, that of forms of identification, clearly the major differences are those that exist between the Hindi-speaking areas and the rest of the country.

First of all, in the Hindi-speaking areas there tends to be less of an identification with the state governments as such than in the non-Hindi-speaking states. Hindi is, after all, the language of several states, while each non-Hindi language (except Urdu) coincides with only a single state. Moreover, while Bengalis, Tamils, Kannadigas, Maharashtrians, and Gujaratis identify with their states and are known for their regional pride, they typically see their region as one of a number of regions within the Indian Union. In contrast, many Hindi-speaking politicians see the Hindi region as the "heartland" of India and Hindi as the natural candidate for the national language.

Beneath the controversy between the Hindi and non-Hindi regions over what ought to be the national or official language lie divergent images of the character of the Indian Union. As Brass points out in his analysis of Uttar Pradesh, in the Hindi-speaking region many politicians conceive of India as a unitary culture as well as a unitary state, with Hinduism—as these individuals define it—pervading cultural and political life and with Hindi not simply as an official language linking the states, but as a national language which all would speak, and finally, perhaps even as a unitary political system. Although these views can be found most commonly in the Jan Sangh, a party known for its pro-Hindu views, variations of these views, especially on Hindi can be found in the Socialist party in Uttar Pradesh, and within sections of the Congress party.

Much of the opposition to the establishment of Hindi as an official language stems from practical considerations. Were Hindi (rather than English) to be the exclusive official language and the language of examinations for the administrative services, then clearly those who speak Hindi as a mother tongue would have an advantage over those who learned Hindi as a second language. Moreover, the areas in which English is now reasonably well taught (particularly Madras and Bengal) would lose their present advantage. As a practical matter not only would such a shift mean a decrease in employment opportunities for non-Hindi-speaking people, but the influence of the non-Hindi-speaking states within the national administrative services would presumably decrease.

But beyond these practical employment and political considerations lie deeply held convictions which intensify the opposition of many non-Hindi speakers to the adoption of Hindi as an official language. There is considerable fear that the Hindi-speaking area views itself as the Prussia of India with the intention of dominating other regions culturally and politically. In contrast, the non-Hindi speakers view India as a country of divergent regions, each of which has the right to develop its own cultural traditions. While the Jan Sangh, which functions almost exclusively in northern India, advocates a unitary state, no significant political party exists in the South or in West Bengal with such a position. On the contrary, one can find in the South some political groups, especially the Dravida Munnetra Kazhagam (DMK) in Madras, advocating the disintegration of the union (though they have now officially withdrawn their demand for secession). The Jan Sangh and the DMK thus represent extreme statements of the unitary and regionalist image of India, and both advocate views which find emotional support in other parties in their respective regions.

POLITICAL PARTICIPATION IN THE STATES

It is commonplace to speak of changing participatory patterns in the new nations. Indeed, some scholars suggest that it is at the very heart of the process of political development. In India, increasingly large numbers of people have come to participate in some level of politics during the past few decades so that the Indian political system at almost all levels has become increasingly representative of the Indian social system. This increase in political participation is quite striking since in many new nations there has been a growing concentration of authority in one-party systems and in military oligarchies. Moreover, the governments of many new nations have limited political participation through legal constraints. Thus in only a handful of new nations is there complete freedom of speech and assembly, and in only a handful have there been free elections. Consequently, the number of open competitive party systems has diminished. In many new nations, moreover, participation has come to mean mobilization, that is, the organization of the populace to support the actions of the government elite, rather than participation as an act of selecting and influencing governmental personnel.

In contrast, India has had four national general elections for the national Parliament and for state assemblies. Elections are highly competitive as large numbers of individuals stand for public office. Social groups which hitherto had been politically passive are now participating in local, state, or national politics. The number of parties and interest groups is substantial, and efforts of individuals to organize so as to influence the making or implementation of public policy have grown within the last decade or so. In this section we shall describe some of these changes in the Indian states through the 1962 elections, both at the elite and at the mass level, focusing on such questions as how and why rates of participation vary from state to state, who are the new groups now participating in politics, and what forms this participation takes. Finally, we shall examine the extent to which political participation has become institutionalized in political parties and other groups.

How Much Participation?

Slightly more than half of the Indian population takes part in parliamentary and assembly elections, but the variation among the states is considerable. In the 1962 general elections, 55.4 per cent of the qualified electorate voted in parliamentary elections. Eight states were above this average and six below. Of the states with a high voting turnout, five of the eight have cast 45 per cent or more of their vote for Congress in two out of three general elections for the state assembly—Gujarat, Maharashtra, Mysore, Madras, and West Bengal—and none of the states with a low voting turnout has been as pro-Congress. The variables which seem most highly related to voting turnout are urbanization and literacy. The states with literacy rates above the national average of 24 per cent are typically those with above-average voting turnout. Only Andhra Pradesh and Kashmir of the high-voting states are below the national average in literacy, and of the low-voting areas, only Assam ranks among the above average in literacy. The correlation coefficient for literacy in relation to voting turnout by state is .43. The most urbanized states are also among the high voting. Only Kerala, Kashmir, and marginally Andhra Pradesh of the highly participant are not highly urbanized, and all the low-voting states are below average in urbanization. (See Table 1.8.) The correlation coefficient for urbanization and voting is .58.

TABLE 1.8

POLITICAL PARTICIPATION: VOTING, LITERACY, AND URBANIZATION

Ranked according to highest % of electorate voting	*% of Electorate voting for state assembly 1962*	*% Literate population*	*% Urbanization*
Kerala	84.4[a]	46.2	15.0
Kashmir	72.9	10.7	16.8
Madras	70.7	30.2	26.7
Punjab	65.5	23.7	20.1
Andhra Pradesh	64.0	20.8	17.4
Maharashtra	60.5	29.9	27.1
Mysore	59.0	25.3	22.0
Gujarat	58.0	18.4	26.0
West Bengal	55.6	29.1	23.2
Assam	52.8	25.8	7.5
Rajasthan	52.4	14.7	16.0
Uttar Pradesh	51.4	17.5	12.8
Bihar	49.0	18.2	8.4
Madhya Pradesh	44.5	16.9	14.3
Orissa	35.6[b]	21.5	6.3
India	56.3	24.0	18.0

[a] Assembly elections held in 1960.
[b] Assembly elections held in 1957.

SOURCES: Election data from *Report on the Third General Elections in India, 1962*, Vol. II (Statistical), Election Commission (Delhi, 1963); literacy and urbanization data from *Census of India, Paper No. 1 of 1962* (1961 census).

The high-voting states also rank high in other indices of communication. They tend to have a higher circulation of newspapers (correlation .38), more roads (correlation .45), and more radio receivers (correlation .59). (See Tables 1.9 and 1.10.) It should be noted, however, that the higher voting turnout is not simply a function of urbanization since the rural areas of the highly participant states have a higher voting turnout than the rural areas of the low participant states. We do have evidence, though, that the voting turnout is higher in urban areas than in the countryside. The Election Commission

TABLE 1.9

POLITICAL PARTICIPATION AND COMMUNICATION

Ranked according to highest % of electorate voting	*% of Electorate voting for state assembly 1962*	*No. of broadcast receivers*	*No. of persons per receiver*
Kerala	84.4[a]	68,506	2,467
Kashmir	72.9	—	—
Madras	70.1	275,009	1,224
Punjab	65.5	254,005[b]	799
Andhra Pradesh	64.0	158,009	2,277
Maharashtra	60.5	364,997	1,083
Mysore	59.0	137,464	1,715
Gujarat	58.0	222,867	925
West Bengal	55.6	349,332	999
Assam	52.8	39,143[c]	3,033
Rajasthan	52.4	70,551	2,856
Uttar Pradesh	51.4	215,079	3,428
Bihar	47.0	96,922	4,793
Madhya Pradesh	44.5	70,647	1,899
Orissa	35.6[d]	28,780	6,097
India	56.3	2,598,608	1,690

[a] Based on Kerala Assembly elections held in 1960.
[b] Punjab includes Jammu and Kashmir and Himachal Pradesh.
[c] Assam includes Manipur, Tripura, Nagaland, and NEFA.
[d] Based on Orissa Assembly elections held in 1957.

SOURCES: Election data from *Report on the Third General Elections in India, 1962,* Vol. II (Statistical), Election Commission (Delhi, 1963); Broadcasting information adapted from *India 1964,* Publications Division, Ministry of Information and Broadcasting, Government of India, 1964.

Report of 1957 provides us with both a breakdown of urban and rural legislative assembly constituencies and a male-female breakdown (since men and women voted in separate ballot boxes). Male turnout is exactly the same in urban and rural areas—56.4 per cent of the eligible voters, but among women the differences are very great—52.4 per cent of urban women vote as against 37 per cent of rural women.

Apart from these quantitative indices there appear to be several non-quantitative factors strongly related to political participation among the states. In general, the areas which were historically part of British India have wider political participation than those areas which were governed by maharajas. Until the late 1930s the nationalist movement was confined largely to British India so that the princely states did not experience any mass mobilization until the forties and in some

TABLE 1.10

NEWSPAPER CIRCULATION BY LANGUAGE

	No. of daily newspapers	*Regional language*	*No. of regional language dailies*	*Circulation (in thousands)*	*No. of persons per regional daily*
Andhra	28	Telugu	9	162	2,037
Assam	4	Assamese	1	7	7,126
Gujarat	30	Gujarati	28	420	388
Kerala	43	Malayalam	29	626	213
Madras	35	Tamil	22	670	396
Maharashtra	76	Marathi	28	505	535
Mysore	37	Kannada	19	177	817
Orissa	7	Oriya	5	71	1,852
Punjab	26	Punjabi	6	33	6,153
West Bengal	25	Bengali	12	305	823
Bihar	11	Hindi and Hindustani	84	752	1,513
Madhya Pradesh	43				
Rajasthan	19				
Uttar Pradesh	68				
—	—	Urdu	48	243	551

Unfortunately, data are not available for the circulation of all newspapers by state. This table indicates the circulation of the regional language newspapers, almost all of which (except for Hindi and Urdu) are distributed in a single state. An approximate rank order of states by readership of the regional language press would be as follows:

1. Kerala
2. Gujarat
3. Madras
4. Maharashtra
5. Mysore
6. West Bengal
7. The Hindi-speaking states of Bihar, Madhya Pradesh, Rajasthan, and U. P.
8. Orissa
9. Andhra
10. Punjab
11. Assam

Since the Punjab is also a Hindi- and Urdu-speaking area and also contains a substantial English-reading public, a rank order of states by newspaper circulation would probably place the Punjab higher on the list. Similarly, since Assam and Andhra both have substantial Urdu-reading publics, they too might rank higher.

SOURCE: *India 1964*, Publications Division, Ministry of Information and Broadcasting, Government of India, 1964.

instances not at all. One consequence is that in much of princely India, party organization was not developed at the time of independence. There are large parts of Madhya Pradesh and Orissa, for example, where no nationalist movement existed and no parties functioned until after 1947.

The linguistic agitation of the early 1950s was another vehicle for mass mobilization, and it is interesting to note that the states that are high on the participant list were among those most active in the states' reorganization movement. The low participant states—without exception they are all in northern India—were hardly affected by the linguistic agitation. In short, the nationalist and linguistic agitations were important vehicles for elites to mobilize non-elites—areas which took part in such movements are today among those which are high participant, and those which did not take part are generally among those which are low participant. These factors must be included in a list of conditions for high participation along with literacy, urbanization, and other communication and transport considerations, for otherwise it would be impossible to understand why such states as Andhra Pradesh and the Punjab, though low in literacy and among the middle ranking urbanized states, are so high in voting turnout.

Still another variable affecting voting turnout is the relationship between voting and concentrations of power. As a tentative hypothesis we might suggest that low levels of political participation (i.e., voting) are generally accompanied by high levels of power concentration at the local level in rural India. It has often been suggested that at the rural level there exists in India a ruling elite or ruling class—usually the term "dominant caste" is used, meaning that those who have the greatest access to wealth, status, and power come from a single social group. The dominant caste theory suggests that a high caste controls the land, is in a patron-client relationship to lower castes, is ritually dominant and socially ranked as the highest group, is influential in local administration, and possesses the important power to adjudicate local disputes. It is also suggested that dominant castes vary from one section of the country to another.

The theory of the dominant caste thus assumes that a single local elite controls all the important values. A related hypothesis is that there is a growing trend in rural India toward differentiation among the elite, and that this differentiation is increasing particularly in areas in which there is a high rate of political participation. Thus in Madras, second only to Kerala in voting turnout, the Brahman caste, once described as the dominant caste in the state, has been replaced in government and to some extent in administration but still holds considerable wealth, actively engages in business, and holds important positions in cultural and educational institutions in the state.

The dominant caste theory also assumes a stratification model of politics which suggests that the political elite is recruited from a single social class, that this single elite makes decisions without regard for the demands and interests of others, and that it is generally united in its actions. There is no evidence to suggest that these assumptions hold for any of the state governments in India, and it is doubtful that all of these assumptions would hold for very many districts, talukas, or even villages. In some rural areas it would be correct to say that those who have power—measured, say, by control over the village panchayat or access to and influence upon local and district administration—belong to one or two castes, and that under such circumstances there is often little mass participation. However, even when the elite is recruited from a single caste, intra-elite conflicts are commonplace in rural India, and these conflicts have important consequences for mass participation. One consequence is that there exists a structural incentive for bringing new social groups into political life and even into elite status. Thus factions within castes, often cutting across castes, struggling for control over the Congress party in a state may each try to win the support of lower castes and non-activists. The establishment of adult suffrage thus provides not only an opportunity for political participation by individuals who had previously not engaged in politics but also an incentive for competitive elites to try to activize and win support from new political participants. If, therefore, the local elites were united, the introduction of adult suffrage would not necessarily have important consequences for changing the composition of the elite; but where the elite is divided, adult suffrage is likely to loosen the power structure.

If we ask not who has power but rather who has power over whom and in what respects, then the stratification theory is of limited utility in India, and a pluralistic theory may more satisfactorily describe the real situation. As one student of community power studies writes: "Stratification theorists ask, 'Who runs this community?' while pluralistic theorists first ask, 'Does anyone at all run this community?' " Posed in this way, one can say that concentrations of power do exist in very many villages, but at the state level the problem has never been one of concentrated power in the hands of a single elite, but rather of competitive elites that have often not learned to share power. Although the Congress party easily won control over almost all of the state assemblies in the first three general elections, it has not always been able to manage stable governments. Moreover, even at the village panchayat level it is not unusual for conflicts to be so intense that the local governments are unable to function at all.

Types of Participatory Changes

It is important to distinguish among different kinds of social groups and how their patterns of political participation have changed. It is a common error to associate political participation exclusively with membership or involvement in the nationalist movement; to do so is to neglect significant types of political involvement. Indeed, as we speak of changing patterns of political participation it is rare that we see shifts from total non-involvement to involvement, but we find rather changes from one form of political action to another. Using this framework we can discern at least four major social groups whose pattern of political activity has changed in recent years.

1. In the pre-independence period there existed in many parts of the subcontinent powerful local elites who can be said to have had a virtual monopoly over both political authority and land—maharajas, zamindars, watandars, jagirdars, and other titled powerholders. These elites exercised power in the village, the taluka, the district, and the state, and their influence was felt mainly in administration and upon executive authority. In recent years, though most of these men have lost their titled power and much of their landed property, many have shifted from closed administrative politics to open electoral politics. In Orissa and Rajasthan, for example, Congress has absorbed many of the ruling families, and in other regions ex-rulers and large landholders have joined opposition parties.

2. A second type of political elite includes the urban professional classes—the journalists, lawyers, academics, and administrators. These were among the earliest supporters of the nationalist movement and, indeed, could be described as the initial organizers of the movement. Sections of this class joined the British administrative structure and, in a sense, shared power with the British, while other sections sought to undercut British power. As the nationalist movement under Gandhi's leadership grew in mass character and reached into the countryside, the influence of the urban elite upon the movement and subsequently upon government has declined.

3. By the mid-1930s the small landholding rural gentry in the countryside and the bazaar merchants in the towns became increasingly active in the nationalist movement. This group had often exercised considerable power in panchayats, municipal councils, and quasi-governmental cooperatives, but not until the mid-1930s in many areas did they extend their political participation into the nationalist movement and into the state government. We speak today of "rising castes," that is, of the Reddis and Kammas in Andhra Pradesh, the Nadars and other non-Brahman in Madras, and the Jats in Rajasthan as if they were new to politics. The important point, however, is that these "new" elements at the state level had always been politically active at the local level. They

are "new" political participants only in the sense that the level of their participation has changed, and that they are now engaged in party, not simply personal, politics.

Among these groups it has been the rural gentry with massive electoral backing that has moved readily into state politics, gradually displacing the more educated urban classes. The critical factor in this development is the growing importance of numbers in an open electoral system, particularly when the numerically large groups are also in possession of some economic means. Thus, neither the numerically large, poor lower castes nor the small, wealthy upper castes are now as important as the large and moderately prosperous middle castes.

4. The last type of political activists can appropriately be described as traditionally non-activist at any level of politics. Here we have in mind the lowest castes, the landless laborers, the tenant farmers, the unskilled factory laborers, the sweepers, and others in the city performing menial tasks. Unlike the rural gentry and bazaar merchants who took an active role in local affairs even before they moved into state politics, these social groups rarely participated even in local affairs. These elements are now prodded into political life by the establishment of adult suffrage, which has made them a target of political parties and ambitious politicians. In the general elections special seats are reserved for members of Scheduled Castes and Tribes, and the Congress party and the Communists have made a special effort to win electoral support from these communities. In a few instances, these communities have produced their own political leadership, though rarely in proportion to their size; but they have become sufficiently influential to make their support, or lack of support, a critical factor in some states. In Andhra Pradesh, for example, the selection of a Harijan chief minister by the Congress party was an important factor in the movement of Harijan landless laborers away from the Communist party in the 1962 general elections for state assembly and for Parliament. And in Gujarat, the Swatantra party succeeded in attracting the leadership of the Bariya community, a group of lower castes, away from Congress, thereby winning enough seats to establish itself as a formidable opposition party in the state.

Where the so-called lower classes enter politics, they often do so not by moving into the local political arena but by leapfrogging directly into state politics. Landless laborers may hesitate to oppose their employers for control over local government but need not fear sanctions by supporting opposing candidates for more remote state assembly and parliamentary seats. Thus in Andhra Pradesh the landless laborers have almost never fought for control over village panchayats, but have often given their votes to Communist assembly and parliamentary candidates. Finally, it should be noted that the lower classes like other communities do not necessarily enter politics as a cohesive force, but typically split into factions which in turn are allied to existing factions within political parties.

Institutional Versus Personal Power

Not only have the levels of political participation changed; there has also been a shift from personal to institutional power. Compared to many other developing nations, India, in virtually all of its states, has a more institutionalized political process. Politicians work through organized political parties and pressure groups, and all but a handful—less than 10 per cent—of all persons elected to the state legislative assemblies and less than 5 per cent of those elected to Parliament were independents. Party membership has remained high even for candidates to local offices, such as municipal councils and village panchayats. It would be accurate to say that personal leadership in India is being displaced by party leadership.

This has occurred to some extent even at the local level where in the past it was customary for a man to wield power because of his personal position as a man of property and high caste. Power was not associated exclusively with office. If, as traditional folklore has it, individuals did not fight for control over village councils or panchayats, it was because they held power without holding office and so one readily gave offices to individuals who already wielded personal power.

The establishment of popularly elected officers at the state level and of local government officers in the villages, talukas, and districts based upon adult suffrage has often resulted in an incongruity between personal and institutional power. Local men of personal power often disdained running for local offices in competitive elections, but soon discovered that the office itself provided independent power. The result was an enormous scramble for office that has made all elections in India, especially for local offices and for state assembly seats (interestingly enough, less so for parliamentary seats), highly competitive. It was not simply that men ran for office to gain power, but often that men who held personal power at the local level recognized that unless they now won office they would lose their power. Moreover, men who wielded personal power at the local level were often poor judges of how far their influence extended and were led by their supporters to assume that they had greater power and influence than they really did have. The result is that an extraordinarily large number of candidates for state assembly positions ran for office with so little support that they lost their deposits for failing to win one-eighth of the total vote. This point may be clearer if we rank the states in accordance with the number of candidates who forfeited their security deposits in relation to the number of seats contested for the state assembly election in 1962. (See Table 1.11.)

TABLE 1.11

PERCENTAGE OF CANDIDATES LOSING DEPOSITS IN STATE ASSEMBLY ELECTIONS, 1962: AN INDEX OF INSTITUTIONALIZATION

Ranked according to largest % of deposits forfeited	*No. of candidates*	*No. who forfeited deposits*	*% who forfeited deposits*
Uttar Pradesh	2,620	1,614	61.6
Punjab	736	420	57.1
Rajasthan	889	498	56.0
Madhya Pradesh	1,333	686	51.5
Bihar	1,592	811	50.9
Maharashtra	1,161	590	50.8
Kashmir	140	69	49.3
Madras	740	330	44.6
Assam	409	178	43.5
West Bengal	960	411	42.8
Orissa[a]	508	209	41.1
Mysore	677	251	37.1
Gujarat	521	189	36.3
Andhra Pradesh	982	353	35.9
Kerala[b]	312	57	18.3
Totals	13,580	6,666	49.1

[a] Figures for the 1957 general elections.
[b] Figures for the 1960 mid-term elections.

SOURCE: *Report on the Third General Elections in India, 1962,* Vol. II (Statistical), Election Commission (Delhi, 1963).

If we view the number of candidates who failed to retain their deposit (indicating the number of individuals unable to judge their capacity to translate personal influence into electoral votes) as one measure of institutionalization, then we can rank states along this simple index. Using these criteria, Uttar Pradesh was the least institutionalized state and Andhra Pradesh and Kerala the most institutionalized. In Uttar Pradesh as many as 1,614 candidates lost their deposit for 430 seats in the state legislature, and among the other least institutionalized states there were as many as two candidates for each seat who forfeited deposits. In contrast, only 353 candidates lost deposits for 294 seats in Andhra Pradesh.

It is interesting to note that the four most institutionalized polities appear also on the list of those who have above-average political participation, and of the least institutionalized states, four out of five (Uttar Pradesh, Rajasthan, Bihar, and Madhya Pradesh) are also among the least participant. It is also of interest that among the institutionalized polities, the bulk of the candidates who forfeited deposits were independents, not party candidates. In these states the parties were reasonably adept at assessing the prospects of their nominees, but in the non-institutionalized systems, even the political parties were poor judges of their capacities. Thus, in Uttar Pradesh there were nearly a thousand party candidates who lost their deposits.

This index matches well with how many votes are given to independent candidates or to candidates of "minor" parties, by which we arbitrarily mean all parties except Congress and the largest opposition party in each state. In Uttar Pradesh for example, 47 per cent of the voters cast their ballot for independent candidates or for some party other than Congress (which won 36.1 per cent), or the largest opposition party, Jan Sangh (16.5 per cent). At the other end of the continuum, only 28 per cent of the voters in Kerala supported independents or any party other than Congress or the Communists in the 1960 elections. In the six least institutionalized states in our table, from 41 to 47 per cent of the population voted for independent or "minor" party candidates, an average of 44 per cent. In the six most institutionalized states independent and minor party candidates typically won 33 per cent of the vote.

Charismatic figures who rise to office without organizational support and whose mass popularity is independent of organizational support have almost disappeared from the Indian political scene. Neither Gandhi's nor Nehru's standing depended upon continued organizational support, but Shastri's did, and so does Indira Gandhi's. And while a few years before Nehru died there was talk of selecting as his successor a popular Gandhian socialist, Jayaprakash Narayan, who no longer played an active role in any political party, when the time came to select Nehru's successor, attention was in fact given only to men with long records of participation in Congress party politics. The rise of organizational leadership in India thus probably accounts for the decline of the charismatic leader.

At the state and local level political leadership is now increasingly professionalized. Congress and many of the opposition parties now maintain full-time party cadres, and typically, members of the state legislative assemblies have spent a lifetime in politics. One can say that India now has a class of professional politicians. It is increasingly common for the office of chief minister to be held by men who have spent their careers exclusively in the party organization without ever having had non-political careers. Thus, Kamaraj has spent his entire career in Congress, first as a party worker in a district organization, then as secretary to the state organization, then after a struggle for control over the state, as chief minister, a post he held for a decade before moving into national office. Similarly, the chief ministers of most of the states have devoted their lives to first working within the party and then entering government. The party has indeed become an institutionalized vehicle for gaining public office.

The institutionalization of political participation through political parties seems most pronounced in states with large-scale political participation, least in those with the least participation. This suggests (but does not prove) that institutionalization may precede rather than follow large-scale participation in India. In short, perhaps it is because there are well-organized parties in Andhra Pradesh, Gujarat, Madras, Kerala, and West Bengal (the evidence is less clear with respect to Mysore and Assam) that participation in elections is high, for in these states organized political parties seek to mobilize mass electoral support.

We have already suggested that low political participation may be accompanied by high levels of local power concentrations, and now we are suggesting that high participation is associated with the presence of organized parties at the local level. It follows, therefore, that where traditional power concentrations continue to exist, one is not likely to find a well-organized political party; to put it another way, the party organization is a substitute for traditional power structures. So long as the local elite commands support by virtue of its traditional ties with the peasantry through control over land, patron-client relationships, and so on, little attention need be paid by local elites to the establishment of an effective party organization.

Since India is one of the few developing countries in which political participation at the constituency level is institutionalized into a party system, let us take a closer look at the types of parties and party systems which exist within the Indian states.

STATE PARTY SYSTEMS

India has been described as having a dominant one-party system because a single party has for a lengthy period been in control of the national government with no serious threat from the opposition. This description, though accurate for describing the national scene before 1967, could not even then be applied to all the states, for there were several states in which Congress had failed to win a majority of seats or where the majority (or plurality) had been precarious. Before 1967 there were five states in India in which party competition had been so great that Congress had failed in at least one of the three general elections to win a majority of seats and had either formed a government with a plurality of seats or actually failed to form a government. These are:

Kerala, which has been successively governed by Congress, Socialist, and Communist parties and has been under President's Rule;

Madhya Pradesh, which has had two Congress minority governments;

Orissa, which failed to give Congress more than a plurality of seats in two elections and has had coalition governments;

Rajasthan, where Congress has won slightly under a majority in two of three elections; and

Andhra Pradesh, which has had a Congress-led coalition government and which on one occasion was under President's Rule.

As far as the popular vote is concerned, Congress has rarely received more than 50 per cent of the popular vote in either assembly or parliamentary elections in any state. Only in Gujarat, Mysore, Assam, and Maharashtra has Congress ever passed the 50 per cent mark in popular vote for state assembly elections. Moreover, even in states in which Congress easily won majorities in the first three elections, a large number of seats were won with a bare plurality. In short, party competitiveness increases as we move from national politics to state politics and down to constituency politics.

Another significant disparity between the national and state party systems is in the character of the parties participating. Opposition to Congress at the national level comes from parties with explicit ideological and programmatic differences with Congress: the two Communist parties; the Jan Sangh (a Hindu-minded party); the Swatantra party (a conservative party); and the two socialist parties, the Praja Socialist party and the Samyukta Socialist party. In the 1962 elections these national opposition parties won 73 seats in parliament as against 353 for Congress and 59 for other parties and independents. In the 1967 elections, they won 156 seats as against 280 for Congress and 76 for other parties and independents.

In addition to national opposition parties competing for both national and state elections, there are also a number of parties which function exclusively in one or two states. (For a list of the major opposition parties in each of the state assemblies as of 1962 see Table 1.12. For the state Congress vote see Table 1.13.)

TABLE 1.12

CONGRESS AND OPPOSITION PARTIES IN THE STATE ASSEMBLIES, 1962

	Assembly seats	*Congress seats*	*% of Congress seats*	*% of Vote for Congress*	*Largest oppo-sition*	*% of Vote for largest opposition*	*No. of opposition parties*
Andhra Pradesh	294	171	58.2	47.3	Communist	19.5	2
Assam	105	79	76.7	48.3	PSP	12.7	2
Bihar	318	185	58.2	41.4	Swatantra	17.3	5
Gujarat	154	113	73.4	50.8	Swatantra	24.4	2
Kashmir[b]	41	36	87.3	67.0	Praja Parishad	17.4	2
Kerala[c]	127	63	49.6	35.5	Communist	36.8	3
Madhya Pradesh	285	139	48.8	38.5	Jan Sangh	16.7	5
Madras	206	139	67.5	46.1	DMK	27.1	3
Maharashtra	264	215	81.4	51.2	Peasants and workers	7.5	4
Mysore	206	136	66.0	50.2	PSP	14.1	2
Orissa[d]	140	56	40.0	38.2	PSP	10.4	2
Punjab	154	90	58.4	43.7	Akali Dal	11.9	4
Rajasthan	175	87	49.7	40.0	Swatantra	17.1	4
Uttar Pradesh	430	249	58.0	36.3	Jan Sangh	16.5	6
West Bengal	251	156	62.2	47.3	Communist	25.0	3
Totals	2,842	1,759	61.9	44.4			

[a] Includes only opposition parties which won over 3% of the popular vote.

[b] Congress does not function in Kashmir. In the Congress columns we have listed the seats and votes for the National Conference.

[c] Kerala figures are from the 1960 mid-term elections.

[d] Orissa figures are from the 1957 general elections.

SOURCE: *Report on the Third General Elections in India, 1962*, Vol. II (Statistical), Election Commission (Delhi, 1963).

TABLE 1.13

CONGRESS STATE ASSEMBLY VOTE, 1952–62

	1952		1957		1962	
	% of vote	*% of seats*	*% of vote*	*% of seats*	*% of vote*	*% of seats*
Andhra Pradesh[a]	29.7	28.1	41.3	62.1	47.4	59.0
Assam	43.8	72.3	52.4	72.3	48.3	75.2
Bihar	41.4	72.7	41.9	66.0	41.3	58.1
Gujarat	54.9	86.3	48.7	73.4	50.7	73.3
Kerala[b]	34.3	32.8	37.8	34.1	34.1[c]	50.0
Madhya Pradesh	48.1	77.4	49.8	80.5	38.6	49.3
Madras	40.0	50.4	45.3	73.6	46.1	67.4
Maharashtra	45.2	82.1	48.7	51.8	51.2	81.4
Mysore	51.5	84.2	52.1	72.5	49.8	66.3
Orissa	38.8	47.8	38.2	40.0	43.3[d]	58.5
Punjab	34.8	65.0	47.5	77.9	43.8	58.4
Rajasthan	39.7	50.0	45.2	68.7	40.0	44.8
Uttar Pradesh	47.9	90.6	42.4	66.5	36.1	57.9
West Bengal	38.9	63.2	46.1	60.3	47.3	62.3
India	42.2	68.4	45.5	68.6	44.4	61.6

[a] The 1957 figure for Andhra Pradesh is a composite made up of the results from the mid-term election in Andhra in 1955 and in Telengana in 1957.

[b] By-elections were also held in the old state of Travancore-Cochin in 1954 in which Congress won 45.3% of the vote and 45 out of 117 seats.

[c] This figure is for by-elections held in 1960. In by-elections held in early 1965, Congress won 32.5% of the vote and 36 out of 133 seats. A splinter Congress group, the Kerala Congress won 23 seats with 12.4% of the vote.

[d] This figure is for by-elections held in June 1960.

SOURCE: Compiled from the reports on the three general elections published by the Election Commission.

In the February 1967 elections the dominant position of the Congress party, both in the states and in the center, was broken. Congress again won a majority (but a much reduced majority) of seats for parliament, and Congress failed to win a majority of seats in eight of the states. The proportion of Congress seats and votes for each of the state assemblies can be seen in Table 1.14. These eight states—Bihar, Kerala, Madras, Orissa, Punjab, Rajasthan, U. P., and West Bengal—contain some two-thirds of the Indian population. With support from independents Congress was able to form a government in Rajasthan, but in the new state of Haryana where Congress did win a majority, a split after the elections led to the formation of a non-Congress coalition government. In Kerala the Communists formed a government and a Communist-supported left government was formed in West Bengal. In Madras, much to everyone's surprise, Congress was overwhelmingly defeated (in seats not votes) by the DMK, and in the Punjab, another regional party, the Akali Dal, emerged as the largest group in a coalition government. In Orissa a Swatantra-dominated coalition was formed, in Bihar a coalition led by the SSP (the Socialist party) was created, and in U. P. the Jan Sangh was the largest group in the coalition government. In short, after the 1967 elections half of the Indian states had non-Congress governments and in almost every instance these were coalition governments. This new pattern clearly has far-reaching consequences both for political stability in the states and in the relationship between the states and the central government.

TABLE 1.14

Congress State Assembly Vote, 1967

	% of vote	*% of seats*
Andhra	42.9	57.5
Assam	43.4	58.0
Bihar	32.8	40.2
Gujarat	43.2	55.1
Haryana	41.4	59.3
Kerala	35.4	6.8
Madhya Pradesh	40.7	56.4
Madras	41.8	20.9
Maharashtra	47.9	74.8
Mysore	48.0	58.3
Orissa	30.4	21.4
Punjab	37.4	46.1
Rajasthan	41.4	48.4
U. P.	32.1	46.8
W. Bengal	40.2	45.4

SOURCE: These are unofficial figures compiled from newspaper reports. In several instances the returns were not complete.

Several features of the party systems in the Indian states deserve attention. First of all, it should be noted that the party systems which exist at the state level are not simply continuations of pre-independence politics. For one thing, the ex-princely areas had virtually no experience in popular government, and in most instances, no parties, not even Congress, existed in the princely states until the late 1930s or later. Thus, in large parts of Orissa, Madhya Pradesh, Rajasthan, Kerala, and portions of Mysore, no party organizations existed at the local level before 1947. It should also be noted that in West Bengal and the Punjab, partition disrupted existing party organizations. In the Punjab, Congress was never very strong since a collaborationist party, the Unionist party, now defunct, and later the Muslim League dominated pre-independence politics. Similarly in Bengal, the Muslim League was the dominant force. Moreover, Congress was truncated by partition since much of its leadership came from areas transferred to Pakistan. Both in Bengal and in the Punjab, therefore, Congress had to be organized from scratch in many areas.

A transformation also took place in the composition and position of Congress elsewhere. The movement of rural politicians into dominant positions in the party was accelerated with the establishment of adult suffrage and with the expansion of rural development programs which increased the patronage available to rural leadership. Some opponents of the nationalist movement joined Congress—the Unionist group in the Punjab, many of the ex-princes in Madhya Pradesh, Rajasthan, and Orissa and many of the large zamindars, jagirdars, and watandars (landlords) throughout the country.

Moreover, some political parties disappeared from the national scene at independence, particularly the Muslim League, which then became a Pakistani party. Several groups within Congress separated from the nationalist movement to create their own political parties, particularly the Socialists and several smaller Marxist left groups.

Though few parties could have any realistic hope of displacing Congress at the national level at the time of independence, the situation in many of the states was sufficiently fluid to offer the hope of victory to opposition parties. In the first general elections of 1952, therefore, a spate of parties and independent candidates stood for state office, and opposition expectations were so great that few electoral alliances were made. The result was that Congress won a large number of seats with a plurality vote.

But political competition in the states has not been confined to competition for assembly seats among contending parties. Some of the most intense political competition in the states occurs within the governing Congress party. The result is that even in states in which the Congress hold is secure—as in Mysore—there is in fact substantial political competitiveness. This competition takes the form of conflict for posts within the government but it also affects, as Brass notes in his study of Uttar Pradesh, legislative politics. Modifications in land reform legislation or taxation bills are more likely to result from pressures within the Congress party and from conflicts within the Congress Legislative party than from pressures from the opposition.

The basis for this competitiveness within Congress varies from state to state, and its impact on governmental performance also varies, but the institutional forms it takes are remarkably similar. Congress dissidents typically attempt first to win control over the party organization, particularly the Pradesh (state) Congress Committee (PCC) which has, in effect, the power to determine who will receive party nominations for assembly and parliament seats, though, as we have noted, ultimate authority is in the hands of the national organization. Intra-party competitiveness, therefore, is typically manifested by a struggle for control over the Pradesh Congress Committee and then between the PCC (the "organization") and the members of the government (the "ministerialists"). The politically most successful (and most durable) chief ministers, therefore, are those who have retained control over the party organization. Among the most skilled chief ministers—and therefore the most stable states ("stable" in terms of the length of time a single chief minister has held office)—have been those from Madras (Kamaraj), Maharashtra (Chavan), West Bengal (B. C. Roy), Punjab (Kairon), Rajasthan (Sukhadia), and Kashmir (Bakshi). From time to time there have also been "strong" chief ministers in Assam, Mysore, Andhra Pradesh, Orissa, and Gujarat. (See Table 1.15.) In a few states, notably Madhya Pradesh, Kerala, and Uttar Pradesh, no chief minister in recent years has been able to establish himself in effective control of the party organization—that is, in control of the PCC and party offices with something more than a precarious majority.

Confronted by contending groups within the party, some chief ministers have followed the strategy of attempting to achieve a balanced government in which all groups are represented. Under such circumstances, ministers belonging to opposition factions within the party may not deal with one another, and the chief minister is forced to retain under his own personal control some of the politically most sensitive portfolios—such as Home and Agriculture. Other chief ministers have established for themselves "strong" images by pursuing an alternative strategy of rewarding their own supporters and punishing, or at least denying patronage to, their opponents within the party. Ministerial posts and patronage, therefore, are provided only to their own supporters, and every effort is made to deny representation in the state assembly to opposing factions.

The Social and Economic Basis of Conflict

As we move from an examination of the forms taken by intra-party and inter-party conflict to the substance of these conflicts, the patterns are more varied.

1. Sub-regional conflicts, as we have noted earlier, can be found in

TABLE 1.15

CHANGES IN GOVERNMENT, 1947–65

	No. of chief ministers 1947–65	*Longest tenure*	*Name*
Andhra Pradesh (since 1954)	6	1956–60	Sanjiva Reddi
Assam	3	1950–58	B. R. Medhi
Bihar	3	1947–60	S. K. Sinha
Bombay (1947–61)	3	1947–52	B. G. Kher
Gujarat (since 1961)	2	1963–65	Balwantrai Mehta
Kashmir	4	1953–64	Bakshi Ghulam Mohammed
Kerala	7	1960–62	Pattom Thanu Pillai
Madhya Pradesh[a]	4	1947–56	R. S. Shukla
Madras[b]	5	1954–65	Kamaraj Nadar
Maharashtra (since 1961)	3	1960–62	Y. B. Chavan
Mysore[c]	7	1947–52	K. C. Reddi
Orissa	6	1957–61	Harekrushna Mehtab
Punjab	4	1956–64	Partap Singh Kairon
Rajasthan	4	1954—	M. L. Sukhadia
Uttar Pradesh	4	1946–55	G. B. Pant
West Bengal	3	1948–62	B. C. Roy

[a] Madhya Pradesh was enlarged in 1956.
[b] Madras was reduced with the creation of Andhra in 1954.
[c] Mysore was enlarged in 1956.

If we exclude the newly formed states of Gujarat and Maharashtra, the rank order of states by average tenure of chief ministers is as follows:

1. Andhra	1.8 years	8. Punjab	4.5 years
2. Kerala	2.6	9. Rajasthan	4.5
3. Mysore	2.6	10. Kashmir	4.5
4. Orissa	3.0	11. Assam	6.0
5. Madras	3.6	12. Bihar	6.0
6. M. P.	4.5	13. W. Bengal	6.0
7. U. P.	4.5		

almost all the states. In states composed of discrete sub-cultural regions or in those which are aggregates of previously existing political units, there are, typically, conflicts over the distribution of posts within the Congress governments and the allocation of state funds for education and for development programs. Sub-regional competition, particularly within Congress, but also among the opposition parties, is particularly common in Maharashtra, the Punjab, Madhya Pradesh, and Uttar Pradesh.

2. Caste conflicts exist within almost every state, though less so in West Bengal and the Punjab than elsewhere. Caste identifications take many forms, from caste associations functioning as interest groups

pressing for jobs in administration and for educational benefits to merely a sense of camaraderie among caste fellows. Only a few parties are explicitly organized to represent castes: the Republican party which seeks support among members of the scheduled castes, and the DMK in Madras and the Peasants and Workers party in Maharashtra which seek support among non-Brahman castes (but whose appeal is so broad that it would be misleading to label them as simply caste parties). In practice however, almost all parties, especially Congress, are concerned with applying ethnic arithmetic, that is, with balancing tickets among a variety of castes.

3. Occupational interests play a stronger part in state than in national politics, but since caste and occupation often overlap considerably, it is difficult to distinguish between caste and occupational conflicts. Among the more industrialized states, urban business interests play an active though covert role in state politics and are especially concerned with exercising influence upon administration. In the non-industrial states, the trading interests are particularly important, especially in Uttar Pradesh and Madhya Pradesh. We have suggested earlier that rural landholders, especially the middle peasantry, are actively concerned with community development programs, the government-sponsored cooperatives with their control over the allocation of credit, fertilizers, and seeds, and on the legislative side, the land reform and agricultural taxation policies of the state governments.

One can also discern in many states tensions between urban and rural areas as each seeks greater allocation of state development funds, and between the urban intellectuals and the business community, particularly in Calcutta and Bombay. Trade unions are also becoming an increasingly important force in state politics although, in the main, unions are hostages of national political parties.

4. The tribal, linguistic, and religious conflicts we have discussed earlier are often manifest through the organization of competing political parties and interest groups, as well as through groups within the Congress organization. The political force of cultural minorities is often muted by their internal divisions. In the Punjab, for example, the majority of the Sikhs have voted for Congress, and only a minority have voted for the Akali Dal. Similarly, the Muslims and the scheduled castes and tribes are divided among several political parties.

5. Although there are many group conflicts within party organizations—generally known in India as factionalism—it is rare that such conflicts are based exclusively upon regional, caste, or other ethnic attachments. and rare indeed for such conflicts to be based exclusively

upon class and occupational interests. There is some disagreement as to whether factional conflicts in village politics are more pronounced today—the consequence, some argue, of introducing party politics into the village—or are simply more visible. In any event, it is clearly a pervasive feature of both village and party politics. Although there is a hard core to most factions, there is also a floating element that shifts from one faction to another, and coalitions among factions are rarely durable. While caste and religious conflicts thus tend to be intense and unbargainable, factional conflicts are fluid with more flexible relationships. The opportunities for skillful leadership capable of coalition building are, therefore, greater in a situation of factional politics than in a situation of conflict based upon intense, primordial religious and cultural attachments.

Conditions for Political Stability

It is a truism that stability within government is a function not of the degree of conflict within a system but rather of the relationship of conflicting groups. The stability of the Indian states has varied considerably, and this provides us with an opportunity to explore a number of hypotheses concerning the conditions for governmental stability.

There have been at least two kinds of instabilities in the Indian states. There are situations in which no one party has been able to win enough votes in the assembly to form alone, or in stable coalitions with others, an enduring government. The most extreme situation has been in Kerala where there has been a succession of party and coalition governments. For a brief period in the mid-1950s the situation in Andhra Pradesh was sufficiently unstable to warrant President's Rule.

In the second kind of instability the chief ministers have been unable to sustain support within the Congress party, and conflicts within Congress have been so intense and overt that there have been frequent changes in ministries. Such situations have existed in Uttar Pradesh, Mysore, Madhya Pradesh, and from time to time in almost every state, with the exception of Madras and West Bengal.

By-elections in Great Britain and off-year elections in the United States are often an indication of shifts in national politics. Shifts in a number of mayoralty elections in large cities, or in several state legislative elections, may suggest a shift in presidential voting. The United States and Great Britain, however, are relatively well-integrated systems, so that election results in one locale may indicate a shift in voting patterns throughout the country. This is not so in India. A Congress defeat or intense factionalism within Congress in a single state has thus far been no indication of the state of Congress elsewhere in the country. Thus, repeated Congress defeats in Kerala have had no significant impact on the strong Congress positions in neighboring Mysore or Madras. Similarly, the growth in the secessionist DMK party in Madras in the 1962 elections took place at a time when the Akali Dal in the Punjab and the Jharkhand party in Bihar declined in strength.

India can be described both socially and politically as a segmented political system. To a remarkable degree those political developments which occur in one segment do not affect developments in another. The segments are not only states, but the states themselves are often divided into segments. Caste or factional turmoil in one district resulting in a series of Congress defeats for assembly seats often has little effect upon neighboring districts.

One consequence of segmentation is that discontent is localized and instabilities are often quarantined. This feature of the Indian system may help us understand why it is that at any one time many of the Indian states are unstable, but the national government is unaffected and unperturbed. Were all the states unstable simultaneously, the national Congress organization and the national government could hardly remain stable. But typically only four or five states at any one time are seriously disturbed: one may be under President's rule, in another a Congress-opposition coalition is in danger of collapsing, and in two or three others dissident factions threaten to overthrow the Congress ministry. It is not uncommon for most of these problems to be resolved in one group of states and to occur thereafter in others. An analogy might be made to a large twelve-wheel truck with four tires on each of three axles. A flat on one tire does not create a flat on another, and it is possible for the vehicle to keep moving even if one or two tires are not functioning. In any event, the driver carries enough spares to keep the vehicle working so long as he does not have a large number of flats simultaneously.

It remains to be seen whether the 1967 elections marked the entrance of national factors into the elections—some observers have suggested that the food shortages and steep rise in prices throughout the country accounted for the Congress decline—or whether the defeat of Congress in many states simply reflected the more effective coalitions among the non-Congress parties. In any event, it is interesting to note that there was not a uniform shift either to the left or to the right throughout the country. In the Punjab and Madras regional parties grew in strength; in West Bengal and Kerala it was the left; in Orissa, Rajasthan and U. P. the right wing parties; and in Bihar both the left and right!

What factors make for stable state governments? The factors which affect voting for various parties are too complex to explore here, but one generalization might be suggested: electoral defeat for Congress at the state-wide level has almost always been associated with internal party factionalism. Since Congress typically has strong support from the rural gentry, has greater access to transportation (such as jeeps), and by controlling the government is able to dispense patronage, it clearly has an advantage over other political parties. Moreover, the very openness of Congress has meant that those who are discontent with policy or with administration can seek redress through attempting to join and exercise influence within Congress. In many states therefore, opposition parties have been continuously weakened by accretions to Congress. Thus, Congress moved into a solid majority position in Andhra Pradesh after it absorbed the state's Socialist party.

Congress governments have frequently been weakened when dissident Congress factions have covertly given their support to opposition candidates in order to undercut the ministerialists. There is, therefore, a close relationship between a low Congress vote and a high degree of internal party factionalism.

The single most significant variable, then, in the establishment of stable governments thus far has been the political skill of the Congress leadership—the skill to build coalitions of factions or to place their own faction in a dominating position both in the government and in the Congress party simultaneously. No other variables therefore—degree of urbanization, literacy, the patterns of social organization, or for that matter, the speed of economic growth—correlate with stability of government.

Whether a state can produce a skillful leadership is not simply a random matter. The scale of a state is one consideration, for it is quite difficult for a politician to establish control in a state which has a vast territory and where communication and transportation is unusually underdeveloped. Perhaps this is why the chief ministers of the large states of Madhya Pradesh, Rajasthan, and Uttar Pradesh have found it particularly difficult to establish unified, stable Congress regimes. On the other hand, one should not conclude that large states must necessarily be unstable, since Maharashtra is not; we are simply suggesting that scale makes the task of organization more difficult for political leaders.

It is also interesting to note that many of the states in which Congress is weakest—those where the Congress vote is low or where internal party factionalism has led to governmental instability—are those which contain ex-princely states. The Congress assembly vote has dropped below 40 per cent in one or more elections in Kerala, Madhya Pradesh, Orissa, and Rajasthan, all containing ex-princely states. Congress developed late in the princely states with the result that there are generally fewer party cadres and less developed party loyalties. Moreover, since the administrative services are generally less developed in the ex-princely areas and social services not as well established, less patronage is readily available to the Congress government. Finally, in the states which have been amalgamated out of discrete political units, political loyalties and associations have been largely parochial and personal, thereby making it difficult to create powerful party factions traversing the entire state.

Now that coalition governments have been formed in half of the Indian states, the establishment and maintenance of stable state governments will increasingly depend upon the skill of the Chief Ministers of those states to satisfy the elements which make up their coalitions. In several states the new coalition governments cover a spectrum of interests and ideologies even wider than those which existed within the Congress governments, and it is hard to see how several of these governments can survive for long. What little leverage the Congress Chief Ministers had in keeping their own dissidents in line—they could at least threaten expulsion and the denial of renomination—is not available to the Chief Ministers of coalition governments. It is quite likely that the defeat of the Congress party in many states will soon be followed by a succession of unstable state governments.

CONCLUSION: GOVERNMENTAL PERFORMANCE

In the final analysis, it is relevant to ask whether a system works or not, or how it works, not simply whether it survives or is stable. We do not have any hard indices of governmental performance. This is one reason why social scientists have more readily considered stability. which can be measured, and have been reluctant to consider performance, which not only can less easily be measured but involves conflicting norms on the part of the analyst. We tend, therefore, to fall back upon the judgment—admittedly not always based upon the same standards—of those who know the states well.

One standard is governmental competence. Wilcox points out that so few members of the Madhya Pradesh government can competently prepare legislation that the state has had difficulty preparing constitutionally acceptable panchayat legislation. Wilcox also suggests that in Madhya Pradesh the energies of the government are literally devoted to the task of building a governmental machinery—an effective administrative framework and even a capital city. In Uttar Pradesh, according to Brass, factional conflicts within the Congress party are so great that the state government is in a state of paralysis since almost any governmental action is likely to disturb the balance of power among the party factions. Factionalism, lack of commitment, and a low degree of loyalty pervade Congress politics in Uttar Pradesh, but one can argue that to some degree the same factors are at work in other states with less injurious consequences for governmental performance. There is a similar situation in Andhra Pradesh, but there the dominant faction has ruthlessly refused to share power with the dissidents. In Uttar Pradesh no faction has been able to really win and consolidate its power; no single group has been able to extend its sway over the entire administration of the state so as to capture sufficient control over patronage to punish or provide rewards to party factions.

As we ask, then, what are the factors which affect the performance of the state governments, we must ask what are the kinds of loads or challenges confronted by these governments. In short, what are the standards for determining governmental performance? A government faced with the task of creating an effective administrative system to penetrate the territory and economy is hardly in a position to perform more than a minimum of functions. Similarly, a state government confronted with divergent and conflicting social and cultural groups that do not have a common political bond and are fearful of encroachments on their way of life, their language, their status, and their occupations can do little more than provide a sense of reassurance in order to build an effective political community. Insofar as initiative for economic development activities must come from government (obviously, this statement does not apply to regions of the subcontinent such as the Punjab where initiative for economic development lies outside of government), then there are only a handful of states in India whose governments have so far been able to play an active and successful role. In one sense, of course, the state governments mirror the kinds of societies in which they function. In regions where individuals are not accustomed to exercising initiative, where rigid hierarchies have paralyzed the initiative of the lower strata, where there is little sense of organization, where goals are personal or limited to one's kinsmen, where individuals are concerned more with sharing an existing economic pie than with expanding it, and where few individuals are motivated by a passion for modernization, one can hardly expect the personnel in government and administration to behave in markedly different ways. The more open and the more participant the Indian political system is at the state level, the more likely is there to be a congruence in values between political leaders and the public at large. But while this may facilitate the growth of legitimacy and integration, will it facilitate the development of a modern innovative government prepared to pursue, as Wilcox puts it, alterative as well as accretive policies?

Thus far, the states have not played an innovating role in development. Some powers constitutionally shared by the states and the central government are exercised almost exclusively by the central government because of lack of interest and skill on the part of state leaders. Industrial relations policies, for example, are virtually set by the central government, and state ministries of labor often do little more than enforce central government legislation. Agricultural development policy is a state matter, but initiative in this area has rested almost exclusively with the central government. There has been some initiative in the area of local government policy, but even here the main outlines have been set by the central government. In the area of land reform much of what the states have done has resulted from pressures from the central government, and much of the energy of the state governments has gone into watering down proposed legislation. Finally, state economic plans are typically collections of projects proposed by ministries rather than careful analyses of the economy of the state; no state government has a planning commission.

Much of the power of the center in dealing with the states rests not only upon superior financial resources or legal powers, but also upon the superior skills and initiative exercised by central leadership. Should state leaders become more skilled and more enterprising, we might find a wider range of policies pursued by the states, and though this might at first diminish central authority, it would have the desirable effect of facilitating a more experimental approach to development. At present, policies prescribed by the center often do not readily take into account varied conditions in the states. Thus, in the field of agriculture where development depends so much upon a recognition of extraordinarily diverse conditions within the subcontinent and upon the development, therefore, of varied policies, it is difficult to bring about a rapid rate of growth without innovative state policies.

It is possible that the establishment of non-Congress governments in half the states will result in greater innovative state policies but it is also possible that as the resources of the state governments shrink (which they are likely to do if some of the state governments drop land revenue taxes as they have promised), their demands upon the central government will grow. If the states do press for a new formula for mechanically allocating central government funds to the states, there is likely to be a major clash between the center and the states and among the states themselves.

So far, the political struggles within the state are more often concerned with control over administration, access to funds for development projects, access to patronage, permits, influence in the colleges, and the like. Although the issue of jagirdari abolition continues to be important in Rajasthan, and controversies over land legislation persist in many state governments, in the main, public policy controversies within the states are not common. The main issues are those of allocation and administration of state development projects.

It is tempting to conclude, as some have, that India ought to move toward a more centralized system in which the states become little more than administrative arms of the center, that education and agriculture be made central subjects and the center be given the power to tax the agricultural sector. Apart from the obvious political difficulties in pursuing such a proposal—it is hard to see how the states would give up such powers unless they were forced to do so by a dictatorial center, presumably a military government—it would result in many of the burdens now being shared by the states being transferred to the central government. Thus there would be an overburdened center with, to use a biological analogy, a strong head and heart but a weak circulating system and ineffectual limbs.

In any event, it is most unlikely that the center will be able to take powers away from the states. Indeed the trend has been just the reverse: the states have tended to become politically more autonomous and to accept central advice reluctantly. Increasingly therefore, the issue for the central government is whether it can take steps to encourage greater developmental initiative within the states, and whether it can use its financial and legal powers to be supportive of modernizing tendencies. The issue for India is not, as some would put it, whether central authority will be powerful enough to develop India despite the limits imposed by the states. Political power is not after all a fixed commodity to be rationed among an ever-expanding number of claimants. The political problem of a modernizing system is how to expand the capabilities of a wide variety of governmental units, at the local, state, and national levels.

UTTAR PRADESH

UTTAR PRADESH
ADMINISTRATIVE DIVISIONS
NATIONAL BOUNDARY
STATE BOUNDARY
DISTRICT BOUNDARY
STATE CAPITAL
DISTRICT HEAD QUARTER
DISTRICT HEAD QUARTERS BEAR THE NAME OF THE DISTRICTS UNLESS OTHERWISE MENTIONED
HIMACHAL PRADESH
CHINA
NEPAL
PUNJAB
DELHI
RAJASTHAN
MADHYA PRADESH
BIHAR
UTTARKASHI
DEHRADUN
TEHRI-GARHWAL
Narendranagar
CHAMOLI
Pauri
PAURI-GARHWAL
PITHO-RAGARH
SAHARANPUR
ALMORA
MUZAFFAR-NAGAR
BIJNOR
NAINITAL
MEERUT
MORADA-BAD
RAMPUR
PILIBHIT
BULAND-SHAHR
BAREILLY
BADAUN
LAKHIMPUR-KHERI
Lakhimpur
SHAHJA-HANPUR
ALIGARH
MATHURA
ETAH
BAHRAICH
Fategahr
HARDOI
SITAPUR
GONDA
AGRA
MAINPURI
FARRU-KHABAD
GORAK-HPUR
BASTI
LUCKNOW
BARABANKI
DEORIA
ETAWAH
FAIZABAD
UNNAO
KANPUR
RAI-BAREILLY
SULTANPUR
JALAUN
Orai
FATEHPUR
Bela
AZAMGARH
BALLIA
JHANSI
HAMIRPUR
PRATAPGAHR
JAUNPUR
GHAZIPUR
BANDA
ALLAHABAD
VARANASI
MIRZAPUR
0 50 100-MILES
0 80 160-KILO.

II

Uttar Pradesh

PAUL R. BRASS*

IN RECENT YEARS, politics in Uttar Pradesh (U. P.) has entered a state of political crisis and instability, the signs of which have appeared in the party system, in the government, and in the processes of policy making and policy implementation. The maintenance of a stable party system has been placed in doubt by persistent Congress factionalism and continued opposition fragmentation. The persistence of internal divisions in the Congress has made it increasingly difficult for the party to provide stable and effective government. Finally, the crises in the party system and in the government have made it more difficult for planners and politicians to formulate, enact, and implement policies designed to accelerate economic development. The last problem has become more serious as it has become clear that there has been little economic progress in the state since independence. This chapter will focus on the origins and development of these three crises in the state's political process—the crisis in the party system, in the government, and in the policy-making process.

THE ENVIRONMENT**

Area and Population

The area of U. P. is 113,654 square miles,[1] almost exactly that of the state of Arizona. The population, according to the 1961 census, was

* Most of the material in this chapter is entirely new. However, in order to provide information for comparison with the other studies in this volume, I have drawn in some places from material previously prepared for and published in my article "Factionalism and the Congress Party in Uttar Pradesh," *Asian Survey*, IV (September 1964), 1037-47, and *Factional Politics in an Indian State: The Congress Party in Uttar Pradesh* (Berkeley: University of California Press, 1965).

Preparation of the manuscript was made possible by grants from the Committee on South Asian Studies of the University of Chicago and the Madge Miller Research Fund of Bryn Mawr College. I am grateful to Professor W. H. Morris-Jones, who read the first version of the manuscript and made helpful suggestions for its improvement. However, I am solely responsible for all statements, opinions, or errors.

** Some portions of the material in this section have been adapted from Paul R. Brass, *Factional Politics in an Indian State: The Congress Party in Uttar Pradesh* (Berkeley: University of California Press, 1965), Chap. ii.

[1] *Census of India, 1961, Paper No. 1 of 1962: Final Population Totals*, p. 348.

close to 74 million[2]—a figure surpassed only by the largest and most populous countries of the world. In parts of the state, the land has passed beyond the point of population saturation—rural densities exceeding 1,000 per square mile in many districts—and yet the growth rate continues to increase. The decade from 1911 to 1921 saw the last population decline in this state. Since 1921, the population has increased decennially by 6.7 per cent, 13.6 per cent, 11.8 per cent, and in the last decade, by 16.7 per cent.[3]

The population of the state is overwhelmingly rural; only 12.9 per cent of the people live in urban areas.[4] The urban population is unimpressive only in relation to the total population of the state. The 1961 census lists 244 cities and towns with a combined population of approximately 9.5 million. Even excluding most of the small towns, which lack real urban characteristics, there are 17 cities with a population of more than 100,000, 7 with more than 250,000, and 3 with more than 500,000.[5]

Administratively, U. P. is divided into 54 districts, ranging in area from under 1,000 square miles to over 4,000 and in population from 100,000 to 2.7 million. Rural population densities range from 41 in the hill district of Uttar Kashi to 1,138 per square mile in Deoria district. All districts, even those with large urban centers, are predominantly rural; only Lucknow district is almost evenly balanced between urban and rural areas. Literacy varies from under 10 per cent in Badaun district to close to 40 per cent in Dehra Dun.[6]

Geographic and Historical Regions

In broad terms, there are three major geographical areas in U. P.—the northern mountains, the central plains, and the southern hills. The central plains account for close to 70 per cent of the area of the state and 90 per cent of the population. The northern mountain region, Kumaon, forms the central part of the central Himalayan range, with Himachal Pradesh on the west, Tibet on the north, and Nepal on the east. The southern hill and plateau districts—including Mirzapur on the southeastern tip of the state and Jhansi, Jalaun, Hamirpur, and Banda on the southwest—lie on the fringe of the Vindhyan mountain range which separates North India from the Deccan.

[2] *Ibid.*

[3] *Ibid.*, p. 349, and *Census of India, 1951*, Vol. II: *Uttar Pradesh*, by Rajeshwari Prasad, Pt. I-A: *Report* (Allahabad: Superintendent, Printing and Stationery, 1953), p. 25.

[4] *Census of India, 1961, Paper No. 1 of 1962*, p. 349.

[5] *Ibid.*, pp. 236-44.

[6] *Ibid.*, pp. 348-51.

The southwestern districts belong historically to the region of Bundelkhand, the greater part of which lies in Madhya Pradesh.

All of the central plains area of U. P. forms part of the Gangetic basin, but there are some important geographic differences within the area. Spate divides it into two portions—the Upper Ganges Plain, comprising all of the western and central plains districts, and the Middle Ganges Plain, made up of the eastern districts of the state and more like the plain of Bihar.[7] The Upper Ganges Plain generally has a light rainfall, is irrigated primarily by the canal systems of the Ganges and Jumna rivers, and is mainly a wheat-growing area, with sugar an important cash crop in the northwestern districts. The eastern districts of the state have a heavier rainfall and grow rice and sugar, a major cash crop in several districts.

Within the central plains area, there are five regions which have had some historical importance and sometimes separate political identities. The Doab, between the Ganges and Jumna rivers, has been the scene of warfare where empires have been founded and destroyed.[8] Three of the state's five great cities are located in the Doab, each representing a different civilization. Agra, in the northern part of the Doab, was the capital of the Mughal Empire during its greatest period; further south, Kanpur, a modern industrial city, was created by British entrepreneurs in the late nineteenth century; finally, Allahabad, at the confluence of the Ganges and the Jumna, is the oldest of the three and one of the most sacred of Hindu cities.

North of the Jumna, there are four other distinguishable historical regions—Rohilkhand, Oudh, Gorakhpur, and Banaras. Rohilkhand includes seven districts in the west—Bijnor, Moradabad, Rampur, Badaun, Bareilly, Pilibhit, and Shahjahanpur. The region takes its name from the Rohilla Afghans who rose to dominance here in the eighteenth century. Rohilkhand has the heaviest concentration of Muslims in the state; in three of the districts, the proportion of Muslims is more than a third of the total population. Rampur district remained an autonomous Muslim princely state until 1949.

Oudh, the north-central portion of the plains tract, containing twelve districts, is the area in U. P. with the longest historical identity. The borders of Oudh have fluctuated throughout its history, the twelve being only the last to be annexed by the British in 1856. Oudh was an

[7] O. H. K. Spate, *India and Pakistan: A General and Regional Geography* (2nd ed.; London: Methuen and Co., Ltd., 1957), pp. 495-521.

[8] On the importance of the Doab (particularly the "Delhi-Agra axis") in Indian history, see *ibid.*, p. 150.

important province under both the Delhi Sultanate and the Mughal Empire. The annexation of Oudh in 1856 and the land settlement which antagonized the talukdars were among the most important causes of the spread of the Mutiny of 1857. Lucknow, the last capital of Oudh, is now the capital of U. P.

Finally, on the eastern borders of the state are the regions of Gorakhpur and Banaras. The Gorakhpur region was sometimes part of Oudh, sometimes part of the old province of Bihar under the Mughal Empire. The Banaras region has more historical individuality. Jaunpur, in this region, was the seat of an independent Muslim kingdom which challenged the authority of the Delhi Sultanate in the fourteenth century. Later, the area became a part of Oudh; but by the time of the British arrival, the Raja of Banaras had become effectively independent of Oudh. The city of Banaras is the most important center of Hindu pilgrimage for all of India.

Uttar Pradesh is largely a collection of geographic and historical regions. Yet for the most part, the differences between regions are shadings rather than sharp distinctions. Moreover, the borders of the state are in hardly any respects natural. On all sides, U. P. merges into the physical and cultural environment of its neighboring states and countries. Kumaon merges into the central mountain belt, Bundelkhand into Madhya Pradesh, the eastern districts into the plain of Bihar. Even the northern boundary of the state is artificial, for there is *tarai*[9] on both sides of the Nepal border. The Jumna forms a natural boundary between U. P. and the Punjab in the northern districts of the Upper Doab, but the same river cuts the districts of Mathura and Agra in half. The desert of Rajasthan encroaches on the tip of Agra district.

Historical Background

Uttar Pradesh is essentially an artifact, put together by the British gradually, by conquest and annexation, over a period of three-quarters of a century. The British first acquired formal sovereignty in a portion of the area of present-day U. P. when the province of Banaras was ceded to them in 1775. Wellesley acquired the lower Doab, Rohilkhand, and the Gorakhpur region in 1801. The upper Doab and Bundelkhand were acquired next, in 1803, as a result of the Anglo-Maratha War. Kumaon, except for Tehri Garhwal, was added after the Anglo-Nepalese War of 1815. Other small enclaves were added in piecemeal fashion. The last major territorial acquisition in the area of U. P. was the province of Oudh, annexed in 1856. The states of

[9] The tract of marshy and jungly land between the Himalayas and the plains.

Rampur and Tehri Garhwal retained their autonomy until after independence.

The territories acquired by the British in the area of U. P. were not administered as a single unit until 1902 when, after several administrative changes, Oudh was merged with the rest of the area (then called the North-Western Provinces) into the United Provinces of Agra and Oudh. The name of the province was changed to Uttar Pradesh ("Northern Province") after independence.

A general consequence of the way in which the state was formed and administered is that regional identification with U. P. as a cultural or linguistic unit is weak. People there, particularly Hindus, tend to think of U. P. as the heart and center of Hindu India, but their identifications are generally either wholly parochial and sub-regional or supra-regional, embracing the whole of the Hindi-speaking area or Hindustan.

The Land System

The British established two entirely different systems of land revenue administration in Oudh and in the North-West Provinces. In Oudh rights of revenue collection and ownership over the land were granted primarily to a small body of talukdars, most of whom controlled areas comprising a large number of villages. Their control was both economic and political since the talukdars of Oudh retained some of the attributes of petty local chiefs. In the rest of the province, the land was settled with individual zamindars or with joint zamindari bodies[10] where the latter existed. Some of the individual zamindars farmed the revenue of hundreds of villages, as did many of the talukdars. The big zamindars also tended to wield both economic and political power. In the joint zamindari areas, economic and political control tended to be exercised over small areas, comprising a *mahal* or estate of one or a few villages. The joint proprietors generally belonged to a single caste lineage which maintained economic and political dominance over other caste groups in the villages under their control.

Altogether, there were more than two million zamindars in U. P.,

[10] In Oudh and the North-West Provinces before British rule, "the talukdar was the large-scale revenue farmer and semi-independent political chief," whereas "the zamindar was a local political power and the manager of a few villages, a single village, or a part of a village." Walter C. Neale, *Economic Change in Rural India: Land Tenure and Reform in Uttar Pradesh, 1800-1955* (New Haven: Yale University Press, 1962), p. 42. Under British rule, while this difference between the two categories of landholders remained largely valid, some of the talukdars became revenue farmers and landlords of only a few villages, while some zamindars acquired rights over many villages.

most of them collecting only a few rupees in revenue from tenants to whom their small holdings were rented. However, there were also many large zamindars and talukdars collecting tens of thousands of rupees in revenue from hundreds of villages. After independence, the entire system of intermediaries was abolished by the Congress government of U. P. under the terms of the Zamindari Abolition Act of 1951. The act has had very little effect on the condition of the former tenants and the petty zamindars, except that the tenants now pay their land revenue directly to the state and they have greater rights of ownership over the lands they cultivate. The large landlords were deprived of their rights to collect revenue, but they retained lands in their private possession and received compensation for the lands taken away from them. Consequently, although the economic and political power of the big zamindars has been reduced, many of them retain considerable influence in the countryside. The continued influence of the former big zamindars and talukdars in the countryside is an important factor in contemporary party politics in U. P.

The Economy

Despite two Five Year Plans, the economy of Uttar Pradesh is characterized by agricultural stagnation and industrial decline: although agricultural and industrial output increased in the decade of the first two plans, production failed to keep ahead of population growth.[11] In agriculture, the pressure of a dense population, cultivating the land by primitive technological methods, has produced a situation in which the small holdings of most peasants can barely sustain them and their families. U. P.'s agricultural problems are most severe in the eastern rice-growing districts of the state where population densities are over 1,000 per square mile, landholdings are very small, and few industries exist to absorb the increasing numbers of unemployed.[12] Villagers from the eastern districts are often forced to leave their homes and seek employment in the big cities of Kanpur, Calcutta, and Bombay. Those who remain live under the constant threat of famine.

The state's industrial base rests very heavily on two old and declining industries—the sugar refining industry and the textile industry. These two industries together provide 57.4 per cent of the total value of indus-

[11] Government of Uttar Pradesh, Planning Department, *Third Five Year Plan* (Lucknow, 1961), I, 5; problems of economic development in U. P. are discussed in more detail below.

[12] For a poignant account of conditions in a village in Ballia district in eastern U. P., see Kusum Nair, *Blossoms in the Dust* (London: Gerald Duckworth and Co., Ltd., 1961), Chap. x ("Poverty Unlimited"), pp. 81-87.

trial production in the state and 62.4 per cent of the employment in large-scale industries.[13] Employment in large-scale industries of all kinds in U. P. during 1962 was only 217,148. Small-scale industries provided employment for another 51,371 persons.[14]

Economic development in U. P. has failed by almost every standard of measurement to keep pace with the rest of the country. Increases in income, in agricultural production, in industrial production, and in the number of students in schools have all been much smaller than the average for the country as a whole.[15] The state's planners and government leaders are very much aware of the problems of economic development. The political problems faced by the state government in increasing the pace of economic development in U. P. will be given special attention in this chapter.

Caste and Community

Caste and religion are the two basic social divisions in U. P. During the nationalist period, the most bitter social and political conflicts in the state were those which divided Hindus and Muslims. Muslims form only 15 per cent of the population of the state, but their historical position in the province was much more important than their numbers both before and during the British period. The Muslim aristocracy remained important in British administration in the United Provinces. Some elements reminiscent of the Muslim period of dominance in North India were retained by the British. For much of the British period, Urdu in Persian script remained the only court language in the United Provinces. In addition, Muslims received more than their share of government jobs in the administrative services as a whole[16] and held dominant positions in certain departments (for example, the police) until independence. U. P. is also a center of Muslim culture for all of India. The two most prominent Muslim educational institutions in the country are in U. P.—Aligarh Muslim University in Aligarh district and Deoband in Saharanpur district.

[13] *Times of India Directory and Yearbook 1963-64* (Bombay: Bennet, Coleman and Co., Ltd.), pp. 956-57.

[14] *Ibid.*

[15] For example, national income increased by 41.6 per cent, state income by only 20.6 per cent in the decade 1950-51 to 1960-61; foodgrains production increased by 52 per cent in India, but only by 22 per cent in U. P.; the index of production increased by 94 per cent in India, by 1.7 per cent in U. P.; the number of students in schools increased by 85.5 per cent in India, by 56.6 per cent in U. P. Figures from Government of Uttar Pradesh, *Third Five Year Plan*, I, 5, Table iv.

[16] Ram Gopal, *Indian Muslims: A Political History (1858-1947)* (Bombay: Asia Publishing House, 1959), p. 83.

A tradition of Hindu-Muslim conflict, primarily over the issues of language and jobs, developed in the nineteenth century in U. P. Of particular importance was the controversy which arose in 1883 to replace Urdu in Persian script with Hindi in the Devanagari script as the official court language.[17] It was only in 1900 that Hindi acquired official status in U. P. along with Urdu. The special privileges which Muslims in fact enjoyed made the demands of Muslim leaders for separate electorates and special representation in administrative services appear unjust to some U. P. Hindus, even though Muslim grievances existed in other provinces. Conflict and tension increased during the late nineteenth and early twentieth centuries. The Aligarh Muslim University soon became the Muslim center of opposition to the main current of Indian nationalism represented by the Congress. Hindu communalism grew and found its organizational expression in the Hindu Mahasabha, and conflict became increasingly violent. Hindu-Muslim riots, often resulting in many deaths, became a common occurrence in the life of the province. The bitterness which developed between the two communities in this period has continued to be an important element in U. P. politics.

In contrast, caste conflict has been less marked than in many other provinces. Caste identifications in the state remain very largely restricted to local caste groups. State-wide caste associations exist only among the low caste (Scheduled Caste) groups and these are often paper organizations. The strongest caste movement so far has been that of the Chamars, a low-caste group of leather workers and field laborers in the countryside and of menial laborers in the cities and towns. Discontent among the Chamars, the largest caste group in the state, over their social status and economic position has been reported in a village in eastern U. P.,[18] in Kanpur City,[19] in Delhi district[20] (on the U. P. border), and in the western districts of the state.[21] Clearly, the potential for a state-wide caste movement exists among the Chamars, but so far the protests of local Chamar castes have not been coordinated in such a movement.

17 *Ibid.*, pp. 40-41.

18 Bernard S. Cohn, "The Changing Status of a Depressed Caste," in McKim Marriott (ed.), *Village India: Studies in the Little Community* (Chicago: University of Chicago Press, 1955), pp. 53-77.

19 Arthur Niehoff, *Factory Workers in India* ("Milwaukee Public Museum Publications in Anthropology," No. 5; Milwaukee: Board of Trustees, Milwaukee Public Museum, 1959), p. 68.

20 Oscar Lewis, "Peasant Culture in India and Mexico: A Comparative Analysis," in Marriott, *op.cit.*, p. 165.

21 See below, pp. 95-97.

The dominance of the traditional landowning castes continues in both economic and political life. The "dominant castes" are Brahman and Rajput in most parts of the state, but other landowning castes are important in certain areas, for example, the Jats in western U. P. and the Bhuinhars in eastern U. P. Between the dominant landowning castes and the usually landless low castes, such as the Chamars, there exist thousands of cultivating and artisan castes, most of them very small and known only in particular areas. Two large caste groups in the state are the Ahirs and Kurmis, the major cultivating castes of central and eastern U. P. Generally called "backward," they were often tenants of Rajput and Brahman zamindars before zamindari abolition; they are behind the Brahmans and Rajputs in education, and have only recently begun to show their potential importance in politics.

In the cities and towns, two important caste groups are the Kayasthas and Banias. Kayasthas are prominent in all modern professional occupations and are generally given the status of elite castes. Banias predominate in trade and commerce. Members of both caste groups have occupied prominent positions in the political life of the state.

According to the last caste census (1931), the largest caste groups in the state were, in descending order, Chamars, Brahmans, Ahirs, Rajputs, and Kurmis. These five caste groups accounted for over 40 per cent of the total population of the state. The Chamars accounted for 13 per cent of the state's population, while the Kurmis, the smallest caste group of the five, accounted for only 3.5 per cent of the population.[22] Other caste groups constituted only 2 or 3 per cent or less of the total population.

The Nationalist Period

The Congress in U. P. The Congress was the dominant force in U. P. politics throughout the nationalist period. Like its counterparts in other states and like the Indian National Congress as a whole, the U. P. Congress organization integrated diverse social and economic groups, personalities, and viewpoints. In other words, the Congress before independence was a movement rather than a political party.

In social and economic composition, the Congress represented a fusion of the professional and business classes in the cities and towns with the middle class of petty and middle zamindars and the more prosperous tenants in the countryside. Disputes arose within the Congress over the extent to which the organization should take part in agitations by the tenants against their landlords. Many prominent Congress-

[22] *Census of India, 1931,* Vol. XVIII: *United Provinces of Agra and Oudh,* by A. C. Turner, Pt. I (Allahabad: Superintendent, Printing and Stationery, 1933), p. 535.

men, including Pandit Nehru, did participate in such agitations, particularly against the talukdars of Oudh, where tenant grievances erupted in peasant agitations in the early 1920s and again in the early 1930s. However, Congressmen in U. P. generally worked through separate *kisan* (peasant) organizations on such occasions and tried to avoid identifying the Congress with a role of promoting class conflict. Even the proponents of peasant agitation stressed the integrative character of the kisan movement. Acharya Narendra Dev, the U. P. Socialist leader, advocated an alliance of kisans and "the smaller zamindars," arguing that the interests of the latter were with the kisans rather than with the big zamindars.[23]

The Congress also integrated diverse viewpoints and personalities during the nationalist period. Hindu revivalists, like Purushottamdas Tandon, worked side by side with secularists like Pandit Nehru. The Congress Socialist party also occupied a very important position in the U. P. Congress before independence. In addition to Congressmen who held more or less pronounced views on cultural and economic issues, there were many leaders in the Congress whose positions were based on their skill in politics rather than on their beliefs. That is, there were personal groups as well as ideological tendencies in the U. P. Congress. All of these groups and tendencies existed in a state of balanced tension in the period before independence. Only the common desire for independence united Congressmen; after its achievement, many found that they could no longer work together.

Political conflict in the pre-independence period. Although the Congress was an integrative movement in the pre-independence period, it did not succeed in uniting all classes and groups in the society. The big zamindars and talukdars only rarely joined the Congress. Congressmen, as has been mentioned, supported the tenants in their struggles against the landlords. The latter, in turn, supported the government against the Congress and organized political associations for the purpose. During the Non-Cooperation movement of 1921-22, the zamindars and talukdars, with the assistance of administrative officials, organized "loyalty leagues" to combat Congress influence.[24] In the 1936 elections to the provincial legislative assembly, many landlords fought against Congressmen on the platform of the National Agriculturalist party. However, largely because of internal divisions among the landlords,

[23] Acharya Narendra Dev, "Kisan Movement in the U. P.," in *Socialism and the National Revolution* (Bombay: Padma Publications, 1946), p. 58.

[24] Peter D. Reeves, "The Politics of Order: 'Anti-Non-Cooperation' in the United Provinces, 1921," *Journal of Asian Studies*, xxv, No. 2 (February 1966), 261-74.

landlord associations and parties were never very effective in U. P. politics.[25]

A more serious problem for the Congress in U. P. was its failure to integrate most Muslims into the organization during the nationalist period. The Congress did win the support of some Muslims, both secularists like Rafi Ahmad Kidwai and the more traditionalist Muslims of the Deoband School.[26] However, most modern, Western-educated Muslims, particularly those trained in the Aligarh Muslim University, remained aloof from the Congress for some time, and most of the politically minded among them eventually supported the Pakistan movement. In fact, U. P. was one of the most important areas in the mobilization of support for the Pakistan movement. The Muslim League, which had polled poorly in the 1936 elections in U. P., reorganized itself after the breakdown of Congress-League unity negotiations in 1937, and succeeded finally in winning the overwhelming support of U. P. Muslims in the 1946 elections.[27]

Thus, the U. P. Congress, despite its secularism and despite the fact that some Muslims occupied important positions in the party organization, was very largely a Hindu organization. Nor did the Congress have the support of all Hindus. The pre-independence leadership of the U. P. Congress came largely from elite castes, such as Brahmans and Kayasthas. The 1936 provincial Congress ministry was called the "all-Brahman Ministry" because all of its Hindu Cabinet ministers—there were two Muslims in the Cabinet—were Brahmans. The Congress never seriously attempted to organize the low castes, which remained largely outside the mainstream of nationalist politics in U. P.

Thus, although the U. P. Congress before independence may be characterized as an integrative movement, it must be recognized that the Congress failed to integrate many important groups in the society. In some cases, those who opposed the Congress formed other political organizations. The National Agriculturalist party (NAP) and the Muslim League were two such organizations. Neither of these organizations exists in contemporary U. P. politics, but a tradition of opposition to the Congress continues among both landlords and Muslims. Other groups in the society remained relatively unorganized during the

[25] P. D. Reeves, "Landlord Associations in U. P. and Their Role in Landlord Politics, 1920-1937," n.d. (mimeographed).

[26] A recent and important book on the Deoband School and its role in Indian politics during the nationalist period is *The Deoband School and the Demand for Pakistan* by Ziya-ul-Hasan Faruqi (Bombay: Asia Publishing House, 1963).

[27] Ram Gopal, *op.cit.*, pp. 247 ff., 304. The League won only 27 out of 66 Muslim seats in the 1936 elections, but won 54 of these seats in 1946.

nationalist movement. For the most part, the low castes did not form a significant political force in the pre-independence period and their demands were not clearly articulated.

In the development of political parties after independence, three processes have been at work, which clearly derive from the pre-independence situation. First, a process of disintegration began in the Congress, which led to the development of new political parties. Second, old political parties like the NAP and the Muslim League disappeared, with the result that their supporters had to form new political allegiances. Third, with the adoption of adult franchise and the spread of education, groups which were inarticulate and unorganized in the pre-independence period began to find leaders to voice their demands. The operation of these three forces will be examined in the next section.

THE POLITICAL PROCESS: POLITICAL PARTIES

Table 2.1 shows the relative strength of the various political parties in U. P. in the three elections since independence. A number of general features of the party system are immediately apparent from the table. First, the major parties in the 1962 election were "national" parties (Congress, Jan Sangh, PSP, Communist, Swatantra),[28] or at least had strength outside of the state (Socialist, Republican). There are no parties in the state which operate exclusively in U. P. Second, since independ-

TABLE 2.1

UTTAR PRADESH ASSEMBLY ELECTION RESULTS

	1952		1957		1962	
Party	*% of Vote*	*No. of Seats*	*% of Vote*	*No. of Seats*	*% of Vote*	*No. of Seats*
Congress	47.9	390	42.4	286	34.9	249
Jan Sangh	6.4	2	9.8	17	15.3	49
PSP[a]	17.8	20	14.5	44	11.9	38
Socialist[b]	—	—	—	—	8.5	24
Communist	0.9	0	3.8	9	5.4	14
Swatantra	—	—	—	—	4.8	15
Republican	—	—	—	—	3.8	8
Others	27.0	18	29.4	74	15.3	33
Total	100.0	430	99.9	430	99.9	430

[a] The 1952 PSP vote is the combined vote of the old Socialist party and the KMPP.
[b] In 1957, the Socialists ran as Independents and won 25 seats.
SOURCE: *Indian Affairs Record*, VII (April 1962), 117.

[28] Parties which receive 3 per cent or more of the total national parliamentary vote in a general election are given official recognition as "national" parties.

ence there has been a multi-party system with one party, the Congress, dominant. Although it has experienced a steady decline in its voting strength in the state, no opposition party by itself has acquired sufficient strength to represent a threat to the Congress. Only the Jan Sangh has experienced steady and significant growth in electoral support over the three elections. Third, a considerable proportion of the total vote in the state in every election has gone to independents and minor parties. The large independent vote affects the stability of the party system as a whole. Thus, the party system in U. P. is characterized by single-party dominance, opposition fragmentation, and continued evidence of an absence of allegiance on the part of many politicians and voters to any party.

The Congress

The growth of factional politics.[29] From a movement, the Congress after independence became a political party. The most important consequence of this transformation in the Congress party organization in U. P. has been the growth of personal and factional politics. Personal politics and factional politics existed in the U. P. Congress before independence alongside a politics of issues. However, internal quarrels and antagonisms were subordinated to the struggle for independence; since independence, personal and factional politics have come to dominate the internal affairs of the state Congress.

In the first years after independence, conflicts which had arisen earlier among Congressmen in U. P. but had been contained during the struggle for independence, developed into major internal political crises. The first crisis was the defection of some of the Socialists from the Congress in 1948. Their departure brought an end to ideological conflict over social and economic issues as a factor in U. P. Congress politics. The second crisis was the great struggle of 1950-51 over the election of Purushottamdas Tandon as the President of the Indian National Congress. Tandon, who came from U. P., was the symbol in his home state and in the country of Hindi and Hindu culture, of Hindu revivalism as opposed to secularism. The resignation of Tandon under pressure and the assumption of the presidency by Pandit Nehru in 1951[30] had an important effect on the Congress in U. P. In effect, Hindu revivalism came to be prohibited in the U. P. Congress party, and the cause of

29 The material in this section has been adapted from Paul R. Brass, "Factionalism and the Congress Party in Uttar Pradesh," *Asian Survey*, IV (September 1964), 1037-47.

30 For the details of this struggle, see Myron Weiner, *Party Politics in India: The Development of a Multi-Party System* (Princeton: Princeton University Press, 1957), Chap. IV.

Hindi and Hindu culture was left to the communal opposition parties. The departure of the Socialists in 1948 and the defeat of the Hindu revivalists in 1951 removed the political extremists from the Congress organization in U. P. A moderate consensus emerged, more or less faithful to the principles which Nehru represented, i.e., a moderate approach to questions of language and culture and a gradual, non-dogmatic approach toward "socialist" ideals. With no issues of substantial importance left to fight about, politics in the U. P. Congress more and more revolved around personalistic group or factional politics. Moreover, as the Congress demonstrated its strength in by-elections and in the general elections of 1951-52, defeated factions became less inclined to leave and more inclined to continue their struggles within the organization than to risk defeat in opposition to the Congress.

In the period of conflict and crisis in the years immediately after independence, a generational change in political leadership also took place. The leaders of the nationalist movement from U. P. either withdrew from the Congress and went into opposition or joined the central Cabinet. However, the final change of generations did not take place until 1955, when Pandit Pant left for the center. His departure marked the end of an historical period in U. P. politics. Pant had been the dominating personality in the U. P. Congress since 1937, when he became the state's first chief minister. He was an authoritative leader with great personal prestige, which enabled him to mediate and arbitrate internal conflict in the U. P. Congress. After he left, the whole tenor of U. P. politics changed. Authoritative political leadership was replaced by group and faction leadership.

Since 1955, there have been three new Congress chief ministers[31] within a shorter period of time than that of Pant's tenure of office. The internal politics of the Congress party in U. P. has revolved around a struggle to gain or control the office of chief minister by dominating the party organization. Two broad groups with a fluctuating membership have grown up inside the Congress organization; the group in power is called the Ministerialist group and the group out of power the dissident group. The Ministerialist and dissident groups have the same structure and the same ends. Both are collections of factions, coalitions of district faction leaders who seek position and power in the state government. The dissident group, the minority, becomes a majority group through gradual accretions of supporters, most of whom switch allegiances for personal reasons. The pro-government forces at any time are

[31] Dr. Sampurnanand, from 1955 to 1960; Chandra Bhan Gupta, from 1960 to 1963; and the present incumbent, Mrs. Sucheta Kripalani.

similarly composed of a number of faction leaders. Each group will have a leader, the chief minister or his heir apparent on the government side and the aspirant for the chief ministership on the dissident side. The groups are often called by the name of the leader, that is, the Gupta group or the former Sampurnanand group, after the last two chief ministers of the state. Dissident faction leaders are permitted by the looseness of Congress discipline to form alliances freely to replace the party leadership. When a dissident group succeeds in becoming the majority group, the process of factional alliance to replace the new leadership begins again. Congress factions play an important role in the political process in U. P., as well as in the internal politics of the party organization. The role of Congress factions in elections and in political conflicts with opposition parties will be described below.

Leadership and sources of support. The leadership of the Congress in U. P. comes very largely from the locally dominant rural communities in the countryside and from the middle class of professional people, merchants, and businessmen in the cities and towns. In the districts, the Congress organizations generally are led by coalitions of the "dominant castes" in the local communities—often Brahmans and Thakurs. However, electoral support for the Congress has been broader than its leadership. The Congress generally does not try to rely only upon its influence with the "dominant castes" to win elections, but seeks to form coalitions of caste and community groups. After independence it was particularly successful in winning the support of Muslims and Scheduled Castes in most districts. However, there is evidence of growing discontent with the Congress among some Scheduled Caste and Muslim voters.[32]

The Congress has benefited in the last three elections from the financial support of the industrialists and big merchants in Kanpur and the mill owners in sugar-producing districts. Another factor of great importance in maintaining the Congress organization both during and after elections is government patronage. In the countryside, villagers have come to expect favors and services from their elected representatives. Villagers want their MLAs to intercede with local administrators on their behalf, to provide jobs and scholarships for their children, and to bring schools and irrigation facilities to their villages. Congressmen are, of course, in the best position to satisfy such requests. Finally, the Congress benefits from opposition fragmentation. The Congress polled only 35 per cent of the Assembly vote in the 1962 election, but the next strongest party, the Jan Sangh, polled only 15 per cent. Opposition fragmentation

[32] See below.

makes the position of the Congress relatively secure in U. P. and allows Congressmen to compete among themselves, rather than against others, for the rewards of politics.

Table 2.1 shows a sharp overall decline of support for the Congress in U. P. in the last two general elections. Although the Congress organization in U. P. is now the weakest state unit of the Congress in India, the decline does not necessarily indicate that the party organization in the state is disintegrating. An analysis of the election results by district indicates that many of the district Congress organizations are able to arrest electoral decline and even increase their votes from election to election. Most districts, 44 of the 51,[33] do show a decline in the Congress vote from 1952 to 1962. Moreover, 25 of the 44 districts show a continuous decline from 1952 to 1957 and from 1957 to 1962. However, in 7 districts, the Congress proportion of the total vote increased over the decade, and in 15 districts, the Congress organizations increased their proportions of the total vote—albeit, in most cases only slightly—from 1957 to 1962.

In general, the Congress vote in U. P. is marked by considerable instability from election to election (see Fig. 1).[34] The instability of support for the Congress is a measure of the low degree of party loyalty in U. P. politics. Habit, tradition, and ideology, factors which tend to produce some stability in voting patterns in older democracies, are relatively unimportant in U. P. elections. In urban centers, there are educated voters who vote Congress for ideological reasons. In the rural areas, ideology is hardly a factor. Neither in urban nor in rural areas are there many people who vote Congress because of habit or family tradition. Partly, of course, the absence of habit and tradition as factors in U. P. elections reflects the relative newness of elections in the state and in the country based on universal adult franchise.[35] However, even among the firmest supporters of the Congress, such as the headmen and panchayat presidents in the villages, very little attachment to the Con-

[33] Although there are 54 administrative districts, there are only 51 electoral districts. The three new defense districts of Uttar Kashi, Chamoli, and Pithoragarh are combined by the state election office with the districts of Tehri Garhwal, Garhwal, and Almora, respectively, from which they were separated for defense purposes.

[34] The wide scattering of dots in Fig. 1 demonstrates the absence of any consistency or of any degree of evenness in the patterns of change in the Congress vote from 1957 to 1962 in the districts of U. P. The conclusion supported by the diagram (and by the analysis in the text) is that local factors primarily determine the variations in the Congress vote. Compare the diagrams (figures 8 and 9) in V. O. Key, Jr., *Southern Politics in State and Nation* (New York: Alfred A. Knopf, Inc., 1949, Vintage Book edition), pp. 50-51.

[35] The writer is indebted to F. G. Bailey, who first made these same points about voting behavior in Orissa in "Politics and Society in Contemporary Orissa," in C. H. Philips (ed.), *Politics and Society in India* (New York: Frederick A. Praeger, 1962), p. 101.

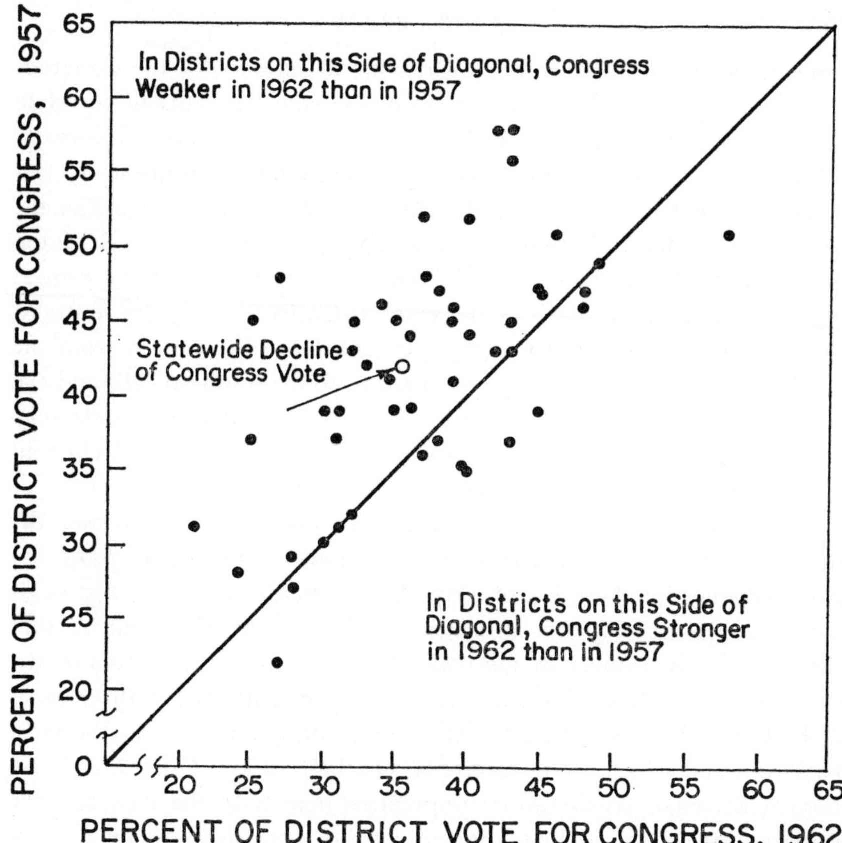

Fig. 1. Instability of Support for Congress: Relation between Percentages of District Vote Polled by Congress Candidates for Legislative Assembly in U.P. in General Elections of 1957 and 1962

gress as a party is detectable. The locally influential vote Congress because the Congress is the government and one always votes for the government; sometimes it is considered safer to vote Congress because one knows how bad the Congress is but not how bad other parties are; finally, one votes Congress because it has done something for the village or for the voter himself.

In addition to the general pattern of instability of support for the Congress, there are frequent cases of very pronounced changes in particular districts from one election to another. Internal party factionalism may transform a very strong Congress district into a very weak one. In addition, sudden changes in the allegiance of a class of voters (such as a particular caste or community) or the acquisition or defection of powerful leaders (such as ex-Rajas) who control large blocs of votes may completely transform voting patterns in a district. The important point about such sudden and often extreme fluctuations is that they indicate that factors are at work in such districts which cause a deviation from the state-wide pattern of slow decline in support for the Congress.

Because of the instability of the Congress vote, attempts to correlate support for the Congress with various environmental factors generally yield ambiguous results. For example, the regional distribution of Congress strength has shifted over the three general elections (see Fig. 2). In the first general elections, the Congress was strongest in all of the northwestern districts, in most of Kumaon, and in parts of the central plains area. It was weakest in the eastern districts and in the southern hills. By 1962 the areas of Congress strength had shifted away from the northwestern districts and the central plains to the southern hills and the eastern districts. The shift in Congress strength is, of course, only relative since it has taken place simultaneously with an overall decline in support for the Congress in the state as a whole.

Nevertheless, the regional distribution of Congress strength and the shift in areas of support over the decade indicate that there is no apparent connection between poverty and opposition to the Congress. If anything, the distribution indicates exactly the opposite, that is, that the Congress is stronger in the poorer and more backward areas of the state. Kumaon, Bundelkhand, and the eastern districts are three areas of U. P. which have been selected by the state government as the most backward and which are to receive special help in the Third Plan.[36] Although Kumaon has the lowest population density in the state and the eastern districts the highest, the problems of both areas relate to pressure on the cultivable land—a result of overpopulation in the eastern districts and a relative lack of cultivable land in Kumaon. In Bundelkhand, where population densities are also very low, agricultural productivity suffers from a severe shortage of irrigation facilities.

Thus, the wide differences in the characteristics of the three regions in which the Congress has its strength, combined with the instability of voting patterns, makes it difficult to find state-wide patterns of support for or opposition to the Congress. The Congress, as has been noted above, tends to get its support from the dominant peasant proprietary body in each district. In addition, it seeks to build caste coalitions which tend to vary not only from district to district but from constituency to constituency. The Congress has somewhat greater strength in the few urban constituencies in U. P. than in the rural constituencies and is stronger in the Scheduled Caste constituencies than in the general constituencies. However, there is no apparent correlation between the vote for Congress and such factors as rural density, literacy, or the proportion of various ethnic groups in each district. Thus, the decline of the

[36] Government of Uttar Pradesh, *Third Five Year Plan*, I, 47-61.

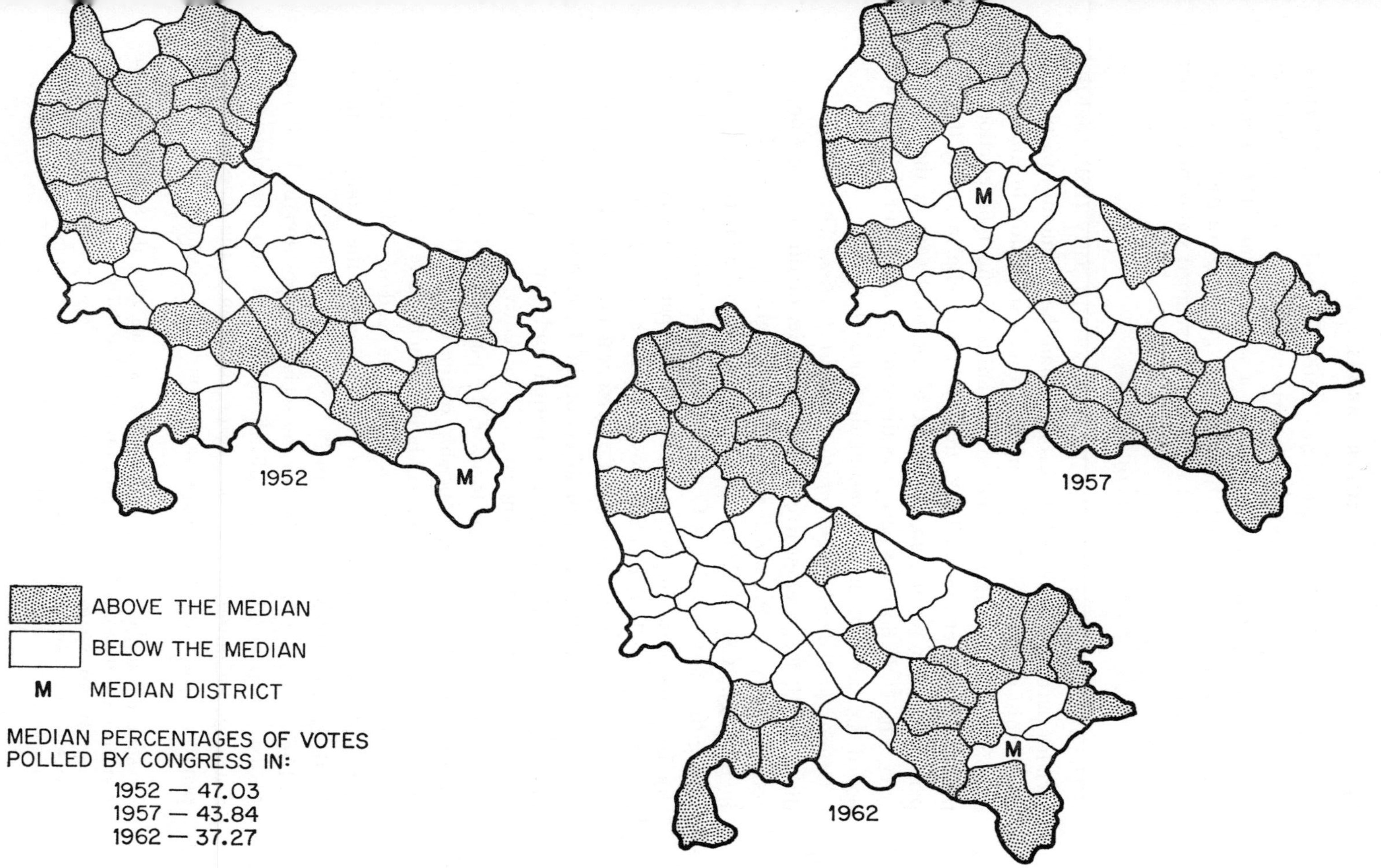

Fig. 2. Distribution of Support for Congress in U. P. Elections for Legislative Assembly

Congress is not clearly related to any state-wide environmental factors. Rather, it is the product of internal party factionalism in both the local and state Congress organizations and of a series of unrelated or loosely related changes in individual districts or in groups of districts. In some areas, in fact, the vote for the Congress has remained stable or has even increased.

Leftist Parties

The socialist parties in U. P.—the Praja Socialist party (PSP) and the Socialist party (SP)—have been stronger than the Communist party. The Communist party in U. P. is among the weakest state units in India. The combined vote of the PSP and the Socialists in the 1962 election was proportionately greater in U. P. than anywhere else in India, the two parties together polling 20.4 per cent of the total vote in the state in 1962. The U. P. Socialist party was the strongest state unit in India and polled 8.5 per cent of the vote in the 1962 elections.[37]

Origins and development of the socialist parties. The socialist tradition in U. P., as elsewhere in India, has its origins in the Congress Socialist party (CSP), which was formed as a group within the Congress in 1934. The CSP in U. P. was always very strong, and its leaders were among the most prominent Congressmen in the state.[38] Acharya Narendra Dev, the most important leader of the party in U. P. was a respected Congress leader in the province, with a large personal following. When the decision to leave the Congress was taken by the national executive of the CSP in 1948, members of the U. P. unit occupied important positions in the party organization and some had been offered offices in the Congress government. Consequently, most members of the CSP in U. P. were reluctant to leave the party. It is estimated that less than 20 per cent of the membership of the CSP in U. P. left the Congress in 1948.[39] In the U. P. legislature, where there were thirty-five to forty CSP MLAs, only twelve followed the lead of Acharya Narendra Dev and resigned their seats to contest against the Congress in by-elections. All twelve were defeated.

The second major addition to the socialist opposition in U. P. came from a group of followers of Rafi Ahmad Kidwai who were defeated in a struggle for power in the Congress organization in the years after independence. In December 1949 twenty-one Congressmen, led by Tri-

37 Since the abortive merger with the PSP in June 1964, the Socialist party has been known as the Samyukta Socialist party (SSP). See below.

38 See Weiner, *op.cit.*, p. 61; and Sampurnanand, *Memories and Reflections* (Bombay: Asia Publishing House, 1962), p. 82.

39 Interview in Lucknow on October 12, 1961.

loki Singh, crossed the floor of the house. These twenty-one MLAs formed a Jan Congress, which merged with Acharya Kripalani's Kisan Mazdoor Praja party (KMPP) in June 1951. The Socialist party and the KMPP fought the elections separately in 1952 but merged into the PSP after the election. In 1955 the Lohia split occurred, again creating two socialist parties in the state and in the country—the PSP and the Socialist party. The split was most serious in U. P., where Lohia's followers controlled the Executive Committee of the PSP.[40]

The socialist parties, like the Congress, have been afflicted with factionalism and with the struggles of individual leaders for personal prestige. The leadership of both the socialist parties originally came out of the Congress, partly because of ideological differences but also because of factional quarrels within the Congress. The state leaders of the socialist parties took with them out of the Congress party local leaders in the districts who had been defeated in factional conflicts for control of the district Congress organizations. The result is that neither socialist party has strong district organizations throughout the state. Both parties are essentially coalitions of local politicians in the districts, politicians who have influence in a very restricted area—enough to win an Assembly election perhaps, but not enough to build a district-wide organization. Moreover, throughout the post-independence period, there has been a constant movement of political leaders from the Congress to the PSP, from the PSP to the Socialist party, and very often from one of the socialist parties back to the Congress. Both the socialist parties were weakened in recent years by the return of many important district leaders to the Congress. Since 1950, there has been no major defection from the Congress to the socialist parties.

Socialist unity. Socialist politics in U. P. and in the country and the political balance between the two socialist parties in U. P. were fundamentally altered in the period between December 1962 and January 1965. In December 1962, a major attempt at the reunification of the two socialist parties in India was begun with the merger of the PSP and the Socialist party in the U. P. Assembly into the United Socialist party. The merger of the two parties in the U. P. Assembly proved to be the beginning of a long process of reunification of the two parties throughout the country, culminating in the merger of the PSP and the Socialist party at the all-India level in June 1964 into the Samyukta (United) Socialist party (SSP). The merger lasted only seven months until January

[40] On the role of the U. P. Executive Committee of the PSP in the split, see Hari Kishore Singh, *A History of the Praja Socialist Party* (Lucknow: Narendra Prakashan, 1959), pp. 211-15.

1965 when the PSP re-established its separate existence. In U. P., the PSP was seriously weakened by these events, for those who opposed unity with the Lohia Socialists joined the Congress in June 1964 and those who favored unity remained in the new SSP.

It is not possible to examine here all the events leading to the reunification and subsequent split of the two socialist parties in the country as a whole. However, an examination of the course of events in U. P. will provide some insights into the nature of the political process in the state. The decline in PSP strength from 1957 to 1962 (see Table 2.1), the stagnant condition of the Socialist party in the state, and the emergence of the Jan Sangh as the largest opposition party in the new Assembly had led to thoughts of a fresh attempt at the merger of socialist forces in U. P. after the 1962 election. It was reported in the press as early as March of 1962 that merger negotiations were taking place between the leaders of the PSP and the Socialist party in the U. P. Assembly.[41] The demand for merger came from many in the rank and file of both parties and from some of the leaders of the PSP. Most of the state and national leaders of the Socialist party, however, remained hostile to the idea of merger with the PSP except on terms set by the Socialist party. Consequently, when the merger of the two parties in the U. P. Assembly was announced in December 1962,[42] it came as a surprise to the national leadership of both parties. The merger was welcomed at first by the state and national leadership of the PSP, but was greeted with shock and anger by the national leaders and by some state leaders of the Socialist party.

There was some logic in the move for unity originating in U. P., but fortuitous circumstances were also involved. Both parties had been disappointed by the election results in U. P. in which only the Jan Sangh had benefited from the decline of Congress strength. Second, the PSP and the Socialist party were more closely balanced in strength in U. P. than elsewhere. Third, a merger in the U. P. Assembly promised the immediate benefit of recognition, in place of the Jan Sangh, as the main Opposition in the Assembly. These three factors were present as a background to the merger negotiations, but the merger itself took place suddenly after an unexpected change in the leadership of the PSP in the Assembly. Genda Singh, a senior PSP MLA and the leader of the party in the Assembly, had resigned his leadership of the party early in December after an agreement he had made with government leaders was disapproved by the rank and file.[43] Genda Singh was replaced as leader

41 *National Herald,* March 4, 1962.

42 *Ibid.,* December 14, 1962.

43 See below, pp. 106-107.

by a younger man who had once been a follower of Lohia. The merger of the PSP and the Socialist party in the Assembly took place a week after this change of leadership in the PSP. The terms of the merger were the acceptance by the PSP legislators of the Socialist Manifesto of 1962, but not the constitution, basic principles, and discipline of the Socialist party.

Although the national leadership of the Socialist party had been consistently opposed to merger with the PSP except on terms of a complete acceptance by the PSP of the Socialist party program and discipline, the announcement of the creation of the United Socialist party in the U. P. Assembly presented Lohia and his closest associates with a *fait accompli*. The U. P. merger was a major topic of debate at the annual conference of the Socialist party in Bharatpur held at the end of December 1962. Strong opposition to the merger was expressed at the conference, but a resolution was nevertheless passed accepting (but not approving) the formation of the United Socialist party and authorizing further steps toward socialist unity.[44]

Contradictory trends soon developed in U. P. Socialist politics, with divisions developing *within* both parties on the question of unification. Doctrinally, the lines of division were over Socialist policy on language (immediate replacement of English) and caste (60 per cent reservation of seats in government and legislatures for "backward castes"). There were also disputes over the Socialist policy of alliance with the Jan Sangh and Communists in opposition to the Congress and on the use of militant tactics by the Socialists to oppose the Congress. The merger in the U. P. Assembly soon broke up on the latter issue. In March 1963, the Socialist legislators engaged in disruptive tactics in the U. P. Assembly in opposition to certain rulings by the Speaker of the House. Twenty-two members of the United Socialist party were expelled and suspended from the House. However, only two PSP legislators joined in the disorderly scenes. Ugra Sen, the leader of the United Socialist party, thereupon announced the dissolution of the merger, on the grounds that the PSP members had refused to join in a struggle with the Socialist party members. Ugra Sen's action was opposed by most PSP legislators and some of the Socialists as well. Consequently, the leadership of the United Socialist party was reconstituted and retained a separate existence in the Assembly. There were now two socialist groups in the Assembly again, a Socialist group under Ugra Sen and a United Socialist party composed of most of the old PSP members and some of the old Socialist party legislators.

[44] The text of the resolution may be found in the *Indian Affairs Record*, IX, No. 1 (January 1963), 47.

Despite the new split in the U. P. Assembly, considerable support continued to be expressed among U. P. socialists for further efforts at unification. Socialist unity conferences were held in several districts. In June 1963, a major conference of socialists of both parties was held in Lucknow at which an appeal was made to the leadership of both the PSP and the Socialist party "to take note of the mass urge for the unity of the socialist forces in the country."[45] These unity moves were soon complicated, however, by the development of an opposite trend among PSP members for unity with the Congress rather than with the Socialist party. The move among some PSP members to join the Congress received impetus with the acceptance by Asoka Mehta, the national PSP leader, of the position of Deputy Chairman of the Planning Commission in September 1963, an act which was followed by his forced resignation from the party and his formal joining of the Congress in June 1964. The PSP was now split three ways, with some members favoring unity with the Socialists, some favoring joining forces with the Congress, and a hard core favoring the continued existence of the PSP as a party of democratic socialism in opposition to the Congress.

In U. P., the party did in fact split three ways. In June 1964, Genda Singh and several other PSP legislators joined the Congress. Genda Singh himself was made Minister of Agriculture, replacing a "dissident" member of the U. P. government in that position. In the same month, the Samyukta Socialist party was formed. When the PSP reestablished itself in January 1965, it was reported that many former PSP members in U. P. chose to remain in the SSP.

The merger and subsequent split of the two socialist parties demonstrate some important features of the party system in U. P. They demonstrate first the fluidity of the system. The movements of socialist politicians in these two years represented a major readjustment in the party system, but the pattern itself of movement of politicians from party to party is a persistent feature of the party system. The adoption by the Congress in 1964 at Bhubaneshwar of a commitment to "democratic socialism" has facilitated such movements from a doctrinal point of view. However, there is much pursuance of personal political advancement beneath the doctrinal cloaks. The second point which these party maneuvers demonstrate is the intimate connection between conflict in the dominant party and conflict within and among opposition parties. Just as opposition parties provide a haven for discontented Congress politicians, so the Congress in turn provides a haven for dissatisfied opposition politicians. Faction leaders in the Congress are eager to recruit sup-

45 *National Herald,* June 3, 1963.

porters wherever they can be found. Third, the Congress clearly has greater strength than its low popular vote would indicate because of its absorptive capacity. If one wishes, therefore, to gauge the strength of the Congress, it is not sufficient to examine merely the party membership figures or the popular vote. One must also consider the continued ability of the Congress to integrate and absorb new members directly from the ranks of the opposition, which by the same token must be considered much weaker than it appears in election figures.

Communist party. The Communist party has made no significant progress in U. P. since independence. Although its share of the popular vote in the state has increased from 0.9 per cent in 1952 to 5.4 per cent in 1962, the increase mainly reflects the larger number of candidates which the party ran in the last election. Divisions within the Communist party in U. P. on the Chinese issue have not been significant. The overwhelming majority of the U. P. Communists belong to the Dange wing of the party, which is now the CPI (Right). The U. P. leadership responded to the Chinese aggression of October 1962 with a quick and unequivocal condemnation of the Chinese.[46] A few U. P. Communists, however, have been accused of pro-Chinese sympathies. The U. P. government arrested twenty-three allegedly pro-Chinese Communists after the Chinese invasion.[47] Even though most U. P. Communists publicly condemned the Chinese invasion, the party has been damaged in the public mind by the Chinese action. One Communist in Kanpur claimed that the party had been set back fifteen years by the Chinese invasion. However, except in Kanpur and two eastern districts, the party had not made much progress in the state in the past fifteen years.

Party programs. The programs of the three leftist parties have been addressed to specific policy issues which have developed as a result of Congress action or inaction. The 1962 election manifesto of the PSP in U. P. called for the granting of *bhumidhari* rights of land ownership to *sirdars* without payment of ten times their land revenue as required by the Zamindari Abolition Act of 1951,[48] for a land ceiling of twenty acres (as opposed to the forty-acre ceiling established by the Congress

[46] *Ibid.*, October 23, 1962.

[47] *Ibid.*, February 14, 1962.

[48] The Zamindari Abolition Act created two classes of landholders in U. P. One class, called *bhumidhars*, acquired full rights of ownership over lands they cultivated and a 50 per cent reduction in land revenue by paying the state government a fee ten times their current annual land revenue. The second class, called *sirdars*, essentially became state tenants and continued to pay land revenue at the old rate. The state government required the payment of a fee for the right to become a *bhumidhar* in order to raise money to compensate the former zamindars. However, most tenants were unwilling or unable to make the payment and remained *sirdars*.

government in 1960), for the nationalization of the sugar and power industries, for encouragement of small and medium industries and their protection against competition from large industries, and for the protection and encouragement of Urdu.[49] The Socialist party has also expressed some specific demands—abolition of land revenue for peasants who cultivate uneconomic holdings, annulment of "fictitious" partitions of land carried out by large landholders to avoid loss of land under the Land Ceilings Act, fixing of prices of manufactured goods within a narrow range, and the like. The Socialist party has distinguished itself by its approach to two other issues. On the question of language, the party has militantly opposed the official use of English in government, in the courts, and in the schools. The language issue, however, is not very significant in U. P. where most official transactions already are carried on in Hindi. A second distinctive aspect of the Socialist party program has been its demand for the reservation of 60 per cent of positions in administrative services and seats in the legislatures to the "backward castes." In some parts of U. P., the Socialist party made a direct appeal to the "backward castes"—particularly the Ahirs and Kurmis—in the 1962 election. In some of the districts, the Socialist party tried to implement the 60 per cent policy for its own party positions and gave prominent posts in the party to members of these middle castes. The Communist party in U. P. has been less active and less articulate in making demands and framing policies than the PSP and the Socialist party. Occasionally, it has joined with other opposition parties in agitation against Congress policies, but the Communists have been more inclined to support the Congress on many issues than have either the PSP or the Socialists.

Party tactics. All of the leftist parties consider *satyagrahas* or nonviolent agitations and demonstrations to be not only a legitimate way of expressing demands and mobilizing public opinion, but also a fundamental right.[50] The Socialist party has been the most militant in this respect. Two large-scale civil disobedience movements were carried out by the Socialist party in U. P. in 1957 and in 1960. In the 1957 satyagraha, carried on over the issues of stopping the use of English and removing public statues and monuments to British figures, approximately 5,000 party members were arrested.[51] In the 1960 satyagraha, somewhat over a thousand party members were arrested. Neither of these agitations posed a serious threat to law and order in U. P. In addition to agitations

[49] *National Herald*, January 19, 1962.

[50] See, for example, statements by PSP leaders and others in *ibid.*, June 25, 1962.

[51] *Pioneer*, September 25, 1957.

and demonstrations, the Socialist party legislators in the U. P. Assembly have sought to disrupt the proceedings of the House by defying the chair and then refusing to leave unless carried out by the sergeant at arms. The Socialists, sometimes with the aid of other opposition parties and independents, effectively blocked normal parliamentary procedures throughout most of the winter session of 1963. Disorder in the House reached its peak in March when a full day was devoted to the suspension and expulsion of twenty-two members of the Socialist party; fifteen members had to be carried out.[52]

The PSP legislators and party members have been less disrespectful toward parliamentary procedures than the Socialist legislators. One of the first major disagreements between the two parties after their merger in December 1962 occurred when PSP members refused to participate in the disorders in the Assembly in March 1963. However, the PSP leaders have also engaged in satyagrahas, demonstrations, and fasts on specific issues. In Deoria district, Genda Singh, formerly a prominent PSP leader, was identified with various agitations for increases in the price of sugar cane paid to cane growers. In the past he also led agitations on the issue of starvation deaths in the eastern districts and in 1958 engaged in a fast on this question. The Communists too have sometimes sponsored peasant agitations in the eastern districts of the state.

Agitations, demonstrations, and fasts sometimes lead to concessions by the Congress government on specific issues. When the government finds it impossible to satisfy specific grievances, it usually offers the demonstrators or fasters the face-saving concession of appointing an inquiry commission. The government thus indirectly encourages future demonstrations. Agitations, demonstrations, civil disobedience movements, and fasts of prominent leaders must be considered a permanent part of the political process in U. P., as in other Indian states.

Leadership and electoral support. A major weakness of the left parties is that their leadership and sources of support come partly from the same elements which support the Congress party. The similarities between the left parties and the Congress are understandable since all the left parties grew out of the Congress. For the most part, the party offices of the PSP, the Socialist party, and the Communist party in U. P. have been run by Western-educated intellectuals, while the MLAs have come from middle peasant or petty zamindar backgrounds.

However, both the PSP and the Socialist MLAs have attempted to organize new sources of support. One PSP MLA from Deoria district in eastern U. P. remarked that most government services are

[52] *National Herald,* March 23, 1963.

> given to friends of the Congress, to the headman and important people of the village. Thus, we have to galvanize the support of those who are below the *chaudhuri* [headman]. The traditional vested interests in the villages exploit the landless laborers and the common villagers. If the *chaudhuri* is a good man, we become weak. If he is a bad man, we thrive because of his evil and generally they are bad men.[53]

In the same district, the Socialist party in the 1962 elections sought the support of the middle agricultural castes, such as the Ahirs. These middle castes were generally tenants of Brahman or Rajput zamindars in their villages, but became landowners after zamindari abolition. The Socialist candidates in the district attempted to exploit this economic difference and to organize support from these middle castes that oppose the ex-zamindars in the villages.

The leftist parties have had some success in identifying themselves with peasant discontent. For the most part, the PSP, the Socialist, and the Communist MLAs were elected from high density districts (see Fig. 3) where landholdings are very small and where there have been frequent agitations on various economic issues. The backbone of support for the parties of the left is in the eight eastern districts of Deoria, Gorakhpur, Ballia, Azamgarh, Ghazipur, Jaunpur, and Allahabad. In most of these districts, densities are over 1,000 persons per square mile, landholdings are usually an acre or half an acre per person, the resource base is very narrow, and flood and famine conditions are recurrent. Forty of the seventy-six left party MLAs were elected from these eight districts. The Communist party has its only significant rural strength here in the two districts of Azamgarh and Ghazipur, which returned eight of the fourteen Communist MLAs in the 1962 general elections.

Jan Sangh and Swatantra

The parties of the "right" in U. P. politics—Jan Sangh, Hindu Mahasabha, and Swatantra—polled a combined popular vote of over 21 per cent and won 66 seats in the Assembly in the 1962 general elections. The Hindu Mahasabha polled only a little over 1 per cent of the vote and won only 2 seats. The Jan Sangh emerged after the 1962 election as the largest opposition party in the state, polling more than 15 per cent of the vote and winning 49 seats in the Assembly. The U. P. Jan Sangh is the second strongest state unit in India after the Madhya Pradesh party. Swatantra had very limited success in U. P., polling less than 5 per cent of the vote and winning 15 seats in the Assembly.

[53] Interview in Lucknow on May 18, 1962.

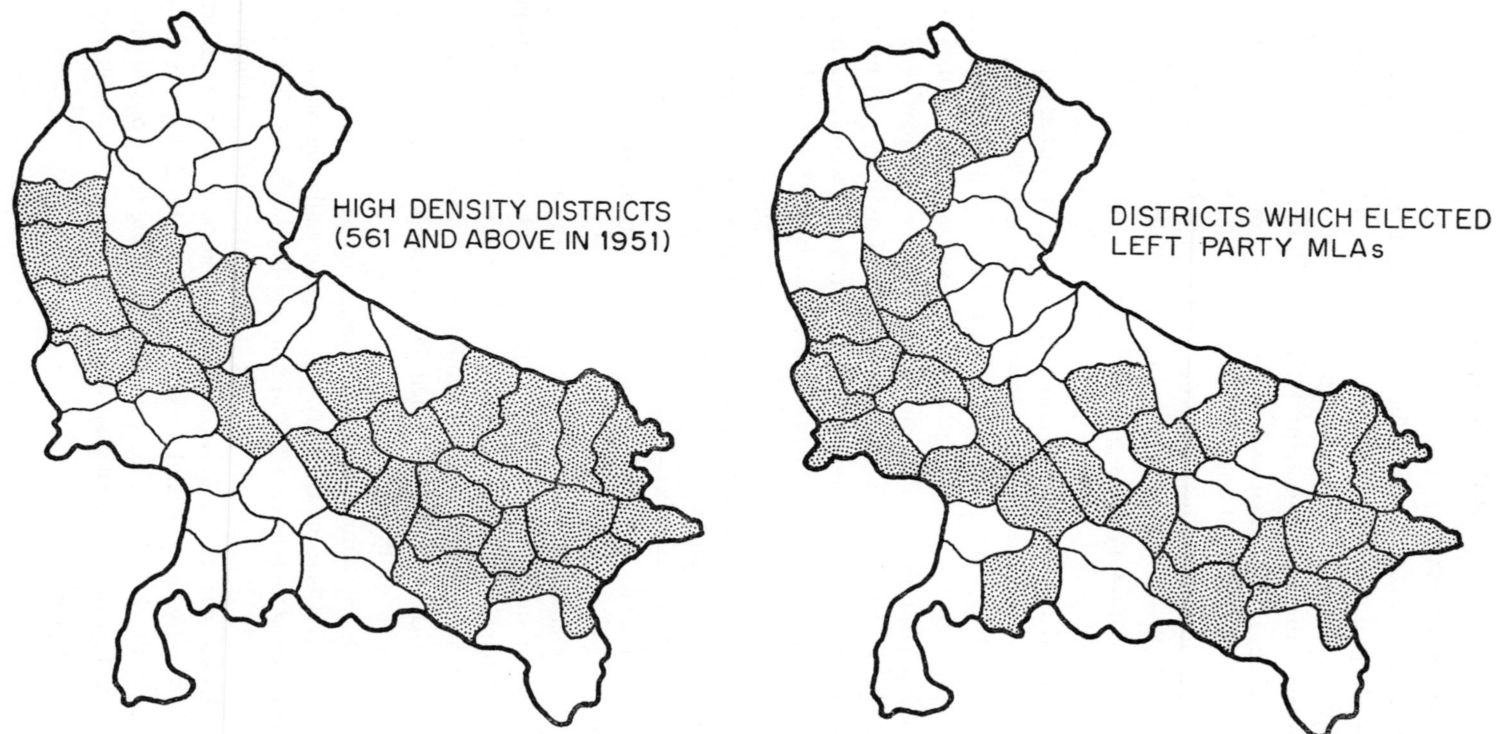

Fig. 3. High Rural Density and Support for Left Parties: U.P. Districts with Highest Rural Densities and Districts which Elected PSP, Socialist, or Communist MLAs, 1962 General Elections

Origin and development of the Jan Sangh. The Jan Sangh is one of three Hindu communal parties which have fought the post-independence general elections. The other two, the Hindu Mahasabha and the Ram Rajya Parishad, have faded into insignificance and left the Jan Sangh alone as the only important Hindu political party in India. A major reason for the survival and success of the Jan Sangh, at a time when other Hindu political parties have declined, is the support which the Jan Sangh has always had from the Rashtriya Swayamsevak Sangh (RSS). The RSS was originally a non-political youth organization, organized on semi-military lines and maintaining rigid discipline.[54] It became active politically in the period between 1947 and 1951 when its workers provided assistance to Hindu refugees from Pakistan and "defended" Hindus in the communal riots of this period. The Jan Sangh was formed by RSS leaders in 1951 to fight the general elections. The RSS maintains a continuing interest in the Jan Sangh; RSS members are in controlling positions in both the legislatures and the party organization. The RSS does not tolerate factionalism either in its own organization or in the Jan Sangh. Members of the Jan Sangh who break party discipline are quickly and permanently expelled from the organization.

The Jan Sangh differs from the other major opposition parties in U. P. in that it did not develop out of the Congress. Many Jan Sangh leaders did not participate in the Congress movements for independence. Most Jan Sangh members have joined the party because they feel that Congress policies since independence have threatened Hindu cultural and religious values.

The development of the Jan Sangh in U. P. since its formation in 1951 has been one of steady growth. The party has increased its percentage vote in the general elections from 6.4 per cent in 1952 to 15 per cent in 1962 and its representation in the Assembly from 2 to 49 members. The number of districts which have elected Jan Sangh MLAs has increased from 2 in 1952 to 22 in 1962.

Swatantra. The Swatantra party was formed on an all-India basis in 1959. It acquired a base in U. P. by winning the affiliation of some ex-Congressmen of conservative views and a few big landlords. The Swatantra party in U. P., like the socialist parties, essentially has brought together in loose coalition a group of district leaders who have left the Congress generally for personal reasons related to local disputes. Swatantra, unlike the Jan Sangh, does not have a strong party organization in the state. Ten of its fifteen Assembly seats in 1962 were won from

[54] Weiner, *op.cit.*, p. 78.

the three adjacent districts of Bahraich, Basti, and Gonda, where the party was dependent upon landlord support.[55]

Party programs. Both the Jan Sangh and Swatantra tend to be conservative on economic issues. In the 1962 election campaigns, both parties strongly opposed government schemes for cooperative farming. Both parties are against state control over most aspects of the country's economic life. However, the two parties are divided by their attitudes toward traditional Hindu society and toward non-Hindus. The Jan Sangh in the past has been concerned primarily with communal and cultural issues whereas Swatantra has been concerned primarily with economic issues. Many Swatantra party members consider the Jan Sangh a communal party, whereas the Jan Sanghis tend to consider Swatantra a party composed merely of right-wing Congressmen. Many Swatantra party leaders are open admirers of Western institutions and Western ways, whereas many Jan Sanghis favor the maintenance of traditional Hindu institutions such as the joint family, the caste system, and traditional Hindu law. A major demand of the Jan Sangh is for the replacement of English, wherever it is still used officially both in U. P. and at the center, by Hindi. The Jan Sangh favors a Sanskritized Hindi, as free as possible of words of Persian origin.

What most prevents cooperation between the Jan Sangh and Swatantra or other parties is the feeling that the Jan Sangh is anti-Muslim. The Jan Sangh has been extremely critical of the role which Muslims have played in Indian life. In U. P., for example, the Jan Sangh has criticized the functioning of the Aligarh Muslim University and has demanded the affiliation of the three predominantly Hindu colleges of Aligarh town with the University.[56] It has been alleged that the Jan Sangh participated in the Hindu-Muslim riots of October 1961 in Aligarh.[57] In the election campaigns, it is generally believed that, although Jan Sangh candidates publicly espouse Hindu-Muslim unity, their workers appeal to anti-Muslim sentiments in private.[58]

[55] For an analysis of Swatantra organization in Gonda district, see Paul R. Brass, *Factional Politics in an Indian State: The Congress Party in Uttar Pradesh* (Berkeley: University of California Press, 1965), Chap. iv.

[56] See the *Organiser*, XVI, No. 47 (July 8, 1963), 8; XVII, No. 6 (September 16, 1963), 6; XVII, No. 8 (September 30, 1963), 7. The affiliation of the three Hindu colleges with the University would make it a Hindu-majority institution. At present, the majority of students and faculty members of Aligarh Muslim University are Muslims.

[57] *National Herald*, November 15, 1961.

[58] See, for example, Harold A. Gould's report on the 1962 election campaign in Faizabad constituency in U. P. in "Traditionalism and Modernism in U. P.: Faizabad Constituency," *Economic Weekly*, XIV, No. 33 (August 18, 1962), 1347.

There is evidence of some ambiguity of attitudes among Jan Sangh members in the districts on the question of the role of Muslims in contemporary Indian society. One successful Jan Sangh candidate for the Assembly in 1962 from Gonda district claimed that he appealed to and won the support of Muslims, who constituted about 40 per cent of the population of his constituency. Yet he has been a member of the RSS since 1951; he feels that Hindus should not show weakness before Muslims; and he distrusts the loyalty of Muslims to India.[59] Many Jan Sanghis are concerned more with protecting their view of Hindu culture against perceived threats from the Congress than with attacking Muslims. Increasingly, the Jan Sangh has given its attention to economic issues. Participation in electoral politics has forced the Jan Sangh to devote attention to the demands and needs of peasants and other villagers, who are often less concerned with Hindu culture and the loyalties of Muslims than with the price of sugar cane, relief loans for flood damages, and securing intervention with administrative officials.

The Jan Sangh has also adopted a militant anti-Communist posture since the Chinese invasion of 1962. In March 1963, Jan Sangh and RSS members played a leading role in the organization of a public exhibition, called "Maa-ki-Pukar" ("Call of the Mother"), in a Lucknow park. The exhibition was designed to arouse patriotic feeling against the Chinese, but it created a public furor because many Congressmen and others felt that Pandit Nehru had been ridiculed and defamed in posters for his handling of the Sino-Indian dispute.[60]

Party tactics. The Jan Sangh, like the leftist parties, engages in agitations and demonstrations to oppose government measures. For example, in October 1962 Jan Sangh party members picketed the Council House of the state government in protest against government tax proposals. Nearly 400 Jan Sangh members were arrested during the month for obstructing the entrance of legislators to the chamber.[61] The Jan Sangh has not, however, launched any major civil disobedience movements in the state. On the whole, it appears less inclined toward agitational methods than the socialist parties and more inclined toward propaganda and education. Jan Sangh and RSS members are active in educational activities of all sorts. Many RSS members teach in schools and some have founded educational institutions. The Jan Sangh is attempting to establish in U. P. a network of private schools, controlled

59 Interview in Gonda on August 14, 1962.

60 *National Herald,* March 3, 4, 5, 1963.

61 *Ibid.,* October 6, 1962.

by party members and sympathizers, where the values which the party supports may be taught.

Leadership and electoral support. The leadership and the main sources of support of the Jan Sangh in U. P. come largely from the merchants, shopkeepers, and businessmen in the towns and from the big landlords in the countryside. Although the party does have support among Hindu businessmen in the towns, almost all of its successes in the 1962 election in U. P. were in rural constituencies. Of the forty-nine seats won by the Jan Sangh in 1962, only one constituency was wholly urban, two were partly urban, and the rest were rural constituencies. Swatantra is even more dependent upon rural, landlord support than the Jan Sangh and has little strength in the towns. Swatantra had no successes in urban or semi-urban constituencies in the 1962 elections.

Most of the MLAs elected on Jan Sangh and Swatantra tickets in 1962 in U. P. came from districts where the great estates were located (see Fig. 4). Jan Sangh and Swatantra successes were greatest in Oudh, where the talukdars have traditionally dominated in the rural economy and in local politics. Ten Oudh districts returned 32 of the 64 Jan Sangh and Swatantra MLAs elected in U. P. in 1962.

In post-independence politics, all the political parties in U. P. have tried to win the support of individual ex-zamindars and talukdars and have offered the former landlords party tickets to contest the general elections. Although it has been over a decade since the abolition of the zamindari system in U. P., most of the ex-zamindars retain considerable prestige in their former estates. Many of the ex-zamindars have used their traditional influence to build political bases for themselves. The conservative economic policies of the Jan Sangh and Swatantra have an appeal to the big landlords. Moreover, Jan Sangh and Swatantra probably benefited from the discontent among landlords who have felt threatened by the new Land Ceilings Act passed in U. P. in 1960. The Land Ceilings Act is, in some respects, a greater threat to the landlords than zamindari abolition. Zamindari abolition deprived the zamindars of their revenue, but the Land Ceilings Act threatened to deprive them of their personal landholdings.

Some ex-zamindars and talukdars have occupied important positions in both Jan Sangh and Swatantra. The Raja of Jaunpur was for a while after the 1962 election the leader of the Jan Sangh in the Assembly and was elected President of the U. P. Jan Sangh in 1963.[62] The first leader of the Swatantra party in the U. P. Assembly was the Raja of Mankapur, a former talukdar of Gonda district.

62 *Organiser,* XVI, No. 26 (February 4, 1963), 14.

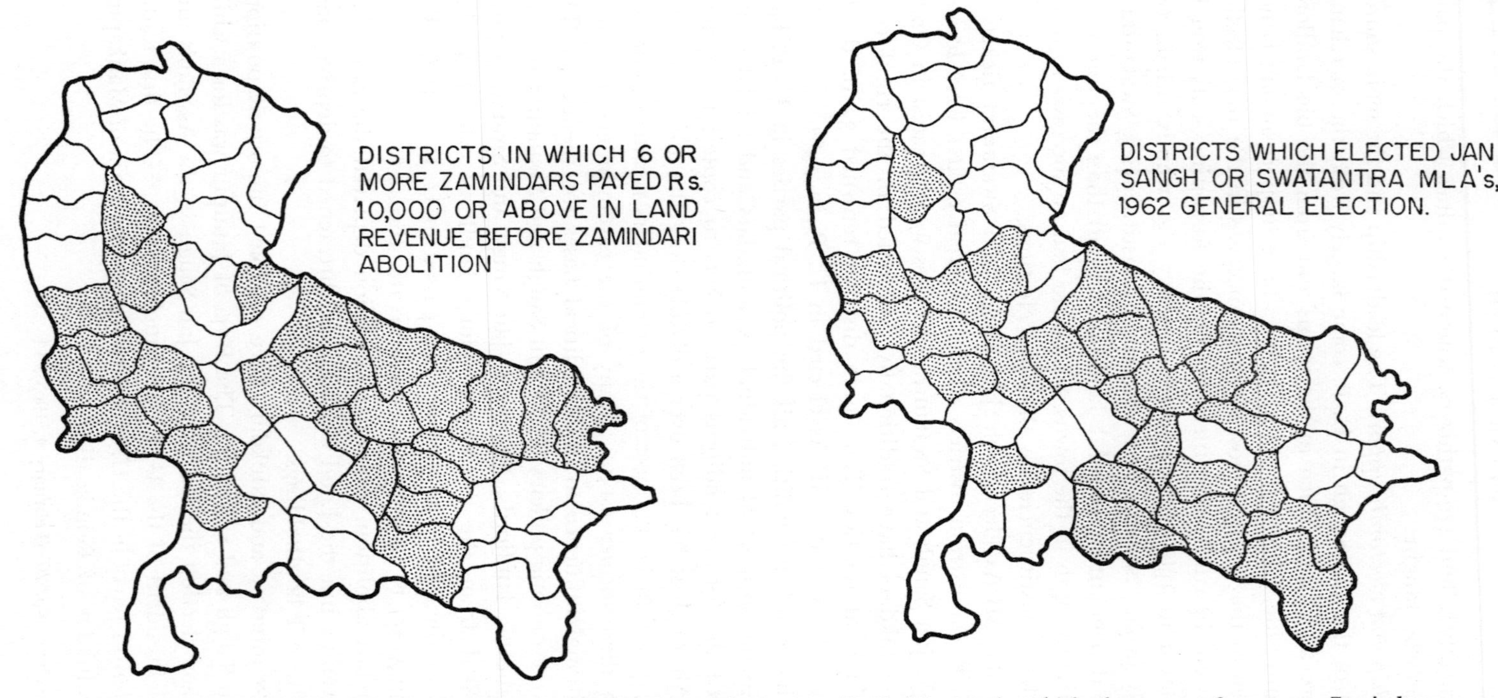

Fig. 4. Large Landed Estates and Support for Jan Sangh and Swatantra: U. P. Districts in which there were 6 or more Zamindars Paying Rs. 10,000 or above in Land Revenue before Zamindari Abolition and Districts which Elected Jan Sangh or Swatantra MLAs, 1962 General Election

Republican party[63]

The Republican party, the political vehicle in U. P. of the militant Scheduled Caste movement founded by Dr. B. R. Ambedkar, polled slightly under 4 per cent of the vote in the state in the 1962 election and won 8 seats in 4 districts. The development of the political consciousness and effectiveness of the Scheduled Castes as a group has been hindered by the continued educational backwardness of most low castes and by the diversity among the hundreds of low-caste groups which come under the legal definition of Scheduled Castes. The center of Scheduled Caste political activity has been in and around Bombay city and has only recently spread to other parts of the country. In U. P. the Chamars or Jatavs are the best educated and the most politically conscious group among the Scheduled Castes, and they dominate the Republican party in U. P. The Chamars are invariably close to the very bottom in the economic and status hierarchies of rural U. P. Throughout the state, they are employed in the rural areas primarily as agricultural laborers, and in the urban areas, in inferior menial occupations—as leather workers, factory hands, coolies, or bicycle-rickshaw drivers.

Until fairly recently, the Chamars in U. P., although they are the largest single caste group in the state, have lacked dynamic political leadership. However, in the last decade, a young lecturer of Aligarh Muslim University, B. P. Maurya, has risen to prominence as the leader of the Chamars in Aligarh district. Maurya comes from the small town of Khair in Aligarh district. His father was a field laborer on a farm in Khair, but Maurya was able to attend high school and then the Aligarh Muslim University. He took a B.Sc. and an LL.M. degree from the University and then joined the Faculty of Law as a Lecturer in 1960. Maurya has led the movement in Aligarh, begun earlier in Bombay, for the conversion of the Scheduled Castes to Buddhism.[64] In 1957 Maurya and one of his followers contested two Assembly constituencies in the district unsuccessfully. As a result of his work among the Chamars and his education, Maurya has become the hero of his community. In May 1961 a criminal case was registered against him for allegedly assaulting a policeman who, Maurya claims, had been beating a rickshaw driver in a dispute over a traffic violation. During the Hindu-Muslim riot of 1961, Maurya acquired some popularity among Muslims also for his criticisms of the Hindu community and for carrying out relief work among

[63] Portions of the material in this section have been adapted from Brass, *Factional Politics in an Indian State,* Chap. v.

[64] The conversion to Buddhism by some Scheduled Castes represents a protest against the inequalities of Hindu society.

Muslims.[65] In the University, Maurya has been sponsored by the Dean of the Faculty of Law, a leading member of a group of conservative Muslims in University politics.

The Scheduled Caste vote has been a mainstay of the Congress in U. P. since independence. Until the 1962 election, the Republican party and its predecessor, the Scheduled Caste Federation, achieved no successes in U. P. politics. For the most part, the Scheduled Castes in U. P. have accepted the patronage of the Congress government[66] and have given their votes to the Congress party in return. The Scheduled Caste leaders who have been given Congress tickets in the reserved constituencies are non-militant and have no power in the local or state Congress organizations. The numerous organizations in U. P. for the advancement of the Scheduled Castes have been content to serve as agencies for the distribution of Congress patronage.

The Republican party leaders feel that Scheduled Caste members who join the Congress betray the aspirations of the low castes. The Republicans are militant opponents of the Congress, which, they claim, is dominated by the elite Hindu castes. To oppose the Congress, Republicans are willing to seek alliances with any parties or individuals whose principles are not opposed to their own.

In 1962, the Republicans formed alliances with conservative Muslim leaders in the western districts of the state. The alliance of Muslims and Chamars in the western districts of U. P. in 1962 was made possible because of the development of a feeling of bitterness among some Muslim leaders toward the Congress and the government after the Hindu-Muslim riots of 1961 in these districts. The riots of October 1961, which originated in the scuffle between Hindu and Muslim students at the Aligarh University, spread to the neighboring districts of Meerut and Moradabad and led to the death of thirty-six people,[67] most of them Muslims. One Muslim who successfully contested an Assembly constituency on the Republican party ticket described his disenchantment with the Congress after the riots:

> I continued to be a member of the Congress till now; but, I found that the Congress was not playing fair game to the minorities and

[65] *National Herald,* October 29, 1961.

[66] Under the Constitution of India and various acts of legislation, members of Scheduled Castes are entitled to certain privileges and special concessions, such as reservation of seats in the legislatures, posts in the administrative services, scholarships in colleges and universities, and so on.

[67] A report on the riots was presented to the U. P. Assembly by the Home Minister in November 1961 and was published in the *National Herald,* November 15, 1961.

> the downtrodden classes. [Before the Aligarh riot, there were the Jabalpur riots]; . . . justice was not done there and there was a report by some MPs which indicated this. . . . Then, these riots spread and the Government did nothing to stop it. If the Government wanted to stop it, there would be no riots.[68]

In areas where the Muslim-Chamar alliance was in operation in the 1962 election campaign, communal antagonisms were aroused. Slogans were reportedly used extensively by Republican party workers referring to Muslims and Jatavs as brothers and attacking Hindus, particularly the elite Brahman and Thakur castes. An election tribunal in Aligarh overturned the election result in Aligarh City Assembly constituency, where a Muslim candidate had won on the Republican ticket, on the ground that communal propaganda had been used by the successful candidate.[69]

Republican party successes in the 1962 election in U. P. were confined to the four western districts of Aligarh, Agra, Moradabad, and Badaun. All four districts have large Muslim populations; in three of the districts, Chamars are the largest Hindu caste group and, in the fourth, Chamars are the second largest Hindu community. Of the eight MLAs elected, three were Muslim and five were Scheduled Caste. Four of the five Scheduled Caste MLAs were returned from general constituencies. The strength of the party in the four districts rested heavily on the urban Muslim vote. Three of the constituencies won by the Republicans are urban constituencies and two others are partly urban. In the huge rural state of U. P., the success of the Republican alliance of Chamars and Muslims largely in urban constituencies is a relatively insignificant matter. However, the limited success of the Republican party in 1962 did reflect the fact that there is considerable discontent with the Congress among members of the state's most important religious minority and its largest Hindu caste group.

Independents

Independent candidates play an important role in U. P. elections. There are always far more aspirants for each seat in the Legislative Assembly than there are party tickets. Many of the independent candidates in every election in U. P. have applied for the ticket of one of the parties in their districts, have been rejected, and have then filed nominations as independents. In the 1952 election, there were over 1,000 independent candidates. The number of independents has been smaller

[68] Interview in Aligarh on September 14, 1962.

[69] *National Herald*, July 21, 1963.

in the last two elections—549 in 1957 and 694 in 1962. However, the independents contribute significantly to the splintering of the opposition vote. In the 1962 election, there were three independent candidates for every two constituencies. The total vote for all independent candidates in the state was close to 14 per cent, a proportion higher than that for any opposition party except the Jan Sangh.

The large number of independents in each election largely reflects the low degree of party loyalty in U. P. politics. The Congress has found that rejected candidates for party tickets, even those who have signed the party pledge not to oppose the official candidate if they are rejected, do not hesitate to contest against the official candidates of the party. In 1952, 343 Congressmen contested against the official Congress candidates in U. P.; the figures for 1957 and 1962 were 122 and 166, respectively.[70] Some of these Congress "rebels" contested on opposition party tickets, but most filed their nominations as independents.

In 1962, 31 independent candidates were returned to the Assembly. Of the 31 MLAs, 13 were Congress rebels. The number of independents in the Assembly is usually reduced during each term as opposition parties and factions within the Congress try to win new adherents. For example, in March 1963 five independents (as well as nine opposition party members) were admitted into the Congress.[71] Successful independent candidates thus find that, even though they have contested against and defeated the official candidates of the major parties, the parties are willing to forget their opposition and bargain for their allegiance.

Party Politics in Uttar Pradesh

Political parties in U. P. differ in many important respects. Ideologically, there is a distinction between the secular, non-communal parties (the Congress, the socialist parties, the Communist party, and Swatantra), whose programs and policies are oriented primarily toward the issues raised by economic planning and development, on the one hand, and parties whose programs are oriented more toward cultural and communal issues (Jan Sangh and the Republican party) on the other.[72]

[70] *Ibid.*, February 2 and 13, 1962.

[71] *The Statesman*, March 24, 1963. The admissions caused considerable controversy in the Congress, particularly because one of the independent MLAs admitted was a Congress "rebel" in the 1962 election.

[72] This kind of division is used by Norman Palmer in *The Indian Political System* (Boston: Houghton Mifflin Co., 1961), pp. 186 ff. The division cannot be considered a very rigid one; for one thing, since economic issues have legitimacy in Indian politics and communal issues do not, communal issues are often phrased in economic language; second, certain cultural issues are raised by the secular parties, e.g., Socialist militancy on the issue of the use of English.

Organizationally, there is a division between the loosely organized parties in which discipline is weak and factional loyalties are often stronger than party loyalties (Congress, the socialist parties, and Swatantra) and the tightly organized parties which attempt, albeit not always successfully, to maintain firm discipline and to eliminate factionalism (Communists and Jan Sangh).[73] Another common distinction between democratic and non-democratic parties divides the parties in exactly the same way as does the distinction based on party organization. The Communists certainly and the Jan Sangh in many respects are both non-democratic parties.

Another division, which has been followed here, distinguishes the parties in terms of their leadership and popular support. The leadership and the major sources of support for the Congress in U. P. come from the locally dominant peasant proprietor castes. Opposition parties, to defeat the Congress, must either win influence among the dominant peasant proprietors for themselves or they must organize alternate sources of support. In U. P. the moderate leftist parties, led largely by ex-Congressmen, compete with the Congress for the support of the peasant proprietary body. Other opposition parties, such as Swatantra, Jan Sangh, and the Republicans have different social bases. Swatantra and Jan Sangh rest heavily upon the support of the ex-talukdars and the former big zamindars, whose influence in the countryside continues to be substantial. The Republicans, in contrast, draw part of their support from the landless, the field laborers who depend economically upon the peasant proprietors. A third alternative source of support for opposition parties lies with the "backward classes" such as the Ahirs and the Kurmis, who became proprietary castes after zamindari abolition. In many cases, these middle castes occupy a secondary position in Rajput or Brahman-dominated villages. In such villages, conflict tends to be organized around differences between the Rajput and Brahman ex-zamindars and their former tenants. The PSP and the Socialists, in some areas, have both attempted to exploit these differences.

Thus, there are many ways of distinguishing the political parties which operate in U. P. Not all political parties are equally interested in the same kinds of issues nor are all organized in the same way. Some are less devoted to the democratic process than others. Some appeal to certain communities, others appeal to economic classes. Nevertheless, there are certain common features which often blur distinctions. Most of the parties use similar tactics; all of the parties are affected in

[73] This division is used by Weiner, *op.cit.*, p. 244.

some degree by factionalism and the low degree of party loyalty in the state; parties like the Jan Sangh and the Socialist party, which differ on most issues, are equally militant on the language issue; most parties tend, at least in party manifestos and on the public platform, to speak in the language of economic development. As in other aspects of life in U. P. and in India, there are unifying elements as well as diversities in the party system.

Political Conflict in Uttar Pradesh: A Case Study

The Third Five Year Plan for Uttar Pradesh called for an expenditure of Rs. 497 crores, of which Rs. 350 crores was to be provided by the central government and Rs. 147 crores by the state government from its own resources. In formulating the plan, the state government was aware that the bulk of the resources would have to be raised by new taxation.[74] It was estimated that Rs. 109 crores of new taxes would have to be raised, most of it from the agricultural sector.[75] State governments in India have been reluctant to resort to rural taxation, even though a very small proportion of the value of agricultural output is taken by taxes on the land and even though rural taxation provides a very small proportion of total tax revenues in the country.[76] State governments have feared the political repercussions that would result from an attempt to increase taxes on land. Nevertheless, in 1962 the Uttar Pradesh government (and other state governments) reluctantly decided that there was no alternative, if the Third Plan expenditures were to be met, but to find new revenues by increasing taxes on the land. Conflict over the passage of a land tax bill in U. P. dominated the political life of the state throughout most of 1962. The conflict over the passage of the bill provides material for a case study of the political process in U. P.

The tax bills. The U. P. government's first proposal for a tax on landholdings in the state was introduced in the Assembly on September 4, 1962 as the U. P. Landholding Tax Bill. The bill was introduced only after long deliberations among government leaders and senior administrative officials of the state. The bill, in its original form, called for a 2½ per cent tax on the capitalized value of landholdings in the state or, more simply, for what amounted to a 50 per cent increase in the land revenue. All landholdings in the state were to be taxed, except

[74] Government of Uttar Pradesh, Planning Department, *Third Five Year Plan,* I, 44.

[75] *The Statesman,* September 29, 1962.

[76] For precise figures, see Myron Weiner, *The Politics of Scarcity: Public Pressure and Political Response in India* (Bombay: Asia Publishing House, 1963), p. 163, citing Ayodhya Singh, "Land and Agricultural Taxes," *Economic Weekly,* XIII (January 21, 1961), 91.

those of one acre or less. The provisions of the bill aroused such opposition among both Congressmen and opposition party members that debate on the bill had to be postponed. The Planning Commission in New Delhi was consulted and the bill was altered. The new bill raised the exemption from the tax to exclude landholdings of eight acres or less, an exemption which eliminated 90 per cent of landholdings in the state from the tax. The altered bill removed the objections of some Congressmen, but all opposition parties in the state and some Congressmen as well remained hostile to the bill and voiced some important criticisms of its new provision for an increased exemption. Opposition remained so bitter that the government was reluctant to use its majority in the Assembly to force the passage of the bill. However, a new spirit of compromise arose in the state after the Chinese invasion of India on October 20th, leading to meetings between the Congress and opposition leaders. As a result of the meetings, an entirely new bill was framed and presented to the Assembly as the U. P. Emergency Surcharge on Land Revenue and Rent Bill. The new bill eliminated the larger exemption and reverted to the previous exemption of one acre or less; but the Surcharge Bill provided for only a 25 per cent increase in the land revenue rather than the original increase of 50 per cent. The Surcharge Bill was passed by the Assembly on December 10, 1962.

The controversy over the tax bill agitated political life in the state for more than half a year. The controversy involved both state and national government leaders, Congress factions, and all opposition parties. Some insight into the state's political process can be gained by examining the roles of the various groups involved in the dispute, the methods which they used, and the influence which they were able to exert in modifying the tax proposals.

Division within the Congress. Division within the Congress over the land tax bill existed at every level in the Congress party organization and the government in U. P. and in Delhi. The controversy rekindled factional rivalries among state Congress leaders, but it also involved rank and file MLAs from the districts. In addition, conflict developed between Congress leaders in U. P. and Congressmen from U. P. in the central government and in Parliament.

The course of the controversy indicated that the concept of the collective responsibility of the Cabinet for policy decisions operates only in a very limited way in U. P. That is, state ministers will not openly express their disagreements with Cabinet decisions on policy matters, but their views are well known to politically informed people in the state and the existence of differences among Cabinet members is publicized by the newspapers. Thus, it was announced in the press in July that the state Cabinet had completed the formulation of its tax proposals, and it was reported, but denied by the chief minister, that differences of opinion existed over the proposals among members of the Cabinet.[77] In September, after the introduction of the bill into the Assembly, it was reported that the Finance Minister and the Agriculture Minister, both identified with the "dissident" group in the Cabinet, sharply opposed the land tax proposals. The Agriculture Minister, Charan Singh, prepared a forty-page memorandum which was circulated only privately. However, direct quotations as well as paraphrases from the memorandum appeared in the press. It was reported that the land tax bill was described by the Agriculture Minister as a measure "spelling breach of faith with the masses"[78] and one which was unjustified in view of the fact that the per capita income of the peasantry had not increased in the last fifteen years.[79]

Opposition to the government's tax proposals was widespread also among rank and file Congress MLAs. Some of this rank and file opposition was expressed openly in breaches of party discipline. One Congress MLA voted with the Opposition against the introduction of the Landholding Tax Bill in the Assembly on September 4th. Other Congressmen expressed their discontent in private letters to the chief minister.[80] Opposition to the bill among Congress MLAs was sufficiently widespread to prompt the government to hold meetings of the Congress Legislature party to discuss the bill. At the meetings, during which seventy speakers participated in the discussion, opinions ranged from complete support for the government's proposals, to qualified support, to complete opposition.[81] The government announced after the meeting that the basic principles of the bill had been approved by the Legislature party, but that the bill had been referred back to the Cabinet for amendments which would take into consideration the views of the members.[82] Despite this announcement of agreement, open opposition was expressed by some Congress MLAs during the Assembly debates.[83] Even after the

[77] *National Herald*, July 13, 15, 1962.

[78] A charge commonly made against the government was that the tax proposals were a breach of the promise made to one category of peasants (*bhumidhars*) at the time of zamindari abolition that their land revenue would not be increased for forty years. The government replied that its proposals were for taxes on the capitalized value of landholdings, not for an increase in the land revenue.

[79] *National Herald*, September 11, 1962.

[80] *The Statesman*, September 6, 1962.

[81] *National Herald*, September 18, 1962.

[82] *Ibid.*, September 19, 1962.

[83] *Ibid.*, September 4, 6, 17, 1962.

Cabinet revised the bill to provide for an increased exemption, discontent continued. On October 18, two days before the Chinese invasion, sixty dissident Congressmen sought permission to vote according to conscience if the Land Tax Bill was not withdrawn.[84] In a government move to close debate on the bill on October 20, one Congressman voted against the motion and another abstained.[85] Mass rank and file opposition within the Congress ended after the Chinese invasion, but one Congressman opposed even the final Surcharge Bill when it was introduced into the House for discussion in December.[86]

A third source of opposition to the state government from within the Congress came from Congressmen from U. P. in New Delhi. The leadership of the New Delhi Congressmen from U. P. was provided by Keshav Deo Malaviya, a central minister at the time, and Mahavir Tyagi, a prominent MP. Both of these men had old quarrels with Chief Minister Gupta, dating back to the years when they were followers of Rafi Ahmad Kidwai. A signature campaign against the state government's tax proposals was carried on among Congress members of Parliament from U. P. Thirty MPs signed a letter which was sent to the chief minister, urging him to withdraw the Land Tax Bill.[87]

The chief minister of U. P. was thus under great pressure from members of his own party, both from prominent ministers in the state and central governments and from rank and file Congressmen from the districts, to withdraw his tax proposals. Some of this opposition was based upon a fear of popular discontent over the imposition of new taxes. Some of the rank and file opposition came from Congress MLAs in the eastern districts where landholdings are very small and where any new tax might be a serious hardship for most peasants. The opposition of the Agriculture Minister, Charan Singh, was to be expected since he has been an ardent advocate of the peasant proprietor and has argued in his writings that most landholdings in U. P. are uneconomic in size.[88] Thus, some of the opposition to the tax proposals from within the Congress was based both upon principle and upon a fear of popular discontent. However, much of the opposition to the government's proposals came from factional rivals of the dominant group in the state government. For many prominent Congressmen, the controversy over the Land Tax Bill was a convenient issue to embarrass the dominant group in the state Congress.

[84] *The Statesman*, October 19, 1962.

[85] *Ibid.*, October 20, 1962.

[86] *National Herald*, December 8, 1962.

[87] *The Statesman*, October 20, 1962.

[88] See, for example, Charan Singh, *Abolition of Zamindari: Two Alternatives* (Allahabad: Kitabistan, 1947), pp. 210-16.

The Planning Commission. The central government has tended to intervene in state disputes when intractable controversies have arisen which threaten the stability of the state government. Three days after the Land Tax Bill was introduced into the U. P. Assembly, Prime Minister Nehru himself intervened in the dispute by announcing in Parliament, in response to an adjournment motion on the U. P. situation, that he was referring the question of increases in land taxes in U. P. and other states to the Planning Commission.[89] Five ministers of the state government, including two ministers who opposed the measure, left for New Delhi to discuss the Land Tax Bill with the members of the Commission. The results of the discussions were not made public. The chief minister announced that the idea of a land tax had been accepted by the Commission "in principle."[90] However, it was reported that the Commission had added its weight behind those who favored the exemption of small landholdings.[91] Thus, both the Planning Commission and the "dissidents" in the Congress influenced the state government toward a major modification in the bill.

The role of opposition parties: Tactics. If the Land Tax Bill created division in the Congress, it also impelled the usually fragmented opposition parties toward a high degree of unity. Opposition pressure against any increase in land taxes began even before the Land Tax Bill was introduced into the House. Throughout the month of August, opposition parties in the Assembly attempted to force the government into discussions on the proposed tax measures. Opposition parties displayed some ability in embarrassing the government, both through parliamentary devices and by creating unparliamentary disturbances in the Assembly. During the month, opposition parties succeeded in forcing the discussion of a motion to *reduce* the land revenue, a motion of no-confidence in the government, and a motion that no new tax and no increase in existing taxes be imposed during the current year. All opposition parties engaged in a protest walk-out when the Land Tax Bill was finally introduced into the Assembly in September.[92]

Opposition agitation against the tax proposals reached its peak after the bill was taken up for discussion at the end of September. Agitations and demonstrations were carried on both inside and outside the Assembly throughout the first three weeks of October, until the news of the Chinese invasion. Although some parties threatened mass civil disobedience movements, these never materialized. The focal points for agitation remained inside and outside the Council House. Inside the Assembly, the

[89] *National Herald,* September 8, 1962.
[90] *Ibid.,* September 13, 1962.
[91] *The Statesman,* September 12, 1962.
[92] *National Herald,* September 5, 1962.

Socialists played the leading role (although other parties contributed) in disrupting the proceedings of the House by shouting, disobeying the Speaker, engaging in walk-outs, and the like. Outside the Council House, the Jan Sangh played the most prominent role by picketing the entrance to the Assembly. The intent of the picketing was not wholly clear since Jan Sangh MLAs continued to participate in the proceedings of the House. Jan Sangh activity outside the House forced the government to station a police detail at the entrances. Some incidents of manhandling of MLAs (both Jan Sangh MLAs and others not involved in the picketing) occurred.

PSP and Communist activities were mild in comparison with those of the Jan Sangh and the Socialists. Leaders of both the PSP and the Communist party were critical of the more extreme tactics of other opposition parties.[93] The major activities of the PSP and the Communists were simultaneous (but not cooperative) processions on September 10 of peasants from various districts through the streets of Lucknow to the Council House where speeches were heard by party leaders.[94] The processions of September 10 were the only important instances of mass participation in the opposition agitations against the government's tax proposals. Of the major opposition political parties in U. P., only Swatantra did not participate in agitations either inside or outside the House, although Swatantra party members did participate in the protest walk-out of September 4th.

Thus, the major opposition parties in U. P. agreed in opposing the government's tax measures but adopted different methods to express their opposition. Jan Sangh and the Socialists adopted militant (although non-violent) agitational methods, the PSP and the Communists favored peaceful public demonstrations, while Swatantra made only symbolic protests.

The role of opposition parties: Issues. Three major issues were discussed during the debates on the government's tax proposals—the exemption issue, the question of the possible fragmentation of landholdings, and the issue of rural versus urban sources of revenue. All opposition parties were at first agreed that "uneconomic" landholdings should not be taxed at all. In the discussion on the opposition motion to reduce the land revenue in the state, PSP, Communist, and Swatantra spokesmen all argued that uneconomic landholdings should be exempt from land revenue altogether. There were differences among the

[93] For example, see the PSP criticism of Jan Sangh methods in *ibid.*, October 16, 1962.

[94] *Ibid.*, September 11, 1962.

opposition parties as to what constitutes an uneconomic landholding. Swatantra and PSP spokesmen thought that any landholding below ten acres was uneconomic, whereas a Communist spokesman thought that three acres should be the dividing line.[95] This kind of debate is obviously a sterile one both because of the difficulties in determining what is an economic holding,[96] and because most holdings in U. P. are uneconomic by every standard so far proposed.[97]

Opposition party spokesmen thus added their weight to those in the Congress who favored a higher exemption limit. However, even after the eight-acre exemption was added to the government's Land Tax Bill, all opposition parties continued to oppose the tax. In fact, opposition spokesmen succeeded in raising a very cogent objection to the eight-acre exemption, despite the fact that most had previously favored such an exemption. During the debates on the Land Tax Bill, opposition leaders pointed out that an eight-acre exemption might encourage peasants with large holdings to partition their lands, thus adding to the fragmentation of landholdings.[98] The government was bound to be particularly sensitive to this argument since it was then engaged in major land consolidation proceedings throughout the state. It is possible that the government was prompted by opposition arguments on this question, as well as by a desire to be accommodating in the wake of the Chinese threat, in withdrawing the Land Tax Bill. It was after consultation with the leaders of all opposition parties in the state that the U. P. government decided to eliminate the exemption and to propose instead the Emergency Surcharge Bill, which sought to increase the land revenue by 25 per cent on all landholdings above one acre.

The Emergency Surcharge Bill did not win the support of all opposition parties when it reached the House, but it did succeed in breaking the opposition front against the tax proposals. In presenting the new bill, government spokesmen claimed that all opposition leaders had agreed to the measure. The Socialist and Jan Sangh leaders denied that they had agreed to the new bill and continued their opposition in the House. The leader of the PSP in the House admitted that he had agreed to the new bill, but resigned his leadership of the party because of continued rank and file PSP opposition to the tax. However, Swatantra, the Communists, the Republican party, and most independents supported the new Surcharge Bill. The division among opposition parties on the

95 *Ibid.*, August 3, 1962.

96 For an interesting discussion, see Charan Singh, *loc.cit.*

97 Nearly 56 per cent of the landholdings in U. P. were under 2 acres in 1949; see pp. 109-111 below.

98 *National Herald,* October 6, 19, 1962.

final bill did not reflect differences of ideology; both Swatantra and the Communists agreed to support it. The division reflected more the general tactical differences among the parties. That is, both the militant parties, the Jan Sangh and the Socialists, remained opposed to the tax proposals until the end. The PSP finally split on the issue and a new, more militant leadership was elected. A week after the PSP change in leadership, the party merged with the Socialists in the Assembly. The Communists and Swatantra, who are generally less militant than the other parties—the Communists partly for tactical reasons, Swatantra for temperamental reasons—were willing to reach a compromise with the government. Thus, the real differences among the parties were not over the tax bills, but over their general attitudes toward the party in power.

A third issue discussed during the debates on the tax bills was the issue of rural versus urban sources of revenue. All opposition parties agreed that it would be preferable to raise new tax revenues from the urban areas. The government passed, before the land tax proposals came up for discussion, a bill imposing new taxes on urban lands and buildings, as well as increases in sales and passenger taxes. Nevertheless, many speakers on the land tax bills argued that cultivators were discriminated against under the present tax structure as compared to town dwellers. Other speakers pointed to the fact that there were large arrears of taxes due from "capitalists and industrialists" and argued that these arrears should be collected before the peasants were taxed. Swatantra spokesmen vied with the Communists in urging that urban residents and big capitalists should be taxed rather than the peasants. All opposition spokesmen seemed to agree with a PSP leader who argued that a land tax "would amount to subordinating the interests of the majority for the benefit of a small minority of town dwellers and capitalists."[99]

Conclusion. The course of the land tax controversy in U. P. in 1962 provides some insight into various aspects of the political process in the state. Some general conclusions emerge from the case study about the capacity of the state government to govern, about the ways in which policy is influenced in U. P. politics, and about the roles and attitudes of Congress factions and opposition parties in the state's political process.

The state government knew very well that considerable opposition would be aroused by its tax proposals. The chief minister was certainly aware of the division in his own Cabinet on the issue. Moreover, opposition parties had given the government clear warning that all peaceful methods, including agitations, would be used to oppose any proposals

[99] *Ibid.*, October 19, 1962.

to tax the peasants. Since much of the opposition both from within the Congress and from opposition parties was designed only to embarrass the government on a sensitive issue, it might be argued that there was no choice for the government but to meet the opposition head on. However, the government did not exhaust all possibilities of winning advance support for its tax proposals. For example, the meetings of the Congress Legislature party were held only after pressure from rank and file Congressmen made the meetings unavoidable.

Throughout the controversy, the government appeared vacillating. It was handicapped in meeting opposition attacks by division within the Congress party. However, the government also feared the possibility that opposition parties might be able to use the tax issue to arouse popular discontent. It twice made major revisions in its tax proposals, the first time largely as a result of pressure from within the Congress, the second time largely as a result of opposition pressures.

Opposition parties showed that, despite the comfortable majority of the Congress in the Assembly and despite the fragmentation of opposition forces, they could seriously embarrass the government and disrupt the process of orderly parliamentary government. Not all the opposition parties were equally militant or equally disrespectful toward parliamentary procedures; nor did they all work together out of choice. There were important differences among them, but these were subordinated throughout most of the struggle because it would have been politically disastrous for any opposition party not to oppose the government's tax proposals. Ideological differences were not important in the debate. All opposition parties opposed the land tax, and all favored taxing urban residents rather than the peasantry. There were differences in tactics, however, which reflected more basic differences in the degree of militancy of the opposition parties.

The ineffectiveness of the Congress government in U. P. in the face of internal factionalism and determined opposition was further demonstrated in September and October 1963 when the land tax controversy was resumed. In September 1963, the U. P. Assembly was again disrupted by the controversy in connection with a misunderstanding over the application of the tax. Opposition party spokesmen and many Congressmen as well interpreted the Emergency Surcharge Bill as a measure which was to apply for one year only. The government argued that the bill was meant to apply for the duration of the national emergency, which had not yet officially ended. The U. P. Assembly was forced to adjourn three days ahead of schedule because of the dispute, and opposition parties began to make plans to launch agitations throughout the state for a withdrawal of the tax. The Congress government was even more divided than usual at this moment because a change in chief ministers was about to take place under the famous "Kamaraj Plan."[100] A meeting of the executives of the Congress Legislature party on October 16, 1963 found a consensus among its members in favor of withdrawal of the tax. The next day, the new chief mininster, Mrs. Sucheta Kripalani, announced that the surcharge would be withdrawn. The chief minister's statement, announcing the withdrawal, reflected fully the dilemma of a government in need of resources, but unable to use its majority to maintain a necessary but unpopular measure:

> Financial commitments arising out of the Emergency, as well as the Plan, do not admit of any curtailment in expenditure. Nevertheless, it has been decided that the surcharge on land revenue will not be levied for the second year. It cannot, however, be overlooked that our financial commitments still continue and may even increase in the implementation of the Plan and defense schemes. The gap between the resources and the requirements of funds is bound to increase by this decision.[101]

GOVERNMENTAL POLICIES AND PERFORMANCE

Governmental policies in U. P. since independence have had four major objectives—the abolition of all intermediaries between the cultivator and the state and the creation of a system of peasant proprietorship, increases in agricultural productivity and output, the provision of more nonagricultural sources of employment and income, and the decentralization of government through the readaption of old institutions of local self-government and the spread of new ones.

Agricultural Problems, Policies, and Achievements

Since independence, the Congress government in U. P. has attempted to deal with three distinct problems in the agricultural sector of the economy—land reform, the existence of fragmented and uneconomic

[100] The "Kamaraj Plan" emerged out of a meeting between Kamaraj Nadar, then chief minister of Madras state, and Prime Minister Nehru in July 1963. The plan was designed to restore unity to the Congress organization and put a stop to factional strife, which had become severe in many states by that time, by asking all central ministers and all chief ministers to resign. The resignations provided the national leadership of the Congress a rare opportunity to reorganize central and state governments. In U. P., the resignation of C. B. Gupta was accepted and Mrs. Sucheta Kripalani was elected chief minister in his place. The plan by no means succeeded in stopping factional conflict in the U. P. Congress.

[101] *National Herald*, October 18, 1962.

holdings, and low productivity. In the area of land reform, the government has sought to abolish the system of intermediaries and to substitute in its place a system of peasant proprietorship. The government passed two important acts to implement these objectives—the Zamindari Abolition Act of 1952 and the Imposition of Ceiling on Land Holdings Act of 1960. The first act eliminated all intermediaries between the cultivator and the state but left the former landlords in possession of their private lands. It thus essentially substituted the state government as zamindar in place of the landlords[102] and confirmed all cultivators in the possession of their lands on a new legal basis.[103] The act did not attempt to strengthen the economic position of the peasant proprietors by redistributing land. It was not until 1960 that a Land Ceiling Act was passed which ostensibly sought to bring about "a more equitable distribution of land" by limiting the size of landholdings in the state to 40 acres and redistributing all individual landholdings above the limit.[104] In fact, the Land Ceilings Act offers little prospect of significant land redistribution in U. P., since a 40-acre limit frees at most only 1.3 per cent of the cultivable area in U. P.[105] for redistribution and will certainly free much less than this amount because of provisions in the act permitting landholders to retain grovelands.[106]

The most serious limitation upon the efforts to create a large and prosperous body of peasant proprietors in U. P. has been the existence of fragmented and uneconomic landholdings. According to the 1948 Report of the Zamindari Abolition Committee, 56 per cent of all cultivators in U. P. held less than 2 acres of land; 86 per cent less than 6¼ acres; 94 per cent less than 10 acres.[107] Since there has been no significant land redistribution and population has increased rapidly, it is certain that the number of small holdings has increased. The problem of uneconomic holdings has been compounded by fragmentation, i.e., by the splitting and separation of the holdings of most cultivators into many tiny plots, adding to the labor of the cultivators and decreasing the efficiency of their operations. The government of U. P. has attempted to solve the

[102] Neale, *op.cit.*, p. 240.

[103] P. D. Reeves, "Zamindari Abolition in Uttar Pradesh: An Investigation Into Its Social Effects," n.d. (mimeographed), p. 16.

[104] The Uttar Pradesh Imposition of Ceiling on Land Holdings Act, 1960.

[105] Baljit Singh, *Next Step in Village India: A Study of Land Reforms and Group Dynamics* (Bombay: Asia Publishing House, 1961), p. 85.

[106] In addition, the land to be redistributed is intended to go to landless laborers rather than to the existing small holders, thus creating new peasant proprietors rather than strengthening the old.

[107] Neale, *op.cit.*, p. 272, citing Z. A. C. *Report*, 2, Statement 5, p. 6.

problem of fragmented landholdings by a massive program of land consolidation, currently being carried out under the terms of the U. P. Consolidation of Holdings Act of 1953. At the end of 1961, consolidation operations had begun in 37 districts, and the work of consolidation had been completed in 30 tahsils, with a combined area of 5.6 million acres. Consolidation in half of the state was expected to be completed at the end of the Third Five Year Plan.[108]

Consolidation of landholdings may increase the efficiency of agricultural operations on small holdings but in itself can only mitigate in part the increasingly acute problem of uneconomic landholdings. There are at least three possible approaches toward a solution of the latter problem—extensive redistribution of land, some form of joint or cooperative farming, or a combined program to increase agricultural production (thus making small holdings more economic) and to provide alternative sources of employment to ease the pressure on the land. The Zamindari Abolition Committee rejected extensive land redistribution on both economic and political grounds, i.e., because there is proportionately very little land that could be made available for redistribution and because any large-scale scheme of land redistribution would cause considerable discontent and opposition. Experimental schemes of cooperative farming have been implemented in various parts of U. P., but the state government has not shown any intention of substituting a large-scale scheme of cooperative farming for the prevalent system of peasant proprietorship. The only practical solutions, in terms of both economic and political considerations, appear to lie, first, in increasing the productivity of the available land, and second, in creating non-agricultural sources of employment through the development of industries.[109]

Unfortunately, progress in both the agricultural and industrial sectors of the state's economy has been disappointing to U. P. planners. The Third Five Year Plan Report notes that "Per capita output of agricultural commodities has increased only nominally in the State [in the decade from 1950-51 to 1960-61], while per capita output in the industrial sector shows a decline."[110] Economic development in U. P. has not been faster than the rate of population growth in the state and has lagged behind the national average by most measures. For example,

108 Interview with the Joint Director, Consolidation in Lucknow, on December 20, 1961.

109 For a more complete statement of economic problems in U. P., see Neale, *op.cit.*, parts iv and v.

110 Government of Uttar Pradesh, Planning Department, *Third Five Year Plan*, I, 6.

population increase in U. P. during the decade 1950-51 to 1960-61 was 16.7 per cent compared to 21.1 per cent for the whole of India, while the increase in state income was 20.6 per cent compared to 41.6 per cent for the country.[111] Foodgrains production increased by only 22 per cent in U. P. compared to 52 per cent for the country as a whole.[112]

The state government has steadily expanded the system of national extension and community development throughout U. P. Progress has been made in some programs designed to increase agricultural production, particularly in the construction of irrigation works. Seed multiplication farms have been developed, chemical fertilizers are being distributed, and improved agricultural practices are being adopted. However, progress has been slow in most programs and unforeseen obstacles have arisen. A general factor which appears to be partly responsible for the slow rate of economic progress in U. P. compared to much of the rest of the country is the low rate of public investment in the state. Per capita expenditure in U. P. in the first two plans was the lowest in the country and will again be behind all other states during the Third Plan.[113] The *Third Five Year Plan Report* of the U. P. government, published in 1961, saw no solution to the problem of economic development in the state, except through "a bold policy of raising resources to the maximum even at a sacrifice to the present generation, and making the best possible use of the outlays available for accelerating the growth of the State's economy."[114] The land tax bills of 1962 represented an attempt to implement that "bold policy." The controversy aroused by the tax bills throws into sharp relief the political problems of economic development in a stagnant economy. It is politically difficult for the state government to raise additional tax resources when the economy is stagnant or in decline, but the decline is likely to continue unless new tax resources are found to implement the state's Five Year Plans.

Employment

The Five Year Plans in U. P. have not been able to provide adequate alternative sources of employment to those who are being forced off the land. The number of unemployed in U. P. has been increasing very nearly in geometric proportion in each plan period.[115] Em-

[111] *Ibid.*, p. 3. [112] *Ibid.*, p. 5. [113] *Ibid.*, pp. 8, 15. [114] *Ibid.*, p. 42.

[115] *Ibid.*, p. 66. The unemployment problem is described in the following terms:

"(a) the backlog of unemployment at the commencement of the Third Plan (18.67 lakhs) was about two times as high as the backlog when the Second Plan was launched (9.46 lakhs);

"(b) the fresh entrants to the labour force in the Third Plan approximately number 21.5 lakhs, and 40.17 lakh jobs will be needed for achieving full employment by 1965-66."

ployment opportunities sufficient even to absorb the new entrants to the labor force are not being created by the plans.[116] The state government has declined to "undertake any sizeable programme of industrialization itself" because of "its limited resources." The state government must therefore "depend on the initiative of the private sector, and on the establishment of industries under the public sector by the Government of India."[117] Despite the generally favorable attitude of the U. P. government to the desires of entrepreneurs for licenses, permits, and state loans, very little new industrial development has been undertaken in the private sector. Nor has the government of India established many new large industries in U. P., a fact sometimes resented by U. P. planners and politicians. The state government has increasingly turned to the development of small-scale industries both in rural areas and in urban "industrial estates" to provide new income and employment opportunities. In the Third Plan an effort is being made to integrate the small industries program with the community development program and thus create an industrial "cluster" for approximately every ten community development blocks. However, the total number of persons for whom the village and small industries program is expected to provide employment in the Third Plan is less than 58,000.[118] There appears to be no prospect in the immediate future that either government or private enterprise will provide anything but a small fraction of the employment required to absorb those forced off the land.

Political Problems

There are no easy solutions to the problems of economic development in U. P. The state government has many programs in hand and has many achievements to its credit in terms of the goals which it has set for itself. If progress has been slow in terms of the usual indices of economic development, much of the difficulty has been the nearly intractable character of the problems. However, there have been some obvious political difficulties in the efficient functioning of the state government which certainly have had an impact upon its ability to carry out programs of economic development.

The factional structure of the U. P. Congress party has affected the orientation of government leaders, the efficiency of government departments, and the functioning of local administration. The constant struggle for power within the Congress has caused most state government ministers to be concerned primarily with questions of patronage and political support rather than policy. Ministries have fluctuated

[116] *Ibid.*, pp. 66-67. [117] *Ibid.*, p. 157. [118] *Ibid.*, p. 70.

greatly in size; they tend to be huge when unity moves are taking place and "composite" governments are formed and small when factional conflict is intense and resignations are being submitted. The result is that portfolios are shifted about frequently; departments are joined together when governments are small, separated when governments are large. At all times, the chief minister tries to keep as much power and patronage as possible in his own hands and those of his closest associates, while giving as little as possible to the less reliable members of the government. When a prestigious portfolio must be given to a political rival, the patronage power is taken away to make the position less dangerous politically. The result is often a fragmentation of authority and responsibility, which leads to confused lines of administrative control in the districts. In addition, factional conflicts between opponents in the government often involve the administrative staff in the districts. Ministers will sometimes clash over appointments and transfers of local officials. Local administrative officers have even been drawn directly into factional disputes, gathering information about the activities of local politicians and preparing charges of corruption against them on the orders of ministers. It is not possible to measure precisely the impact of such political maneuvering on the administration and implementation of government programs, but it is clear that the preoccupation of ministers with problems of gaining and maintaining political support and the consequent politicalization of the administrative staff interfere with the processes of rational, orderly planning and plan implementation.

Panchayati Raj

The introduction of "panchayati raj" or "democratic decentralization" in U. P. is likely to increase the difficulties in the way of economic development and rational planning. Government planners are aware that the granting of greater powers to local bodies will probably lead to administrative inefficiency, but they consider local self-government a value worth pursuing for its own sake. It is also hoped that, in the long run, democratic decentralization will create public enthusiasm for and participation in the planning process and will thus contribute to the progress of economic development programs.

Under the U. P. scheme of democratic decentralization, begun in 1961, a three-tiered structure has been introduced into the districts. The three tiers are the local village panchayats, the *kshetra samitis* (block development committees), and the *zila parishads* (district boards). Great powers over planning and administration have been vested in these local bodies. At the lowest level, the village panchayat is directly elected by the villagers. The higher bodies are composed of indirectly elected members, government appointees, nominees of local municipal, cooperative, and educational institutions, and MPs, MLAs, and MLCs from the area.

The program has barely been launched in U. P., but some tentative hypotheses about the probable impact of these institutions on economic and political development may be stated. Insofar as the local bodies are given major roles in the planning process and control over local administration, it is likely that demands for allocation of scarce government resources will lead to increased political participation and competition. Unless the allocation of government resources is linked very strictly to local production plans, the emphasis of the whole planning process may well become even more heavily oriented to the distribution of patronage, which may not always go to those who would use it for purposes of planned development. Another likely effect of the decentralization of government on the political process in U. P. is an increase in the strength of the local Congress organizations. The use of indirect elections, nominations, and appointments to the local bodies above the village guarantees that most of these bodies will either be controlled directly by Congressmen or at least not easily fall into opposition hands. Of course, continued Congress control over the new institutions of local self-government in turn depends upon the maintenance of Congress control over the state government.

CONCLUSION

This chapter has focused upon three interrelated problems of political development in U. P.—the problem of factionalism in the ruling party, the problem of the fragmentation of opposition parties, and the consequences of both conditions for the effective functioning of the processes of policy making and administration. It has been demonstrated that the effectiveness of the Congress majority in U. P. politics is limited by the persistence of internal divisions within the Congress. In contrast, opposition parties, despite their fragmentation, are able to exercise more influence than is warranted by their actual strength in the legislature. The effectiveness of opposition parties in limiting the freedom of Congress action is partly a consequence of the divisions within the Congress. In addition, some opposition parties have acquired greater influence than their popular support warrants because of their militancy and their willingness to disrupt the normal working of the parliamentary process to prevent government action. Finally, it has been shown that factionalism in the Congress and the aggressiveness of opposition parties both tend to make it difficult for the government to pass desired legislation and to administer efficiently programs designed to accelerate economic development.

The problems discussed in this chapter are likely to become even more difficult in the immediate future. There is no prospect of an end to factionalism in the Congress party in U. P. unless the party is somehow transformed into a mass totalitarian party. There are two more likely patterns of development for the U. P. Congress. One possible pattern is a drift into anomy and the consequent continuation of the disintegration of the Congress organization in the state. A second possible pattern is the stabilization of factional struggle in the U. P. Congress and its containment within bounds which will permit the Congress to regain some of its lost electoral strength. Experience in other states and in some U. P. districts suggests that the latter possibility is the more likely one. However, it is also likely that anomic tendencies will continue to operate in the U. P. Congress indefinitely even if factional conflict becomes stabilized, and it is possible that the Congress may experience a further decline in electoral support before it begins to rebuild its strength.

The possibility of a further decline in Congress strength must be viewed in the context of the continued fragmentation of opposition parties. No opposition party in U. P. can by itself provide an alternative government to the Congress in the foreseeable future. The alternative to Congress rule in U. P. is either coalition government or an unstable minority government supported by the Congress. The most likely prospect for the immediate future, i.e., for the 1967 election, is either a slight decline or a slight increase in Congress strength. A slight increase in the Congress vote would leave U. P. politics much as it is today. A slight decline would accentuate present problems and would probably make it necessary for the Congress to rule either with a precarious majority or in coalition with another opposition group. In either case, the frustrations of a permanent minority status are likely to continue to force some independents and opposition party members to join the Congress and to force those who remain in opposition to continue to use militant tactics to draw attention to themselves and to their demands.

Finally, the likelihood of a continuation of or a further disintegration in the present structure of the party system in U. P. makes it difficult to foresee any significant changes in the policy-making process or in the process of plan implementation. The economy of U. P. may continue to stagnate or even decline in some respects in relation to the needs of an increasing population. Economic discontent is bound to grow under such conditions. The pressure of increased economic distress in a population where some social groups are just beginning to enter the political process and to make demands is likely to place great strains on the political system as a whole.

Demands for change in the political or social system are not likely to take the form of a violent mass revolution. The state is too large and diverse and the degree of political organization is too low for such a movement to take place. Rather, the threats to the system lie in the continuance of drift, the spread of anomy, and the growth of sporadic violent movements in restricted areas among deprived social and economic groups.[119] The danger to the system of politics in U. P. is the threat of utter chaos and the possibility that outside intervention by the central government may eventually be required.

POSTSCRIPT

The 1967 general elections and their aftermath have brought about a regime change in the political system of Uttar Pradesh. After twenty years of unbroken Congress rule, the Congress for the first time failed to win a majority of the seats in the legislative assembly. Although the Congress at first succeeded in forming a government by attracting a few defectors from opposition parties and by winning the support of most of the independents in the legislature, the government was brought down after seventeen days as a result of a major defection from its own ranks. The motion of thanks to the Governor's address was defeated on April 1, and the Congress government resigned immediately thereafter. Chaudhuri Charan Singh, the leader of the defectors from the Congress, was unanimously elected leader of the Samyukta Vidhayak Dal, a joint legislative organization of all opposition parties in the assembly, and was invited to form the government the next day. The new chief minister was sworn in on April 3 and his council of ministers on April 6. With the formation of a non-Congress coalition government on April 6, the one-party dominant system in U. P. politics came to an end.

Although a fundamental change in the state's political system has

[119] This writer heard of one case in an eastern district where an opposition MLA with a long police record for dacoities and other offenses was characterized by a prominent fellow party member as "a staunch peasant worker" and a "mass hero," whose "dacoities" had really been attacks on the former zamindars of the district. One case means little, but it is suggestive. The extent to which dacoity provides "employment" for those forced off the land is a subject on which it would be difficult to do research. However, if discontent in the rural areas becomes violent, an increase in dacoities might well be the first sign.

taken place, there are important elements of continuity as well as a change in patterns of political behavior in U. P. The defeat of the Congress in the elections and the success of all opposition parties in achieving a united front after the election can be attributed in part to the growth of discontent among several well-defined groups in the state's population. This discontent developed into what one correspondent characterized as a general "climate of hostility" against the Congress, especially among the middle class groups in the state. However, the Congress continued to suffer from intense internal factionalism, which in itself was at least as important as any other factor in the defeat of the Congress at the polls. Moreover, the underlying instability of the party system, a result of the uncertain loyalties of the independents and many members in most of the parties, continues. In fact, the political entrepreneurs and independents now hold the balance in the state's political system and can, at any moment, decide the fate of the coalition government.

With respect to the non-Congress parties, the most significant aspect of the 1967 elections is the continued rise of the Jan Sangh to a position of pre-eminence among the non-Congress parties in the state. A comparison of Tables 2.1 and 2.2 shows that the Jan Sangh has benefited not only at the expense of the Congress, but to an even greater extent at the expense of the combined socialist strength in the electorate. The Jan Sangh increased its popular vote by over 6 per cent and thereby nearly doubled

TABLE 2.2

UTTAR PRADESH ASSEMBLY ELECTION RESULTS, 1967

Party	*Votes Polled*	*% of Vote*	*No. of Seats*
Congress	6,862,030	32.10	198
Jan Sangh	4,602,257	21.53	97
SSP	2,178,845	10.19	44
Swatantra	1,011,770	4.73	12
PSP	859,937	4.02	11
Republican	856,727	4.01	9
Communist (R)	732,776	3.43	14
Communist (L)	254,704	1.19	1
Independents	4,020,631	18.80	37
Total	21,379,677[a]	100.00	423[b]

[a] There were, in addition, 1,507,439 invalid votes.

[b] The 1967 delimitation of constituencies reduced the total number of seats in the U. P. Assembly from 430 to 425. Elections in two constituencies were not held at the time of the general elections.

SOURCE: *National Herald*, March 1, 1967.

its representation in the assembly. Although the SSP vote shows a slight increase between 1962 and 1967, this increase stems solely from the additional strength it acquired at the expense of the PSP in the aftermath of the PSP-SP merger and subsequent split. However, the present electoral strength of the SSP is less than that of the PSP in 1962, and there has been an absolute decline in both the combined vote of the two socialist parties from 20.4 to 14.2 per cent and in the number of seats they hold in the assembly from 62 to 55. The PSP has been relegated to the position of one of the minor parties in U. P. politics, along with Swatantra, the Republican party, and the two Communist parties. In fact, the separate votes of these parties is so insignificant as to be even smaller by a wide margin than the number of rejected ballots; and the combined vote of all the minor parties is less than that of the independents. Nevertheless, the present tenuous balance in the state assembly gives real power to every party, in fact to every member. Although there is no doubt that the Congress has become extremely unpopular among many educated people and among significant sections of middle class voters in the cities and towns, it remains the strongest political force in the state. The Congress popular vote declined by only 2.8 percentage points, although it lost 88 seats.

The wide discrepancy between the relatively small drop in the popular vote and the number of seats lost by the Congress cannot be fully explained without a detailed analysis of the elections by district and constituency. However, there are a few obvious factors. Probably the most important factor in the Congress decline was again intense internal party factionalism, rebellion, and sabotage in the constituencies and districts. There was a record number of applicants for the Congress tickets in the state in this election, over 2,300 compared to 1,838 in 1962. Far from reflecting the popularity of the Congress ticket, however, the large number of applicants in 1967 reflected the fact that three groups were competing for Congress tickets instead of two. Mrs. Kripalani, in her three years in office, succeeded in establishing a Congress group separate from both the Gupta and Tripathi groups. The leaders of both groups were eager to replace Mrs. Kripalani and absorb or eliminate her group followers, but they were prevented from doing so by their own continued group rivalries. A superficial air of cordiality and unity was established at the state level before the elections among the leaders of the two main groups in the Congress, but this failed to have an impact on the local level where the number of Congress "rebels" contesting against the official Congress candidates was higher than ever before and some sabotage was nearly universal in the constituencies. Seventeen Congress "rebels" were returned either as independents or on opposition party tickets, but the effect upon the Congress in the state was much greater and contributed to the defeat of many more Congress candidates.

The second factor of obvious importance was the impact, especially upon the middle and lower middle class of salaried employees in the cities and towns, of the great increases in the prices of food and other commodities in the state in the last three years as a result of the food shortage created by three successive bad monsoons. The last monsoon, in fact, resulted in the worst drought and famine in living memory for several parts of the state. The drought and food shortage were, however, largely indirect factors which affected the middle class through rising prices.

The most articulate expression of discontent over rising prices came from the 500,000 state employees, many of whom were on strike throughout most of the election campaign, agitating for an increase in dearness allowance. Teachers in the privately managed colleges and in the secondary schools of the state were also agitated over the rise in prices and were demanding a similar increase in allowances. Finally, there was widespread student unrest, indiscipline, and vandalism in the cities and towns of the state in the months preceding the elections. Student grievances were extremely diverse, but there is some evidence that the student unrest may have been instigated in part by the teachers themselves. The state employees and the students engaged in organized disruption of Congress election meetings and, in some places, physically attacked the cars of Congress candidates and even the candidates themselves. It is probable that most of the votes of the state employees and the teachers went against the Congress. The students had few votes, but they did support and canvass for opposition candidates in many constituencies as well as engage in harassment of the Congress candidates.

The third factor of some importance in this election was the articulation of Muslim discontent over the problem of Urdu and other matters, and the formation of an openly anti-Congress Muslim organization, the U. P. Majlis-e-Mushawarat, which supported non-Congress candidates of various parties in constituencies throughout the state. Muslim discontent began to express itself in 1962 in a few areas of the state, but it was much more widespread this time. Again, it will require detailed constituency analyses to determine how many seats were lost by anti-Congress Muslim sentiment, but even a 20 or 30 per cent shift of Muslim votes, especially if concentrated in constituencies where Muslims are in large numbers, could have lost a large number of seats for the Congress.

There were other issues which may have affected some voters in the state: the food shortage; peasant antagonism to the 25 per cent surcharge on the land revenue (which was re-imposed after the Indo-Pakistan War in 1965);[120] business antagonism to the Congress among goldsmiths and jewelers over the Gold Control Order and among traders over police raids for hoarding, profiteering, and black-marketeering; the cow slaughter issue; and the ever present administrative corruption. However, the slight decline in the Congress vote and the continued strength of the Congress in the countryside will not support the argument that there has been a significant change in rural voting behavior, which seems still to depend upon a combination of local caste and factional alignments.

Nevertheless, the hostility towards the Congress which has developed in recent years among both opposition politicians and the politically conscious segments of the population propelled all opposition parties in the state from Swatantra to the Left Communist party to join together to form a united legislature party called the Samyukta Vidhayak Dal (SVD) on March 6, with a 33-point minimum common program. The program promised abolition of land revenue and certain other taxes, concessions to the various interest groups agitating for increased dearness allowance and other favors, increased irrigation facilities, and provision of fertilizers, among other points. The combined strength of the parties comprising the coalition on that day was 188, but the leadership claimed the support of 27 independents and a total strength of 215, a majority in the assembly. However, the Congress claimed the support of 34 independents on March 9, giving it a claimed strength of 223. The Governor was placed in a delicate position since it was quite obvious that many of the independents had committed themselves to both sides. The Governor concluded that the Congress claim was the more valid one and invited Mr. C. B. Gupta to form the government on March 12. In the first test of strength in the assembly on the election of the speaker, the Congress won by 226 to 188 or a margin of 38 votes, clearly indicating that almost all the independents had voted for the party called to power.

The Gupta government, however, had its difficulties from the beginning. Gupta's main rival in Congress group politics, Kamalapathi Tripathi, had been defeated in the elections and did not create any significant obstacles to the formation of the Congress government. The downfall of the Gupta government was brought about by Chaudhuri Charan Singh, a senior minister in the previous Congress governments and a man who has been consistently discontented with the functioning of the Congress gov-

[120] And abolished again after the formation of the Congress government in March 1967.

ernment and the Congress party in U. P. for more than a decade. Negotiations were carried on between the Gupta group members and Charan Singh, but they failed to bring about an agreement on the composition of the new government. Gupta made the fatal mistake of forming a government composed predominantly of his closest followers. Charan Singh refused to join the government, and negotiations between the two sides finally broke down completely on March 31. On April 1, Charan Singh crossed the floor of the House with sixteen other discontented Congressmen. The motion of thanks to the Governor's address was defeated on the same day by 215 to 198 votes, the margin of 17 made possible by the shifting of allegiance of a number of independents.

The position of the coalition government formed on March 6 is obviously precarious. As of that date, a shift of nine votes would bring the government down. However, it is equally likely that shifts of allegiance may favor the new government.

There is no point in speculating on the future of the present government, which may last anywhere from a few months to five years. However, certain features of the system as a whole do stand out. No matter how long the government lasts, the present party and government structure is essentially unstable. It is an extremely fluid system which depends for its maintenance upon the actions of political opportunists. The two relatively stable components of the system are now the Congress and the Jan Sangh. The Jan Sangh is the dominant party in the present cabinet, with five members in a cabinet of sixteen. The second largest contingent in the cabinet is the Jan Congress, which is a new legislative party formed from the Congress defectors, who now number twenty-one, of whom four, including the chief minister, are in the cabinet. For the rest, the SSP has contributed three members; the Communists (Right), the PSP, and Swatantra, one each; and there is one independent in the cabinet. Barring a wholesale defection from the Congress to the Jan Congress, the latter party has no future. The SSP suffers from severe internal divisions and poor local organization, which have so far prevented it from becoming a stable force in the party system. None of the other parties can hope to increase its strength significantly in the foreseeable future. Thus, U. P. at present has an unstable multi-party system.

Ideological differences have yet to make an impact on the functioning of the party system in U. P. Ideological differences or, at least, fundamental differences of approach do exist in the manifestos of the parties in U. P. However, there are four factors which currently prevent them from operating in a significant way. The first is the present determination of all the parties to make a non-Congress government a reality and to compromise or put aside their fundamental differences. The second is the danger to the popular esteem of the first party to break away for any reason. The third is that the immediate problems of food shortage and inflation are so severe that pragmatic action has become inescapable. Finally, ideology cannot come into prominence in a system which depends for its functioning on appeals to independents and political entrepreneurs.

Policy differences do exist, however, within the present government, and they received public expression on the first major task undertaken by the government—that of procuring surplus foodgrains from the surplus districts and prosperous farmers in the state. Conflicting policy statements were issued, especially from Jan Sangh party leaders, whose party manifesto opposes grain levies on the peasants. The controversy was resolved and a compromise was reached among the parties in the cabinet. The danger to the government still exists, however, for there is a continuing possibility that discontented members of various parties and the independents may make use of such an issue to bring down the government.

The problems before the present government are formidable. Promises and concessions have been made by the government simultaneously to increase the dearness allowance of state government employees and to abolish land revenue and other taxes levied in recent years. The problem of resources has now become even more acute than before. The dominant partners in the coalition government, especially the chief minister and the Jan Sangh leaders, are pragmatic—if socially conservative—men who could reach workable compromises if left to themselves. However, any bold decision taken to face the problems of this state will always raise the possibility of defections which could bring the government down. Yet, the fact that the present government has a program, even though it is a minimum program, is bound to give a new policy orientation to politics in the state and force a confrontation with the basic problems of food and resources for development. In that confrontation, the prospect of a breakdown and the imposition of President's Rule on the state is not the least likely possibility.

Kasauli, Himachal Pradesh
June 13, 1967

REFERENCES

Baljit Singh. *Next Step in Village India: A Study of Land Reforms and Group Dynamics*. Bombay: Asia Publishing House, 1961.

———, and Misra, Shridhar. *A Study of Land Reforms in Uttar Pradesh*. Honolulu: East-West Center Press, 1965.

Brass, Paul R. "Factionalism and the Congress Party in Uttar Pradesh," *Asian Survey*, IV (September 1964), 1037-47.

———. *Factional Politics in an Indian State: The Congress Party in Uttar Pradesh.* Berkeley: University of California Press, 1965.

Charan Singh. *Agrarian Revolution in Uttar Pradesh.* Uttar Pradesh: Publications Bureau, Information Department, n.d.

Cohn, Bernard S. "The Changing Status of a Depressed Caste," in McKim Marriott (ed.), *Village India: Studies in the Little Community.* Chicago: University of Chicago Press, 1955.

———. "The Initial British Impact on India: A Case Study of the Benares Region," *Journal of Asian Studies,* XIX, No. 4 (August 1960), 418-31.

Crooke, W. *The North-Western Provinces of India: Their History, Ethnology, and Administration.* London: Methuen and Co., 1897.

Dharma Bhanu. *History and Administration of the North-Western Provinces (Subsequently Called the Agra Province, 1803-1858).* Agra: Shiva Lal Agarwala and Co. (Pvt.) Ltd., 1957.

Neale, Walter C. *Economic Change in Rural India: Land Tenure and Reform in Uttar Pradesh, 1800-1955.* New Haven: Yale University Press, 1962.

Reeves, Peter D. "The Politics of Order: 'Anti-Non-Cooperation' in the United Provinces, 1921," *Journal of Asian Studies,* XXV, No. 2 (February 1966), 261-74.

Retzlaff, Ralph H. *Village Government in India: A Case Study.* Bombay: Asia Publishing House, 1962.

Sampurnanand. *Memories and Reflections.* Bombay: Asia Publishing House, 1962.

Weiner, Myron, and Kothari, Rajni (eds.). *Indian Voting Behaviour: Studies of the 1962 General Elections.* Calcutta: Firma K. L. Mukhopadhyay, 1965. Chap. iii, "Class and Community Voting in Kanpur City," by Paul R. Brass, and Chap. x, "Traditionalism and Modernism in U. P.: Faizabad Constitutency," by Harold A. Gould.

MADHYA PRADESH

MADHYA PRADESH

III

Madhya Pradesh

WAYNE WILCOX*

MADHYA PRADESH, as its name denotes, occupies the middle country of India between the Gangetic plain and the northern reaches of the Deccan. Its rich eastern districts are lowlands drained by the Mahanadi River as it moves through the Eastern Ghats to Orissa. The western part of the state is dominated by the Malwa plateau, which offers relief to the plains of Gujarat, while the southern zone of the state is dominated in the west by the Narbada valley and in the east by the forests of Bastar. In its central position athwart India's internal lines of communication, the state has borders with seven others: Uttar Pradesh, Bihar, Orissa, Andhra Pradesh, Maharashtra, Gujarat, and Rajasthan. It is the largest state in the Indian Union with an area slightly larger than California: 171,217 square miles. By Indian standards, the state's population of slightly more than 33 million does not signify a densely populated region, and the man/land ratio is more favorable in Madhya Pradesh than in most adjoining states.

A geographer might describe Madhya Pradesh as an Africa-shaped mass between latitudes 17°48′N and 25°52′N and between longitudes 74°2′E and 84°24′E. The boundaries reflect the linguistic and cultural features of the population rather than topographical relief, and hence the outline of the state is extremely irregular. Within Madhya Pradesh are important mineral and forest resources, and perhaps no state in India offers so much promise in terms of food production, energy sources, and the iron and steel industry.[1]

Madhya Pradesh is also rich in the relics of the past, in the echoes of stilled kingdoms caught at Ujjain on the sacred Kshipra, the eroticism of Khajuraho, and the puritan grace of Sanchi. The wanderings of all

* The research for this study was undertaken as part of a comparative study of public policy and the rural sector in India, Pakistan, and Ceylon. Field research was conducted in 1962-63 and 1964 under grants from Columbia University and the Rockefeller Foundation for which I am grateful. Craig Baxter and Richard Von Glatz made helpful comments as did the other contributors to this volume, but the conclusions are solely my responsibility.

[1] For an earlier assessment, see National Council of Applied Research, *Techno-Economic Survey of Madhya Pradesh* (Bombay, 1960). Recent discoveries of larger deposits of coal emphasize its power potential.

of the Indian peoples are catalogued in the lore and literature of central India, and the anthropologist finds their reflection in the contemporary social mosaic of the state. This is the region eliciting Forster's dark truths of India, the meeting ground for a hundred imperial epochs.

The student of Indian history finds literally dozens of separate histories for the cluster of kingdoms in Malwa, Gondwana, Bundelkhand, Baghelkhand, and Chhattisgarh. The ebb and flow of the largest empires in both north and south washed against central India and left their human and social residues. Following the break-up of the Mughal empire and the destruction of Maratha power by the British, the area had no master until the settlement of Sir John Malcolm in 1818. He decided to legitimize the rule of seventy-three semi-sovereign princes, and to place a major part of the southern zone of the state under direct British administration. When he had completed the work, Madhya Pradesh, as it would later be called, "presented the appearance of a sea suddenly petrified while in a condition of stormy unrest and disquietude."[2] And in such a curious condition it remained until Sardar Patel and his successors enforced a higher degree of administrative unity on grudging princes and politicians in the period from 1947 to 1956.

No state in India has fewer bonds underlying its unity, and it can with truth be argued that the parts of Madhya Pradesh are greater than their sum. The dominant characteristic of local politics is that no coherent state political community with well-worn practices and an intrinsic "spirit of the house" has yet emerged. With adequate allowance for spatial and temporal differences, a suggestive comparison might be drawn with the German states before their unification. The principal bond of unity in both cases was language rather than a common history. Both had the misfortune of straddling the middle ground between imperial rivals. The resource base of both was considerable, and each had its Prussia (for Madhya Pradesh, read Mahakoshal) to take the lead in unification against the will of smaller constituent states. There was also a shared "Austrian" problem (for Madhya Pradesh, read Malwa). The history of the German states must be read with that of Europe of the time, so important were external stimuli; so too with Madhya Pradesh and its interested neighbors in Delhi and the bordering states.

[2] Sir William Lee-Warner, quoted approvingly by V. P. Menon, in *The Story of the Integration of the Indian States* (London: Longmans, Green and Company, 1956), p. 224.

THE SOCIAL AND ECONOMIC ENVIRONMENT OF POLITICS

In 1961 the population of Madhya Pradesh was slightly more than 32,370,000 and was growing at a rate of 2.42 per cent a year after having trailed general Indian growth rates for fifty years.[3] Less than 9 per cent of the population lived in cities of more than 20,000, and only eight cities in the state had a population of more than 100,000.[4] Over 80 per cent of the population lived in villages of less than 2,000, and 44 per cent in settlements of less than 500.[5] The high proportion of rural population in the state poses severe problems in communication and contact, especially in view of the topography and the lack of railroads and roads. In 1961 the state had only 13,000 miles of hard-surfaced roads, some of them impassable during the monsoon season. Even with a relatively well-developed road transportation system, it takes several days to travel from Bastar in the extreme southeast to Bhopal, the state capital. Most of the state's population would have to spend additional hours getting to a road or city served by buses. The British-built railway system is irrelevant to many of the needs of Madhya Pradesh as it was constituted in 1956, and the former princely state areas are particularly ill-served.

A second striking characteristic of the state's population is the abnormally high proportion of Scheduled Tribe (20.6 per cent), Scheduled Caste (13.1 per cent), and Backward Class (2.1 per cent) groups. The importance of this socially and educationally backward bloc is enhanced by its concentration in certain regions of the state, notably the south and east, and by the political practice of reserving seats for members of these communities in schools, government offices, and the state legislature.

The state literacy is 17.1 per cent, but as with all state-wide statistics it masks glaring regional disparities. As might be expected, literacy and educational facilities are heavily concentrated in the larger cities of the state, and broad areas of tribal and rural country are possessed of neither. In 1963 the education department reported the total student body of high and higher secondary schools as 278,100 and the college and university population about 53,000.

The economy of the state is overwhelmingly agricultural. Agriculture accounts for between 61 and 63 per cent of the gross state income, with

[3] This data is taken from the excellent analysis prepared by the Directorate of Economics and Statistics, *Demographic Study of Madhya Pradesh*, Part I (Bhopal, 1962).

[4] In decreasing order: Indore, Jabalpur, Gwalior, Bhopal, Ujjain, Raipur, Durg (Bhilai), and Sagar.

[5] *Techno-Economic Survey of Madhya Pradesh*, pp. 2, 181.

mining and manufacturing adding only 10-11 per cent, commerce, transport and communications another 11-12 per cent, and all other services the remaining 16-18 per cent. Of the 12 categories of industrial employment enumerated in 1960, four food and plant processing classifications, which included 1,198 factories employing 54,191 workers, constituted more than a third of total industry. Textiles accounted for 60 factories employing 46,224 workers, and the rest of the industry of Madhya Pradesh employed only 41,562 workers. In the entire state in 1960 there were only 96,184 trade union members.[6]

TABLE 3.1

STATE WORK FORCE BY CENSUS CATEGORY

Total population	32,372,408
Total workers	16,929,177
cultivators	10,611,508
agricultural labor	2,815,200
mining, livestock, forestry	492,287
household industry	841,395
manufacturing	336,845
construction	172,258
trade and commerce	403,637
transport and communication	157,920
other services	1,098,127
non-workers	15,443,231

SOURCE: *Census of India, 1961*, VIII (Madhya Pradesh), Part II-A (Delhi, 1963).

Mineral production, however, is steadily rising. In 1960 Madhya Pradesh produced every resource needed for the huge Russian-built public sector steel complex at Bhilai, although production must increase to meet total requirements. Electrical power consumption has also increased rapidly to 476,966,000 KwH in 1960-61. But both the Heavy Electricals (HEL) in Bhopal and the Bhilai steel complex are isolated examples, the more so because they have a minimum "linkage" to the smaller scale industries and markets of the state. They have yet to produce significant social and political "multiplier" effects outside their immediate region.

While it has the flavor of a truism, a summary statement of the political effects of the historical, social, and economic development of the state would testify to the lack of a single political community in

[6] These statistics are from *Statistical Digest, 1962-63, Indicators of Regional Development* (Bhopal, n.d. [1962?], mimeographed), and *Estimates of State Income of Madhya Pradesh, 1950-51 to 1961-62* (Bhopal, 1963). The trade union figure is a state government estimate. (See Table 3.1.)

Madhya Pradesh. It would be impossible to define various state class and party interests without making a prior unrealistic assumption of a high degree of political integration. The society of Madhya Pradesh is characterized by low levels of communication and a near absence of state-wide functional and institutional processes growing out of an urban-industrial economy. A study of the important associations and practices of groups in the rural, agricultural, and tribal society, however, requires a systematic series of microcosmic studies that do not now exist for the state.

This study is based on a not altogether satisfactory search for a middle range of political transactions in the important regions of the state, directed toward analyzing the state political process as an interactive system, with the principal units of action the regional components. Such anthropological evidence as is available is used, and government performance is also carefully assessed in an attempt to measure the capacity of the state *apparat*. The bulk of the evidence, however, is processed as part of regional politics.

THE FORMATION OF THE STATE

Madhya Pradesh was formed in 1956 on the basis of the recommendation of the States Reorganization Commission Report. The "essential unity" of the central Indian region was based on the common usage of Hindi, and its administrative organization was justified on the grounds of economic size and efficiency. The constituent parts of Madhya Pradesh were (1) Madhya Bharat, a union of princely states in the Malwa plateau region, (2) Vindhya Pradesh, a union of states in the Vindhya mountain region, (3) Bhopal, a centrally administered princely state, and (4) the Hindi-speaking portion of the Central Provinces plus the previously amalgamated Hindi-speaking states of Chhattisgarh.

Each of the constituent portions of the new state, except Bhopal, were themselves composite entities. The Madhya Bharat union, the Vindhya Pradesh union, and the Mahakoshal region had been created after independence. While the agitation for linguistic states and states reorganization had been dominated by forces not important in the region (except for Vinharbha, the Marathi-speaking zone of the Central Provinces), the central government was forced to change political organization in central India to conform with national patterns. In no small measure, Madhya Pradesh was formed because there seemed to be nothing else to do with its constituent parts. The princely state unions were financially weak and politically unstable, and the central government thought that safety and stability lay in amalgamation. What is important to note is that the state was not created on the basis of an indigenous demand, and that its constituent units in fact possessed almost no political affinity.

Regional Profiles: Madhya Bharat/Malwa

The westernmost slab of the state is Malwa, a plateau of 1,500-2,000 feet, which before independence included 25 princely and feudatory states. Three-quarters of the territory of Malwa was included in the domain of either Gwalior or Indore, the two foremost Maratha princely houses in the state. Gwalior, heir to the Scindia fortunes, lay in the north and was the wealthiest state in the British Central India Agency. Indore, founded by the Maratha Holkar family, lay in the south, surrounded like Gwalior by its lesser allies. Few rivalries have matched the raging quarrels of the Scindia and Holkar rulers, and Malcolm's settlement in 1818 was praiseworthy if only because it ended the open violence of their enmity.

The settlement established three categories of semi-sovereign rulers: those who were subordinate to no other prince (such as Gwalior, Indore, Dhar, and Dewas); those Rajputs who claimed independence from Maratha courts (the "mediatised states"); and the smaller Rajput landlords who were given "guaranteed estates" with some governmental powers in local affairs.[7] This settlement, largely unchanged until India's independence, established a semi-feudal order between the cultivator and the intermediary agents of the state. In Madhya Bharat, for example, there were 1,329 jagirs distributed by caste or community as follows: Maratha 92, Rajput 720, Brahman 249, Kayastha 32, Vaisya 14, Muslim 60, Mahant 90, and others 72.[8] But while the total area of Madhya Bharat was about 46,166 square miles, only 8,449 square miles were administered by jagirdars. In a series of acts beginning as early as 1948, the various governments in the region passed legislation eliminating or restricting the power of the rural intermediaries, but with compensation for revenue and rights lost. However, the thakurs and jagirdars remain an important force in regional politics.

Another important factor in the politics of Madhya Bharat are the princely houses and the historic effect of governments on local economies. Both Gwalior and Indore, with British administrative assistance, stimulated the growth of industry, Gwalior through two state investment

7 An excellent study of the tenure-cum-authority system in Madhya Bharat is the *Report of the Rajasthan-Madhya Bharat Enquiry Committee* (New Delhi, 1950), p. 4 *et seq.*

8 *Ibid.*, pp. 29, 30.

trusts[9] and Indore primarily through attracting private investment from Bombay and Ahmedabad in the textile industry. So successful were the two states that Gwalior boasts three cotton textile mills, engineering facilities, pottery works, and manufacturing plants for shoes, sugar, paints, matches, biscuits, and vegetable shortening. Indore has one silk and seven cotton textile mills, numerous oil pressing and processing industries, and light engineering works fabricating such diverse products as diesel engines and glass.

Indore, like most of the large cities of the state, is essentially new, drawing its configuration in part from the plans of Patrick Geddes and much of its population from Rajasthan and the Bombay region. In 1921 the district census officer reported that 45 per cent of the city's inhabitants were born outside the Indore region. In 1961, Indore's population was nearly 400,000, making it the largest city in the state, and its industrial work force was over 26,400.[10] Commerce employed 22,448 workers, and the amorphous services sector employed another 32,793 persons. This thriving economy produced the highest per capita income in the state, 352 rupees, but it was only slightly higher than the Indian national average of 329 rupees, as measured at current prices.

Gwalior, smaller than Indore by a quarter, is one of the four most industrialized and urbanized districts in the state. With a total population of 324,448, the industrial labor force employs about 14,100 workers,[11] commerce and trade 15,709, and the general service sector 27,750. Gwalior ranked fourth in the state in per capita income in 1961, with the district average one rupee less than the national average of 329 rupees.[12]

Within Madhya Bharat region, however, contrasts are much sharper between city and countryside than between cities. In part this is a reflection of statistical problems in comparing monetized and nonmonetized sectors of the economy, but it also reflects differential rates of development. Dhar, a former princely state immediately south of Indore, has an urban/rural ratio of 10.3/89.7 compared with Indore district's 60/40. Indore district literacy is 38.2 per cent compared to Dhar's 13.5 per cent. The per capita income of Dhar, where 51.1 per cent of the

[9] See Menon, *op.cit.*, p. 225, for a brief description.

[10] The census figure and the figures given for employment in factories registered under the factories act differ by almost 15,000. The lower figure is given here as an index to employment in large undertakings. See *Census of India, 1961, Paper No. 1 of 1962*, and *Indicators of Regional Development.*

[11] See footnote 1, page 160, for method and source of calculation.

[12] *Regional Income Atlas of Madhya Pradesh* (Bhopal, 1960), p. 4.

population is classified as Scheduled Tribe, is only 266 rupees. Even greater contrasts exist in the style of living of the people of these two districts, separated by a few miles in space but several centuries in time. This extreme disparity in social and economic conditions poses serious analytical problems, not the least of which results from the fact that radically dissimilar districts frequently comprise one parliamentary constituency or one development bloc.[13]

Yet in spite of great differences in their condition, the residents of fairly extensive regions are, as Adrian Mayer points out, "conscious of being inhabitants of a specific region of India which they consider to be superior to all others in climate and culture."[14]

In areas completely rural in political setting, a different set of factors are important, and the levels of politics shift. The best-mapped portion of the entire state, thanks to the work of Adrian Mayer,[15] is Dewas, 22 miles from Indore. It need only be said here that rural politics tend to be more particularistic than urban politics, and that caste membership, the tenure system, and kin groups play a crucial role in the countryside. It is important to determine the relative strengths of factions and dominant castes and the character of political competition as it develops in rural life around the nexus of land and government policy. In each different setting, especially in a state as ethnically and socially diverse as Madhya Pradesh, these factors must be empirically mapped. It would be misleading to suggest that there are general themes in rural politics which continuously impinge upon and dominate state public policy. And it is important to recognize the many levels of political action in the society, only some of which are affected by policy made in Bhopal.

Five unique factors of political importance characterize public life in the Madhya Bharat region: (1) A tribal bloc in the south which tends to maintain in office experienced political leadership (Non-tribal moneylenders also play an important brokering role); (2) A continuous struggle between village headmen and ex-intermediaries for local power, and a struggle between former ruling houses for status and power; (3) A modern elite rivalry for business and political power between Indore and Gwalior elites; (4) A powerful and well-financed trade union move-

[13] For an amplification of this point, see my "Trade Unions, the Middle Class, and a Communist M.P.: The Indore Parliamentary Election of 1962," in Myron Weiner and Rajni Kothari (eds.), *Indian Voting Behaviour* (Calcutta: Firma K. L. Mukhopadhyay, 1965), pp. 68-84.

[14] Adrian Mayer, *Caste and Kinship in Central India* (Berkeley: University of California Press, 1960), p. 13.

[15] See the bibliography for this chapter.

TABLE 3.2

REGIONAL PROFILES: MADHYA BHARAT/MALWA

District	*Population*	*Scheduled Caste/ Scheduled Tribe, %*	*Urbanization (% in places of 5000+)*	*Literacy, %*	*Per Capita Income Rs.*	*Factory Workers*
Gwalior	657,876	19.0/2.1	49.3	27.9	328	14,100
Bhind	641,169	21.0/0.1	7.4	17.4	206	—
Morena	783,348	21.0/5.1	8.6	14.9	222	900
Shivpuri	557,954	17.5/9.8	7.0	11.6	252	400
Guna	595,825	18.2/7.2	12.6	13.8	259	300
Datia	200,467	18.5/1.2	14.7	14.9	303	—
Indore	753,594	13.6/0.1	60.0	38.2	352	26,400
Ratlam	483,521	13.5/12.0	28.6	21.4	300	4,900
Ujjain	661,720	23.5/—	32.4	23.4	302	12,900
Mandsaur	752,085	15.1/0.1	21.2	22.4	335	4,100
Dewas	446,901	18.2/7.8	15.1	17.3	302	2,300
Dhar	643,774	7.4/51.1	10.3	13.5	266	1,600
Jhabua	514,384	2.9/84.7	6.9	6.0	216	600
West Nimar	990,464	10.7/40.6	13.9	15.3	293	4,700
East Nimar	685,150	8.9/7.9	22.5	24.5	262	9,500

The present Indore Division includes East Nimar, which was not part of Madhya Bharat. It is included in this table for convenience.

SOURCE: Compiled from *Census of India, 1961, Paper No. 1* (New Delhi, 1962) and *Indicators of Regional Development* (District-wise) (Bhopal, 1962[?], mimeographed).

ment in Indore; and (5) a large Jain commercial class[16] with historic, commercial, and religious ties to Gujarat, and with a rivalry for regional dominance with a Brahman-dominated coalition.

Each of these factors allows for political factionalism and fluid coalitions, and they both reflect and contribute to rivalries which exist in the state government. Moreover, they tend to fragment the politically articulate groups of western Madhya Pradesh and diminish the voice of Madhya Bharat in state policy. This is a curious outcome considering the financial and industrial vitality of the region: its similarity to the role of Catalonia in pre-Civil War Spain is striking.

Regional Profiles: Bhopal and Central Madhya Pradesh

Bhopal stood alone as the premier Muslim princely state in central India, and its ruler played an important part in pre-independence Hindu-Muslim politics. Geographically a part of eastern Malwa, the

[16] In 1951, over 180,000 Jains were listed in the census of Madhya Bharat and Bhopal, a number exceeded only by undivided Bombay and Rajasthan.

state had unique qualities because of its Muslim rulers, a Muslim-Sikh army and police force, and a number of Muslim jagirdars and charitable trusts. The state administration was generally progressive, and the rulers enjoyed prestige within their order, but Bhopal was little touched by industrialization before independence.

In 1947 Bhopal was logically an integral part of the new Madhya Bharat union, but because of its heritage and the bitter communalism of partition, it posed special problems.[17] The state *praja mandal* (people's organization, Congress party affiliate in the states) agitated for both liberalization and amalgamation with Madhya Bharat, but the States Ministry decided to keep Bhopal under central control for at least five years.[18] The primary factor in the decision was the insecurity of the Muslim population which was concentrated in Bhopal, one of the few safe islands in a stormy North India.

The old state was about 6,900 square miles, divided into two districts: Sehore, where the capital was located; and Raisen, to the east. In per capita value of agricultural output Sehore and Raisen rank second and third behind Indore's lead, in spite of the fact that cash crops account for only 13.2 per cent of the total cropped area.

Industrialization is relatively new in Bhopal. Before the establishment of Heavy Electricals (HEL) in the public sector, the contribution of industry to income was only 2.86 per cent, most of it in textiles.[19] Nonetheless, HEL, by virtue of its size, organization, and trade unions, is a significant new factor in the political life of the region.

Of more importance than the establishment of HEL, however, was the decision to make Bhopal the capital of Madhya Pradesh. Its special isolation from Madhya Bharat, and its extra-Mahakoshal, extra-Vindhya Pradesh status, made it a relatively neutral ground for regional politics. The States Reorganization Commission recommended Jabalpur as a suitable capital,[20] but there was so little agreement in the region that Prime Minister Nehru was given Solomon's task, and he picked Bhopal. His reasoning must have been conditioned by the quarrels within the state, especially between the smaller regions and Mahakoshal, by unseemly land speculation in Jabalpur, by Bhopal's unique isolation in the state and by its proximity to Uttar Pradesh. The effect has been to continue to make Bhopal's politics foreign to other regions in the state,

[17] An overly brief and discreet account is given in Menon, *op.cit.*, pp. 303-06.

[18] The details are given in *Report of the States Reorganization Commission, 1955* (New Delhi, 1955), pp. 126-27.

[19] See *Economic Survey of Madhya Pradesh Agriculture, 1959-60* (Bhopal, 1964), p. 6 and *Regional Income Atlas of Madhya Pradesh*, pp. 40-48.

[20] *Report of the States Reorganization Commission, 1955*, para. 486, p. 132.

and to build into what was a fairly prosperous part of Malwa a much greater capital development.

Under the present administrative organization, Bhopal is divisional headquarters for five districts in addition to Sehore and Raisen, all of them in central Madhya Pradesh but with considerable variations in social composition, degree of urbanization, per capita income, and industrial working force.[21] The division has little political unity, and

TABLE 3.3

REGIONAL PROFILES: BHOPAL AND CENTRAL MADHYA PRADESH

District	*Population*	*Scheduled Caste/ Scheduled Tribe %*	*Urbanization (% in places of 5000+)*	*Literacy, %*	*Per Capita Income Rs.*	*Factory Workers*
Sehore	754,684	15.6/4.0	36.0	21.5	344	7,700
Raisen	411,426	15.2/14.1	5.3	13.4	313	—
Vidisha	489,213	20.9/4.3	13.1	13.5	241	200
Hoshangabad	613,293	10.1/7.5	19.3	22.9	299	1,500
Betul	560,412	9.4/32.0	8.4	16.5	243	—
Shajapur	526,135	22.7/—	10.1	14.1	275	2,300
Rajgarh	516,871	18.9/0.2	9.5	10.0	241	1,300

SOURCE: Same as in Table 3.2.

district profiles simply reflect conditions in east-west contiguous areas rather than mark Bhopal as a unique unit.

The political life of Bhopal and its immediate locality is conditioned by three unique factors: (1) the presence of a hundred thousand urban Muslims; (2) the development of the state capital and its effect in stimulating heavy immigration into the city and district; and (3) the establishment of HEL in an outlying satellite town, which introduces a new industrial dimension to local politics. The land tenure system and the Muslim jagirdars do not appear to have been a major problem, nor even a Muslim problem,[22] even though there was controversy concerning their abolition.

Regional Profiles: Vindhya Pradesh

In the north and northwest portion of Madhya Pradesh is the region

[21] See Table 3.3.

[22] Three-quarters of the state was under a system of peasant proprietorship (*ryotwari*). Of the remaining one-fourth, half was either uncultivable or held by Gonds and Solanki Rajputs. The remaining half was held closely within the dynasty. Jagir-

of Vindhya Pradesh, with an area of about 24,600 square miles and a population in 1951 of 3,574,690. By 1961 the population had grown to 4,251,042. The region is a product of a forced union of two antagonistic areas, Baghelkhand and Bundelkhand, and their 35 constituent princely states. The most important state in the region was Rewa, which was as large as all of the Bundelkhand states combined,[23] but because of dynastic quarrels based on Rajput caste disputes, the regions had never accepted one another as political allies. Indeed, the rivalry in the region was as great as between the Scindia and Holkar Marathas in Madhya Bharat.

Vindhya Pradesh took its name from the Vindhya range, which sets Baghelkhand and Bundelkhand apart from the plains of Uttar Pradesh. Although Allahabad is only about 65 miles from Rewa, the two localities are radically different. Vindhya Pradesh is the most backward part of central India. In no district is the literacy rate more than 15.6 per cent, or the urbanization, minimally defined, more than 9.6 per cent. No district in Vindhya Pradesh has a per capita income higher than the state average, and in a population of four and a quarter million, there are only 3,500 factory workers. In every district except Chhatarpur the tribal population is important.

In the absence of urban forms of political association, the politics of Vindhya Pradesh is closely tied to agriculture and the traditional and tribal orders. Before the passage of land reforms, there were thirteen variant forms of intermediary offices possible between the government and the tenant. In 1952 there were 21,700 intermediaries who had rights on 5,657,391 acres and in addition wholly owned another 384,206 acres.[24] The 1952 land reform act began assuming jagirdari rights with compensation, in 1953, of almost 20 million rupees.

The region is politically inchoate, in part because there was no organized political life prior to 1947 and very little thereafter. When the Vindhya Pradesh union was organized, for example, Bundelkhand and Baghelkhand were given separate assemblies with a common Rajpramukh (governor), the Maharaja of Rewa. The two ministries concept, according to Menon, was "an utter failure."[25] When a common ministry was formed, even more problems developed. Within less than a year after its formation, Vindhya Pradesh was brought under govern-

---

dari was abolished in August 1953 by the Bhopal Legislature. See H. D. Malaviya, *Land Reforms in India* (2nd ed.; New Delhi, 1955), pp. 401-07.

[23] The account of the union of the states is given in Menon, *op.cit.*, pp. 211-12.

[24] See Malaviya, *op.cit.*, pp. 362-71.

[25] Menon, *op.cit.*, pp. 219-22.

ment control through an I.C.S. regional commissioner. The lack of financial viability was less a factor than the lack of organized government, and it was therefore decided that Vindhya Pradesh should be divided between the United Provinces and the Central Provinces. When the provincial governments failed to agree on the distribution of the region, the central government assumed direct control on January 1, 1950.

The political life of Vindhya Pradesh seems to be strongly influenced by (1) tribal and caste loyalties, (2) the continuing strength and mutual hostilities of jagirdars, mostly Rajputs, and (3) the continuing power and rivalry of princes. In the absence of large-scale economic change in the region, it is difficult to imagine new forces emerging in the politics of Vindhya Pradesh in the immediate future.

TABLE 3.4

REGIONAL PROFILES: VINDHYA PRADESH

istrict	*Population (1961)*	*Scheduled Caste/ Scheduled Tribe %*	*Urbanization (% in places of 5000+)*	*Literacy, %*	*Per Capita Income Rs.*	*Factory Workers*
ewa	772,602	12.1/13.3	5.6	14.9	213	300
idhi	580,129	9.6/33.7	.9	7.8	157	—
hahdol	829,649	5.7/51.4	7.0	10.3	191	400
atna	649,370	12.6/14.6	9.1	15.6	236	2,800
anna	331,257	17.4/14.6	5.0	10.4	258	—
hhatarpur	587,373	22.1/2.9	9.6	11.2	240	—
ikanigarh	455,662	20.7/4.7	4.5	9.7	236	—

URCE: Same as in Table 3.2.

Regional Profiles: Mahakoshal and Chhattisgarh

The "Prussia" of Madhya Pradesh is the region which was part of the former state of Madhya Pradesh, itself formed by a union of the former Central Provinces, Berar, the state of Makrai, which had been part of Bhopal agency, and the chiefs and princelings of Chhattisgarh. Its total area, before the 1956 reconstruction of the province, was 130,323 square miles of which 80,766 had been part of the Central Provinces.

The Chhattisgarh region is the extreme eastern portion of the state on the Orissa border. Of the 15 chiefs of the area, the one with the largest state was the ruler of Bastar, who ruled an area of 13,000 square miles. Most of the states were much smaller, having been founded either by Rajputs or Marathas, and some having been feudatories to the Mughal empire. Immediately after independence, the rulers of the Orissa Hill states and the Chhattisgarh chiefs formed the Eastern States Union.[26] Because of the rich mineral deposits which had been discovered throughout the Chhattisgarh region and for obvious political reasons, the government of India was unwilling to see it split off solely as a princely union. An equally important consideration was the need of Orissa to incorporate the hill states in its political life. In a somewhat devious fashion, the Indian government utilized the state *praja mandals* and capitalized on the inroads being made by Communists in the region to divide the states between the Central Provinces, soon to become Madhya Pradesh, and Orissa.

The Mahakoshal region is that part of the state which was under direct British administration in the Central Provinces. With Nagpur as its capital, the Central Provinces in 1947 was, after the amalgamation of the Chhattisgarh states and the end of the "lease of Berar" from Hyderabad, a large and viable but bilingual state of 21,247,000 people.

Alone of the regions of Madhya Pradesh state, Mahakoshal's population had had opportunities for ongoing political experience. The Congress party had a long history in the Central Provinces, and the Nagpur session of the party was in many ways the seminal period for the state's public life.[27] Although Nagpur was stripped away from Madhya Pradesh in 1956, it proved to be a good school for party politicians.

The States Reorganization Report of 1955 recommended the separation of Marathi-speaking districts south of the Satpura range and considered it desirable that they should go to Bombay (Maharashtra), with the residual Hindi-speaking districts to be amalgamated with Madhya Bharat, Vindhya Pradesh, and Bhopal. This recommendation was in support of the Mahakoshal Pradeshik Congress Committee's stated views. The *Report's* authors admitted that the new area "has never been administered together, at any rate long enough for a tradition of common loyalties and sentiment to have come into existence" but argued that reorganization "should be determined primarily by economic and administrative considerations and not by the history of

[26] See Menon, *op.cit.*, pp. 151-74 for a description of the entire process. For Chhattisgarh alone, see pp. 168-74. There is also a valuable description of *Adivasi* (tribal) politics through the eyes of a senior civil servant, p. 174.

[27] See D. P. Mishra (ed.), *The History of the Freedom Movement in Madhya Pradesh* (Nagpur: Government Press, 1956), pp. 299-494. The editor is presently (May 1967) chief minister of the state.

individual principalities."[28] There was also a candid admission that Mahakoshal and the eastern districts would probably dominate the union, but that in the long run a larger economic unit was in the best interests of all parts of central India.

The Mahakoshal-Chhattisgarh region of Madhya Pradesh accounts for about 40 per cent of the population and includes a part of the iron ore, manganese, and limestone resources of the state. It is also the rice belt and enjoys a surplus production. Both the mineral and agricultural wealth are barely exploited, and the forest products of Bastar have not yet been utilized, in part because of important political disputes over forest rights. The political strength of the region comes not so much from economic potentials, however, as from political and organizational skills and experience. Numbers also help.

The unique characteristics of Mahakoshal are (1) its numerical dominance compared to three other heterogeneous units, (2) the importance of the tribal population and leaders in Chhattisgarh region, (3) the development of heavy industries, and (4) the existence of a trained cadre of party workers. While caste and tribal loyalties are still important, this region has an experienced political elite, and the style of life of rice/paddy cultivators, tied to regional markets as they are, is quite different from that of subsistence farmers in Madhya Bharat. Moreover, the potentials of the region are such as to encourage growth and urbanization, thereby further emphasizing the dominance of Mahakoshal in the life of the state.

THE POLITICAL PROCESS

The political life of the state is dominated by the Congress party in its various factional *avatars*. To a high degree, it exhibits the characteristics of a one-party system in which the struggle for power takes place between rival factions within the same party. This is reflected in a three-way rivalry: between the ministerial and party organization wings, between factions having strength in both wings, and between regional rival groups within the party. In the period immediately following the second general elections, political immobilism led to the appointment of a chief minister from Uttar Pradesh and his governance, with the support of the central government, for five years.

While the Congress party dominates the exceedingly broad middle path of politics in the state, parties of the "right" tend to constitute the opposition. Jan Sangh has increased its strength in the state Legislative Assembly to a quarter of all members, and the milieu of central

[28] *Report of the States Reorganization Commission, 1955*, p. 126.

TABLE 3.5

REGIONAL PROFILES: CHHATTISGARH AND MAHAKOSHAL

District	*Population (1961)*	*Scheduled Caste / Scheduled Tribe %*	*Urbanization (% in places of 5000+)*	*Literacy, %*	*Per Capita Income Rs.*	*Factory Workers*
Raipur[a]	2,002,004	14.9/15.5	13.4	18.5	283	8,400
Durg[a]	1,885,236	11.0/11.1	12.5	17.8	271	7,200
Bastar[a]	1,167,501	5.5/72.3	2.3	6.9	254	800
Raigarh[a]	1,041,226	11.1/45.9	5.7	14.9	221	3,000
Bilaspur[a]	2,021,793	18.2/18.2	8.3	18.2	246	5,000
Surguja[a]	1,036,738	5.8/55.6	4.2	9.2	255	200
Jabalpur	1,273,825	9.4/12.2	37.1	28.5	287	15,200
Mandla	684,503	3.8/61.8	4.8	14.2	211	—
Balaghat	806,702	3.2/10.8	5.7	20.6	233	600
Chhindwara	785,535	9.1/33.3	12.5	16.3	265	600
Sagar	796,547	20.7/—	22.7	20.5	247	1,800
Narsimhapur	412,406	7.9/12.2	11.9	21.5	259	1,100
Seoni	523,741	4.3/38.4	5.8	17.1	204	400
Damoh	438,343	18.3/—	12.7	18.4	198	500

[a] Denotes Chhattisgarh region.
SOURCE: Same as in Table 3.2.

Indian politics is dominated by Hindu political-religious sloganeering. Both the Hindu Mahasabha and the Ram Rajya Parishad are active in the state, but are much less important than the Jan Sangh. It might therefore be fair to suggest that neo-traditional party platforms have more appeal than the conservative platform of the other two parties. The Swatantra party managed to win only 2 seats in the 1962 election and its 1967, 7-seat performance was also weak.

In part the strength of the religious "rightist" parties is attributable to strong communal tensions in the state. The presence of Muslims and of Christian missionaries in certain areas of the state has served as a focus for Hindu politics. In 1956 the state government appointed Dr. M. Bhawani Shankar Niyogi, an ex-Chief Justice from Nagpur, to lead an enquiry into Christian missionary activities.[29] The report did not calm troubled waters. In early February 1961 large-scale communal rioting, which had previously been confined to isolated instances, broke out in Jabalpur. The army had to be called to restore order, and more than 20 people were killed.[30] The disturbances spread and flickered on, erupting again in

[29] Government of Madhya Pradesh, *Report of the Christian Missionary Activities Enquiry Committee* (Nagpur, 1956).

[30] See *Hindustan Times* (New Delhi), February 13, 1961, for an account.

August in Bhopal district.[31] The concern with religious minorities on the part of the rightist parties reinforced minority group feeling. The *Hindustan Times,* in reporting on the anti-Muslim character of politics in Jabalpur, argued that

> communalism is a defence mechanism with which a group of people with identical interests arms itself. . . . The first group loyalty is to his religion rather than the weaver's guild because whereas he does not feel that weavers as a group are threatened, he cannot confidently say the same thing about Muslims as a group.[32]

The attitudes of Hindu parties toward Christians, especially missionaries "with foreign money" was tactically the same as toward Muslims.

The parties of the left are much weaker. The Praja Socialist party is caught between the Congress on the one side and the Communists on the other. Because issues tend to be regional rather than state-wide, the scattered bases of voting strength of parties of the left are a disadvantage. The Communist party of Madhya Pradesh is especially weak, having some strength in the trade union movement but little or none in the peasantry. Only a broad coalition-type party can function in socially diverse, single-member constituencies, and the CPI has neither inclined toward a popular front nor been able to make the necessary matches.[33]

Party behavior is more understandable if regional histories are kept in mind. Every part of Madhya Pradesh had experienced some form of representative government prior to the creation of the state in 1956. Each had established branches of the Congress party which had sustained independent ministries. It was inevitable that these organized subordinate communities should be semi-independent, especially since substantive interests support them. In addition, the constituencies of the state reflect such a wide spectrum of social organization that their representatives could hardly share more than offices in the Legislative Assembly.

Party unity, or lack of it, has also been a function of the degree to which the ministerial wing of the Congress has been able to use its prerogatives and fishes and loaves to support state-wide coalitions. The smaller parties are much less able to deliver benefits to would-be partners, and hence remain unattractive as vehicles for group or regional interests.

[31] *Times of India,* August 6, 1961.

[32] *Hindustan Times,* June 19, 1961.

[33] In fact, Communists candidates sometimes find it necessary to run as independents, so weak is party appeal.

Party Strengths Before the Founding of the State

The Madhya Bharat union was inaugurated in Gwalior on May 28, 1948 by Prime Minister Nehru. In January 1950 the state became full party to the constitution and accordingly organized for the first general elections. The region had 11 parliamentary seats and a Legislative Assembly of 99 members. In the hustings, the Congress secured 9 of 11 Lok Sabha seats, the remaining two falling to the Hindu Mahasabha, and won 46.4 per cent of all votes cast. In the state Assembly the 99 seats were divided as follows: Congress 75, Hindu Mahasabha 11, Jan Sangh 4, Ram Rajya Parishad 2, Socialist 4, and Independents 3. The Congress won 45.3 per cent of the Assembly vote, but the former union chief minister, the law and revenue minister, the speaker of the Assembly, and a Scheduled Caste deputy minister all lost to candidates of the Hindu Mahasabha. On the other hand, the presidents of the state Hindu Mahasabha and Jan Sangh were defeated. These defeats demonstrate an often pronounced trend of the Indian voter to unseat his elected representatives after a short time in office.[34] The Muslim population of approximately half a million lost 3 of the 5 seats they had held in the previous Assembly, two to the Jan Sangh,[35] and hence were underrepresented as a religious minority.

The importance of communalism in Madhya Bharat was evident, but another arresting aspect of regional politics was the contrast of voting behavior in Gwalior and Indore. In Gwalior the Congress majority was 25/37 seats, whereas in Indore its proportion was 50/62. Similarly, 11 of the 12 seats lost in Gwalior went to rightist parties while those in Indore were divided between rightists and socialists. This apparently reflected, at least in part, the continuing hostility between the two states, even with settlement of the state capital issue.[36]

In *Bhopal* the 1952 elections were the first held in the state. Two seats in Parliament and 30 seats in the Bhopal state Assembly were at stake. The Congress had overwhelming strength, its primary opposition coming from a faction which had spun off under the name of the Kisan

[34] This is a curious factor in the subcontinent's politics; see the essay by Myron Weiner, "Struggle Against Power. Notes on Indian Political Behaviour," in *Political Change in South Asia* (Calcutta: Firma K. L. Mukhopadhyay, 1963), especially pp. 153-59.

[35] These figures are taken from S. R. Sharma, "Madhya Bharat" in S. V. Kogekar and Richard L. Park, *Reports on the Indian General Elections, 1951-52* (Bombay: Popular Book Depot, 1956), pp. 188-203.

[36] One of the important controversies in the creation of the Madhya Bharat Union was the location of the capital. In Prime Minister Nehru's award, the summer capital was to be Indore, the winter capital Gwalior.

Mazdoor Mandal (peasant and workers association). Its president, Shakir Ali Khan, and its leftist trade union base continued to be a factor in Bhopal through the elections of 1967. In the polling, the Congress won both parliamentary seats, and 25 out of 30 of the Assembly seats. The other seats fell to independents, except for one member of the Hindu Mahasabha. The Kisan Mazdoor Mandal lost heavily, being forced to forfeit deposits on 8 out of 12 candidates.[37] It is interesting to note that the Bhopal Congress party defended the state's independence from Madhya Bharat, and that the primary issues in the election stemmed from substantive measures such as the abolition of jagirs or the nationalization of industries.

During the course of the first general elections, *Vindhya Pradesh* was in an anomalous position. The experiment with democratic government had worked out badly, and the state had a class "C" status (directly administered by the central government) before the elections. The people, however, voted for 6 MPs and 60 members of the Legislative Assembly, even though the latter had restricted powers. The Congress, which had a brief and checkered history in the region, won 4 of 6 parliamentary seats and 40 of 60 legislative contests. The Socialist party won 11, and all other parties won only 7, leaving two independent MLAs. It was reported that caste bloc voting was important in the election as was personal and local leadership.[38]

The *Mahakoshal* region and the former Madhya Pradesh (including Vidarbha) state showed great loyalty to the Congress. Of 29 parliamentary seats in the state, the Congress won 27, leaving only two for independents. Of the 149 Mahakoshal seats in the state Legislative Assembly, the Congress swept 118 of the 140 seats it chose to contest. The Chhattisgarh region was characterized by the victory of independents, most of them princes. Parties capitalizing on communal issues did poorly in the region, in part because the Muslim population was not more than 5 per cent of the state's population, and because the increasing popular concern with the proposed Hindu Code Bill was locally less marked than elsewhere in central India. The Congress strength, however, lay not in the absence of an opposition but in the smooth and efficient operation of the Mahakoshal Congress organization in turning out the voters.[39]

Parliamentary Party Strengths, 1957–62

In the first elections after the organization of the state in 1956, the

[37] The account as given by Kogekar and Park, *op.cit.*, pp. 261-65.
[38] *Ibid.*, pp. 316-22.
[39] *Ibid.*, pp. 68-86.

Congress won 35 of 36 parliamentary seats, losing only Shivpuri to the Hindu Mahasabha. Five years later, however, the Congress won only 24 seats, losing three each to the Praja Socialist party and the Jan Sangh, one each to the Socialists and Ram Rajya Parishad, and four to independents.[40]

However, it is clear that the parliamentary elections follow a different course than elections to the state Legislative Assembly. The skills of members of the Lok Sabha, for example proficiency in English, and the nature of their representation in New Delhi make a parliamentary election much less sensitive as an index to popular opinion than the state legislative elections. Nonetheless, MPs often are important party figures who attempt to make the jump from provincial to national status. Very few succeed; indeed, one looks in vain for important ministers in the union government from the state.

A survey of the 1962-67 Madhya Pradesh MPs shows an average age of slightly more than 48. One is struck by the infrequency of the return of incumbents except among the Scheduled Caste and Tribe constituencies and in the case of the princes. The biographies of the members of the Lok Sabha seem to indicate six (often overlapping) political bases of power, or at least appeal: (1) leadership of a trade union, a cooperative society or mortgage bank; (2) leadership in a caste or ascriptive group, such as the Rajputs or Harijans, or of a Scheduled Tribe; (3) fame by birth, either into the princely order or as the son of an outstanding local man; (4) success in law, business, medicine or education; (5) service in the nationalist (Congress) cause, and especially a prison record under British rule, and (6) past political experience, either in the party or in municipal and state legislative councils. It would seem clear that among the younger group, prior political experience in local organizations has become a *sine qua non* for election at least in the general constituencies. It is also clear that independents and opposition candidates won only because they either had an impregnable local base (tribe, caste, business, cooperative, trade union) or were successful in breaking party discipline by campaigning against the designated candidate while themselves little more than renegade Congressmen.[41] The fact remains that the party organization is the most important common institution in the state, but it can serve the political demands of a heterogeneous state only by maintaining an exceedingly broad coalition.

40 Including the Communist/independent, Homi Daji, from Indore.

41 These observations are based on 33 of 36 biographies of MPs from Madhya Pradesh published in the *Lok Sabha Who's Who 1962* (New Delhi, 1962).

State Legislative Assembly Party Strengths, 1957-62

In the first state-wide Legislative Assembly elections, the Congress won 232 of 288 seats, with the Praja Socialists winning 12, the Jan Sangh 10, the Hindu Mahasabha and the Lohia Socialists 7 each, Ram Rajya Parishad 5, Communist and Communist/Independent 3, and independents 12. The Congress was weakest in Vindhya Pradesh and Madhya Bharat, but strong in Bhopal and almost unchallenged in Mahakoshal where it won 128 of 147 seats.

Five years later, however, the Congress fell short of an absolute majority, winning only 142 of 288 seats. Every opposition party benefited from the Congress debacle except the Hindu Mahasabha and the Communists, both of whom lost seats. The four-fold increase in the strength of the Jan Sangh (to 41 seats) was most evident in the Madhya Bharat region. In Vindhya Pradesh the Congress held only a one seat majority over the combined opposition strength, and in Mahakoshal the Congress delivered less than 60 per cent of the winning candidates.

Only by bringing independents and dissident Congressmen back into the parliamentary party did the Congress organize the state government with 153 members, but it was a weak government in a state without settled administration or a strong potential state party organization. The pressure of the opposition parties was also increasingly important.

TABLE 3.6

RELATIVE PARTY STRENGTHS, 1952–67, STATE LEGISLATIVE ASSEMBLY

	1952	1957	1962	1967
Indian National Congress	260	232	142	167
Jan Sangh (JS)	6	10	41	78
Ram Rajya Parishad (RRP)	7	5	10	—
Hindu Mahasabha (HM)	13	7	6	—
Socialist Party (Mehta)	16	—	—	—
Kisan Mazdoor Praja party (Kripalani)	10	—	—	—
Independents	27	12	39	24[a]
Praja Socialist party (PSP)	—	12	33	9
Communist party of India (CPI)	—	2	1	1
Socialist party (Lohia)	—	7	14	10
Communist party–Independent	—	1	—	—
Swatantra	—	—	2	7
Totals	339	288	288	296

[a] Including Ram Rajya Parishad and Jana Congress

POLITICAL LEADERSHIP

The tale of political leadership in the state is a tangled skein of personalities, factions, local "dynasties," and external influence. Before India's independence, the political life of the Central Provinces was dominated by the rivalry between Pandit Ravi Shankar Shukla and Seth Govind Das. Shukla had been chief minister of the Central Provinces after K. B. Khare in 1938, and became the first chief minister of the reconstituted Madhya Pradesh in November 1956. Less than two months later, however, he died, and in the absence of a readily acceptable successor, Prime Minister Nehru sent Dr. K. N. Katju, a Kashmiri Brahman with experience in the central government, to Bhopal to form the Congress government. Although Dr. Katju had been born in Madhya Pradesh, he normally resided in Allahabad. In addition to his "alien" quality, his political effectiveness was reduced because he was elderly and almost deaf.

The Katju ministry was installed in January 1957, and its five years in power were marked by recurrent political crises. As an outsider, the chief minister was above regional parochialism, but his tasks were to orchestrate a provincial party which was a coalition of local interests. The three branches of the state Congress party—ministerial, legislative assembly, and organizational—had to be balanced or won over if any viable government was to exist in the province. Repeatedly the central government exerted its weight to rescue its endangered magistrate and to maintain stability in the new state.

The primary opposition to Dr. Katju and consequently to national dominance in the political leadership of the state was from the Pradesh Congress Committee president, Moolchand Deshlehra. Deshlehra's faction pitted the non-Brahman organizational wing of the party against its ministerial wing in the contest for control of the legislative party. Internal crises were therefore clustered in periods of either party or general elections, and the capital was constantly rife with rumors of the most dire disunity in the party, the more so after the Congress sweep in 1957.

The base of support for the Katju and Deshlehra factions of the Congress party is difficult to ascertain. The ministerial wing, regardless of composition, has certain advantages accruing because of patronage which cuts across particular political communities. The following groups, however, seem to be involved: (1) the former governing elites of the four regions of the state, and Brahman-Bania factions within the Congress; (2) the business community, composed of indigenous, Gujarati, and Marwari capitalists; (3) representatives of the central government, and (4) princes, tribal leaders, and other petty "kings" in the state.

The most easily identified groups in the political process are the former regional Congress leaders. In the Madhya Bharat area, there were two important factions: the Taktmal Jain group and the Kanhaiyalal Khadiwala group.[42] Both are largely based in Indore, with the former having more continuous importance in state politics. The weak Gwalior Congress organization has less influence. In Bhopal the primary political figure is Dr. Shankar Dayal Sharma, who at 34 was called as chief minister in the 1952 Bhopal popular ministry. He is hardly a ward-heeling boss, however, having a doctorate from Cambridge and having been a fellow at the Harvard Law School. He has been a minister since 1957, but Bhopal's weight in the regional politics of the state is slight.

Regional politics in Vindhya Pradesh revolve about Rewa state, and Captain Avadhesh Pratap Singh and Shambu Nath Shukla, the former chief minister of the state. Rewa's lead was not universally respected in Vindhya Pradesh, and influences from Uttar Pradesh were often strong, but the "Rewa bloc" is the most important group in the region. In Mahakoshal the Jabalpur region continued to be dominated by the personality of Seth Govind Das, MP, who dominated the Mahakoshal Pradesh Congress Committee well before the creation of the state. The Chhattisgarh region has many masters, and hence very little of the bloc strength possessed by more unified regional parties, and Rajput-Brahman and Brahman-Bania conflicts also undermine unity.

It is much more difficult to document and label the forces and influence of the business community. At the outset, however, it must be borne in mind that there are at least three distinct business communities—Gujarati Bania, Marwari, and indigenous groups. The large bulk of business volume is controlled by the first two groups, with the Gujarat Banias strongest in western Madhya Pradesh. As with almost every business community, the emphasis is on being on the winning side of policies rather than on contesting state leadership, so the ministerial wing has broad support. The so-called rice kings of Chhattisgarh contribute generously to all campaign war-chests in return for state protection of their interests. On the other hand, dominant business groups seek to use their influence to keep rivals out of the state, or to ensure more favorable terms in the conduct of their business. The Deshlehra faction in the Congress seems to draw heavy support from the Marwaris, while the present ministerial wing has the support of Gujarati Jain finance.

At a lower level the indigenous commercial interests play an important role. In the eastern part of the state rice mill owners are active,

[42] As with most state factions, the Brahman-Bania rivalry is evident.

and in Jabalpur and elsewhere the *beedi* (cheap cigarettes) manufacturers are important.[43] The industry of western Madhya Pradesh is largely owned by interests active in state-wide politics, and local small industry has a weak voice in politics. It must be noted, however, that there are no studies and no way in which to study the role of money in state politics despite the general consensus of informed observers that business exercises an "extraterritorial paramountcy"[44] in Madhya Pradesh. Precisely how rival business groups finance their client-politicians while keeping free of harassment from political rivals is an interesting area for further research.

A third force in state politics is the central government, which played a key role in the selection of Dr. Katju and his two successors. The power of the central government is exercised through different agencies. Prime Minister Nehru chose Dr. Katju; and his daughter, Indira Gandhi, who would later become prime minister, had much to do with Dr. D. P. Mishra's rise to power. One might even conclude that the chief ministership of Madhya Pradesh was something of a fief for famous Brahman politicians loyal to New Delhi. The state bureaucracy, the top posts in which are filled with IAS officers, is in a position to exert more than marginal power. The All-India Congress Committee and its agents play an oftentimes crucial role in blunting inner-state party rivalries and facilitating the dominance of a given group. The Governor of the state holds formal but quite real powers which are exercised upon instruction from Delhi. The Home Ministry plays an important, though veiled, role in the princely order since it controls accessions to contested *gaddis* (thrones) and the amount of the privy purses of rulers. The AICC has been most important, in part because the state rivalries have been largely fought within the Congress caucus. Delhi's agents are repeatedly called to mediate conflicts between groups in the state Congress, and can favor their allies.

Outside the purview of regional leadership, strong economic interests, and Congress party politics are the remnants of the old order—men with great strengths independent of modern political organization. The princes, tribal leaders, and aristocracy of the old order have a personal latitude in politics which minimizes party control. Since the state has been in almost continuous crisis since its formation, and especially be-

[43] Indeed, Seth Govind Das (see p. 43) is known as the "beedi king" of Jabalpur, as well as the incumbent member of Parliament.

[44] This phrase is from Sunanda K. Datta-Ray in *The Statesman* (Calcutta) in two articles, "Madhya Pradesh," May 5 and May 12, 1964, which are very useful. The writer is indebted to Richard Von Glatz for directing his attention to it.

tween 1962 and 1967 when the Congress majority was narrow, they exerted an influence out of proportion to their small numbers because the importance of marginal groups was maximized.

This pattern of politics carried explicit limitations on the power and freedom of governmental and party leadership and produced a pattern of "balancing and brokering" characteristic of the state since its formation. It is clear that state leadership does not monopolize the channels for political recruitment, but rather must form coalitions of groups and interests that have attained importance in various public arenas. This, too, minimizes the purposive role of state leadership.

Political Leadership in the Opposition

Opposition parties are also strongly affected by regionalism and other parochial forces in the state. While they offer open and uncrowded channels of recruitment, the most direct paths to power are dominated by the Congress, and consequently none but the ideologically committed, the Congress-expelled, and the foolhardy join other parties. In the Communist party, Shakir Ali Khan in Bhopal and Homi Daji in Indore are the only men who have been able to withstand more than one electoral struggle against the Congress. Homi Daji's 1962 election to Parliament, moreover, was more a function of Congress "Bull Moose" politics than of his intrinsic organizational strength and in 1967 he was defeated. Shakir Ali Khan combined a long history of dedicated public life in ventures of the left with his Muslim faith, maximizing his own electoral base in Bhopal but being unable to extend it to party colleagues.

The Jan Sangh has grown steadily, especially in western Madhya Pradesh and in the small cities and towns of the province. The party has grown partly at the expense of the Hindu Mahasabha, and a considerable portion of its organizing ability and funds comes from the RSS.[45] It is difficult, however, to establish continuing patterns of leadership or fixed patterns of recruitment other than through the RSS. Two of the three Jan Sangh MPs elected in 1962 were freshmen to the House, and lacked political experience elsewhere. One was a lawyer from Khargone, educated at Indore Christian College and active in tribal affairs, and the other an RSS-graduate mill worker elected from a Scheduled Caste constituency dominated by the Koli caste. The third Jan Sangh MP, U. M. Trivedi, had been a member of the first parliament but not the second. Opposition party representatives are vulnerable to the intense campaigns which the Congress can organize to recapture lost seats,

[45] Rashtriya Swayam Sevah Sangh, a militant Hindu organization largely for the young which supplies much of the volunteer strength to parties of the religious right.

and except in most unusual cases of strong local strength are powerless to maintain their control of a constituency.[46]

The same general problem confronts the Socialist and Praja Socialist parties (since the summer of 1964, the combined Samyukta Socialist party-SSP), whose strength is pocketed in various districts, generally in the eastern parts of the state. The history of the party is filled with electoral disasters, the first of which was experienced in the 1952 elections when Archarya Kripalani's Kisan Mazdoor Praja party (KMPP) won only 10 of 339 seats. Later, Dr. D. P. Mishra, who organized the state government in 1963, joined the Praja Socialist party but was defeated. The socialists in the state have lacked able and imaginative leadership, and their commitment to socialist ideology has repelled the primary sources of financial support open to the other parties.

The Ram Rajya Parishad leadership is drawn largely from the former ruling houses or the jagirdars, and most independents in politics claim the same type of local base of personal influence resistant to the Congress organization and strength. In many cases, the Congress has nominated a local figure who has strength independent of the Congress in the interests of its majority, while in other cases it has sought to defeat or humble the local man. This calculation is apparently based solely on expediency and the risks involved. In other cases, the Congress has used local aristocrats, with scant regard for party label, against other parties. Datta-Ray quotes the Congress high command in the state as being "convinced that the Princes will never join hands with the banias behind the Jan Sangh."[47]

Change and Continuity in Political Leadership

Unlike Punjab and Maharashtra, the political leadership in Madhya Pradesh has changed very little since the founding of the state. New faces have been recruited into old factions, and D. P. Mishra has returned from about a decade in the wilderness (or at least Saugor University) to become the state's chief minister. Mishra's return, however, was not unlike Dr. Katju's advent. He was ushered in after Moolchand Deshlehra had been sacked for the 1962 electoral debacle and after the Kamaraj plan and Delhi's blessings had empowered him.

Mishra's opportunity came when Dr. Katju lost his bid for election in the state in 1962, and when B. R. Mandloi was edged out of power after

[46] U. M. Trivedi, for example, was returned from Mandsaur in which his Gujarati training and background served him in good stead.

[47] *The Statesman,* May 12, 1964. Perhaps they realize that it would be imprudent to needlessly alienate a Congress-controlled central Home Ministry.

having moved closer to the Deshlehra group as a compromise candidate in an effort to bring a measure of unity to the narrowly dominant Congress legislative party. D. P. Mishra had once been a strong man supporting the Katju ministry, but had gone to Delhi as head of the public relations office of the Central Citizen's Council in the wake of the Chinese invasion. His aberrant record of loyalty to the Congress cause, his reputation as a "boss," and Nehru's approbation had brought his expulsion from the party earlier, but he used his Delhi stay to good advantage, apparently convincing the "High Command" that Mandloi's victory in the succession struggle would consolidate the position of the Deshlehra faction.[48] In fact, Mandloi had the support of the bania trinity, Seth Govind Das, Takhtmal Jain, and Moolchand Deshlehra, the latter having been forced to resign the presidency of the state congress two weeks earlier. The decision of the Congress Disciplinary Action Committee to set aside Mishra's expulsion and his forceful re-arrival on the scene in a by-election in Raipur district in May 1963 set the scene for the next year's politics. On September 23, 1963 the Congress legislative party cast 84 votes for Dr. Mishra and 62 for Takhtmal Jain, Mr. Mandloi's candidate in the House. On the next day Dr. Mishra became chief minister of Madhya Pradesh.

The fluidity of state politics was demonstrated between September 1962 and September 1963. Mandloi was almost invulnerable at its outset, enjoying the support of three pillars of the Congress in Madhya Bharat and Mahakoshal. D. P. Mishra was apparently worried about his electoral appeal in Jabalpur, the home constituency of Seth Govind Das, and took a safer course in a Chhattisgarh election. Within a year, even though Mandloi controlled the ministry, D. P. Mishra succeeded in taking over the legislative party. Yet the actors in the changed political scene were roughly the same with the exception of Dr. Katju, and Mishra's victory was in part a result of the Kamaraj plan, Delhi's intervention, and Brahman unity in state factions.

The party organization also underwent considerable change. After the 1962 near-defeat of the Congress, an Inquiry Commission was appointed to investigate charges that the Deshlehra group had sabotaged electoral efforts of the ministerial wing candidates.[49] After the inquiry,

[48] There is some reason to believe that the contact within high party circles was through Indira Gandhi. In the succession struggle following Lal Bahadur Shastri's untimely death, it was in D. P. Mishra's Delhi house that the first suggestion from a major state leader that Indira Gandhi should be the party candidate was made. Since that time, Mishra's star has steadily risen in Congress party politics.

[49] A *Times of India* reporter wrote, in the aftermath, that "There was tragedy in Katju's exit. As he drove out after the meeting on August 9th to catch a train

Moolchand Deshlehra was asked to resign as Congress president, and the Pradesh Congress Committee was superseded. Rameshwar Dayal Totla was appointed to convene an *ad hoc* Congress committee. After the announcement of the Kamaraj plan, Mandloi was made chairman of the *ad hoc* committee, apparently on Mishra's recommendation. After Mishra's electoral victory and almost a year of maneuver, Mandloi was removed and Kanhaiyalal Khadiwala installed. This action established the Khadiwala (Brahman) faction in control in Madhya Bharat, brought in an abundance of Chhattisgarh ministers, and mobilized support from Vindhya Pradesh. In June 1963, Mishra had to expand his cabinet to stave off the opposition, adding several new deputy ministers (2 Mahakoshal, 2 Vindhya Pradesh, 2 Bhopal, and 1 Madhya Bharat).[50] Dr. Katju's ministries often were as large as 30, and an apocryphal story has it that when he was once on tour in Rewa, he asked this host, a deputy minister in the state, his name. When he replied, Katju said, "How interesting. I have a minister by that name."

The Mishra cabinet in 1964 was unusually young, with only three ministers, including Mishra, over 60. Only four ministers were in their fifties, the rest in the late thirties and forties.[51] The regional balance in August 1964 was Mahakoshal 8, Madhya Bharat 5, Vindhya Pradesh 4, and Bhopal 1. The biographies of the ministers indicate their past positions, for or against regional factions, so that the composition of the coalition is clearly linked to regional rivalries. In some cases, the same figure stays in the ministry, straddling factional loyalties, but these men are not entrusted with political, as against technical, portfolios.[52]

While it is generally true that "Almost every issue is decided on the basis of regional considerations. Ministers, Deputy Ministers and legislators all represent 'regions' . . ."[53] Dr. Mishra is not the *roi fainéant*, nor the deaf moralist, nor the lowest common denominator of regional unity. If any of the state leaders since Ravi Shankar Shukla have a personal mystique, it is Mishra. He is probably the most experienced politician and public man in the state, having begun politics at 19, journalism (*Amrit Bazar Patrika*, Calcutta) the same year, and was arrested by the British at 21. In 1922 he returned to Jabalpur to

---

for Allahabad, the former Chief Minister mumbled, 'what would Jawahar think.' Eleven more votes would have secured his position."

[50] See the article on Madhya Pradesh in the *Economic Weekly* (Bombay), xv, 12 (June 1, 1963), especially p. 875.

[51] This analysis is made on the basis of the biographies of 20 ministers, *Life Sketches of the Madhya Pradesh Ministers* (Bhopal, 1964, mimeographed).

[52] See *ibid.*

[53] *The Statesman*, November 7, 1961.

found the magazine *Sharda*. While studying for the law in 1926, he successfully contested a seat to the Indian Legislative Assembly. In 1930 he founded the daily *Lokmat* in Jabalpur and modeled it as a militant anti-British sheet. He was arrested and while in jail was elected president of the Jabalpur municipality. From 1930 to 1942 he was imprisoned four times (in 1930, 1932, 1940, and 1942) during which time he composed a Hindi epic novel, *Krishnayana*.

In 1937 he successfully campaigned for a seat in the Central Provinces Assembly, being appointed Minister for Local Self Government. His study and recommendation for a system of decentralization won him considerable fame. When in 1946 the Congress again formed a ministry, he became Home Minister and introduced the "Janapada system" of local self-government. After his short flirtation with the Opposition, first with the Bharatiya Lok Congress and then the PSP, and his fall from grace in the Congress, he left active politics and in 1956 became Vice-Chancellor of Saugor University, resigning only in 1961 to join the Central Citizen's Council.[54] No other man in the state had so much experience, so much prestige as a political "realist" like Sardar Patel, and so much political energy. With central support he parlayed these attributes into a chief ministership. From the outset, he conceived of his tasks as reassertion of the independence and position of Madhya Pradesh in the councils of state in India. He enjoyed his image of a tough professional state boss with the ear of Delhi. The rampant disorder in the Congress party organization enhanced his relative strength, and Indians began talking about "the beginning of political and administrative stability" in Madhya Pradesh, a tendency confirmed by the Congress victory of 1967.[55]

But given the organization of the state and the continuing strength of regional sub-systems, Mishra's position was tenuous. He had managed, under highly artificial circumstances, to subordinate four of the state's leading politicians. They could hardly avoid bearing him a grudge, the more so because he included only one of their "clients" in his ministry. Previous cabinets had reflected the approximate strengths manifested in the legislative party, strengths which in 1963 would have given Mishra 8 and his colleague-rivals 6. Moreover, the chief minister brought most of the district Congress organizations under his control, increasing factional rivalry at the local level.

From this aggressive and purposive style of leadership—a style new to

[54] These events, other than references to the non-Congress period, are given in his "life sketch," *op.cit.*, p. 1.

[55] See, for example, *Link* (New Delhi), July 5, 1964, p. 28.

Madhya Pradesh—arose the feeling that Mishra was more than a strong leader. Charges that he was "dictatorial, intolerant and vindictive"[56] were made, and his own ministers wryly labeled him the "headmaster." His direct contact with civil servants at the operational level without the cognizance of the responsible minister increased the pique within the government group. It has often been charged in Madhya Pradesh as elsewhere that the civil servants were a state within the state, and the chief minister's notions of increasing administrative action were often considered simple disregard of political direction by the responsible ministers.

The second fundamental problem faced by the chief minister in his second year, after the end of the honeymoon of the Kamaraj plan and a waning personal mystique, was the indictment of his client president of the Pradesh Congress Committee, Khadiwala, by the Indore High Court.[57] While the case against Khadiwala was self-evident, there were many potential *amici curiae* interested in reopening the PCC as a vehicle for competition with Dr. Mishra.

Whatever the appearance, therefore, regionalism and the Brahman-Bania conflict continue to power state political life, as manifested in the factionalism of the Congress. Viable coalitions within the state rely upon the cooperation of Mahakoshal (Jabalpur or Chhattisgarh) and of Madhya Bharat. Within both of these regions, there are alternative sets of elites who have generally developed out of a local political community, having worked together in various local ministries before the creation of the state. Since the state was organized so that the Congress was dominated by the four regional committees, political recruitment and training took place at a level of political community dictated neither by state loyalties nor by a state party. The monopoly of the Congress over posts of real importance and power further limits recruitment of political leadership and particularizes the political style.

Political Conflicts in the State

Political conflicts take two forms in Madhya Pradesh: the struggle for power between factions in the Congress party, both at local and regional levels, and competition between interests in the public policies of the government. The two conflicts are often indistinct since factions fre-

[56] See *Times of India*, August 3, 1964.

[57] The charges were that Khadiwala had misused his personal position as chairman of the reception committee of the Indore session of the Congress in 1957. He disposed of sheet steel and jeeps in irregular fashion with poor accounting and on a partisan basis. The timing of the case, six years after the fact, is adequate measure of its special qualities.

quently represent competing interests at the local level, and their debate of public policy issues is often dictated by verbal postures which are motivated primarily by political rather than programmatic disagreement. This is generally true in representative systems, and to disentangle political from functional or interest competition requires an intimate knowledge of the issue, the policy process, and the workings of the Congress legislative party in caucus. It is also necessary to understand administrative implementation or erosion of such policies as are established in the Cabinet.[58]

The range of public policy/political disputes might follow the following classifications: (1) regional demands; (2) group and interest demands; (3) state development demands and (4) ideological or "national" demands. The political system must handle two functions, balancing competitive demands to maintain a political equilibrium, and altering present relationships to effect change in the long-range interests of the state, the ruling elite, and the nation.

It is clear that the primary problem in maintaining a short-run equilibrium in the state is in brokering competitive demands for regional development, especially as the intensity of competition within the government has increased. When the Russian-aided Bhilai steel complex was built in Durg, the western zones of the state demanded an equally gigantic project in their own region and were assigned HEL, Bhopal. This system of balancing regional demands does not always accord with efficient economic planning, nor does it meet the needs of the depressed areas of the state most in need of economic development. It is, in the American sense, a case of "Them that has, gets." In this system, one can expect Mahakoshal and Madhya Bharat to continue to use their political power to see that their regions are given the fruit of the "socialist pattern of society." It will also intensify the regional basis of party loyalty since the distributive function is politically critical, and champions of zonal development can have a meaningful impact on public policy.

A second category of equilibrium politics is the balancing of competing groups and interests in the state. It is clear that the three business groups in the state are active in the policy process, both at the political and the administrative levels. It is also clear that the Congress party's various factions receive support from all of them, sometimes in support of local as well as state-wide interests. The task of running a broad coalition one-party system is to avoid alienating any significant group by parceling out varying parts of the "pie." Trade union interests are simi-

[58] As far as this writer is aware, there has not been a study of this type undertaken in the state. Most of the information available is inferential.

larly best managed by blunting the direct competition between labor and capital with the use of arbitration, tri-partite bargaining, and state-subsidized economic adjustments. The low levels of current interest articulation in the state have ensured that the government, thus far, has been capable of brokering a modicum of social harmony. The interest base is sufficiently narrow as to be manageable.

The two primary equilibrium demands of regional and group interests, however, run counter to the alternative bias of the politics of planning and change. A good example of the frustration of state development in the face of articulated interests is the revocation of the Madhya Pradesh Land Rationalization Act in 1963. This act was scrapped by Dr. Mishra soon after election, when he was at his strongest in domestic politics, at a cost of nearly $3.8 million per year in state revenue. The Jan Sangh had been active in mobilizing the peasantry against the new act, but it was pressure from within the Congress that frustrated a technically appropriate rural land program. Another index to the competition between state investment policies and group interests is the cost of electrical power and the degree to which the fee schedule reflects a profit/reinvestment bias or a loss/subsidy bias. In Madhya Pradesh, power rates have been progressively reduced, contrary to the advice of the technicians in the ministry. This is not to champion the virtues of one position as against the other. It is rather to demonstrate the conflict of interest between articulated interests and planning priorities adopted by the state government.

Another cluster of demands which run counter to short-run political equilibrium in the state are those external to the articulated and substantive state interests. On the one hand, these demands are often "ideological," corresponding to problems in the adjustment of widely held ideals and social reality. The Jan Sangh-Hinduist ideology has a considerable appeal within the Congress as well as other parties. The ban on cow slaughter and other commitments to infuse Hindu values into public policy are potent demands, and yet they tend to undercut the strength of the Congress with the religious minorities, with secular groups in the society, and even among various Hindu groups, especially the Scheduled Castes. Another variety of "external" demand is the constant need in India for national unity and a common approach of the state governments in economic planning.

The food zones plan is an interesting example of the conflict between state interests and Indian national interests. The food zone plan was designed to link production and consumption areas in such fashion as to ensure a steady supply at reasonable prices, insulated from the regional imbalances which result in short-run scarcity conditions and the resultant hoarding/price spiral problem. Given the general rural-urban capital flow of the Indian price system (as enhanced by U.S. Public Law 480 wheat), the food zone plan essentially benefited urban areas by preventing unrestricted inter-regional movement of foodgrains to areas where market prices were highest. Madhya Pradesh was in the western food zone with Bombay its principal market. With the high purchasing power of Bombay, and the pronounced shift of Gujarati and Maharashtrian farmers to cash crops, mostly cotton and sugar, the wheat of Madhya Pradesh, under relatively lower prices, flowed into Bombay. This tended, however, to create higher prices in Madhya Pradesh, where there was not so much purchasing power. The grain traders, an important group in the state, also demanded the right to maximize their profit by wider speculative operations. The producers were essentially competing against American wheat while other zonal farmers shifted to non-foodgrain products. In 1960 it took Prime Minister Nehru at the Raigarh AICC meetings to mend broken fences.[59] In the food crisis of 1964, Madhya Pradesh would not support a revised zonal plan, and the chief minister rather boastfully (it is said) reversed Food Minister Subramaniam's policy statement on agricultural and marketing organization.

Again it should be mentioned that this is not a normative question with truth reposing in Delhi and narrow self-interest in Bhopal. It is rather an example of a relatively strong chief minister, who reflects substantive political interests in the state, refusing to sacrifice his own position on the altar of external demands. Moreover, this example is unrepresentative of the characteristically passive role of Madhya Pradesh in the tug and pull of federal politics in India. In general, most western zone Indian leaders have considered Madhya Pradesh an agricultural hinterland, providing raw materials and foodgrains for a rapidly industrializing Gujarat and Maharashtra. It is fortuitous that Madhya Pradesh is rich in resources, but it is a great problem when it seeks to keep them at home for state advantage.

Gujarat, for example, is especially eager to see the lower Narbada River exploited in a manner unlike the Bhakra-Nangal scheme in which the upper Riparian state maintains control of electrical power and water. Madhya Pradesh, needless to say, has other interests. This is an example of the external demands made by a neighboring state, demands which have been regularly on the increase in the past decade. The cynic might well conclude that the cause of Indian national unity would be best served

[59] See the account in *The Hindu* (Madras), November 28, 1960.

by the weakest possible provincial leadership, and yet under a federal system, state leadership exercises a crucial role in mobilizing popular support.

On balance, the state government has been relatively unable to significantly modify the articulated interests of the state, but it has been able to move in areas not already developed. It has acted as an equilibrium system with some large investments, heavily financed by the central government, in infrastructural development.

Techniques of Political Action

Political parties win power in Madhya Pradesh in much the same way they do in other parts of the country. All of them try to maximize group support, earn the confidence of independent-minded voters, and lure supporters into expenditures of time and money. All of them seek to present programs of the most catholic appeal, melding programmatic themes with popular clichés. In Madhya Pradesh, the appeal of Hindu philosophy and popular religion gives local politics a flavor not unlike the American South in the fabled "Bible Belt." All parties manage this theme, some better than others, in rural constituencies.

Local epics, issues, and unique histories are also part of electoral politics, often completely dominating the appeal of a party's local candidates.[60] But more often, local conditions are taken into account in the selection of candidates with appeal in their constituencies. The elaborate calculations of party bosses of the caste, clan, and village relations in a given district are probably the most accurate social statistics in the state. As Adrian Mayer argues:

> The allocation of the ticket is the result of a complex interbalancing of forces, into which personal qualifications, connections and ambitions, government policies, alternative positions of power, and the degree to which the electorate is thought to be influenced by various leaders, all enter. It is not necessarily the direct measure of the power of any one section in the constituency.[61]

What seems to be most important is that the community power structure of the rural areas is relatively independent of manipulation on terms other than its own. The Congress party's organizational skills are important, but they need not be dominant in regions in which Congress leadership seems to be part of an alien, generally urban, and not always

[60] See S. R. Sharma, "Madhya Bharat," in Park and Kogekar, *op.cit.*, pp. 190-91, for a discussion of party symbol and local history in Gwalior.

[61] "Rural Leaders and the Indian General Election," *Asian Survey*, I (8), October 1961, p. 28.

very palatable, society. But just as the rural leaders are politically independent of Congress management, they are vulnerable to governmental policy which is mostly under the control of the urban Congress leadership. As rural works programs, community development, and various social and economic welfare policies play an increasingly important role in the rural community, its leadership becomes less able to assert independence from urban elites because they can exploit new resources to overcome traditionally dominant groups.

The rising importance of "locals" in state politics was marked after the 1957 second general elections and was carried further in the third and fourth general elections. Moreover, new groups of old leaders with potential political power began asserting influence. This group, manifested in the form of dominant caste leadership and the former princes, became important in electoral politics. As Balroj Madhok has observed: "The personal influence of the candidates, particularly of those belonging to the ruling party or princely families, has been more decisive than any other factor in these elections."[62] The entry of ex-ruling princes as important factors in electoral politics did not change the fundamental problem for political parties in search of support at the hustings, however. There remained the task of building *ad hoc* coalitions of groups, personalities, names, and ideas to command a simple plurality in an electoral district. Even the Congress has never won a clear majority of popular votes in any of the four elections.

Politics changes its character when popular elections are not in prospect. The struggle for power then takes place within the ruling coalition for control of public policy. At this stage, well-organized interest groups are active, although not with public knowledge or official sanction. In Madhya Pradesh at least, these groups have in the past dominated political life. One important lobby is the organized grain traders, people whose economic interests and influence in party finance constitute a strong voice to protect their interests against what one observer has called "a growing consciousness of power in Indian rural society,"[63] as well as against national interference. But all democratic systems have at their heart the balancing of competing interests, and it only needs to be said that this is very much a part of state political life in Madhya Pradesh. What is unique is that non-electoral competition is generally unrecognized in the public debate or, when it is identified, is condemned. In the general "socialist pattern" verbal commitment of the Congress,

[62] Balraj Madhok, secretary of the Jan Sangh, writing in *Seminar* (New Delhi), 34 (June 1962), p. 37. See also "The Princes" by Urmila Phadnis, *ibid.*, pp. 43-46.

[63] The farming correspondent of *The Statesman*, August 31, 1964, in "Political Life in Indian Rural Society."

any interest group is believed to be "impure," just as Dr. D. P. Mishra has branded dissident Congressmen "corrupt capitalists."[64] When the state counter-elite is led by Banias, this line of argument is all the more effective.

In a broader sense, politics returns to its urban base of articulated interests in those years when it does not have to mobilize the countryside. This is true of all of the parties uniformly under urban leadership. In the cities are found the various competing interests which are the stuff of politics. This helps to explain what appears to be a paradox—the ability of the Indian governments to legislate in such sensitive areas as the Hindu Code Bill and land tenure in the face of rural "traditionalism." It is clear that such policies reflect the urban bias of the dominant groups in politics and, as such, are extraneous to political competition except in election years and except in their administrative implementation.

GOVERNMENTAL PERFORMANCE

Problems of state political integration in 1956 were paralleled with those in administration. On three levels the state bureaucracy faced problems: the creation of a state cadre from the various amalgamated units of Madhya Pradesh, Vindhya Pradesh, Bhopal, and Madhya Bharat; the expansion of traditions of orderly rural administration in princely and tribal areas, and the creation of new administrative forms to match programs of decentralization and development. These problems were complicated because of the underdeveloped state of administration and the absence of trained local administrators in central India. Commenting on one aspect, Datta-Ray observes that "Official society consists of Punjabis, Parsees, Goans, South Indians and Bengalis; their medium of communication in this state whose only *raison d'être* is the common bond of Hindi has, of necessity, to be English."[65]

The primary load on the administration since the creation of the state has, in fact, been the transformation of the administration and its development as an instrument of state. This is not unlike requirements faced by other states and the central government,[66] but it was much more difficult in states like Rajasthan and Madhya Pradesh than in Bengal or Madras.

One of the most troublesome aspects of the amalgamation of dissimilar

[64] Quoted by Datta-Ray, *op.cit.*, May 12, 1964.

[65] Datta-Ray, *op.cit.*, May 5, 1964.

[66] See, as an assessment of the need, Ralph Braibanti, "Reflections of Bureaucratic Reform in India," in R. Braibanti and J. Spengler (eds.), *Administration and Economic Development in India* (Durham, N.C.: Duke University Press, 1963), pp. 3-68.

political units was the meshing of existing cadres of civil servants sharing little in common training, outlook or even salary. Datta-Ray suggests that the inevitable adjustments of salary and seniority "has left behind it a trail of bitterness that hampers work in the Secretariat."[67] So serious were these problems that the central Home Minister was brought into the quarrels and from all accounts appeared to be irritated by delays in integration and the exaggerated seniority claimed by bureaucrats from the various regions.[68] As V. P. Menon once put it,

> Similarly, while it was expected that the Union's ill-qualified employees would receive the same salary as their counterparts in the neighbouring provinces, it was claimed that their performance should be judged in the light of their own particular experience and that the standards to be prescribed should not be such as to exclude employees from the least-developed States from finding jobs under the new regime.

In Madhya Pradesh the largest number of trained administrators were to be found in Mahakoshal, particularly those men who had previously served the former Madhya Pradesh in Nagpur. Bhopal presented few problems in administrative integration, having been a Chief Commissioner's charge since independence. With few political restrictions, the central government could weed out incompetents, rationalize administrative practice, and establish strong administrative discipline. In the state unions of Vindhya Pradesh and Madhya Bharat, however, administrative reform was subject, at least in part, to political control.

The system evolved by the Union States' Ministry was to depute four or five senior officials to the new units. One would act as liaison between the new ministries and the administration, and between the union and New Delhi. The chief secretary of the new union would also be seconded from the central government, as would the Finance Secretary, Inspector-General of Police, and often a senior revenue official. The judge of the new High Courts would be experienced from service on another bench, and the chairman of the Public Service Commission would similarly be "alien" to the new union. In the set of practices established by the States' Ministry, it was required that in each new union a minister was made responsible for administrative integration, and that important administrative post appointments were subject to the approval of the central government.[69]

[67] See, for an account, *Times of India*, November 3, 1960.

[68] Menon, *op.cit.*, p. 444.

[69] An excellent account is given in *ibid.*, pp. 435-45.

The system of central supervision and control was integral to the power of the central government over the princes in the immediate post-independence period, but it did not exist in the same measure at the time of the states reorganization in 1956. Moreover, the reconstituted Madhya Pradesh was not unlike the state unions of 1948-49 in which political considerations blunted technical dominance in the creation of an administration fitted to the states' needs. On the other hand, the state services cadre was inadequate to meet its needs, and "outsiders" including the Chief Secretary commanded key posts.

But four years after the creation of the state many of the problems remained, so many in fact that V. P. Menon, writing in the *Hindustan Times,* entitled his article "Failure in Madhya Pradesh." In summarizing his arguments, he noted that "In reorganizing what is now Madhya Pradesh, all administrative, financial and political principles were ignored. . . . In short, Madhya Pradesh today is a collection of left-out portions of different states jumbled into one heterogeneous unit."[70]

Critical to the understanding of the importance of this problem is its relationship to patterns of British administration in India in which the higher national administrative cadre was a very small elite holding loyalty to the Crown, while an amorphous and sprawling subordinate bureaucratic community was indigenous to its area. The inherent weakness of this system was in the cooperation and coordination between the two sets of administrators. During British rule, overwhelming power lay with the central services, but after independence and with the rise of democratic government, especially in the provinces, the authority within the services began shifting. Moreover, the state cadres recognized that their future might well depend upon cooperation with state politicians quite as much as upon technical competence within the service. This in turn facilitated contact between the regional politician and his regional peer in the bureaucracy for support and information. When regions were integrated, patron-client relationships between civil servants and politicians were set in a larger political community and constituted factional cells. These factions were then faced with adjusting their inner-administration position with "alien" supervisory personnel. The senior officials were charged with ensuring efficiency and morale as well as discipline, and with simultaneously acting as responsive tools in the implementation of public policy as enunciated by the popular ministries.

The result of this pattern of administrative problems was that the energies of administrators in large measure turned inward. Menon

[70] *Hindustan Times,* August 19, 1960. See also the rejoinder of the state Director of Publicity and Information in *ibid.,* September 1, 1960.

charged that the collection of land revenue in Mahakoshal, the most settled region in Madhya Pradesh, was only 50-60 per cent of optimum standards.[71] And leaders of the opposition in the state Legislative Assembly charged that two-year delays in getting information from the state civil administration were not unusual. Of 800 "assurances" given to the Legislative Assembly of 1959, its members still awaited information on 150 of them a year later.[72] While one can appreciate the difficulties of finding reliable information about many aspects of state life, these charges indicate that administrative organization is less effective than in most of the Indian states. A former chief secretary of the state told the author that almost all of his efforts were directed toward "establishment" affairs and the development of effective personnel procedures.[73]

The second general need of the state's administration was to extend orderly public authority into the less developed former princely states in Madhya Pradesh. The nature of the problems attendant on the abolition of zamindari rule and the tightening of control over revenue collection by the state government can be illustrated by many examples. For instance, in June 1962, a group of tribal families in search of land occupied a cultivable area in the Balaghat district which was administered by the Forest and Revenue Departments as state land. The Forest Department had restricted portions of the land in the interests of soil conservation and development, but the tribal people cut down trees for fuel and buildings, thereby incurring the wrath of the police. Both the Jan Sangh and the Kisan Sabha (a pro-Communist local organization) organized opposition to government policy in the interests of discrediting the state government by discrediting the local administration.[74]

The same pattern was prevalent in areas under the control of zamindars because many landless laborers had plots under cultivation which, rather than being listed in the land records, were part of the "harmonious inefficiency" of the zamindars' administration. When more formal administration was implemented, social justice and equity were often secondary aims or were simply irrelevant to the "reforms." In such cases, political parties often organized local dissent and forced state politicians to interpose political power in the path of administration. And this pattern characterized noble as well as selfish causes wherever the old order was being changed to more nearly resemble what had once been British India.

71 V. P. Menon in *ibid.*, August 18, 1960.

72 An account is given in *ibid.*, November 15, 1960.

73 Interview, summer 1964.

74 See *Times of India*, July 2, 1962.

The third fundamental need of the state administration was to expand its operation into new fields occasioned by democratic decentralization and an enhanced state planning operation. One of the few truly significant innovations indigenous to Madhya Pradesh was the Janapada system of rural politics developed by Dr. D. P. Mishra while he was a member of the pre-independence Central Provinces Legislative Assembly. Many Indians had begun to think of revitalization of the ancient authority in the Indian village under the stimulus of British orientalist writing, nationalist populism, and Gandhi's notions of *gram raj*. In part, this activity was forced by the obvious disintegration of that authority and the effects (some said invidious) of the urban impingement on rural life.

The Janapada scheme was introduced to the former Madhya Pradesh on July 1, 1948 and was essentially an enhanced district council system with no more than 40 members in the *sabha*. It combined the representation of urban and rural areas and aimed at supervision of local administration by committees of the *sabha*, both at the technical level and at the village panchayat level. The executive officer of the *sabha* was to be a member of the state administrative service, and his posting to a local representative body would more fully integrate local needs and control with technical and administrative procedures, at least in theory.[75]

These developments were elaborated in the growth of the panchayati raj pattern throughout India. Unhappily, all regions of the state had passed different legislation before consolidation,[76] and it took six years after the creation of the state to develop acceptable common patterns. Even then, two versions of the system were supported. The problems encountered in the legislation give some idea of the difficulties in establishing common institutions and practices throughout the state. In 1960 the proposed legislation would have enfranchised only the heads of families in contrast to the adult suffrage provided in most of the regional plans.[77] The finally accepted legislation[78] was returned by the

[75] For a more detailed statement, see "Janapada Experiment in Madhya Pradesh," appendix I, *The Pattern of Rural Government*, report of a seminar at the Indian Institute of Public Administration, New Delhi, 1958, and Government of Madhya Pradesh, *Report of the Janapada Enquiry Committee, Madhya Pradesh, 1952* (Nagpur, 1953).

[76] All are described in Ministry of Community Development and Cooperation, *A Digest on Panchayati Raj* (New Delhi, 1962), pp. 27-29.

[77] *Times of India*, August 29, 1960.

[78] See *Report* of the Select Committee on the Madhya Pradesh Panchayat Bill, 1960 (no. 17 of 1960) and the bill as amended by the Select Committee, Bhopal, 1961.

President of India because samiti membership was by nomination,[79] and the final bill provided for the continuance of Adimjatuja and Pargana panchayats in the tribal area while maintaining village, janapada and zilla panchayats in settled areas.[80] It is too early to make general statements about the work and importance of the scheme, although the government has conducted some preliminary surveys in the interest of considering amendments to existing institutions.[81]

In all programs of democratic decentralization, the fundamental aim is to maximize popular participation in local affairs. This implies not only mobilization of the population, but also its procedural capacity to take advantage of its political power. The adjustment of administration from the externally imposed to the intrinsically responsive pattern is extremely difficult. Administrators are often in conflict with locally felt needs, either because those needs run counter to the "rules," legislative or procedural, or because to accommodate them would be to run counter to state policy and to central control by local agents of the administration. Since democratic decentralization schemes almost always are rural in inspiration and control, and since state political life is generally dominated by the cities, the administrator often has to speak with the bias of the urban dominant groups.

The second area in which the bureaucracy has been stretched is in the planning and management of economic development. The state was handicapped by the absence of reliable or comprehensive statistics but quickly established a directorate of economics and statistics which has done commendable work.[82] The major problem has continued to be the absence of adequate numbers of well-trained personnel, a problem faced by the entire country.

Implementation of Public Policy

While it is clear that thus far the great problems of administration have concerned consolidation and internal discipline and efficiency, the state government has had to "run to stand still" because of externally stimulated problems. In the rural areas, as Tarlok Singh has written, "The pursuit of individual interests within and outside the

79 *Hindustan Times*, November 8, 1961.

80 *The Hindu*, June 5, 1962.

81 See, for example, *A Sample Survey of Village Panchayats in Madhya Pradesh* (Bhopal, n.d. [1960?], mimeographed).

82 Their catalog of publications lists sources on everything from public finance to in-plant training. They also produced district plan handbooks for aid in implementation at the local level, and publish in both English and Hindi. See *Some Publications of the Directorate of Economics and Statistics, Madhya Pradesh* (Bhopal, 1964).

village has become more common [and] the influence of the community over its members has diminished. . . . In this situation conflicts of interest within the village community have sharpened."[83] These conflicts and demands place heavy burdens upon both the law and order and the revenue functions of the rural bureaucracy. In the first five years after the creation of the state, over 5,000 police were added to the force to maintain what was initially inadequate coverage.[84]

In the developmental activities of the state government, the administration has had to manage larger and more complex operations, with the 1958-59 expenditure about $70.7 million and the same expenditure in 1963-64 more than doubled to $151.8 million.[85] These expenditures are on the revenue account, capital expenditure account, and loan and advance system of the state. No matter what the competence of the government at the outset, its place within the context of national development has forced it to become more deeply involved in planning and financial administration.

On the other hand, the state is among the slowest in India in implementing the plan and in efficiently taxing the population. The proportion of tax revenue to general revenue has steadily declined from 70.9 per cent in 1951-52 (Mahakoshal primarily), to 61.7 per cent in 1956-57, and to 56.8 per cent in 1964-65 (by budget). This has led to larger demands for state aid and for the increase in indirect taxation. Madhya Pradesh had the second largest deficit budget of any Indian state in 1963-64, amounting to $9.4 million. These characteristics testify to problems in taxation as well as in administration and mark the state government, both bureaucracy and politicians, as one of the least well developed (by developmental criteria) in India. On the other hand, the state government is probably the least settled in India, and its constituent parts were at the outset among the most backward in the country. Every country has its "Snopes" region, and such regions change slowly.

The implementation of public policy has also been delayed by "political" legislation that has reflected group interests but is difficult to implement. An example of an area in which the administration has been caught in a difficult position is in the organization of road transportation. In various regions of the state, bus transportation was well developed, and in others it was not. Many Indian states brought it under

[83] Cited by Hugh Tinker, "The Village in the Framework of Development," in Braibanti and Spengler, *op.cit.*, p. 101.

[84] *Madhya Pradesh Police Statistics, 1956-61* (Bhopal, 1961), p. 2.

[85] Figures taken from "Trends in Finances of State Governments," *Economic Times* (Bombay), June 11, 1964. See also *Budgetary Trends in Madhya Pradesh, 1957-1958 to 1964-65* (Bhopal, 1964).

government control because transportation is seldom in the private sector and also because there was a public demand for state transportation with its greater reliability and low cost. In the winter session of the 1960 Legislative Assembly, the controversy erupted because only the Gwalior sector of the state transport was "nationalized." The Communists demanded full nationalization and especially the nationalization of the companies in the Chhattisgarh region where several Congress ministers and deputy ministers controlled the company. The Finance Minister, M. L. Gangwal (Indore, Madhya Bharat), replied that nationalization would be delayed and gradually implemented because of financial implications.[86]

Gradualism prevailed, even though *The Statesman* felt a better statement might be that "apathy and drift reign supreme."[87] When Dr. D. P. Mishra became chief minister in 1963, he pledged to nationalize the bus companies in three years. This was a remarkable statement since the half dozen bus companies of Chhattisgarh, operated as a combine, were in part owned by the Congress chief whip, Shyama Charan Shukla, a supporter of Dr. Mishra who himself held a Chhattisgarh seat in the Assembly.[88] It was even more baffling since Shukla's father, Ravi Shankar Shukla, was Mishra's *guru* and since they shared caste and other associational ties. The real question appears to be whether the buses are indeed nationalized.

The road transportation controversy illustrates the difficulty faced by the state government in undertaking state operations against local interests. It is equally clear that where a broad political consensus does not exist, the bureaucracy is hard put to resist pressures for administrative erosion.

Both politicians and senior officials are aware of the weakness of their sources of strength and their operational efficiency and have set very limited goals. Even Dr. Mishra, who seemed to be cut of different cloth, had to cancel the unpopular land rationalization legislation. His direct contact with civil administrators charged with implementation gives evidence of his concern with more efficient government, but not of its present existence. Under such conditions the state administration is embarrassed by central pressure for radical legislation, though like most state governments it is ready to issue verbal commitments to what is desired. In those areas such as agricultural taxation[89] where the central

[86] See the slightly different accounts in *Hindustan Times*, November 12, 1960 and the *Delhi Hindustan Standard* of the same day.

[87] *The Statesman*, April 10, 1964.

[88] See Datta-Ray, *op.cit.*, May 5, 1964.

[89] Expert opinion suggests that direct and indirect taxation on agriculture in India

government has believed considerable revenue could and should be raised, the state government has lacked both the political power and the administrative capacity to undertake broader commitments. This may not be objectively true, but the state government considers it to be true and consequently has not borne the load assigned by central leadership.

Impact of Public Policy

The best measure of the efficiency of governmental organization is the degree to which it has successfully reshaped its environment in accordance with its intentions. With only a decade of actual experience from which to judge, and in light of the extremely difficult conditions in which the government found itself, it is difficult to take the measure of government performance in Madhya Pradesh. The greatest need of the state in its leaders' eyes is probably regional integration and the creation of a state-wide political community. This is an even more pressing problem to Congress politicians, since any change in the organization of the state would probably result in a non-Congress government in the new setting. While it is true that this sense of community has not yet emerged, the integrative agencies of the state are working toward it, and if the state is not partitioned, there is every reason to believe that a higher degree of political unity will emerge. The linguistic basis of the state helps very little, unfortunately, since Hindi is both the North Indian and the national language, rather than a unique language drawing the people of Madhya Pradesh together. More lively federal politics would also serve the needs of state unity well but at a greater cost to the national government than it would be willing to pay. It would be unrealistic to expect a much higher degree of integration before a generational change in government.

Public policy has not been very effective in protecting and forwarding the ideal of a secular and modernist style of life in the state, partly because governments have been representative of the Central Indian milieu and partly because the primary opposition to the Congress has been the Jan Sangh. In order to maintain a centrist coalition, the Congress has had to incorporate a significant amount of rightist leadership in its ranks. As urbanization, education, and economic development take place, the party can perhaps begin to move further in the direction of the national political consensus.

Similarly the government has been unable to move the economy of

---

is not much more than 20 per cent of total tax revenue, whereas in China it may be as high as 60 per cent. See Ashok Mitra, "Tax Burden for Indian Agriculture," in Braibanti and Spengler, *op.cit.*, especially pp. 293-95.

Madhya Pradesh along quickly because of its own limitations in knowledge, will, and administrative ability, and also because the state economy is overwhelmingly agricultural at subsistence levels. Private sector investment has been slow to move into the state, in part because of public sector prerogatives in iron, steel, and power development, and in part because the economic development of Maharashtra and Gujarat consumes most of the available local west Indian capital. Moreover, economic development in the state is inhibited by the absence of a well-developed infrastructure of transport and power and a trained labor force. The state does not have a surplus population; indeed, statistics on female employment show how pressing is the need for even agricultural labor. The great potential of the state speaks well for its future, but not for its present.

CONCLUSION

It has been said that "Ultimately, it is a question of 'good will' whether the laws and regulations of political authority are implemented effectively by the officials and sustained by public compliance and initiative."[90]

The future of Madhya Pradesh, like the rest of India, is bound up in the developing struggle between the forces of order and development and those of chaos and disruption. Isolated as it is from the great urban crucibles of change in the subcontinent, Madhya Pradesh is nonetheless increasingly tied to the fortunes of its neighbors, and a shock in Kerala or Assam produces its effect in Bhopal. The national commitment and contact of the state links its fortunes, for perhaps the first time in history, to all of India. In part, therefore, the fate of some Indians is bound up with the fate of all Indians.

The more immediate problems concern the integration of the regions of the state and of the various classes and groups in the state. The process of economic change, the monetization of agriculture, the development of industry, and the lacing together of the districts by road and rail tend to achieve the first purpose but to inhibit the latter. In the future, class divisions and the division between town and countryside will probably grow, interacting with an increasing awareness of difference and social inequality.

The growth of political participation, competition, and economic rivalry in the rural areas will severely strain the forces of law and order and may make more difficult the work of political parties in building a state social and political consensus. In the absence of general agreement on goals, state governmental leadership will continue to exercise a de-

[90] Reinhard Bendix, "Public Authority in a Developing Political Community: The Case of India," *European Journal of Sociology*, IV (1963), 39.

ciding vote in a fragmented political system, and the votes will become increasingly important. If, in the face of the need for more austerity, a higher measure of authority is given to the government, the slender basis of popular participation in local affairs could be ruptured. On the other hand, the continued low levels of popular contribution to national savings and investment will provoke an economic disaster. It is unlikely that Madhya Pradesh will be the first state to experience either unhappy choice, given its potential for development and low population pressure, but it is not an island secure from the tides on its shores.

The Congress party, therefore, faces an unenviable future. The cause of economic and social change in the state is progressing so slowly that the creation of new groups and values in support of its secular, modernist creed are but a fraction of the new inputs in the political society. If agricultural development creates an articulate but backward rural class, or if the lower middle class of the towns and cities witness bleak prospects for the future, the parties of the right may well challenge Congress monopoly control of the state government. The creation of huge complexes like Bhilai and HEL is no substitute for the development of a Punjab-style entrepreneurial pattern, offering new incentives to many people for self-expression in a modern culture.

The Congress does reflect local interests and perspectives inevitably, and in the tug and pull of federal politics the state apparatus can reflect both rightist sources of strength and more centrist policies cast in Delhi's image, but it is no mean task. A better hope lies in the continuing division of the state's public into all shades of opinion, with only the Congress offering a common denominator adequate to mobilize a plurality. In the next decade, it will be less important to lead than to parlay competing interests into winning performance, the more so because the primary task will be in eliciting public cooperation.

The civil service of the state will "shake down" in due course, but it must also establish the high levels of administrative efficiency which will be required in ever more comprehensive social planning. There will be an interplay between politicalization and professionalization as there is in most bureaucracies, and this will not be an evil. The administrators must come to reflect and serve an intimately understood constituent society. No doubt there will be opportunities for corruption and nepotism, but these are less serious problems than would be the failure to mesh the state administration with popular aspirations.

Madhya Pradesh is also in a position, at least potentially, to cease its parasitic economic life and begin making a major contribution to the national economy. While it is true that agriculture suffers from pricing disincentives, it is also true that the vast resources of the state could be developed with a marginally greater effort. Until this indigenous impetus to development is created or evolves, the state will continue to be justly characterized as backward.

The Tribal and Scheduled Caste population poses a severe social problem for the state. In the 1967 Legislative Assembly, these two groups have 100 of 296 seats.[91] These peoples still have not achieved parity with the majority of the state population in social and educational standards and, if energized as a bloc, will be in a position to command any government, given the narrow party majorities likely in the state. While this might well do more for their cause than the "benevolent majority," it also poses the threat to orderly accommodation of diverse interests. In any case, this seems a distant prospect, because the underprivileged in any society by definition lack the capacity for social action possessed by other groups.

On balance, it seems unlikely that Madhya Pradesh will overcome its birth defects in time to exploit its potential successfully before facing severe "second phase" problems of village conflict, hyper-urbanization and the violence accompanying rapid change. The capacity to live with change and institutionalize its effects is probably beyond the present resources and practices of a society like that prevailing in Madhya Pradesh. It is viable now because of the limited change and the unarticulated interests of its people. If internal or external crises impinged upon the state, its government would be hard pressed to survive at any but the lowest level, as has been demonstrated in communal rioting in the state.

Madhya Pradesh, like the rest of India, must find ways to make the Congress party more than a broker of extant interests, a device for blunting social conflict. It must in part stimulate new patterns of organizational and corporate behavior which will undergird the society with a social fabric increasingly independent of the hard-pressed power of the state. The party, or its successors, must develop linkages between an increasingly technical and powerful bureaucracy and the manifest public will, both to capture public cooperation and energy and to maintain the order on which all future progress depends. These are exceedingly difficult tasks, but the record of the last two decades, while a discouraging one, can be improved if economic and social development proceeds fast enough to give politicians and bureaucrats the time to consolidate a modern political system.

91 *Times of India*, August 18, 1964.

REFERENCES

ETHNOLOGY

Central Provinces. *District Gazetteers.* 22 vols. Nagpur, 1908.

Mayer, Adrian. *Caste and Kinship in Central India.* London: Routledge and Kegan Paul, 1960.

———. "The Dominant Caste in a Region of Central India," in *Southwestern Journal of Anthropology*, XIV (1958), 407-27.

Russell, R. V., and Hiralal, Rai Bahadur. *The Tribes and Castes of the Central Provinces of India.* 4 vols. London, 1916.

Saxena, Ranvir. *Tribal Economy in Central India.* Calcutta, 1964.

ECONOMICS

Government of Madhya Pradesh. *Demographic Study of Madhya Pradesh.* Bhopal, 1962.

———. *Regional Income Atlas of Madhya Pradesh.* Bhopal, 1960.

———. *Statistical Abstract of Madhya Pradesh.* Annual.

National Council of Applied Economic Research. *Techno-Economic Survey of Madhya Pradesh.* Bombay, 1960.

HISTORY

Aberigh-Mackay, G. R. *Central India.* 2 vols. London, 1878.

Malcolm, Sir John. *A Memoir of Central India.* London, 1824.

Mishra, D. P. (ed.). *The History of the Freedom Movement in Madhya Pradesh.* Nagpur, 1956.

POLITICS

Datta-Ray, S. K. "Madhya Pradesh," *The Statesman* (Calcutta) (May 5, May 12, 1964).

Mayer, Adrian. "Rural Leaders and the Indian General Election," *Asian Survey*, I:8 (October 1961), 23-29.

Wilcox, Wayne. "Trade Unions, the Middle Class Intelligentsia and a Communist M. P.; The Indore Parliamentary Election," in Myron Weiner and Rajni Kothari (eds.), *Voting Behaviour in India.* Calcutta: Firma K. L. Mukhopadhyay, 1965.

MAHARASHTRA

MAHARASHTRA

IV

Maharashtra

RAM JOSHI

THE STATE of Maharashtra was created on May 1, 1960, with the break-up of the bilingual state of Bombay. Covering a major part of the western side of the southern peninsula, it is one of the largest states in the Indian Union. With its area of 118,717 square miles and population of 39,553,718, Maharashtra ranks third among the seventeen states in both area and population.[1]

The state extends from the Arabian Sea in the west to the Eastern Ghats in the east. To the south, the Krishna River forms part of the boundary and in the north, it is formed by the Tapi trough and the Satpura hills. The state has common borders with four states: Gujarat in the northwest, Madhya Pradesh in the north and east, Andhra Pradesh in the southeast, and Mysore in the south.

Geographically, the area has a distinct physical relief, brought about by the underlying Deccan trap, whose surface coverage is almost coincident with the boundaries of the state. The low mountain range known as the Western Ghats runs as an almost continuous range from the northern limits of the state for about 400 miles north-south. These mountains appear as steep ranges, rising to elevations of between 2,500 and 4,000 feet, when looked at from the coastal strip. The west-facing slopes are scoured by numerous short, swift-flowing rivers which have cut deep ravines in the slope. On the eastern side, the ranges are flatter. Their gentle eastward slopes are cut by wide river valleys through which flow several large and long-winding rivers like the Godavari, Krishna, and Bhima.

Culturally, the area has a high degree of individuality as the homeland of the Marathi-speaking people. Economically, this is a region of dry cultivation, only 5.4 per cent of the net sown area being irrigated as against the national percentage of 17.9.[2] Although still predominantly agricultural—some 64 per cent of the people are dependent on agriculture, of whom only 2 per cent are non-cultivating landowners—Maharashtra is also one of the most industrialized states in India.

[1] *Census of India, 1961, Paper No. 1 of 1962: Final Population Totals*, pp. xi and 340.

[2] Bureau of Economics and Statistics, *Statistical Abstract of Maharashtra State* (Bombay, 1960), p. 3.

THE SOCIAL AND ECONOMIC ENVIRONMENT

Historical Background

The areas now included in Maharashtra, with the exception of Bombay city, were a part of the Maratha empire until its conquest by the British. The political revolution that stirred this area in the sixteenth and seventeenth centuries culminated in the establishment of the Maratha power whose sphere of influence extended throughout western India. The establishment of this power is viewed by historians as the political expression of a strong feeling of nationalism among the people of this region. As the late Justice Ranade—a widely read Maharashtrian historian—has written, "The rise of the Maratha Power was due to the first beginnings of what one may well call the process of nation-making. It was not the outcome of the successful enterprise of any individual adventurer. It was the upheaval of the whole population, strongly bound together by the common affinities of language, race, religion and literature, and seeking further solidarity by a common political existence."[3]

In 1818, the empire fell into the hands of the British who dismembered it by apportioning parts of it to various other provinces under their control. Nationalist leaders of Maharashtra throughout the twentieth century yearned for reunion, for which, however, they had to wait till 1960. Thus, unlike many other states of the Indian Union, Maharashtra had been a single political community long before it was made a single political unit of the Union. This historical context must be borne in mind in understanding the process by which the different regions of the state like Vidarbha and Marathwada were integrated with Western Maharashtra to form a homogeneous state. It is not suggested that regional tensions do not exist or that local pulls are not exercised, but leaders of regional lobbies appear to be aware of the larger context of the state interest in which local demands of development and representation must be viewed. The Nagpur Pact (September 1953) signed between the protagonists of Samyukta Maharashtra and Vidarbha leaders in an attempt to forge a common front during the linguistic agitation for the creation of the state is a case in point.

Social Configuration

The population of Maharashtra represents Aryan as well as Dravidian elements. This mixture is best illustrated by the peculiarities of the

[3] M. G. Ranade, *Rise of the Maratha Power* (New Delhi: The Publications Division, 1961), p. 3.

language, whose base is Dravidian, but whose growth and structure have been fashioned by Aryan influences. The people are neither as fair or broad-built as those in the north, nor are they as dark as the southern Dravidian races. Caste differences persist, but there have also been strong anti-caste movements. In the fifteenth and sixteenth centuries, there was a religious, social, and literary revival and reformation in Maharashtra led by saints and prophets about half of whom were non-Brahmans. They protested against ritualistic practices and ceremonies and class distinctions based on birth. Dnyaneshwar, who wrote his famous commentary on the Bhagavadgita in the vernacular language, was the first saint and prophet to represent the new spirit of protest against the established order. He was followed by a succession of some fifty saints and prophets for the next five hundred years. "A few of these saints were women, a few were Mohamedan converts to Hinduism, nearly half of them were Brahmans, while there were representatives in the other half from among all the other castes—Marathas, kunbis, tailors, gardeners, potters, goldsmiths, repentant prostitutes, slave girls, and even the outcaste Mahars (i.e. Harijans). Much of the interest of this religious upheaval is that it permeated deep through all strata of society."[4]

There is a parallel between the history of the Protestant Reformation movement in Europe and that of the work of these saints and prophets who flourished about the same time in Maharashtra. Like the Reformers who protested against papal authority and objected to the intermediation of the clergy between God and man, the saints in Maharashtra protested against the ancient authority and tradition which had been petrified in the monopoly of the Brahman caste.

Two contributions of the saints have had an enduring impact. The saints broke down the dominance of Sanskrit, the language of the superior classes, by using the vernacular in both speech and writing. This brought the hitherto inaccessible classical knowledge and learning within the reach of the average man. The social impact of this literary struggle between Sanskrit and Marathi was revolutionary. It ended the dominance of Sanskrit and with it the dominance of the Brahman class and inaugurated a cultural and religious renaissance among the lower classes.

The second significant contribution of the saints was their stress upon *Bhakti* (devotion)—as opposed to ritualism—as the path of salvation. There is no saint of any importance who has not emphasized the superiority of Love and Faith over all other forms of worship, such as performance of rites and ceremonies, pilgrimages, fasts, or meditation. They

[4] *Ibid.*, p. 65.

also stressed the essential equality of all men regardless of their birth and social rank. The abiding contribution of the saints to the social practices of the people is found in the near absence of ritualism and orthodoxy among the people and the generally prevalent climate of equalitarianism. This enabled many Maharashtrians to be receptive to the new ideas of liberalism, secularism, individualism, and socialism as they came one after another from the West.

The work of the social reformers in the past one hundred and fifty years is a second factor responsible for introducing social reforms among the lower castes. From Balshastri Jambhekar in the first quarter of the nineteenth century to Dr. B. R. Ambedkar in the second quarter of the present century, there has been a galaxy of reformers: Lokhitwadi, Phule, Ranade, Gokhale, and Agarkar. With the exception of Phule, they were all scholars who reinterpreted the Hindu scriptures and declared that these did not permit caste differences based on birth or provide any religious sanction for the many social disabilities to which lower castes were subjected. They preached equality among castes and classes and between men and women. They demanded the abolition of child marriage and campaigned for remarriage of widows. This, they said, required education among women and so they started schools for women's education. More than a hundred years ago, Phule educated his wife, and the two then opened schools for women as well as for the outcastes.

Justice Ranade gave a new prestige and importance to this movement. Under the impact of Western ideas, he and his followers carried on a struggle for the recognition of equal rights of women and of the Harijans. They stressed the primacy of social reform over political struggle: in the absence of social reforms, they maintained, political freedom would degenerate into a privilege of the upper strata of society. This view brought them in conflict with Tilak, who laid stress on political independence and believed that only after India was politically free could she tackle the problems of social custom and tradition.

The reformers did not succeed in eliminating caste as an institution, but they did free the lower castes from the hegemony of Brahmanical power. By making the lower castes conscious that the disabilities to which they were subjected were no part of divine dispensation but were perpetrated by other classes, Ranade and his followers created the necessary will and organization to resist those injustices.

Economy of the State

As stated earlier, Maharashtra is the third largest state in India, with 9.02 per cent of the country's population and 10.08 per cent of its area.

It is the most urbanized state: as against an urban population of 18.0 per cent in India as a whole, Maharashtra's population is 28.2 per cent urban. What is of further significance is that of this urban population, 23.3 per cent live in cities larger than 20,000. The census of 1961 lists 265 cities and towns, with a combined population of 11.16 million. There are as many as 62 towns with 20,000 or more inhabitants. There are also 12 large urban complexes with population over 100,000, Poona and Nagpur having more than 500,000 and Metropolitan Bombay more than 4.1 million.[5]

Production other than cultivation absorbs about 14 per cent of self-supporting persons as compared with 10.6 per cent in India as a whole. Cultivators of land constitute 47.2 per cent in Maharashtra as compared with the national figure of 55.8 per cent. Agriculture contributes about one third of the state's income, but 64 per cent of Maharashtra's inhabitants are dependent upon it.

The gross produce per acre of net sown area is only about 70 per cent of what it is nationally because of (1) low fertility of soil and (2) inadequate irrigation facilities. Only about 6 per cent of the net sown area in the state is irrigated as compared with the national average of 17 per cent.

The state is a study in contrasts. There are pockets of highly developed industrial centers and also large areas of agricultural backwardness. Prior to independence, the country's economy was geared to the export-import trade, and this aided the growth of Bombay city as an entrepôt center. In contrast, other regions of Maharashtra like Konkan, Vidarbha, and Marathwada have remained relatively backward. These areas lacked the entrepreneurship as well as the private capital required for utilizing the indigenous resources for industrialization.

Owing to the high level of development of non-agricultural activities, the per capita income of the state works out to be significantly higher than the national average. As compared to Rs. 261 per capita income for the country as a whole, it is Rs. 292 in Maharashtra.[6] However, if the contribution of the Greater Bombay area is excluded, the state is as backward as any other part of India.

Regional Profiles: Western Maharashtra

Maharashtra state consists of four divisions: namely, Bombay, Poona, Aurangabad, and Nagpur. The Bombay division includes Greater Bombay, the three coastal districts of Konkan, and the three districts of

[5] *Census of India, 1961, Paper No. 1 of 1962,* p. li.

[6] National Council of Applied Economic Research, *Techno-Economic Survey of Maharashtra* (New Delhi, 1963), p. 211.

northern Maharashtra. The Poona division includes six southern districts of the state. These two divisions comprise thirteen districts and the area covered by them is called Western Maharashtra.

Bombay and Poona are the two main cities in this region. The former is the political capital, and the latter is the educational and cultural center of the state. The growth of cities, particularly of Bombay, has brought in its wake problems of congestion and slums, diminution of open spaces, and continuous pressure on essential civic amenities. With its area of 169 square miles and population of 4.1 million, Bombay has a density of 24,568 persons per square mile. Being the country's leading industrial center, its prospects of industrial employment attract people from every part of the country. About one-third of the inhabitants of Bombay were born in the city, the rest having immigrated during their own lifetime. Of the city's working population, 35 per cent are engaged in manufacturing, 24 per cent in trade and commerce, 8 per cent in transport and communication, and 32 per cent in other services. The population of the city has increased from 927,994 in 1901 to 4,152,056 in 1961; it was 2,994,444 in 1951. Percentage decade variation was the lowest in 1921-31 (+1.26) and highest in 1941-51 (+66.23).

Large-scale migration from rural areas in the state has combined with an enormous influx of immigrants from other states to produce large slums and areas of poverty in Bombay. There are 144 slums in the city; at least 100,000 people have no homes except the pavements and sidewalks of the city; 8 per cent of the family dwellers have no latrines at all. Three-quarters of the population have no bathroom facilities.[7] Of the 148,659 households selected by the census staff in 1961 on a 20 per cent sample, it was found that 3,591 had no regular room, 107,512 had only one room, and 24,488 had two rooms. In the first category were 15,373 persons, in the second 534,525 persons, and in the third 139,612 persons out of an enumerated 783,733 persons.[8] The influx into Bombay, however, continues unabated. The attractions of city life, an uneconomic man/land ratio, land reform legislation, underemployment, disguised unemployment, and lack of alternative sources of employment are some of the causes of the staggering rate of urbanization. Immigration has given the city a heterogeneous character. There is hardly a region, religion, or language in India which is not represented in the population of the city.

[7] See Asoka Mehta, "The Future of Indian Cities" in *India's Urban Future*, ed. Roy Turner (Bombay: Oxford University Press, 1962).

[8] *Census of India 1961, Maharashtra*, Part X (1-3), p. 298.

TABLE 4.1

POPULATION OF GREATER BOMBAY, ACCORDING TO RELIGION, LANGUAGE, AND STATE OF ORIGIN

(Total Population: 4,152,056)

Religion		*Language*		*State of Origin*	
Hindu	2,869,276	Marathi	1,775,114	Gujarat	450,832
Muslim	538,389	Gujarati	792,771	U. P.	320,266
Christian	288,023	Urdu	401,616	Mysore	171,806
Buddhist	192,717	Hindi	330,529	Andhra	90,133
Zoroastrian	70,065	English	48,509	Madras	85,304
Jains	155,747	Tamil	104,387	Goa, Daman, Diu	82,985
Jews	12,366	Telugu	97,997	Kerala	73,593
Sikhs	25,440	Kannada	82,832	Rajasthan	51,815
		Malayalam	65,673		

SOURCE: *Census of India 1961, Maharashtra,* Part X (1-8), Greater Bombay Census Tables, pp. 185, 193, 202.

Bombay has always been the center for the diffusion of new ideas and for the activities of leftist parties. The Communist party of India, the Praja Socialists, and the Socialists have been very active in city politics for many years and have recently been joined by the Jan Sangh and the Swatantra parties. There were unprecedented scenes of mob fury and violence during the Samyukta Maharashtra agitation for creating a Marathi-speaking state, and since then there have been many militant trade unions and leftist party struggles such as the Municipal Workers' strike and the Port and Dock Workers' strike. The large numbers of unemployed, rootless, unmarried, and disturbed persons in the city can be easily provoked to violence. Many of the youth in Bombay are turning cynical and destructive and are suspicious of every political faith and organization. The city youth also has an unwholesome influence on young men and women in rural areas.

The quality of politics in the city of Bombay has steadily worsened. Men without any experience of social service and without personal integrity are finding it easier to secure election to the City Corporation or State Assembly. Political campaigns often degenerate into personal vilification and character assassination; and some of India's most sensational newspapers are published in Bombay.

Western Maharashtra, excluding Bombay, is nearly as backward as Vidarbha and Marathwada. Only the Bombay-Poona belt, where new industries are rapidly coming up, and the sugar cane districts of Ahmednagar, Sangli, and Kolhapur have prospered to some extent in the past ten years. In fact, more areas of scarcity are to be found in this region than in any other part of the state for the agricultural output is low. The three coastal districts of Konkan, except for the Thana and Kolaba areas adjoining Greater Bombay, have the lowest density of population, low literacy rates, and marginal industrialization. The poor mineral resources position also puts serious limitation on the growth potential of this area.

Regional Profiles: Vidarbha

This region is made up of the four districts of Berar and the four districts of Mahakoshal which together formed part of the former Madhya Pradesh. The States Reorganization Commission recommended the separation of these Marathi-speaking districts south of the Satpura range and proposed that they be constituted into a separate state.[9] The Parliament, however, by its act of 1956 included the area in the bilingual Bombay state. After the break-up of Bombay state to form two unilingual states of Gujarat and Maharashtra, the area became part of the state of Maharashtra.

The area of Vidarbha is 36,880 square miles and its population 9.2 million of which 21.4 per cent live in urban areas. It has a population density of 273 per square mile and a literacy rate of 27.8 per cent. From 1905 onwards, the separation of the Marathi-speaking districts from the Hindi areas of the Central Provinces and their formation into a separate province was demanded by the people of this area, as they felt that they were unjustly treated by the government in the matter of jobs, political representation, and facilities for the development of Marathi. The surplus yielded by this cotton-growing tract also lent viability to the proposed province. The historical rivalry between Nagpur and Poona was perhaps another reason for demanding a separate state. Attempts were therefore made to reconcile the differences between the protagonists of a single province of the Marathi-speaking people and the advocates of a separate province of Maha Vidarbha and to press unitedly for a separate province with adequate guarantees for Vidarbha. On August 7, 1947, an agreement was reached for the creation of sub-provinces. This was embodied in what came to be known as the Akola Pact.

However, the fears of discrimination, ill-treatment, and transfer of the resources of Vidarbha for the development of the poorer regions of Hindi-speaking Madhya Pradesh which had given rise to the separatist demand were not fully allayed. Another apprehension in the minds of the people of Vidarbha was in regard to the status of Nagpur. Nagpur had been the

[9] *States Reorganization Commission's Report* (New Delhi: The Manager of Publications, 1956), p. 125.

capital of a large province, and it was feared that it might lose importance since Bombay was to be the capital of Maharashtra. The Akola Pact was drawn up before the constitution of India came into effect, and the notion of sub-provinces had no legal basis. So on September 28, 1953, a comprehensive agreement assuring the people of the region fair and just treatment and the continued importance of Nagpur was signed, with the result that the spokesmen for a separate Vidarbha now became supporters of a united Maharashtra. This agreement, known as the Nagpur Pact, is an important document determining the nature of government policies affecting this area. The text of the pact is as follows:

THE NAGPUR AGREEMENT

1. Now that a high power Commission is being appointed to report on the question of reorganizing and regrouping of the States in India, we the people residing in the various parts of the Marathi-speaking area, have reached the following conclusion as a basis for the formation of a single State comprising all such areas.
2. This State should be formed of the contiguous Marathi-speaking areas of the present Bombay, Madhya Pradesh and the Hyderabad States. There should be no enclaves within the limits and boundaries of this State. It shall be called Maharashtra or Marathi Pradesh and the city of Bombay shall be its capital.
3. The State will comprise the three units of Maha Vidarbha, Marathwada and the rest of the State for the purposes of all types of development and administration.
4. Subject to the requirements of a single Government, the allocation of funds for expenditure over the different units will be in proportion to their population but in view of the undeveloped conditions of Marathwada special attention shall be given to promote the all-sided development of that area. A report in this behalf shall be placed before the State Assembly every year.
5. The composition of the Government shall reflect the proportion of the population of the units.
6. Fair and adequate facilities in proportion to the population of these units shall be assured for admission to all educational institutions having training facilities in vocational and scientific professions or other specialized training.
7. The High Court of the new State will have its principal seat at Bombay and a second seat at Nagpur. The Bench at Nagpur will ordinarily function for the Maha Vidarbha area. While making

recommendations for High-Court Judges it shall be seen that the Maha Vidarbha area gets adequate representation in respect of appointments from the services and the bar. This paragraph will also apply to Marathwada area *Mutatis Mutandis.*

8. In the matter of services under Government or Government-controlled enterprises of all grades recruitment will be in proportion to the population of the respective units.
9. We believe in decentralization as an effective means of better associating the people of the different units with the administration.
10. We realize the long association of the people of Maha Vidarbha with Nagpur as a capital of their State and the various advantages consequently derived by them from it. We are anxious that subject to the efficient conduct of administration of a single State those advantages should be preserved to the extent possible. All steps necessary to implement this clause will be taken on the advice of experts. The Government shall officially shift to Nagpur for a definite period and at least one session of the State Legislature shall be held every year in Nagpur.
11. The district boundaries shall be adjusted on the basis of the latest Census, with village as the unit so as to include all the contiguous Marathi-speaking areas in the New State.

The assurances contained in the Pact have been carried out. A bench of the state High Court sits in Nagpur, functioning primarily for the Vidarbha area. In recruitment and promotions to higher cadres, due representation is given although no formal quota has been fixed. One session of the legislature is held every year at Nagpur. The region has 63 members in the state legislature. There are 5 ministers and one deputy minister from the area in the state Cabinet of 25. The present chief minister comes from the region. The first presidentship of the unified Maharashtra Pradesh Congress Committee was also given to a leader from this area.

In spite of all this, relations between this region and Western Maharashtra are not always cordial. In the first two years after the formation of Maharashtra, they were particularly strained. Inconveniences faced by government servants and difficulties arising out of differing legal and revenue structures and traditions of administration created a sense of frustration and bitterness which manifested itself in the revival of the demand for a separate Vidarbha and in violent demon-

TABLE 4.2

INDICATORS OF REGIONAL DISPARITIES IN MAHARASHTRA

(A) Regional figures, or (B) Regional figures as percentage of the total for Maharashtra

	Aurangabad Division	*Nagpur Division*	*Poona Division*	*Greater Bombay*	*Bombay Division excluding Greater Bombay*	*Total*	*Maharashtra*
Population (B)	20.8	23.8	26.1	9.3	20.0	29.3	100.0
% of population in each region engaged in							
Primary Sector (A)	76.5	69.3	68.1	0.8	68.6	47.0	63.9
Secondary Sector (A)	7.9	13.5	11.3	34.5	10.4	18.1	13.1
Tertiary Sector (A)	15.6	17.2	20.6	64.7	21.0	34.9	23.0
Number of factories (B)	5.9	16.1	23.2	44.1	10.7	54.8	100.0
Average no. of workers engaged in factories (B)	4.1	10.9	12.2	65.4	7.4	72.8	100.0
Average no. of workers engaged in factories as % of population in each region (A)	0.4	0.9	0.9	14.2	0.8	5.0	2.0
Consumption of electricity (B)	0.4	6.9	5.3	68.0	19.4	87.4	100.0
Per capita consumption of electricity (in KWH) (A)	1.0	17.5	12.2	437.7	58.5	179.2	60.2
No. of persons per car operating in each region (A)	8829	1628	1514	–	–	287	734
% of literate persons in population (A)	13.4	19.0	19.4	49.3	49.3	29.2	20.9

SOURCE: *Basic Statistics of Maharashtra*, Bureau of Economics & Statistics, Bombay.

strations. An effigy of the then chief minister, Y. B. Chavan, was burned, there was mob violence in many places, and in Nagpur a tense situation was created by the secessionists, who installed in the center of a busy thoroughfare an image of the goddess Chandika, a symbol of their determination to fight. Although violence ceased after some time, the feeling of resentment did not. On the eve of the general elections of 1962, it found an outlet in the formation of the Nag-Vidarbha Andolan Samiti, which put up four candidates for the Parliament and 19 for the State Assembly and secured 1 and 2 seats respectively. However, in the elections of 1967 the Samiti put up only one candidate for Parliament and 6 for the State Assembly. As a matter of fact, key figures in the Samiti joined the Congress on the eve of the fourth elections and the Samiti has become a spent force.

Relative economic backwardness and an injured political ego may be said to be the principal causes of tension between Vidarbha and Western Maharashtra. Vidarbha has an urban population of 21.4 per cent as against 50.7 in Western Maharashtra including Bombay. As many as 72 per cent of the people depend on agriculture, of which 49 per cent are owner-cultivators, 9 per cent tenant-cultivators, and 39 per cent landless laborers.[10]

To correct these imbalances and to push the developmental activities ahead, the state's Third Plan was formulated in such a way that the regions of Vidarbha and Marathwada should receive greater support. Thus the per capita outlay for these regions is kept at a high figure of Rs. 95 and Rs. 98, respectively, as against Rs. 88 for each of the other two divisions excluding Greater Bombay. The same applies to irrigation and primary education, as shown in Table 4.3.[11]

TABLE 4.3

EXPENDITURES FOR IRRIGATION AND PRIMARY EDUCATION IN VIDARBHA AND MARATHWADA

Region		*Allocation in proportion to population*	*Actual Allocation*
Vidarbha	Irrigation	Rs. 19.48 crores	Rs. 21.37 crores
	Primary education	Rs. 3.12 crores	Rs. 5.65 crores
Marathwada	Irrigation	Rs. 13.31 crores	Rs. 24.49 crores
	Primary education	Rs. 2.13 crores	Rs. 4.16 crores

[10] *Third Five Year Plan, Maharashtra State* (Bombay: Government Central Press), p. 130.

[11] *Ibid.*

Regional Profiles: Marathwada

Unlike Vidarbha, Marathwada showed from the beginning a strong and unequivocal desire for merger with Maharashtra. Its five districts formed a part of the Muslim state of Hyderabad until the latter's disintegration following the reorganization of states. Under Nizam's rule, the area was neglected. The introduction of Urdu as the language of the court and administration left little opportunity for the regional language to develop. As a consequence, literacy of the Muslims rose from 12.5 to 77.1 per cent between 1911 and 1941 while Hindu literacy rose from 3.8 to only 17.1 per cent.[12] The struggle against the Razakar misrule preceding the take-over of Hyderabad brought the people still closer to those in Western Maharashtra, thus strengthening the historical ties between the two regions. Linguistically and culturally Marathwada had been an integral part of Maharashtra. The saints of Maharashtra, who came primarily from Marathwada, have been symbols of the spiritual and cultural unity of the people of the state. Later, when the cultural center shifted to Poona, Bombay, and Nagpur, the literary life of Marathwada began to draw inspiration from these centers.

The area of Marathwada is 25,740 sq. miles and its population 6,297,373. It has a population density of 244 per sq. mile. Only 12.5 per cent of its inhabitants live in urban areas, which indicates how predominantly rural the region is: 86.9 per cent of the people are dependent on agriculture. The area has a literacy rate of only 16.1 per cent, the lowest in the state. Not only is it the least developed part of the state, but its unfavorable resource position and inadequate basic facilities augment the difficulties of developing the region. The low level of development has created a feeling in Marathwada that no adequate measures are being taken by the state government to correct the imbalance. Table 4.4 gives some measures of the regional disparities.

There is some feeling in Marathwada that Vidarbha, by being vocal and periodically raising the threat of separation, has been able to gain more than proportional advantages while Marathwada, because it is mute, is neglected. The region has 43 seats in the state Legislative Assembly and it has 3 ministers and 2 deputy ministers in the state Cabinet. In the first three years of the third Five Year Plan, development expenditure for the region has lagged behind by as much as 17 per cent. No major industry has been established in this area either in the public or

[12] *Reorganization of States in India with particular reference to the Formation of Maharashtra* (Bombay: Samyukta Maharashtra Parishad Publication, 1964), p. 95.

TABLE 4.4

REGIONAL DISPARITIES

	Bombay Division excluding Greater Bombay	*Poona Division*	*Nagpur Division*	*Aurangabad Division*
Gross value of agricultural produce per acre (average 1955–56 to 1958–59)	130	111	104	74
Percentage of irrigated area to gross cropped area	4.6	9.9	5.1	3.2
Railway mileage per 100 sq. miles	2.6	2.7	2.7	2.2
Road mileage per 100 sq. miles	32.9	29.2	11.3	7.4
Consumption of Electricity (million KWH)	391	110	142	3
Factory employment per 100 population	7.3	8.9	7.7	2.3
Primary education (no. of pupils per 1,000)	119	124	82	54
Employment in factories in 1957 (in thousands)	472.7	77.9	69.8	26.5

SOURCES: *Third Five Year Plan, Maharashtra State*, p. 130, and National Council of Applied Economic Research, *Techno-Economic Survey of Maharashtra* (New Delhi, 1963), p. 235.

private sector. The fact that there are only 39,815 factory employees in a population of 6.2 million is a measure of the industrial backwardness of Marathwada. Marathwada is also very poor in agriculture, education, transport and communication, and public health. Economically it is the least developed region, and because it lacks vocal leadership it continues to suffer from neglect at the hands of the politicians of Western Maharashtra and Vidarbha.

Western Education

Along with Bengal and Madras, Maharashtra was the first to feel the impact of Western contact, especially of Western education. During the term of Governor Mountstuart Elphinstone, education in English was begun. In the first few years these efforts were spasmodic in character, and since the schools were manned by missionaries, many parents withdrew their children from these schools. Jagannath Shankarshet, a social leader and philanthropist, then took the initiative in founding in 1822 the Bombay Native School Book and Society. The name was later changed to the Bombay Native Education Society, and under its guidance several schools were started in the city and elsewhere in Bombay. The Bombay Education Board was an amalgam of the Elphinstone College and the Native Education Society created in 1837. In 1848 the Students' Literary and Scientific Society was founded with the object of holding discussion meetings, reading papers on literary and scientific subjects, and conducting schools for men and women. In 1857 Bombay University was founded. From this university, as from Calcutta and Madras universities, came the new Western-educated class, possessing English as a common language and sharing the liberal ideas of nineteenth-century writers. The graduates of these universities joined the civil service, the commercial firms, and the professions of law, medicine, education, and engineering.

After independence, there was an unprecedented growth of educational facilities in Maharashtra. In 1951, there were 2.4 million students attending primary schools in the state. They constituted about 44 per cent of the population in the age group of 6-14 years. Free primary education was instituted, and all the towns and two-thirds of the villages have schools. The number of schools has increased from 22,422 in 1951 to 32,995 in 1960, and the number of students from 2.4 million to over 4.1 million during the same period. There are another 86,000 children attending secondary schools. There are six universities and 343 technical institutions in the state.[13]

Social Restratification

Among the major changes brought about by Western contact, it was the changes in social stratification that had the most profound effect on the whole process of political change. A new class of Western-educated elite arose and took their place in civil service, trade and commerce, the professions, and politics. The national struggle for independence was led by this middle class, which drew its inspiration from the liberal democratic ideas of the West. The adaptation to Western ideas by leaders and reformers in Maharashtra was, however, conditioned by the concepts and social practices then current in society. As elsewhere in the country, the Brahmans were in the forefront in every walk of life and were sustained in their superior position by the prevailing social stratification based on caste.

In the past one hundred years or so, increased emphasis has been placed on the attainment of status by achievement. Education has now become an important instrument for acquiring status. The British

[13] *Third Five Year Plan, Maharashtra State*, p. 30.

made education accessible to all, irrespective of caste or community, who could pay for it. In spite of its distortions and limitations this education remained liberal in content. It propagated such principles as the equality of men before the law, equal rights of all citizens, equal freedom to follow any vocation. It was based on European liberalism. Although the British rule was an alien rule, still the education organized by it was secular and basically liberal, in contrast to the education in pre-British India which endorsed Hindu caste distinctions and upheld privilege.[14]

Brahmans retained political leadership until the death of Tilak in 1920. Although for another fifteen years or so they dominated the provincial Congress, they lost their national position since none of the Brahman leaders after Tilak had the scholarship, political acumen, and popularity which had given him such a commanding position in the country's politics. The leadership gradually passed into the hands of non-Brahman upper castes, especially the Marathas. Because of the historical rivalry between the Peshwas, who were Brahmans, and their Maratha chieftains, and the anti-Brahman movements of the first quarter of this century, the relations between these two important castes became increasingly estranged, and a struggle for political power ensued in which the Marathas emerged victorious. In the democratic set-up, this was inevitable since the Brahmans constitute less than 5 per cent of the population while the Marathas are the largest single social group, with about 45 per cent of the population. The Brahmans have now reconciled themselves to playing a secondary role. Congress leadership in the state is mainly Maratha by caste, and the new institutions of local government known as panchayati raj are contributing to a further strengthening of the political power of this caste.

A development of the most far-reaching significance has been the conversion of Harijans to Buddhism. In 1956 B. R. Ambedkar, the acknowledged leader of the Scheduled Castes in India, led this movement by embracing Buddhism. His example was followed by thousands of his followers. According to the 1951 census, the Scheduled Castes population in Maharashtra was 4 million; in 1961 it dropped to 2.2 million while the Buddhist population, which was only 2,487 in 1951, shot up to 2.8 million. Although the state government has, by appropriate notification, continued the educational, service, and other facilities previously given to the Scheduled Castes, it has reduced Scheduled Caste representation in the Parliament, the state legislature, and the zilla parishad. Only 3 seats are now reserved for Parliament and 15 for the state legis-

14 A. R. Desai, *Social Background of Indian Nationalism* (Bombay: Popular Book Depot, 1959), p. 232.

lature as against 6 and 33, respectively, in the 1962 elections. For zilla parishads (district councils), there are only 72 seats in 26 districts reserved for the Scheduled Castes out of a total of 1,271.[15] The social and economic hardships to which the Scheduled Castes were subjected prior to their conversion to Buddhism are only gradually disappearing; the seething discontent about this and the tardy ameliorative efforts of the government manifested itself in a nation-wide satyagraha in which 32,000 men and women in Maharashtra alone courted arrest.[16]

THE POLITICAL PROCESS

Until the death of Tilak in 1920, Maharashtra was always in the forefront of the national movement. The first conference of the Indian National Congress was held in Bombay, and Maharashtrians were prominent among the moderates who provided leadership to the Congress in the early years. Along with Bengal, Maharashtra was also a center of terrorist activities in the beginning of this century, and it was here that leftist thought later found receptive ground. Marxist ideology and the image of Soviet Russia had a great hold over the minds of educated youth, and from their ranks came several of the Socialist and Communist leaders. However, in Maharashtra, unlike Bengal, the sway of leftist ideologies did not last long among the intelligentsia.

Maharashtrians were prominent in early nationalist politics, but with the advent of Gandhi their role subsequently declined. This shift had important consequences for their attitude toward the nationalist movement, for many Maharashtrians did not accept the new leadership until a decade or two later. The bitter memories of the opposition and of the eventual split and the ouster which Tilak, their hero, had to face in Congress did not permit his followers, and the members of the Brahman classes from which he came, to take kindly to the new leaders. Many of them tried to rally under the flag of the Democratic Swaraj party led by N. C. Kelkar, a colleague of Tilak. Later they supported Savarkar, a leader of the terrorist agitation in the region and an ardent advocate of militant Hindu ideology. The Hindu Mahasabha was a powerful force in the state's politics in the late thirties. The Westernized urban intelligentsia, though divided ideologically between adherence to Western liberal democracy and Russian Communism, were too rationalistic and scientific in their attitudes to be able to comprehend and accept Gandhian ideas. They disdained Gandhi's traditional outlook and modes of behavior—his asceticism and non-violence, his advocacy of hand-spin-

[15] *Census of India, 1961, Maharashtra,* Part V-A., p. 25.

[16] Stated by Home Minister in State Assembly on December 12, 1964.

ning, and his opposition to machinery. They considered his philosophy outdated and rejected his program, which was based primarily on a concern for the rural masses. Instead, the urban middle classes were interested in Western education and administration, which increased their chances for lucrative professional careers; a few were enchanted by the vision of a sovietized India whose economy and government would be in their hands. In any case, they had no interest in a philosophy couched in religio-ethical terms or a drab reform program which could neither stimulate their intellect nor excite them to revolutionary action.

As the Maharashtrian intelligentsia refused to accept Gandhi's leadership, they gradually receded to the background of the nationalist movement. The resurrection of the Congress in the region had to await the arrival of Maratha political leadership. With the support of a few Brahman Gandhians they revitalized the organization by bringing the rich and middle-class peasantry into its fold. The century-old rivalry between Brahmans and Marathas was aggravated and extended to almost every field of life and activity. In the end, the Marathas triumphed, their grip over the organization was complete, and they won mass rural support. Beaten and frustrated, many Brahmans turned against Congress and joined the opposition. The Hindu Mahasabha and the RSS became Brahman strongholds, but their power declined after independence.

Since 1935, the political life in the state has been dominated by the Congress party, with little electoral fluctuation except in the 1957 elections when the upsurge of linguistic agitation nearly overwhelmed it. By 1962, however, the party had more than regained its lost ground and won an easy victory over all the opposition parties. To a high degree, political life exhibits the characteristics of a single-party system wherein the struggle for power and influence is conducted within the Congress party. The rivalry runs generally along regional lines, with groups of Congressmen from each of the three regions of Vidarbha, Marathwada, and Western Maharashtra bargaining hard for political gains. Unlike some other states, however, there is hardly any rivalry between the ministerial and organizational wings. This is undoubtedly because the two are conscientiously maintaining harmonious relations, and also because the ministerial wing is far too powerful. Outside the ministry, there are no senior and outstanding Congress leaders who could organize groups against the ministry. Y. B. Chavan was both the chief minister of the state and the accredited leader of the party. The latter position is retained by him even after his elevation to the center. Factions persist, and many influential individuals have broken away from the party, but so far no one, either from inside the party or from outside, has been able to make any dent in the solidity of the Congress position in the state. In fact, the Congress organization as well as the Congress ministry in Maharashtra are among the most stable in the country today. The dominance of the Congress in the politics of the state is proved once again in the February elections of 1967, in which the party secured 203 seats out of 270 in the Assembly.

While the Congress dominates the broad middle, there are several parties of both "left" and "right." Without being electorally powerful, they are, nonetheless, quite effective in exerting popular pressures through meetings, demonstrations, satyagraha, and other similar peaceful democratic methods. In fact, at the present moment, the state has supplied leadership to many all-India parties. The leaders of both the right and the left Communist parties, the chairman of the Praja Socialist as well as the Samyukta Socialist parties, the president of the Jan Sangh, the chairman of the Republican party, and the general secretary of the Swatantra party come from Maharashtra.[17]

Besides the state units of national parties, there are local or state parties. Some of them, like the Samyukta Maharashtra Samiti and the Nag-Vidarbha Andolan Samiti, have their origin in the state's reorganization movement.

The major opposition to Congress in Maharashtra is a regional party known as the Peasants & Workers party, which has backing among the peasantry—both landlords and tenants. The party originated out of personal feuds between its leaders when they were in the Congress and other top leaders of that organization. "Partly it also represented the growing leftist trend in rural areas. In order to take on a radical complexion this dissident group took more and more to Marxian thought and in its well-known *Dabhadi Thesis* publicly avowed its acceptance of the 'cominform' line."[18] The party did not, however, merge with the Communists nor did it enter into any electoral alliance with it. This led to the first of a series of splits. A splinter group left to form another party which worked in close collaboration with the Communists and with the left socialist group which broke away from the Socialist party.

[17] Chairman of the Rightist Communist party is S. A. Dange from Bombay; leader of the Leftist Communist party is B. T. Ranadive from Bombay; chairman of the Praja Socialist party is N. G. Goray from Poona; chairman of the Samyukta Socialist party is S. M. Joshi from Poona; last year the president of the Bharatiya Jan Sangh was Bachhraj Vyas from Nagpur: he is now (1966) treasurer; general secretary of the Republican party is R. Khobragade from Nagpur; and general secretary of the Swatantra party is M. R. Masani from Bombay.

[18] S. V. Kogekar and Richard L. Park, *Reports on the Indian General Elections, 1951-52* (Bombay: Popular Book Depot, 1956), p. 33.

The party had a pronounced communal orientation. It was opposed to the Brahmans and appealed to the non-Brahman to oust the Brahmans from positions of power and influence. A Marxian interpretation put on the Brahman-non-Brahman struggle took the form of identifying the Brahmans with the bourgeoisie and the non-Brahman peasantry with the proletariat. This was all the more remarkable in view of the fact that most of the Brahmans in Maharashtra live by serving in government and private offices or by following the liberal professions whereas many of the "peasants" from whom the party received support were substantial landowners. The opposition to the Brahmans had a ready appeal in the rural areas against the historical background of the anti-Brahman movement in Maharashtra.[19]

In the 1952 general elections, the party won 26 seats; in 1957, 30 seats; in 1962, 15 seats; and in 1967, 19 seats. Its percentage of votes has been 9.1, 9.4, 7.5, and 7.2 respectively. The party has a fairly good following in certain districts of Western Maharashtra and in Marathwada; in the elections of 1957 it captured 25 seats in Western Maharashtra. But after the formation of the state in 1960, its influence waned and that of the Congress increased. In fact, with the re-emergence of the Congress as the strongest party after the formation of the state, the strength of the PWP has gone down. The main reason for its decline seems to be that the Maratha community, which was the backbone of the party, was attracted to Chavan, who has become a national leader. Then, too, in a system of one-party dominance, relations between the administration and the party in power are very close; and through the program of community development projects, the national extension service and the panchayati raj institutions, the ruling party is in a position to influence the implementation of welfare activities. It is also in a position to see that opposition parties are not given opportunities to undertake such activities. The result is that those who are excluded from power also get excluded from the benefits of it. In rural areas, to oppose the party in power often amounts to being cut off from patronage. One hears complaints that the supporters of Congress have used their positions in panchayat samitis and zilla parishads to penalize whole villages which voted for opposition candidates by delaying or denying them approach roads, dispensaries, co-operatives, fertilizers, or corrugated sheets.

The Praja Socialist party (PSP) is caught between Congress on the one side and the Samyukta Socialists and the Communists on the other. The

[19] *Ibid.*, p. 34.

leaders of the Congress Socialist party had left Congress in 1948 to found the Socialist party. The Socialists hoped to dislodge the Congress from power in several provinces in the very first elections after independence. It was a party of young nationalists looking toward the establishment of a socialist society through peaceful and democratic means. In industrial areas in the state they were very active among the working classes and were particularly popular with the middle class. An aura surrounded the leaders of the party for their active role in the underground Quit India Movement. However, the party had little contact with the peasantry, and the leaders of the party in the state, predominantly Brahmans, were unable to win popular support. The present name of the party was acquired after the merger in 1953 of the Socialist party and the Kisan Mazdoor Praja party founded by Acharya Kripalani just before the elections of 1952.

The party later split into two sharply divided factions led by Asoka Mehta and Dr. Rammanohar Lohia. The former advocated closer association with the Congress, perhaps even joining a coalition government. The success of long-term plans of economic development required, according to Mehta, continuity; under a democracy, this could be ensured only by unity of the middle-of-the-road political forces, driving "left" and "right" opinions to the fringes. The faction led by Dr. Lohia opposed this thesis on the ground that it would destroy democratic socialism and instead called for an accentuation of the struggle against the party in power. This factional struggle was carried on intensely in Maharashtra because Bombay was the center of Asoka Mehta's activities, and the followers of Dr. Lohia were also active in Maharashtra. It resulted in the weakening of both groups, and many active cadres left the party out of disillusionment and joined Congress.

The adoption by the Congress of a resolution calling for a "socialistic pattern of society" at its Avadi session in 1954 precipitated another crisis in the PSP. Madhu Limaye, Keshav Goray and others in Bombay and Bagaitkar, Naik and Vinayak Kulkarni and others in Maharashtra, took an active part in consolidating the group within the party supporting Dr. Lohia. The bitter factionalism ultimately ended in disciplinary action, and the Lohiaites were asked to leave the party.

Agitation over the report of the States Reorganization Commission, the violent nature of that agitation, and the formation of a united front with Communists and other leftist parties (called the Samyukta Maharashtra Samiti) produced another serious crisis. This alliance with the extreme left resulted in the defection of whole groups of workers to the Congress and brought the state unit of the party to the verge of disaffiliation by the National Executive. S. M. Joshi, the chairman of the state PSP, accepted the general secretaryship of the Samiti and, in the face of opposition from his colleagues, subordinated party interests to the cause of the alliance. In the Samiti, Joshi was outmaneuvered by the CPI and its leftist allies, and this led to further dissensions in the party. The failure to combat Communist tactics inside the Samiti cost the party dearly, and in 1960 when the PSP eventually broke away from the alliance, it had to face a hostile public. The PSP fought alone in the elections of 1962 after there had been large defections from the party. It can be said that no party has given to the Congress as many active workers as the PSP.

Disciplinary action taken against Asoka Mehta for accepting the deputy chairmanship of the Planning Commission in 1963 produced the next crisis. There was a wide gulf between the cooperationist views of Mehta and the strong antipathy to Congress felt by the majority. The party suffered a major jolt, not only because its principal theoretician and spokesman joined the Congress but also because hundreds of workers from every state did the same in support of Mehta. In desperation the party amalgamated with the Lohiaite faction of the Socialist party to form the Samyukta Socialist party. However, in less than eight months the unification was annulled and the PSP began to function once again as a separate party. The party won 8 seats in 1952, 33 seats in 1957, 9 seats in 1962, and 8 in 1967, with 13.4, 10.7, 7.04 and 3.98 per cent of votes, respectively.

Another political party of significance in Maharashtra is the Communist party. Except for a few strongholds in some districts like Bhir, Ahmednagar, and Nagpur, the party has little support in the rural areas. Its main source of strength is the urban industrial proletariat. But in the past fifteen years its former unchallenged position has steadily weakened and it has lost ground to the Socialist party and the Praja Socialist party. Even the Congress-dominated Indian National Trade Union Congress has made deep dents in what were previously strong pockets of Communist influence. The textile workers in Bombay, whom the Communists had organized as early as 1926 and out of whose struggles had emerged the Communist leadership which later dominated the party at the national level, are no longer solidly with the Communists.

Lohia Socialists have been most active in the trade union movement. Bombay's municipal labor, bus transport workers, taxi drivers, and similar employees in public utilities have been organized by George Fernandes, a militant union organizer in the Socialist party. His militant unions have organized a number of successful strikes. Fernandes is often invited by labor in different industries to organize them, and his influence has begun to spread. He has also organized state bus transport workers, hospital workers, and hotel workers. Fernandes caused a big political upset in the 1967 elections by defeating S. K. Patil, Bombay's Congress party boss. The PSP is strong among port and dock workers and silk mill laborers, while the CPI retains its traditional hold in the cotton textile industry, though the Congress-dominated Indian National Trade Union Congress has been functioning as the "representative union."[20]

It is interesting to note, however, the failure of the leftist parties to win the political loyalties of workers. In spite of militant ideologies and their trade union activities, they have so far failed in making the workers follow their parties, with the result that Congress continues to get a substantial vote in predominantly labor constituencies.

The anti-national record of the Communist party is perhaps the most important single reason for its stagnation. People have not forgotten the role of the party in the Civil Disobedience and Quit India movements. Support for the Muslim League's demand for Pakistan and its equivocal stand on the border dispute with China are the two other main reasons why the party continues to be in disfavor. The recent split in the party over the China issue has had a paralyzing effect on the organization. In spite of all the advantages of rigid discipline, sound finances, an ideology tailored to all levels of comprehension, and a well-designed program of action, the party has failed to make much impression on any section of the society except to some extent upon the discontented fringe of the middle classes in urban communities. The inability of the party to develop as a truly national party without subordination to either Moscow or Peking incapacitates it for extensive growth, and even its united-front politics loses in appeal because of the extremely embittered relations between its right and left wings.

However, the skillful manner in which the party managed to jockey for positions of power inside the Samyukta Maharashtra Samiti helped it to improve its earlier position and make some significant gains. S. A. Dange, the leader of the party and chairman of the parliamentary board of this united front, was able to win the election to the Lok Sabha from Bombay in 1957 with the largest majority of votes in the country. He lost in 1962 but has been elected again in the 1967 elections. The

20 A union which, under the Bombay Industrial Relations Act of 1947, has the largest membership provided it is at least 25 per cent of the total labor force in the industry.

party also secured a number of seats in the state Assembly. It won 7 seats in 1952, 19 seats in 1957, and 6 seats in 1962 with 3.4, 6.4, and 6.0 per cent of the votes, respectively.

Politics in Maharashtra, as elsewhere, suffers from fragmentation. Besides the parties mentioned there are others like the Republican party, Jan Sangh, Hindu Mahasabha, and Swatantra party. The Republican party is the successor to the Scheduled Castes Federation and represents the neo-Buddhists. Since the death of Dr. Ambedkar, the party has been riven by personal groups and their rivalries, but its hold over the new converts to Buddhism is substantial as was revealed by a mass satyagraha launched by the party to draw the government's attention to the economic hardships of its followers. In 1952 the party won 3 seats to the state Assembly; in 1957, 13 seats; in 1962, 3 seats; and in 1967, 5 seats.

There are three large factions in the party, each led by a powerful associate of the late Dr. Ambedkar. During the period of agitation for United Maharashtra, two of the three factions—those led by Gaikwad and Professor Bhandare—worked inside the Samyukta Maharashtra Samiti in close collaboration with the Communists. The third faction, led by Kamble, worked with the Praja Socialist party (PSP). The debacle of the 1962 general elections produced disenchantment among the followers of all the three factions. Their leaders moved further away from each other, and since then an acrimonious debate among the feuding factions has been going on in the party press and on party platforms.

The election reverses of the party have sombered the ebullient Gaikwad, who started making overtures to the Congress for an electoral understanding between the two parties. He leads the largest faction and commands wide support among the followers of Dr. Ambedkar. His association with the left parties enabled the Communists, the Peasants and Workers party, and others to return several of their candidates to the Parliament and the state legislature in constituencies having a large number of neo-Buddhist voters. But this association has not benefited the Republican party since the high-caste Hindu followers of the left parties did not vote for the neo-Buddhist candidates of the Republican party. Recently Gaikwad sought an electoral adjustment with the Congress party. Chavan and the state's Chief Minister responded, but the Congress High Command turned down the proposal. The faction led by Bhandare has joined the Congress.

Although the Jan Sangh has grown steadily in organization and influence, its appeal is largely confined to the militant Hindu communalists. It is a party of Hindu communalism, traditionalism, and social conservatism. Its main source of strength in Maharashtra lies in the Brahman middle class from urban localities, in contrast to Uttar Pradesh, Rajasthan, or Madhya Pradesh, where the party has some rural support.

The Swatantra party started with a flourish. Its founding conference in Bombay was well attended. Support, in the main, came from the business community—both Gujarati and Parsee. Even the urban intelligentsia appeared interested in this new party, which called for the lifting of government restrictions on trade and commerce and for greater freedom for private enterprise. The leadership of C. Rajagopalachari, the financial backing of a section of the business community, and its laissez-faire philosophy brought initial support, but very soon the party was involved in personal feuds, and several members, including the general secretary of the Bombay branch, left the organization. The exclusive use of English even in mass meetings limited its appeal and has made it difficult to obtain grass-root party workers. Its state leadership is drawn from the Westernized, upper-middle-class intellectuals and rich businessmen, and this handicaps it in building a mass base. Although local branches have been established in a few district capitals, its activity is confined almost entirely to the city of Bombay, but even there its influence is negligible. In the 1962 general elections the party put up 9 candidates to the state Assembly—4 in Bombay and 5 in the rest of the state. All of them were defeated and lost their security deposit. In 1967 the party put up 138 candidates but none of them was successful.

Strangely enough, the leaders of the opposition parties are older than the Congress leaders and have been in their party positions for a very long time, while the Congress has produced new leadership. The Communists (both left and right), Praja Socialists, and Samyukta Socialists have leaders in their sixties who have been party leaders for over twenty-five years. The leadership of all the parties except the PWP and the Republicans is drawn mainly from the upper castes including the Brahmans.

In the pre-election period of 1966 the opposition parties gave attention to a number of critical economic issues: the scarcity of food, the high unemployment, the rise in prices, and the devaluation of the rupee. However, on a number of other issues, such as the production of the atom bomb, the dispute over the proposed Indo-U.S. Educational Foundation, and the "nuclear umbrella," the opposition parties were quite divided.

Regional issues have received more public attention than economic issues in Maharashtra. Both Congress and the opposition have been agitating for the inclusion of certain Marathi-speaking areas of Mysore into the state of Maharashtra. In all the elections held in the disputed areas since 1956, candidates favoring inclusion in Maharashtra have been returned with substantial majorities, but the Mysore government remains opposed to any major readjustment of its state boundaries. Recently the central government announced the appointment of a one-man commission to examine the dispute.

Another regional issue which has come to the fore in a particularly forceful way is the demand for preferential treatment to Maharashtrians in the matter of housing and employment. In Bombay an organization called Shiva Sena (Shivaji's army) has recently come up. Its aim is to speak and act for the interests of the "sons of the soil" against outsiders in the state. Shiva Sena's slogan is "Maharashtra for Maharashtrians," and its program is to create mass sanctions to Maharashtrians in employment and housing in the state of Maharashtra. Its main target is the South Indian community, which is accused of gaining a disproportionate share of jobs in the state through clannishness. Its repeated accusations against that community and its use of intemperate language have created feelings of insecurity among linguistic minorities in the city and state. In India, as elsewhere in conditions of poverty and unemployment, resentment of the outsider can be an explosive political force. Virulent campaigning by leaders of the Shiva Sena in the fourth general elections bears ample testimony to the deep-seated resentment in a section of the Maharashtrians against immigrants from other states.

There has also been public concern in Maharashtra over the relationship to neighboring Goa. The Congress high command in Delhi recommended to the central government that an opinion poll be held in Goa in 1967 to ascertain the wishes of the people of the territory on the question of their merger with Maharashtra. Goa is currently governed by the pro-mergist Maharashtrawadi Gomantak party and is opposed by the United Goan's party, which advocates maintaining Goa as a Union territory. An opinion poll was conducted in Goa on January 16, 1967, in which the people of the territory were asked to decide whether they favored merger with Maharashtra or continuance of the present status of Union Territory. Out of an electorate of 388,392, as many as 317,633 (81.8 per cent) actually favored the continuation of the Union Territory status and 128,170 (43.5 per cent) opted for merger. The result of the opinion poll came as a big disappointment to people and parties in Maharashtra, but they have accepted it as a democratic verdict of the Goan people. It also did not affect the trend of the general elections in the state which were held within a month. In Goa, elections for the territory's legislative assembly were held in March and the pro-mergerist Maharashtrawadi Gomantak party has once again formed the government.

In summary, we can say that at present none of the opposition parties in Maharashtra threatens to replace Congress and that for the foreseeable future this situation is likely to continue.

TABLE 4.5

REGIONWISE SEATS WON BY PARTIES IN MAHARASHTRA 1957 AND 1962 LEGISLATIVE ASSEMBLY (264) & 1967 (270)

		Bombay City		*Western Maharashtra*		*Vidarbha*		*Marathwada*	
Party	*Year*	*Put up*	*Won*	*Put up*	*Won*	*Put up*	*Won*	*Put up*	*Won*
Congress	1957	24	13	135	33	63	55	40	33
	1962	24	21	135	116	65	47	40	31
	1967	28	20	136	102	63	48	43	33
PSP	1957	8	3	35	27	29	2	6	1
	1962	11	1	72	6	7	2	11	–
	1967	17	1	46	7	4	–	–	–
CPI (both wings)	1957	2	2	15	9	4	–	10	2
	1962	10	1	29	3	7	–	10	2
	1967	9	3	22	3	9	1	11	4
PWP	1957	–	–	35	25	6	1	14	4
	1962	1	–	52	7	8	1	18	7
	1967	1	–	37	16	5	–	16	3
Jan Sangh	1957	–	–	4	4	19	–	3	–
	1962	18	–	72	–	36	–	1	–
	1967	24	1	76	1	41	2	27	–
SSP	1957	–	–	–	–	–	–	–	–
	1962	8	–	5	1	1	–	–	–
	1967	5	–	27	1	9	–	6	3
Swatantra	1957	–	–	–	–	–	–	–	–
	1962	5	–	4	–	–	–	–	–
	1967	22	–	13	–	2	–	2	–
Republican	1957	3	3	14	7	25	3	5	–
	1962	5	–	30	–	25	3	6	–
	1967	8	1	21	1	44	3	7	–

Political Leadership in the Congress

Maharashtra has the unique distinction of having two Pradesh Congress committees, one for Bombay city and the other for the rest of the state. Under the Congress constitution there can be only one state party unit in a state. Exception has, however, been made in the case of this state in view of the great importance of Bombay. Historically, the reason for it can be traced to the status of a separate regional unit accorded to the city in the thirties. The agitation for the break-up of Bombay state into two unilingual states of Gujarat and Maharashtra and the opposite positions taken by the two committees provided additional reason for retaining the Bombay Congress as a separate entity. While the Maharashtrians unitedly demanded the inclusion of Bombay in the state, other linguistic and regional groups and particularly the Gujarati business community strongly opposed it. Their opposition was spearheaded by the Congress Committee in the city (BPCC).

The BPCC organized all the groups which were opposed to the inclusion of Bombay in Maharashtra, and took the initiative in organizing citizens' committees and protest meetings, publishing literature, challenging the Maharashtrian claim, and finally drafting and presenting memoranda to the States Reorganization Commission.

The tempo of Maharashtrian militancy frightened linguistic minorities, which now aligned themselves even more strongly behind the city Congress and its leadership. In the elections of 1957 they voted en bloc for the Congress candidates, which enabled the party to win 13 out of the 24 Assembly seats and two of the four parliamentary seats in the face of the united opposition of the Samiti. At a time when in adjacent Western Maharashtra, Congress won only a meagre 33 out 135 seats, in Bombay city Congress won a majority of seats.

The arguments put forward by the Maharashtra Pradesh Congress Committee (MPCC) and other parties and groups for including the city in the state were ultimately convincing. The city was geographically within the area that was to be included in the new state, and in 1961 Maharashtrians constituted the largest single linguistic group in the city (1.77 million out of 4.1 million as against 0.7 million Gujarati, 0.4 million Urdu, 0.3 million Hindi, and 0.9 million others speaking one of the remaining fourteen national languages of India).

Since Maharashtra was formed with Bombay city, the leadership of the BPCC has remained in the hands of non-Maharashtrians. S. K. Patil, former Union Railway Minister, who is the undisputed leader of the BPCC, is a Maharashtrian. But he stoutly opposed both the demand for a unilingual state and the claim for Bombay's inclusion in Maharashtra. Except for Patil, the city unit has no Maharashtrian leader of any public stature.

Patil's unrivalled position in the organization is due, in part, to the common cause he has made with the non-Maharashtrian groups, particularly the leading Gujarati traders and industrialists. They constitute his principal base of support. His close association with them dates back to the early 1940s when, as the general secretary of the BPCC, he showed uncommon tact and organizational skill and made the local unit a strong and efficient political machine operated by men who would be personally loyal.

Although Nehru had made no secret of his dislike for Patil's views and methods, he nonetheless invited him to join his Cabinet after the second general elections. Patil served in various capacities until he went out under the Kamaraj Plan, but he was later taken into the Shastri Cabinet and also into the first cabinet of Mrs. Gandhi.

There is little evidence to show that Patil has lobbied for the state with the center. He has avoided involvement in such state problems as the border dispute between Maharashtra and Mysore or the river water dispute with Andhra Pradesh. In the dispute over whether Goa should be merged with Maharashtra he issued a statement, at the behest of the national Congress leadership, that Goa should remain a union territory for ten years. On the whole, his presence in the Union Cabinet did not strengthen the hands of the state government; there seems to be very little, if any, prior consultation between him and the state leadership, and it is said that it is because of Patil's opposition that the BPCC–MPCC merger does not take place.

Patil has a major rival in Y. B. Chavan, presently Home Minister in the Union Cabinet. There was little in Chavan's previous performance, either as a minister in the old Bombay state or as a secretary of the Pradesh Congress, to suggest that he possessed the potentialities for becoming a national leader, but he emerged in the political crisis of 1956. Morarji Desai, who was then chief minister of the state, joined the Cabinet in Delhi, and Chavan was elected to lead the legislature party by a vote of 333 to 111. On November 1, 1956, he became the chief minister of bilingual Bombay state at the early age of 43 and conducted its affairs so well and so astutely that he won wide acclaim. He gained the confidence of Nehru and other senior Congress leaders by his efficient and tactful handling of the state's problems. Chavan has disarmed even the most partisan critics by his candor and his knack of giving the impression that he values their point of view. He has avoided entanglement in issues with which he is not directly concerned, and although he rose to national stature by identifying himself with the aspirations of his state, he is conscious of the national context in which state problems must be viewed. In his own words: "My present responsibility is Maharashtra. But my approach, background, everything is absolutely all-India. As a member of the Congress Working Committee I have to take the larger view. Even my thinking for Maharashtra flows from my thinking about national problems."[21]

GOVERNMENTAL PERFORMANCE

The new state of Maharashtra was required to continue tackling the problems of administrative integration and legislative uniformity which were begun after the formation of the bilingual Bombay state in 1956. With their different traditions of law and administration, Vidarbha and Marathwada presented numerous difficulties in determining the position and seniority of personnel. In the beginning, these difficulties caused widespread dissatisfaction and consequent delay and inefficiency. The existence of different, and often conflicting, laws in the various regions presented even greater problems. Land reform legislation, secondary education law, labor laws, and co-operative laws were some glaring examples of laws with regard to which the three regions of the state differed widely, in both approach and detail. A series of new legislation has since been enacted, and has been applied to the entire state. Integration in this area has now been nearly completed.

The basic objectives of governmental policies have been (1) to undertake legislation to make the tiller the owner of his land through a system of peasant proprietorship and then to introduce voluntary cooperative farming; (2) to increase agricultural productivity and output; (3) to provide for more employment and generate more income outside the agricultural sector; and (4) to decentralize power and authority through the revision of existing institutions and the creation of new institutions of local government.

Agricultural Problems and Policies

In 1948 the Government of Bombay passed the Bombay Tenancy and Agricultural Lands Act. The main purposes of this act were (1) to protect the tenant against eviction from his land; (2) to restrict the transfer of agricultural lands and to encourage the transfer of agricultural lands into the hands of tenants; and (3) to fix the maximum rent payable by a tenant to a landlord.

The act was further amended in 1951, 1952, 1953, and again in 1955. Although the objects of this legislation were laudable, it was so poorly implemented that instead of helping the tiller to become the owner, many tenants were forced to surrender tenancy to their landlords who wanted it for personal cultivation. Of those who belonged to the category of "protected tenants" (that is, those who held their land continu-

[21] Welles Hangen, *After Nehru Who?* (London: Rupert Hart Davis, 1963), p. 144.

ously for a period of not less than six years) in 1947-48, only 78 per cent remained in the following year. This percentage dwindled further during the successive years to 71, 67, 64, and 57 in 1952-53. As a consequence the proportion of plots cultivated by protected tenants also declined. In 1948-49, 52 per cent of the tenant-cultivated plots were under protected tenancies. This declined to 41 per cent in 1952-53.[22] In Marathwada alone, for example, the area of tenant-cultivated plots in 1950 was more than 2.8 million acres. By 1958, 1.7 million acres had been resumed by the landlords, depriving 101,000 tenants of their tenure out of 150,000 tenants.

From these figures, it can be seen that the implementation of the land legislation in Maharashtra has favored the landlord. Its impact on agriculture has been quite contrary to the professed aims of the legislation. There has been alienation of tenants, and a parcelling and fragmentation of land in order to evade the operation of the law.

Two other problems connected with agriculture are low productivity and a significant shift from food crops to cash crops. Although Maharashtra has 12.8 per cent of the country's gross cropped area and 13.9 per cent of net sown area, it produced in 1960-61 only about 9.5 per cent of the value of India's agricultural output. Partly because of scanty and unevenly distributed rainfall, output is low. There is not much opportunity for improving irrigation facilities. Even if Maharashtra spends Rs. 200 crores in the next fifteen years on irrigation, it has been estimated that the cultivated area that would come under irrigation would be only between 20 and 22 per cent.

In those districts where perennial irrigation is available and the soil is fertile, there has been a marked shift from cereals and pulses to cash crops like sugar cane and cotton as can be seen from the table below.

TABLE 4.6

TRENDS IN AGRICULTURAL GROWTH, 1952–53 TO 1959–60

(Base: 1952-53 = 100)

	Cereals	*Pulses*	*Ground-nut*	*Sugar cane*	*Cotton*
1955-56	120.0	98.8	144.7	123.5	98.4
1956-57	118.5	94.3	133.5	137.9	104.5
1957-58	127.1	92.1	137.2	153.8	131.4
1958-59	125.7	88.8	133.5	157.9	115.3
1959-60	133.4	95.2	140.3	161.8	125.6

SOURCE: *Third Five Year Plan, Maharashtra State*, p. 25.

22 Dandekar and Khudanpur, *Working of Bombay Tenancy Act, 1948*, Report of Investigation (Poona: Gokhale Institute of Politics & Economics, 1957), p. 38.

This trend has further aggravated food shortages in the state and has led to a steep rise in prices resulting in considerable disquiet in the countryside. The state government has fixed minimum procurement prices for jowar (an important millet in the state) and has banned open market sales in it. In spite of monopoly procurement, the state has not been able to get more than 34,000 bags of jowar as against the target of 500,000. In August-September 1964 rice, wheat, and sugar were not available at all for several days in certain areas of the state. The call of the opposition parties for a day's token strike received wide support in both rural and urban areas in 1964 and again in 1966.

Cooperative farming continues to receive lip service but nothing tangible has been done in this field. No cooperative farming societies have been started in the state in spite of the Nagpur resolution on Cooperative Farming adopted by the Congress in 1958. The leaders of the Pradesh Congress, being of rural background, view the proposal as an expression of urban middle-class ideology. As Chavan told the editor of the Communist-line Bombay weekly *Blitz*, "So far as the question of agriculture is concerned, this is a sector of economic activity where the incentive to produce is very vitally linked up with the idea of ownership. . . . That is why to take this idea of taking ownership from the peasants without giving them the proper idea about it would naturally take away that incentive to production."[23]

The abrupt withdrawal of the monsoon in August 1965 caused considerable damage to Kharif crops. The drought was the worst in thirty years and it further aggravated food scarcity. The state of Maharashtra suffers from a chronic food deficit amounting to roughly 2.2 million tons annually but in 1966 the shortage was expected to be on the order of 3 to 3.3 million tons. The state government declared scarcity conditions in 16,012 villages in 22 out of the 26 districts of the state. The total population affected by scarcity has been estimated at 13.2 million. The government opened 5,561 scarcity works providing employment to about 600,000 people.

A three-pronged strategy to overcome the agricultural backwardness of the state and to make the state self-sufficient in two years has been planned and is being currently implemented. The government has launched a vigorous campaign among agriculturists to persuade them (1) to grow a second crop making use of water in village tanks, rivulets, and wells (lift irrigation schemes involving pumping directly from streams and ponds and the construction of jack wells have been encouraged); (2) to use hybridized seeds, chemical fertilizers, and other

[23] Quoted by Hangen, *op.cit.*, p. 140.

scientific means of increasing per acre yield; and (3) to take full advantage of the guaranteed remunerative prices announced by the government before the sowing season every year. Through these three methods the government hopes to wipe out the deficit in food output.

While the food situation remains unsatisfactory, there have been improvements in the area of rural industries. State funds have been used to encourage investment in rural industries and in a few districts there has been a relatively successful program. In the district of Sangli, for example, a cooperative sugar mill has benefited the entire area, and other cooperatives have been started—in dairy, poultry, paper milling, and oil milling.

Employment

Although the problem of unemployment is not as acute in Maharashtra as it is in Kerala, Uttar Pradesh, or Madhya Pradesh, it is nevertheless sizable. It has been estimated that the extent of unemployment in the state at the beginning of the Second Five Year Plan in 1956 was 446,000. During the plan period the addition to labor force in the state was expected to be 1,055,000, and additional employment opportunities as a result of plan outlays by the state and the center as well as on account of investment in the private sector would be 717,000. The state, therefore, started on the Third Five Year Plan with a backlog of 784,000 unemployed.

During the Third Plan period the expected addition to the labor force is 1,650,000 and additional employment opportunities 1,450,000. Thus the state will launch its Fourth Plan with a backlog of nearly one million unemployed. In spite of the declared policy of industrial dispersal, new industrial ventures and therefore more labor continue to be attracted to the traditional centers of industry—Bombay, Poona and, to a certain extent, Nagpur.

Panchayati Raj

The introduction of the new system of local government known as panchayati raj in May 1962 was an event of tremendous political significance. Following the report of the Central Government Committee chaired by Balwantrai Mehta, the state government studied the question through the Naik (presently chief minister of Maharashtra) Committee and enacted the Zilla Parishad Act (District Councils Act) of 1961. The Mehta Committee had observed that one of the least successful aspects of the community development and national extension service program was its attempt to evoke popular initiative, that few local bodies at a level higher than the village panchayat had shown any enthusiasm or interest in this work, and that even village panchayats had not provided support to any appreciable extent. To create public enthusiasm for and participation in the planning process the Mehta Committee suggested a three-tiered institutional framework in which only the base, that is, the village panchayats, would be elected and the upper two tiers (block and district councils) would be indirectly elected from the base.

The scheme of decentralization adopted in Maharashtra, however, differs from the recommendation of the Mehta Committee. According to the Maharashtra legislation the district council—the zilla parishad—is the basic unit, and the legislation provides for direct elections for that level instead of indirect elections as recommended by the Mehta Committee. The legislation also seeks to revitalize the village panchayats by placing larger funds at their disposal and by making them executive agencies for Plan projects decided upon by zilla parishads.

Panchayati raj has thus far had some important political consequences. First, the position of the Congress in rural elections has proven to be very great. Out of a total of 1,271 seats in the 25 zilla parishads, the Congress has secured 827 seats. Second, devolution of authority has created new seats of power in the rural areas and has thereby provided an outlet for local political ambitions. More aspirants can be accommodated, thereby moderating faction rivalries inside the Congress party. This may not only help to satisfy local party workers, but also train them for higher responsibilities. Finally, the panchayati raj institutions have resulted in competitive rural politics. Casteism is in some respects on the ascendancy in many rural communities. It is further buttressed by the democratic logic of numbers. Insofar as the sanction behind political power is the backing of a majority, castes which form a major or a substantial part of a community enjoy political power. Holding together thus becomes necessary for power, and this results in the solidifying of caste loyalties.

CONCLUSION

The foregoing discussion has focused attention upon three interrelated aspects of political development in Maharashtra—the socialist slant of the Congress organization, the fragmentation of opposition parties, and the effect of both of these upon the formulation and implementation of state policies. It has been shown that the Congress organization in the state is strong and does not suffer from organized factionalism. Its leadership is young and receptive to new and progressive ideas. The programs of rural industries, free primary education, free education at all levels to the children of citizens whose annual income is below Rs. 1,200, and the various social, economic and educational concessions given to the neo-Buddhists have already had an impact on the rural society.

The opposition parties are in disarray and are likely to form even more splinter groups. In Maharashtra, there is no possibility in the near future that any of the existing parties will be able to successfully challenge the Congress. What role then will the opposition parties play? Even today opposition parties are, on the whole, more effective than their legislative strength suggests. First, the tradition of parliamentary government, although new, is powerful enough to prevent the gagging of opposition inside the legislature. Second, freedom of political action and freedom of the press create mass pressures which the government cannot easily disregard. When opposition parties organize mass demonstrations or strikes or undertake some such direct action, the press publishes it widely. The Congress will probably remain in power for a long time, but it will have to meet with steadily mounting opposition pressure and an articulate public opinion.

The overwhelming strength of the Congress party in the state and the absence of effective alternatives, far from spelling danger to the democratic process, may in fact be a boon. It has ensured political stability and continuity in administration, two of the most important prerequisites of peaceful economic and social growth. By being inclusive, the Congress has given representation to regional and sectional interests, thereby minimizing social discord which might have threatened the integrity of the new state. Finally, the preponderance of one party, along with a small but active opposition, has also resulted in making the administrative apparatus relatively efficient and responsive.

REFERENCES

Chavan Abhindan Granth. Nagpur: Chavan Birthday Celebration Committee, 1961.

Dandekar, V. M., and Jagtap, M. B. *Organization of Rural Society in Maharashtra.* Poona: Gokhale Institute of Politics and Economics, 1957.

Desai, A. R. *Social Background of Indian Nationalism.* Bombay: Popular Book Depot, 1959.

Hutton, J. H. *Caste in India.* Bombay: Oxford University Press, 1961.

Karve, Joglekar, and Joshi (eds.). *Introduction to Maharashtra* (in Marathi). Poona: Prasad Prakashan, 1954.

Mangudkar, M. P. *Liberalism in Modern Maharashtra.* Poona: Sangam Press, 1958.

Masani, M. R. *The Communist Party of India.* London, 1954.

Morris-Jones, W. H. *The Government and Politics of India.* London: Hutchinson University Library, 1964.

Nalini, Pandit. *Growth of Nationalism in Maharashtra.* Bombay: Pandit Nalini, 1955.

Overstreet, Gene D., and Windmiller, Marshall. *Communism in India.* Berkeley: University of California Press, 1959.

Problems of Maharashtra. Bombay: Indian Committee for Cultural Freedom, 1960.

Ranade, M. G. *Rise of the Maratha Power*. New Delhi: Publications Division, 1961.

Sahyadriche Vare (Winds from Sahyadri), in Marathi, a collection of Y. B. Chavan's speeches. Bombay: Government of Maharashtra, Publication Department, 1962.

Sirsikar, V. M. *Political Behaviour in India, A Case Study of the 1962 General Elections in Poona*. Bombay: Manakyalas, 1965.

Srinivas, M. N. *Caste in Modern India*. Bombay: Asia Publishing House, 1962.

Stern, Robert W. "Maharashtrian Linguistic Provincialism and Indian Nationalism," *Pacific Affairs*, Spring 1964.

Turner, Roy (ed.). *India's Urban Future*. Bombay: Oxford University Press, 1962.

JAMMU AND KASHMIR

WEST PAKISTAN
CHINA
50 MILES
N
JAMMU AND KASHMIR
MUZAFFARĀBAD
SRĪNAGAR
BĀRAMŪLA
PŪNCH
ANANTNAG
MĪRPUR
RIĀSI
UDHAMPUR
JAMMU
KATHUA
LEH

V

Jammu and Kashmir

BALRAJ PURI

JAMMU AND KASHMIR, the most controversial and strategic state of India, has a total area of 53,665 square miles and a population of 3.5 million,[1] half of whom live in an area of approximately 6,000 square miles in the lovely Valley of Kashmir. Bordering Pakistan, Afghanistan, Russia, and China, Kashmir is the only predominantly Muslim area that became a part of India when the subcontinent was partitioned in 1947. The state is as diverse as any area in the subcontinent. In fact, its three main regions—Jammu, Kashmir, and Ladakh—are distinct in their geography, culture, language, and dominant religion.

No state in India has been more affected by international events than has Kashmir. Pakistan's efforts to gain support within Kashmir have had important consequences for the state's internal political development. Moreover, the internal politics of the state, marked by interregional tensions, has influenced the attitude of the people on the question of their external affiliation. Divergent reactions of its regions and communities to the changing relationship of the state to the Union of India have further complicated internal politics. An analysis of the development of local nationalism in each region of the state and its attitude on the issue of accession should, therefore, be a good starting point for a study of the politics of Kashmir.

THE DEVELOPMENT OF KASHMIR NATIONALISM

The state of Jammu and Kashmir owes its existence in its present form to an historical accident. In 1846 the Sikh rulers of the Punjab sold the Valley of Kashmir to Raja Gulab Singh of Jammu for Rs. 7.5 million in order to earn part of the money needed to pay reparations to the British East India Company after their defeat in a war. Earlier, Zorawar Singh, a general of the Raja, renowned for his exceptional skill and ruthlessness, had annexed Ladakh after a series of battles on what is often called the roof of the world, 17,000-21,000 feet above sea level.

[1] These figures relate only to the Indian part of Kashmir. Out of a total original area of about 86,000 square miles, more than 32,000 square miles are occupied by Pakistan, while some 2,000 miles of Kashmir's northern district of Ladakh were recently annexed by China.

Ladakh, the only citadel of Buddhism in India, with 350 miles of common border with Tibet and 450 miles of border with Sinkiang, was again a battleground between Indian and Chinese armies in 1962. Incidentally, the treaty of 1842, entered into by Raja Gulab Singh and the Lama of Tibet and ratified by their respective suzerains, the Sikh Durbar of Lahore and the Emperor of China, defined the international boundary of Ladakh and is one of the important bases of India's legal claims over the territory.

TABLE 5.1

POPULATION AND AREA OF JAMMU AND KASHMIR STATE

District	*Area (Sq. miles)*	*Population*
Kashmir Valley	6,364	1,901,438
Anantnag	2,097	656,368
Baramula	2,536	604,659
Srinagar	1,205	640,411
Jammu Province	10,073	1,572,877
Doda	4,380	268,403
Jammu	1,249	516,932
Kathua	1,024	207,420
Poonch	1,689	326,061
Udhampur	1,731	254,061
Ladakh	37,754	88,651
Totals	53,665	3,562,966
Occupied by Pakistan	32,358	—

TABLE 5.2

POPULATION OF JAMMU AND KASHMIR BY RELIGION

Religion	*Population*
Hindu	1,013,193
Buddhist	48,360
Christian	2,848
Jain	1,427
Muslim	2,432,067
Sikh	63,069
Others	12
Scheduled castes	268,530
Density of population per sq. mi.	66
Per cent literate	11 (17% males and 4.3% females)

Raja Gulab Singh belonged to the Dogra family of Jammu, which ruled over Kashmir and Ladakh for over a century. It is interesting to note that before the Dogras assumed power Kashmir was ruled by other outsiders—by the Mughals for 167 years, by the Afghans for 66 years, and then by the Sikhs for 27 years. Although it would be difficult to say how far the Kashmiri population reacted to these rulers in a nationalist way, it is important to note that the present generation of politicians dates the freedom movement to about four hundred years back when the Valley first came under outside domination and seeks inspiration from any incidents of resistance that occurred against any of these rulers.

Since much of the agitation against the non-Kashmiri rulers by Kashmiris was against Muslim rulers—the Mughals and Afghans—a genuine, non-communal Kashmiri nationalism was able to develop. It is true, of course, that the last ruler of Kashmir was a Hindu, and the movement against him in the 1930s started as an uprising of the Muslims. But it is also important to note that the Muslim political organizations of Kashmir were not even accommodated in the mainstream of Muslim politics of India before independence. First, the strong regional aspirations of Kashmiri Muslims made them quite distinct from the Muslim League led by M. A. Jinnah with much emphasis on Muslim solidarity. Second, the struggle against the Maharaja of Kashmir did not receive support from the Muslim League, for the League did not oppose as a matter of policy rulers of the princely states, many of whom were Muslims. Third, the League had no sympathy for the Muslim peasants of Kashmir in their conflicts with the landlords, even though a majority of the landlords were Hindus. On the other hand, the Indian National Congress, the nationalist movement in India, was quick to provide support to the political and economic aspirations of Kashmiri Muslims. Since Muslim leaders in Kashmir drifted away from the Muslim League, they turned readily to accept the influence of the Indian nationalist leaders, notably Gandhi, Nehru, Azad, and Abdul Ghaffar. This influence further shaped the intellectual life of political cadres in the Valley.

The Communist party of India also played an influential role in Kashmiri politics before independence. It may be recalled that on the crucial Hindu-Muslim question the CPI took a position midway between the Congress and the League. While it did not subscribe to the League's demand for partition on religious lines, it did not accept the Congress conception of a united India. Instead the Communists pleaded for the right of self-determination for each nationality, and this had a special appeal for Kashmiri nationalists. In fact, the leading political party of the state, the Kashmir National Conference, passed a resolution on these lines in 1945 even before such a position was formally adopted by the Communist party. The same session of the National Conference approved a blueprint of its economic objectives, entitled *New Kashmir,* which had marked Marxist overtones. Having acquired a radical economic content and an ideological rationale, the movement of Kashmir nationalism tended to assume a self-righteous and militant tone. Echoes of self-determination slogans are still reverberating in Kashmir.

The Accession

The divergence between the Kashmir National Conference (predominantly Muslim) and the Indian Muslim League was further sharpened by their respective attitudes in 1947 toward the question of Kashmir's future affiliation. The Muslim League conceded the right of the rulers to decide the issue of accession. The All-India Congress Committee, on the other hand, resolved on June 15, 1947, that the "people of the state must have a dominating voice in any decisions regarding them."

On August 15, 1947 the Maharaja of Kashmir offered a standstill agreement to the new dominions of India and Pakistan. Pakistan readily accepted the proposal while India did not. Instead, the Indian leadership exerted pressure on the Maharaja to release Sheikh Abdullah and his colleagues in the National Conference, who were then in jail, and to seek their advice.

Gandhi visited Kashmir in early August and categorically stated then that the question of Kashmir's accession "should be decided by the will of the Kashmiris." According to Gandhi, the treaty of Amritsar, under which sovereignty over Kashmir was transferred to Raja Gulab Singh and his successors in 1946, was a sale deed which lapsed on August 15, 1947. The state, he added, then reverted to the people.[2]

Pakistani leaders were upset by the enthusiastic emotional response that Gandhi received in Kashmir during his visit. They also had reason to distrust the leaders of the Kashmir National Conference. Upon his release from jail in September 1947, Sheikh Abdullah sent two of his emissaries to Pakistan for talks on the future of Kashmir, but no solution was found. The next month hordes of tribesmen, with support from Pakistani authorities, launched an invasion of Kashmir. This further infuriated leaders of the National Conference, who endorsed the Maharaja's decision to accede to the Union of India on October 26, 1947.

[2] Pyarelal, *Mahatma Gandhi: the Last Phase* (Ahmedabad: Navajivan Publishing House 1956-58), pp. 355-58.

Kashmir was soon granted what was called a special status in the Union of India. Under the Instrument of Accession the state ceded to the Union only in defense, foreign affairs, and communications. Article 370 of the Indian constitution exempted the state from the application of most of its provisions. This gave a much-needed emotional satisfaction to the Muslims of the Valley. But it also meant that the state was not covered by the liberal provisions of the Indian constitution such as the sections on Fundamental Rights. Nor did the statutory autonomous Union institutions like the Supreme Court, the Election Commission, the Public Service Commission, and the Auditor General have any jurisdiction in Kashmir.

Constitutionally, therefore, Kashmir was without a system of checks and balances. Under the charismatic leadership of Sheikh Abdullah, politics, religion, culture, and administration were blended to build up a monolithic structure in what was almost a one-party state. From 1947 to 1951, the government ruled without a legislature. In 1951 it convened a Constituent Assembly in which the ruling National Conference won 73 uncontested and 2 contested seats in the House of 75.

The new regime started with a revolutionary program. Kashmir was the only state that abolished landlordism without any compensation. A maximum ceiling of 22¾ acres was fixed on all agricultural holdings. Eight hundred thousand acres of land, in excess of the ceiling, was distributed free among 247,000 tillers. Debts of the rural population were scaled down by more than half. These measures evoked dissimilar responses among various regions and communities, and serious difficulties were encountered in their implementation all over the state. Corruption in the distribution of land and a shortage of resources robbed the land reforms of some of their usefulness. Compulsory procurement of foodgrains—the classical Marxist method of extorting agricultural surplus for capital formation—introduced by the Kashmir government was generally unwelcomed. The network of cooperatives proved on the whole to be inefficient and corrupt.

By the early 1950s there was already considerable discontent in the Valley. But meanwhile a more explosive situation was brewing in Jammu, whose political leaders had not reconciled themselves to living under what they considered to be Kashmiri rule. Jammu's population of 1.6 million is 300,000 less than that of the Valley, but its area (10,000 square miles) is more than 1½ times larger. It constitutes the only physical link between the Valley and the rest of India. While the population of Kashmir is predominantly Muslim, the population of Jammu is predominantly Hindu. Since the Maharaja belonged to Jammu, he could appeal to its local patriotism while the National Conference, which was struggling against his rule and was inspired by a sense of militant Kashmiri nationalism, could not gain much influence within Jammu. When the constitutional monarchy was abolished in 1952, it appeared to many that a shift of power had taken place from Jammu to Kashmir. When the Dogras of Jammu lost their political privileges, the National Conference began to extend its organizational network into Jammu. Third- and fourth-level workers from the Valley entered Jammu to manage its affairs, and there was considerable feeling there that these workers were ignorant and arrogant. Sheikh Abdullah did not know many people in Jammu whom he could trust except the Communists, who he thought were the only non-communal group there.

Similar dissatisfaction was simmering in Ladakh, the third important region of the state. With an area of 32,000 square miles, it is larger than the other two regions combined. It is, however, very sparsely populated, with only 88,000 people. The leaders of Ladakh did not seem to be satisfied with their share in the new political power and their links to Kashmir. Protesting against what he felt was a Srinagar-dominated administration, Kushak Bakula, the religious and secular leader of Ladakh, pleaded in a press statement in 1953 that "on the transference of power from the present descendant of Raja Gulab Singh (the founder of the state) to the National Conference of Kashmir, the constitutional link, which tied us down to this state, was shattered and from that time we were morally and juridically free to choose our own course independent of the rest of the state."

Many voices were also raised in Jammu for its separation from the Valley. But to avoid the charge of being secessionist or sectarian the protest of Jammu eventually crystallized into a seemingly patriotic slogan of "full accession." By pleading for a transfer of more powers to the Union government, Jammu leaders hoped to reduce the extent of Kashmiri domination. The clash between Jammu and Kashmir has both communal and ideological overtones. The two regions were different not only in language and culture but also in their predominant religion. Moreover, the abolition of the monarchy and landlordism did not have the same emotional appeal in Jammu that it did in Kashmir. Soon the popular unrest in Jammu was articulated by a newly formed party—the Praja Parishad—which received support from and was later merged with the Jan Sangh, a Hindu nationalist party in India.

Sheikh Mohammad Abdullah, the hero of Kashmiri nationalism, reacted with self-righteousness to what he felt was the "communal and reactionary" revolt in Jammu and Ladakh. The means his government used to deal with the situation were not always fair and included almost wholesale rejection of the nomination papers of the entire Opposition in the election to the Constituent Assembly in 1951.

The Constituent Assembly started its work on constitution making in an atmosphere of fierce controversy over the issue of full or limited accession. Abdullah in a challenging speech delivered in a town of Jammu in 1952 asserted his determination to defend limited accession of the state to the Union. Mirza Afzal Beg, the then revenue minister, declared in the Constituent Assembly that Kashmir would be a republic within a republic. These statements provoked a storm of protest in Jammu.

Pressure was put on Kashmiri leaders by New Delhi to concede partially to Jammu's demands. After a crucial round of talks, Sheikh Abdullah agreed in July 1952 to enter with the government of India into what was known as the Delhi agreement. The substantial further concessions that Kashmir made, having already conceded defense, foreign affairs, and communications, included the acceptance of the national flag, along with the state flag, and the original jurisdiction of the Supreme Court in certain matters. It was also agreed that the emergency powers of the Union could be applied to the state in the event of external aggression, but "in regard to the internal disturbance at the request or with the concurrence of the government of the state." The right of the Constituent Assembly to frame a constitution for the state on all other subjects had already been conceded by the constitution of India and was not changed. While speaking on this agreement in the Kashmir Assembly on August 11, 1952, Sheikh Abdullah warned, "Any suggestions of altering arbitrarily this basis of our relationship with India would not only constitute a breach of the spirit and letter of the constitution, but it may invite serious consequences for a harmonious association of our state with India."

Abdullah received a hero's welcome in the Valley for his agreement with New Delhi, but the agreement was not completely acceptable in Jammu. At the end of 1952 the Praja Parishad launched a massive agitation for "one constitution, one flag and one president" for Kashmir and the rest of India. While the ostensibly patriotic objectives of this agitation evoked sympathetic response in much of India, it caused fresh misgivings among many Kashmir Muslims who began to feel that their entity, which they had defended against Muslim invaders from Pakistan, seemed again in danger. What further unsettled many Kashmiris was the report that India and Pakistan were now negotiating on various alternative solutions to the Kashmir problem. Mohammed Ali, the Prime

Minister of Pakistan in 1953, gave the impression that a settlement on Kashmir was possible. Even the appointment of a plebiscite administrator and a date for a plebiscite were being considered. This gave the Kashmiris an opportunity to reconsider their future affiliation. For the first time a pro-Pakistan political party came into existence. It was led by G. M. Karra, a dissident senior leader of the National Conference who, in his dispute with Sheikh Abdullah, could not secure support in India. Several Kashmiri Hindus, anticipating the results of a possible plebiscite, joined the Political Conference, the new party, which continued to profess faith in secularism. The members of the new party often called themselves Gandhian Pakistanis. Sheikh Abdullah was thus under attack from Jammu where a movement had developed for full integration into India, and within Kashmir from a group which advocated merger with Pakistan. Abdullah responded to these challenges by declaring his determination to resist Indian domination as much as he had resisted that of Pakistan. This equivocation on accession and his equating India with Pakistan created doubts as to Abdullah's loyalty.

Meanwhile, around May 1953, Nehru is reported to have sought the opinion of Kashmiri leaders on various alternative solutions which he could discuss with Mohammed Ali during their scheduled meeting in July. Thereupon an eight-man committee of the National Conference, headed by Sheik Abdullah, after prolonged deliberations, submitted the following four proposals "as possible alternatives for an honourable and peaceful solution of the Kashmir dispute between India and Pakistan":

a) Overall plebiscite (including choice for independence);
b) Independence of the whole state;
c) Independence of the whole state with joint control by India and Pakistan of foreign affairs; and
d) Dixon Plan with independence for the plebiscite area.[3]

Nehru invited Sheikh Abdullah to Delhi to discuss the implication of these proposals. The latter expressed his inability to come in view of the prevailing tension in the Valley. In an atmosphere that was already crowded with misgivings, Abdullah's refusal added further suspicions

[3] Sir Owen Dixon, United Nations representative, had, after his mediational efforts in India and Pakistan, recommended in August 1950 as follows: "Some areas were certain to vote for Pakistan and some for accession to India. Without taking a vote therein, they should be allotted accordingly and the plebiscite should be confined only to the uncertain area, which I said appeared to be the Valley of Kashmir and perhaps some adjacent country." Report of Sir Owen Dixon to the Security Council quoted in *Kashmir Affairs*, No. 1, Delhi, p. 34.

concerning his motives. In the following months a number of factors were at work which undermined Sheikh Abdullah's position in the state.

First of all, Bakshi Ghulam Mohammed, the deputy prime minister of the state, while publicly protesting loyalty to his leader, joined the conspiracy to replace him. Moreover, the Communist party of India and the Communists within the National Conference soon turned against Sheikh Abdullah. This was surprising since the Communists had thus far been encouraging a "progressive Kashmir" to defend itself against a "reactionary India" and had, in fact, provided most of the ideological rationalization for Kashmir's independence.

The idea of an independent Kashmir was originated by the Communists. For "it reflects the innermost desire of the Kashmiri people" (*Cross Road*, May 20, 1949). The same paper, the official organ of the party, on January 6, 1950, called on the people of Kashmir to "concentrate on mass struggle for the realization of freedom, democracy and peace, for the end of monarchy, for a people's democratic state, and for friendly relations with the Soviet Union, the People's Republic of China and other neighbouring countries." Again on July 27, 1952, the paper regretted that the Kashmir delegation was being forced to accept the Indian government's terms on Kashmir's constitutional position in the Union, agreed upon in the Delhi agreement.[4]

By the time the leaders of Kashmir started shifting toward independence, the Communists had, ironically, developed their own doubts about it. They were upset by Adlai Stevenson's cordial talks with Abdullah during his visit to Kashmir in May 1953 and reported U. S. support for Kashmir's independence. Moreover, by now post-Stalin Russia was coming to terms with India, necessitating a more nationalist orientation on Kashmir policy for the CPI. Accordingly, on August 2, *Cross Road* published the text of the party resolution which "viewed with grave concern reports from Kashmir that some leading personalities of the Sheikh Abdullah group and its supporters had made public declarations that the state of Kashmir should be independent of India."[5]

Another factor that might have precipitated the crisis in Kashmir was the death in Abdullah's jail of Dr. Shyama Prasad Mookerjee, a great Hindu leader and president of the All-India Jan Sangh, who had gone to Kashmir to lend his support to the Praja Parishad agitation. His

[4] See Balraj Puri, *Communism in Kashmir* (Calcutta: Institute of Political and Social Studies), pp. 31-37.

[5] *Ibid.*, p. 32.

death resulted in mass resentment not only against Abdullah but against Nehru as well.

Rafi Ahmad Kidwai, Nehru's trusted Muslim colleague in the Cabinet, is often credited with the decision to dismiss and arrest Abdullah without Nehru's prior approval. The formal order was issued by Dr. Karan Singh, the young Sadar-i-Riyasat (head of the state) on August 9, 1953. The government of India described it as an internal event with which they could not interfere. Sheikh Abdullah was to remain in jail for a decade as the popular martyred hero of many Kashmiris.

THE GOVERNMENT OF BAKSHI

Bakshi Ghulam Mohammad, the new prime minister supported by the leftist group in the party, ruled the state for over a decade with an artful blend of corruption and tyranny. He skillfully manipulated his adversaries and by appointing his cousin, Abdul Rashid, as General Secretary and his close supporters to other key positions, he reduced the National Conference to a personal handmaid.

Within two months after Abdullah's arrest, Bakshi secured a vote of confidence from the Assembly. He arranged great rallies of the National Conference which had previously been presided over by Sheikh Abdullah. He also replaced Abdullah as the president of the Auqaf, a Muslim religious organization. In addition, Bakshi patronized art and culture and became the chairman of a newly formed academy. In short, he centralized the entire political, administrative, and social activity of the state. Appointments to government jobs, promotions and transfers, admissions to educational institutions, grants of licenses, quotas, and loans and contracts for business were invariably made by him. Through the use of such patronage Bakshi created a cadre of thousands of men who were personally loyal to him. He created a private army, paid from the state funds, called the Peace Brigade, which was used to disrupt political meetings of opponents.

With the help of generous central financial aid, Bakshi also paid attention to winning popular political support. On assumption of power, he took steps to increase the supply of cheap rice, subsidized by the state to the tune of 75 per cent of its cost. Liberal state loans were given for agriculture, industry, and higher education. There was also a phenomenal expansion in social services. The number of schools, for instance, increased from 2,000 in 1952 to 6,500 within a decade, and the number of colleges from 4 to 23. Engineering, medical, agricultural, and other technical institutes were established for the first time. Kashmir was the only state to introduce free education at all levels with provisions for scholarships and loans. Literacy increased from 3.6 per cent to 10.6 per cent under the Bakshi regime. The budget allocation for education increased tenfold in ten years from Rs. 4 million to Rs. 40 million. In the same period capital expenditure on public health increased sixfold. Between 1956 and 1961 alone the capacity of the hospitals increased from 1,262 to 9,829 beds.[6]

There was considerable economic growth within the state. Bank deposits and assessed income tax more than doubled in less than half a decade. There was a fivefold increase in the number of radio sets and motorcycles during this period and an eightfold increase in the consumption of petrol.

Total disbursements by the state in various categories rose from Rs. 95 million in 1953-54 to Rs. 400 million in 1962-63. The rise in development expenditures in the same period was from Rs. 16 million to Rs. 108 million. The per capita plan expenditure was among the lowest of the Indian states in the early 1950s, but it equalled the all-India average by the Second Five Year Plan (1956-61) and doubled this average thereafter. Furthermore, the per capita budget revenue of the Kashmir government was the highest: Rs. 48 in 1961-62 as against Rs. 23 for the average of all the states. Revenue receipts increased from Rs. 52 million in 1953-54 to 220 million in 1961-62. In spite of these vast increased expenditures, however, Kashmir remained the least taxed state of India. In 1958-59 per capita taxes in Kashmir amounted to Rs. 4.23 in contrast to the average of all states in India of Rs. 9.17. In fact, taxation in Kashmir had fallen from Rs. 6.10 per capita in 1951-52, whereas the average for all of India had risen from Rs. 6.51 in the same period.

The secret of this fiscal and economic miracle was aid from the government of India. The financial integration of Kashmir with the Union, which Sheikh Abdullah had resisted and which was readily accepted by Bakshi, brought great financial benefits to the state. Over and above the formal agreement, the Union government seemed to be quite generous in meeting the needs of Kashmir, obviously for political reasons. Per capita financial assistance to Kashmir for the Second Plan (1956-61) was, for instance, Rs. 50 against the average of 33 for other states. In the Third Plan beginning in 1961, the figures were Rs. 117 and Rs. 57, respectively. Again, the central grant-in-aid formed 30.7 per cent of the revenue of Kashmir whereas for other states it averaged

[6] *A Brief Review of Progress* published by Department of Information, Jammu & Kashmir Government (Srinagar, 1963).

just 10 per cent. Indeed, the per capita statutory grant-in-aid to Kashmir of Rs. 41.7 for the five-year period from 1957-58 to 1961-62 was almost seven times the Rs. 6 average of all the states. A food subsidy, road building, and border development were among the other items financed by the central government.

There was indeed expansion in revenues from internal resources of the state as well, principally due to the multiplier effect of the central aid. The income from the forests rose from Rs. 7 million to Rs. 40 million from 1953 to 1961 while the number of tourists increased from 21,000 to about 100,000.[7]

How did economics and politics interact on each other? Political loyalty to the regime was of course a key to personal prosperity. The expansion and diversification of the economy on the other hand affected the class character and social status of many people and consequently influenced their attitudes toward and relations with authority. Enlargement in the administrative apparatus, for example, not only raised the positions of the existing staff, but also absorbed practically the entire educated class of the state. Writers and artists found job opportunities in the Departments of Information, Broadcasting and Culture. As government appointments and promotions were based on patronage rather than upon merit and as there was ample opportunity for corruption, the demoralized bureaucracy became an instrument of politics.

Kashmir also became the most cooperativized state in India, with 50 per cent of the families in the Valley and 15 per cent in Jammu covered by the cooperative movement. This was because generous state loans on easy terms for rural activities were granted through the cooperatives. This too was a highly politicalized sector of the state's economy, first, because the Cooperative Department was legally armed with drastic powers over the affairs of cooperatives, and second because in practice the cooperatives functioned as an economic adjunct of the National Conference.

The story of other sectors of the economy was not much different. The role of the state in financing, regularizing and licensing economic activity as part of the planned development of the country was in the case of Kashmir guided by the political interests of the chief minister and his supporters rather than by a defined economic policy. The pattern of economic development thus furthered the process of regimentation in the state.

[7] All statistics relating to the budget and economy of the state are quoted from the bimonthly *Kashmir Affairs*, Nos. 4, 9 and 11, 4A-4, B.S.A., Delhi-9 edited by Balraj Puri.

Patterns of Political Control

Bakshi devised a wide variety of schemes for establishing effective political control in the state. Having appropriated the anti-Abdullah appeal of the Praja Parishad, he succeeded in splitting and buying a part of its leadership and in demoralizing the rest. By his often repeated slogan of "irrevocable accession" he acquired a sufficient patriotic halo to challenge the bona fides of his possible critics in the rest of India. Within Kashmir he continued to be a champion of its special status. He also enlisted the support of the remnants of the Pakistani group against Abdullah, who had suppressed them.

In making political nominations for the ministry, the State Assembly, and Parliament, the Bakshi government kept in view the claims of each caste and area. For the first time Ladakh was represented in the ministry by Kushak Bakula. Greater representation was also given to Jammu in the government and in the leadership of the National Conference. This too was distributed on the basis of the importance of every caste and district, thus making them conscious of their entity and their rights. The revival of caste struck at the solidarity of the Dogra front that the Parishad was able to put up against Abdullah.

The political skill of the government was reflected in the performance of the Praja Parishad in the general elections. In the second general elections in 1957, the party was able to win only four seats out of the thirty allotted for Jammu in the State Assembly. In the third elections in 1962 its strength was further reduced to three. Though elections in Kashmir do not entirely measure the strength of the political parties, in the Hindu areas, which were the strongholds of the Parishad, irregularities were, on the whole, fewer, and the results broadly indicate a decline in the influence of the Parishad.

One measure of the growing importance of caste in the politics of Jammu is the role that Harijans increasingly acquired in politics. The Harijans constitute a little more than a fourth of the total Hindu population of the state (268,000) and are concentrated in the prosperous plains of Jammu, where they had become landowners after the passage of land reform legislation. The Harijans divided their allegiance between the ruling party and the Harijan Mandal, but they always opposed the upper-caste-dominated Praja Parishad, which had opposed the land reform legislation. Bakshi also increased the representation of other non-Brahman castes to various positions in the party and government in an effort to wean them away from the Parishad.

Bakshi was thus able to demonstrate in the Valley that he was more successful than Sheikh Abdullah in containing the Parishad threat. And in Jammu he sought to create the impression that he alone could curb the "anti-national" activities of Sheikh Abdullah. However, Bakshi had a vested interest in ensuring a minimum strength for the Parishad and for Abdullah so that Bakshi could arouse fears against them in Kashmiris and Dogras, respectively, and emerge as their protector. He did not want the Parishad to be replaced by a non-communal group in Jammu and Abdullah to be replaced by a pro-India group in Kashmir. For in the peculiar circumstances of the state, only a non-communal and pro-India group could wrest power from Bakshi. He therefore needed Abdullah and the Parishad to divert all anti-government sentiments into anti-India and communal channels so that he could retain a monopoly of loyalty to India. How conscious he was of the potential danger of pro-India rivals was indicated by the way in which he dealt with the two pro-India challenges in the Valley, that of the Socialists and the Communists.

Socialist Opposition

The Praja Socialist party, the third largest party in India at the time, made a bold bid to penetrate the power Bakshi had built up in the Valley. As the only all-India party to start direct functioning in the state, the Socialists had an initial appeal for the Hindus of Jammu, particularly the Harijans. By raising its voice against the detention without trial of Sheikh Abdullah and by calling for the restoration of civil liberties, the party also aroused some emotional response in the Valley. The party was led by the former Jammu National Conference leader, Om Prakash Saraf, and was the first to offer an interregional and inter-communal challenge to the ruling party.

However, the attempt failed. One of its respected leaders, Asoka Mehta, who had gone to Kashmir to inaugurate a unit of the party, was physically beaten along with many of his local colleagues in a busy street of Srinagar in broad daylight. Arrests, intimidations, and assaults prevented organizational activities of the new party, and Bakshi condemned it as an instrument of Indian interference in Kashmir. He also confronted the party with extremist elements in Kashmiri politics by releasing a number of pro-Pakistan and pro-Abdullah leaders, thus ironically meeting in part the Socialist demand for civil liberties. It was during this release that Mirza Mohammed Afzaf Beg, who continues to be Abdullah's trusted lieutenant, formed the Plebiscite Front in August 1955. He invited the PSP workers to disband the party and join the Plebiscite Front. Beg and his supporters almost succeeded in shattering the PSP before he was rearrested.

Bakshi condemned the Socialist party outside the Valley as Sheikh Abdullah's agent, since it demanded his release. To lend credence to Bakshi's charge, Nehru also criticized the Kashmir PSP for "joining hands with the enemies of the country." The debacle in Kashmir and the aspersions cast on its patriotic role so unnerved and confused the leadership of the party that it never again launched or supported any major political move in the state. Thus victimized in the state, maligned outside, and devoid of organizational and material resources, the Kashmir PSP fared poorly in the general elections. The party polled only 1.9 per cent of the vote in 1957 and 2.3 per cent in 1962. Its importance, however, lay in the fact that it was the only party to oppose the National Conference in Muslim constituencies. And in the Hindu areas, the alliance of the PSP, the Harijan Mandal, and the Akali Dal emerged as a third political force, after the National Conference and the Praja Parishad. The PSP has continued to function as a small nucleus trying to provide an emotional and intellectual bridge between divergent political and communal pulls.

The Communist and Left-Wing Challenge

A leftist group, led by G. M. Sadiq, defected from the National Conference in the fall of 1957. In Jammu the group won control over the National Conference party when Abdullah was in power, for he considered them to be "at least non-communal" in what he called "communal ridden" Jammu. In Kashmir their role in the coup of August 1953 gave them still more power in the state government. In the five-man cabinet of Bakshi the group had three members. The presiding officers of the two Houses of the state legislature also belonged to it. All policy statements of the party and the government were drafted in the Communist phraseology by Communist intellectuals. Though he had initially made concessions to this group, Bakshi reversed his position after the 1957 elections and refused to give them the share of power which they had previously held.

G. M. Sadiq led the group of dissidents out of the party to form the Democratic National Conference, which provided the most effective constitutional opposition the state had yet had. Having been elected on the National Conference ticket, it had a group of 15 in the 75-member Assembly and had attracted its best debating talent. The party filled a near vacuum that existed in the opposition politics of the state. It had the advantages of the stature of its leadership, wide contacts, and resources, all of which it had earned by sharing power for a decade. However, events were soon to bring about sharp setbacks in the DNC. The release of Sheikh Abdullah in January 1958, perhaps deliberately timed, drastically changed the pattern of polarization. The DNC faced the same predicament as the PSP had faced after the release of Beg in 1955. Abdullah swept away much of the influence that the new party had built up which it was not able to recover even after his rearrest three months later.

The shift in the Kashmir policy of the Communist party of India, in response to its international requirements, had handicapped the Communists within Kashmir. Having once encouraged aggressive trends in Kashmiri nationalism, it had now become a champion of Indian nationalism. The party, which had called accession to India treacherous in 1950,[8] pleaded for a "de jure recognition of the present frontiers in Kashmir" in 1956,[9] and by 1957 demanded abandonment of Pakistani aggression.[10] Likewise, the Communists first favored full independence, then later supported limited accession,[11] and finally advocated full integration into the Union.[12]

When the DNC, taking the Communist position, demanded in the State Assembly the extension of the jurisdiction of the Supreme Court and the Union Election Commission to the state, Bakshi condemned it as a pro-merger party trying to "sell Kashmir to India." In fact, the DNC stand helped him to appear a champion of Kashmir's autonomy. In Jammu the DNC group, in its effort to outbid the Praja Parishad, championed Dogra chauvinism and demanded a greater share for Jammu in services and in developmental expenditure. This further isolated the party in the Valley and led the National Conference to spread the rumor that the DNC was an agent of Hindus conspiring to get the state merged with the neighboring Hindu majority state of Himachal Pradesh. The DNC was further weakened by fundamental ideological divisions within the organization. The Jammu group, led by Ram Piara Saraf, was categorically committed to the discipline of the CPI and the principles of Communism, while the Sadiq group of Kashmir had a broader base and was nationalistic and less doctrinaire. On issues like the Tibet and Sino-India disputes, the divergence between the two groups became very marked.

At this stage, the leaders of the government of India successfully inter-

[8] *Cross Road*, January 6, 1950.
[9] *New Age*, April 15, 1956.
[10] Ziaul Haq, in *New Age*, October 6, 1957.
[11] P. Sundarayya, *Cross Road*, July 13, 1952.
[12] *New Age*, August 30, 1960.

vened to bring about a rapprochement between the two pro-India parties of Kashmir. On December 5, 1960, after three years of opposition, the DNC working committee overwhelmingly resolved that the "D.N.C. be and is dissolved" and directed its "members and sympathizers to reunite with the parent organization." Only six members of the working committee dissented and five of these belonged to Jammu. The Kashmir provincial unit of the party ratified the merger decision. The Jammu unit, on the other hand, considered the decision "undemocratic, anti-people and highly opportunistic."[13] The Kashmir unit was thus dissolved while the Jammu group retained the DNC and continued its opposition to the government of Bakshi and now of Sadiq. Its leader, Saraf, was nominated to the Central Committee of the CPI and after its split joined the left section of it. In the process, Sadiq, who had cited the danger from the north as one of his reasons for merger, was for a while believed to have pushed away from the Communist movement. He gradually grew close to the central group in the Indian National Congress. In contrast, Bakshi was closely associated with both the extreme right- and left-wing leaders of Congress led by Morarji Desai and Krishna Menon, respectively, both of whom favored a tough line on Kashmir. After coming to power, however, Sadiq again mended his fences with Communists and Menonites.

The Decline of Bakshi

Bakshi seemed to emerge stronger after every challenge to his position. A measure of his command over the situation was the fact that when a popular hero like Sheikh Abdullah was rearrested in 1958, no protest took place. Moreover, during Abdullah's trial, about 200 witnesses, mostly Kashmiris, including his former followers were brought to court to testify against him.

India's tough international line on Kashmir also had a demoralizing effect on the secessionists. Krishna Menon declared in the Security Council debates in 1957 that Kashmir was as irrevocable a part of India as Madras and the Punjab. Pakistan's international prestige was at a low ebb. The merger of several linguistic states in West Pakistan into a single province and the imposition of martial law were not inspiring events for the Kashmiris. Sham Lal Yachu, publicity secretary of the Political Conference, the only professedly pro-Pakistan party of Kashmir, declared in a lengthy statement that serious rethinking had started in his camp. He spoke of the advantages of Kashmir's willingly becoming a part of India.[14] Yachu was not disowned by his party. Similarly, Prem Nath Bazaz, the first vocal exponent of Pakistan's case in Kashmir, expressed

[13] See Puri, *Communism in Kashmir,* p. 26.
[14] *Kashmir Affairs,* No. 1, Delhi.

his disillusionment with Pakistan.[15] In Abdullah's camp, too, pressure for a settlement with India was growing, and possible solutions for Kashmir within the Indian framework were discussed.

Meanwhile opposition to Bakshi began to grow in New Delhi. Bakshi had agreed to the extension of the jurisdiction of Union institutions such as the Supreme Court, the Auditor General, and the Election Commission. But in practice he managed to circumscribe the role of these institutions. Dissatisfaction in Jammu again increased over half-hearted measures at integration and what its leaders considered an inadequate share in services, development activity, and political power.

The liberal conscience in India had been aroused by the excesses of Bakshi. Criticism against him began in the press and in Parliament. And demands for central action were more frequently made. A movement for a rapprochement with Abdullah also gained ground, following conciliatory overtures on his behalf by his supporters in New Delhi. In September 1963, 50 members of Parliament demanded the withdrawal of the conspiracy case against Abdullah and his supporters. In late 1963 the Congress party approved what is known as the Kamaraj Plan, under which a large number of ministers in the center and in the states were asked to submit their resignations to Prime Minister Nehru in order to enable him to draft some of them for party work. A large number of prominent politicians thereupon submitted their resignations and at the last moment Bakshi too resigned. It was reported, moreover, that Nehru received a promise from Bakshi that Sadiq would be elected the new leader of the government in Kashmir.

Throughout the state Bakshi supporters openly protested against the resignation of their leader and refused to elect Sadiq. It was obvious that neither Bakshi nor his supporters wished to turn power over to an opponent within the party. Bakshi ultimately reported to Nehru his inability "despite his best efforts" to get Sadiq elected as his successor. The fact is that almost the entire party organization, legislature, and administrative machinery were manned by loyal supporters of Bakshi. In the fall of 1964 Bakshi nominated Shamusuddin. With the transfer of power to a new leader, the opposition parties now began to revive. Jammu's pent-up resentment burst out in a violent demonstration while a more explosive situation was about to follow in the Valley.

THE MIRACLE OF THE HAIR

A hair of the prophet Mohammed, enshrined and worshipped on the outskirts of Srinagar for three centuries, was found missing one day

[15] *Radical Humanist,* Calcutta, August 23, 1959.

near the end of 1963. Within hours, there was an unprecedented demonstration throughout the Valley. Thousands of Muslims, hysterical over the loss of the sacred relic, thronged into the streets of Srinagar. The movement soon turned into an angry attack against the Bakshi family and the government. The movement, led by Maulana Mohammad Saeed Mussoodi, demanded the recovery of the relic and the naming of the culprit. On the third of January, the Director of the Central Intelligence Bureau announced that the relic had been recovered. For a month, however, the government refused to have the relic identified by Muslim leaders, lest its authenticity be doubted. The Home Secretary declared that those who were demanding identification were in fact Pakistani agents. As unrest, doubts, and tensions increased, the authorities sought to suppress the movement with force. This resulted in a score of deaths and injuries, and as a reaction there were riots in East Pakistan against Hindus, which caused a chain reaction in the eastern towns of India where Muslims were victims.

There was little goodwill left for the Indian government in Kashmir. Lal Bahadur Shastri, who was then a minister without portfolio in Nehru's cabinet, was sent to Kashmir on February 3, 1964 to seek a compromise. He resolved the conflict very simply by allowing Muslim leaders to examine the relic. The relic was unanimously identified as genuine by Muslim divines selected by Mussoodi, for no Muslim could commit the sacrilege of doubting the authenticity of a holy relic. The culprits, however, were not named for another fortnight so that the three unimportant names disclosed by the Home Minister did not receive any credence. Nothing was heard of the culprits and the mystery of the theft after that, and the relic episode continued to be a sore point among Kashmiris.

But on the political front the retreat of the Kashmir government continued. Shamusuddin was forced to relinquish office, and on February 28, 1964, he was succeeded by Sadiq. The new government released all political *détenus* within a month. The trials against Sheikh Abdullah, Mirza Afzal Beg, and others were withdrawn, and civil liberties were fully restored. The Preventive Detention Act of the state was liberalized and brought in line with the law in force in the rest of India. The period of maximum detention provided by the law was reduced from five years to one, and provision was included for a judicial review. The government's Peace Brigade, used as an instrument of repression, was disbanded. Administration was toned up and anticorruption measures strengthened, and recruitment and promotions within the services were regularized.

Were these developments merely an internal set of reforms or did they signal a new determination in New Delhi to resolve the problem of Kashmir? Was the change in the Kashmir government meant to strengthen the center's hold on the state or to assuage popular feelings? Were political leaders released as an act of belated justice or out of weakness? Was the new policy of liberalization and the restoration of freedoms a gesture of generosity and goodwill or was it forced by the popular pressure of the relic agitation after it took a political turn?

Though it is difficult to answer these questions, the important point is that Abdullah and his supporters treated these developments as their own victory. Elaborate state arrangements were made for Abdullah's journey from the Jammu jail to Srinagar. Moreover, he received the red carpet treatment both in New Delhi, where he was Nehru's personal guest, and in Pakistan. An impression was created that Abdullah held the key to the solution of the Kashmir problem and that in a short time he might reassume power. There was considerable hope that his talks in New Delhi and in Rawalpindi would result in a settlement. Unfortunately, these prospects diminished with the sudden death of Nehru on May 27, 1964.

Abdullah meanwhile extended his influence further into Kashmir. Bakshi handed him back the presidentship of the Aukaf, the Muslim religious organization. He patronized the Plebiscite Front and spoke frequently from mosques to large Muslim audiences. He based his appeal on the promise to secure for Kashmir the right of self-determination without elaborating how it should be exercised and he created an impression that the right would be conceded soon. Beg, his lieutenant, predicted on the basis of "his faith in the mass struggle that a plebiscite would be held in Kashmir in 1965."[16] But as the prospects of fulfillment of the promise receded, after Nehru's death, Abdullah found it increasingly difficult to maintain his grip over the situation.

However, the most formidable challenge to Abdullah within the Valley was posed by a young boy of twenty, Maulvi Mohammad Farooq. Farooq became known when he served as president of the Action Committee, which led the relic agitation. He owed his importance to the fact that he was Mir Waiz (head priest) of Kashmir and a nephew and successor of Maulvi Yusuf Shah, the former President of Azad Kashmir, the Pakistan-held area of the state. Yusuf Shah, supported by the Muslim League, had been unsuccessfully but continuously challenging Abdullah's supremacy in Kashmir politics during the 1930s and 1940s.

[16] *Front*, Srinagar, December 9, 1964.

The hard core of his religious following, which Farooq now inherited, had remained dormant after 1947 in the absence of a leader on the Indian side of the border. Bakshi had managed to enlist the support of some of them during Abdullah's incarceration. Now, Abdullah accused Farooq of being an agent of Bakshi.

The emergence of Farooq onto the political scene with a following that had never been reconciled to Abdullah revived the old family-cum-ideological feud. He too demanded a plebiscite, but he ruled out independence as one of the alternatives. This stand, combined with his family background, projected a pro-Pakistan image of him. After he was ousted from the Action Committee, at Abdullah's insistence, he formed the Awami (People's) Action Committee to carry out his political activities.

Though there had been a number of pro-Pakistani political groups in Kashmir after independence, none of these had an organizational base and a genuine Pakistani ideology. In 1947 a group of Hindu intellectuals led by Prem Nath Bazaz demanded accession to Pakistan and carried on a campaign for some years. But they were not able to build a substantial organization among Muslims. In 1953 G. M. Karra formed the Political Conference, a professedly pro-Pakistan party, but it continued to endorse Gandhism, socialism, and secularism—the broad Indian values—and to reject the two-nation theory based on religion which was the political philosophy of Pakistan. Farooq's Awami Action Committee was, therefore, the first genuine pro-Pakistani group of importance and it attracted militant sections of the population, among the youth in particular, and especially in parts of Srinagar. Abdullah and Farooq soon clashed with one another. Rival meetings were disturbed, processions stoned, offices ransacked, and workers assaulted. In their bids to isolate each other, Abdullah and Farooq took extreme positions, and each charged the other with being soft toward India. But the internecine quarrel weakened the anti-India camp. There was, therefore, considerable pressure on both Abdullah and Farooq to resolve their conflict. The angry popular reactions to the measures announced by the government of India to further integrate the state with the Union added urgency and force to the unity moves. On the first anniversary of the relic theft, December 27, 1964, the two leaders announced that they would work together under the leadership of Abdullah for their common long-term objective of securing for Kashmir the right of self-determination and the immediate objective of resisting the integration measures. Farooq continued to maintain his Awami Action Committee while Abdullah supported the Plebiscite Front of which Beg was the president. But now for the first time these two antagonistic leaders worked together for common objectives.

In Delhi Shastri was accused of pampering Sheikh Abdullah and providing him facilities for an anti-national role. In Jammu the Jan Sangh, which had replaced the Praja Parishad, threatened to begin an agitation to end the special status of the state. Bakshi, with a majority in the state legislature, threatened to dislodge the Sadiq government and thus to upset the new Kashmir policy of India. For a variety of such reasons, therefore, the government of India began to tighten its constitutional grip over the state.

Toward the close of 1964 the President of India issued an order, on the recommendation of the state government of Kashmir, to extend Articles 356 and 357 to the state. These articles provide emergency powers for the President of India to assume direct responsibility for governing a state if in his judgment there has been a breakdown in the state's constitutional machinery. Previously these powers of the President could be exercised in Kashmir only with the concurrence of the state legislature, but this concurrence was no longer necessary. Several other provisions of the Indian constitution were also extended by the President to the state of Kashmir in late 1964.

The Kashmir government also announced its intention to change the nomenclature of the Sadar-i-Riyasat (head of the state) to Governor and of the state Prime Minister to Chief Minister to make them uniform with the rest of the country. To cap these measures of integration, the All-India Congress Committee decided in the beginning of 1965 to extend the party to the state and to replace the National Conference. This was done at the request of the National Conference. On January 26, Republic Day for India, the new party unit was formally launched by Sadiq and the National Conference was dissolved.

In opposition to these moves the Plebiscite Front called a protest day on January 15. Abdullah and Farooq addressed a joint meeting in Srinagar to condemn India for starting a "process of tightening its tentacles over Kashmir."[17] On January 29 the Action Committee gave another call to protest against "attempts to end the identity of Kashmir."[18] At a protest rally, Beg warned that the present measures were preliminary to merging the state with the neighboring Hindu majority state of Himachal Pradesh.[19]

Abdullah's patience with New Delhi was exhausted. "It was futile," he

[17] Weekly *Front*, Srinagar (official organ of the Plebiscite Front), January 20, 1965,
[18] *Ibid.*, February 3, 1965.
[19] *Ibid.*

said, "to expect anything from them or to appeal to them on the grounds of justice, humanity or morality. Time for such things has passed."[20] He urged his followers to treat all those who joined Congress as untouchables. "No one should have any relations or dealings with them and no one should talk to them. If they refused to see reason, they deserved no mercy."[21] He announced that he was leaving Kashmir for a tour of several foreign countries including a pilgrimage to Haj. Before he left he said, "I have prescribed social boycott of the Congressmen as a test for you. If you succeed in this, I will know your capacity to carry out the future programs that I will disclose on my return from the sacred country."

Tension soon mounted between the government and the opposition, between Congressmen and the Plebiscite workers, and between Hindus and Muslims. In the areas of Kashmir in which the Plebiscite Front was strong, they would not permit the dead bodies of Congressmen to be buried. In some areas Hindu businessmen complained that the boycott movement was taking a communal turn. Religious minorities began to develop a feeling of insecurity, business activities slowed down, and the flow of tourists—the mainstay of Kashmir's economy—began to diminish.

In the first week of February Sheikh Abdullah left Kashmir for a foreign tour. He announced that he would seek world support for his cause and "pray for deliverance of the suffering Kashmir at Mecca."[22] Although Abdullah and Beg had left Kashmir, their supporters continued the social boycott movement. On March 7, about a week after Abdullah's departure from Kashmir, the Kashmir government arrested 200 Plebiscite Front workers all over the Valley under the Defense of India rules to "ensure that the normal life of the community was not interfered with." Official spokesmen charged the Front with "inspiring and instigating activities highly prejudicial to the maintenance of public order, including the promotion of ill will and hatred between different sections of the people." Mussoodi, Karra, and Farooq, who had been overshadowed by the Plebiscite Front's militant politics, publicly condemned the arrests and revived the Action Committee, set up at the time of theft of the relic.

In a country where foreign travel is subject to very rigid restrictions, Sheikh Abdullah and Mirza Afzal Beg surprisingly got easy permission to go abroad on what was essentially a political mission, in no sense favorable to India. Abdullah's passport—which he applied for not as an

[20] *Ibid.*, January 20, 1965. [21] *Ibid.*, February 10, 1965.
[22] *Front*, Srinagar, February 10, 1965.

Indian citizen but as a Kashmiri Muslim—was endorsed, not only for Mecca but for all Muslim countries in the Middle East and for most of Europe. He proved to be no more discreet in his statements abroad than he was at home. At Algiers he met with the Chinese Prime Minister, who, as Abdullah reported to Reuters (April 1), "reiterated China's support for the right of self-determination to the people of Kashmir" and invited him to visit China. The Kashmir leader was "most gratified by the reaffirmation of China's support for our cause." Taking a grave view of the matter, the emergency committee of the Union Cabinet decided on April 4, 1965, to cancel all endorsements on Sheikh Abdullah's passport and directed him to return to India after completing his pilgrimage to Haj. Abdullah and Beg were taken into custody in the early hours of May 8, 1965, as soon as their plane landed at Palam airport in New Delhi to prevent them "from acting in a manner prejudicial to the defense of India, civil defense, public safety, and the maintenance of public order." Later Beg was removed to Srinagar and kept under house arrest while Abdullah was confined to the hill resort of Kodaikanal in South India.

A little later India and Pakistan resumed their dialogue, not at a conference table, but on the battlefield. On August 5, 1965, armed infiltrators from Pakistan-held areas of Kashmir—estimated between 6,000 and 10,000—crossed into the state. Soon the entire cease-fire line along which India and Pakistan had divided the state on January 1, 1949, became alive. By the end of the month, the Indian army had captured several vital passes across the line to stop the further entry of raiders. On September 1, 1965, Pakistan's heavy tanks crossed the international border between the two countries at Chhamb and threatened to cut off the supply lines of the Indian forces in Kashmir. India retaliated on September 6 by opening another front at Lahore, the nerve center of West Pakistan. Fighting stopped on the morning of September 22 at the intervention of the Security Council. After a few months of an uneasy cease-fire, Soviet Prime Minister Kosygin invited Shastri and Ayub Khan to Tashkent and on January 10, 1966, persuaded them to sign an agreement which provided for the return of the two armies to the positions they held on August 5, 1965, and to abjure war as a means of settling their outstanding disputes.

POSTSCRIPT

The civil disobedience movement—on the Gandhian pattern—launched by the Action Committee for the release of Abdullah and for the right of self-determination fizzled out as the war began. Mussoodi, Karra, and

Farooq tried to revive the movement after the war, but they were put under detention, and the agitation for self-determination that had continued in one form or another for a year and a half thus came to an end.

The war and the Tashkent agreement demonstrated the irrelevance of external force in altering the political status of the state and consequently caused in Kashmir a sense of disillusionment with Pakistan and a tendency to reconcile with the status quo. It was in this period that the supporters of Chief Minister Sadiq were for the first time able to organize public meetings and processions in various parts of the Valley. The curbs imposed during and after the war on civil liberties further paralyzed the opposition to the government. Most of the opposition papers were banned, and under the Defense of India Rules over 1,200 political workers were jailed, most of whom were later gradually released when the new regime had stabilized itself.

Sadiq had already taken care of the possible challenge from a pro-India rival. Bakshi Ghulam Mohammad was arrested on September 22, 1964, just in time to prevent him from calling for a motion of no confidence against the Sadiq Ministry, signed by a majority of members in the state legislature. When the National Conference was converted into a branch of the Indian National Congress in January 1965, all posts were filled by nominations, thereby purging the party of Bakshi's supporters. Bakshi on his release in December 1964 announced retirement from politics. But he was soon to face an inquiry on charges of corruption and irregularities allegedly committed when in power. After two and a half years the quasi-judicial commission of inquiry held him guilty of the substantial charges, which included "undue financial advantage of the value of Rs. 54 lakhs to his family."

Bakshi has offered to face a legal trial on these charges which far from sealed the process of his political recovery. In March 1966, he announced his decision to return to active politics and by July he revived the National Conference at a convention of about 5,000 delegates at Srinagar. Commending the role of constitutional opposition, Bakshi said, "If any such opposition had emerged in the state, neither Sheikh Abdullah nor I would have committed mistakes."

In an election year, Bakshi was the only available focal point of discontent against the Sadiq regime in Jammu as well as Kashmir. His party was able to announce a list of candidates for all the Assembly and Parliament seats in both the regions. The general elections in February 1967 were the first seriously contested elections in the state, particularly in the Valley. In the first elections in 1951, 73 out of 75 candidates were returned unopposed. In 1957 the contest was confined to 32 seats while in 1962 the number rose to 41. Most of these contests were in the Jammu area, which had 30 seats.

For a while the thrill of challenging the authority not only of Srinagar but also of New Delhi, through constitutional means, seemed to be more absorbing than the call of the secessionists. For the first time the people of Kashmir found a real opportunity to change their government through elections. On the eve of the fourth general elections, the public politics of the Valley tended to be polarized between parties owing allegiance to India. All those who questioned the finality of Kashmir's accession to India were never so isolated.

The discomfiture of the once formidable Plebiscite Front was increased by a split in its ranks on what attitude to take toward election. A section led by its former general secretary, Ali Mohammad Naik, defected and contested the election in defiance of the official decision to boycott. But excepting Naik, all candidates of the group were routed. Shabir Mussoodi, son of Maulana Mohammad Saeed Mussoodi, was trounced in the prestige parliamentary constituency of Srinagar by Bakshi Ghulam Mohammad with a big margin. The full impact of the poll activity on Kashmir politics was, however, missed by the way elections were conducted. Nomination papers of 118 opposition candidates were rejected in 39 out of 75 constituencies, including 22 unopposed returns. Whatever might be said in defense of the Returning Officers, who rejected the papers, it was obviously their decision and not that of the people which mattered in the formation of the government. As further doubts spread about the fairness of elections, the voter lost confidence in the value of his vote. In Jammu region, the leaders of which were not in the race for power, people became reconciled to the *fait accompli* more readily. The Congress bagged 28 out of 31 seats in the region, conceding 3 to the Jan Sangh and 1 to the National Conference. In the Valley, the National Conference put up a stiffer resistence and scraped through, getting 7 seats out of 42, half of which were uncontested.

The unprecedented upsurge of constitutional opposition in the Valley, which provided a pro-India outlet to the frustrating secessionist sentiment, itself had a frustrating experience. Apart from denying it some of its democratic rights, during and after the elections, Sadiq also made an attempt to cover up the ground that Bakshi was occupying between him and Abdullah. Soon after re-election as Chief Minister, Sadiq defended special status for Kashmir, which he had all along opposed and taken measures to erode. An opportunity to align with popular Muslim sentiments was offered to him during the West Asia war in June 1967. Following inflammatory anti-Israel statements by him, violent anti-West and even anti-India demonstrations were staged on June 7. The degree of official connivance may be debated. But the political atmosphere did become more favorable to the ideology and power of Sadiq. In the past also, the security and stability of the regimes in Kashmir have paradoxically depended on the revival of anti-India forces that divert popular attention from the question of making and unmaking governments to questions of accession and secession.

Meanwhile, a move for Abdullah's release gained ground in the country. In the first week of July 1967, 125 members of Parliament endorsed the move mainly on grounds of civil liberties. But they were encouraged by an indication of Jaya Prakash Narain—who had met Abdullah in detention—that Abdullah was realistic enough to take note of the changed context of the station following the Indo-Pakistan war of 1965 and might agree to a solution by which Kashmir might be included within the Indian framework with a substantial measure of autonomy.

Will the Union of India give back to Kashmir all the powers it enjoyed under Abdullah until 1953? Will the original accession, in the three areas of defense, foreign affairs, and communications, be able to satisfy all political sections in the Valley? How will Jammu and Ladakh react to such alteration in the state's status? The idea of autonomy does appeal to the sentiments of Kashmiri regionalism. And in the context of renewed country-wide debate on the revision of center-state relations and the demand for greater autonomy for the states by non-Congress Chief Ministers (notably of Madras and Kerala), pro-India sections in the Valley no longer consider an autonomous status as a step toward secession. Like Sadiq, the Communist party of India, too, gave up the demand for "full integration of Kashmir with the Union" and joined the campaign for the release of Abdullah, whom it had been branding as an imperialist agent. This incidentally follows Soviet Russia's overtures to Pakistan and her somewhat less unequivocal support of India's case on Kashmir.

Can claims of Kashmiri regionalism be reconciled with those of Indian Nationalism through constitutional devices? Will an autonomous status within India absorb all the secessionist sentiments?

For fear of the secessionist challenge in the Valley, India's policy-makers denied the people of Kashmir free expression of their pride, their linguistic and cultural loyalty, their aspirations for a good and free life. The secessionist challenge itself was magnified by the dissatisfied Kashmiri aspirations, which have been trying to assert themselves in this India framework. Their success depends on the fate of the secessionist forces.

The two-party system, which for the first time operated in the February 1967 elections, has already shown its potentiality in diverting popular discontent into constitutional and pro-India channels. A fairer election and a more vigorous confrontation of pro-India parties may unfold further possibilities. Likewise, the search for regional identity, through revision of Kashmir's relations with the center as well as with other regions of the state, might make it a more contented part of the country.

This context adds significance to the fierce controversy that is raging throughout the state over the proposal for a federating relation among its three regions, namely Jammu, Ladakh, and Kashmir. In Jammu in particular, the movement for regional autonomy assumed the form of a popular upsurge around mid-1967, for it promised to answer its urge for sharing political power.

Hitherto, Hindu Jammu sought security in the transfer of power from Srinagar to Delhi, which only provoked Kashmiri Muslims to seek security in secessionist channels. But as six lakh Muslims of Jammu, also deprived of an adequate share in power, sought a regional sense of belonging, Jammu's protest changed from communal to regional. Instead of negative demands for reducing Kashmir's powers, the new movement positively demanded a status of equality and autonomy within the state. Limitations of communal politics (the Jan Sangh could win only 3 out of 31 seats of Jammu), the promise of a secular opposition party like the National Conference, and the entry into politics of a noncommunal leader of the stature of Maharaja Dr. Karan Singh helped this process of the secularization of Jammu politics, which is not without its sympathizers in the Valley.

There are still many imponderables in Kashmir politics. The constitutional form regional relations take and the way the party system evolves would undoubtedly shape it. But it has also been sensitive to distant events, including India's international position and its relations with a country like Pakistan. Conversely, whatever has happened in Kashmir has had a profound effect on national politics and on the external relations of India, notably with Muslim countries and the Soviet Union.

REFERENCES

Abdullah, Mohammed, Sheikh. "Kashmir, India, and Pakistan," *Foreign Affairs*, April 1965.

Bamzai, Prithvi Nath Kaul. *A History of Kashmir*. Delhi: Metropolitan Book Co., 1962.

Bazaz, Prem Nath. *History of Struggle for Freedom in Kashmir*. New Delhi: Pamposh Publications, 1954.

Bhutto, Z. A. "The Kashmir Case," *Pakistan Quarterly*, Summer 1962.

Birdwood, Christopher Bromhead, Baron. *Two Nations and Kashmir*. London: R. Hale, 1956.

Dutt, Raijni Palme. "Kashmir—The Only Solution," *New Age*, New Delhi, Oct. 31, 1954.

Korbel, Josef. *Danger in Kashmir*. Princeton: Princeton University Press, 1954.

Madhok, Balraj. *Kashmir—Centre of New Alignments*. Delhi: Deepak Prakashan, 1963.

Narayan, Jayaprakash. "Our Great Opportunity in Kashmir," *Hindustan Times*, April 20, 1964.

Noorani, A. G. *The Kashmir Question*. Bombay: Manaktalas, 1964.

Puri, Balraj. "The Challenge of Jayaprakash Narayan," *Janata*, Bombay, Feb. 28, 1965.

———. *Communism in Kashmir*. Calcutta: Institute of Political and Social Studies, 1962.

———. *Jammu—A Clue to the Kashmir Problem*. Published by the author. Delhi, 1966.

———. "Kashmir Perspectives," *Seminar*, New Delhi, August 1963.

———. "Sheikh Abdullah's Re-arrest and After," *Janata*, July 3, 1958.

———. "State of Kashmir's Finances," *Eastern Economist*, New Delhi, June 17, 1966.

———. "What Should Be Done With Abdullah," *Radical Humanist*, Calcutta, May 10, 1964.

Puri, Balraj, editor. Bimonthly *Kashmir Affairs*. Nos. 1 to 12. Delhi.

Sufi, Ghulam Muhi-ud Din. *Kashmir: A History of Kashmir*. Lahore: University of the Punjab, 1948.

Symposium on Kashmir. *Seminar* (58), June 1964.

WEST BENGAL

WEST BENGAL, 1966

VI

WEST BENGAL

MARCUS F. FRANDA*

IN A COUNTRY that is overwhelmed with problems, West Bengal has a special reputation for being "a problem state." The difficulties facing all of India—poverty, underdevelopment, population growth, and their resultant complications—have been compounded in West Bengal by a series of historical factors and events that have not affected other areas of the subcontinent, or at least not to the same degree. Unlike most other regions, which have been moving toward linguistic unity, the Bengali-speaking linguistic unit has been constantly partitioned during the past century.[1] Less than one-third of Bengali-speaking people now live in the Indian administrative area controlled by Bengalis, and West Bengal is now smaller than all the Indian states except Kerala and tiny Nagaland. Yet this tiny, truncated state maintains a population larger than all but four Indian states, and the average population density in 1961 (1,032 people per square mile) was exceeded only in Kerala.[2] Population density in Calcutta is unrivalled in South Asia—more than 90,000 people per square mile—and some parts of the city are as crowded as any other part of the world. To complicate the poverty and underdevelopment that is common to all of India, West Bengal has had to contend with a series of events which have seriously disrupted its

* Research for the present study was carried out under the auspices of the Foreign Area Training Program, jointly administered by the Social Science Research Council and the American Council of Learned Societies. The following pages do not, of course, reflect the views of the Foreign Area Training Program. This study is highly dependent on the work of many other persons who are interested in Bengal, and especially on the research that has been conducted by Myron Weiner. I am deeply grateful to the Foreign Area Training Program for encouragement and support, and particularly indebted to Professor Weiner, both for the insights furnished by him in his courses at the University of Chicago and for his generosity in allowing me to draw so heavily on his own studies of West Bengal.

[1] In the first Indian census of 1872, the area of Bengal was 248,231 square miles; by 1901 it had dropped to 189,837 square miles; by 1941 to 82,876 square miles; and by 1951 to 33,524 square miles. The partition of 1947 was thus the last of a long series of partitions that have left the state of West Bengal less than one-seventh the size of Greater Bengal a century ago.

[2] Population figures are taken from the provisional census statistics, 1961, as published in *India: A Reference Annual, 1963*, compiled by the Research and Reference Division, Ministry of Information and Broadcasting, Government of India (New Delhi: Publications Division, Ministry of Information and Broadcasting, 1963), pp. 5-24.

economy. In the past twenty years alone, West Bengal has had to withstand the wear and tear of major Allied war operations in and around Calcutta, has suffered one of the largest famines ever to occur in India, and has witnessed communal riots that began in August 1946, culminated in the partition of 1947, and led to the subsequent influx of more than four million refugees. The partition of Bengal in 1947 cut off the supply of food grown in East Bengal, creating serious shortages in the West; the supply of jute to West Bengal dwindled to a trickle, leaving the jute industry without raw materials; transportation and communication networks were disrupted to such an extent that there is still no rail or road link between the northern and southern districts of the state (except by a circuitous route through Bihar or by a more direct route which involves riverine transshipments and transfers). To complicate the problems of West Bengal still further, all of this happened in an area that already had a tradition of terroristic politics, and during a time when Bengal was losing its political, economic, and perhaps even cultural hegemony over the rest of India.

Despite the magnitude of its problems, and the rapidity with which they have occurred, West Bengal has remained a fairly stable and integral part of the Indian Union, and it continues to be an area of crucial importance to the future development of India. One of India's four major ports lies within its boundaries; it is rich in coal, copper, iron, and other minerals; it is still one of the leading centers of industry and commerce; it remains a major center of higher education; and its writers, artists, and other intellectuals are prominent in cultural and scientific fields. If West Bengal has had more than its share of the strains, tensions, conflicts, and general disorder found in a developing nation, it also has a rich cultural, social, and political background that has shaped the lives of people who are finding ways to grapple with, if not solve, unprecedented problems.

THE SOCIAL AND ECONOMIC ENVIRONMENT

Historical Background

Lying at the eastern end of the Gangetic plain, and extending from the Himalayan mountains to the sea, Bengal has been subjected to a variety of influences from diverse sources. Bengal's closest links are with the north, its language being related through Sanskrit to the languages of northern India, and its culture being infused with the Brahmanic culture that spread along the course of the Ganges to the delta. The Bengali region also has links with the south: it has at times been under the rule of southern dynasties, and has been a source for the spread of Brahmanic culture to southern India as well as to Southeast Asia. Thus, some Bengali cultural traits—religious practices and rituals, methods of food preparation, and some forms of clothing—indicate a cultural development in some spheres that is more akin to the south than to the north and west.[3]

But despite basic affinities with other parts of India, Bengal has always been a definite cultural region in its own right, distinct from both north and south. Since Bengal is located in the northeastern corner of India, far from the Hindu Kush mountains, it managed to escape to some extent the far-reaching influences which the earlier invaders had on the Hindu heartland. Bengal was always on the periphery of the great Hindu empires; it was generally the last area to come under, and the first to break away from, central control. Though Brahmanism spread to Bengal, it did so by fits and starts, and in the process was altered in basic ways by the tribal and folk cultures that already existed in this region. In its earlier history Bengal was also deeply influenced by the teachings of the Buddha, who was born on its borders about six hundred years before Christ. In fact, Buddhism remained the dominant religion of Bengal until the ninth century, when the Sena kings, in contrast to their predecessors, attempted to establish the "pure" religion and social organization of the midlands, and to purge Bengal of its non-Brahmanic cultural traits. But although the Sena dynasty did effect a solidly caste-based social structure which was to survive for centuries, the work of the Senas was never completed, and in the thirteenth century they were overthrown by the Pathans, who were in turn overthrown by the Mughals, who were later replaced by the British.

Social Configurations

The social composition of West Bengal today still reflects the distinctive and variegated background of this region. Bengal is largely Hindu (see Table 6.1), but the Bengali Hindu differs in many important respects from the non-Bengali Hindu. Hindus in Bengal have their own beliefs, rituals, ceremonies, and caste lineages, borrowed from the tribal, folk, and tantric cults and legends that influenced Hinduism in this region but did not affect other areas of the subcontinent. There also exists in Bengal a tradition of unorthodoxy, practiced by a number of sects—Sahajiya, Nath, Baul, and others—which grew up in Bengal dur-

[3] The affinities between Bengal and other parts of India are explored in Nirmal Kumar Bose, "Culture Zones of India," *Geographical Review of India*, Vol. XVIII, No. 4 (December 1956), 1-12.

ing the past six hundred years, in almost all of which the emphasis is on a more direct and humanistic relationship with god than that common to Brahmanic ritualdom. These unorthodox Hindu cults have been a major factor in the creation of a distinctively Bengali literature and culture.[4] The Bengali language itself, which flourished under the patronage of both Pathans and Mughals as they attempted to build up support among the Hindu nobles, is one of the most highly developed in the subcontinent and sets the Bengali-speaker apart from his Hindi-speaking brethren.[5]

TABLE 6.1

SOCIAL CONFIGURATIONS IN WEST BENGAL

Religion	*Number, 1951*[a]	*Number, 1961*[b]
Hindu	19,462,706 (78.45%)	27,542,794 (78.92%)
Muslim	4,925,496 (19.85%)	6,971,287 (19.98%)
Other[c]	422,106 (1.70%)	383,198 (1.10%)
Totals	24,810,308 (100.0%)	34,897,279 (100.0%)
Language (Mother Tongue)	*Number, 1951*[d]	
Bengali	20,994,374 (84.62%)	
Hindi	1,574,786 (6.34%)	
Santali	663,503 (2.67%)	
Urdu	457,635 (1.84%)	
Oriya	182,271 (0.78%)	
Nepali	174,017 (0.75%)	
Other	763,722 (3.00%)	
Total	24,810,308 (100.0%)	

[a] Figures taken from *Census of India, 1951,* Vol. VI, "West Bengal, Sikkim and Chandernagore," Part II "Tables," p. 445.

[b] Figures taken from provisional totals, 1961 census, as published in *India: A Reference Annual, 1963* (New Delhi: Publications Division, Ministry of Information and Broadcasting, 1963), p. 18.

[c] Includes Sikhs, Jains, Buddhists, Zoroastrians, Christians, Jews, Animists, and Atheists.

[d] Figures taken from *Census of India, 1951,* Vol. VI, Part II. Only those languages spoken by more than one lakh (100,000) people in the state of West Bengal in 1951 are included in the table. Figures for 1961 were not available.

[4] The unorthodox nature of Bengali religious cults is analyzed in Shashibhusan Dasgupta, *Obscure Religious Cults* (2nd ed. rev.; Calcutta: Firma K. L. Mukhopadhyay, 1963), pp. 346-55. For the influence of these cults on Bankim Chatterjee, Tagore, and others, see pp. xlvii-l, 186 ff; the development of Bengali literature is also discussed in *The Thief of Love: Bengali Tales from Court and Village,* (ed. and trans.), Edward C. Dimock (Chicago: University of Chicago Press, 1963), pp. 1-17.

[5] The development of the Bengali language is analyzed in S. K. Chatterji, *The Origin and Development of the Bengali Language* (Calcutta: Calcutta University Press, 1926), Vol. I.

Another result of the distinctive social and cultural background of this region is the diversity of the population. West Bengal contains the second largest Muslim minority of any Indian state (second only to Uttar Pradesh), a result of the Mughals' successful policy of spreading Islam in an area that was not closely tied to the Hindu heartland. It also contains a large number of the lower-caste Hindus who are now placed in the category "Scheduled Castes,"[6] primarily former Buddhists who were relegated to the bottom of the social hierarchy by Hindu forms of social organization. The two other large minority communities—the tribals[7] and the non-Bengali Hindus—are of more recent origin, both having migrated to Bengal for the most part after the introduction of British rule. The tribals come primarily from the states of Madhya Pradesh, Bihar, and Orissa, and now work in Bengal either as agricultural laborers or as factory hands. Most of the non-Bengali immigrants come from neighboring Bihar, from Uttar Pradesh, or from Orissa and are also employed as common laborers or factory workers. Finally, there is a small, but influential, minority of people from Rajasthan, Madras, Punjab, Gujarat, and almost all other states, who have established themselves in business and commercial ventures.

Patterns of Change

Because of its geographical location on the periphery of the subcontinent, Bengal was one of the first regions to be subjected to British penetration, and one of the first to accept and assimilate the process of change that has characterized the last two hundred years of Indian history. The traditional cultures in West Bengal have thus been deeply affected by, and interwoven with, ideas and forms of social organization resulting from contact with the West; and the economy of this area has of course been seriously altered. The most fundamental changes, and those which set the Bengali area off from the rest of India, are related to developments in the land tenure system; to political, commercial, and industrial developments associated with a high rate of urbanization; and to developments in the field of education.

Permanent Settlement

Prior to 1765, the land tenure system in Bengal revolved around the *zamindar*, a hereditary rent-collecting and magisterial official, who col-

[6] The "Scheduled Castes" in West Bengal in 1951 numbered 4,696,205 (18.93 per cent of the total population), a figure which rose to 6,950,726 (19.92 per cent of the total population) in 1961. *India: A Reference Annual, 1963*, p. 118.

[7] The "Scheduled Tribes" in West Bengal numbered 1,165,337 in 1951 (4.69 per cent of the total population), and 2,063,883 in 1961 (5.91 per cent of the total population). *Ibid.*

lected a certain amount (usually one-third) of the cultivator's gross produce and turned over most of it to the state, retaining some for his labor. Although each individual zamindar paid a fee to secure his position, his family usually acquired an hereditary right to that position, even to the extent that it was necessary for a zamindar to get state permission should he wish to be relieved of his duties. Because the zamindar was responsible for public order and economic development in his district, the land tenure system was an integral part of the political, economic, and social systems. But because land was not as highly valued as it is today, the eighteenth-century zamindars were not always the wealthiest members of their community, nor were they always the political rulers, or even the highest in social status. The wealthiest members of the community were those involved in private moneylending and business ventures, the political rulers of the localities were the panchayat members, and the most prominent in social status were the higher-caste members. Indeed, social position in eighteenth-century Bengal depended largely upon caste ranking and wealth, and not upon one's position in the land tenure system.[8]

When the British began experimenting with new land tenure and assessment systems in 1765 and finally decided upon the Permanent Settlement of 1793, they produced a change in traditional Bengal which was to have profound effects on the structure of the society. The most immediate consequence was the replacement of the old set of hereditary zamindari families with a new set of landlord families. British land tenure methods brought about this transfer of positions by introducing into the system confiscation as the primary punishment for failure to pay the *juma* (assessment). Whereas previously the zamindars suffered fines, imprisonment, or flogging for failures to pay the assessment, they were now in many cases deprived of their right of collection and were replaced by other people, usually wealthy merchants from Calcutta. Because British assessments in the early nineteenth century were often quite high, instances of confiscation were numerous and the transfer of zamindari rights to a new set of zamindars took place on a large scale.

The nineteenth-century zamindars came to occupy positions of far more wealth and influence than those held by their eighteenth-century counterparts. Because of the introduction of the concept of land ownership and because of the disintegration of Bengal's indigenous handi-

[8] H. T. Colebrooke, *Remarks on the Husbandry and Internal Commerce of Bengal* (Calcutta, 1806), pp. 31-50. See also Ronald B. Inden, "The Localization of the Hindu Elite of Bengal and Its Effects on the Polity of the Southeastern Bengal Chiefdoms" (unpublished Master's Thesis, University of Chicago, 1963), pp. 53-55.

crafts and commerce, the value of land assumed prominent proportions in nineteenth-century Bengal. Moreover, the revenue collected by the government from the landholders was fixed on the basis of eighteenth- and early nineteenth-century standards. When the amount of cultivated land increased, and land values and agricultural prices subsequently soared during the nineteenth century, the landholders were left with substantial surpluses after they had collected rents from the cultivators and had paid what was due to the government. In addition, land ownership came to entail increasingly less responsibility as British law-enforcement and administrative powers expanded, and the British rulers usurped the administrative functions of the zamindar.

In this atmosphere, land became an increasingly attractive investment. Earnings from business and commercial activities, government services, and the legal profession went into the purchase of zamindaris and other rent-collecting rights; and the late nineteenth century witnessed the growth of an extremely influential landed gentry. Along with the growth of this landed gentry, the number of intermediaries in the land tenure system multiplied: zamindars sold their rent-collecting rights to subsidiary interests; more prosperous peasant cultivators gave up agriculture, turned their land over to tenants or sharecroppers and became members of the landed class; the increasing indebtedness and impoverishment of small peasant proprietors led to foreclosures and sales of holdings on a large scale, and a further increase in the number of noncultivating landholders and intermediaries.[9]

But the growth of a landed aristocracy and a large number of intermediaries in Bengal in the nineteenth century proceeded apace with the development of other factors which worked to simultaneously limit the ability of landed Bengalis to live solely, or even primarily, from their landholdings. While subinfeudation expanded at a rapid rate, agricultural productivity remained nearly constant, and the population of Bengal grew at a faster rate than at any previous time. The number

[9] Although there are no accurate statistics on the number of intermediaries in Bengal at any one time, estimates made before the Land Revenue Commission in 1939 ranged as high as ten million. These figures would include the area that is now in East Pakistan, which would mean that the number of those in the area that is now West Bengal would be somewhat less than half of this figure. See *Report of the Land Revenue Commission, Bengal* (Alipore: Bengal Government Press, 1940). When the Zamindari Abolition Act was passed in 1954, the West Bengal government announced that proclamations had been served to 1,300,000 intermediaries. But of course a large number of intermediaries retained their interests in land through a variety of devices. See Myron Weiner, *The Politics of Scarcity* (Bombay: Asia Publishing House, 1963), p. 141; and S. K. Basu and S. K. Bhattacharya, *Land Reforms in West Bengal: A Study of Implementation* (Calcutta: Oxford Book Company, 1963).

of intermediaries therefore increased at the same time that their profit from land diminished.[10] Many of the intermediaries were forced to turn to urban occupations—government service, the professions, and commerce—to supplement their incomes. And this resulted in the growth of a large urban middle class.[11] In this century, the size of the urban middle class has been enlarged by recent land reform legislation, which abolished some of the large zamindari holdings, and by the fact that partition cut off a number of the large zamindari estates that were included in the area that is now East Pakistan. The size of this class has also been augmented by the addition of a large number of refugees from East Bengal, many of whom were members of the middle class before coming to West Bengal.

The growth of a landed gentry and a large middle class was also accompanied by the growth of a high rate of tenancy and sharecropping. Some idea of the number of tenants and landless laborers in West Bengal can be gained from the 1951 Census Report, which estimated the percentage of West Bengal's landless agricultural population at 42.4 per cent.[12] Twenty-one per cent of the cultivators in the 1951 census were listed as tenants or sharecroppers, meaning that they either rented their land from a landholder or his intermediary at a flexible rate, or they shared the profits of the land with the landholder and his intermediaries.[13] Another 21.4 per cent were listed as agricultural laborers: either day laborers, hired by the day and paid in food and cash; or *kishan*

[10] In 1921, the census report estimated the average gross income for rent-receiving families at only 620 rupees per year ($125.00). As W. H. Thompson, the census commissioner, commented: "When it is remembered that not less than 10 per cent [of gross income] has to come off for land revenue and the cost of collecting rents, though the small middlemen usually collect their rents themselves, and that a small number of great landlords take a large proportion of the assets of the land to themselves, it will be realized that most of the landlord and middlemen class in Bengal are by no means well-to-do." *Census of India, 1921*, Vol. v, "Bengal," Part I "Report," p. 385.

[11] The term "middle class" is now defined by Bengalis as those people who have at least a secondary education, or whose families have such education; who do not do manual labor; but who depend on occupational earnings for their livelihood. While this class is referred to as "middle class" (*nimna-moddhabitta*) in the urban areas, it is still called the *bhadralok* (gentleman or "a man of good breeding") class in the rural areas.

[12] However, Asok Mitra, the author of the 1951 West Bengal census, reports that tenants and *bargadars* (sharecroppers) often claimed proprietorship, while landlords claimed cultivating status. The 42.4 per cent figure should therefore be viewed as a very poor approximation of reality. See *Census of India, 1951,* Vol. VI, Part IA "Report," pp. 345-51.

[13] Under the terms of post-independence legislation, the landlord's crop share in West Bengal is not to exceed 50 per cent of the produce if the landlord contributes the cost of cultivation, and 40 per cent if he does not. Even these high limits are not always enforced, however. See *India: A Reference Annual, 1963*, p. 221.

laborers, employed on a yearly, monthly or daily permanent basis and sometimes provided with living quarters.

The high rate of tenancy in West Bengal, combined with other factors, has resulted in the deterioration of the economic and social position of Bengal's peasant cultivators. Since the Permanent Settlement did not encourage development of land, the Bengali peasant was subject to a host of factors which contributed to his decline—fragmentation of holdings, the introduction of cash crops dependent upon a world market, the growing power of a moneylending class, an increase in tenancy—at the same time that he was unable to overcome these factors by increasing his own production. Moreover, the pursuit of liberal economic policies by the British meant the duty-free importation of mill-made cloth from England and the subsequent destruction of a number of handicraft industries that had previously provided substantial rural employment for the landless in Bengal.

Another result of the economic forces of the last century is a rural economy that remains close to the subsistence level. In 1952-53, more than 95 per cent of the cultivated area was under crops intended for consumption in the state itself. Almost 80 per cent of the cultivated land was under rice, and more than 10 per cent was under pulses (rice and pulses being the two primary staples of the Bengali diet). Yet, because of the low unit yield and the fact that the population is growing at a faster rate than production, West Bengal is still chronically deficient in rice, and must depend on supplies from the center, from neighboring states, and from foreign areas, to feed its population. Farming techniques have progressed very little: in 1952-53 there were only thirteen ploughs for every one hundred acres of cultivated land, and the ratio of iron ploughs to wooden ploughs was four to a thousand.[14]

Urbanization

The poverty of the rural areas, combined with the growing commercial, cultural, educational and governmental activities of the cities, has given rise to a large urban population in West Bengal. Urban growth has thus far centered around Calcutta, which was not only the political and administrative capital of British India until 1911, but also the commercial capital, a principal port, the trading center of the eastern region (both for internal and foreign trade), and a center of industrialization and cultural activities. Originally a cluster of villages, Calcutta began to grow rapidly after the victory of the English East India Company at the battle

[14] *West Bengal: Land and People*, ed. Sushil Kumar Sen and Rabindra Nath Sengupta (Calcutta: City College Commerce Department, 1956), pp. 34-39.

of Plassey in 1757. By the end of the eighteenth century, the population was estimated to have risen to 140,000; by 1850 to 413,182; by 1901 to 847,796; and by 1931 to 1,163,771. Since 1931, Calcutta's population has more than doubled, and the population of the Calcutta Metropolitan Area (which extends about 45 miles on both sides of the river Hooghly) is fast approaching 6 million. West Bengal contains other large urban complexes (large by Indian standards), but they are still minute in comparison with Calcutta. Asansol (168,689 in 1961), Kharagpur (147,255 in 1961), and Burdwan (108,224 in 1961) are the only cities outside the Calcutta Metropolitan Area that contain populations of more than one lakh (100,000).

Large-scale migration from the rural areas has combined with the influx of refugees from East Bengal after partition to produce large pockets of poverty in Calcutta.[15] But in spite of this poverty, the rush into Calcutta from the surrounding rural areas has continued unabated for more than a century. Overcrowding on the land, the increase in rural debt, tenancy, underemployment, and a lack of rural handicrafts to provide alternative sources of employment, all have driven, and continue to drive, the peasant to the city. Some urban immigrants, especially in the past, have come because of the attractions of city life: the intermediaries from the land tenure system were attracted by opportunities for education or for positions in government administration, or by the cultural milieu; immigrants from other states have come for business opportunities, or again for education. But the vast majority of the urban immigrants have always been villagers driven by rural pressures to seek work in the city, who return to their homes in the countryside as soon as it is financially possible. The 1951 census estimated that less than one-third (33.1 per cent) of the total population of Calcutta was born in the city; the rest (66.9 per cent) having migrated in during their own life-

[15] It is estimated that over 300,000 people now live on the pavements and sidewalks of the city with no homes at all. Only 5 per cent of the city's families live in separate flats, and only 2 per cent in complete houses. Thus, only 7 per cent of the families live in exclusive dwellings. Most families live either in *bustees* (huts made of sticks, corrugated tin, oil drums, and other cheap building materials), or are crowded with other families into one or two rented rooms of an old house. Using forty square feet as the minimum amount of space needed for one person, it has been estimated that at least 77 per cent of the people of Calcutta live in overcrowded rooms. The conditions found in Calcutta's households are among the worst in the world: 30 per cent of the families have no water tap attached to their residence; 12 per cent have no latrine; 61 per cent have no bathroom; 78 per cent have no separate kitchen; and 45 per cent have no electric connection. See Richard L. Park, "The Urban Challenge to Local and State Government: West Bengal, with Special Attention to Calcutta," in *India's Urban Future*, ed. Roy Turner (Bombay: Oxford University Press, 1962), pp. 382-96.

time. One study, conducted by Calcutta University in 1954-58, estimated that of the migrants in Calcutta, 13 per cent were displaced migrants (primarily refugees from East Pakistan) and rural migrants accounted for the remaining 87 per cent.[16] The same study estimated that more than half (56.3 per cent) of the households in Calcutta were single-member units, most of which consisted of male migrants who left their families in their villages to come to the city to make money which they could send home. This accounts for the fact that 65 per cent of the city's population is male, making Calcutta one of the most male-dominant cities in the world.

Large-scale rural to urban migration has conditioned the character of both the economy and the social structure in Calcutta. In 1957-58 it was estimated that only 6.3 per cent of the gainfully employed in Calcutta's population were engaged in the manufacture or repair of machine-made goods,[17] and only another 4 per cent were engaged in the distribution of such goods; only 2.4 per cent were engaged in construction. The majority of wage earners were employed in the manufacture and distribution of hand-made consumer products (44.2 per cent) and in the various services which keep the city operating: 18.8 per cent were employed in the public services (government departments, police, government banks, and corporations) and in public utility concerns; 11.6 per cent were employed either as domestic servants or in the domestic services (barbers, cobblers, and so on); 7.6 per cent were in the professions. These figures point to a low level of industrialization: the proportion of people engaged in manufacturing and related occupations is quite small, and those so engaged are employed in the so-called "unorganized sector": in small cottage industries, in handicrafts, and in shops that employ few people who are not members of the owner's family.

The low level of industrialization and the preponderance of small-scale enterprises, in combination with a very inefficient capital market, an overall low level of saving, and pressures which drive people from the rural areas into the city, have produced a situation in which urban growth continues unabated but with a very small accumulation of industrial capital. What results is a relatively slow rate of economic development, and one which is unable to keep pace with the growing population.[18] Migrants from rural areas find it increasingly difficult to find

[16] S. N. Sen, *The City of Calcutta: A Socio-Economic Survey, 1954-55 to 1957-58* (Calcutta: Bookland Private Limited, 1960), p. 207.

[17] *Ibid.*, pp. 60-62.

[18] Based on the article by Bert F. Hoselitz, "The Role of Urbanization in Economic Development: Some International Comparisons," in *India's Urban Future*, pp. 157-81. In this article Hoselitz compares the rate of industrialization in India's urban

jobs in the city, and the poverty and discontent that already characterizes the bulk of the urban population increases at a rapid rate.

These factors, many of which are common to other parts of India, were accentuated in West Bengal by the disruption of the economy resulting from partition, and by the influx of large numbers of refugees from East Pakistan. Urban discontent in Calcutta has also been aggravated by the propensity of the urban middle classes to organize the malcontents. The growth of a volatile urban middle class in Bengal has in turn been due largely to the imbalances that have resulted from the nature and the intensity of Westernized education.

Westernized Education

As in other matters relating to Western contacts, Bengal was among the first regions in India to feel the impact of English education. Organized and effective attempts by missionaries in the field of education were begun at the Serampore Baptist Mission in 1800, and the first British college to bring English officers and Bengali scholars together was established at Fort William in Calcutta in the same year. The first college designed to teach Indians in the English language (Hindu College) was founded in Calcutta in 1817, and the University of Calcutta was the first Indian University to be established (in 1857) on the subcontinent. Expansion of the educational system coincided with the growth of the number of intermediaries in the land tenure system, and gave rise to an increasing number of opportunities for the middle class to secure education and to enter the growing commercial and professional order, and government service. In the nineteenth century Bengali "babus" thus became the backbone of the British administration throughout most of northern India, from Assam to Uttar Pradesh and Orissa, and they dominated the staff of the British administration in the capital at Calcutta. During the nineteenth century Bengalis also dominated the leadership of educated India in almost every sphere. Bengal was the center of the great reform movements, of the growth of Westernized schools, of the "renaissance" in literature and the arts, and of the growth of political consciousness. Bengalis were prominent among the leaders of the Moderates who founded Congress in the latter half of the nineteenth century, and at the forefront of the terrorists who emerged at the beginning of the twentieth. No other province can produce so formidable a list of Indian leaders of the nineteenth and early twentieth centuries, in almost every sphere of activity, as can Bengal.

---

areas with the rate of industrialization in Western urban areas at a similar stage of population growth.

With the growth of education in other areas in this century, however, the position of Bengal as the leader of educated India has definitely declined. Whereas Bengal once boasted the highest percentage of literates in India, the state of West Bengal now ranks fifth in literacy (29.3 per cent in 1961). The number of colleges, universities, and research institutions in West Bengal (193) in 1961 was also less than that in four other states: Maharashtra (265), Madras (231), Madhya Pradesh (215), and Uttar Pradesh (209).[19] But while Bengal's position as the leader of educated India has declined, it has still shared in the problems associated with Westernized education to a greater extent than most other regions. English education in India emphasized liberal arts, the Western humanities (especially literature), and the speaking of English, with little or no emphasis on scientific and technical training. The extent to which this system has affected education in Bengal (where the traditional social system also valued training in literary and cultural activities) can be seen from the fact that as late as 1959-60, the number of students in technical colleges (i.e., engineering, agriculture and veterinary, and technical schools) was still only 4,002, or approximately 3.2 per cent of the total number of students in colleges in West Bengal.[20] The vast majority of Bengal's students have been, and continue to be, trained in the arts and in general education, prepared primarily for clerkships in private commercial firms or in government, or for cultural pursuits.

As a result of the rapid expansion of education in Bengal, education in most schools, colleges, and universities has become notoriously poor, the object of general opprobrium. Classrooms are crowded far beyond capacity, teachers receive extremely low remuneration, and libraries are very unsatisfactory. The result is often a very low level of instruction, and an even lower level of performance demanded. Thus many Bengalis refer to their schooling as "under-education," and to themselves as "educated unemployables." Yet the number of schools, colleges, and universities continues to grow at a rapid rate (often at the further expense of quality). Most Bengalis still feel that the expansion of education will result in greater modernity and industrialization, and in addition, education is considered essential for obtaining jobs and for maintaining social status. Educational institutions are multiplying so rapidly that, despite the growth in commercial and governmental activities, the universities and colleges are producing far more graduates than there are jobs. Moreover, the rapid growth of educational institutions, combined

[19] Figures taken from *India: A Reference Annual, 1963*, pp. 69, 73.

[20] Government of West Bengal, State Statistical Bureau, *Statistical Abstract, West Bengal, 1960* (Alipore: West Bengal Government Press, 1963), pp. 118-19.

with the low level of educational instruction provided by them, has created a situation of imbalance between the educational system and the needs of the larger community. In 1953 the number of matriculates and graduates in West Bengal who were without full-time employment and were seeking jobs stood at 125,000, a figure that has been rising rapidly since.[21] In Calcutta alone in 1956-57, it was estimated that 22 per cent of the unemployed possessed matriculate or graduate qualifications, while another 37 per cent had read up to the tenth standard. Ten per cent of the unemployed in Calcutta in 1956-57 claimed to possess some experience of mechanical work, while another 2 per cent were mechanical or technical diploma-holders.[22] Yet, in the face of these apparently adequate "paper" qualifications of many employment seekers, industries continue to cry out for skilled workers and educated executive and office personnel. Business and industry, even schools and hospitals, contend that, despite the existence of so many unemployed diploma-holders, they are unable to find competent employees for a large number of posts.

That Bengal was among the first regions in India to be subjected to a widespread Westernized educational system and that its position has now declined in this sphere, together with the problems of maintaining educational standards and coping with large-scale educated unemployment, are factors that have shaped the social, economic, and political life of the state of West Bengal. In the following discussion we shall attempt to explore the ways in which the educational system, the system of land tenure, and the commercial and industrial activities of the past two hundred years have combined with the social system associated with the traditional society to produce the system of social stratification, social structure, and the patterns of social and political conflict which are characteristic of this area.

Social Stratification

The major changes introduced by the British in Bengal were clearly modeled after Western patterns of social, political, and economic development. The British assumed that the Permanent Settlement would lead to the growth of a landed gentry similar to that which grew up in Britain

21 Government of West Bengal, *Survey of Unemployment in West Bengal,* State Statistical Bureau, First Interim Report, Vol. 1, Part I, 1953, p. 7. This figure, like most estimates of educated unemployment in West Bengal, serves to disguise the extent of educated unemployment, however, since a large number of Bengali graduates are not included as unemployed even though they are seeking work. No attempt has yet been made to determine the number of people who have part-time and temporary positions as tutors; who call themselves writers; or who attend college or university classes while looking for permanent jobs.

22 Sen, *op.cit.,* p. 120.

in the seventeenth and eighteenth centuries—a landed aristocracy that would develop the land and furnish an elite around which the foundations of orderly rule could be built. The system of Westernized education in English was designed to create a class of South Asians who would become committed to Western ideas and institutions and who could purge their society of such non-British institutions as idolatry and caste. The British attempted to found a rational-legal administrative system, and to base recruitment into the civil services and into British firms on achievement criteria with which they were familiar. The thrust of British interference in the social sphere thus revolved around the attempt to establish completely new (and basically Western) criteria for social stratification.

The manner in which Bengal adapted to these new social ideas and forms of social organization was conditioned, however, by a host of ideas and practices which prevailed in this area prior to British rule. Bengal had been infused with Brahmanic forms of social organization which based social status largely on the ascribed position of caste, and even Buddhism and Islam, despite their egalitarianism in other areas, had in large part been drawn into the caste system. Within the caste system in Bengal, moreover, there was an elaborate refinement known as Kulinism,[23] whereby each of the castes was divided into various classes on the basis of such factors as learning, wealth, and family background. The traditional social system of Bengal was also conditioned by the fact that Bengal had been divided politically among a number of noblemen, chiefs, and petty princes who remained relatively independent of one another, and relatively free from the control of the Pathan and Mughal emperors. Social and economic relationships varied from one part of Bengal to another, depending on the policies of the prince and on such factors as the caste composition of the area, the nature of settlement, and the economic interdependence or lack of interdependence of the villages.[24] Social practices and forms of organization which prevailed in Bengal prior to British rule were thus highly developed and extremely complex.

[23] According to Bengali traditions, a king of Bengal named Adisura invited five learned Brahmans of Kanauj in Uttar Pradesh to settle in Bengal sometime in the ninth century. In the twelfth century, tradition has it, one of the Bengali kings, Vallalasena, used these families as the basis for the introduction of the Kulin system. Originally Brahmans were divided into classes on the basis of their learning and character, but later this system extended down among other castes in the social hierarchy. Thus far there has been no historical evidence that would either prove or disprove this widely accepted version of the introduction of Kulinism. See R. C. Majumdar and A. D. Pusalkar, *The Struggle for Empire*, Vol. v of *The History and Culture of the Indian People* (Bombay: Bharatiya Vidya Bhavan, 1957), p. 38.

[24] In this regard see the interesting article by Ralph W. Nicholas, "Ecology and Village Structure in Deltaic West Bengal," *Economic Weekly* (Bombay), Vol. xv (July

The system of social stratification that has resulted from the collision of these two highly developed social systems reflects the diversity and complexity of the traditional society at the same time that it incorporates ideas and forms of social organization associated with the process of change. Thus, while many of the caste taboos and regulations, and even many caste organizations, were weakened or abolished by changes resulting from the British impact—travel abroad, the necessity of increased public contacts, the movement of caste members to urban areas—caste as a basic unit of social organization has remained. The vast majority of the members of all castes in West Bengal—even those who have given up their traditional occupations and have widely subscribed to Western education—still remain members of an endogamous social unit.[25] While the Kulin system has disappeared in name, the basic features of that system—the emphasis on learning, wealth, and family background as a basis of social stratification—have survived. The number of families in Bengal who can trace their family origins back to the Kulin system is now quite small, but the importance of educational and cultural attainments in the determination of social status, both for the individual and for future generations of the individual's family, is still widely accepted by Bengalis.

The land tenure system which was introduced into Bengal did create a landed aristocracy, but this landed aristocracy was in large part drawn from members of the traditional society who already formed an elite. Because Bengal's zamindars were drawn primarily from the Brahmans, Kayasthas, and Vaidyas—the three high-caste groups—the changes introduced by the land tenure system served to widen the social gap between the high and the low castes.[26] The Permanent Settlement also reinforced

1963), 1185-96, in which an attempt is made to demonstrate ways in which the geographic environment of certain areas of West Bengal has affected the social system in these areas.

[25] Nirmal Kumar Bose, "Some Aspects of Caste in Bengal," *Man in India*, Vol. XXXVIII, No. 2 (April-June, 1958), 84-85.

[26] A number of village surveys have shown the extent to which the landed gentry is still dominated by the high castes in West Bengal. In one village, Shona Palasi, in which a survey was conducted in 1960, 90 per cent of the upper-caste families owned land, and the average holding per family was fifteen *bighas*. In this same village, only 20 of the 131 low-caste households owned any land, and the average holding per household among the lower castes was less than one (0.93) *bigha*. See Kusum Nair, *Blossoms in the Dust* (London: Gerald Duckworth and Co., 1961), p. 157. For similar findings, see Jyotirmoyee Sarma, "A Village in West Bengal," in *India's Villages*, ed. M. N. Srinivas (2nd ed. rev., Calcutta: Asia Publishing House, 1960), pp. 180-201; and H. D. Malaviya, *Village Panchayats in India*, Chapter XII "West Bengal" (New Delhi: All India Congress Committee, 1956), pp. 330-43.

the position of some people within the Kulin system (initially the zamindars or revenue-collectors, but later other people who could afford to buy zamindaris) by providing them with additional sources of wealth and leisure which they could use to further their positions. Even the new members of the landed gentry subscribed to many of the same ideals and values which had characterized the social elite before the advent of the British: they valued learning and cultural activities; they pursued landed wealth and other occupations which did not require manual labor; and they used their wealth to promote, either directly or indirectly, literature and the arts. They attempted to strengthen their positions in the land tenure system by adherence to caste practices.

The ideals established by the landed aristocracy were maintained or adopted by those members of the middle classes who were later cut off from the land, and who entered the professions and urban occupations. These people were also drawn primarily from the three high castes in Bengal and they were also extremely conscious of maintaining their positions in the traditional social hierarchy. They came to describe themselves as "middle class" in English, but continued to use a more expressive word, *bhadralok* ("gentleman" or "a man of good breeding") when referring to themselves in Bengali. Like the landed aristocracy the middle classes pursued certain kinds of occupations which were in keeping with their family traditions. In fact, Bengalis came to define middle-class occupations as those in which a man does not do physical labor, and the lower-class occupations as those in which manual labor is required. Westernized education did become a new criterion for social status which was widely accepted, but this too served to reinforce the social position[27]

[27] The following table, taken from the *Census of India, 1931,* Vol. v, Part II "Tables," p. 184, indicates the extent to which the three high castes have predominated in English education (1931 was the last census in which caste statistics are available).

Caste	Total Number	Literate	Literate in English
Brahman	1,456,180	542,832 (37.3%)	208,573 (14.3%)
Kayastha	1,558,442	512,699 (32.9%)	207,078 (13.2%)
Vaidya	110,739	57,380 (51.7%)	31,227 (28.1%)
Mahisya	2,376,302	363,552 (15.3%)	49,336 (2.1%)
Namasudra	2,094,936	139,016 (6.6%)	20,372 (1.0%)
Bagdi	987,315	18,973 (1.9%)	1,172 (0.1%)
Santal	796,634	5,686 (0.7%)	217 (0.03%)
Other Castes	12,832,521	1,411,253 (11.0%)	224,211 (1.8%)
Total Hindus	22,212,069	3,051,391 (13.7%)	742,184 (3.3%)
Muslims	27,810,100	1,583,710 (5.7%)	264,877 (1.0%)
Other Religions	1,065,169	108,180 (10.2%)	58,746 (5.5%)
Total Bengal	51,087,338	4,743,281 (9.3%)	1,065,807 (2.1%)

In the 1931 census, the Brahmans, Kayasthas, and Vaidyas were the only Hindu castes of the three high castes and the landed classes.[28] Moreover, because the kind of education that was imparted, and was valued most highly, was one which emphasized liberal arts and the humanities, and especially English and Bengali literature, the educational system served to reinforce traditional notions which attached high status to cultural attainments.

Changes in the criteria for social status which were introduced by British rule in Bengal also served to benefit the Bengali Hindu community, to the detriment of the social position of the Muslims. The Permanent Settlement in Bengal converted Hindu revenue collectors into landlords, which meant that the landed aristocracy which grew up was almost exclusively Hindu. Moreover, Muslim families in Bengal responded to Western ideas and institutions at a much later date than did the high-caste Bengali Hindus, and, as a result, opportunities for entering positions in government or the professions were considerably fewer for Muslims than for Hindus. Finally, the Muslim community in West Bengal lost the bulk of what leadership had arisen in the twentieth century, when many of the Muslim leaders opted for Pakistan after partition. The extent to which these factors have affected the social position of the Muslim community today can be seen from the predominance of Bengali Hindus in both educational and occupational pursuits. In 1959, for example, only six Muslims (0.6 per cent of the total) received degrees from Jadavpur University in Calcutta, while the number of Hindus was 938 (98.2 per cent of the total). At Visva-Bharati University (the university founded by Tagore at Santiniketan), which prides itself on the "universality" of its student body, the number of Muslims who received degrees during the period 1958-60 was 25 (2.3 per cent of the total) while the number of Hindus who received degrees was

that were more than 2.1 per cent literate in English. Although no state-wide statistics have been available since that time, some village surveys would indicate that the predominance of the three high castes in education is continuing. In the Shona Palasi survey, for example, 59 per cent of the upper castes were found to be literate, while only 5 per cent of the lower castes could read and write. This pattern of education was being accentuated by the education of the younger people. In this same village in 1960, 40 per cent of all boys and 35 per cent of all girls in the age group six to eleven were attending school. But the corresponding figures for the *choto-lok* (literally "little people"), or lower castes, was still only 5 and 4 per cent, respectively. See Nair, *op.cit.*, p. 157.

[28] Some idea of the extent to which the landed classes still predominate in education can also be gained from census statistics. In 1951, the last census for which data are available, literacy rates were highest (28.45 per cent) for non-cultivating owners of land; next highest (15.8 per cent) for cultivators who owned their own land; much lower (8.95 per cent) for cultivators whose land was wholly or mainly unowned by them; and lowest (5.05 per cent) for cultivating laborers. See *Census of India, 1951*, Vol. VI, Part IC "Report," p. 161.

1,005 (92.1 per cent of the total).[29] Lacking educational opportunities, the Muslim population of West Bengal continues to occupy the lower occupational positions. For example, in Calcutta in 1957-58 it was estimated that 82.1 per cent of the Urdu-speakers (almost exclusively Muslims) earned less than 100 rupees per month, while only 57.4 per cent of the Bengali-speakers (and this includes both high- and low-caste Bengali Hindus) earned less than that figure.[30]

The introduction of new commercial and industrial occupations did serve to introduce new elements into Bengal's population—a non-Bengali factory and commercial class—but these new elements maintained their traditional ties. Because the Permanent Settlement encouraged investment in land rather than in commerce and industry, business in Bengal came to be dominated by European merchants and by non-Bengali Indians (especially Marwaris from Rajasthan), whose tradition was more receptive to trade and commerce and whose wealth in fact depended on new business ventures.[31] Because of the aversion of many Bengalis to manual labor, the laboring class in West Bengal's urban areas came to be dominated by non-Bengali immigrants, largely from Bihar, Uttar Pradesh, and Orissa.[32] For a variety of reasons, however, these non-Bengali immigrant groups were not absorbed into the Bengali social hierarchy. Differences in language, in manners and customs, and in historical traditions, have been maintained by the majority of the members of each of these communities, with the result that relationships between people tend

29 *Statistical Abstract, West Bengal, 1960*, pp. 131-33.

30 S. N. Sen, *op.cit.*, p. 100.

31 In 1957-58 the people speaking minor languages (largely Punjabi, Gujarati, Marwari, English and Chinese) had incomes far out of proportion to their numbers, indicating the extent to which they dominated high-income occupations. Although they constituted only 4.5 per cent of the total earners in Calcutta, they made up 28.5 per cent of the upper-income groups (those receiving more than 750 rupees per month) and 14 per cent of the middle-income groups (those with incomes between 201 and 750 rupees per month). While only 11.3 per cent of the Bengali-speakers, only 2.1 per cent of the Hindi-speakers, and only 2 per cent of the Urdu-speakers earned more than 200 rupees per month, the corresponding figures for the minor language groups was 26.2 per cent. See *ibid.*, pp. 100-01.

32 The predominance of the two largest groups of non-Bengali immigrants in Bengal, the Hindi-speakers from Bihar and U. P. and the Oriya-speakers from Orissa, is dramatically demonstrated in Sen's study of Calcutta. More than 88 per cent of the Hindi-speaking earners and more than 92 per cent of the Oriya-speaking earners in 1957-58 had estimated incomes of less than 100 rupees per month. These two communities also had the highest male-female ratios among language groups, the ratio being 3,952:1,000 among the Hindi-speakers and 10,204:1,000 among Oriya-speakers, indicating the extent to which these groups consist of male migrants from the rural areas who have come to Calcutta only to earn money at menial occupations in order to supplement their village income. See *ibid.*, pp. 16, 100-01.

to be circumscribed by cultural and social backgrounds and by community and caste affiliations.

Because of the importance attached to caste and community affiliations, the social stratification system in West Bengal is extremely disjointed. It would perhaps be more accurate to speak of a number of sub-stratification systems, rather than of one system which applies to all people. Wealth is a criterion for social status among all people in West Bengal, but even the wealthiest member of one community may be socially unacceptable to the vast majority of the members of another community. Educational and cultural attainments are highly valued and are an important source of status for Bengalis, but except insofar as they afford an accumulation of wealth or lead to occupational attainments, they are less highly valued among the non-Bengali communities. High-paying jobs, regardless of their nature, will be coveted by the members of some Bengali low castes and by non-Bengalis, but if they entail manual labor they will result in a loss of social status among high-caste Bengalis.[33]

In addition to the important differences that have grown up between castes and communities in West Bengal (which have resulted as much from the ability of castes and communities to change as they have from their ability to resist change) other developments which affect the stratification system are occurring. Because the dominance of the Bengali high castes over the low castes has come to be based as much on the educational, occupational, and cultural attainments of high-caste Hindus as it is on caste and family background, a relaxation of the laws of endogamy is taking place among some (but by no means all) members of the three high castes. Families are increasingly willing to marry their sons or daughters to partners not within the sub-caste, and at least in the urban areas, an inter-caste marriage between people of two high (but different) castes is not rare. The distinction between the high and low castes, however, remains. Marriages between a person from a high caste and a person from a low caste are still almost unheard of, even in those areas where the individuals concerned, and not the families, select the marriage partner.

To say that the majority in West Bengal remain tied to closed social groups is not to say that the administrative, economic, and social changes of the last two hundred years have not profoundly altered the relatively ordered and isolated environment of social life. Large-scale com-

[33] Where high-caste Bengalis take positions as taxi drivers, bus conductors, and small shopkeepers, which provide higher incomes than many clerkships and many teaching and tutoring jobs, this action is viewed, by the individual concerned as well as by his neighbors, as one which involves a considerable loss of social standing.

munication and transportation networks and the growth of urban areas of unprecedented size have led to an increased number of social contacts and have made possible the influx of large numbers of people from outside communities who have taken their place in the social structure of West Bengal. Westernized education has inculcated new ideas and forms of social organization which have served to weaken the authority relationships between the members of some families, castes, and communities, and even led some individuals to completely sever their ties with these social institutions. The introduction of new criteria for social status has led to new ambitions and aspirations, and made possible more upward and downward mobility than existed in the previous social system. Class divisions (based on economic and educational criteria for social status) have arisen at the same time that older institutions—caste and the joint family—have taken on new functions. Many new organizations based on economic and social interest have emerged. The result has been the widespread extension, and the ramification throughout the society, of opportunities for the expression of differences, the making of demands, and the struggle for benefits.

Social Conflict

The effect of the political, economic, and social forces of the last two hundred years has been more far-reaching among Bengali high castes than among other communities. The three high castes were deeply influenced by Westernized education and are highly urbanized;[34] their traditional social institutions have been subject to a greater degree of disintegration than other social groups;[35] and they have experienced a number of cultural and economic shocks—the partition of Bengal, educated unemployment, the loss of the cultural and political hegemony of Bengal over India—which have not affected other communities to the same extent. The result has been the creation of numerous divisions and distinctions among the Bengali high castes, and a high level of discontent and dissatisfaction. In addition to a class division which is ap-

[34] In the 1931 census, the last census in which caste statistics were compiled, the three high castes—Brahman, Vaidya, and Kayastha—accounted for 28.9 per cent of the population of Calcutta, compared to only 6.1 per cent of the population of Bengal as a whole. See *Census of India, 1931*, Vol. v "Bengal and Sikkim," Part II "Tables," pp. 225-32.

[35] See, for example, Sunil Sengupta, "Family Organization in West Bengal: Its Nature and Dynamics," *Economic Weekly* (Bombay), March 15, 1958, pp. 384-89. Sengupta reports that the joint family (defined as kinship plus common kitchen) holds together among Mahisya, Sadgop, Ugra Kshatriya, and Pundra Kshatriya castes in the three villages studied in Bankura, Birbhum, and Howrah districts, but has deteriorated among the older well-established Brahman, Vaidya, and Kayastha families.

pearing,[36] the Bengali high-caste community is divided—across caste lines—between intellectuals and businessmen, between the more traditional-minded and the more Western-minded, between those with rural interests and those with urban interests, and on a variety of other issues. The problems of the Bengali high castes have been intensified by the fact that many of those who now live in West Bengal are refugees from East Pakistan, many of whom have suffered a loss of social position as a result of the forced move to a new area. Consequently, the Bengali high castes have organized for social conflict on a broad geographic scale, and on the basis of a host of ideas and interests. They now dominate all of the peasant organizations in the state, all four of the large trade union federations, one of the four major chambers of commerce, almost all student groups and refugee movements, and all of the minor and major political parties.

Not all West Bengalis have been affected to the same degree. Many of the villages, for example, still remain relatively isolated social units. The vast majority of the peasants and rural cultivators have imbibed very little education at all, much less a Westernized education that would inculcate a belief in the legitimacy or necessity of egalitarian or class forms of social organization. Most peasant cultivators remain deeply committed to a hierarchical social system in which authority relationships between individuals and classes are well defined; in which the area of legitimate individual ambitions and aspirations is carefully circumscribed; and in which the weight of almost all symbols of authority is on the side of obedience to caste, family, and village superiors. These factors are in turn reinforced by the wide economic gap that exists between the peasant-cultivator low castes and the non-cultivating high castes.[37] The existing man/land ratio and the short supply of land in relationship to demand reinforce an economy of high rents and a high rate of tenancy, and encourage attitudes of acquiescence on the part of the landless and tenant farmers.[38] This accounts for the fact that conflicts

[36] Bengalis in Calcutta now distinguish between the upper class (*dhani*); the upper middle-class (*uccho-moddhabitta*); and the lower middle-class (*nimna-moddhabitta*), a distinction based almost entirely on the criterion of wealth.

[37] For a more detailed analysis of village conflict in West Bengal, see Ralph W. Nicholas and Tarashish Mukhopadhyay, "Politics and Law in Two West Bengal Villages," 1963. This article has now been published in the *Bulletin of the Anthropological Survey of India*.

[38] This is being increasingly recognized as a primary difficulty in the implementation of plans in the countryside. See, for example, the statement by Gulzari Lal Nanda, summarizing from the report of the Tenancy Committee of the Land Reforms Panel of the Planning Commission: "Even where the tenants are aware of their rights they are generally in too weak a position—both economically and socially—to insist on their rights. In some states, there are no village records from which a tenant can

between landholders and peasant cultivators have not developed to any significant degree in the countryside, for the failure of the Communist party to promote a "class struggle" in the rural areas, and for the propensity of most villagers to do little more than assent to the plans made for them by non-villagers.

The same is true for some members of the urban population. Despite the high rate of urbanization in West Bengal, there is a substantial segment of the urban population which is culturally—i.e., in attitudes, values, and behavior—rural. Many of the urban dwellers maintain their closest ties with their village: they return to their village at regular intervals; they marry within their village; their pattern of living is the same as that of the villagers, and their contacts are often confined, despite their urban residence, to people from their own community and caste, and sometimes do not even extend outside their own family. They remain illiterate and uneducated, and they identify only with the social organization that has its center in their place of birth.[39] Their position is also reinforced by economics—by the difficulty of finding jobs and housing—and if the problems of urban life become too much for them, they return to their village rather than engage in social conflict in the city.

This is not to say that people in the rural areas, or the working classes in the city, do not engage in social conflict. Villages in West Bengal, like villages in all of India, are prone to numerous controversies and conflicts which center around various kinds of factions. Since the social system emphasizes hierarchical arrangements and notions of prestige, the

---

establish his possession. Even where his name is entered the landlord has so much influence in the village that frequently it is very difficult for the tenant to establish his possession. In some cases the attitude of the Revenue Officers may at times be unconsciously against the tenants. . . . After all, ideas about the evolution of tenants' rights as against the landlord have been of a comparative recent growth. The conception of land as property and the rights and privileges of the owner of property is deeply rooted. The rights and privileges of the actual cultivator of the land are not yet fully comprehended." Gulzari Lal Nanda, "Progress of Land Reforms in India," *All-India Congress Committee Economic Review*, Vol. IX, No. 10 (September 15, 1957), 17; quoted in Weiner, *Politics of Scarcity*, p. 161.

39 This is true, for example, of factory gangs who are recruited in the villages. The way in which this process works is described by Asok Mitra: "A *sirdar*, whose home is in one of these districts brings down to a factory a gang recruited from among the poorer of his co-villagers, maintains some sort of control over them while they are employed and generally looks after them till he takes or sends them home again. This explains how it is that in one factory a large body of labourers often comes from a very closely circumscribed area, often a few adjoining villages only, in some up-country districts." See *Census of India, 1951*, Vol. VI, "West Bengal, Sikkim and Chandernagore," Part IA "Report," pp. 318-19.

disputes and divisions that can arise are many and varied. Individuals, families, and cliques vie with one another for social prominence and social benefits, and try to rally around their own faction a group which will support the faction leader. To do this they depend on those who are tied to them in various ways—fellow caste-members, relatives, friends, employees, tenants, borrowers, and many others. The point is that in the rural areas such conflicts are still confined largely to local communities and local geographic areas, and in some of the urban areas they are confined to a neighborhood or to an alley, or are an outgrowth of village factions and village conflicts.

The sphere in which peasant cultivators and the urban laboring classes are willing to engage in social conflict is, of course, expanding. Organizations of peasants have existed since the 1920s, and they do engage in agricultural activities, movements for the abolition of landlordism, and protests against the high price of consumer goods. But these organizations are still dominated almost exclusively by upper-caste, middle-class families, and the membership in such organizations is still relatively small. The All-India Kisan Sabha, the largest of these organizations, reached a peak in 1955-56 when its membership was only 219,000. Trade union leadership has been somewhat more successful in organizing the urban laborers. The three largest trade union federations in West Bengal estimated their combined membership in 1957 at 500,000. And, although these federations are also organized by the Bengali middle classes, and though they are often beset by organizational difficulties, the success of some unions in pressing their demands before management and in staging strikes and protest movements indicates a greater willingness on the part of workers to articulate their own interests.

The sphere of social conflict is widening in another sense, in that it is increasingly coming to involve caste and community loyalties across wide geographical regions and inclusive of wide social groupings. Many of the personal group and class conflicts which arise in the present social system can now be expressed through community and caste associations in a way that was not possible earlier in this century. Because the lower classes who compete for jobs and housing in the urban areas are highly conscious of their community identities, the competition for economic benefits ofttimes results in an increase in inter-community tensions (between Bengalis and non-Bengali laboring classes for example) and sometimes even in violence (especially between Hindus and Muslims). Because business and industry is dominated by Europeans and Marwaris while trade unions are led by the Bengali middle classes, the conflict between management and labor extends to a conflict between communities.

Because some castes organize and vote on the basis of caste loyalties—the Mahatos in Purulia, the Ugra-kshatriyas in parts of Burdwan, the Subarna Baniks in Calcutta, and the Panda-kshatriyas and Mahisyas in south 24-Parganas—local caste and factional conflicts are often expressed as parts of wider political issues.

The extension of social conflict to wider and wider spatial and social areas has led to an increase in the demands which individuals and groups place before government. Government, at both the state and central levels, is being depended upon more and more to satisfy the increasing demands of the diverse social groups in West Bengal: for jobs, for education, for goods and services, and for economic development. The necessity of reconciling diverse communities and solving the problems of a "problem state" is becoming more acute. At the same time, the ability of government to meet the demands of the people and to overcome the difficulties that have arisen in the state is conditioned by the nature of the political process, which gives effect to the demands made on government at the same time that it determines the kind of government that is elected to meet those demands. In order to understand the limits and capabilities of the government to cope with demands, it is therefore necessary to first gain some understanding of the political process.

THE POLITICAL PROCESS

Until this century, Bengal was always one of the focal points for the development of modern Indian political movements. Beginning in the early part of the nineteenth century, a number of organizations—the Brahmo Samaj, the Indian League, the Indian Association, and others—came into being in Bengal as forums for the expression of views by Hindu reformers and the newly created intelligentsia, and these organizations were later instrumental in providing a background of leadership for the Indian National Congress. The first Congress president was a Bengali, and Bengalis were prominent among the leaders of the Moderates who led the Congress in its infant stages. Bengalis were also at the forefront of the revolutionary agitation in India in the twentieth century. The successful early terrorist organizations—the Jugantar and the Anushilan Samiti—were founded in Bengal, as were most of the Marxist left parties which sprang up in India after the Russian revolution. Not until the early 1920s, when Gandhi and a new national leadership arose, did the position of Bengal in the nationalist movement recede.

Bengal's prominence early in the nationalist movement, and its subsequent decline with the advent of Gandhi, lie at the heart of an understanding of Bengali politics. For, unlike most other regions of the subcontinent, the Congress party in Bengal did not accept the leadership of Gandhi and the central Congress party organization until after independence, a fact which was to have profound repercussions on future events. A number of people and groups in Bengal, especially in the countryside, did accept Gandhi even in the 1920s, and a number of centers—the Khadi Pratisthan of Satish Das Gupta, the Abhoy Ashram of P. C. Ghosh, the Arambagh group of P. C. Sen, and others—promoted Gandhian ideas. But the Westernized urban intellectuals who dominated the Congress party in Bengal during most of Gandhi's lifetime—Chittaranjan Das until his death in 1925, and then Subhas Bose and his followers—were almost constantly in active opposition to the Congress center.

The antipathy between the Gandhian-dominated center and the Congress leadership in Bengal appears to have derived from several sources. (1) In part it was a struggle over the methods to be used in the nationalist movement. The Bengali leadership was constantly prodding Gandhi and the Congress party to move faster and to intensify its activities. They urged complete independence even while the Congress leadership was prepared to accept Dominion status; and they urged civil disobedience movements when the Congress leadership still hoped that further negotiations would bring concessions from the British rulers. Gandhi's faith in non-violence, negotiation, and moderation contrasted sharply with the Bengali belief that terrorism and violence had been successful in revoking the partition of 1905 and in gaining other concessions from the British, a point-of-view romanticized in Bengali literature. (2) The Westernized urban intelligentsia, in Calcutta especially, experienced what Subhas Bose has called "a rationalist revolt against the Mahatma and his philosophy." The Bengali middle class tended to look with disdain upon Gandhi's traditional outlook and modes of behavior, and cynically rejected his asceticism, his antagonism to cow slaughter, his advocacy of hand-spinning, and his opposition to machinery. (3) Perhaps most important, Gandhi had little feel for the problems of the urban middle class. His main concern was with the rural areas, and his attention was focused primarily on programs—spinning, the removal of untouchability, and communal unity—which provided little satisfaction to a class which was most concerned with the extension of education and the opportunities for professional and governmental jobs.

For whatever reasons, the antagonisms between Bengali political leadership and Gandhian leadership of the central Congress party grew, even up until independence. In 1923 C. R. Das broke with the Congress to form the Swaraj party, having differed with Gandhi over the wisdom of joining the Legislative Councils. At both the 1928 and 1929 Congress sessions, Das's successor, Subhas Bose, brought his disagreements with Gandhi to an open vote, and both times Bose was defeated by only a narrow margin. As Bose continued in opposition to Gandhi, and as he attempted more and more to effect a leftist coalition within the Congress capable of overcoming Gandhi's position of dominance, Gandhi became more and more intent upon ousting Bose. This conflict reached a climax in 1939 when Bose won the elections for Congress president against Gandhi's own candidate, but was unable to form a Working Committee because of Gandhi's lack of cooperation. Bose then resigned, and, later in the same year, organized demonstrations against two central Congress party directives. The All-India Congress Committee (A.I.C.C.) used this as the opportunity to oust Bose as president of the Bengal Pradesh Congress Committee (PCC) on the charge of "indiscipline," and to disqualify him from any elective office in the party for three years.[40]

The expulsion of Bose in 1939, coupled with his flight from India in 1942 and the partition of 1947, virtually destroyed the urban coalition that had dominated the Congress organization in Bengal from the 1920s. During the war, the coalition remained shakily intact, led by the Jugantar group, an old and famous terrorist organization that had joined the nationalist movement under Gandhi's leadership. Suren Ghosh, the leader of the Jugantar, was the Pradesh Congress Committee president, and Kiron Shankar Roy, a Jugantar supporter, was the leader of the Bengal Assembly Congress party. The Jugantar group drew its membership, however, primarily from east and north Bengal, areas which were absorbed into East Pakistan as a result of partition, and shortly after independence a number of the Jugantar supporters (including Kiron Shankar Roy himself) opted for East Pakistan.

Independence thus ushered in a serious political crisis in West Bengal. The urban coalition that had dominated the Congress until the expulsion of Bose in 1939 no longer existed; a number of the Congress supporters had followed Bose out of the Congress and joined the leftist parties; a number of Congress strongholds had been cut off by partition, and the party faced the prospect of contesting elections in an area where a Muslim Ministry had been in power before independence. With no single group in control of either the Assembly or the Bengal PCC, the Congress high command stepped in and gave its support to Prafulla Ghosh, a member of the Congress Working Committee and an ardent

[40] The conflict between Bose and the central Congress party is dealt with in some detail in Michael Brecher, *Nehru: A Political Biography* (London: Oxford University Press, 1959), pp. 133 f., 142 ff., 245 ff.

supporter of Gandhism. But Ghosh also lacked support within West Bengal. He was the leader of a Gandhian group centered in the Abhoy Ashram at Comilla (in East Bengal) and without a large following his support dwindled. The Assembly party did not support him, and Congress members soon began agitating for a new leader, forcing him to resign.

The instigation for the present Congress organization in West Bengal therefore came from the state itself and not from the center.[41] In January 1948, the Congress members of the Legislative Assembly threw their support to Bidhan Chandra Roy, a respected West Bengali, and Roy quickly turned for support to the organized groups and factions centered in West Bengal, notably the Arambagh group of Prafulla Sen and the Hooghly group, which derived its strength from the area north and west of Calcutta. Sen was appointed to a ministry in the Roy government, and members of the Hooghly group were likewise placed in a number of ministerial posts. Several important ministries were either kept in Roy's hands or turned over to his supporters not associated with any of the Congress factions. Several ministers, for example, had almost no record of participation in the nationalist movement. Of no small importance to Roy's survival was the capacity of the Hooghly group and of Roy to win the financial backing of Calcutta businessmen as well as the tacit approval of Sardar Patel and of Nehru in New Delhi.

The coalition which B. C. Roy effected in 1948 has remained remarkably stable. Factions persist, and influential individuals have broken with the Congress party organizations, but thus far no one, either from inside the party or from without, has been able to challenge the dominant position of the Congress. The driving force of the organization at present is Atulya Ghosh, who was originally elected General-Secretary of the PCC in 1948 and who was able to cement his hold on the party organization during the thirteen years that B. C. Roy was Chief Minister. Largely because of Roy's wish to remain aloof from the day-to-day affairs of politics, Ghosh was left free to organize the state along his own lines, generally with the backing of the Chief Minister. As a result of his long and intense involvement in party affairs, Ghosh is now the only man in the entire state who has knowledge of, and access to, virtually all party matters. Moreover, the present Chief Minister, Prafulla Sen, is a friend of long standing who is in basic agreement with Ghosh on most issues. And Sen, like Roy, also operates in such a way as to leave Ghosh free to manage party affairs. It should also be mentioned that Ghosh has

[41] K. P. Thomas, *Dr. B. C. Roy* (Calcutta: West Bengal Pradesh Congress Committee, 1955), p. 225.

gained a great deal of respect within West Bengal from his increasing importance in the Congress party at the all-India level.

Considering the state of disrepair in which the Congress party found itself immediately after independence, its success at the polls has been almost startling. It has won all three general elections, in each case winning more than 60 per cent of the seats in both the Legislative Assembly and the Lok Sabha. Moreover, the number of seats it has held in the Legislative Assembly has been steadily increasing (see Table 6.2) while the percentage of the vote that it has been able to gain has jumped from 38.9 per cent in 1952 to 46.1 per cent in 1957, and to 47.3 per cent in 1962.

Figures in Table 6.2 indicate the extent to which the Communist and leftist parties have come to dominate the opposition in West Bengal. Like the Congress, the Communist party (CPI) has also steadily increased the number of seats it holds in the Legislative Assembly. Similarly, the percentage of the vote it has received has constantly risen, from 10.8 per cent for its Legislative Assembly candidates in 1952 to 17.8 per cent in 1957 to 25.2 per cent in 1962. Moreover, the Communist party has been able to unite, at least for electoral purposes, with other leftist groups to form leftist electoral fronts which have increased the electoral efficiency of the Opposition. In 1952 the Communist-dominated leftist front (which included the CPI, the Revolutionary Socialist party, the

TABLE 6.2

SEATS WON IN WEST BENGAL, 1952-62[a]

Party	*Legislative Assembly* 1952	1957	1962	*Lok Sabha* 1952	1957	1962
Congress	150	152	157	24	23	23
Communist	28	46	50	5	6	8
Forward Bloc (M)	14	8	13	2	2	1
PSP[b]	15	21	5	0	2	0
Jan Sangh	9	0	0	2	0	0
Hindu Mahasabha (HM)	4	0	0	0	0	0
Independents	18	25	26	1	3	3
Totals	238	252	251	34	36	35[c]

[a] Figures for the 1952 and 1957 elections are taken from the reports of the Election Commission; Figures for 1962 are taken from *India: A Reference Annual, 1962* (New Delhi: Publications Division, Ministry of Information and Broadcasting, 1962).

[b] The Praja Socialist party was not founded until 1953. Thus figures for 1952 are those of the Krishak Praja Mazdoor party which eventually merged with the KMPP and the Socialist parties at the national level to form the Praja Socialist party.

[c] There were 36 Lok Sabha seats filled in 1962; one was won by the Revolutionary Socialist party.

Marxist Forward Bloc, the Socialist Republican party and the Bolshevik party) won 42 seats and gained 27.5 per cent of the vote for the Legislative Assembly. In 1957 the leftist front (which was called the United Left Election Committee in that year) consisted of essentially the same groups with the addition of the Praja Socialist party, and its percentage of the vote increased to 36.8 per cent while the number of seats it gained also rose (to 75). In 1962 the leftist coalition was known as the United Left Front, and the Praja Socialists now remained outside the coalition (largely over the China issue) with the result that the percentage of the leftist vote declined slightly (to 36.1 per cent) while the number of seats it won declined considerably (to 63).

The Communist party of Bengal has its origins in the Indian terrorist movement and the Marxist influence which emanated from the British universities in the 1920s and 1930s. The earliest Bengali Communists —Virendranath Chattopadhyay, Bhupendra Nath Dutta, Abani Mukherjee, and M. N. Roy—were terrorists who had either been forced to emigrate by British security measures, or who had gone abroad to secure weapons for future terrorist activities. Once outside the country they were attracted to Marxist revolutionary groups or to the Comintern—in Mexico, in Germany, in Moscow and other centers—by the similarity of their interest in freeing India with the advocacy of these same objectives by Communist groups. Later, in the 1920s and 1930s, they were joined by intellectuals who had been attracted to Marxism at Oxford or Cambridge—Jyoti Basu, Renu Chakrabarty, Rajani Palme Dutt, Hirendra Nath Mukherjee, and others—or by young men in Bengal who had come into contact with Bengali Marxists who had returned. Muzzafar Ahmed imbibed Marxist teachings from Indians returning from Tashkent in the early 1920s; Ajoy Ghosh became interested when he came in contact with Indian Marxists in the trade union movement; and Ranen Sen and Somnath Lahiri were attracted as students of Indian Marxists at Calcutta University.[42]

The Communist party of India became a formal organization in 1924, but it remained a small band of revolutionaries until the middle 1930s, being opposed to the Indian National Congress and the mainstream of the nationalist movement. In 1934 the party was banned by the government of India for its revolutionary activities, although later in the decade it joined with the Congress Socialists in a popular front. Being allied with the Congress, the CPI first opposed the Second World

42 Biographies of leading Communists in India, including many Bengalis, have been collected in Gene D. Overstreet and Marshall Windmiller, *Communism in India* (Bombay: Perennial Press, 1960), pp. 555-79.

War as imperialist, but completely switched its policy within the first year of the war when the Japanese began to make advances in Southeast Asia. By supporting the war effort, the Communists gained the favor of the British, who immediately lifted the ban on the party, but at the same time they alienated themselves from the Congress, which was at the time opposing war and engaged in a "Quit India" movement. At the end of the war the Congress expelled the Communists from the coalition they had effected in the 1930s, on the ground that the Communists had violated Congress policy.

With the coming of independence in 1947, the CPI, which had always been revolutionary, was faced with the necessity of formulating a program that would allow it to survive in a parliamentary system. The first reaction among most Communists in West Bengal was to continue with a policy of violence in an attempt to create a revolution.[43] Numerous instances of bank robberies, train robberies, bomb and acid-bulb attacks at public meetings, looting, destruction of factory equipment, and murders of police, rival labor organizers and other enemies were attributed to the activities of the CPI in Bengal immediately after independence.[44] As a result of these activities, the government of West Bengal banned the party in March 1948, suppressed the party newspaper in West Bengal, and arrested a number of Bengali Communist leaders.

Since their release in 1951, one section of the CPI has been attempting to move farther and farther away from revolutionary violence (at least so far as the public image is concerned). The Central Executive Committee of the party was in fact pleasingly surprised with its showing in West Bengal in the 1952 elections, and since that time the pro-central CPI faction in West Bengal has offered itself as an "alternative government" in both the 1957 and 1962 elections. The decision of the national party at its Amritsar session (in 1958) to accept constitutionalism as the means to attain democracy and socialism was in fact brought about by the prospects of being able to win elections in West Bengal, as well as in Kerala and other states. At the same time the CPI has been faced with a number of problems in West Bengal, some indigenous to the state, some resulting from conditions in the national and international party. Electorally, the Communists have failed to create a class struggle in the countryside and their votes in rural areas have suffered as a result. Like

[43] The Bengal Provincial Committee of the CPI, for example, issued a circular calling upon the Indian Army to "turn your guns and bayonets and fire upon the Congress fascists" and "fraternize with the revolutionary laborers in the factories and the students in the streets." See *ibid.*, p. 279.

[44] *Communist Violence in India* (New Delhi: Ministry of Home Affairs, Government of India, 1949), pp. 3-7.

all Communist state parties in India, it has suffered from a lack of funds, and in fact has been placed in some extremely embarrassing positions because of the necessity to raise large amounts of money in order to contest elections.[45] The party has also suffered, like the CPI elsewhere in India, from the lack of a clear and unambiguous connection with the Communist movement in Moscow and Peking, and, as a result of this and other factors, has been prone to intense factionalism. The revolt of the majority of the party in West Bengal against the decision of the National Council of the CPI to support India in the face of Chinese aggression was in fact one of the most significant and large-scale violations of discipline in the party's history.

The Chinese aggression in 1962 created serious disunity within the CPI in West Bengal. The majority of the West Bengal unit voted against the National Council resolution, but two powerful district committees (Calcutta, led by Jolly Kaul, and Midnapur, led by Biswanath Mukherjee) endorsed it. The State Council of the party was thus disbanded; over one hundred Communists from West Bengal were imprisoned; and the State Council's powers and functions were delegated by the CPI central executive to a seven-member "Provincial Organizing Committee (POC)." The POC, run by the pro-Dange (or pro-central) wing of the party, functioned throughout 1963. But in early 1964 the pro-Peking leaders of the CPI were released from jail and immediately held a meeting to re-establish the State Council under their dominance. At this point the Rightists (pro-Dange faction) walked out, and the Leftists (pro-Peking) became divided among themselves. One section of the Leftists, led by Jyoti Basu, was in favor of some form of compromise with the Rightists, in an attempt to prevent a schism. But the stronger Leftist faction, led by Harekrishna Konar, was not favorable to a compromise and immediately branded Basu and his group as Centrists.[46] Since 1964, then, the Communist party in West Bengal has been seriously divided, and has shared in the intense factionalism that has characterized the party at the national level.[47]

In addition to the Communist party, there are a number of other Marxist-left parties in West Bengal, parties which claim to be Marxist

45 Some of the monetary problems of the CPI in West Bengal are traced out in N. C. Bhattacharya, "Leadership Problems in the Communist Party of India; With Special Reference to West Bengal." Paper prepared for the International Political Science Association Convention, Bombay, January 1964 (mimeographed), p. 9.

46 *The Statesman* (Calcutta), February 4, 1964.

47 See Ralph Retzlaff, "Revisionism and Dogmatism in the Communist Party of India," in *The Communist Revolution in Asia: Tactics, Goals, and Achievements*, ed. Robert A. Scalapino (Englewood Cliffs: Prentice-Hall, 1965), pp. 309-42.

or socialist but which are organizationally separate from the Communist and Socialist parties. Although they supported the Congress party prior to independence, they have all since defected, and can now either trace a long history, tradition, and organization of their own, or are factions which broke away from the older and larger leftist parties.[48] A number of factors are responsible for the growth of these parties in Bengal. Because of the intensity and duration of the Western impact, a large number of Bengalis became discontented with traditional forms of social organization quite early in the history of British India. The tendency for these people to refuse adherence to the rigors of both caste and family was encouraged by a tradition of religious unorthodoxy in Bengal,[49] and by the teachings of Bengali religious leaders who were attempting to effect some "synthesis" of East and West at the turn of the century.[50] The forerunners of the present Marxist-left parties

[48] The four largest Marxist-left parties are also the four oldest: the Revolutionary Socialist party (RSP) arose out of the Anushilan terrorist organization, which changed its name in 1930 to the Hindustan Republican Army, then to the Hindustan Republican Socialist Army, and finally in 1938, to the Revolutionary Socialist party. The Revolutionary Communist party of India (RCPI) was founded in 1934 by Saumyendranath Tagore, the grandnephew of the great poet, when he broke with the CPI. The Bolshevik party of India had as its predecessor a group called the Bengal Labour party, created in 1933 by N. Dutt Mazumdar, a young Bengali who had been deeply impressed by Marxist ideas as a student at the London School of Economics. The Forward Bloc, the largest of the Marxist-left parties, was founded in 1939 by Subhas Bose in an attempt to unite all leftist groups in Congress against the Congress party policy of the day. For a detailed description of the Marxist-left parties in Bengal, see Myron Weiner, *Party Politics in India* (Princeton: Princeton University Press, 1957), pp. 117-38.

[49] Because of the willingness of Bengalis to subscribe to Westernized education, for example, a fairly large network of Anglo-vernacular schools, maintained by private subscriptions, had sprung up in a large number of towns and villages in Bengal around the turn of the century. This network of schools, not found in other provinces until much later, was mentioned by the Sedition Committee of 1918 as one source for the spread of ideas which led to the terrorist movement in Bengal. See *Sedition Committee Report* (Calcutta: Bengal Secretariat Press, 1918), p. 15.

[50] The synthesis of Swami Vivekananda advocated a "European society with India's religion"; the synthesis of Bankim Chandra Chatterjee attempted to explain Puranic religion and culture by means of European logic, philosophy and history; and the synthesis of Aurobindo Ghose attempted to combine Western forms of social organization with the "beautiful and sweet and gracious" spiritualism of Hindu life. See the foreword by Sankar Roy Chaudhuri in Bankim Chandra Chatterjee, *Anandamath*, translated by Aurobindo Ghose and Barinda Kumar Ghosh (Calcutta: Basumati Sahitya Mandir, n.d., pp. i-xii). The terrorist movement and the leftist parties which resulted from it were clearly linked to these religious movements. The terrorists justified their use of violence by reference to the works of these three leaders. They adopted the aims and forms of revolutionary organization advocated by Chatterjee and Ghose. And, although the terrorist organizations were formed after the death of Swami Vivekananda, they were actively supported by Vivekananda's main

in Bengal were a large number of small social groups, scattered throughout Calcutta and other large towns and cities—groups of writers, artists, students, and teachers, or just groups of friends who came from the same ancestral village or the same school or neighborhood—composed of people who had common ideas about life and who were deeply affected by the attempts at a cultural synthesis on the part of Bengali reformers. Social intercourse among these groups was very limited and there was little active recruitment, yet within the groups, warm, affectionate, and genuinely intimate relationships developed.

It was from among these groups that the Marxist-left parties developed. The fact that these social groups turned to politics stems both from the nature of their education and training and from the economic and cultural dislocations which severely affected the Bengali middle class in the twentieth century. The rise of these social groups coincided with the rise of educated unemployment in and around Calcutta at the turn of the century, and with the partition of the province of Bengal in 1906. Bengali intellectuals and a large number of the middle class turned to revolutionary and terrorist activities, and two of these early revolutionary organizations—the Jugantar and the Anushilan Samiti—laid the groundwork for the later left-wing parties. Leftism was encouraged in Bengal during this century by economic and cultural dislocations of a magnitude not found in other areas of the subcontinent. The capital of British India was shifted from Calcutta in 1911; business in Calcutta became increasingly dominated by non-Bengali Indians and British industrialists; the leadership of the nationalist movement shifted from Bengal to the Hindi-speaking Brahmanic heartland; the dominance of the Bengalis in the Indian Civil Service receded as other areas gained in higher education; educated unemployment continued to grow in Bengal, and finally in the 1940s Bengal witnessed in rapid succession the famine, the activities of war, partition, communal riots, a trade war between East and West Bengal, and the influx of millions of refugees.

In this atmosphere, Communism and Marxism had an ever greater appeal. Marxism promised a modern society in which the intellectual would have a more prominent position; it appealed to intellectual classes because it denied the usefulness of *banyas* (traders) and merchants; it promised the overthrow of the hated British and the anglicized ruling and commercial groups who were guided by their ideas. It promised the liberation of colored men from white men, who were equated with capi-

---

followers—Swami Saradananda and Sister Nivedita—and by Vivekananda's brother, Bhupendranath Dutta. See Nemai Sadhan Bose, *The Indian Awakening and Bengal* (Calcutta: Firma K. L. Mukhopadhyay, 1960), pp. 190 ff.

talists and foreigners; and it derogated those who clung to orthodox Hindu ideas and behavior. A number of the small, closed social groups that had sprung up in Bengal turned to Marxist doctrines and Marxist forms of group organization during the 1920s and 1930s. Attracted by the possibility of winning mass support they first supported the Congress party, rallying behind Subhas Bose and the Bengali wing of the party. Though Marxist in orientation, they developed separately from the CPI when it failed to give complete support to Bose in his quarrel with the Gandhian center. Similarly, the leftist parties broke with the Congress left-wing when the Congress Socialist party failed to give complete support to Bose between 1938 and 1940. When Bose left the Congress in 1939, the Marxist-left parties of Bengal followed him out, and ultimately dissolved into their constituent parts.

Despite the fact that these parties are now organizationally separate, they have a number of points in common, and they cooperate with one another on certain occasions in a way that they do not cooperate with the Congress or communal parties. They all claim to be socialist: they advocate nationalization of industry, confiscation of land without compensation and land to the tillers, withdrawal from the Commonwealth, confiscation of foreign capital, planning, and government welfare programs. Without exception they do not accept Gandhi's principle of non-violence; in fact, they have a positive attraction to, almost a fascination for, militancy and violence. All of the Marxist-left parties claim to be "revolutionary" and to reject the principles of parliamentary democracy. They do not, therefore, measure their strength or their prospects by electoral results, but rather by their ability to lead mass demonstrations, rallies, boycotts, and processions.[51] Although they partici-

[51] The differences that develop between these parties point to the highly personal and ideological interests of these groups, a factor that keeps them organizationally separate. "The Revolutionary Socialist Party leaders, for example, feel that the Bolshevik Party, the Socialist Unity Center (which broke off from the RSP), and the two wings of the Forward Bloc either have large pro-Communist groups or are actually pro-Stalinist parties. The RCPI, they feel, is a highly sectarian party and Saumyen Tagore, its leader, a very difficult person to work with for personal reasons. On the other hand Saumyen Tagore criticizes the RSP and other leftist groups for their willingness to work in united fronts with the Communists. In contrast he justifiably points to his record of unwillingness to collaborate with the Communists. The Bolshevik Party feels that it has 'systematically and correctly followed the paths of Marx, Engels, Lenin and Stalin by upholding the banner of . . . socialism and by trying to consolidate the leadership of the working class in the Indian political movement.' The Bolshevik leaders declare that theirs is a national communist party, and that neither the CPI nor other leftist parties are true working class parties with a working class, trade union composition like that of the Bolshevik Party." Weiner, *Party Politics in India*, p. 187.

pate in elections, they tend to view the electoral process only as an opportunity for building mass strength, or for registering social protest, but not as a means for bringing about a social transformation. Only one of these parties, the Marxist Forward Bloc, has had any degree of success in winning seats in the Legislative Assembly.

Aside from the Congress party and the Communist and Leftist opposition, other political parties are of fairly recent origin in Bengal and have not fared well. The Praja Socialist party had its origin in West Bengal when in 1948 Prafulla Ghosh resigned from the Congress party shortly after he had resigned as Chief Minister. Taking 100 Congressmen with him, Ghosh formed the Krishak Praja Mazdoor party (Peasants, People's and Worker's Party), which eventually combined with the KMPP and the Socialists to form the Praja Socialist party (PSP) at the national level. But the position of the Socialists in West Bengal, never solid, has been constantly dwindling: in 1952 the Socialist party and the KMPP combined won 15 seats in the Legislative Assembly with 11.9 per cent of the vote; in 1957 the PSP won 21 seats with 9.5 per cent of the vote; and in 1962 the PSP won only 5 seats with only 5 per cent of the vote. The Socialists' weakness has resulted from their growing emphasis on Gandhism, a reactionary outlook in the minds of most middle-class Bengalis. Some idea of the extent to which the PSP has declined in West Bengal can be gained from the fact that two of their senior leaders, Atindra Nath Bose and Suresh Banerjee, died in 1962, while three other major PSP figures left the party. In fact the PSP was in such a state of disrepair in 1962 that it failed to even contest many of the constituencies that it had won in 1957.

The other major all-India parties have fared no better. The Jan Sangh did win 9 seats in the Legislative Assembly in 1952, and the Hindu Mahasabha four. But since then neither of them has been able to win any seats in the state of West Bengal. The Jan Sangh vote declined from 6.1 per cent in 1952 to less than one per cent in 1957, and the Hindu Mahasabha vote from 2.8 per cent to less than one-half of one per cent. Some idea of what happened to the communal parties can be gained from the fact that Congress increased its vote from 38.9 per cent in 1952 to 46.1 per cent in 1957, an increase of 7 per cent, while the percentage of the vote which the communal parties drew declined by almost the same amount. Moreover, Congress increases in 1957 were highest in those areas where the Jan Sangh and the Hindu Mahasabha had been highest in 1952 but had slipped in 1957.[52] It would thus appear that no

52 Asok Mitra, "West Bengal Elections," *The Economic Weekly* (Bombay), XIV, Nos. 4–6 (February 1962), p. 156.

one in West Bengal was sufficiently concerned with the issues raised by the communal parties to vote for them in the face of the opportunity for securing benefits from the Congress. The reasons for a lack of appeal of the communal parties in West Bengal again stems from the history of the province. The defense of Hinduism in Bengal largely centers around the teachings of Ramakrishna Paramahimsa, and Swami Vivekananda, which was as much a revolt against Hindu orthodoxy as it was against Western ideals. The Hindu Mahasabha, which adheres to orthodox ideals (and which also advocates Hindi as the national language), was thus unacceptable to most Bengalis. The Jan Sangh, which was founded by a Bengali (Shyama Prasad Mookerjee), had more of an appeal while its founder was alive, and did manage to gain a fairly large percentage of the vote in 1952. But with the death of Mookerjee in 1954, and with the increased emphasis which the Jan Sangh places on the adoption of Hindi as the national language, the party has had little appeal for Bengalis.

Political Leadership

Despite the existence of different parties and the real differences between those parties, politics in West Bengal continues to be the preserve of the very limited number of people who dominate the social structure. Few of the state's political leaders, across the party spectrum, are non-Bengalis. Fewer still come from the lower classes, from among those people who have done manual work. In a study conducted in 1957-58,[53] Weiner gathered background data on 408 political leaders in West Bengal, drawn from all parties. Of these, only six had ever done manual work (all peasants, there were no factory laborers). Of the others, the largest category by far (169) were those who could afford to be full-time political workers, devoting all their time to trade union organization, social work or other public activities, while the rest, in descending order of frequency, were landowners, lawyers, teachers, businessmen, doctors, and journalists. Few of the politicians in Weiner's sample lacked formal education, and 76.3 per cent had been to college or beyond. Nearly half (46 per cent) of the sample came from the three high castes of Bengal—Brahmans, Kayasthas, and Vaidyas—and the majority (58.5 per cent) were born between 1900 and 1920. It would thus appear that politics in West Bengal continues to be dominated by the upper and middle classes—by the wealthy, by the upper castes, by those with education, by those who entered politics during the nationalist movement.

[53] Myron Weiner, "Changing Patterns of Political Leadership in West Bengal," in *Political Change in South Asia* (Calcutta: Firma K. L. Mukhopadhyay, 1963), pp. 177-227.

Within this limited range, however, there are important differences in the social backgrounds of political party leaders in West Bengal. The most striking difference between the parties is in age: a substantial majority (60 per cent) of the Congressmen in Weiner's sample were born before 1910 (making them at least in their fifties), while the bulk (73 per cent) of the Communists and leftists were born after 1910. Some members of the leftist parties argue that the youth of its leadership indicates a tendency on the part of the younger generation to support the leftists, and some look forward to an eventual large-scale shift from the Congress party to the left. Although no detailed study of political recruitment practices in present-day Bengal has been conducted, there is evidence which would indicate that such a shift is not likely to occur in the near future. While the Congress party leaders are presently older than other party leaders, the Congress has been more successful than other parties in appealing to the rising rural leadership and to low-status group leaders.[54] The rise of this new leadership, which is younger than the present leadership, has not yet been adequately reflected in the executive committees of parties or in party front groups, but it is gaining in prominence in the Legislative Assembly and in Parliament, and is likely to be an important source of political recruitment in the future. The age difference between the leadership of the leftist parties and the Congress party at present would thus appear to stem largely from the fact that the leftists recruited their present leadership in the late 1930s when the younger elements of the Congress party turned against the conservative wing of the party and advocated a more militant line against the British, while the greatest period of recruitment for the Congress came in the early 1920s, when Gandhi launched his first civil disobedience movement, and again in the 1930s when the second nonviolent movement occurred.

Weiner's study also indicates the extent to which the Congress leadership is representative of those who dominate the social structure in West Bengal—the older, well-established, "solid citizens"—while the Communists and Marxist-left parties draw their strength largely from those who have been alienated from the community. Most Congressmen (77 per cent of Weiner's sample) are employed members of their localities, in a wide variety of occupations, carrying on political work on a part-time basis, much as do political workers in American or British political parties. In contrast, 68 per cent of the Communists and 78 per cent of the Marxist-leftists in Weiner's sample were full-time professional revolutionaries, devoting all of their energies to political work. While

[54] *Ibid.*, pp. 209-27.

32 per cent of the Congressmen were in business and commerce, or were landlords, only 3.3 per cent of the Communists and only 7.3 per cent of the Marxist-leftists fell into one of these three categories. In addition, the vast majority of Congressmen are deeply involved in local government, local civic activities, and various caste, religious and tribal bodies. They are active in school boards, village panchayats, charitable organizations, tribal and untouchable organizations, Muslim associations, temple boards, and a host of other bodies in their community. In Weiner's sample, for example, 103 (61 per cent) of the 167 Congressmen for whom information was available were active in local government, while only 9 out of the 100 Communists and Marxist-leftists were involved in such activities. Eighty-four (50 per cent) of the 167 Congressmen were involved in civic activities, while again only 9 of the 100 Communists and Marxist-leftists were so involved. Whereas 29 of the Congressmen were members of a caste, religious or tribal association, none of the Communists and only two Marxist-leftists were members of such organizations. These bodies, public and private, are the structure of power and influence in India, especially in the rural areas, and it is in these that the Congress party demonstrates so clearly the source of its voting power in West Bengal.

While the Congress dominates in civic activities and bodies which undertake "constructive work," the Communists and Marxist-leftists are represented in organizations intended to intensify "class conflict": trade unions, peasant organizations, student groups, and refugee organizations. Thus far, however, the groups in which the Congress party predominates have been the best established, in terms of income, occupation, community leadership, and in some cases caste, and few individuals active in class conflict organizations have been elected to public office. It would thus appear that any changes in the character of the present party alignment would depend largely on the ability of the Communist and Marxist-left parties to either (1) adapt to the existing social structure and entrench itself in "constructive" bodies; or (2) to increase significantly its ability to promote class conflict and to create class organizations strong enough to function as a base for gaining electoral victories. Failing either of these developments, the Congress is likely to continue in power, and its leadership is likely to become increasingly dominated by those well entrenched in the rural areas.

Strategies and Techniques of Political Action

The ability of the opposition parties to adopt an electoral strategy based only on class conflict and class organizations is extremely unlikely, however, in view of the nature of the social system and the economy. Because the social system is hierarchically structured, and because the willingness and ability of some groups to engage in social conflict is both spatially and socially limited, people in the higher levels of the local stratification systems are able to wield political power and influence far out of proportion to their numbers. Tenants and sharecroppers are almost entirely dependent on landowners for their livelihood; small tradesmen control the supply of credit which often determines who shall have money for seeds and whose land may be taken away in default of payment; petty officials such as the *patwaris* (official keepers of land records) or land-settlement officers determine how official documents will record the ownership of land plots; managers of *bustees* or *dhobi khannas* in Calcutta determine rent-rates and have the power to evict tenants; and many others exercise a similar kind of control over the public and private facilities and services upon which large numbers of people depend for their livelihood. Moreover, economic power is often reinforced by other factors in the social system. Especially in the rural areas, some men have influence over large numbers of people because they are members of a leading caste in their locality, or because they occupy hereditary positions of authority within their castes.[55] The *sirdar* of a factory gang of Calcutta maintains authority over almost all spheres of the lives of those under his charge, an authority which derives largely from his place in a village social structure. A large measure of influence may also rest in men who are highly respected in their community: leaders of tribal and untouchable associations; members of the Bengali middle class who are deferred to because of their cultural attainments, or the cultural attainments of their family; leaders of the *para* (neighborhood) organizations who organize and provide funds for neighborhood *pujas* (religious festivals); and patrons of literature and the arts who provide facilities and funds for dramas and cultural events.

Because these men hold positions in which they control the economic fortunes of a large sector of the local population, or because their positions of authority and respect command deference from a large number of people, they have become exceedingly important politically. As mentioned above, it is men drawn from influential social positions who dominate the leadership of all political parties. And, during the

55 The political importance of caste in West Bengal's villages has been documented in a number of studies. See especially Ralph W. Nicholas, "Village Factions and Political Parties in Rural West Bengal," *Journal of Commonwealth Political Studies*, Vol. II, No. 1 (November 1963), 17-31; see also Prabodh Kumar Bhowmick, "Caste and Service in a Bengali Village," *Man in India*, Vol. XLIII, No. 4 (October-December 1963), 277-327.

election campaigns, it is these "key men"[56] who are the cogs that drive the electoral organization of all political parties. To be sure, political parties do attempt to appeal to people who do not occupy influential positions in the existing social structure: the Communist and Marxist-left parties depend on the members of their trade unions and peasant organizations for votes; campaign literature and speeches are filled with slogans and generalities which promise benefits for the non-influential masses; party leaders do canvass door-to-door for votes and offer services and material goods in exchange for votes. But all of these tactics are pursued through the "key men" in the constituencies, who are in turn tied to the political party largely on the basis of a series of *ad hoc* arrangements. The success of a political party in the elections is thus largely determined by the inducements, ranging from offers of ministries to outright bribes, which it can offer to either attract or retain these "key men."

In this atmosphere, the Congress party has had a distinct advantage. As the party most closely linked with the nationalist movement, it could initially draw on an immense amount of prestige and glory to attract local leaders and influential solid citizens. In addition, it also had a widespread organization intact when independence came. Although a number of the urban supporters of the party had broken with the Congress in the 1940s, the party could still find influential people in almost every locality of West Bengal who had organized non-violent protest movements or who were social workers who had long been linked with the Congress cause.

Being the party in power also gave the Congress a lever of patronage which, in West Bengal, it has used with increasing skill.[57] The Con-

[56] This is the phrase coined by Rajni Kothari, "Some Problems of Articulation in Indian Politics," paper prepared for the International Political Science Association Convention, Bombay, January 1964, mimeographed, p. 2. It is also used by Nicholas in "Village Factions and Political Parties in Rural West Bengal," p. 10.

[57] The identification of the Congress with the government was especially crucial in winning the support of certain "key men" at the beginning of Congress rule. As Nicholas has observed: "For the village headmen the transition to Independence was a very smooth one; there was no break in the continuity of their relations with rural administrative officers. . . . The local bureaucracy was still in the service of the Government, as the headmen saw it, but now the Government of the Congress rather than of the British. The headmen supported the bureaucracy in the expectation of achieving a favoured position, and it did not matter to them whether the bureaucracy supported the British or the Congress. As soon as it was seen that (a) the Block Development Officer encouraged Congress supporters (with an eye towards promotion), and (b) that he had development funds to distribute to individual villages, the headmen cheerfully indulged him by bringing their supporters into the Congress camp." Nicholas, "Village Factions and Political Parties in Rural West Bengal," pp. 27-28.

gress patronage machine operates in a variety of ways. At one level it attracts men who are already influential in their localities, and men who can sway large portions of the electorate. To them it offers administrative rewards, influence with ministers, seats in Parliament or the Assembly, or perhaps even a ministry. At the same time the Congress acts to enhance or maintain the prestige which a Congressman already has in his locality, thus making him even more powerful in winning or influencing votes. Congress attracts funds from businessmen in Calcutta because it is the party in power, and it uses these funds to run its widespread organization. Although there is a statutory limit on contributions to party funds, the enforcement of the limit is by no means effective; and, in addition, the Congress collects money from wealthy people in the city for its relief campaigns (money which is not legally considered a political contribution) and parcels it out through influential Congressmen in the localities of both the rural and urban areas. In periods of famine and flood, or after a riot in Calcutta, the Congress thus often takes on the character of a relief organization in the localities affected. Finally, of course, Congress personnel have jobs to distribute, from peons to office secretaries, and they have a great deal of influence in the administration—in schools and colleges, and in private and public business concerns—which they can use to the benefit of their supporters.

The Communists and leftists also base their electoral strategies partly on the attempt to work within the existing social structure, but in this endeavor they are at a distinct disadvantage. Because they have always been relatively small revolutionary groups, they developed no widespread organization which they could use for electoral purposes. In 1952 the Communist party could run only 79 candidates while Congress contested all of the 238 seats. In 1957, the CPI in West Bengal ran fewer Assembly candidates (100) than the number of *incumbent* Congress Assemblymen (104) that ran in that year. Even in 1962 when the Communists were able to run 145 candidates, they offered fewer candidates than the number of Congressmen in the Assembly at any given time. The Communists and leftists can still boast of, and attract, some leading individuals in a number of localities, but these are confined almost entirely to the urban areas, and certainly to a much smaller number of constituencies than the Congress. In addition, the Communists and leftists lack the funds and patronage necessary to improve their electoral organization and their electoral position. In fact, when a Communist or leftist wants to get something done in West Bengal—if he wants a theater permit or funds for a cultural event, or a recommendation for his son to be admitted to a college—he will frequently have to call on a local Congressman for support and assistance.

The Communist and Marxist-left parties are also hampered in electoral skirmishes by the commitment of their members to ideological positions and by factional loyalties. Especially in recent years a number of the leaders of these parties have been attempting to cultivate the leadership of various local bodies, such as credit societies, cooperatives, and village panchayats. The difficulty, however, is that other leftist party leaders and workers are more disposed to cultivate class struggles than such civic activities, and the differences between leaders on this issue often lead only to factionalism and disunity. Moreover, as a result of its adherence to the Communist party line laid down in Moscow or in Peking, the CPI has taken a number of unpopular positions in West Bengal, which have seriously hampered its ability to attract some leading citizens: it supported the British war effort during the "Quit India" movement; it was in constant opposition to Subhas Bose; and it supported the Muslim League before independence, as well as the proposal to partition Bengal. Recently, the failure of the majority of the CPI in West Bengal to support the Indian government in the face of Chinese attacks on India resulted in the defeat of the party in six by-election races, and the loss of two CPI municipal strongholds.[58]

Although the opposition parties in West Bengal have thus far been unable to achieve a position which would present an electoral challenge to the Congress party, the importance of these parties for the political process is nevertheless considerable. The strength of the major opposition parties—the Communist and Marxist-left—in fact rests on their success in pursuing two non-electoral political strategies, one of which is "revolutionary" and the other, "influence through protest." The Communist party especially has been highly successful in initiating, or taking advantage of, processions, hartals, strikes, boycotts, and, on numerous occasions, riots and violence. By the adoption and support of these methods of political action, the CPI is sometimes consciously attempting to foster a "revolutionary spirit" among the people, and to increase the commitment of large sectors of the population to these methods.[59] Similarly, both the Communists and the Marxist-leftists have made frequent use of the legislature—particularly the question hour, adjournment motions and budget debates—to reveal instances of corruption and inefficiency on the part of the government, and at least in some cases to undermine the legitimacy of the present regime. At the same time,

[58] *The Statesman* (Calcutta), February 24, 1964.

[59] Based on interviews with CPI leaders in January 1964.

however, a number of the actions of the CPI, and almost all of the actions of the Marxist-left parties, are intended less for the promotion of a future revolution than simply to organize and give vent to the dissatisfaction of certain sections of the population who the leftists feel are inadequately represented in the electoral process.

The adoption of revolutionary and protest strategies has been in large part responsible for the success of the Communist and leftist groups in attracting a large section of the Bengali urban middle class.[60] Middle-class trade unions are the best organized of all trade unions in West Bengal, and have secured the greatest concessions from both government and private industry. Organized demonstrations have been the most violent and the most effective when they have involved Bengali middle-class students. And the Communist and leftist parties have gained their most sweeping electoral successes in areas of Calcutta populated for the most part by Bengali middle-class residents. The widespread support of revolutionary and protest strategies on the part of the urban middle class stems both from the weakness of this class in the electoral process and from the nature of political attitudes and inter-

60 The dependence of the Communist party on urban votes for its seats in the Legislative Assembly can be illustrated by the following table. It will be noticed that the CPI gained 75 per cent of its seats in 1952 from the seven most urban districts; 78 per cent of its seats in 1957 from these districts; and 70 per cent of its seats in 1962 from these districts, while the Congress has depended almost equally on the urban and the rural districts.

District	*% Urban Population 1951 Census*	*Congress Seats*			*Communist Seats*		
		1952	*1957*	*1962*	*1952*	*1957*	*1962*
Calcutta	100.0%	17	8	14	4	10	8
Howrah	32.41	8	5	9	2	4	2
24-Parganas	29.64	23	20	33	8	14	8
Hooghly	24.61	7	11	10	4	3	4
Darjeeling	21.22	1	1	2	1	2	1
Nadia	18.18	9	10	6	0	0	2
Burdwan	14.78	13	10	10	2	3	10
	Totals	78	65	84	23	36	35
Murshidabad	7.86	14	15	8	0	0	1
Midnapore	7.53	12	22	27	6	5	3
Cooch Behar	7.48	7	7	1	0	0	1
Jalpaiguri	7.23	9	7	7	0	1	0
Bankura	7.17	10	13	9	0	0	4
Purulia	6.71	–	4	6	–	0	0
Birbhum	6.47	8	5	4	0	3	2
West Dinajpur	.22	6	8	6	0	1	2
Malda	3.75	6	6	5	1	0	2
	Totals	72	87	73	7	10	15

ests of a large section of this class. The introduction of adult franchise after independence meant a shift of political power from the urban middle classes to other groups and communities throughout the state. Since the Congress party has come to depend on business finances and rural votes for its electoral success,[61] it has tended to undertake projects which benefit business and the rural areas, while it has avoided or postponed large-scale undertakings in Calcutta. Similarly, the distribution of educational, public health, and social welfare funds, has gone largely to people and communities who are numerically superior to the urban middle class.

Confronted by a situation in which they secure fewer benefits because they are outnumbered, a large portion of the urban middle class has been alienated from the electoral process.[62] The present state and central governments are viewed by these people as being representative of a less cultured, less refined group of people than those who governed in Bengali before independence, and certainly than those who should govern ideally.[63] The efforts of politicians to attract votes, to appeal to caste and communal ties during election campaigns, and to use patronage as a political weapon do not conform to their ideas of how a democracy should operate ideally or how it operates in some Western countries; and the electoral process is thus viewed as a sign of the "decadence" and of the "backwardness" of those in power.

The adoption by the Bengali middle class of a revolutionary or protest strategy also stems in large part from the attempt by some members of this class to preserve and extend what is viewed as a distinctive Bengali culture. The Bengalis consider their language to be the most highly developed of all of India's languages; Bengali literature, art, drama,

[61] In 1957, for example, the Congress party secured 75 per cent of its seats from rural constituencies. Sufficient data for an analysis of other elections was not available.

[62] In a recent study conducted by the author, a sample of 102 graduates, selected at random from 20 colleges in West Bengal, were interviewed in 1963. The purpose of the study was to determine those factors in the environment which would lead graduates to be either predisposed toward or opposed to what they perceive to be the structure of political authority in India. Although it would be impossible from such a small sample to determine the extent to which Bengali graduates have been alienated from the electoral process, it is significant that 36 of the 102 graduates interviewed indicated a predisposition to fundamentally alter the electoral process: 23 were in favor of abolishing elections entirely, and 13 were in favor of a restricted franchise, usually restricted on the basis of educational qualifications.

[63] This attitude is succinctly summarized in Flibbertigibbet, "The Euthanasia of English," *Economic Weekly* (Bombay), Vol. xv, No. 20 (May 18, 1963), 807. "As in so much else, what we are witnessing is the passing of power not from a few to the many but from an enlightened few to a slightly larger class uninhibited by those constraints on thought and behavior that come from a liberal, rational, humanistic education. If that is democracy, India has it."

and films are considered to be far superior to those of other regions; and Bengalis consider it evidence of the Bengali "genius" that Tagore has been the only Indian to win a Nobel prize, that Presidency College was once called "the Harvard of India," and that Gokhale once said, "What Bengal thinks today, India thinks tomorrow."[64] The Bengalis still attach great importance to cultural achievements and intellectual and educational attainments, and the majority of the middle-class families insist on activities and customs which are in keeping with the traditions of the *bhadralok* class. While trying to maintain their cultural superiority, however, the Bengali urban middle class has met with a high degree of frustration and hardship in recent years. Educated unemployment, common in India, has been augmented in West Bengal by the dislocations of the economy resulting from partition, and by the rapid expansion of the middle class in the past twenty years. The struggle for middle-class jobs, educational opportunities, and housing has become seriously acute since partition when the size of the middle class was considerably enlarged by the influx of refugees, and by the abolition of *zamindari* rights for 1.3 million intermediaries. Since independence, the economic position of the urban middle class has further deteriorated with the rising cost of living, and with the neglect of the mounting urban problems of Calcutta as a result of electoral realities. The shift of political power to the Hindi-speaking areas, and the cultural and social developments in those areas, has led to the adoption of a policy by the central government which favors the promotion of Hindi and a Hindi-speaking culture. And, at the same time, the dislocations of Bengal, combined with the heavy demand for education, has created an educational system far from adequate to maintain the level of cultural activities previously attained in Bengal.

A wide section of the urban middle class interprets these events in terms of almost conspiratorial activities on the part of the British government, the state and central governments, and the non-Bengali and foreign businessmen.[65] A significant portion of the urban middle class is

[64] A great number of Bengalis feel that Bengal's cultural "genius" is inherent in the Bengali people. Three "theories" which attempt to account for this "genius" are especially prevalent: one attributes it to the fertility of the land, which allowed Bengalis to spend more time on the luxuries of life; another attributes it to the climate, which encouraged the pursuit of leisure; and a third attributes it to the racial composition of the Bengali people.

[65] The following statement of the CPI, for example, is one with which many Bengalis would agree: ". . . the Council of Ministers of West Bengal . . . has foisted upon this state a blatant misrule, marked by cynical disregard of fundamental rights and vital interests of the citizens, by insatiable lust for power and party and personal gains, by deceit and dishonesty, by graft, and enormous corruption. The sole bene-

now fundamentally opposed to what they perceive to be the existing structure of political authority.[66] And at the same time, they have subscribed to an almost fanatical belief in the greatness of Bengal's past, and of the virtues of the heroic tradition in Bengal's politics. It is now widely believed that only a strong man, or a group of strong men, can deal with India's problems, that this man (or men) must possess certain definite characteristics which are highly valued in Bengali culture,[67] and that he (or they) must come to power under a regime which is fundamentally different from the one which presently exists.

Because of the widespread acceptance of such attitudes, a considerable portion of the Bengali middle class has refused to partake in electoral politics, or when they have joined in, have done so largely in the spirit of protest. The Communist and leftist parties have encouraged these attitudes and given expression to them by the tactics they use and by the policies they adopt. Moreover, a protest strategy in West Bengal has been encouraged by the success of that strategy in gaining concessions from government, and sometimes in initiating governmental action. Through the organization of violent and non-violent demonstrations (or sometimes only because of the threat of such organization), the leftist parties have succeeded in vetoing proposed legislation and administrative acts: they have successfully prevented proposals to merge Bihar and Bengal; to increase tram fares; to prohibit refugees from squatting on private property; and to increase college fees. Their actions in 1959-60 significantly affected the administrative procedures of the government in controlling the distribution of rice paddy and in rationing rice and other scarce essential commodities.[68] The threat of organized violence in

---

ficiaries of this misrule and corruption have been, of course, a handful of moneyed exploiters, Ministers and their favourites, the corrupt officials, and some careerists and self-seekers among their partymen." See *West Bengal Accuses*! A Memorandum Containing Charges Against the Congress Government in West Bengal Submitted to the President of the Indian Union by the West Bengal State Council of the Communist Party of India (New Delhi: Communist Party of India, 1959), pp. 1-2.

66 In the study by the author mentioned above, 38 of the 102 graduates interviewed were predisposed to a fundamental change in the regime, and 36 others were predisposed to changes which were less fundamental.

67 The most frequent terms used to describe this man (or men) are *kortabho parayan lok*, meaning "one who is devoted to his duty," or *kortomanus*, meaning a boss or influential person. As used with reference to political leaders these terms imply at least three things for Bengalis: (1) that the man (or men) so described would be willing to make great personal sacrifices; (2) that he (or they) would consider their position as one which imposes certain duties on him; and (3) that he (or they) would be willing to use any means (including force or violence) necessary to carry out his duties.

68 "Mass Food Agitation," *Economic Weekly* (Bombay), Vol. XII, No. 14 (April 2, 1960), 547, 550.

Calcutta has considerably influenced the willingness of the center to provide funds for the rehabilitation of Hindu refugees from East Pakistan; and at least in one case the Communists were successful in placing demands before the government which ultimately resulted in a reduction of the tax assessment on property owners.[69]

The Relationships between Parties and Groups

The different strategies which parties pursue and the different conceptions they have of the political process are most clearly reflected in the relationships they maintain with the important interest groups, and the ethnic and social groupings in the state. While the Congressman conceives of his role as that of a mediator, attempting to draw in "key men" from all groups and social classes, and creating an harmonious society therefrom, the Communists and leftists try to organize groups largely on a class basis. They attempt to promote class conflict, and make groups militantly conscious of class differences, in an effort to use them as instruments for winning power and, in some cases, for destroying the institutions of representative government.

In the trade union field, the Congress party encouraged its trade union section to create a new national federation, the Indian National Trade Union Congress (INTUC) when the older federation had been captured by the Communist party during the war. Once formed, INTUC became a staunch supporter of the basic program of the Indian government: it supported the government policy of compulsory arbitration in industrial disputes embodied in the Industrial Disputes Act of 1947, and it has been dedicated to the principle of avoiding strikes. In contrast, the non-Congress trade unions are much more aggressive and militant: they attempt to make inroads into industries, such as jute, which have undergone little unionization; to build labor membership in existing unions; and to compete successfully against rival unions. All of these objectives necessitate more militant policies: high and often irresponsible demands, radical slogans, and strikes. While INTUC is in principle reluctant to press for strikes and hesitates to embarrass the Congress government, other trade unions feel no such restraints. While INTUC

[69] In March 1964, the local Communist party in Asansol contended that "taxation of the holding-owners only without municipal facilities . . . was unjustified, and the development of this industrial town was not only an obligation of the people but also of the state and the Union Governments which should come forward with a benevolent outlook." After the meeting of local civic leaders, led by the CPI, with Mr. Fazlur Rahman, Minister of Local Self-Government, the Minister announced that taxes would be scaled down from Rs. 16 lakhs to Rs. 13 lakhs. See *Hindusthan Standard* (Calcutta), March 4, 1964, p. 6.

views tribunals as means for settling disputes, the non-Congress unions view them as instruments for furthering union organization.[70]

Similarly, in the countryside the Congress party's adoption of the doctrine of "rural-village harmony," and its attempt to work within the existing social structure, are both in sharp contrast to the Communist attempts to promote class conflict. After independence the Congress generally supported the more prosperous peasantry and rural gentry—the heads of local school boards, the members of union (local government) boards, village headmen, petty merchants, shopkeepers, and professionals. Land reform in West Bengal was postponed until 1954, and when it did come it was in a form largely acceptable to the rural gentry: it provided substantial compensation, and it permitted *benami* transactions (transfer of title to a friend or relative to circumvent ceilings). The introduction of panchayats, which extended the franchise for local elections from taxpayers alone to all adults, was also postponed until 1956, allowing the rural gentry to cement their hold on local government institutions and to plan for the introduction of the new franchise. In addition, the Congress maintained a low rate of taxation in the rural areas, while the state government's planning had a distinctly rural bias. Congress has thus discouraged the organization of landless laborers and tenants, while it has used its patronage to cement its links with the more influential rural inhabitants. In contrast, the All-India Kisan Sabha (AIKS), the Communist peasant-front organization, launched a revolutionary movement designed to overthrow the new independent government immediately after independence, as a result of which it was banned until 1951. Since 1951, the AIKS has continued to organize tenants and *bargadars* against landlords, in the hope of fomenting a class struggle which would change the present social structure in the rural areas and sweep them into positions of power and influence.

On the student front as well, the Congress party has attempted to mitigate conflict between students and turn their efforts to "constructive activities." In 1950, in an effort to depoliticize students, the central Congress leadership took the initiative in creating the National Union of Students, a non-political federation of the various student unions. Later, a youth department was created and placed under direct control of the party organization. The Youth Congress in West Bengal is organized by districts, and each district Youth Congress is now engaged in a number of "constructive" projects, chief among which are the construction of youth hostels throughout the state. Political activity within the Youth

[70] For a more detailed analysis of interest groups and interest group strategies in West Bengal, see Myron Weiner, *Politics of Scarcity*, pp. 80-97, 109-23, 145-55.

Congress is strongly discouraged; in the eyes of Congress leaders its function should be simply to train young people for Congress work, to create study circles, to organize social service work, to canvass during elections, and to sponsor sports and cultural activities. While the All-India Student Federation (AISF), the Communist student-front group, has also done some "constructive" work, it has been most prominent in the revolutionary and protest movements of the CPI. The AISF joined the militant Communist party struggles against the newly independent government immediately after independence, and, like the CPI in general, did not become more moderate in its attitude toward the democratic process and toward the government until 1951. But even since 1951 the Student Federation has pursued a much more militant policy than Congress student groups: it agitated against fee increments in schools and colleges, and was active in the Bengal-Bihar merger agitation, in the teachers' strike, and in the movement against increasing tram fares in 1953 and 1954. In 1964 it was prominent in the agitation protesting against the excesses of the police in killing a student during the January Hindu-Muslim riots.

Aside from the "mass" organizations—peasants, students, workers, and refugees—few other associations are dominated so openly by any political party. This is not to say that associations and social groupings in West Bengal do not take part in politics or form alliances with various political parties. On the other hand, a large number of caste, tribal, linguistic, religious, business, and other organizations do take an active interest in politics in an attempt to secure benefits for their group or association which they could not obtain otherwise. At the same time, all of the major parties—Congress, Socialist, Communist and Marxist-left—attempt to appeal to groups as groups. In a predominantly Muslim constituency they will generally all run Muslim candidates; in a constituency where the majority of the people come from one caste, they will all run candidates from that caste, in a tribal constituency they will all try to find someone from the tribal gentry who can be their nominee.

Congress, the party in power, has a distinct advantage in the competition among parties to attract various segments of the society. The leaders of Tribal and Scheduled Caste associations, for example, are attracted to the Congress for much the same reasons as the other rural gentry. Thus in the 1962 elections, 33 of the 53 reserved seats in the West Bengal Legislative Assembly went to Congress candidates while only 10 went to the CPI and 4 to the Marxist Forward Bloc (six ran successfully as Independents). Aside from the patronage that Congress controls and the benefits that come from joining the party in power, the Congress is also attractive to community association leaders because it is flexible: leading members of the Marwari community, for example, can work with the Congress party without being required to adopt the socialist ideology of some Congressmen, or the more rigorous ideologies of the Communist, Socialist, leftist, or Jan Sangh organizations. In addition, minority groups in West Bengal tend to be widely dispersed: in only one MP constituency (Murshidabad) do Muslims constitute a majority, and in only one MP constituency (Darjeeling) do non-Bengali speakers predominate. The dispersion of minorities diminishes the possibility of their forming effective political parties by themselves, and forces them to rely on the organization of local interest groups which can effectively influence the state government or local administration. Insofar as access to both is largely through the Congress party, such organizations tend to work closely with Congress. An examination of the electoral figures for 1952 and 1957 has shown that on the whole various minority groups in the state—Muslims, non-Bengalis, and members of Scheduled Castes and Tribes—gave Congress a larger vote than did the Bengali caste Hindus.[71]

Because of the increasing interest which the Communist party is taking in the electoral process, and because some members of the CPI now follow the Moscow line of the party, some Communists and leftists have in recent years begun to change their view of the political process. The All-India Kisan Sabha, for example, stated in 1957 its desire to minimize conflicts of interest in the countryside through the "principle of village solidarity":

> The fifteenth provincial conference, meeting in 1957, announced that the Kisan Sabha favored compensation for those small intermediaries whose holdings were confiscated by government. It further declared that the organization would launch agitations for agricultural loans, improved irrigation facilities, manure, education, health, and drinking water, and would continue agitation against excessive irrigation taxes and other taxes, including a proposed development tax. The Sabha also announced that it would work within the existing legislative framework, would take the initiative in forming panchayats under the new Panchayat Act, and would support credit co-operatives, marketing societies, handcraft co-operatives, and even the government's Community De-

[71] Myron Weiner, "Notes on Political Development in West Bengal," in *Political Change in South Asia*, pp. 242-44.

velopment Program and National Extension Service. In short, the Kisan Sabha proposed to minimize agitations and maximize the benefits peasants (and the Kisan Sabha) might receive by working within existing legislation, while at the same time putting pressure on the state government for greater rural expenditures. Rural harmony rather than class conflict was the new theme of the West Bengal Kisan Sabha.[72]

On the student front as well, the All-India Student Federation has undertaken some constructive activities. Beginning in 1951 the AISF, with financial support from the university, the Calcutta municipal government, membership donations, and private contributions, built a student health home, run by the student union in which the AISF is the most active group.

But despite indications that the Communist party is adapting to the electoral process, it still remains most effective in those areas outside of electoral politics. Since the Chinese aggression, for example, it has lost all but one of the state and municipal elections in which it has participated, while it has maintained its effectiveness in staging strikes among tramway workers, mercantile employees and teachers, and in organizing hartals and processions. In mid-1963 the leftist parties staged a successful hartal protesting against food prices, which completely closed down the city of Calcutta for two days, and later in the year they successfully organized processions to protest the proposal to send the Seventh Fleet to the Indian Ocean, and to demand a puja bonus for government employees. They also played a leading role in the agitational activities protesting against alleged excesses of the police during the Hindu-Muslim riots of January 1964 and were prominent in the food shortage demonstrations of 1965-66.

The factors which produce a political process in which two strong party traditions exist, and in which parties pursue widely divergent political strategies, are deeply embedded in the social, cultural, economic, and political background of West Bengal. The present party alignment and political strategies are thus likely to remain for some time as important determinants of the political process. At the same time, the nature of the political process adds to the problems of government, by offering a variety of alternative ways in which demands generated in the social and economic environment can be put, and by offering at least one political strategy in which the use of force and violence is accepted

[72] Weiner, *Politics of Scarcity*, pp. 158-59.

as legitimate. This promises to intensify the already existing pressures on government for meeting increasing demands and for coping with the problems of a "problem state," and to increase the need for government to effect rapid and far-reaching social and economic change. What develops will therefore depend largely on the ability of government to cope with the problems that have resulted from the social and economic environment and from the political process, as well as the performance of government in effecting change.

GOVERNMENTAL PERFORMANCE

The policy decisions of the government of West Bengal and the ability of government to implement those decisions have been conditioned by a number of problems—political, economic, administrative, social and cultural—which confronted the government when it first took office and which have been intensified and complicated by the history of the state since independence. Before turning to an analysis of the state's governmental and administrative apparatus, and a review of the performance of government—in meeting increasing demands, in coping with the problems of a problem state, and in effecting desired changes—it is necessary to review those limitations that set the framework within which the government must operate.

Economic Limitations

The economy of the state of West Bengal was severely disrupted by partition. In 1947, 92 per cent of the jute grown in Bengal was grown in the area which became part of Pakistan, while all of the 108 jute mills were located in the area that is now part of India. In 1947, 61 per cent of Bengal's paddy, 61 per cent of its oil seeds, and 70 per cent of its cotton was grown in East Bengal, while 84 per cent of the rice mills, 80 per cent of the oil mills, and 76 per cent of the cotton mills of Bengal were located in the west. While 80 per cent of the hides and skins tanned in Bengal came from the east, all three of Bengali's tanneries were located in the west.[73] The West Bengal government was thus faced with the task of finding ways to procure raw materials with which to maintain the production of industrial concerns in the state. And at the same time, government was faced with the necessity of finding alternative methods for keeping its industrial complexes intact.

The difficulties of maintaining and expanding industrial production

[73] Bidhan Chandra Roy, "Paving the Way," in *West Bengal Today* (Calcutta: West Bengal Pradesh Congress Committee, 1956), p. 19.

revolved largely around the lack of adequate transportation and communication networks which would allow industry to move raw materials from new sources of supply to the centers of industrial production: from other states in India to the industrial areas of West Bengal; and from the rural areas of the state to Calcutta and the industrial conurbations in the south and west. But independence has also ushered in serious transport problems for the state. Rail communications between the northern and southern districts were snapped by partition, and they have still not been completely restored. A rail link has been established by an all-India route, but the route, chosen by the central government, linked the industrial areas of Bihar and Orissa with the northern districts of Bihar, and this only complicated the problems of shipping from the northern districts of West Bengal to the industrial belt around Calcutta. In addition, the state and central governments have concentrated on the building of the industrial areas in the western part of the state (the Durgapur-Asansol complex) in an attempt to relieve urban crowding in Calcutta, with the result that the communication and transport networks between the western districts and the rest of the country have been improved considerably, but to the neglect of the northern and southeastern districts. The West Bengal government has been pressing the Ministry of Railways for an alternative rail link connecting Jalpaiguri with Alipurduars or Cooch Behar (in the north), but thus far the Ministry of Railways, in the face of other large expenditures in the eastern region, has been unable to grant the request.[74]

Economic problems have been further complicated by the influx of refugees. Unlike the western border of India, where there was an exchange of populations, the flow of refugees in the eastern region has been largely one way. Since Hindus occupied a more prominent position in the society of East Bengal, they have generally been harder hit by communal tensions and have elected in greater numbers to come to the west. Since the bulk of the Muslims in the west occupied lower social positions and since their position in society would be relatively the same regardless of residence, they have elected to stay in the west in large numbers. With every flare-up of communal tension, the flow of Hindu refugees from East Pakistan to West Bengal therefore continues, while the number of Muslims who move east remains almost insignificant. The result has been the influx of more than four million refugees in the past seventeen years, a number which continues to grow,[75] and an in-

[74] *Budget Statement by Shri Sankardas Banerji, Minister-in-charge, Finance, West Bengal, 1963-64* (Alipore: West Bengal Government Press, 1963), pp. 13-14.

[75] On January 10, 1964, communal riots broke out in many parts of West Bengal,

ordinately high rate of population growth (between 1951 and 1961 the population of West Bengal rose by 33 per cent, compared to the all-India average increase of only 21 per cent). Moreover, since the refugees speak Bengali and identify with the past traditions and cultural background of Bengal, they are reluctant to settle anywhere in India except in the Bengali linguistic area.[76] And since a large number of them are members of the middle class, whose landed interests in East Bengal have been severed, they find it necessary to locate in those areas where they can secure middle-class jobs and opportunities. This means that the vast majority of the refugees settle in the urban areas, and especially in Calcutta, thus complicating and intensifying the problems of the urban areas even further. The ordinary demands made on the state and central governments—for jobs, education, housing, urban amenities—have escalated in West Bengal, owing to the addition of this highly discontented stratum of society. In addition, the continuing influx of refugees serves as an irritant which keeps memories of past communal tensions alive and results in continuing tension between the communities.

The partition economy, together with the influx of refugees and rural migrants, has resulted in the deterioration of the city of Calcutta. Density of population has led to a serious scarcity of housing; overcrowding in education; large-scale middle-class unemployment; the concentration of homeless refugees in public places; a serious deficiency in sanitation and health facilities; inadequate transportation; and a lack of maintenance of public utilities. The Calcutta water supply, which was inadequate before partition, has become even more inadequate as a result of population growth. And in addition, the Hooghly River has been silting more rapidly than it can be dredged, with the result that water for agricultural and other purposes has become increasingly saline. The port of Calcutta, which now handles more than 40 per cent of the total export tonnage of the country, is in danger of becoming inaccessible

and throughout almost the entire city of Calcutta, and lasted for nearly a week. Although the exact cause of the rioting was not known, it was clearly related to the rioting that had occurred in Khulna district in East Pakistan during the previous week. The Khulna riots were in turn attributed to the theft of the Prophet's hair from the Hazratbal shrine in Srinagar. Whatever the cause of the communal tension, it did result in the influx into West Bengal of a large number of new refugees in 1964. For a review of the rioting, see Kedar Ghosh, "How the Army Restored Order in Calcutta," *The Statesman* (March 14, 1964), p. 61.

[76] This is given as one of the primary reasons for the failure of the government rehabilitation schemes to live up to original expectations. See S. D. Thapar, "The Dandakaranya Project: Failure of an Ambitious Scheme," *Economic Weekly* (Bombay), Vol. xv, No. 9 (March 2, 1963), 401-02.

to large ships unless something is done either to stop the silting or to increase the flow of water.[77]

The cost of an adequate solution to the problems of Calcutta is indicative of the enormity of the problems facing the central, state, and municipal governments in West Bengal. With regard to housing, for example, one study[78] has estimated that 70 to 80 per cent of Calcutta's resident families need to be rehoused. This means that new housing would be necessary for at least 524,563 families. Assuming a Rs. 6,000 minimum investment per new family tenement-unit (one room), the cost of rehousing Calcutta's present population would amount to Rs. 3,147,378,000. As Richard Park has pointed out, this money cannot be expected to come from rentals alone: "An assumed investment of about Rs. 6,000 per tenement unit and a 5 per cent per annum return from rentals works out to Rs. 300 rent per annum, or Rs. 25 per month. Yet the average monthly rental in those parts of Calcutta most affected is today somewhat less than Rs. 10!"[79] Nor can the money be expected to come solely from the state's own resources. Were the state government to undertake a project which would provide adequate housing for Calcutta's population alone, it would have to spend more than the total amount provided in its third five-year plan proposed budget. And this of course would leave the state with no funds for the building of schools; for the creation of jobs; for the rehabilitation of refugees; for the construction of sanitation and health facilities; for roads; for public utilities; or for the investment by government in any other area outside of Calcutta. But, even if funds for rehousing were available, there are other difficult problems that must be faced, such as the necessity of finding land in an already overcrowded state. It has been estimated, for example, that in order to rehouse only those people now living in *bustees,* it would be necessary to find 2,470 acres (or 7,310 bighas) of land, which is approximately one and a half times the area now covered by *bustees.*[80]

If only because of the financial and physical limitations imposed on the state government, an adequate solution to Calcutta's problems in the

[77] D. N. Sengupta, "The Hooghly River," *The Modern Review* (Calcutta), Vol. CIV, No. 3 (September 1958), 201-05.

[78] Syamal Chakrabartty, *Housing Conditions in Calcutta* (Calcutta: Bookland Private Limited, 1959), pp. 50-51.

[79] Richard L. Park, "The Urban Challenge to Local and State Government: West Bengal, With Special Attention to Calcutta," in *India's Urban Future,* p. 388.

[80] By S. K. Gupta, chairman of the Calcutta Improvement Trust; see *Annual Report on the Operations of the Calcutta Improvement Trust, for the Year 1955-56* (Calcutta: Calcutta Improvement Trust, n.d.), p. 41, quoted in Park, *op.cit.,* p. 388.

near future is obviously ruled out. Thus, interested observers and participants in the situation in the city, who have recommended a large-scale attack on Calcutta's problems, have been intent only on preventing further deterioration of the city in order to pave the way for future plans which could possibly be more adequate. The World Bank Mission, for example, offered a plan which would involve the building of some new refugee settlements outside of Calcutta; some improvements in the systems of drainage, sewerage, garbage disposal, and drinking water supply; the building of a new city south of Calcutta for at least 150,000 people; and the building of a new port at Haldia.[81] Yet the total cost of even these stop-gap measures is unduly high. The cost of the World Bank project, for example, was estimated at 225 crores of rupees, the equivalent of (as the Hoffman report itself stated) "the price of a steel plant."

Administrative Limitations

The difficulties involved in tackling the problems of West Bengal revolve not only around matters of economics. Some observers have argued, for example, that the amount of funds recommended by the Hoffman report could be obtained by the state, but that the projects recommended in the report, if left in the hands of the state administration, would be either ineffectively implemented or not implemented at all.[82] The obstacles to the implementation of plans in West Bengal stem largely from the nature of the administrative apparatus and the ties between the administration and the Congress party. Although the administration of West Bengal has not been adequately researched, most observers agree that most segments of the present state bureaucracy are incapable of innovating new policies or of implementing efficiently policies laid down elsewhere. This inability appears to stem from a variety of factors. To begin with, the administration is to a large extent staffed with middle-class Bengalis who themselves have been alienated from the present structure of political authority. Although they seek positions as administrators and clerks in order to maintain their social positions, they do not identify very closely with the work that they do on behalf of the government. Many clerks even view the circumstances of their own positions—the low salaries, poor working conditions, and

[81] For a review of the report of the World Bank Mission, the so-called Michael Hoffman Report, which was not released for public circulation, see the following articles: "Calcutta and the World Bank Mission," *Economic Weekly*, Vol. XII, No. 40 (October 1, 1960), 1468-74; "Greater Calcutta," *ibid.*, Vol. XII, No. 47 (November 19, 1960), 1668-69; and "Calcutta Scheme 'Under Consideration,'" *ibid.*, Vol. XII, No. 48 (November 26, 1960), 1711.

[82] This argument is made in "Greater Calcutta," *op.cit.*, p. 1668.

the corruption and nepotism which goes on around them (and in which they sometimes indulge)—as an affirmation of their views that the present government is incapable of coping with the problems of the state. The level of morale within the administration is thus extremely low. Moreover, the views of the middle class within the bureaucracy tend to discourage the willingness to innovate, a tendency which is reinforced by other factors in the society that militate against the production of innovating individuals. As Weiner has pointed out, Bengal is characterized by

> . . . the existence of hierarchical and generally authoritarian patterns within all institutions, from the family to schools, universities, administration and government, which serve to inhibit the development of innovating individuals. Men in authority view innovations within their institutions as devices to threaten their positions; they also tend to view new ideas from underlings as intolerable threats to their status. As a result, men with ambition express fidelity and humility to authority. When they attack authority it is not one's personal superior, but rather impersonal institutions, such as government, and in impersonal ways, as in the street demonstration.
>
> Those who are on the top not only discourage innovation from below, but having themselves been nurtured by the system are often incapable of innovating. Furthermore, inaction by men in authority brings no punishment, while action often opens the possibility of antagonizing someone in a still higher position of authority. Action-mindedness therefore is a quality possessed by very few men.[83]

Some administrators of course—the secretaries in ministries and all members of the civil service—do have the skill, and in a few cases the incentive, to innovate policies. But under a democratic regime these men do not have the power. The Commissioner of Calcutta Corporation, for example, is almost invariably a higher civil servant of proven competence, and one who in many cases has the desire and the administrative ability to give effect to new plans and policies. But though the commissioner is theoretically vested with the entire executive authority of the municipal government, he is in fact at the mercy of the state Congress party, the Corporation Councillors, and the government of West Bengal. He is appointed by the state government and may at any time be removed from his office by the state government. He is not a member of the Corporation Council and may not undertake any work uncon-

[83] Weiner, "Political Development in West Bengal," pp. 255-56.

nected with his office without the sanction of the state government and the Council. The Council may also remove him from office by calling a special meeting and passing a resolution approved by a mere majority vote of the Councillors (the meeting and the resolution are, of course, subject to the approval of the state government). The Commissioner can make appointments for positions carrying a salary of 250 rupees per month or less; but appointments for salaries between rupees 250 and 1,500 are made by a state-appointed municipal service commission, and above rupees 1,500 by the state public service commission.[84] These forms of control, exercised by the state government over the administration within the Calcutta Corporation, are repeated in almost every state government agency.

The extent to which the administration is controlled by the state government and the state Congress party can be seen not only from the structure of the administration, but also from the limited powers which rest with many local bodies. Calcutta Corporation, for example, does have the power to issue building permits and regulations; to maintain and repair public works facilities; to control infectious and dangerous diseases; to supervise, maintain, and control markets, foods and drugs; to license dogs, theatres, restaurants and professional groups; to undertake town planning and development (subject to state approval); and to initiate and maintain primary-stage educational institutions. But neither the Corporation Councillors nor the commissioner and his staff have the power (even if they had the initiative) to raise sufficient funds either to cope with the numerous problems involved in maintaining Calcutta's public facilities or to initiate changes that would lead to a massive attack on the city's problems. The Corporation, for example, has no power either to tax or to license commerce and industry; no control over small-scale industries; no power in the sphere of refugee relief and rehabilitation; no power or control over education beyond the primary school stage; no power in the fields of housing and planning and development generally; no power over transport and communications; and no power over fire-fighting and fire services or police and jails. Power in these spheres lies with the state government, and with the Congress party that controls the government. The income of Calcutta Corporation in 1957-58 was 74,297,342 rupees, a figure that

[84] For a review of the structure of Calcutta Corporation see M. M. Singh, *Municipal Government in the Calcutta Metropolitan District: A Preliminary Survey* (Calcutta: Institute of Public Administration, New York, 1963), pp. 17-30. See also Prabuddha Nath Chatterjee, "A Plea for Municipal Self-Government," *The Modern Review* (Calcutta), Vol. CIV, No. 5 (November 1958), 396-99.

includes all licensing and other taxes, as well as receipts from property taxes (about 60 per cent).[85] The Corporation uses 25 per cent of these revenues for the staff needed to run its organization,[86] and the rest (five to six crores per year) is obviously insufficient to even maintain the services that would be adequate for the city. Yet the Corporation is hesitant to attempt to increase property taxes (its main source of income) because it is dependent on property-owners for its votes.[87] Since the funds it can collect are insufficient to cope with the city's needs, the Corporation does not even pretend to use its revenues for the development of the city, but rather undertakes stop-gap measures, such as the cleaning up of the most diseased and unsanitary portions of the city when a situation becomes intolerable to the press or to an important part of the citizenry. The remaining funds provide some Councillors and administrators with a relatively small amount of patronage and graft. It should be noted that because the Corporation is confronted with monumental problems over which it has little or no control, it does tend to attract people interested less in public welfare than in personal and familial gains, and it often repels the most responsible citizens in the community.[88]

Limitations Imposed by the Political Process

While the state ministers and Congress party leaders do have more power than anyone else in the state to instigate and implement new policies, they too are limited by the nature of the administration, and by the nature of the ties between the administration and the party. The Congress government bases its electoral success on a series of alliances with "key men" in the constituencies—businessmen, influential men in the rural areas, group and community leaders, and so forth—who are in many cases party supporters precisely because they can gain administrative concessions or engage in administrative irregularities. The Con-

[85] *Statistical Abstract, West Bengal, 1960,* p. 379.

[86] M. M. Singh, *op.cit.*, p. 20.

[87] While the state government did introduce universal adult franchise in Calcutta municipal government elections in 1965, Congress' success in the Corporation elections still depends on the ties between Congressmen and rate-payers. For a sharp critique of the Congress organization in Calcutta, see Flibbertigibbet, "The Uncleared Garbage: Calcutta Corporation," *Economic Weekly* (Bombay), Vol. xv, No. 22 (June 1, 1963), 879-80.

[88] In February 1964, for example, S. B. Ray resigned as Commissioner of Calcutta Corporation because of "a depressing experience of successive obstructions by Councillors to his plans and proposals." *The Statesman* (Calcutta), February 23, 1964, p. 1. A state government spokesman later intimated that the resignation of Mr. Ray "would make it difficult for the Government to persuade any senior officer to accept a Corporation assignment." *The Statesman*, February 25, 1964.

gress party has, in fact, established a public relations office in Calcutta which is designed to act as a "link between government and the people," meaning that it opens up cracks in the administration through which businessmen and other influentials can penetrate to obtain their wishes more quickly. Only recently the state government decided to set up a similar "advisory organization," comprising representatives of the government and industry, "to review industrial prospects in the state." This proposed organization, the state government has intimated, "should considerably help private enterprise in removing various difficulties now being experienced in setting up new industries and in maintaining and expanding existing industrial units."[89] In the countryside too, the local Congressman often acts as the broker for his constituents and the administration. The ties that link the Congressman broker with the people and the government may, in many cases, rest on the coincidence of interests between the three parties, as well as on personal friendships, kinships, caste affiliations, and sometimes payments. Or the ties between the party, its supporters, and the administration may rest simply on the fact that the party leaders, administrators, and constituents who bargain for benefits in the local areas are often men of high status who have learned to deal with one another in a hierarchically structured social system.[90]

While the system of close constituent-party-administration ties does make for a viable party government, and while it sometimes makes the machinery of government operate more smoothly, it also inhibits the effectiveness of the administration in those areas where a policy of reform is to be implemented. The implementation of policy in this system is influenced as much by the party representative, who must please those who often want to preserve the existing state of affairs, as it is by the administrator, who (in India at least) is often charged with the responsibility of reforming the existing state-of-affairs. The party government does of course attempt to please as many people as possible, and thus legislation and policy decisions are enacted which promise desired changes. But the negation of many government policies is subsequently encouraged by the provision of regularized methods of cancelling out aspects of a policy that are undesirable to persons who are established in the social and political structure.[91] The pervasive acceptance of this

89 *The Statesman,* February 20, 1964.

90 Weiner, "Political Development in West Bengal," p. 233; see also Weiner, *Politics of Scarcity,* Chapter VI "Organized Business," for a more detailed study of close party-administration-constituent ties.

91 Numerous examples of the way in which this system operates in West Bengal are available: the processing, distribution, and transportation of food grown in the state are all subject to government regulations, but state law enforcement and ad-

system in West Bengal indicates the support that has been generated for its continuance. And this in turn indicates the extent to which the Congress government, which is largely based on the system, is limited in the implementation of policies that would go against the wishes of those influential in the system.

In addition to the constraints that result from the nature of the administration, the state government has also felt compelled to enact legislation or promulgate administrative acts that openly favor Congress supporters. The Estates Acquisitions Act, for example, confiscated zamindari landholdings in the state, but was carefully designed to exclude urban property, to permit *benami* transactions, and to provide substantial compensation. The Eviction Bill (later renamed the Refugee Rehabilitation Bill) was clearly aimed at protecting property owners against squatting refugees. The Ministry of Labor in West Bengal has given invaluable aid to the business community, such as the efforts of the Ministry to avoid strikes and the quick application of arbitration proceedings so that pending a government settlement of the dispute strikes are illegal. And the government-appointed labor minister continues to be a man more favorable to business (the present labor minister is a Marwari) than to labor despite pressure by the unions for a labor appointee.

Government policy and planning has also had a distinct bias in favor of the rural areas, from which the Congress receives the bulk of its support. In 1962-63 only 7.3 per cent of the state income came from land revenues (it had been 50 per cent in 1921, and 35 per cent in 1936), and agricultural income tax constituted less than one per cent of state revenues.[92] Yet, in the face of low taxation in the rural areas, most of the state government's planning has still had a distinct rural bias. The second

ministrative agencies are often reluctant to prosecute businessmen for illegal hoarding of food or for misuse of government permits to run price-controlled food shops; the Congress government has established elaborate licensing procedures to control the private sector, but it simultaneously negates the effect of many of these procedures by failing to enforce them effectively, and by establishing bodies designed to mitigate their effectiveness; a city ordinance prohibits cows from loitering in the streets of Calcutta, a state law makes it illegal for non-licensed book dealers to sell government text books, and state building regulations demand that certain housing requirements be met by landlords, but at the same time the system of close party-administrative-constituent ties makes it possible for some people to break all of these laws almost at will. For an illustration of government unwillingness to change this system, even in the face of opposition, see the report of the (1958) food policy enquiry committee as described in "Extra-'ordinary' Ordinance," *Economic Weekly* (Bombay), Vol. x, No. 44 (November 1, 1958), 1383-84.

[92] Government of West Bengal, Finance Department, *The West Bengal State Rupee: From Where it Comes and Where it Goes* (Alipore: West Bengal Government Press, 1964), p. 1.

five-year plan in West Bengal provided for heavy investments in the north and south Lake Reclamation Scheme, the Kansabati Scheme in Midnapore and Bankura districts, the Ganga Barrage Scheme, and the Sewerage Gas and Durgapur projects. These projects reclaim land, improve water supply, prevent floods and provide irrigation to rural areas. Even when a plan is devised to solve the problems of Calcutta, it has often involved investment outside of the Calcutta Metropolitan Area. The bulk of the money for the rehabilitation of refugees has gone to setting up refugee camps outside of urban areas, sometimes for the creation of whole new townships. The solution to the problem of the silting of Calcutta's port has been attacked by schemes—principally the Ganga Barrage scheme and the creation of a new port at Haldia—that simultaneously benefit large parts of the countryside. Recently, the Minister of Commerce and Industries and of Cooperation announced a number of new schemes in progress—a cement factory in Purulia, coal-mining projects, a gas grid under the Durgapur scheme, a sugar mill in the cooperative sector in north Bengal, and spinning mills for almost all of the districts[93]—none of which involved direct benefits for Calcutta. And in the 1964-65 budget, agriculture and economic development in the rural areas received the highest total allotment of all investments, covering over 25 per cent of the total budget expenditures.[94]

The state government has also concentrated on social welfare and public health schemes, most of which are undertaken in the villages and towns. In the first five-year plan, West Bengal spent 42.7 per cent of its allotment on social services (education, medical and public health facilities); in the second five-year plan 37.64 per cent; and it has planned expenditures of 26.71 per cent on these services during the third plan period (see Table 6.3).

The adoption of policies that favor those groups that keep the Congress in power is clearly linked, in the eyes of party leaders, to the effect of these policies in building support for the present government. In 1956, for example, the chief minister justified the state's disproportionately large social welfare expenditures as follows:

> The standard of living of most of our people is so low that better nutrition, better health and better education are necessary preliminaries for efficient production of wealth . . . but there is more to it than that. The provision of drinking water, roads, housing, medical facilities, and mental stimulation can be immediately appreciated by

93 *Amrita Bazaar Patrika* (Calcutta), March 8, 1963.

94 *The Statesman,* February 20, 1964.

TABLE 6.3

DISTRIBUTION OF WEST BENGAL PLAN OUTLAY, 1951–66[a]

	First plan[b]		*Second plan*[c]		*Third plan*	
Agriculture	8.87	(12.56%)	17.86	(11.32%)	54.34	(18.53%)
Cooperation and community development[d]	—	—	16.63	(10.55%)	16.81	(5.73%)
Irrigation and power	15.17	(21.48%)	30.34	(19.24%)	63.85	(21.78%)
Industry and mining	1.20	(1.75%)	9.44	(5.98%)	12.04	(4.11%)
Transport and communications	15.23	(21.51%)	19.47	(12.35%)	26.50	(9.04%)
Social services	30.15	(42.70%)	55.34	(37.64%)	78.28	(26.71%)
Miscellaneous	—	—	8.19	(2.92%)	41.33	(14.10%)
Totals	70.62	(100.0%)	157.67	(100.0%)	293.15	(100.0%)

[a] Figures in crores of rupees (one crore is ten million).

[b] Figures for first plan taken from *Statistical Abstract, West Bengal, 1960,* p. 531.

[c] Figures for second and third plans taken from Hiranmay Banerjee, "Our Third Plan," *West Bengal 1962* (Alipore: West Bengal Government Press, 1963), p. 12.

[d] This heading did not appear in the first plan.

> the people, who will be eager to plan and execute measures which promise these amenities.[95]

In a similar vein, the neglect of Calcutta in the allotment of government funds was recently explained by a leading Bengali Congressman as follows:

> How can the Congress take up all of these schemes to develop Calcutta? The Government does not have so much money that they can make Calcutta a dream place overnight. And if Congress only does some things and not others, then the people of Calcutta will vote them out of office. . . . What can the Congress do? The Congress party has to worry about votes, as every other party must do—if Congress lost two or three per cent of the votes in many constituencies it would be voted out of power.[96]

[95] Bidhan Chandra Roy, *op.cit.,* p. 25.

[96] Based on an interview (January 1964). The statement that Congress electoral victories are often by narrow margins is borne out by statistics provided by Asok Mitra. If an additional 2 per cent of the vote had been cast against Congress and in favor of the major Opposition candidate in a selected number of constituencies in the first two general elections, Congress would have lost 23 of its 149 seats in 1952, and 26 of its 151 seats in 1957, enough in both cases to deprive the party of a majority in the Legislative Assembly. See Asok Mitra, *op.cit.,* p. 155.

From the evidence that is available, it thus appears that the Congress government does feel compelled to channel a major portion of its scarce resources into development and other projects that favor those people and groups who are most willing to cooperate with the existing regime. Insofar as that pressure is real, this acts as a brake on the freedom of the government to formulate and implement plans.

The government is limited by the nature of the political process in another way, in that the pursuance of a successful electoral strategy by the Congress serves to widen the communications gap between the government and certain sectors of the population. Demonstrations, processions, strikes, riots, and boycotts have now become almost everyday occurrences in the city of Calcutta. Led by the middle classes, people have banded together to burn tram cars, hold protest meetings, hunger strikes and sit-down strikes, and stage one- and two-day hartals that still the city. Some members of the Opposition have even thrown eggs or come to blows with Congressmen in the Legislative Assembly. These are all forms of protest which reflect the increasing inability of a certain group of people to get what they want from government, and their increasing willingness to resort to tactics that will not assure them the sympathy of government. Faced with these tactics, the West Bengal government has often reacted in such a way as to further the use of a protest strategy on the part of these groups. A refugee act is bluntly labeled an "Eviction Act"; a merger with a neighboring state is proposed without any prior attempt to test its political feasibility; tram fare and tuition fees in the colleges are raised without notice; and the government has recently been reluctant to stage inquiries into various matters when such inquiries have been demanded by those in protest. This further encourages political groups to use violence and civil disobedience to veto government action, which in turn reinforces the government's image of political groups as being irresponsible and therefore unworthy of consultation. Rather than attempt to appeal to the middle classes, the government has thus become increasingly dependent on restraint by force or the threat of force. On numerous occasions the police have resorted to lathi-charges, tear-gassing, and firing to dispel processions and riots. The Preventive Detention Act, which provides for detention without trial, has been widely used.[97] Assembly of five

[97] The CPI estimates that between 1947 and 1958, over 100,000 people "connected with the democratic movements of different sections of the people" were jailed in West Bengal; and that the government had dismissed during that same period "over 200 government employees on the basis of 'adverse' police reports against them." See *West Bengal Accuses!*, pp. 45, 54.

persons or more has been permanently banned in Dalhousie Square area (where government offices are located), and Section 144 of the Criminal Procedure Code is invoked at least once annually in other parts of Calcutta, sometimes in the whole city, and sometimes throughout the state. When the state police have been unable to cope with riots, the government has not hesitated to call in the Indian military.

Restraint by force is, of course, a necessity in any political system. But insofar as certain people and groups are encouraged to engage in activities that can only be dealt with by the coercive apparatus of government, the support structure of the government is impaired. The continual adoption by some sectors of the populace of protest strategies serves to promote attitudes that lead to a further deterioration of morale within the administration, a lack of willingness to cooperate with the government in nation-building activities, and an increase in the demand for fundamental changes in the regime. These factors in turn detract from the ability of the administration to implement nation-building projects, and they encourage postures of pervasive, almost blind, opposition to all of the plans, projects, and policies that are undertaken by the existing government.

Governmental Implementation

In the face of almost overwhelming problems and severe limitations, the achievements of the state of West Bengal are not inconsiderable. Most of the four and a half million refugees that have come into the state since independence have been resettled. The seriously dislocated economy of the state has not boomed, but it is still perhaps as flourishing and as progressive as any in India. The state and central governments have been able to maintain law and order in the state despite the existence of widespread discontent. And the educational, public health, and social welfare programs of the state are comparable to those of any other region in the subcontinent.

By 1957 more than three million refugees from East Pakistan had been resettled in West Bengal, a large number as a result of the rehabilitation policies of the state and central governments.[98] The state and central governments have established refugee colonies throughout the state, they have in some cases set up whole new townships, and they have established refugee colonies outside the state as well. The state government has advanced loans to industrialists and mill owners for establishing industries to provide jobs for refugees. The bus industry

[98] In 1963 it was estimated that over 656,000 refugees had been rehabilitated by the government; *India: A Reference Annual, 1963*, p. 114.

in Calcutta has been nationalized and refugees have been favored by the hiring practices of that industry. Bengali refugees have also been favored in the issuing of taxi permits. The state government has continued to press the center for monetary and other assistance with which to provide both temporary and permanent rehabilitation of refugees,[99] and the state has received a large sum of money—rupees 200 crores by 1963[100]—from the center for this purpose.

A number of projects have been set up in the sphere of large-scale industrial development. As part of the Damodar Valley Corporation project, West Bengal has a major thermal power station at Durgapur; and numerous other power schemes are now in progress—the Jaldhaka hydro-electric project, the Bandel thermal power station project, the Durgapur coke oven plant station extension, the Durgapur coke oven plant power house extension, and the Calcutta Electric Supply Company extension (private sector). One of India's major steel plants was completed at Durgapur in 1962, and in the third plan period this plant is being expanded. The Hindusthan Cables factory, established at Rupnarainpur, began production in 1954 and has been rapidly expanding since. The National Instruments Factory in Calcutta has been nationalized (it is now called the National Instruments Limited), and its production has also risen. An ophthalmic glass project is to be set up

99 The force with which the state government presents its demands to the center is indicated by the tone of the following speech, delivered by Atulya Ghosh, then president of the WBPCC and MP from Asansol, in the *Lok Sabha* during the debate on states reorganization: "The Honorable, the Prime Minister says: 'we won't bother about what happens about Bengal or Bihar.' I say with due humility that he is going to bother about the condition of Bengal. If 20,000 people come every month to a state, if 2½ *lakhs* of people come every year to a state, the Prime Minister of India will have to bother his head to solve that problem. Our question is not a Bengal question. If one question is not solved, the unity of India will be hampered. This is not a periodical question.

"I do not want to flaunt the sacrifice of Bengal. I do not want to say that Bengal was divided for the emancipation of the teeming millions of India. I will only say, we were a party to that division, because, we wanted to free ourselves also. We made that sacrifice for our emancipation . . .

"But, we want a sympathetic treatment from citizens of India. We want a sympathetic treatment from the other states. We want sympathetic treatment from the Government of India. I want to make it clear that I have not come here with a begging bowl. I do not want to evoke the pity and draw the merciful attention of other states. I want to be at par with other states of India. I want that a solution should be found for those persons who, leaving their herths [sic] and homes, are coming to Bengal every month, who have no future, for whom there is no silver lining in the horizon, those who do not know where they will remain, where they will settle. We have to solve that question." Atulya Ghosh, "Linguistic Affinity Conducive to India's Unity," in *West Bengal Today*, pp. 33-34.

100 *India: A Reference Annual, 1963*, p. 114.

at Durgapur (at a cost of 4 crores) with the collaboration of the USSR. Chittaranjan Locomotive Works is now manufacturing both steam and diesel locomotives, and its production is also increasing. The government is now attempting to establish a heavy steel foundry at Chittaranjan that would be capable of meeting all of the heavy casting requirements for the railways.

The state government has also undertaken and supported a number of smaller projects. It has set up a milk colony at Haringhata; wood industries centers throughout the state; a scheme for the supply of processed clay for sanitary wares and electric goods; numerous brick and tile manufacturing units; an ice and cold storage plant; silk reelers cooperatives; and numerous handicraft industries. It has also experimented with the development of bone china and earthenware industries and has established numerous sales emporia around the state and the country. The state government had constructed more than 6,000 miles of state highway by 1962, and the national highways in West Bengal had accounted for another 286.5 miles, with the result that the miles of roadway in West Bengal had jumped from 1,181 miles in 1947 to over 7,700 miles by 1962.[101]

Because partition created serious food and crop deficits in West Bengal, a great deal of the expenditure by government has gone into the development of land and attempts to improve the efficiency of cultivation. The government has organized and supported cooperatives throughout the state, and through these it has distributed fertilizers, seeds, and other necessities. Agricultural credit given through these societies amounted to 2.27 crores of rupees at the end of the second plan period, and to 7.50 crores of rupees in March 1963.[102] Largely as a result of the Mayrrakshi irrigation project, by 1963 West Bengal had irrigated more acres (650,000) than any other state except Punjab (2,750,000 acres) or Uttar Pradesh (794,000).[103] The government has also initiated a project for the preservation of the port of Calcutta (the Ganga-barrage project) which is expected to irrigate large portions of land during the next eight years, as well as the Kansabati scheme (total cost: 25.2 crores) which is expected to eventually irrigate over 900,000 acres.[104] A number

101 Khagendra Nath Dasgupta, "Highways and Village Roads," in *West Bengal 1962*, pp. 115-18. See also R. C. Roy, "Road Development in West Bengal," *Indian Construction News*, Vol. VI, No. 12 (December 1957), 25-29, for a statement of government transport policy.

102 *Amrita Bazaar Patrika* (Calcutta), March 8, 1963.

103 *India: A Reference Annual, 1963*, pp. 246-47.

104 *Ibid.*, p. 248. Funds for the completion of almost one-fourth of the Kansabati scheme (6.11 crores) have already been allocated.

of other schemes have been instituted to reclaim land. The largest of these—the reclamation of the Salt Lakes to the east and south of Calcutta and the Sonarpur-Arapanch Drainage Scheme—have together converted more than 30 square miles of previously waterlogged land into areas suitable for growing paddy.

In an effort to find new sources of food, the state government has attempted to develop the *beel* (marshy areas) fisheries in the state, and has advanced loans to a number of local owners to improve derelict water areas. Similar loans have been advanced to the tank owners in various parts of the state for the development of intensive pisciculture. Moreover, the state has set up five state nursery units in which small fish and fingerlings are raised to be sold subsequently for liberation in the *beels,* tanks, and ponds throughout the state. To help backward and distressed fishermen, the state government has supplied them with boats, nets, and other equipment at subsidized rates.[105] Attempts have also been made to explore the Bay of Bengal as a source of edible fish. Trawlers have been purchased from both Denmark and Japan, and the Bengalis are being trained to do research in the as yet unexplored field of deep-sea fishing. The state government has also experimented with the cultivation of crops hitherto not grown in this area—principally ipecac, ramie, sisal and wheat—in an effort to find either a crop that could furnish greater yield or one that could be alternated with rice to make better use of the present land area. While the government's concern for more efficient land use and increased yield has not always met with marked success, food production in the state has increased to some extent. In the ten years beginning with 1949-50 (the base year) the rice index of the state fell below 100 only once (in 1951-52), and agricultural production for all crops had risen on the average to 110.87 by 1959-60.[106]

While the state government has been instrumental in providing a stable electoral majority in the state and in undertaking development projects in some spheres, it is also evident that in many areas the state is highly dependent on the center, on private industry, and even on international agencies. The government of West Bengal has in fact flatly stated that it plans to leave major organized industries "to be looked after by the central government on the national level or by the private sector."[107] It has also left the development of the city of Calcutta almost entirely in the hands of the center and of international bodies.

105 *West Bengal: Land and People,* p. 43.
106 *Statistical Abstract, West Bengal, 1960,* p. 161.
107 Bidhan Chandra Roy, *op.cit.,* p. 25.

In September 1960, after the Hoffman report of the World Bank had requested greater help from the center, the Chief Minister of West Bengal approached the United States ambassador in India for a grant from Public Law 480 rupee funds for a scheme of urban improvement in Calcutta.[108] He also established a Calcutta Metropolitan Planning Organization (CMPO) charged with the task of preparing a master plan for the development of the Calcutta Metropolitan area, and asked the Ford Foundation to provide a team of consultants to assist the CMPO in its work. Funds for the redevelopment schemes of the CMPO are expected to come almost entirely from outside sources. The government of India has already allocated Rs. 40 crores under the Third Five-Year Plan, a sum which may be matched from the U.S. Wheat Loan Fund.[109] In addition, it is hoped in many quarters that aid will be forthcoming from other outside agencies: the Agency for International Development, the World Bank, the Development Loan Fund, the World Health Organization, the United Nations Special Fund, and others.[110]

CONCLUSION

Despite the numerous achievements to date and some promise of more in the future, it would appear that the state of West Bengal will remain a "problem state" for a long time to come. In February 1967, the Congress party was defeated in the state Legislative Assembly elections by a fourteen-party coalition that has now assumed responsibility for governing the state.[111] However, even if the Congress party within the

108 "Calcutta and the World Bank Mission," p. 1473.

109 Park, *op.cit.*, p. 396.

110 "Calcutta and the World Bank Mission," p. 1473. On numerous occasions, state government leaders have stated that the plans of the CMPO are in progress, and have pointed to the work of the CMPO as evidence of their interest in Calcutta. See *Budget Statement by Shri Sankardas Banerji*, p. 15; see also *The Statesman*, February 20, 1964, containing the speech of the Governor introducing the 1964-65 budget. At the same time, a number of people within the CMPO have been critical of the government (privately) for not implementing the present plans at a faster rate; publicly the CMPO constantly points out that "plans alone can solve no problems; they must be carried out, to make their effective mark. CMPO is a planning agency; it does not implement the plans." *CMPO First Report, 1962* (Calcutta: Calcutta Metropolitan Planning Organization, 1963), p. 78. Thus far the CMPO has completed a number of short-term, emergency plans, but no organization has been set up to implement them, nor have they been taken up in the legislature. In the meantime, the residents of Calcutta are becoming increasingly critical of the CMPO and its work. See, for example, "CMPO Takes it Easy," *Link* (New Delhi), Vol. VI, No. 31 (March 15, 1964), 16-17.

111 Publication schedules made it impossible to incorporate the results of the 1967 elections into the regular text of this article. It is clear, however, that the Congress defeat in West Bengal in 1967 was a result of the reduction of the Congress percentage

state had been able to prevent factionalism within its ranks (the principal reason for its defeat in 1967), thereby providing a minimal degree of continued coordination between party, government, and administration, it is doubtful that a Congress government would have been able to effect radical changes in the present structure of society. Had the Congress attempted major land reform legislation, effective local self-government legislation, changes in the tax policy of the government, or major alterations in the relationship between the public and private sector or between the administration and the party, it would have risked its already tenuous electoral margin. As it is, the defeat of the Congress party in West Bengal in 1967 promises to increase both political fragmentation within the state and the willingness of more and more laborers and peasants to participate in social and political conflicts.

These factors in turn indicate the extent to which the state of West Bengal will be dependent—for political stability, administrative effectiveness, and leadership in the areas of social change and economic development—on the central government and on outside agencies. The present coalition government, like the Congress government before it, will be heavily dependent on: (1) central government funds for the rehabilitation of refugees and for development projects; (2) central government administrators for large-scale industrial enterprises and for the development of the city of Calcutta; and (3) central government troops for the

---

of the vote (from 47.3 per cent in 1962 to 39.8 per cent in 1967), which was in turn caused by the defection of a number of Congressmen from Congress ranks (into the dissident Bangla Congress Party). Of a total of 280 seats in the West Bengal Legislative Assembly, Congress thus secured only 127 seats, a larger number than any other party, but nevertheless a minority. The fourteen-party coalition that succeeded the Congress was composed of two major blocs of parties: the People's United Left Front, which secured 66 seats (Bangla Congress, 37; CPI, 16; Forward Bloc, 13); and the United Left Front, which garnered 62 seats (Left CPI, 43; SSP, 7; RSP, 6; Socialist Unity Centre, 3; Workers' Party, 2; Forward Bloc-Marxist, 1). In addition, the PSP won 7 seats; the Swatantra, Jan Sangh, and Lok Sewak Sangh, 1 each; and the Gurkha League, 2—each of these parties joining the fourteen-party coalition.

The tenuous nature of the coalition is indicated by the fact that it can muster an absolute majority against the Congress in the legislature only when it is in complete unity and can add the vote of at least one Independent. The problems that can be expected to arise within the coalition are indicated by the wide variety of personal and political differences that separate the members of the coalition cabinet. Chief Minister Ajoy Mukherjee (Bangla Congress) and Food Minister P. C. Ghosh (PSP) are the only members of the Cabinet with previous Cabinet experience, and both are known to be in substantial disagreement with other major Cabinet Ministers on a number of important issues. As of this writing (early May 1967), the principal accomplishment of the coalition government was its ability to unite behind the 1967-68 budget that had been prepared by the outgoing Congress government, presented to the State Assembly by the new Finance Minister, Jyoti Basu (CPI).

maintenance of law and order. Should the present coalition government fall apart, the result would most likely be a return to the Congress party or a Congress coalition government, with all of the problems which that would entail. Equally plausible, in this atmosphere, is the possibility that continued instability might eventually lead either to a millenarian movement that promised a social revolution, or to eventual intervention by the center.

REFERENCES

Bose, Nirmal Kumar. *Modern Bengal.* Calcutta: Vidyodaya Library, 1959. Also published in *Man in India* (Calcutta), XXXVIII, No. 4 (October-December 1958), 229-95.

Bose, Subhas Chandra. *The Indian Struggle, 1920-1942.* Calcutta: Asia Publishing House, 1964. Originally published in two volumes.

Chaudhuri, Nirad C. *The Autobiography of an Unknown Indian.* London: Macmillan and Co., 1951.

Fibbertigibbet, "A Calcutta Diary," *Economic Weekly* (Bombay), 1956-1964.

Gupta, Atul Chandra (ed.). *Studies in the Bengal Renaissance.* Calcutta: National Council of Education of Bengal, 1958.

O'Malley, L. S. S. *History of Bengal, Bihar and Orissa Under British Rule.* Calcutta: Bengal Secretariat Book Depot, 1925.

Park, Richard L. "The Urban Challenge to Local and State Government: West Bengal, With Special Attention to Calcutta," in *India's Urban Future*, ed. Roy Turner. Bombay: Oxford University Press, 1962.

Sen, S. N. *The City of Calcutta: A Socio-Economic Survey, 1954-55 to 1957-58.* Calcutta: Bookland Private Limited, 1960.

Sinha, Narendra Krishna. *The Economic History of Bengal.* Calcutta: Firma K. L. Mukhopadhyay, 1956.

Sur, A. K. *History and Culture of Bengal.* Calcutta: Chuckervertti, Chatterjee and Co., 1963.

Weiner, Myron. "Changing Patterns of Political Leadership in West Bengal," in *Political Change in South Asia.* Calcutta: Firma K. L. Mukhopadhyay, 1963.

———. "Notes on Political Development in West Bengal," in *Political Change in South Asia.* Calcutta: Firma K. L. Mukhopadhyay, 1963.

RAJASTHAN

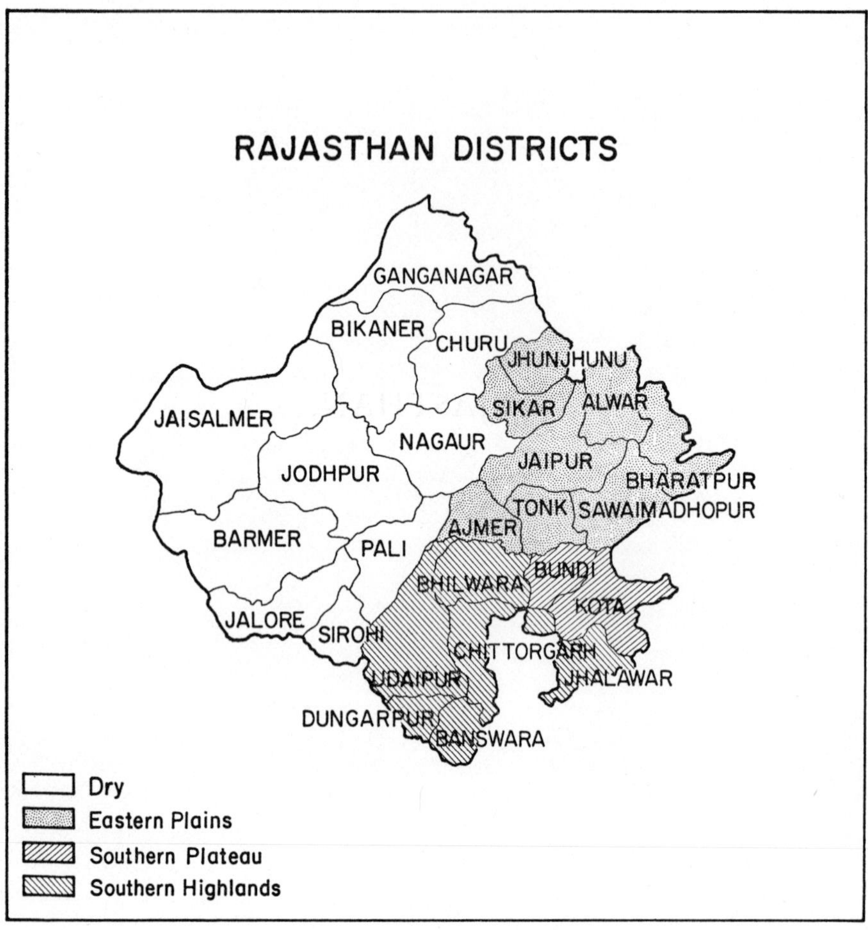
RAJASTHAN DISTRICTS
GANGANAGAR
BIKANER
CHURU
JHUNJHUNU
SIKAR
ALWAR
JAISALMER
NAGAUR
JAIPUR
JODHPUR
BHARATPUR
TONK
SAWAIMADHOPUR
AJMER
BARMER
PALI
BUNDI
BHILWARA
KOTA
JALORE
SIROHI
CHITTORGARH
UDAIPUR
JHALAWAR
DUNGARPUR
BANSWARA
Dry
Eastern Plains
Southern Plateau
Southern Highlands

VII

RAJASTHAN

LAWRENCE L. SHRADER

RAJASTHAN, located in the northwest corner of India, has an area of approximately 132,147 square miles and a population of some 20 million. Because its northern border is contiguous with West Pakistan, it ranks as one of the most strategically important states in the Indian Union. The famous "Pink City," Jaipur, is the capital, lying in the central eastern portion of the state. As the state's capital, Jaipur houses the Vidhan Sabha (Legislative Assembly) and the residences of the Governor and the Chief Minister, as well as the latter's cabinet members. Hence, Jaipur is the focal point of the state's busy politicking.

Most of what is present-day Rajasthan was created in the years 1948 and 1949, following India's independence; the state had no prior history as a political unit. Neither nature nor history had provided substantial support for the maintenance of the state as a political entity, since the area's geographical features, political history, and cultural and social structures were and are all characterized by diversity. Many of the state's political problems can be traced to these diverse objectives and historical conditions, which will be surveyed briefly before analyzing Rajasthan's politics.

The major geographical feature of Rajasthan is the Aravalli Hills, one of the oldest geological formations in India. This range cuts diagonally across the state from south to north, dividing it in half. These hills begin in Sirohi district in the southwest and extend northeastward through Ajmer district, continuing acrosss the state through the northern portions of Sikar and Jhunjhun districts. At this point the Aravalli Hills begin to break up, and finally slope and disappear in the Jumna River's delta area west of New Delhi. South of the Aravalli Hills, spurs extend in a discordant pattern, making much of the southern area of the state a contrast between rugged hills of no more than two thousand feet in altitude and plateau and valleys. Commencing at the southern extension of the hills in the west, the further eastward one continues, the less abrupt and rugged the spurs become, the eastern portion of the state south of the Aravalli Hills consisting of rolling plains, only occasionally broken by outcroppings or spurs. Above the Aravalli Hills lies the flat arid portion of the state; this becomes part of the Thar desert, which extends across the border into Pakistan.[1]

These distinct geographical divisions have influenced the area throughout its history. North of the Aravalli Hills, there have been no significant barriers to mobility except those created by the desert climatic conditions, which were not sufficient to discourage or limit trade and communications or dissuade invading armies. This mobility encouraged the development of similar social and political structures throughout the area. By contrast, the topography south of the Aravalli Hills (particularly in the southwest) has provided numerous barriers to communication and transportation, its rugged hills, high plateaus, and valleys making it possible for diverse peoples and small political units to survive in isolated pockets.[2] Because of these geographical differences there were historically only three autonomous political units north of the Aravalli Hills (the princely states of Jodhpur, Jaisalmer, and Bikaner), while south of the hills there were at least eighteen separate political units in existence at the time the modern state of Rajasthan was formed.

The recent political history of Rajasthan has not yet been able to overcome these basic geographical factors which tend to divide the state. Composed of twenty-one former princely states, Rajasthan's history has been characterized more by competition and conflict than by cooperation. With the exception of Ajmer district (the "eye of the Empire" in both the Mughal and British periods), no area of the state had experienced direct British rule during the colonial period since the region was ruled by traditional princely rulers, who were, in turn, under the surveillance of the British agent. Politically, the three states of Jodhpur, Udaipur, and Jaipur had dominated the history of Rajputana, and each state, was located in a distinctly separate region. Udaipur was the dominant power in the southwestern region south of the Aravalli Hills; and, aided by the ruling family's close ties with the Bhil tribesmen of the region, Udaipur had been able to maintain its political autonomy throughout the Mughal period despite the persistent efforts of the Mughals to conquer it. Udaipur's resistance, and particularly its refusal of offers of intermarriage with the Mughal court, is one of the proudest aspects of its historical legacy in Rajasthan today. However, the

[1] An old but apt description of Rajasthan's topography can be found in *The Rajputana Gazetteer*, Great Britain, Colonial Office (Calcutta: Office of the Superintendent of Government Printing, 1879), I, 10-13.

[2] One student of Indian history has described the region south of the Aravalli Hills as an "area of refuge" for displaced communities from the Gangetic Valley. K. M. Panikkar, *Geographical Factors in Indian History* (Bombay: Bharatiya Vidya Bhavan, 1959), p. 43.

struggle with the dominant power of north India and the later Maratha invaders from the south reduced the state and the ruling house to a condition of destitution, and only the agreement reached with Great Britain in the nineteenth century saved the ruling house from annihilation.

Jodhpur's relationship with the dominant power of north India ranged from open defiance to an alliance with both the Mughal and British governments, depending upon the exigencies of military conditions. Of the three major states, only Jaipur, the dominant power of the southeastern area, entered into a sustained and stable relationship with the dominant power in north India. The rulers of Jaipur served the Mughal rulers with distinction throughout India, and when the British succeeded the Mughals, Jaipur early negotiated a treaty with Great Britain.

Although the twenty-one princely states offer a pattern of diversity, some continuity and similarity were provided by the fact that seventeen of them had been ruled by members of the Rajput caste. In addition, the rulers in each of the three major princely states were also leaders of one of the three most important clans of the caste in the state. The Maharaja of Udaipur led the Seesodia clan, and his clansmen ruled the neighboring states of Shahpura, Pratapgerh, Banswara, and Kushalgarh. The Rathor clan's leadership rested with the ruling house of Jodhpur, and this house had combined with the ruling house of Bikaner to form this clan's domination of the northern half of the state. The Maharaja of Jaipur was the leader of the Kachawaha clan, and the princely states of Alwar and Karauli were controlled by his clansmen. Only the Maharaja of Jaisalmer and Jhalawar represented the Jadon clan in Rajasthan, and although a powerful clan elsewhere in India, it did not play a significant role in historic Rajputana.[3] The overall and general dominance of Rajput political control was, however, broken by the two Jat kingdoms of Bharatpur and Dholpur.

Thus, this Rajput dominance throughout most of the region meant that the traditional political system exhibited broadly similar characteristics. Hinduism was dominant throughout as were the ancient claims to authority contained within its system of beliefs. Each state had a court system composed of the ruler and his immediate family, attended by an aristocracy which was granted control over collection of land revenue in designated areas in return for loyal support to its respective rulers (in

[3] For a clear description of the relationship between clan membership and the ruling houses of Rajasthan, see Thakur S. J. Singhji Seesodia, *The Rajputs: A Fighting Race* (London: East and West, Ltd., 1915), pp. 50-65.

theory, at least), the provision of a specified number of armed men, and the performance of other duties of a semi-judicial and administrative nature. Each court was the center of cultural life, as well as of political power, and the courtly life of Rajputana produced some of the highest forms of north Indian painting and poetry. As centers of culture, however, each princely state encouraged the growth of distinct cultural forms and social customs peculiar to the respective courts, which further added to the cultural and linguistic diversities of the state, buttressed by the divisive geographical factors discussed above.

A similar system of land tenure, called the jagirdari system, was also practiced in the Rajput princely states. The jagirdari system derived from the practice of a ruler assigning land (jagir) to an individual (jagirdar) who, in return for payment of a set fee and/or services, had the right to collect revenue from his jagir. The fee or tribute paid by the jagirdar to the ruler varied, but it was always substantially less than the total revenue collected. The amount of revenue collected by jagirdars varied also, since the amount of revenue was based on specific arrangements each jagirdar made with individual peasant cultivators, ranging from one-eighth to one-half of the crop harvested. Often a large jagirdar would subdivide his jagir with sub-jagirdars who, in turn, might also repeat this fragmenting process. All land was cultivated, therefore, within the context of an elaborate web of agreements which, though their basic outline was restricted by tradition, were subject to frequent renegotiation at the succeeding lower levels.

At the time of Rajasthan's creation, this jagirdari system covered some 60 per cent of the area of the state. Security of land tenure varied according to local traditions and the existing economic and power relationships of the jagirdar to the peasantry. In general, economic factors tended to favor the jagirdar, since the conditions under which he received his jagir tended to be more stable than the conditions under which the peasant agreed to till the land. Thus with the general rise in agricultural prices during the twentieth century, especially during the two world wars, the jagirdars' profits greatly increased as the payments or tributes to their rulers remained constant while the land revenues collected mounted in value.[4]

The disadvantageous position of the peasantry was also evident in terms of land tenure. Of Rajasthan's total population, 77.23 per cent were engaged in agriculture in 1951; 50.3 per cent cultivated their

[4] The best analysis of the jagirdari system in Rajasthan at the time of independence can be found in Government of India, *Report of the Rajasthan-Madhya Bharat Jagir Enquiry Committee* (New Delhi: Government of India Press, 1950), *passim*.

own land and 23.38 per cent cultivated unowned land, while only a small percentage (3.55 per cent) were agricultural laborers.[5] Security of land tenure was lowest in the northwestern area of the state, where, for example, in the four districts of Barmer, Jalore, Jodhpur, and Nagaur in Jodhpur state, only 18.2 per cent of the total population of that region were owner-cultivators of their land. Land tenure was most secure in the southwestern area of the state, particularly in the former small princely states of Banswara and Dungarpur, 88.5 per cent of the latter population being owner-cultivators of the land.[6] Thus, although the security of land tenure varied greatly within the state, conditions of life did not differ as widely for the bulk of the peasantry. With the exception of Ganganagar district in the former Bikaner state, which benefited from irrigation canals constructed in the 1920s, the peasants' efforts to gain a livelihood from the land was a constant struggle, the poor land, inadequate water supply, and harassment of the jagirdar making survival itself an achievement.

Although Rajasthan was created by the merging of the twenty-one formerly *distinct* political units into one modern state political unit, many of the former princely states were broken up or merged together to form the twenty-six districts of the state's political divisions. Even though the disappearance of the historic political units of the state has not meant that they have *in fact* disappeared as effective political forces in the state, for purposes of analysis it is necessary to make more viable divisions which have relevance to regional forces and trends in the state today. For this reason, Rajasthan will be divided into four basic regions, and these have been superimposed on the map of the state.*

The Dry region consists of the ten districts which lie north of the Aravalli Hills and represent primarily the area covered by the former princely states of Bikaner and Jodhpur. The Eastern Plains region consists of the eight districts of southeastern Rajasthan and represents the area in which Jaipur state has historically dominated. The Southern Highlands region consists of the five districts of southwestern Rajasthan, and is the area wherein Udaipur state was the major princely state. The

[5] The figures for owned land are larger than the actual number of cultivators who really owned their own land, since cultivators of unowned land who had the right to bequeath the land to their heirs were included in this category by the 1951 census. For a discussion of the basis of classification in the 1951 census, see *Census of India, 1951*, Vol. I, Part I (New Delhi: Government of India Press, 1953), 95.

[6] For statistical information on land tenure in Rajasthan, see Government of Rajasthan, *A Report on the Panchayat Elections in Rajasthan, 1960* (Jaipur: Government of India Press, 1961), pp. 3-4.

* See Tables 7.13–7.16, pp. 393-395 for the district and regional areas of Rajasthan.

Southern Plateau region is composed of the three districts which represent the southern finger of the state, surrounded on three sides by the state of Madhya Pradesh.

The relationship between the social structure and the political system is fundamental to all political systems. In India the style of politics, the type of political leadership, the question of stability and instability, and the effectiveness of the political system are greatly influenced by the caste structure in most Indian states, where one meaning of the "politics of modernization" is the political mobilization of traditional groups in the society. The historic claims of caste on its members' loyalty make caste an important channel of political action. In a state such as Rajasthan, where little modernization has occurred, caste tends to be of even greater significance. It can be argued, as a general proposition, that if the state's caste structure is characterized by a numerically dominant caste, social supports for political unity will more likely be brought into play as political mobilization proceeds, and the caste structure can be utilized by political leaders in the creation of an effective and stable political system. State-wide leaders will be more likely to develop in such a state, and the legitimacy of the leader will be greater. Firmly supported by a significant section of the dominant caste, the political leaders can actually afford to be more accommodating to smaller caste groups and build a coalition which is multi-caste but which will have a central focus of political power. If, on the other hand, no dominant caste exists in the state, political mobilization will be more likely to activate divisive forces within its social structure, thereby offering less social support for an effective political system at the state level. It will thus be more difficult for political leaders to establish state-wide influence, as well as a high degree of legitimacy. Their political support will lack a focus of power and will have to depend to a greater extent on shifting coalitions of factional groups within and outside of the party. Political control will tend to be based more on political manipulation, a balancing of one group or region against another, and the utilization of influence and corruption techniques, even of violence or threats of violence. The dominant political coalition in both types of states will be based on a multicaste alliance, but states with no focus of power will be less stable and less effective.

Rajasthan's caste structure falls into the second category; and, although it is difficult to obtain reliable information regarding the caste structure of Rajasthan today, sufficient information exists in earlier census data to obtain an accurate *general* picture of its caste structure. As shown in Table 7.1 below, Rajasthan's caste structure lacks any numerically dominant caste. In addition, some of its larger caste groups are concentrated in specific regions. Older census data may well be more reliable in Rajasthan than in other states, since less political and economic development has taken place in Rajasthan than in many other states.

TABLE 7.1

MAJOR CASTES OF RAJASTHAN

Caste	*% of Population*
Jat	9.2
Brahman	7.6
Mahajan	7.4
Chamar	6.8
Bhil	5.8
Rajput	5.6
Mina	5.4
Gujar	4.7
Mali	3.3
Total	55.8

SOURCE: *Census of India, 1931*, Vol. XXVII, *Rajputana Agency*, Government of India (Meerut: Government of India, 1932), p. 124.

The 1931 census reported 13 castes with over 100,000 members; combined, these castes represented 71 per cent of the population at the time. Table 7.1 lists the nine largest castes in the state. Of these, one is a Scheduled Caste (Chamar), two are Scheduled Tribes (Bhil and Mina), three are agricultural castes (Mali, Gujar, and Jat), and three represent the traditional "twice-born" castes (Brahman, Mahajan, and Rajput).[7] Of the nine castes, only four are broadly distributed throughout the state. One is the Chamars, but because of this caste's low social status, level of economic development, and education, they have not acted as an effective state-wide caste. Only the three "twice-born" castes can be considered to be state-wide castes; all the others are concentrated in limited areas of the state. The Jats are the largest single caste in the state, but they are concentrated in the Dry and Eastern Plains regions. In the latter region, they are almost entirely limited to the northern districts of the region.[8] South of this area and in the Southern Plateau and Southern

[7] Almost all of the Mahajans consist of the Agarwals, the Khandelwals, the Mahesris, and the Oswals in Rajasthan.

[8] In Jhunjhunu, Sikar, and Bharatpur districts, as well as in the northern portion of Jaipur district. The northern portion of Jaipur district and Jhunjhunu and Sikar districts have been known as the Shekawati region, and this area will be referred to by this term.

Highlands regions, they form an insignificant caste. The Gujars, a second agricultural caste, is not a significant caste in the Dry region, but in the other three regions they represent between 4 and 8 per cent of the population. The concentration of the Mina and Bhil Scheduled Tribes is even greater. The Bhils live almost exclusively in the Southern Highlands region, where they form approximately 25 per cent of the population. In the former states of Banswara and Dungarpur, they represented 64 per cent and 54 per cent of the population respectively, and in the smaller princely state of Kushalgarh they constituted 84 per cent of the population. The Minas are concentrated in the Southern Plateau region and the southern half of the Eastern Plains region. In 1931 the Minas represented approximately 8 per cent of the total population of the princely states which made up the Southern Plateau region, and with the formation of Rajasthan, this percentage rose to over 10 per cent since the non-Mina areas of the region were incorporated into the adjoining state of Madhya Pradesh. In the Eastern Plains region, the Minas represent the third largest caste group, with approximately 8 per cent of the total population, concentrated for the most part in what is now Alwar, Sawai Madhopur, and Jaipur districts.[9] The Mali caste follows the pattern of the Scheduled Tribes and the agricultural castes to a lesser degree. They form from 2 to 5 per cent of the population in all regions of the state, except the Southern Plateau region, where they are numerically insignificant.

These figures do not represent a complete description of Rajasthan's caste system, for there are many other smaller concentrations of particular castes. Nevertheless, it does serve to indicate the mosaic of castes. None of the peasant and Scheduled Castes and Tribes are state-wide castes; and, above the village level, there are few castes which dominate any area in terms of forming a majority caste. In addition, the non-state-wide castes are distinct autonomous caste groupings, with no historical linkage between or among them, and therefore no traditional basis for mutual cooperation. Their traditional social organization was limited horizontally in terms of regions and vertically in terms of social stratification.

The three "twice-born" castes tend to be much more evenly distributed throughout the state. The Brahmans ranged from 5 per cent to 9 per cent of the population in all four regions of the state, with their

[9] The 1931 census reported that in Karauli state, which was combined with a portion of Jaipur state to form the present district of Sawai Madhopur, the Minas represented 23 per cent of the population. In the former Jaipur state, the Minas represented approximately 10 per cent of the population at the same time. *Census of India, 1931*, pp. 166-68.

highest concentration in the Eastern Plains region, where they represent approximately 9 per cent of the population. The Rajput caste in each region varies from approximately 2 per cent to 8 per cent of the population, with their highest concentration in the Dry region. The Mahajan castes are less evenly distributed throughout the state, but with the exception of the Southern Plateau region, they represent from 3 per cent to 7 per cent of the population. In the Southern Plateau region they are slightly less than 1 per cent of the population. The state-wide castes of Rajasthan have provided most of the political leadership in the state since independence. For the most part, the Brahman, Mahajan, and Jat castes have provided the modernist leadership, and the Rajput caste has provided the leadership of the opposition and of tradition.

Rajasthan emerged as a state in the Indian Union with few of the prerequisites for an effective basis of unity. The continuation of the princely state political system and the jagirdari system of land control in much of the state did little to encourage forces of modernization and social reform. As a consequence, little social mobility or economic development occurred until the last decade. Until its formation, as a state, the area of Rajasthan remained a stronghold of traditional India, divided by ancient loyalties and rivalries. Social and economic change did not come until after a basic political change had occurred, and this coincided with the establishment of the state in 1949. These changes, however, had to be superimposed on a political unit which provided few supports for effective political action. Rajasthan was a challenge to political imagination and political leadership and remains so even today.

THE POLITICAL PROCESS

As of today, after three general elections, a stable political party system does not yet exist in Rajasthan. The Congress party has experienced two major changes in political leadership, and four changes in the post of chief minister. In the twelve years since the first general elections, the party has been characterized by factionalism—a condition which has required frequent intervention from New Delhi. A summary of election results is presented in Table 7.2.

Despite the problems faced by the Congress party and despite a significant challenge from the Rajput aristocracy of the state in both 1952 and 1962, the Congress party has managed to remain in continuous control of the state since its formation. However, in the first and third general elections, its control was based on a bare majority. The largest opposition party in 1962 was the recently formed Swatantra party, led by the

TABLE 7.2

GENERAL ELECTIONS: RESULTS OF THREE GENERAL ELECTIONS[a]

Party	Assembly Seats Won 1952	1957	1962
Congress	82	119	88
Ram Rajya Parishad (RRP)	24	16	3
Jan Sangh (JS)	8	6	15
Socialists	1	0	5
PSP	0	1	2
Independents	35	33	21
KLP	7	0	0
Communist Party of India (CPI)	0	1	6
Swatantra	0	0	36
Hindu Mahasabha	2	0	0
KMPP (Kripalani)	1	0	0
Totals	160	176	176

[a] See Table 7.8 for a regional and district breakdown of the results of three general elections.

Maharani of Jaipur, which won 36 seats in the third general elections. But the Swatantra party's capacity to function effectively as a political party over a sustained period of time has not yet been tested, and this capacity cannot simply be assumed to exist. In 1962 the Jan Sangh was the third largest political party in the state, 15 of its candidates winning Assembly seats in a legislature totaling 176 seats. It was also the only party, outside of the Congress, which had convincingly demonstrated its ability to function effectively over a period of time. Compared to its performance at the polls in the 1952 election, Jan Sangh's representation was nearly doubled in 1962, and its organization had increased in both scope and effectiveness. The formerly significant Ram Rajya Parishad's representation in the Legislative Assembly had dwindled to 3 from a high of 24 MLAs in 1952, at which time this party was the major opposition party. By 1962 it had ceased to be an effective political party in the state. Both the RRP and the Swatantra party were primarily controlled by elements of the Rajput aristocracy, and even though the Swatantra party was the successor party, there was little continuity or overlapping in terms of political leadership or of regions of political strength. The major strength of the RRP had been located in the Dry region of the state, where it had won 10 of its 16 seats in the 1957 elections; the Swatantra party's strength in 1962 lay principally in the Eastern Plains region. Thus, while drawing on the same social strata and traditions, they were two distinct political movements.

Parties of the left, such as the PSP, the Socialist party, and the CPI, as well as the now defunct KMPP and KLP, had not established any distinct political tradition in the state, nor had they shown signs of becoming effective state-wide political parties. None contested a majority of Assembly seats in 1962, and the CPI, the strongest party of the left in 1964 with 6 Assembly seats, had been the weakest in 1952. Nevertheless, despite the failure in establishing a stable political party system, there was some evidence that Rajasthan politics was becoming more institutionalized and that parties were becoming more effective means of aggregating political interests.

Although the total proportion of independent candidates rose from 37 per cent in 1952 to 44 per cent in 1962, the political parties were contesting more constituencies in 1962 than in 1952. In 1952 the RRP contested the greatest number of Assembly seats of any opposition party, sponsoring candidates in 38 per cent of the state's constituencies. In 1962 both the Jan Sangh and the Swatantra party contested more than 50 per cent of the Assembly constituencies. The 1962 election also produced the first Assembly in which independent candidates did not form the single largest group of MLAs. In addition, successful candidates for the Assembly were mobilizing larger blocs of voters behind their candidacy in 1962. Despite a rise in the number of multi-cornered electoral contests in the Assembly elections,[10] the percentage of seats won with 21-30 per cent of the total votes fell from 15.7 per cent of the total seats in 1952 to 1.7 per cent in 1962. Correspondingly, the number of seats won with 41-50 per cent of the votes increased by nearly 11 per cent in 1962. Thus, even though an effective political party system had not yet developed, more candidates ran under party labels and more party candidates were winning at the polls.

Only the Congress party has significant roots in pre-independence political movements in Rajasthan, and while these are not deep, they are important since they are the political roots of nearly all major political leaders in the state. The Congress party was formed out of the Praja Mandals which developed in most of the princely states in the 1930s and 1940s. Each Praja Mandal was an autonomous unit, and even after the formation of the All-India States Peoples Conference in 1933 to co-

[10] Between 1952 and 1962, the number of straight contests for the Assembly declined from 17.4 per cent of the total seats contested to 3.8 per cent, and the number of constituencies with five or more candidates rose from 30 per cent to nearly 50 per cent of the total. This information is based on an analysis of material contained in Government of Rajasthan, Bureau of Statistics, Rajasthan, *A Statistical Study of the General Elections in Rajasthan, 1952*, p. 16; and Government of Rajasthan, Election Department, *Candidates for General Elections in Rajasthan, 1962*, pp. 1-59.

ordinate political activities in the Indian states, there was little cooperation among the Praja Mandalists of the state. It was not until the Rajasthan Congress was formed after independence that a true state-wide political organization came into existence.

In the larger princely states of Rajasthan, nationalist political activity dates back to the 1920s. Jai Narain Vyas formed the *Marwar* (Jodhpur) *Hitkarani Sabha* as early as 1923 in his native state, in order to "promote the political, social and economic interests of the people of Marwar."[11] However, by 1925 the state's government suppressed the Sabha, and Vyas was exiled, forcing him to shift his base of operation to Ajmer where he continued his political activities while publishing a vernacular weekly. In 1929 he returned to Jodhpur to establish the Marwar State Peoples Conference; but he was soon forced to leave Jodhpur again or face imprisonment, whereupon he chose the former course. He later became a secretary of the All-India States Peoples Conference, a position which required most of his time and energies, and during this time he lived in Ajmer and later in Bombay. However, at the time of the formation of Rajasthan, Jai Narain Vyas was one of the few political leaders who was already widely known and respected throughout Rajasthan.

A second major early nationalist leader emerged in Udaipur state—Manik Lal Varma. He was engaged in political and social uplift work by the early 1920s in his home state, and he became the leader of the Udaipur Praja Mandal when it was formed in the late 1930s. He himself never held an elective office in the state government, but he became a major force in the state after 1949, and his protégé, Mohan Lal Sukhadia, has been Rajasthan's most successful chief minister. In Jaipur state leaders such as Harilal Shastri and Gokulbhai Bhatt were active about the same time as Manik Lal Varma and Jai Narain Vyas. They formed the *Charkha Sangh*, a social uplift organization with strong political overtones which later became the nucleus for the Praja Mandal movement in the state.[12]

These early leaders of nationalist movements were the only prominent state-wide political figures in the state after the formation of Rajasthan. However, another stratum of nationalists, a younger generation, emerged during the mid-1930s in the larger states of Rajasthan just about the

[11] Kishen Puri, *Memoirs of the Marwar Police* (2nd ed.; Jodhpur: Jodhpur Government Press, 1938), pp. 145-46.

[12] Much of this information is based on talks the writer held with former nationalist leaders while in Rajasthan and on an analysis of biographical data collected at that time.

time the Praja Mandals were being formed. Born, for the most part, between 1910 and 1920, this second generation of nationalists became politically conscious while obtaining their education (outside their home state in many cases) during the rise of nationalist sentiment in the 1930s. Upon returning home they plunged into political activities. This second generation of nationalists was to produce major political figures in Rajasthan, such as the present chief minister Mohan Lal Sukhadia, Damodar Lal Vyas, and Mathura Das Mathur, who by the mid-1950s were to replace many of the older nationalist leaders.

The Praja Mandal organizations were, for the most part, limited to the towns and cities of the state, and the leadership was well educated and drawn principally from the Brahman and Mahajan castes. Of the 89 MLAs of the first two Assemblies who had been Praja Mandal members, 39 belonged to these two castes. Their control of major government and party posts was even higher than this figure would indicate. Of the 89 Praja Mandal MLAs, 36 held college degrees; 27 held law degrees, and 15 had earned MA degrees. Well-educated, particularly in the context of Rajasthan, the Praja Mandalists represented the non-aristocratic urban elite of the state. Because of their social origins and the difficulties of communication, as well as the oppressive government measures against their political activities, the Praja Mandals did not develop extensive ties in the countryside. The political mobilization of the peasantry was to be a post-independence phenomenon in most sections of the state.

In terms of ideology, the Praja Mandals were influenced by Gandhi and employed non-violent techniques to achieve their goals. Like the Indian National Congress, the Praja Mandals assumed that the primary struggle was the anti-colonial struggle and not the "anti-feudal struggle" against the princely aristocracy. They correctly believed that the abolition of the princely state system would follow as a consequence of ending colonial control, rather than as a result of waging separate political agitations. Thus the Praja Mandalists tended to focus their attention on the broad political goals of the Indian National Congress in British India and on social uplift work at home, particularly among the depressed classes of the states. Their movement was not a conscious class- or caste-based movement, and their techniques and political goals emphasized unity of all classes and castes toward the achievement of their aims.

The only significant break with the Brahman-Mahajan dominance of pre-independence political activity in Rajasthan was in the Jat region of the state. Here a Jat-based leadership emerged during the

1930s and the early 1940s. Led for the most part, by petty functionaries of Jodhpur and Bikaner states, the Jat political leaders tended to emphasize conflict and the anti-feudal struggle, and their strategies were based more on conflict, class and caste. Their immediate objectives were focused more on economic issues and the abolition of the jagirdari land system and the princely state system than were those of the Praja Mandalist leadership elsewhere in the state. This was true whether their organization was within the general nationalist movement in the state, as in Bikaner state where Kumbharam Arya led the Praja Parishad movement, or outside the nationalist movement, as in Jodhpur state, or whether the Jat leadership participated in both the Praja Mandal and the Kisan Sabha movements, as it did in the Shekawati districts of Jaipur state and Bharatpur state. All Jat leaders were carriers of an agrarian radicalism which they have never given up.

The most significant movement outside the nationalist organizations was the Marwar (Jodhpur) Kisan Sabha. Its origins lay in a social reform movement within the Jat caste dating from the 1920s. Its leader was Baldev Ram Mirdha, who rose to the rank of Deputy Inspector General of Police in Jodhpur state but had also devoted much of his attention and energies to uplift work among his fellow Jat caste members. In this endeavor, he utilized his position in the state's bureaucracy to recruit Jats to government posts and sponsored the establishment of Jat student hostels which housed sons of peasants while they gained an education. From his efforts a small but dedicated educated Jat elite group emerged in Jodhpur; such future political leaders as Baldev Ram Mirdha's son, Ram Niwas Mirdha, and his nephew, Nathu Ram Mirdha, and many of their closest political associates lived together in these hostels during the 1930s. During World War II they formed the Marwar Kisan Sabha, which became the major political organization in Jodhpur state and the only organization with close contact with the countryside. The principal aims of the Marwar Kisan Sabha were immediate and economic, not long-term or nationalistic. Its aims were the abolition of the jagirdari system, the ending of the jagirdar's traditional rights of demanding forced labor from the peasantry, and the establishment of legal protections for tenancy rights. It was willing to confront the landed aristocracy in the countryside directly and its agitations led to sporadic armed conflicts between the peasantry and their jagirdars. For this organization the major enemy was the Rajput aristocracy not the British, and the ideology was popularist and conflict-oriented.

During the years preceding the formation of Rajasthan and the first general elections, Jodhpur state presented the most clearly drawn picture of the fundamental conflicts the new state of Rajasthan would have to meet in the future, and the political developments between 1946 and 1951 fundamentally affected the political history of the state. In the first place, the Rajput aristocracy was adamantly opposed to giving up its traditional rights. Against them was pitted the Kisan Sabha, equally insistent on a fundamental change in both the economic and political systems. The nationalist leadership recruited by the Praja Mandal movement under the leadership of Jai Narain Vyas was restricted to the urban centers of the state (principally Jodhpur city) and as the representative now of the Congress party, the Mandal had to face the possibility of being opposed by two political forces over which it had no direct influence.

The Marwar Kisan Sabha leadership had ambitions of serving as the nucleus for a state-wide agrarian movement which would either replace the nationalist leaderhip or become the dominant element within the Congress party. In pursuit of its policy of direct confrontation with the aristocracy and as a protest against the worsening conditions in the countryside which followed the withdrawal of British influence from Jodhpur state, the Marwar Kisan Sabha launched a series of agitations between 1946 and 1949 to abolish the jagirdari system. Meeting limited success in these efforts, however, the Marwar Kisan Sabha supported the formation of a state-wide Kisan Sabha by attempting to unite the Kisan Sabha movements formed earlier in the Shekawati districts of northern Jaipur state and Bharatpur state and to extend its organization below the Aravalli Hills. In addition, the plan envisaged unity with the Bikaner Praja Parishad movement led by Kumbharam Arya. If successful, a state-wide peasant-based movement would have been established and a third political elite would have come into existence, juxtaposed with the existing Rajput elite and the leaders of the nationalist movement in the state.

Several factors defeated these efforts. One was the heterogeneous caste structure of Rajasthan. Although the Marwar Kisan Sabha successfully allied itself with other peasant castes (such as the Vishnoi and Sirvi castes), in the non-Jat areas of the state the Kisan Sabha leaders were unsuccessful in gaining support among peasant castes. Second, the Kisan Sabha movements in such states as Bharatpur and the Shekawati districts of Jaipur state had not remained completely outside the Praja Mandal movement, and the Kisan Sabha leaders were members of both the Kisan Sabha and the Praja Mandal organizations. These men, such as Kumbharam Arya of Bikaner state, automatically gained access to the Congress party when the Praja Mandals became the Congress party and hence were reluctant to leave the Congress, for to do so would have meant casting their future with the new Rajasthan Kisan Sabha.

The challenge represented by the leadership of the Marwar Kisan Sabha and the Rajput aristocracy, the latter organized under the leadership of the Maharaja of Jodhpur, could not be ignored by the new Congress party. The Jodhpur Congressmen, including Jai Narain Vyas, realized that their influence in the countryside was nominal and if the election was to be won in Jodhpur an alliance with at least one of the two powerful rural groups was essential. The history of the jagirdar-Jat conflict in the area made it unlikely that both groups could be accommodated immediately within the Congress party; nevertheless, the Congress party apparently negotiated with both groups. If an agreement could have been reached with the Maharaja of Jodhpur and his supporters, it would have had the effect of placing the Marwar Kisan Sabha outside the Congress party and perhaps drawn other Jat leaders from other areas of Rajasthan out of the party. This would have fundamentally altered the pattern of contending forces in the forthcoming election and perhaps the political history of Rajasthan itself. The negotiations failed, however, for the Maharaja demanded too much in terms of allocation of seats and the Congress was unable to fully satisfy the Rajput demands on the complicated question of the forthcoming resumption of jagirdaris. Working through such Congress Jat leaders as Kumbharam Arya, the Marwar Kisan Sabha leadership reached an agreement with the Congress whereby they joined the Congress party, having been granted the right to select 50 per cent of the candidates for the Legislative Assembly from the Jodhpur state region and also having been guaranteed money and jeeps for use in the election campaign. Through this agreement, the Congress party gained direct contact with the countryside in Jodhpur and the Marwar Kisan Sabha gained access to New Delhi and the national leadership of the dominant political party of the nation; the Sabha merged its political cadre with the old Praja Mandal organization, thereby enhancing its capacity for political organization.[13]

Thus, by the time the first general elections were held, the Congress party had incorporated two types of political leaders into the party. The largest group consisted of the old Praja Mandal members, controlled by a Brahman-Mahajan-based leadership, Gandhian in ideology, and drawn primarily from urban areas of the state. The Praja Mandal group came

[13] This latter consideration was not inconsequential for, according to one of the major leaders of the Marwar Kisan Sabha, their movement had been severely hampered by lack of an educated cadre.

from throughout the state. The smaller group was the Jat leadership of northern Rajasthan, somewhat younger than most of the major Praja Mandal leaders, non-Gandhian, and with a history of agrarian struggle and radicalism.

Political Leadership in Rajasthan

For the most part, the major political leaders of Rajasthan have come from the ranks of the members of the Legislative Assembly, so that an analysis of these men would provide a broad general view of the basic characteristics of the state's political leadership.

Tables 7.3 through 7.7 summarize the most important characteristics of the MLAs. An examination of Tables 7.3 and 7.4 reveals overwhelmingly large numbers of Brahman, Rajput, Mahajan, and Jat MLAs in the first and second Legislative Assemblies. Based on the 1931 census, these groups constituted only approximately 30 per cent of the state's population, and yet the MLAs from these castes comprised 63 per cent of the first Assembly and 57 per cent of the second Assembly. The preponderance of these four castes continued even while wide swings of strength occurred in terms of both political parties and individual caste percentages between these two Assemblies. Although Rajasthan has no numerically dominant caste, these four castes represent the dominant political castes in the state. The proportion of members of the Brahman, Mahajan, Rajput, and Jat castes contrasts sharply with the Mali and Gujar castes. Together, these latter two castes account for approximately 8 per cent of the state's population, but in the second Assembly, the members from these two castes composed only 3 per cent of the Assembly's membership. This figure appears to be an increase over the first Assembly, despite the fact that the data are less complete.

Tables 7.3 and 7.4 also indicate the party affiliation of the MLAs. Dividing the MLAs into those who were members of the Congress party and those who were members of the Opposition, a marked change in the caste composition of the two groups is apparent. Of the 73 Opposition MLAs in the first Assembly for whom information is available 53 were members of the Rajput caste, and only 2 Rajputs were members of the Congress party. However, in the second Assembly the Rajputs accounted for only 13 of the 49 Opposition MLAs, and the number of Rajputs belonging to the Congress party increased to 14. By 1957, while still forming a major part of the Opposition, a substantial influx of Rajputs into the Congress party had occurred.

The time of political recruitment was also affected by caste membership, as is shown in Table 7.5. Approximately 85 per cent of the Brahman

TABLE 7.3

CASTE OF MLAS ELECTED TO THE LEGISLATIVE ASSEMBLY, 1952–57

Caste	*Cong.*	*RRP*	*Ind.*	*JS*	*KLP*	*KMPP*	*HM*	*CPI*	*PSP*	*Caste totals*	*% of Total by caste*
Brahman	18	0	1	0	0	1	0	1	0	21	13.0
Rajput	2	22	23	7	0	0	1	0	0	55	34.0
Jat	11	0	1	0	2	0	0	0	0	14	8.6
Mahajan	11	0	1	0	0	0	0	0	0	12	7.4
Gujar	0	0	0	0	0	0	0	0	0	0	0
Mali	0	0	0	0	0	0	0	0	0	0	0
Kayasth	2	0	0	0	0	0	0	0	0	2	1.2
Scheduled Caste	13	0	0	0	1	0	0	0	0	14	8.6
Scheduled Tribe	5	0	0	0	0	0	0	0	0	5	3.1
Muslim	3	0	0	0	0	0	0	0	0	3	1.8
Unknown	24	2	5	0	4	0	0	0	1	36	22.2
Totals	89	24	31	7	7	1	1	1	1	162	

and Mahajan MLAs were recruited into politics prior to attainment of national independence, as were 50 per cent of the Jat MLAs. Only 14 per cent of the Rajput MLAs were active at a similar date. Many of the Scheduled Castes and Scheduled Tribes MLAs were also active in politics prior to independence, and this reflects the significance of social uplift work carried on by Congress party workers among the depressed castes before 1947.

Social status and education were also important factors in political recruitment. Except for the Jat caste, the politically dominant castes are all high-status castes. As shown in Table 7.6, the MLAs of the politically dominant castes were the most highly educated members of the Assembly. From 47 per cent to 67 per cent had obtained college degrees, a sub-

TABLE 7.4

CASTE OF MLAs ELECTED IN SECOND GENERAL ELECTIONS TO MAY 1960

aste	*Cong.*	*RRP*	*Ind.*	*JS*	*PSP*	*CPI*	*Caste totals*	*% of Total by caste*
rahman	19	1	2	0	1	0	23	13.7
ajput	14	9	3	1	0	0	27	16.1
at	18	0	5	0	0	1	24	14.3
ahajan	18	1	1	1	0	0	21	12.5
ujar	1	0	2	1	0	0	4	2.4
ali	1	0	0	0	0	0	1	.6
cheduled Caste	23	4	2	0	0	0	29	17.2
heduled Tribe	13	1	6	1	0	0	21	12.5
ayasth	4	0	0	1	0	0	5	3.0
uslim	3	0	0	0	0	0	3	1.8
nknown	6	0	2	1	0	0	9	5.4
rvi	0	0	1	0	0	0	1	.5
Totals	120	16	24	6	1	1	168	100.0

stantially larger proportion than any other caste group in the Assembly, with the exception of the numerically insignificant Kayastha caste. Excluding the Rajput MLAs, a large number of the other three castes had obtained law degrees and masters' degrees. For the Assemblies as a whole, there was no marked shift in the level of education, although the number of holders of college degrees fell slightly, from 51 per cent to 45 per cent of the MLAs.

In terms of age, the MLAs are generally young. Table 7.7 shows that 60 per cent of the MLAs in the first Assembly and 80 per cent in the second Assembly were born after 1910. The largest proportion of them were born in the decade between 1915 and 1925: 41 per cent of the MLAs

TABLE 7.5

CASTE AND DATE OF ENTRANCE INTO POLITICS

Caste	*Pre-1942*	*1942–47*	*1947–52*	*1952 or after*	*Date unknown*	*Totals*
Brahman	23 (63.9)[a]	8 (22.2)	0	3 (8.3)	2 (5.5)	36
Rajput	2 (3.0)	7 (10.5)	9 (13.6)	27 (40.9)	21 (31.8)	66
Jat	8 (23.5)	9 (26.5)	4 (11.8)	6 (17.6)	7 (20.6)	34
Mahajan	14 (53.8)	8 (30.8)	3 (11.5)	1 (3.8)	0	26
Gujar	0	0	0	3 (75.0)	1 (25.0)	4
Mali	0	0	0	0	1 (100)	1
Scheduled Caste	11 (32.3)	5 (14.7)	7 (20.6)	4 (11.8)	7 (20.6)	34
Scheduled Tribe	3 (12.5)	6 (25.0)	6 (25.0)	5 (20.8)	4 (16.7)	24
Kayasth	4 (80.0)	0	0	0	1 (20.0)	5
Muslim	2 (33.3)	1 (16.7)	2 (33.3)	1 (16.7)	0	6
Unknown	5 (11.9)	9 (21.4)	5 (11.9)	9 (21.4)	14 (33.3)	42
Totals	72 (25.8)	53 (19.0)	36 (12.9)	60 (21.5)	58 (20.8)	279

[a] Figures in parentheses represent the percentage of MLAs from each particular caste wh[o] entered politics at the time.

in the first Assembly were born during this ten-year period, and almost 50 per cent in the second Assembly. In both Assemblies there was a larger proportion of younger MLAs among non-Congress than among Congress party MLAs: 31 per cent and 51 per cent of the non-Congress MLAs in the first and second Assemblies, respectively, were born after 1921, while the corresponding figures for the Congress MLAs were 29 per cent and 44 per cent. The larger pool of potential candidates in the Congress party requires that capable party workers must either wait longer to become MLAs, or else they must leave the party and run against the official Congress party ticket.

In summary, high social status, a college education, an age of between 30 and 45 years, and experience in pre-independence political activities

TABLE 7.6

EDUCATION BY CASTE OF MLAs
RAJASTHAN LEGISLATIVE ASSEMBLY, 1952–MAY 1960*
(*in per cent*)

EDUCATIONAL LEVELS	CASTE											
	Brahman	*Rajput*	*Mahajan*	*Jat*	*Gujar*	*Mali*	*Kayasth*	*Scheduled Caste*	*Scheduled Tribe*	*Other*	*Muslim*	*Caste Unknown*
No formal education	0	0	7.7	2.9	0	0	0	21.7	17.1	0	0	2.4
Primary and middle schools	8.3	12.1	15.4	29.4	50.0	0	40.0	47.8	37.1	0	33.3	28.6
High school	13.9	16.7	19.2	17.6	25.0	100	0	4.3	25.7	0	0	7.1
College degree**	66.9	65.1	53.8	47.0	25.0	0	60.0	13.0	17.1	100	33.3	45.2
LL.B.	44.4	15.1	50.0	29.4	0	0	40.0	8.7	8.6	100	33.3	28.6
Master's degree	22.2	6.1	30.8	20.6	0	0	20.0	0	5.7	100	50.0	19.0
Medical degree	0	0	3.8	0	0	0	0	0	0	0	0	2.4
Education Unknown	0	4.5	0	0	0	0	0	0	0	0	16.7	9.5
Total Number of MLAs (279)	36	66	26	34	4	1	5	23	35	1	6	42

* The information in this table is based on 279 MLAs, which represent 91 per cent of the MLAs elected between 1952 and May 1960.

** MLAs holding more than one advanced degree are included in each category. The percentages for College degree, LL.B., and Master's degree are therefore based on the total number of MLAs holding each degree.

TABLE 7.7

Age Structure of MLAs Born Between 1910 and 1930

Years of Birth	Total No.	% of Assembly
A. FIRST ASSEMBLY		
1910–14	24	14.2
1915–25	67	41.3
1926–30	10	6.1
Totals	101	61.6
B. SECOND ASSEMBLY		
Years of Birth	*Total No.*	*% of Assembly*
1910–14	17	10.1
1915–25	83	49.4
1926–30	33	13.7
Totals	133	73.2

are the principal prerequisites for political leadership in Rajasthan today.

Changes in Political Leadership

At the time the state of Rajasthan was created, no effective state-wide political leadership existed, and much of the political history of the state is closely related to this central fact. However, two potential sources of leadership existed. One was the recently formed Rajasthan Congress party, and the other the Rajput aristocracy. Although having been politically dominant for centuries in the state, the Rajput aristocracy had been historically divided. Each princely state was officially an autonomous unit, and political loyalty was limited to its boundaries although broader clan loyalties did exist. However, even these clan loyalties were limited to specific regions of the state. Consequently, no ruler could appeal directly to the jagirdari class in another state unless he was supported in his appeal by the ruling family of that particular state. Thus, their political effectiveness on a state-wide basis depended on the element of cooperation among at least the major former ruling families of the state.

Thus far there has been no effective cooperation between any of the major ruling houses of Rajasthan. A brief survey of the political activities of the Bikaner, Jodhpur, Udaipur, and Jaipur ruling families will illustrate this point.

The Maharaja of Udaipur has eschewed politics since independence, and he has not used his influence or position to openly support any political party. Members of the three other major ruling families have been active in politics at least at some time between 1952 and 1962. The Maharaja of Bikaner was elected to parliament in all three elections as an independent candidate. He has refused to associate or lend his support to any political party, although he has from time to time expressed the wish to lead a united front composed of all leftist and rightist parties against the Congress party. In 1952 the Maharaja of Jodhpur was the most significant political figure among the former rulers. In his former state he led a powerful coalition of independent candidates, composed chiefly of jagirdars, which, except for the Jat stronghold in Nagaur district, succeeded in winning nearly all Assembly seats in Jalore, Pali, and Jodhpur districts. Although in loose alliance with other jagirdari forces throughout the state who were supported by the Kshatriya Mahasabha,[14] his political effort was principally an independent one. However, the Maharaja was lost to the state as a potential political leader when he was killed in an airplane crash in January 1952. Since his death, the royal family of Jodhpur has continued to be active in politics, especially the Maharaja's uncle, Ajit Singh, and in 1962 the family sponsored an *ad hoc* united front composed mainly of dissident Congressmen. It had little success, and this is perhaps best indicated by the fact that in the three districts of Jalore, Pali, and Jodhpur where the Congress party was unable to win any Assembly seats against the Maharaja of Jodhpur's candidates in 1952, it won 13 out of the 20 Assembly seats in 1962.

It was only in 1962 that the ruling family of Jaipur became actively engaged in politics, and its initial effort surpassed that of the Maharaja of Jodhpur in 1952. Unlike other political efforts of the Rajput ruling families, the Maharani of Jaipur associated herself with a political party by joining the recently formed Swatantra party. She not only stood for parliament on Swatantra's ticket but also became the party's dominant figure in the state. She also extended the scope of her activities beyond the boundaries of the former Jaipur state, for the Swatantra party ran candidates in over 50 per cent of the state's Assembly districts. Although aided in her efforts by the Maharaja of Dungarpur, who was second in command of the party, the Maharani was unable to gain the support of any of the major ruling houses in the state. They all preferred to continue their independent political activities or remain apolitical. Partly

[14] The Kshatriya Mahasabha endorsed 140 Assembly candidates, and these included all candidates of the Jan Sangh, Hindu Mahasabha, and Ram Raj Parishad parties, as well as numerous independent candidates. Of these, 79 were jagirdars. S. V. Kogekar and Richard L. Park, *Reports on the Indian General Elections, 1951-52* (Bombay: Popular Book Depot, 1956), p. 227.

as a consequence of her inability to rally major ruling families under the Swatantra banner, the party's success, though considerable, was limited primarily to the Eastern Plains region where it routed the Congress party, winning 26 of its total of 56 seats.

By 1962 it was clear that the political center of gravity among the Rajput aristocracy had shifted from Jodhpur to Jaipur; although showing greater political awareness and willingness to associate itself with established political parties than it had earlier, the Rajput aristocracy as a group was still characterized by regional autonomy and an inability and/or unwillingness to cooperate among themselves. There seems little doubt that if they had succeeded in establishing a single political party across the state in either 1952 or 1962, they could have won control of the state's government. It is a telling commentary on the Rajput aristocracy of the state that, despite its great potential for political leadership, it has not succeeded in developing a single political leader who can exert state-wide political influence and respect, or an organizational structure through which their regional strengths could have been combined.[15]

The Congress party was more successful in developing major political leaders. Having control of the state's government throughout this period and backed by the prestige of the national party, the state Congress leaders have been able to exploit the advantage of office, the control of patronage, and the responsibility for implementing programs of economic development and social and political reforms in the development of political leadership. Despite these advantages, Congress leadership has tended to be local and regional in nature. No mass leader who could appeal directly to all sections of the state has emerged; instead, political leaders have tended to be adroit managers of political influence.

Within the rank of the state's top leadership, Mohan Lal Sukhadia, who has been Rajasthan's chief minister since 1954, is the state's major political figure. A second generation Praja Mandalist from Udaipur state and a protégé of Manik Lal Varma, Sukhadia has managed to retain leadership of the Congress party through twelve stormy years, more by his judicious use of political influence, his balancing of competing factions within the party, and his capacity to anticipate the political intrigues of his opponents than through any quality of personal magnetism. Below

[15] The inability of the Rajput aristocracy to develop an organized, united, and programmatically conservative alternative to the Congress party is not restricted to Rajasthan since this has also characterized conservatism at the national level. See the recent discussion of these problems in Howard L. Erdman, "Conservative Politics in India," *Asian Survey*, VI (June 1966), 338-47.

the chief minister there are a series of regional and caste leaders who control local support and who vie with each other for political influence and power within the state government.

The leadership of the Congress party consists of a diminishing group of old-time nationalists, an increasing number of second generation nationalists, Jat political leaders, and a few who entered politics following independence. The emergence of Sukhadia as chief minister coincided with the trend of replacing the old nationalist leaders with younger and less important political figures of the pre-independence period. Prior to Sukhadia's assumption of the state's highest political office, there had been three chief ministers in the brief span of three and a half years, 1951-54. All had been old-time nationalists. One of the oldest Jaipur nationalist leaders, Harzari Lal Sharma, became the state's first chief minister at the request of Sardar Patel, who, faced with the task of supplying leadership for the political unit he had created, turned to the nationalist leadership of the largest princely state in Rajasthan. But Harzari Lal Sharma was unable to form an effective political base in the new state party, and he was replaced by Jai Narain Vyas shortly before the first general election in 1951. Vyas was the best-known nationalist leader at this time, and in 1951 it appeared that he was the candidate most likely to become the major political figure in the state. This bright prospect was badly shaken, however, when he was defeated in the 1951 general election in his native Jodhpur constituency by the forces led by the Maharaja of Jodhpur. A second Jaipur political leader, Tika Ram Paliwal, then became the interim chief minister until such time as Vyas could win a seat to the Legislative Assembly. Apprehensive lest he be defeated in his native Jodhpur, Vyas chose to contest from an Eastern Plains constituency in the summer of 1952. Winning in this election, Vyas resumed the chief ministership once more in the fall of that year. He held this post for two years. However, the young Congress party was in the process of developing blocs of political power which assumed regional configurations for the most part. Vyas was unable to withstand a coalition of Southern Highlands MLAs led by Sukhadia and supported by Manik Lal Varma and the Dry region MLAs led by Nathu Ram Mirdha, Mathura Das Mathur, and Kumbharam Arya, along with secondary Eastern Plains Praja Mandal leaders such as Damodar Lal Vyas and Badri Prasad Gupta. This coalition brought about Vyas' defeat, albeit by a narrow margin, and Sukhadia was voted into the position of legislative party leadership.[16] Most of the state's current leadership op-

[16] *Hindustan Times*, November 10, 1954, p. 9.

posed Jai Narain Vyas, and his defeat is a pivotal date in the contemporary political history of the state. Vyas retained a group of loyal supporters who, even as recently as 1961, were an active and powerful force within the party.

Mohan Lal Sukhadia became chief minister more because he was the least objectionable of the anti-Vyas leaders than because of any personal broad-based support in the state. He was widely known to be a conscientious and capable administrator; he had served in all previous cabinets, and he was regarded as a man who was willing to listen to all groups within the party. He was in the enviable political position of having fewer political enemies, and within the anti-Vyas coalition group he was among the most politically and administratively experienced individuals. In addition, even though he was known as a regional leader of the Southern Highlands (a reputation he has never fully succeeded in overcoming), he was not closely identified with any single caste, as were the Jat leaders of the Dry region of the state. With the Eastern Plains Congressmen split between the pro- and anti-Vyas factions, and having strong support of the Dry region's MLAs in the party, Sukhadia gained control over the largest bloc of regional votes in the party. The anti-Vyas faction within the Eastern Plains region included the old Jaipur nationalist, Ram Kishore Vyas, as well as other younger nationalist leaders. Thus the combination of strong regional support and support of the negative anti-Vyas faction enabled Sukhadia to propel himself into the chief ministership. The importance of the role played by Mohan Lal Sukhadia in Rajasthan's politics is perhaps best indicated by the difficulty he has faced in 1965 and 1966 in leaving the state. Efforts have been made to move him to the national level of the Congress party's organization in preparation for the fourth general elections, but it has been impossible to find another person in the state who would be acceptable as chief minister to the important factions within the Rajasthan Congress party.

The significance of the change in political leadership in 1954, as well as the basic characteristics of the state's top leadership, can best be understood through an analysis of the composition of the major cabinets between 1951 and 1962. Most of the major political leaders have been members of the cabinet, ministerial rank being one of the most coveted posts in the political structure of the state both in terms of power and of status. Tables 7.8, 7.9, and 7.10 present the names of members of the nine major cabinets and summarize each cabinet's caste composition, regional representation, age, education, and political background. Deputy ministers are not included in the data contained in the tables inasmuch as these tend to be added spasmodically and could not be readily analyzed. In addition, a few ministers who were added after the initial formation of each of the cabinets are not included in the tables.

Rajasthan's cabinets have varied in size from 6 to 11 members; all but two cabinets have numbered between eight and ten ministers. All three post-election cabinets (II, VII, and IX) have been smaller in size than the pre-election cabinets. Since Mohan Lal Sukhadia became chief minister, cabinet personnel has become more stable. In the three and a half years prior to the first Sukhadia cabinet (V), sixteen men held ministerial portfolios in four cabinets. In the five Sukhadia cabinets of the next eight

TABLE 7.8

MEMBERS OF MAJOR RAJASTHAN CABINETS, 1951-62

Cabinet code[a]	*Size*	*Initials of Ministers*[b]
I	10	JNV MDM KRA JS TRP YKC NLJ MLS BSM BSS
II	8	TRP RKV RKJ BN NRM MLS ALY BP
III	9	JNV TRP RKV RKJ BN NRM MLS ALY BP
IV	8	JNV RKJ BN KRA MLS BP ALY
		TRP (As of 8 January 1954)
V	9	MLS BP ALY RKV DLV BPG KRA RNM BSS
VI	10	MLS BP ALY RKV DLV BPG BMS RNM RCC BSS
VII	6	MLS RKV DLV BPG HU NRM
VIII	11	MLS BB RKV DLV BPG SR HU RCC NRM HC RCD
IX	8	MLS BB HU BKK MDM NRM BK HC

[a] I April 1951 to First General Elections
II April 1952 to October 1952
II November 1952 to April 1953
IV April 1953 to November 1954
V November 1954 to November 1956
VI November 1956 to Second General Elections
VII April 1957 to November 1960
VIII November 1960 to Third General Elections
IX March 1962

[b] JNV	Jai Narain Vyas	BN	Bhola Nath
TRP	Tika Ram Paliwal	DLV	Damodar Lal Vyas
YKC	Yugal Kishore Chaturvedi	BPG	Badri Prasad Gupta
NLJ	Nattom Lal Joshi	RNM	Ram Niwas Mirdha
MDM	Mathura Das Mathur	BMS	Brij Mohan Sharma
KRA	Kumbharam Arya	RCC	Ram Chandra Choudhuri
JS	Jaswant Singh	NRM	Nathu Ram Mirdha
BSS	Brij Sunder Sharma	BB	Bheeka Bhai
BSM	Balwant Singh Mehta	SR	Sampat Ram
MLS	Mohan Lal Sukhadia	HC	Harish Chandra
RKV	Ram Kishore Vyas	RCD	Ram Chandra Dhariwal
BP	Bhogi Lal Pandya	BKK	Bal Krishan Kaul
ALY	Amrit Lal Yadau	BK	Barkatullah Khan

URCES: (1) Cabinets I–V: Congress Legislative Party, *Three Years of the Rajasthan Assembly,* d (2) Cabinet VI: *Hindustan Times,* 2 November 1956, p. 12. Cabinet VII: *Hindustan Times,* April 1957, p. 1; Cabinet VIII: *Hindustan Times,* 11 February 1960, p. 4; Cabinet IX: *Indian xpress,* 13 March 1962, p. 9.

TABLE 7.9

Decade of Birth, Education, and Entrance into Politics of Ministers in Rajasthan from 1951 to 1962

		Born					*Education*						*Entered politics*					
Cabinet code nos.[a]	*Size*	Before 1900	1900–09	1910–19	1920–24	Unknown	HS	B.A.	LL.B.	M.A.	Private	Unknown	By 1942	1942–47	1947–52	After 1952	Unknown	*Member Praja Mandal*
I	10	10	40	40	—	10	10	80	30	—	—	10	80	10	10	—	—	90
II	8	—	38	50	12	—	25	63	38	13	13	—	78	12	—	—	—	78
III	9	11	33	45	11	—	22	67	33	11	11	—	89	11	—	—	—	89
IV	8	12	25	50	—	12	12	50	12	—	12	—	100	—	—	—	—	100
V	9	—	33	45	11	11	33	67	56	22	—	—	89	11	—	—	—	89
VI	10	—	30	60	10	—	20	80	70	20	—	—	80	—	10	10	—	80
VII	6	17	33	33	17	—	17	83	67	17	—	—	83	—	—	—	—	83
VIII	11	9	18	46	27	—	9	91	64	18	—	—	54	9	18	9	9	55
IX	8	12	12	38	25	12	12	75	38	25	—	12	50	12	12	12	12	62

[a] Cabinet code numbers. See Table 7.8.

TABLE 7.10

CASTE COMPOSITION AND GEOGRAPHICAL DISTRIBUTION IN RAJASTHAN'S MAJOR CABINETS FROM 1951 TO 1962

		Caste composition								*Geographical Distribution (in per cent)*			
Cabinet code nos.[a]	*Size*	Brahman	Mahajan	Jat	Rajput	Kayasth	Sched. Castes	Sched. Tribes	Muslim	Eastern Plains	Dry	Southern Highlands	Southern Plateau
I	10	50	20	10	10	10	—	—	—	30	40	20	10
II	8	63	12	12	—	—	12	—	—	50	12	38	—
III	9	67	12	11	—	—	11	—	—	56	11	33	—
IV	8	63	12	12	—	—	12	—	—	50	13	37	—
V	9	44	22	22	—	—	12	—	—	33	22	33	11
VI	10	50	20	20	—	—	10	—	—	40	20	30	10
VII	6	50	33	17	—	—	—	—	—	67	16	16	—
VIII	11	27	27	18	9	—	9	9	—	45	18	18	18
IX	8	25	12	12	12	12	—	12	12	25	37	25	12
Total %		50	19	15	3	3	7	2	1	44	21	28	7

[a] Cabinet code numbers. See Table 7.8.

years, seventeen men have held the ranks of minister. Of these, seven were members of pre-Sukhadia cabinets, although two, Amrit Lal Yadau and Bhogi Lal Pandya, represented the Southern Highlands cabinet contingent in the period from 1952 to 1960. It is not surprising, therefore, that these two men continued to be included in the cabinet when their regional leader became chief minister. Of the four other ministers who served in both periods, two were the Jat leaders—Kumbharam Arya and Nathu Ram Mirdha—and the third was Mathura Das Mathur, who, although a non-Jat and a second generation Praja Mandalist from Jodhpur, was closely associated during most of this period with the Jat leadership of the Dry region. The only member from the Eastern Plains region to hold ministerial rank in both periods was Ram Kishore Vyas. In the Southern Plateau region, Brij Sunder Sharma was a member of cabinet I and later of the first and second Sukhadia cabinets; but he has not been a member of the last three state cabinets. Clearly, the leaderships of the Southern Highlands and the Dry regions have been the most stable in the state, while there has been little continuity of leadership in the other two regions between the periods prior to and following Sukhadia's chief ministership.

Other general characteristics of the ministerial leadership in the state are evident from the material contained in Tables 7.9 and 7.10. Most of the men who reached the cabinet level had participated in the nationalist movement, most of them were Brahmans, most held bachelor's degrees or higher, they were born between the years 1910 and 1919, and they had entered politics prior to 1942. Beyond these general characteristics, other specific aspects of Rajasthan cabinet members are of particular importance.

It has already been noted that the Brahman, Mahajan, and Jat castes form the three dominant castes in the Rajasthan Congress party. Table 7.9 indicates that their dominance is greater at the ministerial level than within the legislative party: 84 per cent of all cabinet members have been members of one of the these three castes. The Brahmans represent the largest single caste group in the cabinet, and have held 44 per cent of all cabinet posts—more than twice the proportion of the Mahajan or Jat castes, which have been 19 per cent and 15 per cent respectively. The dominant position of the Brahman caste is even more evident if its membership in the cabinet is compared with its membership in the Congress party. Between 1952 and 1957, 20 per cent and between 1957 and 1962, 16 per cent of all Congress MLAs were Brahmans. Thus their membership in the cabinet was more than twice the proportion in the legislative party. The proportion of Mahajans and Jats in the legislative party was identical in both periods—12 per cent in the first and 15 per cent in the second period. This compares much more closely to their overall average membership in the cabinets of the state than does that of the Brahmans. The Brahmans' dominant position in the cabinet cannot be explained solely on the basis of their being better qualified educationally, nor in terms of their political experience. The education of the Mahajan MLAs was comparable, if not superior in some respects, to that of the Brahman MLSs, and both castes had entered the Praja Mandals at an early date. Unquestionably, the very high proportion of Brahmans in the cabinets is, in part, a reflection of their high educational level and their political experience; but the disproportionate size of their representation suggests that the Brahman caste was the dominant political leadership caste in Rajasthan for most of the period covered by this study.

However, while initially the Brahman leadership came from throughout the state, since 1960 it has become limited to the Eastern Plains region. This becomes evident from the material presented in Table 7.11, which analyzes the three major castes in the cabinets in terms of regions. Of the 39 Brahman ministers in the ten cabinets analyzed 30 came from the Eastern Plains region. Until cabinet VII, the Brahmans had a broader representation than any other caste, the Brahman ministers being drawn from at least two regions and in 50 per cent of the cabinets before 1960 from three regions of the state. Their isolation in the Eastern Plains region since that time has been the result of the emergence of leaders in other parts of the state who are capable of demanding cabinet posts. The dominance of the cabinet positions by Brahmans is not the result of "caste politics," for they were not organized in terms of castes; the leadership of the Brahman caste in the state is rather a legacy of Rajasthan's past and a result of its present level of development.

TABLE 7.11

REGIONAL REPRESENTATION IN RAJASTHAN CABINETS BY CASTES

	Cabinets									
Region	I	II	III	IV	V	VI	VII	VIII	IX	
				BRAHMAN						
Eastern Plains	3	4	5	4	2	4	3	3	2	30
Dry	1	—	—	—	—	—	—	—	—	1
Southern Highlands	—	1	1	1	1	1	—	—	—	5
Southern Plateau	1	—	—	—	1	1	—	—	—	3
								Total		39
				MAHAJANS						
Eastern Plains	—	—	—	—	1	1	1	1	—	4
Dry	—	—	—	—	—	—	—	—	—	—
Southern Highlands	2	1	1	1	1	1	1	1	1	10
Southern Plateau	—	—	—	—	—	—	—	1	—	1
								Total		15
				JATS						
Eastern Plains	—	—	—	—	—	—	—	—	—	
Dry	1	1	1	1	2	1	1	2	1	11
Southern Highlands	—	—	—	—	—	—	—	—	—	
Southern Plateau	—	—	—	—	—	—	—	—	—	
								Total		11

The caste composition of the state's cabinets also discloses the relatively weak position of the Scheduled Castes and Scheduled Tribes at the cabinet level of leadership. Although the Scheduled Castes constituted the second largest contingent of Congress MLAs in the first Assembly and the largest contingent in the second Assembly, their membership in the cabinet was only 7 per cent. The Scheduled Tribes MLAs represented a smaller proportion of the Congress MLAs than did the Scheduled Castes MLAs, but their representation was substantially greater than their 2 per cent proportion of all cabinet ministers. In part as a result of the political activity of the large Yadav caste, which dates back to the early 1930s, and in part as a reflection of their more advanced state of development in terms of education and economic position as compared to the Scheduled Tribes, the Scheduled Castes received their own representative on the cabinet much earlier than did the Scheduled Tribes. The most important Scheduled Castes leader has been Amrit Lal Yadau, who was a member of cabinets II–VI. A close associate of both Manik Lal Varma and Mohan Lal Sukhadia throughout his adult life, he joined the Praja Mandal organization in Udaipur before he was 20 years old, and he has been an active worker ever since. In 1947 he founded the Rajasthan Dalit Varga Sangh (Oppressed Castes League), the major Scheduled Castes organization in the state. He was dropped from the cabinet after the 1957 election because the Central Election Committee refused him the party's ticket on the ground that he had promoted groupism in the state party. He later won re-election to the Assembly in a by-election. A Scheduled Tribes member did not serve on the cabinet until 1960, at which time Bheeka Bhai, an MP from Dungarpur from 1952-57, was elected to the Assembly in 1957 and appointed to a cabinet post in 1960. Until that time the Scheduled Tribes portfolio was held almost continuously by Bhogi Lal Pandya, a Brahman MLA from Dungarpur, who had spent most of his life doing uplift work among the Scheduled Tribes.

The decline of Brahman dominance in the cabinet and the emergence of political leaders in the Scheduled Castes and Scheduled Tribes are but two indicators of a general broadening of the caste basis of the state's cabinets. Given the importance of caste in Indian politics in general, it was unlikely that the disparity between social structure and control of ministerial offices could continue indefinitely. Cabinet VIII represents the transition to a broader caste basis, for instead of the typical four-caste base of most of the previous cabinets (i.e., Brahman, Mahajan, Jat, and Scheduled Castes), six castes were represented in this cabinet formed in 1959. This was accomplished by enlarging the cabinet by four members, three of whom were from castes not represented on the previous cabinet, thereby expanding the cabinet to 11 members, the largest in the state's brief history. But the post-election cabinet of 1962 (IX) was again reduced to eight members. However, the number of castes remained the same (six), and in addition, the first Muslim member was brought into the cabinet. Thus the pattern of a broad-based cabinet seemed well established by 1962.

Cabinet VIII was important for other reasons as well. Harish Chandra, the former Maharaja of Jhalawar in the Southern Plateau region, joined the cabinet. Chandra was the first member of the Rajput caste since the first election to become a minister. His entrance into the cabinet represented the culmination of a long process of attempted assimilation of at least a portion of Rajput aristocracy into the Rajasthan's Congress party. Negotiations to this end had been continuing since 1953. Cabinet VIII also included more non-Prajas Mandal members and political leaders who had entered politics after independence than had any previous cabinet. Prior to cabinet VIII, from 78 per cent to 100 per cent of the ministers in each cabinet had been members of Prajas Mandal, but in cabinet VIII this proportion fell to 55 per cent of the total membership. Approximately one-third of the members of the last two cabinets in Rajasthan had not participated in politics prior to independence.

Significant changes occurred in the Congress party's ministerial group during Rajasthan's first ten years of democratic politics. The chief ministership had changed hands from the old nationalists to a representative of the second generation of nationalists. Its caste base had broadened and more closely reflected the state's social structure. This trend coincided with a decline of the earlier Brahman preponderance in the cabinet. A representative of the Scheduled Tribes emerged to replace their *de facto* representative, and the first member of the Rajput aristocracy achieved cabinet status. These changes indicate that significant mobilization and development of new leadership had transpired in Rajasthan and that the political structure, which was imposed rather arbitrarily on the historic area of Rajputana, was becoming more closely integrated with the society. These important changes illustrate as well the capacity of the Congress party to respond to a changing Rajasthan and to adapt itself to new forces and interests in the state.

Political Conflicts in the State of Rajasthan

The changes in political leadership described above took place within the context of two basic political conflicts. One centered around the controversy between the Rajput jagirdari class and the Congress party; the other was centered within the Congress party and focused on the emergence of new leadership groups in terms of both generation and caste. The first has tended to be an open conflict, legitimized by the new political system, and the latter a less open conflict which, although perhaps legitimized by the *de facto* political system, did not conform to the articulated principles and values of the Congress party.

The Congress party's decision to resume all jagirs initiated open conflict with the jagirdari class in the state. The Rajputs' entrance into politics in almost monolithic opposition to the Congress party at the time of the first general elections was triggered by this decision, and they have remained an important, if less monolithic, opposition group in the state's politics ever since. The Resumption of Jagirs Act, 1952, passed prior to the first general election, was opposed by various means. Writs staying the act were secured from the High Court immediately after it came into force in 1952, and the legal controversy continued until 1954 when the Supreme Court of India finally upheld the act. The Kshatriya Mahasabha served as the central co-ordinator for the jagirdari class, extending its support to a broad coalition of candidates from several parties, as well as independent candidates. At a later stage, the Kshatriya Mahasabha served as the institutional means through which negotiations with both the state and national governments were conducted. Although candidates supported by the Kshatriya Mahasabha achieved substantial success in the election, it was not sufficient to dislodge the Congress party from control of the state's government. As negotiations continued between 1952 and 1954, it became evident that the jagirdars were split between the small jagirdars controlling jagirs with income of Rs. 5000 or less and the larger jagirdars. Although extensive negotiations were carried on with the state government over the terms of resumption, it was not until November 1953 that an agreement satisfactory to the large jagirdars was reached through the arbitration of Pandit Nehru.[17] Subsequently, most large jagirdars withdrew their writs pending in the High Court. However, these terms were unsatisfactory and unacceptable to the small jagirdars, who demanded more liberal terms of compensation, an immediate payment of 50 per cent of the compensation at the time of resumption, more liberal rehabilitation grants, and alterations in the definition of *Khudkasht* land which would not be resumed. To achieve these objectives they launched a direct action campaign, organized by the Bhoomswami Sangh and waged throughout the state: they courted arrest and held demonstrations to protest the terms of the settlement. At the height of the campaign, thousands of Bhoomswamis were reported to be in Rajasthan's jails,[18] and law and order was seriously threatened throughout the state, requiring the utilization of the Preventive Detention Act.[19]

In the 1957 general elections, both the Ram Raj Parishad and the Jan Sangh parties took up the cause of the Bhoomswamis and supported their basic demands. The Ram Raj Parishad demanded that no jagirs having

17 Government of Rajasthan, *Report of the State Land Commission for Rajasthan* (Jaipur: Government Central Press, 1959), p. 20.

18 *Hindustan Times*, May 1, 1956, p. 12.

19 *Ibid.*, March 6, 1956, p. 4.

an income below Rs. 5,000 per annum should be resumed, and the Jan Sangh supported a liberalization of terms for the Bhoomswamis.[20] Neither party was able to enhance its position in the state by identifying with the Bhoomswami movement, and in fact, both lost from 25 per cent to 33 per cent of their previous strength. Neither party became an effective channel for resolving the dispute for the negotiations with the government continued to be carried on by the Bhoomswami Sangh representatives. In 1958 Pandit Nehru again entered the controversy at the request of both the Rajasthan government and the Bhoomswamis; and in 1959 he proposed liberalized terms for rehabilitation grants for jagirs with an annual income of less than Rs. 5,000. This proposal was accepted by both sides, thus finally ending this controversy.[21]

Several aspects of the conflict illustrate important characteristics of interest articulation and resolution of conflict in Rajasthan. In the first place, resolution of conflict did not occur within the state political system, but only when the conflict was extended to Pandit Nehru and the center. This is not an unfamiliar pattern for conflicts in India, but it is important to note that neither the formal legal system nor the state government could end the conflict until a final arbitration by Prime Minister Nehru was made. Second, the higher echelons of the Rajput aristocracy were not willing to support violent or direct action, limiting themselves instead to available legal techniques and electoral contests. In general, the Rajput aristocracy has continued this pattern of political behavior ever since. Thus the large jagirdari class and the Rajput ruling families, by limiting their techniques of conflict to those legitimized by a democratic system, have served as a modernizing influence. Third, non-associational organizations, not political parties, served as the most effective means of articulating interests. The Kshatriya Mahasabha was the recognized Rajput organization in the state, and when it refused to support the grievances of the small jagirdars, the latter formed an *ad hoc* organization rather than identify with a political party despite the fact that two existing parties publicly supported their demands. Finally, without the support of the large jagirdars, the protest movement was not effective in gaining popular support, and both political parties associated closely with the Bhoomswami movement lost strength in the second general election. This underlines the fact that no opposition group can expect to gain significant support in Rajasthan unless it has the support of the important members of the Rajput aristocracy. Further, it should be noted that it required seven years to resolve the conflict. Two elections

20 *Ibid.*, February 7, 1957, p. 7.

21 *Report of the State Land Commission for Rajasthan*, p. 21.

were held during this period, but these elections played no significant role in resolving the conflict, the solution only being attained through extensive negotiations, direct action, and arbitration.

Factionalism within the Congress party is the second major force of conflict in Rajasthan; moreover, this has been a constant feature of the party's history. The survival of the Congress party has depended on its ability to keep factionalism within reasonable bounds, so as to prevent such a weakening of the party as to render it ineffective as a political organization. Initially, factionalism assumed the form of regionalism, consisting of three basic groups. One of these was the Udaipur group, headed by Mohan Lal Sukhadia and Manik Lal Varma. The Vyas group, after the first general election, centered in the Eastern Plains region, primarily in the old Jaipur state area. The Jat group consisted of the Jodhpur and Bikaner Jat leaders from the Marwar Kisan Sabha and the Praja Parishad movements, respectively. The coalition which defeated Jai Narain Vyas assumed the form of regional groupings when the Jat and Udaipur groups joined forces with the second-generation nationalist leaders in the Eastern Plains.

Although regionalism has continued to be one characteristic of Rajasthan's factionalism, since 1954 personalism and caste have become more prominent features as well. In part, this represents the more thorough political mobilization of the society; but it is also a consequence of the progressive breakdown of regional loyalties. One of the ironies of Rajasthan's politics is that the more the old regional loyalties are corroded, the greater the tendency for factionalism to shift to a caste and local base. The shift in the style of state leadership which accompanied the change in the chief ministership also encouraged a shift to local and caste-based factionalism. Rooted in the older tradition of the nationalist movement, Vyas's concept of leadership was more functional for agitational and oppositional politics than it was for faction-based politics. Until his death in 1962, Jai Narain Vyas had always had the reputation of being a man who refused to make "deals" and who settled disputes and issues on principles. He carried this attitude so far, in fact, that he is reported to have issued orders that no Congress MLA could visit the Secretariat to present grievances of his constituents without prior permission of the party's leadership. Mohan Lal Sukhadia did not share this view of politics, and when he became chief minister, the MLAs had more freedom to exercise their influence.

At the state level, factionalism is so widespread that an aura of intrigue often hangs over the state capital. Endless rumors of internal conflicts within the cabinet or the legislative party are circulated, and from time to time, major cabinet reshufflings take place in response to the shifting lines of factional strength. No minister dares ignore his own group of followers and his allies for should he become isolated or should his support be undercut, his own position would soon be in jeopardy. The high command has endeavored assiduously to limit factionalism in the state. In pursuit of his goal, it has tried many techniques. In 1957 the CEC refused the Assembly ticket to nearly one-half of the ministers in the Sukhadia cabinet in an attempt to "purge" many of the important supporters of Mohan Lal Sukhadia's rise to power.[22] This effort failed almost immediately. One hundred Congress candidates, supported by all but one member of the state's cabinet, refused to accept the party's nomination unless adjustments were made to accommodate at least some of the "purged" ministers.[23] The high command was forced to compromise: the two ministers from the Eastern Plains were granted the ticket, and five candidates in Bikaner district who had previously been denied the ticket also became the party's candidates.[24] The high command also attempted to remove factional leaders from the state scene by approving their candidacies for Lok Sabha or Rajya Sabha seats. The important Jodhpur leader Mathura Das Mathur was given the parliamentary ticket in 1957 instead of being approved for an Assembly seat as he had requested. The CEC refused to reverse this decision, but it did transfer Mathur's constituency to Nagaur district, the heart of the Jat strength in the Jodhpur area and a safe seat.[25] Mathura Das Mathur, however, succeeded in returning to state politics by 1959, at which time he was elected to the post of PCC Chief. New Delhi's displeasure over this development was evidenced by the controversy which occurred between the newly elected PCC Chief and the high command. Technically, Mathura Das Mathur had violated a party ruling which required that a member of Parliament could not even be nominated for a post in the organizational wing of the party without obtaining prior permission of the high command. When Mathur was asked why he had not sought this approval, he stated simply that his nomination and subsequent election to the post had developed so "suddenly" that there was not sufficient time to seek the national party's permission. It was reported that he was advised to reject the PCC post and continue as an MP, but this he refused, assuring the national party that he would personally

[22] *Hindustan Times*, January 23, 1957, p. 1. With the backing of New Delhi, Jai Narain Vyas had become PCC Chief shortly before as part of a pre-election unity move.

[23] *Times of India*, January 29, 1957, p. 1.

[24] *The Statesman*, January 29, 1957, p. 1.

[25] *Hindustan Times*, January 29, 1957, p. 12.

guarantee that the Congress would win the by-election which would be necessitated by his resignation.[26] Mathur thus returned to Rajasthan's politics, won an Assembly seat in the third general elections, and subsequently became Home Minister in the post-election cabinet.

New Delhi has been no more successful in stopping the general growth in strength of major factions than it has been in purging or removing important factional leaders.[27] Kumbharam Arya, the Jats' principal leader, has been refused the party's ticket in all three general elections. In the first general election he did contest even though Prime Minister Nehru had "advised" him against taking this step. In doing so, Arya explained that although he had been most willing to abide by Nehru's "advice," by the time he had received this communication from New Delhi it was "discovered" to be too late to withdraw his name from the list of candidates. He won his seat handily.[28] A supporter of Mohan Lal Sukhadia, Arya became a minister in Sukhadia's first cabinet. But soon charges of "casteism" against him were heard at an AICC meeting in August 1955,[29] and he subsequently resigned from the cabinet, reportedly at the request of the Central Parliamentary Board.[30] Kumbharam Arya is perhaps the most powerful man in the state next to the chief minister. The high command attempted to remove him from the arena of state politics after the second general elections by approving his candidacy for a seat in the Rajya Sabha to which he was elected.

Events during the third general elections suggest that there is little prospect for the abeyance of factional controversy in the near future but instead that factionalism has become an integral part of the Rajasthan Congress. The political temperature of the state mounted in the months preceding the elections as political maneuvering intensified and focused on the selection of the party's candidates. The chief minister and the new PCC Chief, Mathura Das Mathur, engaged in a running factional fight in Jodhpur district over the selection of candidates. In addition, one Jat minister and two Jat deputy ministers threatened to resign from the cabinet as a protest over the increased influence accorded the Rajput wing of the Congress party during the chief minister's negoti-

26 *Ibid.*, January 3, 1960, p. 12.

27 The clearest illustration of this is the long conflict between the Jat group and the national party organization. Despite the frequent criticism of its two most important leaders, Nathu Ram Mirdha and Kumbharam Arya, by the high command, the group's strength has continued to grow. After the third general election, it held two of the six ministerships and four of eight deputy ministerships in the new cabinet. *Indian Express*, March 11, 1962, p. 6.

28 *Hindustan Times*, December 7, 1951, p. 7.

29 *Ibid.*, August 12, 1955, p. 8.

30 *Ibid.*, October 22, 1955, p. 1.

ations with the princely families over the possibility of political cooperation. As the final stages of the selection of candidates approached, there were reports of growing tension between the Jat wing of the party and Damodar Lal Vyas, the sitting Revenue Minister and an important leader of the Eastern Plains. At the final meeting of the Pradesh Election Committee in October 1961, 160 out of 176 candidates were officially designated and the remaining 16 seats were left to arbitration between the chief minister and the PCC Chief.[31]

When the official party candidates were announced, it was clear that the principal losers among the major groups had been the Vyas supporters from the Eastern Plains region. An outstanding example of this trend was the failure to secure renomination of N. L. Joshi, a former Speaker of the Assembly from Jhunjhunu district and a widely respected member of the Vyas group in the state. The dominant Jat group in the district secured five of the six non-reserved seats and the remaining seat went to Bhim Sen, a Rajput and former leader of the jagirdars in Jhunjhunu. In 1952 he had run successfully as an RRP candidate, but in 1954 he joined the Congress party. Joshi, representing the older urban-based nationalist tradition in the district, could not effectively contend against these two powerful rural forces and hence he was unable to gain the party's ticket.[32] Only in Jaipur district were the Vyas supporters given seats by the Pradesh Election Committee. But in view of the strength of the Swatantra party in this district, these nominations offered little prospect for enhancing the strength of the Vyas group in the forthcoming Legislative Assembly.

As a result of these developments, Jai Narain Vyas injected his personal strength and prestige into the election and led an open fight against "corrupt Congressmen" upon whom he declared "jehad" in the name of the "true Congress" or, as he called it, the "People's Congress." In this effort he was joined openly by numerous old Congressmen, the most notable among whom were the former PCC Chief from Bharatpur, Master Aditendra, and former Chief Minister Harilal Shastri.[33] Vyas charged that Sukhadia was personally profiting from his relations with "capitalists"; that Revenue Minister Damodar Lal Vyas had met with the Maharaja of Jaipur to "pray for clemency" for opposing the Maharani; and he accused Mathura Das Mathur and Nathu Ram Mirdha of using

[31] *Ibid.*, October 16, 1961, p. 14.

[32] *Dainik Lokwani*, November 29, 1961, p. 1.

[33] For a discussion of the support of Vyas' "Peoples Congress," see *Hindustan Times*, October 16, 1961, p. 14; *Dainik Rashtradoota*, February 14, 1962, p. 4; and *Dainik Lokwani*, December 7, 1961, p. 1.

Congress funds against the party.[34] During a tour of the Alwar district, Vyas called upon the people to defeat the entire Congress ticket in the district and singled out the incumbent Congress candidate for the Lok Sabha as an "outstanding example of a corrupt Congressman," charging that he had misappropriated over Rs. 200,000.[35] He pointed to a local Communist party candidate as being "100 times more honest" than the Congress candidates in the district. Vyas also refuted the elaborate charges by Congress candidates against the princely families who were supporting opposition political movements. He denied that they were dreaming of regaining their former empires by bringing about the defeat of the Congress party in Rajasthan. In support of this position, he asserted that he personally knew many progressive princes.[36]

As an example of the "degeneration" of the Congress party in the state, Vyas observed that even while the party was mounting an attack against some princes in the state, it was nevertheless according its ticket to former rulers who had repressed the nationalist movements in their respective former princely states and who had even tortured nationalists for fighting in the nation's cause. The case of the Nawab of Loharu was an especially flagrant example. The Nawab had been nominated for the Assembly seat of Johri Bazar in Jaipur city and had joined the Congress party only pursuant to his nomination. Since a substantial portion of this constituency was Muslim, the Nawab's nomination had been based on Congress' hope that a former Muslim ruler might possibly effectively counteract the strength of the Rajput Jaipur house in this constituency. As an old nationalist, Vyas had not forgotten that there had been a serious gun-firing directed against demonstrators in Loharu in the 1930s in which fifteen Congressmen had been killed and, in fact, he himself had written the report at that time for the Congress, charging that the Nawab himself had been responsible for the firings. The Nawab of Loharu maintained that it had been the British troops and not his own troops which had been responsible for the death of the nationalists. But Vyas circulated photostatic copies of his report which contradicted the Nawab's claim.[37] Irrespective of the validity of his charges, Vyas exposed an obviously dubious effort by the state Congress party to find candidates with special appeal for certain constituencies and an example which dramatically exemplified his charge that

34 For the most extensive coverage of Vyas' charges, see *Dainik Lokwani*, February 5, 1962, p. 3.

35 *Dainik Rashtradoota*, February 12, 1962, p. 4.

36 *Indian Express*, February 8, 1962, p. 5.

37 *Dainik Lokwani*, January 6, 1962, p. 1, and January 10, 1962, p. 1.

the new leaders of the party in the state did not represent the "true" Congress.[38]

It is impossible to determine the effects of Vyas' "People's Congress" movement inasmuch as it was just one among the numerous contending forces in the election. In Alwar district where Vyas had called for the defeat of all Congress candidates, the Congress majority was reduced from 8 to 6 out of the district's total 10 Assembly seats; on the other hand, the Lok Sabha seat was won by a Congressman in a close contest with the "honest" Communist candidate. In Bharatpur district where some 300 Congressmen had joined Vyas' movement by resigning en masse from the party shortly before the election, the Congress party suffered a major defeat. It was able to win only 2 out of the 10 Assembly seats in 1962 as compared to the 6 seats it had won in the election of 1957* The significance of Vyas' efforts to chastise the Congress party for drifting from its "true heritage" was not its electoral effect, which is difficult to determine, but rather that it did represent the final protest of the old Congressmen who had not adjusted to the new "Congress system" of politics necessitated by a mass electorate and the new age of democratic politics. Jai Narain Vyas paid the ultimate "price" for his opposition to official Congress candidates by being expelled from the party after the general elections. His death followed shortly upon the heels of his expulsion from the party, ending the political career of the state's perhaps most widely respected political figure, who, regardless of his position, had never had his motivation nor integrity seriously questioned. In the context of Rajasthan's politics this was indeed a remarkable achievement, and it is doubtful whether it will be equalled in the foreseeable future.

The second major example of factionalism in the Congress party was also linked to the third general election. In contrast to the Vyas revolt, however, this did not manifest itself until after the election and it represents what might be termed "normal factionalism" within the party. The Swatantra party's near-sweep of Jaipur district and its strong showing in most of the Eastern Plains region where it won 36 per cent of the Assembly seats caused great concern within the Congress party. This concern was enhanced by the fact that four members of the cabinet, including the "strong man" of the Eastern Plains, Damodar Lal Vyas,

[38] The strategy of the Congress party did not succeed in winning the Johri Bazar seat for the party. Both Congress and Swatantra ran Muslim candidates, splitting this community's vote, thereby abetting the ultimate victory of the Jan Sangh candidate, who won the seat handily.

* See Table 7.16, p. 395 for a comparison of election results in these districts.

had been defeated in his bid for election. In addition, no member of the ministry was returned from this same Eastern Plains region. The effect of these electoral defeats was that no major leader from the Eastern Plains region who had risen to power with the chief minister in 1954 was available for appointment to the post-election ministry. As a result the new cabinet showed a substantial rise in representation from the Dry region and the Jat group: 25 per cent of the full ministers and 50 per cent of the deputy ministers were appointed from the Jat group, its strongest representation in any ministry.

In order to determine some of the major causal factors contributing to the defeat of the party in the Eastern Plains region and in response to growing charges within the state of "sabotage" of Congress candidates in the Eastern Plains region by the Jat group, the national Congress Working Committee appointed a seven-man subcommittee to conduct extensive examinations into the electoral defeats in Rajasthan. This committee was headed by Khandubhai Desai and included such other prominent national political figures as Lal Bahadur Shastri, Mrs. Indira Gandhi, and G. L. Nanda. Initially the committee was reported to be concerned with the activities of Kumbharam Arya, Nathu Ram Mirdha, and Mathura Das Mathur, the PCC Chief. However, its interest quickly focused upon Kumbharam Arya.

Arya was charged by Eastern Plains Congressmen with having entered into an electoral understanding with "feudal elements" in order to defeat Congress candidates, and it was noted that the only two seats Congress successfully contested in Jaipur district were in the Jat "strongholds" in the northern portion of the district where no Swatantra candidate contested. One of the victors in these two constituencies was Kamla Beniwal, now a deputy minister and strong supporter of Kumbharam Arya. The Jaipur DCC accused Kamla Beniwal and her workers of having openly canvassed votes for the son of the Maharaja, Maharajkumar Prithviraj Singh, the Swatantra party candidate who contested successfully for the parliamentary seat in her area. No official text of the Khandubhai Desai Report was issued, but it was widely reported that it had found evidence to support the charges against Arya even though no immediate disciplinary action was taken against him.[39]

Kumbharam Arya responded to the report and the attacks upon him made within the state by maintaining that the report was biased and that it was only a partial study of the causes of the party's misfortunes

[39] For some major newspaper accounts of the Khandubhai Desai report and the controversy, see *Indian Express*, June 29, 1962, p. 7; July 1, 1962, p. 5; and July 18 1962, p. 5.

in the election. At a special meeting between Arya, Prime Minister Nehru, and Lal Bahadur Shastri, he was reported to have said that before any final decision were reached, a probe of the Congress reverses in his home district of Bikaner should also be conducted, alleging that such an investigation would establish the fact that his own supporters had been sabotaged there. He maintained that the defeat of the ministers in the state was due to their respective unpopularity and not to factionalism within the party.[40] As the final decision regarding disciplinary action approached, Arya supporters in the state maintained that at least 30 Congress MLAs would resign from the party if he were to be disciplined and, shortly before the meeting of the Congress Working Committee in August, Arya supporters organized a joint trip to New Delhi to appear before the Desai committee in Arya's defense. There were 24 MLAs, 12 presidents of DCCs, and 12 Pramukhs of zilla parishads in the state included in this group.[41] Following a "frank talk" between Prime Minister Nehru and Kumbharam Arya, it was reported that Arya had placed himself at the "disposal" of the Prime Minister and that he would abide by Nehru's decision regarding discipline. The issue was finally resolved in mid-August by Arya's resignation from the Executive of the PCC as well as from the Pradesh Election Committee, which represented his posts in the organization wing of the party.[42] Subsequent to the announcement of Arya's resignation from his party posts, the political conditions in the state stabilized and the threatened revolt of MLAs did not materialize. Nathu Ram Mirdha offered his resignation from the cabinet but it was not accepted, and Mohan Lal Sukhadia won a unanimous vote of confidence from the legislative party.[43]

The experience with factionalism of the Rajasthan Congress party during the third general elections only highlights the contending forces which are constantly at work within the party. Traditional group loyalties, Rajasthan's social structure, and political and social mobilization are too powerful a combination of factors in support of factionalism to suggest its decline in the immediate future. Arya's efforts to extend Jat influence into the Eastern Plains region represent the continuing search for strength and support by the Jat group among the rural segments of the state's society. This pursuit is carried on even to the point of threatening the party's continued control of the state for, had it not been resolved, it seems likely that the Congress' precarious position in the state would have been undermined and either President's rule or

[40] *Ibid.*, July 18, 1962, p. 5.
[41] *Indian Express*, July 18, 1962, p. 7.
[42] *Ibid.*, August 6, 1962, p. 9.
[43] *Ibid.*, September 1, 1962, p. 7.

minority government would have followed. It should be noted that while Arya was under attack for factionalism the Jat group attained its strongest position in the cabinet; that although there is less clear evidence, it would seem reasonable to assume that there was some substance to the counter-charges made by Kumbharam Arya; and that the techniques allegedly employed by the Jat faction are by no means unique to this group.

It is also instructive to note the differing fates of Kumbharam Arya and Jai Narain Vyas. The latter was expelled from the party for his open opposition and it is unlikely that he could have re-asserted even a semblance of his former influence in the party had he lived on for a number of years. By contrast, Arya remained within the party fold; within two years he was granted the Congress ticket for a by-election, and having won the seat, he was immediately taken into the cabinet. Arya's case implies that certain unwritten and unarticulated rules of factionalism do exist which allow for wide scope of political maneuvering, just short of open opposition to the party. It further suggests (as does the history of factionalism elsewhere in India) that factional conflict within the party is part of competitive politics within a dominant national party system.

In Rajasthan factional conflict has been the major mechanism through which the "changing of the guard" has occurred within the Congress party. This mechanism has provided the framework within which the process for the replacement of the old political leaders by a new generation of leaders has taken place. It has served to absorb important elements from the diverse social structure of the state and these changes have reflected the varying strength of these elements within the party. It further serves as an established means whereby new groups can seek their place within the Congress party and attempt to assert their influences to achieve their goals. Viewed in this perspective, factionalism loses some of its narrow, crass characteristics, becoming a process whereby a society gropes its way toward greater political mobilization and more accurate bases of representation.

The history of the high command's attempt to control factionalism in Rajasthan indicates that the most it can expect to achieve is to contain factional controversy within reasonable bounds in order to permit the party to continue functioning effectively. In this sense one of the important functions played by the Congress party is that of legitimizer of the winners of factional conflicts in the state within the context of broad policy commitments which are compatible with the aspirations and goals of a large sector of the society. This is perhaps the inevitable fate of a pragmatic political party as opposed to an ideological political party in a new nation, but the significance of this function should not be under-emphasized. It should be remembered that the Congress party represents the most legitimate political institution in India. It is functional for the integration of the society, for ordered change, and for the maintenance of political stability that the Congress channels the conflicts flowing from modernization and contains them within the political institution possessing the greatest claim on its members' loyalties. The party has been forced to assume this role on account of its historic legitimacy as well as its institutional strength, and before students of Indian politics become overly critical of the Indian political scene, perhaps they should examine the political histories of other new nations with either a less dominant party system or a less pragmatic institutionalizing process.[44]

Electoral contests serve not only as one focal point for factional conflict within the Congress party but as an important arena in which the Rajput aristocracy and Congress leadership have clashed. The state party's success in meeting this challenge has been aided greatly by the prestige and organization of the national party and the appeal of Prime Minister Nehru, which were primary supports for the party in Rajasthan during the first general election. By the second general election, the state party could rely to a greater extent on its own organization, its own accomplishments, and the web of influence it had been able to spin during these years. But the primacy of the Rajput threat to its leadership still remained. One may assume that the Congress party has attempted to reduce this challenge through the judicious use of its power over the privy purses of the princely houses, and, in terms of political strategies, it has consistently followed a policy of dividing the Rajput elite where possible by accommodating some of their elements within the party. The first unsuccessful efforts in Jodhpur have already been discussed as has the relationship of the efforts to absorb Rajputs into the party to the defeat of Jai Narain Vyas in 1954. The first actual absorption of Rajputs into the Congress occurred only when the Kshatriya Mahasabha was split between the small and large jagirdars. Twenty-two jagirdar MLAs were admitted as full members of the party in August 1954, on condition that they would no longer oppose the

[44] The writer is indebted to Samuel P. Huntington's discussion of the relationship between social mobilization and political institutionalization in his article "Political Development and Political Decay," *World Politics*, XVII (April 1965), 386-430. For a fine analysis of the role of factionalism in the Indian political system, see Rajni Kothari, "The Congress System," *Asian Survey*, IV (December 1964), 1161-73.

resumption of their jagirs and that their entrance would not "lower the prestige of the party."[45] In the second general election, more Rajputs were recruited as candidates. The most prominent among these was Harish Chandra, the former ruler of Jhalawal. The Rajput members formed a significant group within the ranks of Congress MLAs in the second Assembly, and in 1959 Harish Chandra was appointed to a cabinet post. Until 1962, however, the Congress had not recruited other former rulers into the party. In the third general election, when the forces of the Rajput aristocracy were powerfully mobilized by the Maharani in the eastern portion of the state, the Congress party extended its policy of recruitment among the Rajput aristocracy and actively pursued the recruitment of former princes. The Maharaja of Jaisalmer accepted the Congress ticket, though he had won in the two previous elections, running as an independent candidate. The Raj Kumar of Kota accepted a Congress Lok Sabha nomination, and the Raj Kumar of Karauli ran for the Assembly on the party's ticket. However, the latter's candidacy was strongly opposed by the local party.[46] The PCC Chief announced that Karni Singh, the Maharaja of Bikaner, had been "requested" to join Congress but that no reply had been received from him.[47] Despite this, no Congress candidate contested against Karni Singh. Karni Singh's silence was symbolic of the Congress party's limited success in absorbing the Rajput aristocracy into the party. No member of the four major ruling families in Rajasthan openly associated with the Congress party, although they were unable to cooperate with each other. The Congress party's success in absorbing members of the less important ruling houses did split the state's aristocracy, however, and lessened the threat to the party from that direction. The successful neutralization of major ruling houses, the absorption of Rajputs over the past nine years, and the offering of the party's ticket to those princes who would accept the party's offers were crucial to the Congress' continued, if precarious, control of government following the 1962 general election.

GOVERNMENT PERFORMANCE

Any evaluation of governmental performance in Rajasthan must be viewed in the context of its origins, its history, and the attendant problems of integration. Composed of princely states, with the single exception of Ajmer, Rajasthan lacked the modern political and adminis-

45 *Hindustan Times*, August 7, 1954, p. 6. The latter requirement was insisted upon by the PCC Executive, which was badly split over the entrance of the jagirdar MLAs. See *ibid.*, June 23, 1954, p. 1.

46 *Times of India*, February 5, 1962, p. 1.

47 *Dainik Lokwani*, December 6, 1961, p. 1.

trative experience gained in the areas of former British India. One consequence has been that members of the state's cabinet have often had little and sometimes no previous experience in administration. Although a hybrid form of representative government was established in some of the princely states in the 1930s and 1940s, this came too late to provide effective experience with parliamentary constitutional government and with the problems of administration for most of the men who were to hold high political office in the state's government. Men who did gain experience in the administrations of the princely states were, for the most part, politically disqualified since they had opposed the nationalist movement. Thus, no pool of trained political leaders existed upon which the new state could draw; instead, former participants in the nationalist struggle had to face the burden of responsible leadership with little if any previous experience in positions of administrative leadership.

Second, Rajasthan inherited the princely states' civil service. Although some of these states did borrow ICS personnel to aid them in establishing an administrative system along British lines, these efforts were not markedly successful, and traditional status and family influence, rather than individual merit, were overriding considerations in the recruitment of personnel.[48] Implicit in this situation were numerous problems which could only militate against the growth of an effective administrative service, loyal to the new government and with the high morale needed to assume the tasks it would face in independent India. Civil servants of the princely states possessed old loyalties which would not immediately disappear with the formation of Rajasthan. The state's new leadership included the same nationalist leaders the civil servants had previously restricted or suppressed. To accept the state's new leaders as superiors and arbiters of their professional destinies was difficult, if not impossible, for some. The very process of integration of administrative services involved the extensive reallocation of positions and power. A chief engineer of a small state such as Kishangar would most likely be integrated as a district engineer, and he would undoubtedly feel the loss of status acutely. Since these decisions were often influenced significantly or made directly by the new leaders of the state for whom the civil servant felt little loyalty or respect, morale and efficiency within the administrative service could not be expected to be great. A final im-

[48] One observer in Rajasthan at the time of the first general elections described the state's administrative service as "overstaffed, inexperienced and often unqualified." S. V. Kogekar and R. L. Park, *Reports on the Indian General Elections 1951-52*, p. 225. S. M. Rameshwar describes many of the princely state officers as: "Manifestly unfit for service." *Resurgent Rajasthan* (New Delhi: Apex Publications, 1962), p. 119.

portant consequence for the state of the inheritance of the princely state bureaucracies was that regionalism tended to be perpetuated by old loyalties and associations.

In an effort to meet these problems a Rajasthan Administrative Service (RAS), a Police Service, and a Judicial Service were organized and a Public Service Commission created. The state had to be divided into districts and sub-districts; and district magistrates, collectors, and superintendents of police had to be appointed. To patrol the 750-mile border where "murderers, kidnappers, and smugglers moved with impunity across the sandy wastes,"[49] the Rajasthan Armed Constabulary was created in 1950 to maintain border security. Law and order, always a serious problem in the state, had badly deteriorated, and dacoity and violence in the rural areas were common. The inadequate police forces of the integrating states were brought together to form the Rajasthan Police Force, and slowly a semblance of order was established. By 1960 this force claimed that it had killed 4,000 dacoits in the ten-year period of its existence.[50]

All these tasks of organizing the governmental apparatus had to be accomplished at the same time, and the creation of the administrative base of the state was in itself an impressive achievement. Time and the expansion of the state's functions aided the growth of a more effective administrative service. Rapid expansion of the bureaucracy made possible the recruitment of better-trained public servants and brought into the administration individuals who did not possess the deeply ingrained loyalties of those in the initial pool of public servants. But expansion, retirement, and promotion of new recruits to positions of responsibility required time, and even as late as 1962, a truly integrated state service still did not exist.

Although the administrative service is more integrated and functions more effectively than during its early years, its reputation has not improved commensurately. Corruption is reported to be widespread, and lower-echelon public servants tend to assume that their superiors are engaged in some form of unethical activity. There are indications that administrative secrecy is not as highly practiced as it should be and that other loyalties take precedence over professional norms. Recently, when a new Finance Minister presented his budget to the Assembly, he was embarrassed by dissident Congressmen who were able to point to errors of arithmetic in the budget, knowledge of which could be based only on examination of the document prior to the minister's presentation to the Assembly.

Factionalism takes its toll in other ways as well. On paper, the cooper-

[49] Rameshwar, *op.cit.*, p. 124.

[50] *Ibid.*, pp. 118-31.

ative movement is one of the most successful programs in the state. By 1961 it was officially estimated that 53 per cent of the state's villages and 24 per cent of all rural families were enrolled in cooperative societies.[51] This department has been under the control of successive Jat ministers during much of the time that rapid expansion of the cooperative movement occurred, and it is widely maintained by informed persons in the state that the cooperative movement has been of greater benefit to the Jat faction than to the general peasantry. The Khandubhai Desai report concerned itself with this problem and reportedly charged Nathu Ram Mirdha and Kumbharam Arya with "political profiteering" in the cooperative movement. Thereupon, the report recommended that an inquiry board be established to investigate the alleged embezzlement of cooperative funds.[52]

Prior to integration, the economy of Rajasthan was one of the least developed in India. A state with constant food deficits, inadequate transportation and communication even by Indian standards, no major industry, an archaic land tenure system, large areas of arid and uncultivable land due to inadequate rainfall, and a population whose literacy rate did not exceed 10 per cent, Rajasthan had few prerequisites for a sound agricultural economy, much less for industrialization. Because of these conditions, economic planning has emphasized the development of Rajasthan's agricultural economy and the establishment of the basic overhead capital necessary for future industrialization. In the decade of the fifties the literacy rate in the state as a whole rose to only 15 per cent, but there was a substantial increase in the school-age population. In 1961, 46 per cent (compared to 15 per cent in 1951) of children between the ages of 6 and 11 were in schools, and there was also a substantial increase in the older age groups attending schools.[53] Road mileage expanded 50 per cent in the same period, and a partially nationalized bus system has improved transportation, but less than in many other Indian states. Statistics point to other areas of change and development: medical facilities and care have expanded; three new medical colleges are now in operation; and the state exceeds the national average in numbers of hospitals and hospital beds.[54]

In terms of agricultural development, the significant factor has been the reform of the feudal land system and the installation of irrigation systems. Other land reforms have been made following the decision to

[51] Government of Rajasthan, *Second Five Year Plan: Progress Report, Rajasthan, 1956-61* (Jaipur: Government Central Press, 1962), p. 104.

[52] *Indian Express*, July 3, 1962, p. 5.

[53] Government of Rajasthan, Directorate of Economics and Statistics, *A Decade of Planned Economy*, p. 4.

[54] *Ibid.*, p. 5.

resume jagirs. The Rajasthan Land Tenancy Act of 1955 gave greater legal protection to tenants, enabled them to obtain more secure rights to land, and protected them from arbitrary ejection. However, no ceilings on landholdings had been established by 1961.[55] Nearly 27 per cent of the total funds allocated to the state under the Second Five Year Plan was earmarked for irrigation; and the area of irrigated land increased from 24,000 acres to about 36,000 acres between 1951 and 1959.[56] However, waterlogging has been a serious problem in the state, and irrigation is somewhat less effective than these figures would indicate.

During the Second Five Year Plan the state's net annual income increased by an average of 3.3 per cent a year, slightly more than the national average of 3.1 per cent a year. Its per capita income fluctuated between Rs. 227 and Rs. 249 from 1954 to 1959. The yearly rise in the per capita income during the same period was .9 per cent.[57] Clearly Rajasthan achieved no major economic breakthrough even though its performance did not compare unfavorably with the national performance.

The state's economic future will depend greatly on its two major development projects—the Rajasthan Canal and the Chambal Dam. The Rajasthan Canal is the largest canal project in the world; it is being constructed in Bikaner district and later will be extended westward to Jailsalmer district. Ultimately, it will provide irrigation for some seven million acres of land, and when completed, it will turn the waste lands of these two arid districts into one of the major grain-producing areas in India. The Chambal multi-purpose dam project is located in Kota district in the Southern Plateau region. This is a joint project with the adjoining state of Madhya Pradesh. It is claimed that the availability of power will convert Kota into a "second Kanpur."[58] Although industrial activity in the southeastern portion of the state is on the rise, its industrialization is still a future prospect rather than a current reality.

Land reform, community development projects, the cooperative movement, and other rural development projects have, of course, greatly influenced and altered the countryside. However, officials are still prone to point to the "psychological" change in the peasantry rather than to evidences of economic and objective change. Jagir resumption has been slowly implemented, and this process is not yet complete at this time.

55 *Second Five Year Plan: Progress Report*, p. 75.

56 *A Decade of Planned Economy*, p. 2.

57 *Second Five Year Plan: Progress Report*, p. 17.

58 The city of Kanpur in Uttar Pradesh is one of the most rapidly developing industrial areas in India.

Controversy and resentment have surrounded the entire process. The special concessions for acquiring land opened up by the major irrigation projects in Kota and Bikaner at concessional prices are widely resented by the peasantry. Many jagirdari families escaped the full impact of resumption by evicting tenants and assigning rights of tenancy to various members of their own families.

Factional politics associated with the cooperative movement has lessened its effectiveness and restricted its membership. As factional politics intensified during the 1950s and early 1960s, development activities became increasingly associated with political struggles and divisions in the state. The division between the rural and non-rural political leadership regarding the effectiveness of these programs indicates the extent to which the state is becoming fissured on this question of development in the countryside. Town and urban political leaders of non-agricultural castes confidently maintain that a "revolution" has taken place in the countryside and that the peasantry is substantially better off today. Many rural leaders in all political parties vigorously question the validity of this assertion. There is a growing belief among these leaders that until the urban-based leadership of the state's government is completely replaced by agrarian leadership, there can be no truly effective development of the countryside. The most significant consequence of over a decade of economic planning and of social and political reforms in the state may well be the mobilization of its agricultural population. But because of the deep political cleavages among the populace of the countryside and the low level of literacy, agrarianism has not yet succeeded in forming an effective movement throughout the state.

The establishment of panchayati raj in October 1959 encouraged the growth of ruralism in the state. Agrarian leaders maintain that the urban leaders of the state instituted panchayati raj primarily because they recognized that their programs had not succeeded in changing the living standards of the peasantry significantly. By the devolution of many types of planning to the panchayat level, they hoped to avoid the growing resentment in the countryside. Leaders of the new rural forces in the state maintain that they have subverted this objective and that they are successfully utilizing the new political institutions to develop their own political strength. The Jat and Rajput leaders have proven especially effective in expanding their influence. After the first panchayat elections in 1959, the Rajput and Jat castes held 22.5 per cent and 16.8 per cent, respectively, of all sarpanchships.[59] Their dominance of Pradhanships

[59] Government of Rajasthan, *A Report on the Panchayat Elections in Rajasthan 1960* (Jaipur: Government Central Press, 1961), Appendix C, p. ix. Sarpanchas are the presidents of the local village panchayats.

was even greater: according to the Congress Rajput and Jat leaders these two castes control over 50 per cent of all the state's Pradhan offices. The strength of the Rajputs is greater and their range of influence broader. The Jats predominate in those areas where there is a concentration of their caste, in the Dry and Eastern Plains regions. Many of the Rajput Pradhans appear to be representative of the middle level of the old jagirdari class. This group of Rajputs was not wealthy enough to maintain a house at the court at which they were only infrequently required to attend. They tended instead to spend most of their time in the countryside. This class of jagirdars was better educated than the peasantry, yet remained in close contact with village life and culture and was the focal point of local political power. Rajput effectiveness is limited by traditional caste divisions, and since independence this caste has become divided on the basis of political parties. Especially important for the Rajputs is the division between the Congress and the Swatantra parties. Although limited to specific areas of the state in the third general elections, this division will apparently grow. In many areas of the state, the basic political contest will be between the Congress and Swatantra Rajput factions. The local leaderships of the Jats are less divided by differing party allegiances.

Two problems face the new agrarian leadership in the state. One is the traditional conflict between the two major groups, and the other is the ability of the more experienced, better educated, and town-based leadership, often supported by the capital, to split its support by patronage or other means.

The Jat-Rajput conflict was one of the most important features of pre-independence politics in the state. In the early 1950s the Jat group opposed the absorption of the jagirdari MLAs, and they did not welcome the rise of Harish Chandra to the cabinet. But after the third general elections, there were signs that some degree of rapprochement between the two groups had been reached. Harish Chandra signed a petition supporting Kumbharam Arya in the dispute over the Khandubhai Desai report, and his discontent with the chief minister was growing because of what he felt was insufficient representation in the cabinet.

Although a Jat-Rajput alliance is not a reality, it is a possibility. If such an alliance could be formed, the nucleus of an organized and coordinated rural movement would exist. By successfully challenging the Sukhadia leadership, a pattern more similar to that which has emerged in other states such as Maharashtra and Madras would be created. But the differences between Rajasthan rural leadership and that in other states is instructive for understanding the problems it is likely to face. Where rural-based leadership has emerged in other states and has succeeded in controlling the government, greater political stability and often more positive government performance has resulted. The consequences of these developments have been felt even at the national level of leadership. Rural-based political leadership appears to be more capable of developing political unity and of moderating the inherent conflict between traditionalism and modernization. Although there is not always a significant ideological difference between the two types of leaders, the rural leadership seems to be able to add significant cultural content to the party's ideology. The capacity to formulate more meaningful symbols and an ideology adapted to the state identifies the modernizing institutions more closely with local values and the culture of the traditional peasantry. Rural leadership increases the likelihood that a political figure will emerge who can serve as an integrating force. But these benefits are less likely to occur in Rajasthan even if the rural leadership does gain control of the state's government. The diversity of the state's agricultural castes, their concentration in specific regions, and the historic division between the two main leadership castes would all tend to lessen the benefits that rural dominance of the state has brought elsewhere. A mass leader in Rajasthan would have to depend more on his rural ideology than on traditional support. This suggests that agrarian radicalism would have to be more extreme in Rajasthan to overcome its diversity.

The only other source of leadership for the growing ruralism in the state is one of the major ruling families. The emergence of such a leader could unite the competing factions of the Rajput aristocracy and develop a broad-based mass appeal throughout the state. This could effectively merge the more traditional ruralism with a modernizing elite capable of integrating the state more effectively and creating a more stable political system. In order to succeed, such a movement would have to be organized into a modern political party and its elite committed to a program of modernization. The Maharani of Jaipur has paved the way in organizational terms to some extent, but it is less clear how firmly she is committed to modernization.

CONCLUSIONS

In the period under review, political institution building necessarily was the primary focus of political activities and energies in Rajasthan.[60]

[60] For a brilliant discussion of the relationship between social mobilization and political institutionalization see Huntington, *op.cit.*, pp. 386-430.

Political institutions are normally difficult to establish and imbed in a society. This was especially so in Rajasthan in that the two primary political institutions of a democratic society—the bureaucracy and the political party—had to be established simultaneously where there existed little traditional or natural support for them. Judged in this context, Rajasthan's accomplishments are not as insignificant as it would appear from its post-independence history of conflict, factionalism, and threatened instability.

Concrete and significant progress has occurred in the establishment of an integrated bureaucracy, which today surpasses any system of administration in the state's history. Unlike some areas of former British India, there was no previous system of efficient administration which might have been considered superior in some ways to the present bureaucracy. Improvement in conditions of law and order are only the most obvious fruits of this development. Although the implementation of specific development programs may be criticized, the existence of a bureaucratic structure capable of conceiving and implementing planned development must be recognized as an important development in the political capacity in the state.

Because of the continued control of government by the Congress party, its development has been of greater significance in the second general area of political institution building. It has been the Congress party which has most directly faced the problem of maintaining a balance between social mobilization and political institutionalization in the state. Here the history of conflict and factionalism is less encouraging and more difficult to judge.[61] But in order to gain a proper perspective, it is necessary to look beyond the recurring factional controversies to broader and more significant developments. The Rajasthan Congress party has demonstrated its capacity to serve as the basic institution of integration in the state. It has survived changes in leadership in terms both of personnel and of generations. It has proved itself an adaptive institution which can absorb new elements in the society as they become politically active, and it has shown a willingness to open up its ranks at the higher echelons of authority and control to important forces in the state which are capable of developing political support. The changes in the composition of the state's cabinets clearly demonstrate that govern-

[61] For an outstanding study of the origins, growth and development of factionalism in Nagaur district see Richard Sisson, *Caste, Faction and Politics: A Case Study in the Rajasthan Congress*, Working Paper prepared for the South Asia Colloquium, Center for South Asia Studies, Institute of International Studies, University of California, Berkeley, May 1965.

mental institutions more closely reflect the state's social structure today than in 1952. The Congress party's successful absorption of a portion of the Rajput aristocracy lessened the major threat to the party's hegemony and demonstrates its capacity to absorb groups in the society which had previously been among its major opponents. These developments indicate that the Congress party is not dominated by a closed elite whose primary concern is to cut off the channels of access to political authority, but rather an open elite, pragmatic in approach and responsive to evolving societal demands.

Although factionalism has occurred at all levels of the Congress party, at times threatening the unity of the party as well as its sense of purpose and effectiveness, factionalism has also been the primary technique for meeting the basic problem of social mobilization of new elites in the society. Elite conflict seems inevitable in Rajasthan, and there are many advantages to this conflict occurring within the ranks of the Congress party. As a political institution, the Congress is more legitimate than any other. It consequently has a broader, deeper and stronger basis for appeals to its members' loyalty, and therefore, it is the political institution most capable of absorbing tensions and conflicts. Violence and unregulated conflict is less likely to occur within the Congress party than if it were to take place between parties or local groups unconnected with a state-wide institution. Hence, if factionalism has to occur, it is best that it occur within the Congress party.

Factionalism can be utilized as a means of control as well. Constituency and district-level factionalism can serve the purpose of limiting the existing dominant political groups and elites at the local level, since because of and through factional controversy they are aware that an alternative to their control exists. Although perhaps temporarily outside the Congress party, this alternative elite is likely to regain access to the party if it is successful in defeating the current dominant faction. While this is not the most desirable process of establishing responsibility and maintaining responsiveness in a political system, it is at least one technique of doing so.

It is also important to recognize that factionalism occurs at differing levels and that factional controversy and instability at the local level is not automatically translated into division and instability at the state level. State leaders appear willing to allow substantial factional controversy at the local level, and they may even tend to encourage it while maintaining substantial unity at the state level. Thus although constituency studies of any major group may reveal substantial instability and division on a petty, personal, or traditional basis, this does not mean that the group will be equally divided at the state level. Factionalism at the local level is not a process which must inevitably create the same type or degree of instability at the state level. In fact, it may even be integrated into more highly organized conflicts between political elites at the state level that represent more specific and long-term interests. This analysis does not deny the unfavorable effects that factionalism at all levels has on governmental effectiveness, but it does recognize that it is a technique which attempts to control the often conflicting processes of social mobilization and political institution building.

Rajasthan's political prospects are not substantially different from the experience of the state's immediate past. The continued expansion of effective political participation will most likely mean continued factionalism and conflict. The Congress party will increasingly face more difficult choices between governmental effectiveness and its absorptive and responsive capacities. It would seem likely that its absorptive capacity has not been exhausted as yet and that new groups and new elites can be effectively accommodated within the party's structure. But ultimately, it will face a choice between being a political party attempting to represent all strata of society and a political party representative of only some. At this point it will be faced with the loss of major elites and groups. The point at which this occurs will be dependent in part upon the growth of a society differentiated on a less traditional basis and in part upon increasing demands for effective government. The latter possibility may well arise before the former for, in the long run, the Congress party's legitimacy will rest on its capacity to provide effective and purposeful government.

In terms of the major groups within the Congress today, it would appear more likely that the non-Jat groups will face a greater challenge to their political control because of their greater vulnerability to the appeals of ruralism and because of the character of their social basis, which provides less potentiality for stability. The survival capacity of the non-Jat groups will depend to a greater degree on their political skills and the judicious use of their influence. It would seem likely that elections and the maintenance of their position will depend more on financial resources and that the political elite outside the Dry zone will be more responsive to those elements in the society which can most easily provide these resources. Based upon past experience, it does not seem unlikely that they will succeed, and if this should prove to be the case, the present style of political leadership is likely to continue. Thus it is probable that Rajasthan will continue to be characterized by political leaders who possess little mass appeal, but who have clearly established areas of influence and political strength. It is unlikely that an integrative mass leader will emerge from the Congress party who could appeal to a broad segment of the population throughout the state. Such leaders could arise as spokesmen of an emergent ruralism, and this movement would tend to be a carrier of a radical populist ideology. The other most likely source for an integrative leader would be the traditional Rajput elite whose success may well depend on the ability not only to appeal directly to the rural peasantry, but also to develop significant support within the major business groups in the state and elsewhere. This would bring it into direct competition with the town-based elite now dominant in the state. The continued dominance of the Congress party, and perhaps the political stability of the state, may hinge on the success of the current Congress leadership in devising strategies which guard against the undercutting of its rural mass base and which do not alienate non-rural sources of support.

POSTSCRIPT*

In Rajasthan, as in other parts of India, the fourth general elections produced a greater threat to the dominant party system. However, the threat was neither new nor was the "Congress system" as well established in Rajasthan. Except for the second general elections the Congress party's hold on the state had already been precarious, but never so precarious as after the most recent elections. President's Rule, a possibility before, became a reality and Congress's survival as the ruling party hung in the balance until April 28, some eight weeks after the general elections. Few new actors were involved in the most recent drama of Congress's survival, and the plot was not fundamentally different from previous occasions. However, the performance was gripping and perhaps significant.

The success of the Congress system in Rajasthan has not differed fundamentally from elsewhere in the nation. It depended on the development of conflict resolution mechanisms to contain factional struggles within the party, on the maintenance of an open and adaptive power structure,

* The preceding study of Rajasthan's political development was completed long before the fourth general elections. The dramatic events and significant political developments of the general elections made it necessary to update the study. This postscript on the general elections will be handicapped by the lack of complete information, and its conclusions and analysis are tentative. At the time of this writing (May 1967), only daily Indian newspapers through mid-March 1967 and incomplete election results were available. No attempt will be made to present a comprehensive review of political developments since 1962, but rather the 1967 elections will be treated as a case study.

and on the intricate interrelationship with the center which allowed intervention from the national leadership, usually in support of stability and continuity. By 1966 the assumed stability of the national leadership was more in question than ever before and the Prime Ministership was not predetermined as in previous elections. This difference may have fundamentally limited the center's influence in the states. Furthermore, the dominant party system was in question in many Indian states during the general elections and perhaps even at the national level. This new situation produced a significant change in the attitudes of the opposition parties in Rajasthan, and this, combined with the breakdown of the conflict control mechanisms within the Congress, produced a major post-election crisis and President's Rule.

The Opposition Parties

The opposition parties "smelt blood" in 1967 and their behavior and electoral strategies reflected this. Their hopes of defeating the Congress party and ending Congress rule in the state were based on sound factors. Some had occurred well before the election time approached, and events immediately before the election gave sustenance to their expectations. Such national events as the death of Nehru, an economic recession, inflation, and food shortages were scarcely the most sanguine conditions for the Congress to "go to the people." When the Kumbharam Arya and Harish Chandra factions withdrew from the Congress and formed the Janta party in December 1966, the issue appeared settled and there seemed little hope for a Congress victory. The Jan Sangh and Swatantra parties had additional reasons to approach the election with confidence and high expectations. The Jan Sangh had devoted five additional years to organizational work, and its state political leadership was now more widely known and had increased in stature. The Swatantra party seemed stronger also. The popularity of Maharani Gaytri Devi had not dimmed significantly, and by maintaining its unity and organizational identity during the past five years the Swatantra party had demonstrated that it was a permanent addition to the state's political system. It seemed not unreasonable to hope that the two parties together might achieve a majority and have the opportunity to form the state's government. To do so required that the two parties cooperate and not undermine their individual strengths; and, in addition, they must contest the election throughout the state.

The Jan Sangh–Swatantra election alliance was announced in principle by mid-November, and the allocation of seats between the two parties had been completed by the end of December. Together the parties planned to contest all 184 Assembly seats with Swatantra running candidates in 119 constituencies and the Jan Sangh in 65.[62]

Factionalism and Candidate Selection in the Congress Party

Factional conflict within the Congress party gave a major fillip to the opposition parties' electoral prospects. It had been rumored since 1964 that Mohan Lal Sukhadia would move to the center in 1967 and join the national cabinet, ending his thirteen-year tenure as the state's Chief Minister. The anti-Sukhadia factions apparently based their strategy on this assumption. To avoid an open contest with the Sukhadia group over the selection of candidates and to present a united front against the growing Jan Sangh–Swatantra threat, the anti-Sukhadia factions agreed to allow the Chief Minister to select personally all the party's candidates. They probably calculated that they would have limited success in an open contest over the selection of candidates with the Sukhadia group, since the Chief Minister controlled both the parliamentary wing and the organizational wing of the party.[63] Furthermore, they may have realized that the "rules of the game" had changed since 1962 and that it was less likely that the Central Election Committee (CEC) would intervene to protect minority factions.[64] If the Chief Minister elevated himself to the national level as was expected, they would stand a better chance of exercising their influence in the state. But as the date for the announcement of the Rajasthan list approached, it was still unclear whether the Chief Minister would contest for the Assembly or the Parliament. Four days after the announcement in November of the Jan Sangh and Swatantra electoral alliance, the Rajasthan list was published and Sukhadia was standing for the Assembly.[65] From this point on events moved rapidly, culminating in the largest open exodus from the Rajasthan Congress in its history and in the formation of the Janta party.

The composition of the Janta party illustrates the role of expediency in Indian politics as well as the importance of long-term political and social forces. The leader of the dissident movement was Kumbharam Arya and he was joined by Harish Chandra, the Maharaja of Jhalawar. Thus a quasi Jat-Rajput alliance was realized for pragmatic political

[62] For press reports on the electoral alliance, see: *Hindustan Times*, November 21, 1966, p. 9, and December 27, 1966, p. 11.

[63] A Sukhadia man, Ram Kishore Vyas, had been elected PCC Chief. See pages 346-347 for Vyas's political history.

[64] See Stanley A. Kochanek's "Political Recruitment in the Indian National Congress: The Fourth General Elections," *Asian Survey* (May 1967), pp. 292-304, for an excellent analysis of the politics of candidate selection in the Congress party.

[65] *Hindustan Times*, November 25, 1966, p. 1.

reasons, if not for ideological reasons, five years after this alliance had first been suggested by events after the general elections of 1962.[66] Joining Kumbharam Arya and Harish Chandra in the formation of the Janta party was Ram Karan Joshi, the former Jaipur DCC chief and once an important member of the Jai Nayran Vyas faction, who had spearheaded the attempt to drive Arya out of the Congress party at the time of the Khandubhai Desai committee's investigation. Ram Karan Joshi's revolt was not part of a general exodus of the remaining members of the Vyas factions, for some former Vyas men ran on the official Congress ticket. The Vyas group no longer represented a cohesive group in Rajasthan. Both Kumbharam Arya and Harish Chandra maintained that their respective groups had not been given adequate representation on the ticket, but their major objection was clearly that the Chief Minister was remaining at the state level.[67] The mass exodus from the Congress occurred on December 20 when Arya and Harish Chandra announced their resignations from both the cabinet and the party. Two Jat deputy ministers, Kamla Beniwal (Jaipur district) and Daulat Ram Saran (Churu district) announced their resignations at the same time. The Rajput deputy minister, Bhim Singh (Shekawati) had resigned a week earlier. These cabinet members were joined by at least twelve sitting MLAs making a total of seventeen resignations.[68]

Opposition party leaders claimed that because of the resignations the Congress no longer enjoyed a majority and the government should resign. Sukhadia rejected these demands stating that his government enjoyed a majority, for there were many independents in the assembly who

[66] See page 363.

[67] The relationships of the two ministers with Sukhadia had deteriorated substantially in recent months and Kumbharam Arya's relationship had never been good. Arya maintained that when he had joined the cabinet in 1964 as revenue minister, accompanied by ten independent MLAs who joined the Congress at the same time, it was on the insistence of Mohan Lal Sukhadia, who requested his cooperation in "smashing Maharani Gaytri Devi's plans to become the Chief Minister of Rajasthan." Arya complained that after he joined the government he was not fully consulted and that cabinet decisions were taken before he arrived or after he had left the cabinet meeting. Furthermore, both Harish Chandra and Kumbharam Arya had lost important portfolios in recent months. Arya had lost the important famine relief portfolio and was systematically isolated from any influence over the party's election machinery. *Hindustan Times*, December 21, 1966, p. 1. Harish Chandra's relationship with Sukhadia deteriorated more recently and may have been connected with his refusal to support a Sukhadia candidate for Chief Minister if Sukhadia went to the center.

[68] Some reports maintained that as many as twenty-five MLAs resigned but the seventeen MLAs given above are certain resigners for they were named and later took part in the Janta party. For the conflicting reports on the number of resigners, see *Hindustan Times*, December 21, 1966, p. 1; December 27, 1966, p. 11; and January 15, 1967, p. 8.

were outside the Congress mainly because the Kumbharam Arya group was within it and these supporters could now join the Congress party. The question was really academic since the assembly would not be in session before the general elections but the demands for the government's resignation reflected the eagerness of the opposition to end Congress rule in the state. The "open umbrella" policy of the Congress party, to use Morris-Jones' apt metaphor, had become more like a "revolving door" in Rajasthan.

Because of its formation barely two months before the general elections, the Janta party was unquestionably an *ad hoc* organization to a substantial degree. At the party's founding convention in Jaipur city on December 24, 150 dissident Congressmen attended; and when its manifesto was issued later, it placed the party squarely behind such general objectives as ending the "social, economic and political exploitation" in the state.[69] However, it is also clear that the Janta party was a more institutionalized form of Congress rebellion. At the convention and afterwards, every effort was made to establish the Janta party's identity as a permanent party in Rajasthan's political system. Arya refused to identify with the Jana Congress movements elsewhere in India because he questioned whether Jana Congressmen were true rebels and doubted that they would stay outside the Congress after the general elections. Harish Chandra stressed his loyalty to the new party in an apparent effort to discount his rumoured sympathies for the Swatantra party. Kumbharam Arya also emphasized, reportedly with some anguish, that members of his group who had not followed him out of the Congress and who had accepted the official ticket could expect no quarter from him in the forthcoming elections.[70] Furthermore, the Janta party's purpose was not the reform of the Congress but the defeat of the Congress. Kumbharam Arya expressed this sentiment when he said to a group of party workers that: "I want to expose this Government before the public and for that it is necessary to destroy the Congress. We have to decide that after leaving the Congress once, we shall never return."[71]

Although the party's program was vague, its emphasis on ruralism was clear, and there is little question that its leaders thought of it as being an anti-urban party. But more important for the immediate general elections than the Janta party's programmatic significance was its potential electoral strength, its impact on the election strategies of the opposition parties, and the split it revealed in the state-wide Jat group. The last point is perhaps the most significant.

[69] *Ibid.*, February 10, 1967, p. 6.

[70] *Ibid.*, December 25, 1966, p. 1.

[71] *Ibid.*, December 26, 1966, p. 1.

The Jat group had always been divided into at least two major sections, although as a group it cooperated effectively at the state level. The Bikaner–Eastern Plains group was led by Kumbharam Arya, while the second major Jat group was based in Jodhpur division and was led by Nathu Ram Mirdha. Arya, although his strength had never been tested fundamentally in the Jodhpur area, was reputed to be the more powerful of the two leaders and his influence was state-wide while Mirdha's was regional. The glaring absence of Nathu Ram Mirdha and Jodhpur Jat MLAs from the dissidents' movement clearly indicated that the Jat group was divided at the state level on a basic issue for the first time. Commenting on the dissident movement, Nathu Ram Mirdha stated that only one Congress candidate and two of Jodhpur's twenty-eight seated MLAs would join the Janta party. He predicted that Congress would win twenty-eight of the thirty-nine assembly seats in Jodhpur division and all the Lok Sabha seats. In his own district of Nagaur, he maintained that Congress would win eight or nine seats.[72] Nathu Ram Mirdha's statement and Arya's unqualified opposition to all official Congress party candidates strongly suggest that the lines of battle had been drawn and that the general elections would be the test of the two Jat leaders' strength in Jodhpur division.

More generally, the Janta party's formation seemed to ensure the defeat of the Congress party. It was assumed that the Arya and Chandra factions would seriously hurt the Congress in thirteen of the state's twenty-six districts and that Congress had no chance of winning more than 65 to 75 of the 184 assembly seats.[73] Obviously, the formation of the Janta party improved the prospects of the Swatantra–Jan Sangh alliance's winning control of the state. Perhaps reflecting the improved prospects, the Maharani of Jaipur announced on the day following the mass resignations from Congress that she would prefer to stand for an assembly seat instead of running again for the Jaipur Lok Sabha seat she had won so overwhelmingly in 1962. Because of the timing of her statement, her assurances that she had no interest in replacing Laxshman Singh, Swatantra's state leader, as the opposition's prospective Chief Minister seemed somehow unconvincing.[74]

The Janta party created problems for the opposition parties as well.

[72] *Ibid.*, December 29, 1966, p. 11.

[73] For predictions of Congress' electoral chances, see *ibid.*, December 26, 1966, p. 1, and January 15, 1967, p. 8.

[74] *The Hindu*, December 22, 1966, p. 7. Ultimately the Maharani ran for both the Lok Sabha and the assembly. She was again successful in winning her Lok Sabha seat but was defeated in the assembly contest.

The carefully negotiated distribution of seats between the Swatantra party and the Jan Sangh was disrupted by the prospects of including the Janta party in the electoral alliance. In general the Swatantra party was in favor of renegotiating the allocation of seats to include Janta party members while the Jan Sangh party was opposed. No formal agreement was reached between the parties although local adjustments were made, principally by the Swatantra party. The late formation of the Janta party denied it the opportunity of applying for a state-wide party symbol, and Janta party members were allowed to run under other political parties' symbols as well as running as independent candidates. For example, Harish Chandra and some of his supporters ran under the Jan Sangh symbol in Jhalawar district, although he was not a member of the party. It was reported that as many as 100 Janta party candidates were contesting under various symbols,[75] although this figure is probably an exaggeration. Nevertheless, whatever the actual number of Janta candidates, the total was significantly large; and it is clear that the 1967 election results are not a true reflection of the political parties' strength in the state.

The Campaign and the Election Results

Even by the state's own standards, the election campaign was intense and violent. Jaipur city was particularly unruly, and not only were the Chief Minister's election rallies disrupted by mob action, but such national leaders as Morarji Desai, Kamaraj Nadar, and Y. B. Chavan experienced the wrath of their Jaipur audiences. Indira Gandhi refused to be shouted down by agitators favoring cow protection and lectured her audience on decorum and political history over the din. Despite the highly charged political atmosphere, polling proceeded peacefully on the election days; and no more than normal disturbances were reported. However, once the results were announced the political tensions rose once again—this time to a new high.

Winning 89 of the 184 assembly seats was a remarkable achievement by the Congress. It clearly demonstrated its capacity to withstand the serious challenge to its authority and indicated the deep roots it had put down in the state's arid soil. Its success adds credence to the Chief Minister's statement at the time of the mass resignations in December that: "Congress is a vast organization and its doors are open to every sincere worker. If anybody goes out, the party will not suffer. It is the person who suffers. The organization is supreme, whereas the entity of an individual is a secondary thing."[76] However, while the Congress party's showing was most

[75] *Hindustan Times*, January 15, 1967, p. 8.

[76] *Ibid.*, December 26, 1966, p. 1.

TABLE 7.12

RESULTS OF THE FOURTH GENERAL ELECTIONS

Party	Contested	Won	Percentage of poll
Congress	182	89	41.44
Swatantra	108	49	22.45
Jan Sangh	63	22	11.61
SSP	38	8	4.76
Communist (M)	21	—	1.15
Communist (R)	20	1	0.95
PSP	17	—	0.81
Republican	6	—	0.16
Independents	437	15	16.66
Total	892	184	100

Rejected votes 343,895 (4.85 per cent of total)
Total votes polled 7,093,438.

creditable, it must be remembered that the opposition parties had achieved their major objective—Congress did not have a majority. It was also expected that finding additional support for a Congress government would be more difficult than in the past, since nearly all the non-Congress MLAs were members of opposition political parties.

It is more difficult to assess the relative fortunes of the opposition parties because of the confusion created by the Janta party. Based on the election results, the Swatantra party had increased its representation by thirteen and the Jan Sangh by seven for a total of twenty additional seats. But Kumbharam Arya maintained that thirty-one members of the Janta party had won election and that thirteen were independents, twelve Swatantra, four Jan Sangh, and two had run under the Samyukta Socialist party's label.[77] This would mean that the true increase in seats for the Swatantra party and the Jan Sangh respectively was only one and three and that all but two of the independents belonged to the Janta party.[78]

Even though it is impossible to determine accurately the Janta party's success without fuller information and complete election returns, it is possible to check the electoral fortunes of the MLAs who resigned from the Congress and who are known to have contested the election. Of the seventeen MLAs who resigned, ten are known to have contested the election. Of these ten, four won. Resigning ministers tended to do

[77] *Ibid.*, February 26, 1967, p. 1.

[78] If these estimates are only partially correct, they still give added meaning to the Maharani's post-election statement that Swatantra's showing was disappointing. *Ibid.*, February 24, 1967, p. 4.

better than the known resigning MLAs. All former ministers except Kumbharam Arya contested the election, and of these four, two won (Harish Chandra and Daulat Ram Saran). These figures suggest that the Janta party was only moderately successful in winning electoral contests. Another way of testing the effectiveness of the Janta party is to determine how successful it was in defeating the Congress party candidates. Of the nine known constituencies where resigning Congress MLAs contested the election, only one was won by the Congress party, four were won by Janta party members, two by the Swatantra, and two by independents. These figures suggest that the Janta party was more successful in defeating the Congress than winning elections and that if the Janta split had not occurred the Congress might have done much better in the general elections.

The Janta party's capacity to defeat the Congress was dramatically demonstrated in Nagaur district where it seems likely that a trial of strength occurred between Nathu Ram Mirdha and Kumbharam Arya. Winning eight and six seats out of eight in the 1957 and 1962 general elections respectively, Congress had long had a stronghold in Nagaur district. Results are known for eight of the district's nine constituencies in the fourth general elections. Of these eight, Congress won three; candidates running under the Swatantra symbol won four; and one seat was won by an independent. More importantly, both Nathu Ram Mirdha and his cousin Ram Niwas Mirdha, the speaker of the assembly, were defeated in straight contests. In addition a Swatantra candidate won the Nagaur parliamentary seat. Of the three successful Congress candidates, at least two were non-Jats. These results suggest that Kumbharam Arya most effectively demonstrated his influence in the heart of the Jodhpur Jat group's strength, and perhaps these results illustrate what he meant when he said that he would oppose all official Congress candidates regardless of their past relationships with him.[79] The Janta party thus demonstrated its capacity to win electoral contests as well as its capacity to defeat the Congress party's candidates.

President's Rule

Intense controversy broke out in Rajasthan over the formation of the state's government immediately following the election. Congress' failure to achieve a majority, the greater hope by the opposition parties that they

[79] It should be noted that Kumbharam Arya did not specifically claim he was responsible for the defeat of the Mirdhas, and the argument presented above is based on the "logic of the situation." Arya was reported to have observed only that "some Congressman" sabotaged the Mirdhas in Nagaur. *Ibid.*, February 26, 1967, p. 1.

could control their MLAs, and the parties' common conviction that their primary goal was ensuring that Congress should not become the ruling party were the key elements in the post-election crisis.

In pursuit of their basic goal the opposition parties acted as a united group. The Swatantra state leader Laxshman Singh was elected leader of the United Opposition at a special meeting of all opposition MLAs on February 25, 1967. The Janta party and the SSP announced that they would give full backing to a non-Congress government but would not participate in the cabinet. The United Opposition claimed the support of ninety-four MLAs and noted that only one independent MLA was not with them.[80] Laxshman Singh petitioned Governor Sampurnanand (a former Chief Minister of Uttar Pradesh) to invite the United Opposition to form a government. He maintained that the people of the state had spoken clearly on the point that they did not want another Congress government. In a public statement by the four leaders of the opposition parties (Swatantra, Jan Sangh, Janta party, and the SSP), it was announced that it would be difficult to maintain law and order if the Congress was allowed to take recourse to "corrupt and immoral practices" in its efforts to find a parliamentary majority.[81]

At a meeting of the Congress Legislative party held at the Chief Minister's residence, Mohan Lal Sukhadia was re-elected as leader. Following his re-election, he introduced four MLAs (three independents and one Swatantra party member) to the meeting and they were admitted into the Congress party on the spot. The Chief Minister maintained that the Congress now possessed a majority and the "capitalists'" plan to make Rajasthan an "experimental laboratory" of Swatantra rule had been frustrated.[82] However, in New Delhi, the party's high command disallowed the enrollment of two of the four MLAs because they had been expelled from the party only one month earlier. At the same time the high command sanctioned Sukhadia's efforts to form a government.[83]

The issue of a majority was thus drawn to a fine point and focused on the support of the two recently expelled Congressmen. In separate visits to the Governor, each of the two MLAs was escorted by high Congress officials to profess to the Governor their support of the Congress government. But the opposition had one additional gambit to play. Immediately following the two MLAs' visit to the Governor, Swatantra's deputy leader, Raja Man Singh of Bharatpur, made public a letter of resignation from the Congress of the Maharajkumar Brijendra Pal of Karauli (a neighboring princely state to Bharatpur in pre-independence Rajputana),

80 *Ibid.*, February 24, 1967, p. 4.
81 *Ibid.*, February 26, 1967, p. 1.
82 *Loc.cit.*
83 *Ibid.*, February 28, 1967, p. 1.

which he maintained he had held secret for two days.[84] Brijendra Pal's resignation reduced the Congress support to ninety-one and denied them a majority. Sukhadia claimed that he had additional support for his government among the opposition MLAs but that they were under "surveillance and hence it [was] difficult to contact them personally."[85] The suspense was broken on March 4 when the Governor requested Mohan Lal Sukhadia to form a government. The Governor based his invitation on the fact that the Congress was the largest *single* party.

He argued that the independent MLAs should not be counted for they did not stand for any single program. Thus Congress was the largest single party and, in fact, represented a majority of the MLAs who were identified with political parties.[86]

The Governor's invitation triggered riots in Jaipur city in which at least seven persons were killed in police firings, and the threat of a general breakdown of law and order throughout the state seemed imminent. Sukhadia informed the Governor that under the circumstances he did not wish to form a government, and after a week of uncertainty, during which a twenty-four hour curfew was maintained in Jaipur city, President's Rule was declared as the first act of the new Indira Gandhi government. In order to avoid fresh elections and to ensure that the Rajasthan MLAs could participate in the forthcoming presidential election, the assembly was suspended, not dissolved.[87]

Rajasthan remained under President's Rule until April 28 when Mohan Lal Sukhadia was sworn in as the state's Chief Minister with a verified majority of ninety-four MLAs. During President's Rule, Governor Sampurnanand's term of office expired; and the former speaker of the Lok Sabha, Hukam Singh, was appointed. He carefully scrutinized the lists of supporters submitted to him by both the Congress and the opposition;[88] and, in the twenty-one cases where an MLA's name appeared on both lists, he personally interviewed the MLA concerned and had him write out and sign a statement declaring his support for either the Congress or

84 *Ibid.*, March 3, 1967, p. 1.

85 *The Hindu*, March 3, 1967, p. 7.

86 Governor Sampurnanand alluded to a similar situation in Madras state in 1952. At that time C. R. Rajagopalachari was requested to form a Congress government despite the fact that T. Prakasam, leader of the opposition parties, had a United Opposition majority. Perhaps the Governor hoped to lessen Swatantra's reaction to his invitation to the Congress to form a government by indicating that the current leader of the Swatantra party in India had himself headed a minority government. *The Hindu*, March 5, 1967, p. 1.

87 *Hindustan Standard* (Air Mail Edition), March 18, 1967, p. 5.

88 It should be noted that all the conflicts were over the opposition's list of supporters. The Congress knew precisely who its supporters were.

the opposition. Through this technique the new governor was able to determine accurately the precise support of each group and to avoid any charges of partisanship. Thus Rajasthan's government was formed and the crisis was ended, at least temporarily. The re-enactment of the drama of the survival of the Rajasthan Congress party as the ruling party was completed. Had anything changed?

Some Tentative Thoughts on the Significance of the Fourth General Elections for the Development of Rajasthan's Political System.

Certain broad continuities stand out from the welter of political complexities and the intricate web of personal, factional, and opportunistic conflicts which criss-crossed the election itself. One continuity was the continued inability of the major ruling houses to establish a firm basis for cooperation. Once again the Maharaja of Bikaner contested as an independent. He refused to associate himself with any modern political institution. The Jodhpur house did support some candidates running under Swatantra's symbol in their region of influence, but they were less successful and the candidates' connection with the Swatantra party was tenuous in most cases. Finally, the Maharaja of Udaipur continued his apolitical style, although he was somewhat more vocal in his support of the Congress party. For the first time the head of the Jat ruling house of Bharatpur entered the electoral contest and defeated Rajasthan's major national figure, Raj Bahadur, in a straight contest for the Bharatpur Lok Sabha seat. But unlike his brother, Raja Man Singh, he refused to associate himself openly with the Swatantra party. Harish Chandra continued the tradition of disunity within the Rajput aristocracy by joining the Janta party instead of the Swatantra party when he left the Congress, despite the fact that he was believed to be sympathetic with the Maharani's party.

The Rajput aristocracy gave no further evidence of increasing its capacity of developing an integrative mass political leader. The Maharani of Jaipur did not improve her popularity and stature as a state-wide leader significantly between 1962 and 1967 and may have lost some of her mass appeal. If Swatantra's electoral gain was as small as is suggested by some of the evidence, it is difficult to see that it made any substantial gains over the previous general elections. Although still a potent force in Rajasthan's politics, the Rajput aristocracy seemed still beset by the same set of basic problems it faced in 1962.

One widely publicized and significant event was the entrance of a member of the Birla family into politics. R. K. Birla ran for the Jhunjhunu Lok Sabha seat in his family's home district. Although running under Swatantra's "star," he stood as an independent and won the parliamentary seat handily. The entrance of a member of one of India's major industrial families into politics cannot be taken lightly, but its long-term significance is not clear.

There were other continuities in the political pattern of the state—the steady if unspectacular growth of the Jan Sangh, and the continued division of the leftist opposition parties. The success of the urban-based Sukhadia group within the Congress is another outstanding continuity. However, the greater problems this leadership faced and the loss by Congress of an important segment of its rural-based political elite were significant changes in the state's political system. The emergence of the Janta party raised serious problems for the continuation of the "Congress system" in the state. It highlighted basic long-term cleavages in Rajasthan that may ultimately prove to be the most significant factor in the state's political development.

The threatened breakdown of the Congress system in the pre-election situation was the major immediate change to emerge from the general elections. The breakdown was not so much in terms of greater factional conflict as of the different forms that the conflict took. The formation of the Janta party and its commitment to the goal of destroying the Congress party were major changes in the pattern of factional conflict in the state. As pointed out in the body of the study of Rajasthan's political system, one of the basic advantages of containing factional conflict within the Congress party was that it moderated political conflict and made violence and instability less likely. The eruption of riots and violence in the state following the general elections suggests the potential conflicts which had been avoided in the past by the Congress system. The creation of an institutionalized dissident Congress movement may make the re-absorption of dissident elements more difficult than when Congress dissidents rebelled individually. Also, the institutionalized Congress rebellion added strength to the "anti-Congress ideology" of the opposition parties. Greater significance must be placed on the formation of the Janta party than on the somewhat similar effort of Jai Naryan Vyas in 1962. In the first place the latter was a less institutionalized effort and little progress was made in establishing an effective organization. Perhaps more important was the relative strength of the two movements and their sources of support. The Janta party could claim greater mass support than Vyas's "Jana Congress." The latter was for the most part composed of older generation nationalists of urban origins and did not have direct contact with the countryside. The Janta party, on the other hand, had direct contact with the countryside and could threaten the Congress party more seriously and directly both in the general elections and in the panchayat elections of future years. The Janta party had demonstrated greater unity and discipline than the Jana Congress movement of 1962. The ability of the two major factional leaders to lead a significant portion of their followers out of the Congress party and into the political wilderness, despite the fact that some left high government positions and many gave up the official Congress ticket, was an impressive demonstration of loyalty and unity by the core groups of the Janta party.

It is too early to attempt an assessment of the programmatic significance of the Janta party. It may be but a short-term variant of the more established forms of factional conflicts linked to the unique political conditions in India as a whole at the time of the general elections.[89] If unique national events were the basic cause of the Janta party, then we can expect that the party will disappear when an established, stable leadership is formed at the national level. On the other hand, the Janta party may be the fulcrum of, or an important element in, an emergent rural populistic movement, which will take some time to develop fully. This possibility is suggested by the partial Jat-Rajput alliance the Janta party represented. To grow and develop beyond its current base, which is grounded primarily in expediency, this agrarian alliance would have to be nurtured in concrete political experience over some period of time in which mutual interests of greater specificity, above the current general rural sentiment, could be recognized. The prospects of such a development received a severe blow in mid-March when Harish Chandra died suddenly of a heart attack. His death removes the central figure of the Rajput group from the Janta party, and it will be much more difficult to maintain the party's coherence in the future. At this time all that an analyst can do is make a few comments on the character and composition of the Janta party and examine their implications for the future.

Some evidence exists which suggests that the Janta party represented not only a geographical division between the two major Jat groups but also a generational split. This is even suggested by the geographic split itself. Nathu Ram Mirdha is of the same generation as Mohan Lal Sukhadia and most of his major supporters, while Kumbharam Arya represents the generation of the pre-independence nationalists. Election returns from approximately two-thirds of the constituencies seem to indicate that a similar split occurred throughout the state. Where Jats contested on the

89 See Stanley A. Kochanek, *op.cit.*, pp. 292-304, for an analysis of these national developments.

Congress ticket, they tended to be from the younger generation of political leaders. Jats who rebelled against the Congress party tended to be from older pre-independence generations. This evidence suggests that the split in the Jat community was associated with styles of leadership.[90] The more educated, modernist Jats remained with the Congress party, and the less educated, more traditionalist leadership, who tended to continue to place greater emphasis on community solidarity and "populistic ruralism," tended to leave the Congress party. If this is true, it suggests that the "focus of power"[91] represented by the Jat community's solidarity in the past had been weakened by political, social, and economic developments since independence. In long-term trend analysis this would mean that the pragmatic and manipulative style of leadership represented by Sukhadia and his followers (and increasingly by the younger Jat political leadership) would be more functional to the growing differentiation of the social structure in the years ahead. If this style of leadership proves successful, then the chances of a populist rural movement emerging in the future would be less likely.

Whatever the long-term significance of the Janta party, its current existence raises short-term questions of significance. The addition of the Janta party to the other parties in adamant opposition to the Congress party lessened the ability of the Congress system to function effectively in forming a majority based government. Four votes is not an insurmountable problem for the Congress party in normal conditions. But in 1967 conditions were not normal. Obviously the bargaining process on which the Congress system depends was seriously disrupted in the post-election crisis. The efforts to isolate the opposition MLAs from the bargaining process through party loyalty *or* other means made it more difficult to find a majority base for the government. In this more restricted atmosphere, personal and factional considerations played a greater role. The events of the post-election crisis suggest that the Congress system not only *supports* basic democratic values but *is dependent* on them. When the conditions necessary for the Congress system to function effectively were re-established by President's Rule and the procedure of ascertaining whom the MLAs supported was devised by the new governor, the Congress system worked effectively and resolved the conflict. So, although the Congress system survived, the post-election crisis pointed to possible instability and political deadlock in the future. Thus the potentialities for instability were much greater after the fourth general elections than

[90] For a discussion of styles of leadership in Rajasthan, see pp. 336-337.

[91] See p. 326 for a discussion of this concept.

they had been at the end of the third general elections. In the new political situation there was greater danger that personal loyalties, opportunism, or factional conflict could bring down the Congress government. This situation could place greater emphasis on party loyalty and internal unity within the Congress in the years to come.

The events of the fourth general elections may have established the basis for developing greater coherence within the Congress party. The cleansing of the most disruptive element in the Congress (and, some would argue, the most disreputable) and the growing compatibility of styles of leadership throughout the state could aid the establishment of a stronger political party. If this should occur, it would bring to the fore more clearly the issue of effectiveness of government. In the future the Congress would have to depend more and more on its performance to hold the support of the citizenry rather than the composite of group loyalties on which it has depended to a greater extent in the past. Whether the Congress would succeed in this new venture would depend on many factors, both at the national and state levels; but the results of the fourth general elections at least prepared the ground for this development.

TABLE 7.13

PARTY STRENGTH BY REGIONS—SOUTHERN HIGHLANDS

District	*Parties—1952 Election*							*Parties—1957 Election*					*Parties—1962 Election*				
	Cong.	*RRP*	*JS*	*Soc.*	*Ind.*	*HM*	*KLP*	*Cong.*	*RRP*	*JS*	*Soc.*	*Ind.*	*Cong.*	*Swt.*	*JS*	*Soc.*	*Ind.*
Bhilwara	3	0	1	0	3	1	0	6	2	0	0	0	7	0	0	0	1
Udaipur	7	0	4	0	1	0	1	12	0	0	0	1	5	5	3	0	0
Dungapur	3	0	0	0	0	0	0	2	0	0	0	1	1	2	0	0	0
Banswara	2	0	0	1	0	0	0	2	0	0	0	2	2	0	0	2	0
Chittorgarh	4	0	2	0	0	0	0	7	0	0	0	0	5	1	1	0	0
Totals	19	0	7	1	4	1	1	29	2	0	0	4	20	8	4	2	1
% of seats won by region	58.0		21.0	3.0	12.0	3.0	3.0	83.0	6.0			11.0	57.0	23.0	11.0	6.0	3.0

TABLE 7.14

PARTY STRENGTH BY REGIONS—SOUTHERN PLATEAU

District	*Parties—1952 Election*							*Parties—1957 Election*					*Parties—1962 Election*				
	Cong.	*RRP*	*JS*	*Soc.*	*Ind.*	*HM*	*KLP*	*Cong.*	*RRP*	*JS*	*Soc.*	*Ind.*	*Cong.*	*Swt.*	*JS*	*Soc.*	*Ind.*
Jhalawar	3	1	0	0	0	0	0	5	0	0	0	0	3	0	1	0	1
Kotah	4	4	0	0	0	0	0	5	0	2	0	0	3	0	4	0	0
Bundi	0	2	0	0	0	0	1	3	0	0	0	0	2	0	1	0	0
Totals	7	7	0	0	0	1	1	13	0	2	0	0	8	0	6	0	1
% of seats won by region	44.0	44.0				6.0	6.0	87.0		13.0			53.0		40.0		7.0

TABLE 7.15

Party Strength by Regions—Dry Region

District	Parties—1952 Election					Parties—1957 Election					Parties—1962 Election						
	Cong.	*RRP*	*JS*	*Soc.*	*Ind.*	*Cong.*	*RRP*	*JS*	*PSP*	*Ind.*	*Cong.*	*RRP*	*Swt.*	*JS*	*PSP*	*Ind.*	*CPI*
Churu	3	0	0	0	2	3	0	0	0	3	4	0	0	0	0	2	0
Gangenager	6	0	0	0	0	5	0	0	0	2	1	0	0	0	0	4	2
Bikener	0	0	0	0	3	1	0	0	1	2	1	0	0	0	2	1	0
Jaisalmer	0	0	0	0	1	0	0	0	0	1	1	0	0	0	0	0	0
Sirohi	0	0	0	0	3	1	0	0	0	2	3	0	0	0	0	0	0
Pali	0	0	0	0	7	4	0	0	0	3	5	0	1	0	0	1	0
Jalore	0	1	0	0	4	1	4	0	0	0	4	1	0	0	0	0	0
Jodhpur	0	0	0	0	7	5	2	0	0	0	4	1	0	0	0	2	0
Barmer	0	2	0	0	2	3	2	0	0	0	2	1	0	0	0	2	0
Nagaur	4	4	0	0	0	8	0	0	0	0	6	0	1	0	0	1	0
Totals	13	7	0	0	29	31	8	0	1	13	31	3	2	0	2	13	2
% of seats won by region	27.0	14.0	0	0	59.0	58.0	15.0	0	2.0	25.0	58.0	6.0	3.7	0	3.7	23.0	3.0

TABLE 7.16

PARTY STRENGTH BY REGIONS—EASTERN PLAINS

District	*Parties—1952 Election*						*Parties—1957 Election*						*Parties—1962 Election*						
	Cong.	*RRP*	*JS*	*Soc.*	*Ind.*	*KLP*	*Cong.*	*RRP*	*JS*	*Soc.*	*Ind.*	*CPI*	*Cong.*	*RRP*	*Swt.*	*JS*	*Soc.*	*Ind.*	*CPI*
Ajmer							7	0	0	0	2	0	6	0	2	0	0	0	1
Jaipur	12	4	0	0	1	0	7	4	2	0	4	0	2	0	13	2	0	0	0
Tonk	3	1	0	0	0	0	3	0	0	0	1	0	0	0	4	0	0	0	0
Swai Madhopur	6	1	0	0	1	0	5	0	0	0	3	0	3	0	2	3	0	0	0
Bharatpur	6	0	0	0	0	4	6	0	0	0	4	0	2	0	2	0	3	3	0
Alwar	9	0	0	0	0	0	8	1	0	0	1	0	6	0	0	0	0	2	2
Sikar	4	1	1	0	0	2	5	1	2	0	0	0	7	0	0	0	0	1	0
Jhunjhunu	3	3	0	0	0	0	5	0	0	0	1	1	3	0	3	0	0	0	1
Totals	43	10	1	0	2	6	46	6	4	0	16	1	29	0	26	5	3	6	4
% of seats won by region	69.0	16.0	2.0	0	3.0	10.0	63.0	8.0	6.0	0	22.0	1.0	40.0	0	36.0	7.0	4.0	8.0	5.0

REFERENCES

Chaudhuri, P. K. "Panchayati Raj in Action," *Economic Weekly* (February 1964), pp. 211–18.

Chauhan, Brij Raj. "Changing Phases of Power-Structure and Leadership in a Few Villages in Rajasthan," in Central Institute of Community Development, *Trends of Change in Village India*. Mussoori, India: Central Institute of Community Development, November 9, 1961.

Erdman, Howard L. "Conservative Politics in India," *Asian Survey*, VI (June 1966), 338–47.

Government of India. *Report of the Rajasthan-Madhya Bharat Jagir Enquiry Committee*. New Delhi: Government of India Press, 1950. 84 pp.

Huntington, Samuel P. "Political Development and Political Decay," *World Politics*, XVII (April 1965), 386–430.

Kothari, Rajni. "The Congress System," *Asian Survey*, IV (December 1964), 1,161–73.

Maheshwari, B. "Two Years of Panchayati Raj in Rajasthan," *Economic Weekly* (May 26, 1962), pp. 845, 847–48.

Millman, Harry A. *The Marwari, a Study of a Group of the Trading Castes of India*. Unpublished M.A. thesis. Berkeley: University of California, 1955. 107 pp.

Narain, Iqbal. "Democratic Decentralization and Rural Leadership in India: The Rajasthan Experiment," *Asian Survey*, IV:8 (August 1964), 1,013–22.

Puri, Kishen. *Memoirs of the Marwari Police*. 2nd ed. Jodhpur. Jodhpur Government Press, 1938. 273 pp.

Qanungo, Kalika Ranjan. *Studies in Rajput History*. Delhi: S. Chand and Co., 1960. 111 pp.

Rajasthan, Directorate of Economics and Statistics. *Second Five-Year Plan: Progress Report, Rajasthan, 1956–61*. Jaipur: Government Press, 1962. 177 pp.

Rameshwar, S. M. *Resurgent Rajasthan*. New Delhi: Apex Publications, 1962. 268 pp.

Retzlaff, R. H. "Panchayati Raj in Rajasthan: A Case Study," *Indian Journal of Public Administration*, VI:2 (April–June 1940), pp. 141–58.

Sisson, Richard. *Caste, Faction and Politics: A Case Study in the Rajasthan Congress*. Working paper prepared for the South Asia Colloquium, Center for South Asia Studies, Institute of International Studies, University of California, Berkeley. (May 1965.)

Talbot, Phillips. "E Pluribus Unum or Out of Rajputana, Rajasthan," Report #3, American Universities Field Staff, pp. 1-13.

Tinker-Walker, Irene. "Rajasthan," in S. V. Kogekar and Richard L. Park (eds.), *Reports on the Indian General Elections, 1951–52*. Bombay: Popular Book Depot, 1956.

ANDHRA PRADESH

ANDHRA PRADESH

VIII

Andhra Pradesh

HUGH GRAY

THE PRESENT STATE of Andhra Pradesh was formed in November 1956, by merging the nine Telengana districts of Hyderabad state with eleven that were once part of British India. It has an area of 106,041 square miles and a population (1961) of 35,983,000.[1] Its literacy rate in 1961 was 20.8 per cent.[2]

Andhra, until 1953, was a Telugu-speaking area in multilingual Madras state. In that year the Telugu-speaking districts of Madras were separated by the central Indian government to form a new state, after Potti Sriramalu, a Gandhian advocate of linguistic autonomy, had fasted to death.

The struggle for a Telugu-speaking state was strongly supported by the Communist party, and this fostered the party's subsequent success, combined, as Selig Harrison writes, with "exploiting the rivalry between two rising peasant proprietor caste groups."[3] These were the Kammas and the Reddis, who "before the separation of Andhra from multilingual Madras State were lost in a welter of castes. In Andhra they face each other as Titans."[4] Harrison goes on to say that the "demand for Andhra derived from regional caste factors. Initially the leadership in the Andhra movement came from the Telugu Brahman, who took a reluctant second place to the dominant Tamil Brahman in the cultural and political life of the multilingual Madras State. But by late 1930s the leadership of the Andhra movement and of all Andhra political life had broadened, as more and more of the sons of non-Brahman peasant proprietors broke through the Brahman monopoly on education . . . the Kammas and Reddis became vigorous advocates of an Andhra State in which their place in the power structure was sure to enlarge."[5] Kammas

[1] *Hand Book of Statistics,* Andhra Pradesh, issued by Bureau of Economics and Statistics. Out of the total population of 31,260,000 (1951), the Scheduled Caste population was 4,407,000 and the Scheduled Tribes population 767,000. The density of population in 1951 was 295 per square mile.

[2] *Ibid.*

[3] Selig Harrison, *India: The Most Dangerous Decades* (Princeton: Princeton University Press, 1960), p. 205.

[4] *Ibid.,* p. 106.

[5] *Ibid.,* pp. 110, 111.

and Reddis were once united inside the anti-Brahman Justice party in their successful aim to reduce Brahman power, but "since the founding of the Andhra Communist Party in 1934, the party leadership has been the property of a single subcaste, the Kamma landlords."[6] Meanwhile, Reddi leaders were similarly prominent in the Congress party, and the stage was set for the caste and party battles in Andhra in the general elections of 1954 and 1955.

The history of Hyderabad, a princely state, was very different. Its first Muslim ruler, Asaf Jah, who died in 1748, was a feudal chief who declared himself an independent ruler and founded the state of Hyderabad. Asaf Jah brought with him from Malwa a number of Mohammedans and Hindus, who were attached to his person and fortunes. The Mohammedan nobles were granted jagirs or estates on military tenure and were employed principally in administrative work in the departments of revenue and finance. They were also granted jagirs as a remuneration for their services, and all jagirs, whether granted for civil or military purposes, came to be considered hereditary. There was also a large number of Rajas who were all recognized by the Nizam on payment of tribute and who were allowed to exercise a kind of semi-independent jurisdiction within the limits of their estates.[7]

The total area of Hyderabad state (82,695 square miles) was divided into three distinct portions:

(1) The jagirs, almost one-third of the state.
(2) Sarf-e-Khas lands, 8,109 square miles of territory, reserved for the Nizam's privy purse, which were scattered over the state.
(3) Diwani, or government lands, the revenue of which was devoted to the expenses of the administration.

Although Hyderabad was autonomous, with its own coinage but no foreign relations, British paramountcy was exercised through the British Resident, and the Nizam's attempt to act as an independent ruler was firmly quashed. In 1926 the Viceroy intervened and in a curt letter to the Nizam said: "I will merely add that the title 'faithful ally' which your Exalted Highness enjoys has not the effect of putting your government in a category separate from that of other states under the paramountcy of the British Crown."[8] Following the Viceroy's intervention, the Nizam was always in a weaker position than the rulers of such princely states

[6] *Ibid.*, p. 207.

[7] J. D. B. Gribble, *History of the Deccan* (London: Luzac and Co. [1925?]).

[8] Lord Reading to the Nizam, March 27, 1926. Parliamentary Papers, Hyderabad (1926), CMD 2621, pp. 461-62, quoted in C. H. Philips, *The Evolution of India and Pakistan, 1858 to 1947* (London, New York: Oxford University Press, 1962).

as Mysore and Cochin, and the British government must share responsibility for the slow advance in setting up democratic government.

In 1937 it was announced that the Nizam intended to introduce a representative form of government for Hyderabad by setting up a Legislative Council. A reforms committee was appointed to recommend how "a more effective association of the different interests of the state with the Government" should be brought about. This actually provided an excuse for postponing reforms, and it was not until 1946 that a Legislative Council of 122 members was set up, of whom 38 Muslims and 76 non-Muslims were elected and the rest nominated. The state Congress party by boycotting the elections made an ineffective body completely unrepresentative.

In 1947 power was transferred by the British government to India and Pakistan. The Nizam of Hyderabad asserted that he was entitled to resume the status of his ancestors as an independent sovereign, and refused to accede to India or Pakistan. After protracted negotiations, fully described elsewhere,[9] on September 13, 1948 the Southern Command of the Indian army, commanded by Major General J. N. Chaudhuri, marched into Hyderabad. On September 17 the Hyderabad army surrendered, after 800 casualties among irregulars and a few Indian deaths. After the police action of 1949 the Nizam was allowed to continue as the constitutional head of the government ("Rajpramukh") but exercised no power and little influence. After the formation of Andhra Pradesh in 1956, he refused the offer of the Indian government to become its first governor and retired to private life, dying in 1967.

On August 15, 1949 the Jagir Abolition Regulations were published and the administration of all jagirs was taken over by a government representative; their integration with the state government district administration was completed by March 1950. Some compensation was paid to jagirdars.

The military government of Major General J. N. Chaudhuri continued until 1949 when a civilian government headed by a senior Indian Administrative Service official, M. K. Vellodi, was installed. In 1950 four representatives of the Hyderabad State Congress were taken into the administration as ministers. In 1952 the first and only general election on the basis of universal adult suffrage was held in Hyderabad state, and following a Congress party victory, a Congress ministry was formed. In the cabinet were 5 Brahmans, 2 Reddis, and 1 Muslim. They were

[9] V. F. Menon, *The Story of the Integration of the Indian States* (London: Longmans, Green, 1956); K. M. Munshi, *The End of an Era* (Bombay: Bharatiya Vidya Bhavan, 1957).

all urban professional men, and of the eight ministers of state two were Brahmans.

In November 1956, Hyderabad was absorbed into the new state of Andhra Pradesh.

CASTE, RELIGION, AND PARTIES IN HYDERABAD

The population of Hyderabad was 16 million and of these only about 10 per cent were Muslims,[10] but from this small Muslim minority were drawn 75 per cent of state officials and 95 per cent of the police and military services. The major political struggles in the state were between the Majlis Ittihad-ul-Muslimin, a Muslim organization, the Hyderabad State Congress and the Communist party of India.

The Majlis

The Majlis Ittihad-ul-Muslimin (Council of the Union of Muslims) was founded in 1926 as a cultural-religious organization with the object of uniting Muslims in the state of Hyderabad in support of the Nizam, and reducing the Hindu majority in the state by large-scale conversions. It was an urban-based political movement since the vast majority of Muslims were living in Hyderabad city or in the district towns. Its relationship to the Nizam was always ambiguous, as many of its members maintained that sovereignty was vested in the members of the Muslim community and not in the person of the Nizam. During the war years it became increasingly political and its leadership passed into the hands of Kasim Razvi, a rural lawyer and middle-class intellectual who was always despised as an upstart by members of the Muslim nobility.

Kasim Razvi organized a voluntary group of fighters named "Razakars," who provided protection to landowners and the government administration during a Communist-led uprising. Only they and the Communists offered any resistance to the Indian army at the time of the police action in 1948. Before the police action, it was continually alleged by the Indian government that the Razakars were a threat to the authority of the state and the Nizam was urged to disband them. Whether Razvi was the Nizam's tool and under his control or whether the Razakars were controlling the Nizam is still argued about by Muslims and Hindus in Hyderabad. It is possible that Razvi was leading an upsurge of the urban Muslim class against feudal authority and that this was transformed by events into a movement against integration into the Indian

[10] After the formation of Andhra Pradesh the percentage of Muslims in the new states was 7 per cent; see Theodore P. Wright, Jr., "Revival of the Majlis Ittihad-ul-Muslimin," *The Muslim World*, Vol. LIII, No. 3, July 1963.

Union. The movement also took a communal turn as the Razakars clashed with the Arya Samajists, a Hindu organization. Certainly the Ittihad had a majority in the Ministry of Laik Ali immediately before the police action and was interfering with the day-to-day affairs of the administration.

After the police action in 1948, the Razakars were disbanded. Kasim Razvi was arrested with other leaders; many fled to Pakistan. Razvi was released in 1957 and also went to Pakistan. Before he left, he summoned some members of the executive committee of the Majlis and nominated Abdul Wahid Ouaisi as leader of the movement—a position he still holds.

The Ittihad was not reformed until 1960 and then ostensibly as a non-communal movement standing for the protection not only of an "oppressed Muslim minority" but of all other minorities. It won 18 seats in majority Muslim areas at the Hyderabad municipal elections in 1957, and it was expected to win several Legislative Assembly seats at the general elections of 1962. However, it failed, winning only one, to the relief of the moderates. In 1967 it improved its position by winning another two seats.

The Rise of the Reddis

Under the Nizam of Hyderabad, the castes favored for employment in the administration were local Brahmans, the Khatris, and the Khaists, Urdu-speaking townsmen who claim to have come originally from the north of India with the Muslim conquerors. There were Reddi holders of jagirs (usually of Mutati sub-caste), but Reddis were not prominent in administration or in politics.

One exception, however, was Raja Bahadur Venkat Rama Reddy, who rose from Sergeant of Police to Commissioner of Police in Hyderabad. He was much favored by the Nizam of Hyderabad and became a wealthy man. In 1918 he established the Reddy Hostel, a boarding house for Reddis studying in Hyderabad, financed by subscriptions collected from Reddi landlords. In the 1930s scholarships for poor but scholastically promising Reddis were also provided. As they became academically qualified, the Reddis joined government services and the professions. As a result of attending the University and living in Hyderabad, students became politically conscious and joined the Congress or Communist parties.

Reddis of different sub-castes lived in the hostel together, and this may have been one of the reasons why in the 1940s the Reddi sub-castes began to intermarry. In villages such marriages are rare, but they have become

TABLE 8.1

ELECTIONS TO ANDHRA LEGISLATIVE ASSEMBLY, 1967

Total No. of seats: 287 | Electorate: 21,071,776 | Votes polled: 14,346,366; invalid votes: 625,495

Party	*No. of seats contested* 1	*No. of valid votes polled* 2	*%* 3	*No. of seats won* 4	*% of seats won* 5
Congress	285 (2 unc.)	6,148,941	46.27	165	57.5
	(299)	(5,523,359)	(47.25)	(176)	(58.9)
CPI (R)	103	1,047,307	7.63	10	3.5
CPI (M)	83	1,086,424	7.91	9	3.1
	(136)	(2,282,767)	(19.53)	(51)	(17.0)
Swatantra	90	1,478,917	10.77	29	10.1
	(140)	(1,215,987)	(10.40)	(19)	(6.4)
Jan Sangh	80	308,457	2.24	3	1.0
	(70)	(121,721)	(1.04)	(–)	(–)
Republican	12	47,916	0.34	2	0.7
	(18)	(46,338)	(0.40)	(–)	(–)
SSP	8	49,669	0.36	1	0.4
	(15)	(70,878)	(0.61)	(2)	(0.7)
PSP	2	26,317	0.19	–	(–)
	(6)	(34,732)	(0.30)	(–)	(–)
Independents	226	3,526,923	25.63	68	23.7
Majlis (counted	6	77,513		3	
among Indep)	(8)	(43,527)		(1)	
Indep. 1962	(193)	(2,393,415)	(20.47)	(51)	(17.0)

PARENTHESES: 1962 results

SOURCE: 1: Link, 5.3.1967, 1962: H. Gray, Thesis p. 136. 2,3: table supplied by India House, London. 4: Link, 5.3.67, 1962: H. Gray, Thesis p. 136. Majlis: R. A. Khan, "Some Aspects of Factional Politics and Electioneering in Hyderabad," paper presented at the 4th South Asia Conference at Triberg, June 1967.

common among those living in the city and among the families of rural landlords who have houses in Hyderabad.

In Telengana the Reddi sub-castes[11] are arranged hierarchically: (1) Pakanati, (1a) Mutati, (2) Gudati, and (3) Kapu. There are very few Pakanatis, and some of the Mutatis were of jagirdar class and looked down on the Gudatis as "peasants" even though the economic position of Mutati and Gudati families is often similar. Intermarriages between the educated of these sub-castes do take place. There is much argument as to whether the Kapus (cultivators) are a Reddi sub-caste or not. In any event, the Kapus, although still numerous, are disappearing as a

[11] Dr. R. Anderson says that there are about 10 Reddi sub-castes in Andhra. "Preliminary Report on the Associational Redefinition of Castes in Hyderabad-Secunderabad," Kroeber Anthropological Society Papers, No. 29, Fall 1963.

separate caste, and call themselves Reddi. This demographic influx has strengthened the Reddis politically.

After the police action, the movement of Reddis to the capital, which had started during the Telengana struggle, continued. Many sold part of their land and purchased houses in Hyderabad. Formerly only the sub-caste, wealth, and amount of land owned had been primary considerations in marriage alliances. Now education acquired monetary value, and an educated girl found a husband more easily and at less cost to her father in dowry. In cross sub-caste marriages children take the sub-caste of the father.

The Reddis were always landlords—whether with large, medium, or small holdings—but under the Nizam their power until the 1930s was localized and outside the capital. With the police action and the abolition of jagirs, the powerful Reddis to emerge were the medium landlords. The wealthier ones, particularly the jagirdars, who had been favored by and supported the Nizam, were kept at a distance by Congress during the first years of Congress rule.

The State Congress Party

The first beginnings of Congress can be traced to a district Congress Committee started in Hyberabad city in 1917 or 1918. In 1923 the Kakinada session of the Indian National Congress was held. Hyderabad Congressmen attending it called a meeting of their own and passed a resolution that the administration of Hyderabad should be popularized and a representative assembly established, with the government responsible to public opinion.

At this time there was no open political propaganda against the Nizam, and Congress sympathizers turned to cultural activities, knowing that they would receive no support from the British and should avoid arousing the Nizam's suspicions. The Andhra Jana Sangham was founded for the Telugu-speaking districts of the state. Its activities were outwardly educational and cultural. It established libraries in villages and tried to foster a taste for Telugu literature, in the hope that the reading habit would develop political consciousness later. Three or four years afterwards the Marathi-speaking districts established a similar body, and then a Kanarese-speaking one was formed. These regional movements did have some effect, and R. K. Rao (ex-chief minister and later Governor of Uttar Pradesh) told this writer in July 1962 that British officials were highly suspicious of them, one official having said, "Your libraries are revolutionary centers. You aim to spread disaffection against the Nizam."

Later the Andhra Mahasabha was formed, and Congressmen, Socialists, and Communists were all in it. It split into two movements in the late 1930s, one led by Congress and the other by the Communists. The Andhra Mahasabha, like the library movement, was suspect, and no public meetings were permitted without special permission from the Nizam's government. One such meeting was held in Nalgonda district in 1931, and as a result of the speeches made, no further meetings were permitted for three years.

In 1937 the Hyderabad State Congress was started in defiance of the state government ban. Before launching it, a deputation of Congressmen had seen the chief minister, Sir Akbar Hydari, who had said, "We will allow you to start it but not under the name of Congress." This offer was rejected. The first satyagraha or civil disobedience movement was started, and 700 people were arrested and imprisoned.

At this time the Arya Samaj movement gained in strength and clashed with the Ittihad-ul-Muslimin. Gandhi was alarmed and advised the state Congress to proceed slowly, lest it be identified with communalism. The state Congress went underground and maintained a shadow working committee until 1946, when the ban against it was lifted by the Nizam's government. In the same year a Congress session was held in Hyderabad and a resolution passed asking for representative government. In 1947, with Indian independence, the attitude of the Nizam to the state Congress party stiffened. He encouraged the Ittihad-ul-Muslimin, and the Razakar movement was started.

Since 1945 when the Communists were expelled from Congress, there had been no major splits within the Congress party. Now two factions emerged. One was led by Swami Tirth, the other by R. K. Rao, both Brahmans. Some of those supporting Swami Tirth wished to go outside the state borders in order to carry on a military movement to unseat the Nizam or to obtain representative parliamentary government. R. K. Rao's group wanted to use Gandhian methods and attain its ends by passive resistance. Swami Tirth's group was popularly known as the "Congress of Thieves" (referring to a spectacular bank robbery supposedly carried out by his supporters to obtain funds), and R. K. Rao's group as the "Congress of Capitalists."

Swami Tirth was President of Congress for ten years and his group commanded a majority, but there were two bodies both calling themselves Congress. When the police action took place, an emissary was sent by Nehru to explore the differences between the two wings of Congress, and V. P. Patel, the Union Home Minister, came to settle them. Swami Tirth was asked to step down from the presidency of the Congress; one of his supporters, Mr. Bindu, another Brahman who was acceptable to R. K. Rao's group and to V. P. Patel, was made President, and the two groups of Congressmen reunited. But V. P. Patel considered Swami Tirth and his supporters to be dangerously left wing, and gave his support to R. K. Rao and his friends.

When, in 1949, Mr. Vellodi (a civil servant) replaced the military governor, four ministers were appointed by the government of India and four from the state Congress party. The leader of this group was R. K. Rao, who held the Revenue and Education portfolios. A land reform scheme was prepared and introduced as a pilot effort in Khammam district by R. K. Rao's government. It was anticipated that hundreds of thousands of acres of land would become available for redistribution, as a low ceiling with an income of Rs. 3,600 was fixed. However, after land had been apportioned among different members of the same family and trusted servants, and sales, real and fictitious, had taken place, there were only 19,000 acres for redistribution. This was not very much more than the 12,684 acres which, according to government sources, the Communist party redistributed when it dominated Nalgonda district during the Telengana struggle. Of these, 12,127 had been recovered and restored to their lawful owners. The Congress food reform scheme was widely interpreted as a response to the Communist-led redistribution program for the landless.

When the Andhra Pradesh government decided to introduce its land ceiling legislation, the ceiling was fixed at an income of Rs. 5,400 net or Rs. 10,800 gross, which represents about 27 acres of first-class irrigated land or 324 acres of dry land. Government spokesmen said they were giving owners a chance to dispose of lands owned above the ceiling, and much voluntary redistribution has taken place. In addition to the ceiling, each individual was allowed to retain land up to one-third of the ceiling for grazing purposes. There were many paper partitions, but few real changes in the ownership of land, and the domination of the rural power structure by rural landlords remained unaffected.

With jagir abolition some tenants were converted into peasant proprietors. The Nizam of Hyderabad had been backed by many Hindu jagirdars and wealthier landlords. Jagir abolition and the replacement of the Nizam by the Congress party meant that power in rural areas passed from the wealthier landowners, mainly absentee landlords who lived in Hyderabad, to the medium landlords and wealthier peasants who directly supervised the working of their lands.

In 1952 there were general elections on an adult franchise, and a popularly elected cabinet of Hyderabad state was formed. A majority of the ministers were Brahmans. R. K. Rao became chief minister and held the post until 1956. He told this writer in July 1962 that when he had formed his first cabinet, supporters of Chenna Reddy had gone around Hyderabad writing "Brahman Raj" on the walls, although he had "decided that the different communities should be properly represented." After the general elections of 1967, Reddy was made Minister of Steel, Mines, and Metals in the central government.

In October 1953 Andhra state was formed. Three years later Hyderabad state was carved into three sections, each given to an adjoining linguistic area. The States Reorganization Committee recommended giving the three Kannada-speaking districts to Mysore and the Marathi-speaking districts to Bombay, but had advised that the nine districts of Telengana should remain separate for five years and then merge with Andhra state, if two-thirds of the legislature was in favor.

R. K. Rao, the chief minister of Hyderabad, disagreed with this recommendation. He argued that there should be no probationary period and that the state should be broken up forthwith for two reasons: first, if Telengana were made a separate state for five years, people would acquire a vested interest in its maintenance, and a move for integration with Andhra later would be impossible; and second, Telengana, despite the suppression of the Communist movement, remained a Communist stronghold. In June 1952 there were more Communists from Telengana in the Legislative Assembly than Congressmen. R. K. Rao had been able to form a Congress government with a majority of only six in the Legislative Assembly. He therefore warned the Congress high command that they ran the risk of a Communist government in the heart of India, and this was the view he put before the Chief Ministers' Conference. Eventually only Maulana Azad, the Education Minister, was in favor of the five-year period, which even Nehru opposed, although Nehru was still against the dismemberment of Hyderabad. Surprisingly, the Communists, under the influence of Andhra leaders who had long expected the formation of a Telugu-speaking state, were in favor of an immediate merger and were against the idea of a separate Telengana. At a meeting between the leaders of the Andhra Congress party and the Hyderabad party a gentlemen's agreement was made, and its points listed and signed by Gopal Reddy for Andhra and R. K. Rao for Hyderabad. In this it was agreed that if the chief minister was from Andhra, then the deputy chief minister should be from Telengana, and vice versa.

On November 1, 1956, Andhra Pradesh was formed, and the question arose as to whether Gopal Reddy, Sanjeevah Reddy, or R. K. Rao was to become chief minister. According to R. K. Rao, he was approached by representatives of Gopal Reddy and Sanjeevah Reddy asking him to become chief minister of the new state provided that he could obtain the united support of Telengana Congressmen. For twenty hours he considered accepting, but he was told by Chenna Reddy and Ranga Reddy (who had opposed the disintegration of Hyderabad) that he did not have the support of their group, so he decided to leave the state and accepted a governorship. Chenna Reddy and Ranga Reddy were unwilling to accept R. K. Rao, not only because he was a Brahman, but, more importantly, because he was a townsman and might carry through land reforms in a way which would damage those with landed interests like themselves. The Telengana struggle had made urban Congressmen aware of the necessity for land reform, and they felt more likely to get it from Sanjeevah Reddy than from Gopal Reddy, who was not a peasant proprietor but an extremely rich landlord. This left the field clear to Sanjeevah Reddy and Gopal Reddy. The support of R. K. Rao's group, which held the majority in Telengana, was swung behind Sanjeevah Reddy, and this gave him a majority. Gopal Reddy later went off to the center to become a minister.

During Sanjeevah Reddy's first chief ministership he acquired an iron grip on the political and administrative machinery of the state, and by thus commending himself to the Congress high command, he was subsequently made All-India Congress President. When forming his first cabinet among the Telengana leaders, he took in Ranga Reddy and J. V. Narsing Rao (a Velama), but left out Chenna Reddy. His nominee for the chief ministership, which he had unwillingly vacated, was Brahmananda Reddy. Opposition forces grouped themselves around Alluri S. Raju (a Kshatriya). Neither Brahmananda Reddy nor Alluri S. Raju had a clear majority. After much discussion between the two Congress factions, a compromise candidate was decided on—Sanjiviah, a Harijan from Rayalseema. It was also hoped that his appointment would detach Harijan support from the Communists. In accordance with the gentlemen's agreement, Ranga Reddy became deputy chief minister, as the Telengana nominee. In the chief ministership Sanjiviah proved stronger than had been expected, particularly in introducing welfare measures for his own caste. His introduction of an administrative order reserving positions for Harijans at every level of the civil service, not just in lower ranks, aroused much opposition, and an attempt was made to pass a vote of no confidence in his leadership.

For two-thirds of Andhra Pradesh the election came after seven years. The 1957 election was confined to 105 seats in the nine Telengana districts, while the term of 196 Legislative Assembly members from the eleven Andhra districts (elected in the mid-term election of 1955) was extended by two years, so as to be coterminous with that of the Telengana legislators. The total strength of the state Legislative Assembly is therefore 301, including one member who is nominated by the governor of the state from the Anglo-India community.

In the three regions of Andhra Pradesh, in the circars (the seven wealthy coastal delta districts), the Congress party won 88 out of 176 seats: in the four Ryalseema districts it won 25 out of 57; and in the nine districts of Telengana, 63 out of 106. Of the remaining 43 Telengana seats, the Communist party won 18 (9 of them in Nalgonda district), Independents 19, Swatantra 3, and Socialists 2. The election in one constituency was postponed because of the death of a candidate.

TABLE 8.2

Elections to Andhra Legislative Assembly, 1962

Party	*Seats contested*	*Seats Won 1962*	*(1957)*	*Votes polled*	*Percentage*
Congress	299	176	(238)	5,509,865	47.23
Communist	136	51	(37)	2,257,748	19.35
Swatantra	140	19	(12)	1,239,324	10.62
Jan Sangh	70	—	—	117,029	1.03
Socialist	15	2	—	72,131	0.71
Republican	18	—	—	45,115	0.40
Praja Socialist	6	—	—	34,738	0.32
Independents	193	51	(10)	2,389,692	20.42
Invalid votes				466,330	

In the Andhra Pradesh cabinet after the general elections there were 5 Reddis, 1 Kamma, 1 Kshatriya, 2 Brahmans, 1 Muslim, and 1 Harijan. The ministers of state included 1 Velama, 1 Brahman, 1 Reddi, 1 Kamma, 1 Bania, and 1 Harijan. Following the general elections of 1962 Sanjeevah Reddy returned to the chief ministership. He offered a ministry to Sanjiviah, but refused one to Alluri S. Raju. Sanjiviah said he would not go in without Alluri S. Raju. There was a pause and then the All-India Congress Presidency, which Sanjeevah Reddy had vacated to return to state politics, was offered to Sanjiviah. Alluri S. Raju remained outside the new cabinet.[12] Sanjeevah Reddy contravened the gentlemen's agreement, and did not offer the deputy chief ministership to anybody from Telengana, thus arousing much resentment.

In the early autumn of 1962, an election was held for the internal Congress post of Pradesh Returning Officer. This generally arouses no

[12] Alluri S. Raju has since died.

interest, but a two-thirds majority is required to elect the chief minister's nominee. This was not forthcoming, and Sanjiviah, as All-India Congress President, in accordance with the constitution nominated somebody, choosing a Congressman from Mysore. It was thus publicly demonstrated that Sanjeevah Reddy had been unable to re-establish his hold on the state party machine.

In 1964 Sanjeevah Reddy resigned, following criticisms made of him by the Supreme Court in a case which concerned his action in taking into public ownership a privately owned transport firm for allegedly political reasons. He was succeeded by his close associate and friend Brahmananda Reddy. In late 1964 Sanjeevah Reddy joined Sanjiviah as a minister in the central government. By 1966 open opposition to Brahmananda Reddy at the state level came from a new grouping led by A. C. Suba Reddy, and relations between Sanjeevah Reddy and Brahmananda Reddy were less cordial, and by the time of the 1967 general elections they were declared enemies.

In the 1967 general elections, Brahmananda Reddy triumphed over all his adversaries. Inside the Congress party the Sanjeevah Reddy–Sanjiviah–A. C. Suba Reddy "alliance" was routed. Sanjiviah lost his seat; Sanjeevah Reddy after the election became the Speaker of the Lok Sabha; and, after a suitable pause, in a conciliatory gesture A. C. Suba Reddy was taken into Brahmananda Reddy's new cabinet. Brahmananda Reddy's majority in the Congress party was also strengthened when Congress candidates from his group unexpectedly won in the Communist strongholds of Nalgonda and Guntur, where rival Communist candidates destroyed each other.

In 1964 the Communist party had divided into two new parties—the CPI (Right) and the CPI (Marxist or Left). They failed to reach any working agreement for the general elections of 1967 and set up rival candidates for 53 Legislative Assembly seats and 11 Lok Sabha seats. These rival communists fought each other much more bitterly than they did their Congress opponents, and as a result of their mutually destructive activities their representation in the Legislature declined from 31 Right CPI and 20 Left CPI to 10 CPI (R) and 9 CPI (M).

The Swatantra party slightly improved its position, and the Jan Sangh showed signs of emerging as an electoral force in urban centers. The Majlis Ittihad-ul-Muslimin gained two seats in the city of Hyderabad, and only one Congress candidate, M. M. Hashim, succeeded in winning a seat for the Congress party in a predominantly Muslim constituency. The Congress party emerged from the general elections with a slightly smaller majority but with its power unimpaired.

In the outgoing assembly of 300 members, the Congress party strength had been 177; Right CPI, 31; Left CPI, 20; Swatantra, 19; Ittihad-ul-Muslimin, 1; Praja party, 1; and Independents, 51. After the 1967 general elections, in a new Assembly of 287 members (the strength of the Assembly having been reduced), the Congress strength was 165; Swatantra, 29; CPI (R), 10; CPI (M), 9; Jan Sangh, 3; Republicans, 2; Ittihad-ul-Muslimin, 3; Samyukta Socialist, 1; and Independents, 57.

In 1967 the new President of India, Zakir Husain, a Muslim Hyderabadi by birth, received fewer votes from Congressmen entitled to vote in the presidential election than from any other Congress Legislative Assembly party in India. This may have been due not only to anti-Muslim feeling, but to the desire to hit back at Brahmananda Reddy's prestige as Indira Gandhi's champion.

In the Andhra Pradesh cabinet after the general elections, before it was enlarged to include all the ministers of state, there were 3 Reddis, 1 Brahman, 1 Velama, 2 Backward Classes, and 1 Harijan.

The Communist Party

In the old state of Hyderabad, political parties were prohibited, there was no freedom of the press, and permission was needed to hold a public meeting. In the 1930s the beginnings of today's political parties were seemingly innocuous organizations like the library movement and merchants' associations in the towns. The activists in all these groups, mostly urban politicians and Brahmans, eventually came together in the Andhra Mahasabha. By the late 1930s the Communists were in a majority inside the Andhra Mahasabha, and it split into two organizations, both calling themselves by the parent name.

Fig. 5: The Andhra Mahasabha Split

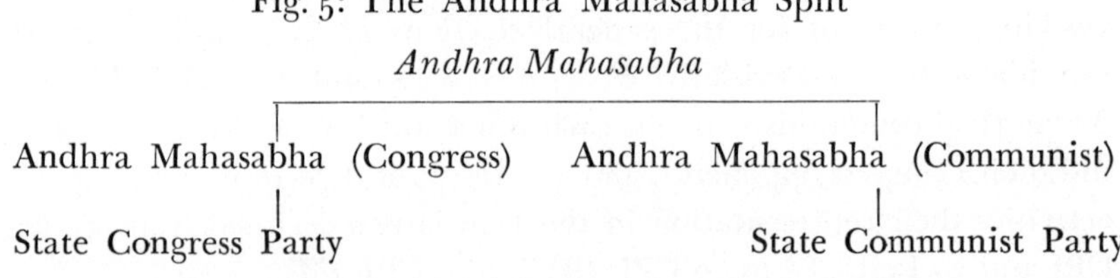

An emissary was sent in 1940 from the Andhra Communist party (Ram Rao, a Brahman from Guntur) to organize formally the Hyderabad party as a district branch of the Andhra party. Its first general secretary was Ravi Narayan Reddy (from Nalgonda district), who also remained a prominent member of the Congress until he was expelled in 1945. In an interview with this writer in September 1962 Ravi Narayan Reddy said: "After the entry of the Soviet Union into the war, when the Communists were released from prison, they started to build up a real and effective party organization in Telengana. From the first we were closely associated with the Andhra Party and leaned on them for ideological guidance."

Ravi Narayan Reddy is immensely respected by Congressmen. He is the only state politician with charismatic qualities, and it is not surprising that in 1952, when standing for the Lok Sabha from Nalgonda, he obtained more votes than any other candidate elected to Parliament from the whole of India (Mr. Nehru was second). He is an excellent speaker for mass, rural audiences, and has acquired Gandhian characteristics in peasants' eyes, having, it is said, given away several hundred acres of his own land. In the 1957 election, when he stood for the Legislative Assembly from his home constituency in Bhonghir (Nalgonda district), the Congress party unsuccessfully opposed him with his brother-in-law, a fellow-landowning Reddy, who had become known by making the first land gift to Vinobha Bhave and by launching the "Bhoodan" movement.

The Telengana Communist leaders were never drawn from one caste. Among them were Maqdoom Mohiuddin (the famous Urdu poet), Badam Yella Reddy (from Karimnagar district), and Raj Bahadur Gowd (a Khaist). The solidarity of the Communist party in Telengana derives from violent struggle, in this case against the landlords and the Nizam's government. The Congress party leaders, urban-based and in and out of prison, never resorted to organized violence or guerrilla warfare, and many left the state of Hyderabad before the police action to return with the Indian Army.

The Telengana struggle can be traced to a spontaneous uprising against a particularly despotic and ruthless landlord, Visnuri Ramachandra Reddy, in what is now Jangaon taluk (Warangal district), but was then Nalgonda. There were demonstrations and processions by peasants from one village to another, followed by physical clashes with the authorities. In 1946 a youth named Komaraya was killed, and his name became a rallying point for revolt.

Communist party leaders say that the Nizam's administration contained party sympathizers who kept them well informed. They knew well in advance when party offices were to be raided, removed all documents and went underground. At this time the emerging peasant movement waxed and waned, but in late 1946 it spread to Suryapet (Nalgonda district), and there was fighting between peasants and police, but without guns. At this time illegal warfare was not yet organized by the party, although its workers were stimulating, and participating in, these forceful demonstrations of peasant discontent; but soon afterwards instructions were received from the Andhra party to set up a military organization for this purpose, and workers were sent from Andhra to help in doing so. The role of party workers was seen as leading a peasant revolt against the jagirdars and deshmuks, who were undisputed rulers of their estates. It was hoped that the movement would spread throughout India. In China the revolution was successfully based on the peasants, so why not in India?

The Communist party's first action was to send couriers to assess and report on peasant strength, identify friendly and unfriendly villages, and instruct the peasants to seize guns from landlords and the police. By 1947, according to Communist party sources, there was an organized guerrilla army of 4,000 peasants, led by a Communist cadre of officers. The Communist high command laid down broad strategies and policies, and mobile squads under Communist leadership were responsible for day-to-day operations.

From 1946 to 1948 the Communist party claims to have administered and ruled over 3,000 villages[13] in Telengana. They say that they organized village panchayats and educated villagers in self-government. They claim to have carried out developmental works, and to have fostered inter-dining between castes though "no attempts were made to encourage inter-caste marriages as there were more important problems." The Communist party claims to have redistributed 1,000,000 acres of land in 2,000 villages to 6,000 peasants.[14] The party was helped with substantial subscriptions from sympathizers living in Hyderabad, because they were seen as fighting against the Nizam rather than as social revolutionaries.

According to ex-Communist party sources, the direction of the struggle was carried on as follows: there was a regional committee of five or six members, one of whom was a military member. Under the regional committee there were zonal committees consisting of three or four members, one of whom was the zonal military commander, under whose command were armed mobile squads consisting of eleven to twenty members. To every ten to fifteen villages there was one full-time worker, many of whom assumed lower caste names, and in each Communist village a cell of ten to fifteen members and probationary members.

Zonal committees were empowered to pass death sentences, but cases on which there was disagreement or which seemed complicated were referred upwards to the regional committee for decision.

[13] It is very difficult to gauge just how widespread their control was.

[14] According to government sources only 12,684 acres were redistributed.

Fig. 6: Chains of Command

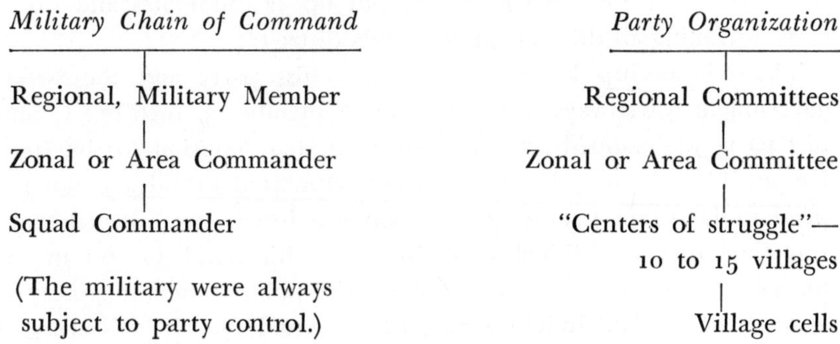

Accounts differ on exact responsibilities and the chain of command. Squads probably enjoyed more autonomy than the above theoretical scheme shows, and there was much decentralized initiative. The Communist intelligence service seems to have been good. In talking about the Telengana struggle, which many villagers in Nalgonda district now seem to consider a golden age, this writer was often told that the Communists always knew the right persons to kill, the real traitors, whereas the government often made mistakes.

Effective resistance to the Communists was made only by Kasim Razvi's volunteers, known as Razakars, and the military situation just before the police action in Nalgonda district was that certain villages were held by the Communists and certain villages by the Razakars. Today those villages which were occupied by the Razakars generally support the Congress party. The Communist-occupied villages generally support the Communist party.

After the police action there was a division of opinion in the Communist high command as to whether the struggle should be continued. Ravi Narayan Reddy and Mohiuddin Maqdoom led the moderates, who wished to end the revolt now that the Nizam's government had been overthrown, while Sundarayya (the Andhra Communist leader) [15] favored its continuance, holding that India would become another China. Instructions were given by the Communist party that nobody was to shelter Ravi Narayan Reddy and Maqdoom. Ravi Narayan Reddy left the area from Bombay, and Maqdoom was arrested. Ravi Narayan Reddy helped to persuade the All-India party to issue orders that the struggle be discontinued. It is said by Communist party leaders that this was done on Stalin's advice, as he discounted the suggestion that the revolt might spread throughout India. The struggle gradually petered out, and the Communist party

[15] In 1962 on the right wing of the party.

leaders gave themselves up and went to prison, to be released just before the elections of 1952 in which they put up 42 candidates and won 35 seats, including all the seats in Nalgonda district.

The relationship between the Communist party and the Nizam's government was always ambiguous. On September 3, 1946 the Communist party was banned since it then advocated accession to the Indian Union. Then in 1947 the Communists supported the idea of an independent Hyderabad state and the ban was lifted. It is alleged that at this time they established local alliances with Razakars and in some places received arms from them. After the police action the party was again banned. The Indian Army, which found the Nizam's army and the Razakars so easy to deal with, had to stay in Telengana until 1951 to put down Communist guerrilla fighters. In 1952 the ban was lifted to enable them to contest the elections. Since 1952 the Communist party has not been banned, and in Andhra Pradesh it has been the main opposition party. At the time when states reorganization was under discussion, the Communists supported the merger of Telengana with Andhra, under the influence of Andhra leaders, even though in an independent Telengana they might well have had the strongest party. Internally the Communist party, as throughout India, is divided into two main groups although their membership fluctuates, and in 1964 they became two separate parties. One is China-oriented and revolutionary, the other is Russia-oriented and reformist, believing that in India a socio-economic revolution can be achieved through parliamentary processes. These groupings in Andhra are not along caste lines.

DISTRICT ADMINISTRATION

Perhaps the single most important change in state politics in recent years—apart from the displacement of the Brahmans by the rural gentry caste—is the new relationship between the bureaucracy and the politicians. This change is apparent at the district as well as at the state level.

Until recently the authority of the government at the district level rested with the district collector and his staff. He was responsible for law and order, exercising magisterial powers and collecting revenue. This authority has been reduced by the establishment of a popularly elected state Assembly and by the establishment of new institutions of local government known as panchayati raj.

Before the introduction of political democracy the collector represented to the people in the district the only channel of communication with the government above the district level. With political democracy, there were now several lines of communication upwards from the district, for the government acquired other eyes and ears in members of the Legislative Assembly and other district politicians. But the government continued to act through the district collector and the line of communication downwards to the district level remained more or less the same. The theory continued to be that the government relied on the collector for an unbiased picture of the state of affairs in the district. The introduction of panchayati raj—the new system of local government—accelerated the democratic trend. These new local bodies were manned by local politicians, and they were given a dual role as independent local governments and as agents of the state government for the execution of certain state programs.

In Andhra Pradesh the collector as chairman of the standing committees of the zilla parishad, the new district council, has a say in both its deliberative and executive responsibilities. At the block level, the block development officer is in a different position; for, in a number of cases, the presidents of the samithis act as the chief executive authorities. If the collector is replaced at the district level by a non-official, a similar situation will arise.

All the officials in a district are on a lower level of the hierarchy than is the collector. The one exception is the district's senior police officer who, although theoretically responsible to the collector, tends to act autonomously. When there is serious conflict between the collector and any other official in the district, it is the other official who generally gets moved, but in the case of serious differences between the collector and the senior police officer in a district, they generally both get moved. If the collector is a strong man, officials will seek his aid in resisting what they consider to be improper demands by members of the Legislative Assembly, the zilla parishad chairman, or the panchayat samithi presidents. If he is a weak man, and he fears being transferred, he will not resist pressures. A transfer which results from a quarrel with a Congress party politician is more feared than one resulting from a quarrel with another more senior officer. Many officials point out that through the Congress party intelligence network, Congressmen generally know in advance that a new man is "uncooperative and difficult."

The collector is responsible for supervising all the officials serving in his district. He in turn is supervised by the Board of Revenue and by the chief secretary of the state. When community development blocks were first formed, the Revenue Department in the district was made entirely responsible for this work. The first officers on the staff of the blocks were taken from the Revenue Department. The collector was the chief planning officer in the district. Through his network of officers, over whom he had control down to the village level, he implemented development schemes. Extension officers at block level were under the block development officer, who was responsible directly to the collector. This situation underwent a sudden change with the introduction of panchayati raj.

The financial and administrative powers connected with planning were transferred to panchayati raj bodies. Only the collector's emergency powers remained. He still coordinates the work of other departments, but his control over the block development officer and the extension officers has changed. He is a member of the zilla parishad and chairman of its standing committees. As chairman of the standing committees, his only statutory duty is to preside at meetings. As a member of the zilla parishad, he has no more rights than any other member, although as collector he has to fill vacancies on it, and act in emergencies and in connection with "no confidence" motions. Although the collector's planning responsibilities have been taken away and transferred to the politicians, he is still responsible for revenue collection, law and order, and for general supervision of the work of all the officials in the district. Where his general authority has become most attenuated is at the samithi level.

Samithi Officials

The senior official at samithi level is the block development officer, who is flanked by a staff of technical experts as extension officers.

Fig. 7: Samithi Officials

The Block Development Officer

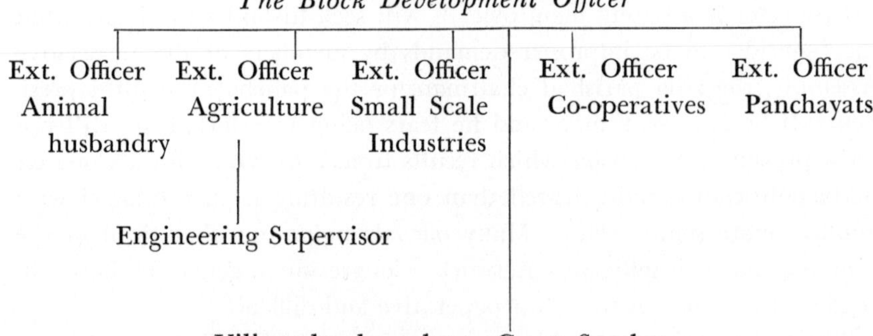

The block development officer is the executive officer of the samithi and is responsible to the samithi for the execution of their decisions. His confidential report is made by the samithi president, at whose discretion he shares the samithi jeep. Meetings of all the extension officers are held monthly to report on their activities and are generally presided over by the samithi president. How the block development officer spends his time depends on the president. In some samithis the block development officer hardly leaves the office. All the touring and inspection work is done by the samithi president. In others the work is more equally divided. Although it was originally said the samithis would only make policy decisions, not execute them, most samithi presidents implement as well as make policy.

Most block development officers in Nalgonda district told this writer that they would like to be posted to Communist samithis. In such cases they would be able to stand up to the samithi president and know that they would be supported by the district collector. In the case of Congress samithi presidents, any sign of independence and strength would probably result in a transfer, unless the block development officer enjoyed support higher up in the Congress hierarchy. The allocation of block development officers within a district also has political implications. In Nalgonda district one block development officer suspected of Communist sympathies was sent to a samithi with a Congress party president while the strongest block development officer was sent to a Communist samithi. In the constituency of the Minister of Small-Scale Industries there were two samithis. In one samithi the block development officer had previously been employed in a Hyderabad Weavers Co-operative Society run by the Minister. In the other samithi the block development officer was not on good terms either with the samithi president (who was also the district Congress president) or with the Minister, and he was eventually transferred.

The block development officers and extension officers are all college graduates. Some are members of the rural gentry themselves; others are urban in origin. Most of them are resentful of their new situation as the executive agents of politicians. In an interview one said:

> The BDO is always responsible for anything that goes wrong, and at Samithi meetings he always has to answer questions and accept responsibility. The President may have forced him to go slow on the developmental work for a certain village. Then there is a question about it in public, and the BDO has to answer as best he can. The President always has the last word. He can say to ministers that the BDO is uncooperative, does not have the right attitude and spirit for Community Development work, gets on badly with people, is a difficult man and unsympathetic to Congress ideals—and he will be moved. He has no channel himself for

> telling the government, in safety, what is going on. It is dangerous to quarrel with politicians. They will black-list you, and the Congress people where you go will be warned against you. It is better for the Block Development Officer to close his eyes to certain things. It is the same for the Secretary in the Zilla Parishad.

This general atmosphere leads to less interest and activity by the block development officer and probably fewer completed projects.

Types of Officials

There are three types of officials: (1) Those who are completely independent, determined to do their duty as they see it, and who do not care where they get sent as a result of displeasing politicians; (2) Those who draw their own conscience line, who are flexible on questions which they consider are only formal or permit choice but will take stands on questions of principle; (3) Those who are identified with the politicians and are recognized members of political sub-groups. Most officials are in category two, and the problem for politicians who are dealing with them is to find out where their individual conscience lines are drawn. Which of these categories officials fit into is known to their fellow officials and all politicians at the different levels concerned. The following are examples of these three types in district politics.

Type 1. A block development officer was involved in a question of back dating a check so that some money could be spent which would otherwise have lapsed. Although instructed to do so, first by the panchayat samithi president and then verbally by the collector, he refused. He told the collector that he would do so if the instruction was given in writing, but this was not forthcoming. This particular official was hoping to be transferred, so he was unwilling to be accommodating.

Type 2. Gram (village) panchayat projects, in which half the contribution comes in cash from the government and half in labor and materials from the village, have to be inspected and certified as completed in accordance with sanctioned specifications. Sometimes the work has been skimped or obviously carried out on government money alone without the public contribution. But the inspecting official concerned told this writer that, provided there was no glaring dishonesty, he generally said that the work had been properly completed.

Type 3. A loan had been sanctioned by a committee of a samithi to one person, while the request of another was refused. By the time the next standing committee took place, the person who had been refused the loan had received it, but not the one whose name had been approved. When this question was brought up, the block development officer accepted responsibility, saying that he knew no shorthand and had made an error in the name. It was decided that the man who had originally been voted the loan should now get it in addition to the one who had got it mistakenly. The block development officer told this writer afterwards that he always did as instructed by his president, who was too powerful a man to be offended.

How conflicts are resolved between politicians and officials depends on the status positions of the individuals involved, and the allies they can call to their defense, both in the hierarchy of officials and that of politicians. At the state level the chief minister has the last word, and the decision in any important power dispute is made by him. He may of course be evasive, but this may multiply his enemies more than would a decision in favor of one person or group. At the samithi level, too, politicians are in supreme command, and the officials are subordinate.

The ex-State Minister of Agriculture, Mr. T. Reddy (in 1967 again a minister), once said: "If you want to understand politics in this state, you must realize that there are two governments. There is the Chief Minister surrounded by his Ministers, and opposed to him is the Chief Secretary surrounded by his secretaries. Everything that happens is the result of interaction between these two groups, the play of pressures on them and the conflict of interests between them." This would seem to be an over-simplification, for power is not equally balanced between the contending sides, and the officials can only fight defensive and evasive actions. The chief threat to politicians comes from other politicians who wish to replace them and ascend the power hierarchy. Nor are officials really grouped around the chief secretary. The inspector general of police is also a power in his own right; and if he is a strong man with political friends, he is not really subordinate to the chief secretary. Here the position at the state level mirrors that at the district level, where the only district officer not really subordinate to the collector, although he is on paper, is the senior police officer.

Since 1959, panchayati raj has been gradually extended throughout India. A decision was made to introduce a three-tier system of local government in all districts. However, the states were left free to make their own decisions about the units that each of the three tiers was to comprise and whether there was to be direct or indirect representation at each level. In Andhra Pradesh there are direct elections only at the village level to the village panchayat. The panchayat members then elect their own chairman, the village sarpanch. The samithi (local government at the middle tier) is formed from thirty to fifty sarpanches of the block (districts are divided into blocks for purposes of community development) along with some co-opted members (who are mostly local politicians) and members of the Legislative Assembly in whose constituency the blocks are situated. Each samithi elects its own president from among its members.

At the district level the top tier, the zilla parishad or district council, is made up of the samithi presidents of the district, plus co-opted members, members of the Legislative Assembly from the district, and Members of Parliament, and in addition also such members of the Legislative Council and the Council of State as are appointed by the government. This device was introduced so that the ruling party could make sure that no zilla parishad need have a hostile majority.

When guiding the Andhra Pradesh Panchayat Samithis and Zilla Parishads Act in 1959 through the Legislative Assembly, the Finance and Planning Minister, Mr. K. Brahmananda Reddy,[16] said that it had been sponsored by the Congress party government with four objects:

1. the transfer of power to people's institutions;
2. development of the initiative of the people;
3. increased participation of people in the implementation of developmental programs; and
4. development of village leadership.

The zilla parishad has its own gazetted officer as secretary, its own engineer and other officials, but the district officials are not its executive agents, nor are they subject to its authority. The collector (the senior district official) in Andhra Pradesh is the chairman of the standing committees of the zilla parishad but not of the zilla parishad itself, which elects its own chairman. The zilla parishad chairman's authority and influence is dependent on the interplay of his personality with that of the collector. The position of the samithi president is much more powerful than that of the zilla parishad chairman. The samithi president has a manageable area to control and has effective sanctions over the officials who work under him. Samithi presidents are often not amenable to direction by zilla parishad chairmen, and it is difficult for the zilla parishad to take action against samithis unless there are glaring irregularities.

The zilla parishad's job is "supervision and co-ordination." Samithi presidents tend to look at it, as one said, "as a post office to which the government sends money for distribution." The zilla parishad's other jobs are running and supervising the high schools and looking after the

[16] Later chief minister (1964).

parts of the district which as yet have no samithis. Unless the zilla parishad is given more power in Andhra Pradesh, it is difficult to see what use it will serve once the districts all have samithis.

The panchayat samithi, the intermediate between the zilla parishad and the village panchayat, has more effective powers than either and is responsible for the execution of development projects. It approves the budgets for village development schemes and supervises rural works programs, irrigation and extension of drinking water facilities, and enforces compulsory education, the organization of community and welfare schemes, the construction of roads, and so on. A samithi is also responsible for the execution of extension programs, the forming and running of cooperatives, and the distribution of improved seeds and agricultural implements and fertilizers.

A panchayat samithi has several standing committees for such purposes as agriculture, cooperation, education, communications and public works, finance and taxation. Every standing committee consists of seven members, and the chairman of every committee is the samithi president. The staff of a panchayat samithi is under the administrative control of the block development officer and all are subordinate to the samithi. The president of the panchayat samithi exercises control over the block development officer "to ensure that the resolutions of the Panchayat Samithi and of its Standing Committees are implemented."

In poor districts like those of Telengana, and unlike those of the circars, cash contributions from villages to community development projects are rare, and contributions are more easily forthcoming in labor and materials. In what are known as "stage-one" blocks, where the public contribution expected is only 25 per cent, much work gets done. But in stage two, the required public contribution goes up to 50 per cent and there is less enthusiasm, particularly for roads and schools. In backward areas village councils collect a smaller percentage of the compulsory taxes because this is politically unpopular. For the same reason, the voluntary taxes which village councils may or may not impose are not—to this writer's knowledge—imposed in any village in Andhra Pradesh. The cumulative effect of possibilities being always taken up by rich villages but only infrequently by poor ones means that the rich villages tend to become richer and the poor poorer. Those on a samithi who are members of the dominant castes seem to do more for their villages—but this may also be a question of education, knowing what one's rights are and how to fight for them, and also having the leisure which wealth gives to do the fighting.

The Recruitment of Samithi Members

The sarpanchas. Most panchayat samithi members are sarpanchas. The members of village panchayats are directly elected from territorial wards by secret ballot on the basis of universal adult suffrage. These directly elected panchas together elect a sarpanch, who becomes the executive head of the gram panchayat and an ex officio member of the panchayat samithi.

The nine districts of Telengana were in the old state of Hyderabad, one-third of which was dotted with jagirs. The villages in the other two-thirds were controlled by landowning agriculturalists called "Doras."[17] These men, like the Hindu jagirdars, were members of the dominant agricultural landowning castes, the Reddis, the Velamas, the Brahmans, and the Kammas.

There was no headman in the Telengana villages, but in the mid-nineteenth century the Nizam of Hyderabad introduced a system of village hereditary offices. The holders of these were called watandars and consisted of the mali patel (who helped in revenue collection), the police patel (responsible for reporting transgressions of the law to the nearest policeman), and the patwari (who kept the land records). The patwari was nearly always a Brahman, and the other two offices were filled by members of the dominant agricultural castes. Farseeing families, not wishing to see alternative sources of power in their villages, ensured that these offices were given to relatives. Subsequently the offices were often farmed out, and today there are many absentee patwaris and patels.

In most landowning families today there is a conscious division of labor among brothers. For example, in a Kamma family it was decided that one brother should look after the land, a second should become sarpanch of their home village and go into district politics, a third should be responsible for affairs in the state capital (perhaps going into the Legislative Asssembly or Legislative Council), a fourth should go into the army and a fifth into the state administration. All the brothers receive a share of the joint family income. It is understood that politics is a full-time occupation, whether directly rewarded as in the case of a Legislative Assembly member who receives a salary, or rewarded by expenses only as in the case of a samithi president.

The largest group of sarpanchas on the panchayat samithi consists of those who have assumed office to protect their village interests only and who are without further political ambitions. They are the followers of

17 "Dora" means "sahib," "sir," "lord of the village."

the political leaders of factions within parties. They expect rewards for themselves and their villages for their loyalty. They join samithis because they feel that their villages are no longer isolated, and it is the only way to resist intrusion by officials and politicians. Threats to their authority from without can be countered only by influencing those who control intrusive agents. Threats to authority from within the village can be countered by using office gainfully for oneself and one's village. If one is on the samithi, one has voice in how government money is to be spent, who is posted to one's village as a primary school teacher, and so forth.

There are some village leaders with larger ambitions. One such man, a Vaisya, had built up a network of clients in his village by moneylending and by carefully playing off two small landlords against each other in a divided village emerged unexpectedly as sarpanch. He then extended his moneylending activities, at lower rates of interest than he charged to villagers, to his fellow samithi members. He hopes eventually to become samithi president.

Leaders are distinguished from followers by education. Politicians, if they are not to be fooled by officials, must be able to read the letters and documents which come from the government. Leaders are also men with enough money and leisure to give up every day to politics, not merely an occasional one. Therefore, they must be rentiers or have relatives looking after the land for them, be full-time party officials, or make a great deal of money outside of politics.

In landowning families it is the custom to send the educated son, the one who knows some English, into politics. Membership in one of the dominant agricultural castes is an almost necessary entrance qualification to the political elite, but a high position in terms of economic ranking, although it helps, does not guarantee political influence and success. A Reddi with fifty acres of land and the appropriate education, personality, and character can be more influential in a district or at the state level than one with five hundred acres, although he will have a harder time getting there.

If it is difficult for a man to become sarpanch of the village in which he lives, through kinsmen he may become sarpanch of another village. The law is not transgressed providing his name is on only one electoral register, and he does at times live in the village concerned. In one such case, villagers said of their sarpanch: "Yes, he comes and stays with his uncle, who is a village officer here, but he owns land and has his wife and children in another village."

Co-opted members. The candidates put forward for co-option are chosen by political parties to strengthen majorities, or to bring in leaders who are not already on the samithi as sarpanchas. The women, who have to be co-opted, are usually relatives of sitting members, or prominent local politicians. In one case the wife of a samithi president was co-opted onto an adjoining samithi, where they owned land. Co-option can also be used to harry political enemies across block boundaries.

Members of the Legislative Assembly. Whether members of the Legislative Assembly play any role directly in block affairs depends on their interests and the party situation on a particular samithi. A few MLAs were panchayat samithi presidents, but this has now been prohibited.

The Role of Samithi President

The samithi president has emerged as the most powerful figure in panchayati raj. He has a manageable area to control. The block development officer is responsible to the samithi through him, and through the block development officer all the other block officers are responsible to him. The samithi president can be curbed effectively only when the samithi passes a two-thirds majority vote against him. From above he is subject only to supersession, a sanction which the collector can use only in extreme circumstances.

The samithi president has several sources of patronage:

1. Taccavi loans. These are given to individuals for development purposes against security of land. A lump sum of money is advanced which is repaid in installments.
2. Well subsidies. A loan of 750 Rs. can be given (against security of 1,500 Rs. on land). After completion of the work the loan becomes a subsidy. Applications for well subsidies and Taccavi loans are examined and reported on by the block development officer, and voted on by a standing committee.
3. The samithi president is responsible for the allotment and transfer of primary school teachers.
4. The location of primary health centers.
5. The allocation of grants to co-operatives, the building of stores for grain, roads, housing subsidies for Harijans, fertilizers, etc.
6. The placing of contracts for development purposes.
7. Estimates.

The decisions as to which people and villages shall receive benefits are taken in the standing committees, of which the president is chairman.

Power at the Village and District Levels

Within the village, responsibility for carrying out community development schemes rests on the gram panchayat in Andhra Pradesh. In villages with a ruling family, where the "Dora" or his nominee is sarpanch, it is with the Dora that the block development officer must come to terms. The block development officer knows that the Dora will accept only such schemes as reinforce, or at least do not endanger, his authority. Officials also rely on Doras for food and hospitality when going on their official rounds, and life can become uncomfortable for them if they offend powerful people. If, on the other hand, power in the village is divided, the block development officer may be able to play the sarpanch off against the village officials and exploit differences among village politicians to attain his ends.

One intruder into villages from the outside world as an agent of change is the village schoolmaster. He is a man who reads newspapers, may own a radio, and tells people about the outside world and conditions in other villages. The panchayat samithi president is responsible for the postings of primary schoolmasters within the community development block and will send to his political opponents those who are likely to disturb their rule or weaken their power positions.

But the chief agent drawing villages into the political arena is the panchayat samithi president, who on his tours of the community development block area visits every village and keeps himself up to date as to the power situation in each village. Moreover, the sarpanchas travel to samithi headquarters for meetings of the samithi and its standing committees. They meet sarpanchas of other villages, go with them to district headquarters on questions of common concern, visit each other's villages, and often become aware of district and state politics. In the general elections of 1962 the support of panchayat samithi presidents was considered extremely important by candidates and their opposition often regarded as a cause of defeat.

CONCLUSION

The introduction of panchayati raj has weakened the position of the collector[18] at the district level for he now shares power with the zilla parishad chairman. Similarly, the block development officer and his staff are responsible to and supervised directly by the panchayat samithi president. In the villages the sarpanch is more powerful than the village

[18] Collectors in Andhra Pradesh are not all members of the I.A.S., and some have been taken over from the Nizam's service.

officers even though the latter continue to be collectors of revenue for the government and intelligence agents for the police. At the same time, the weakening of the power of the bureaucracy has not yet resulted in the emergence of completely new power forces, for panchayati raj has momentarily strengthened traditional authority. It has brought the members of the dominant agricultural castes into the political parties, and conversely the political parties are extending their organization into the villages. Political power resulting from votes has momentarily been joined to socio-economic power and has consolidated the grip of dominant agricultural castes on the rural areas. At the same time, the introduction of democracy and panchayati raj has created the machinery through which new social groups can achieve power and the socio-economic structure can be modified.

At the state level, when different members of a powerful family are in different parties their position is strengthened, as when Sanjeevah Reddy was chief minister and his brother-in-law was general secretary of the state Communist party. Unofficial approaches and conversations between rival parties are often arranged through relatives when it would be embarrassing for anything official to be arranged. But in the districts, if members of a family are in different parties, their power position is weakened.

The distinctive characteristic of Andhra Pradesh state politics was the incidence of central government intervention in crucial situations.[19] This has occurred several times: the initial police action which led to the dismemberment of the old Hyderabad state and the setting up of the Telugu-speaking state of Andhra Pradesh; the replacement of the left-wing Congress party president and leader by a more pliable member of his own group more acceptable to the right-wing Congress group; the order to release imprisoned Communists before the general elections of 1952; the removal first of Mr. Sanjeevah Reddy to the center to become All-India Congress President, then the appointment of Mr. Sanjiviah to fill the same role. All these major changes were provoked in the state by intervention from the center.

The principal problem for Andhra Pradesh is the building up of one stable political system out of many. When Andhra Pradesh was created in 1956, Hyderabad politics merged with Andhra politics. An immediate result was the extrusion of the Brahmans from their dominant position in the Hyderabad (Telengana) Congress and their replacement by Reddis and their allies. Despite their number and politi-

[19] Suggested to the writer by Miss Carolyn Elliott.

cal, social, and economic power, the Reddis did not form a Reddis-against-the-rest front government. The Kammas lost heavily by the amalgamation of Hyderabad with Andhra as there are few Kammas in Telengana. If one tries to analyze situations of political conflict in the Telengana districts in caste terms alone, one may at any one point in time see Reddis opposed to Velamas, or opposed to Brahmans, but these caste alignments rarely last long. When spoils are shared there are always those left dissatisfied who join other alliances.

When this writer was present at a meeting of the Kurnool zilla parishad, a member made an embittered speech in which he attacked the granting of funds by the state government on the basis of population to panchayati raj bodies. This, he said, meant that the heavily populated regions of the delta in Andhra benefited, the richer zones became richer, and the poor zones of Ryalseema, like those of Telengana, became poorer. The feeling of being fellow poor regions has sometimes drawn Ryalseema and Telengana together against Andhra and may have made it easier for a Ryalseema man, even a Harijan, to emerge as a chief minister.

The composition of the various groups within the Congress party at state level is a shifting one. Sometimes the groups may be based on caste affiliations, on economic interests, or on regional, linguistic, kinship, class, ideological or other loyalties. Moreover, the levels of political conflict are now interconnected. In rural areas powerful men are no longer content to remain politically isolated in their villages, for now they try to enter the samithis. The presidents of samithis are on the district zilla parishad. The prominent Congressmen of the zilla parishads are members of the factions within the Congress party at the state level, and the state leaders all have their friends and associates in Delhi.

The foregoing is a description of the interaction of politicians with officials at the level of the samithi. For any complete picture of state politics similar analyses would have to be made at the district, state, and central level. The main problem which Congressmen have to face at the state level is their own reluctance to act against their own economic interests in such matters as increasing agricultural income tax, land taxes, and other taxes which hit rural interests. The agricultural sector is undertaxed, which is one of the reasons for slow economic growth. It is noteworthy that no panchayati raj body in Andhra has chosen to impose any taxes, whether it has the discretionary possibility of doing so or not. The main reason is the unpopularity of such taxes with voters. There is a similar problem with community development schemes where matching contributions are expected from the general public, for the wealthier, forward-looking landlords and villages respond while the poorer villages do not. To provide incentives for the poorer peasants, the Congress government would have to introduce sweeping land reforms, with low land ceilings for all landowners, and of this there is little possibility while Congress is dominated by the men whose interests would be directly affected.

Fragmentation within the Congress party is not as destructive as it first appears. When Congress was confronted with a strong opposition party as in Nalgonda district in 1962, Congressmen united and there were straight party fights. In districts where Congress is supreme, it can afford the luxury of dissident Congressmen standing against the officially chosen candidates.[20] Moreover, dissident Congressmen, when victorious, are usually allowed to re-enter the Congress party. These men, whatever their differences of interest, share common views, and in this sense can claim to be Congressmen whether inside or outside the party. At the state level, provided that Congressmen do not leave the party, internal party democracy is strengthened by the shifting nature of power coalitions, and by ministers' posts changing hands when power shifts from one combination to another. Provided that this does not happen too often—and it does not in Andhra Pradesh—conflict strengthens the party internally instead of weakening it.

Fragmentation is more destructive within the Communist parties. The ideological nature of their internal struggles prevents their factions from coming together effectively to confront the Congress party. The revolutionary China-oriented party cannot bury its differences with the Russia-oriented reformists. In the city of Hyderabad, and in urban areas, the reformists have more backing, but in the rural areas where most Communist party support lies, and memories of the Telengana struggle are still very much alive, the revolutionaries have more support.

In Andhra Pradesh there is a stable party system. The Congress party is likely to remain in power despite its internal dissensions, and the Communist parties are likely to remain the principal opposition in spite of their internal dissensions. Viable state government under the Congress party will probably continue, but there is not likely to be greater clarity of purpose or unity within the state's governmental leadership.

REFERENCES

Anderson, R. T. "Preliminary Report on the Associational Redefinition of Castes in Hyderabad-Secunderabad," Droeber Anthropological Society Papers, University of California, No. 29, Fall 1963.

20 "Each agonistic fight is a contest between opponents who delight in measuring their strength according to certain rules of the game." Hans Speier, "The Several Types of War," *American Journal of Sociology*, Vol. XLVI (1941).

Andhra Pradesh Administration Report 1959-60. 2 vols.

Dube, S. K. *Indian Village.* London: Routledge and Kegan Paul, 1956.

———. *India's Changing Villages.* London: Routledge and Kegan Paul, 1958.

Gray, Hugh. "The 1962 Indian General Election in a Communist Stronghold of Andhra Pradesh," *Journal of Commonwealth Political Studies,* Leicester University Press, Vol. 1, No. 4 (May 1963).

———. "The 1962 General Election in a Rural District of Andhra," *Asian Survey,* Vol. II, No. 9 (September 1962).

Harrison, Selig. *India: The Most Dangerous Decades.* Princeton: Princeton University Press, 1960.

Khusro, A. M. *Economic and Social Effects of Jagirdari Abolition and Land Reforms in Hyderabad, 1958.* Hyderabad: Department of Publications and University Press, Osmania University, 1958.

Maheshwari, S. R. *The General Election in India.* Allahabad: Chaitanya Publishing House, 1963.

Philips, C. H. (ed.). *Politics and Society in India.* London: George Allen and Unwin Ltd., 1963 (particularly v. Fürer Haimendorf).

Wright, Theodore P., Jr. "Revival of the Majlis Ittihad-ul-Muslimin," *The Muslim World,* Hartford Seminary Foundation, Vol. LIII, No. 3 (July 1963).

PUNJAB

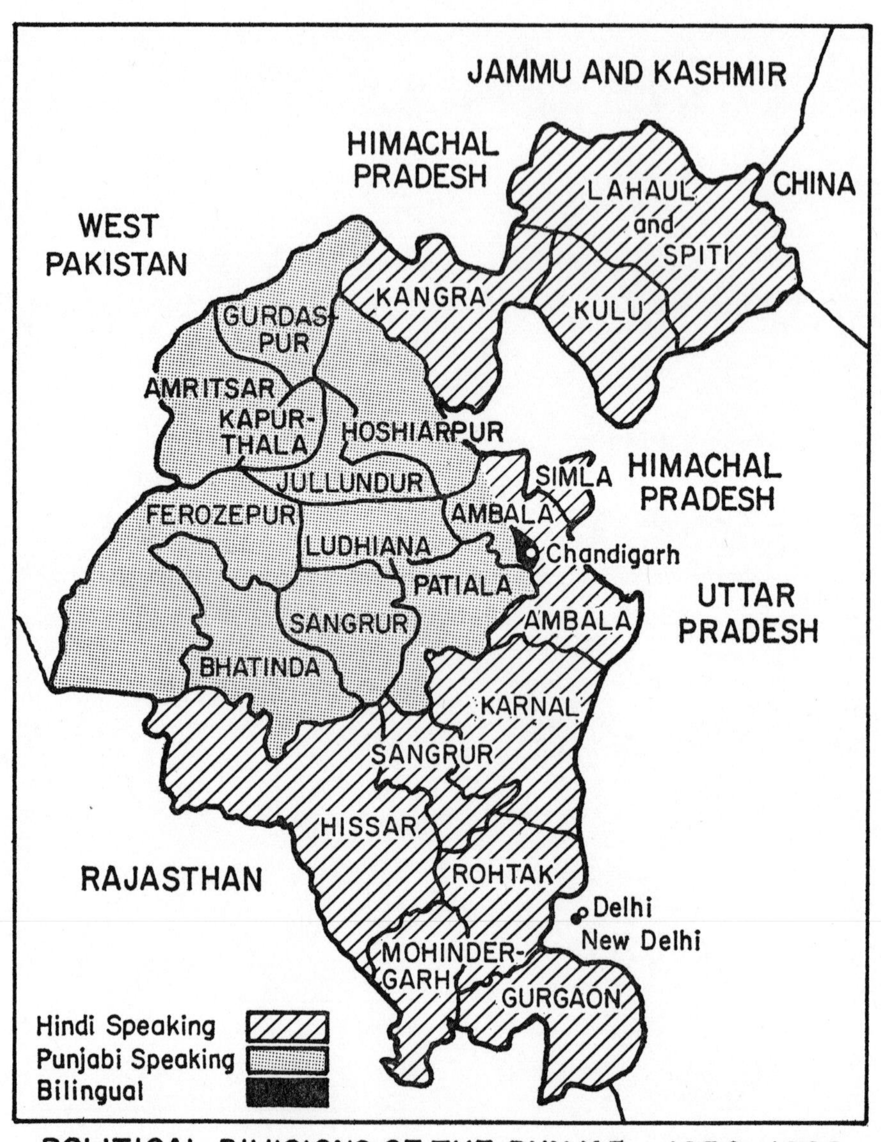

POLITICAL DIVISIONS OF THE PUNJAB, 1956-1966

IX

PUNJAB

BALDEV RAJ NAYAR

THROUGHOUT HISTORY the Punjab region has been subjected to political and social disruption by external forces. Lying on the northwest frontier of the subcontinent, the landlocked region of the Punjab, known as "the shield, spear and sword-hand of India," has been the first to feel the impact of the various invasions into the subcontinent through the northwest. At times the Punjab has even been part of empires and kingdoms outside India. Apart from preventing the evolution of a stable political system in the Punjab and the possibility of cultural achievements comparable to some other parts of India, these repeated invasions and incursions have had an important influence in molding the character of the people. Some authorities maintain that the strategic and historic position of the state led to the development of a "frontier consciousness," a self-image of being the sole defenders of India, and an inchoate regional nationalism. Further, it seems to have imparted to the people of the region a practical outlook on life, a sense of initiative and enterprise, and a general vigor along with a certain coarseness. But politically it has made for a rather turbulent people.[1]

THE POLITICAL HERITAGE OF THE PUNJAB: CLEAVAGE AND CONFLICT

The history of the Punjab has been marked by endemic conflict, with repeated outbursts of violence, among the various groups settled in the region. The invasions from across the northwest frontier made for great ethnic diversity. The various movements of tribes starting with the invasion of the Aryans in the second or third millennium B.C. gave the Punjab basically a tribal social structure, modified later by the growth of the caste system. The continual fights among the various tribes made them easy prey to new invasions through the northwest.

From the thirteenth century onwards, with the coming of Islam

[1] For some interesting descriptions of the character of the Punjabi people, see G. D. Khosla, "The Punjabi Character," *Advance*, v, No. 1 (January-March 1958), 6-8; Khushwant Singh, *The Sikhs* (London: George Allen and Unwin Ltd., 1953), pp. 17-18; L. F. Loveday Prior, *Punjab Prelude* (London: John Murray, 1952), pp. 1-64 and 115-27; and Prakash Tandon, *Punjabi Century 1857-1947* (London: Chatto and Windus, 1961), p. 14.

through the agency of Muslim invaders and conquerors, the internal conflicts among the various groups in the Punjab were cut across by the religious factor. From the time of Aurangzeb's rule, conflict among the religious groups of Hindus, Muslims, and Sikhs became especially intense and violent. In the resulting unsettled conditions, neither life nor property was safe: "every village became a fort," a neighbor "was synonymous with an enemy, and husbandmen ploughed the fields with matchlocks by their side. No man could consider his land, his horse, or his wife secure unless he was strong enough to defend them."[2] When in the mid-eighteenth century a combination of foreign invasions and internal weakness brought the Mughal empire to a near-collapse, the Sikhs established their rule in the Punjab. In 1849 the British conquered the Punjab. Friction among the three religious groups re-emerged in the political sphere in the twentieth century, punctuated by violent communal riots. In 1947 the cleavage between Muslims and non-Muslims became the basis for the partition of the Punjab, with the Muslim-majority districts becoming a part of Pakistan and the non-Muslim majority districts part of India. The partition itself was followed by mass rioting, murder, and mass migration.[3]

Conflict among the religious groups is not the only type that has prevailed in the Punjab. Within each religious group there is a great deal of internal differentiation based on tribe, caste, sect or faction. When there has been no direct threat from an outside group, and sometimes even in the presence of it, various parts of a religious group have engaged from time to time in internecine conflict and warfare. This phenomenon is illustrated by the history of the Sikh community, which is perhaps the most cohesive of religious groups in the Punjab and India.

Sikhism as a religious faith grew in the wake of the impact of Islam in northern India, and there is still dispute over whether it was an attempt to create a new religion, or to reconcile the differing faiths of Hinduism and Islam, or merely a revivalistic movement within Hinduism. At any rate, the Sikhs were a quiet, pacifist group at the time of Guru Nanak (1465-1539 A.D.), the founder and first of the ten Gurus (spiritual teachers) in Sikhism. By the time of the tenth Guru, Gobind Singh (1666-1708 A.D.), Sikhism had become as a result of conflict with the Mughal empire a militant religion and the Sikhs a highly organized military group. To emphasize their importance as a separate, cohesive group, the tenth Guru established a baptismal ceremony and required all Sikhs to wear the five

[2] Lepel Griffin, *Ranjit Singh* (Delhi: S. Chand & Co., 1957), pp. 84-85.

[3] See Penderel Moon, *Divide and Quit* (Berkeley: University of California Press, 1962).

distinctive symbols of Sikhism, the so-called "K's," including unshorn hair on their bodies and a dagger. All baptized Sikhs were to recognize Guru Gobind Singh as their father and receive the surname of Singh. He further invested the Sikh community with a single will by declaring that after his death, the Guru's living presence will be in the Panth—the Sikhs organized as a single entity.

After a long and protracted struggle between the Sikhs in the Punjab, with whom the Hindus were allied, and the Muslim rulers, the Sikhs finally emerged as the sovereign power in the Punjab, but their territories were divided into some twelve principalities or *misls* under different Sikh chiefs. At times these chiefs cooperated in the face of external threat to the Sikh religion and community. However, they "fought against each other more often than against the common enemy," and "even within the borders of each confederacy, the barons were always quarrelling, and first one chief and then another took the lead."[4] When Maharaja Ranjit Singh attempted to create, through war and statecraft, a single Sikh state out of the various *misls,* many of the Sikh chiefs chose to be under the protection of an alien conqueror. The final extinction of the kingdom bequeathed by Ranjit Singh was preceded by "storm and anarchy in which assassination was the rule,"[5] and leaders were not above treason.

Although the internal cleavages within the Sikh community have not erupted into violent activity since the British annexation of the Punjab, they have prevented the Sikh community from acting in politics as a single entity on a sustained basis and have made for competing groups within Sikhism.

While conflict among religious and other groups has been the norm through much of the history of the Punjab, the region has not been without serious attempts to overcome such conflict through the establishment of an inter-communal political framework in which each community would have an important role. The efforts of Emperor Akbar are well known, but there are also some of equal importance native to the Punjab. Though himself a Sikh, Ranjit Singh associated members of other communities in his administration, and "there was an element of partnership with other communities, even if it was only subordinate partnership."[6] In a vague way he attempted to create a Punjabi nationality by repudiating the idea of exclusive political control by the religious community of the Sikhs. He deprived the Panth of any political

4 Griffin, *op.cit.,* p. 83. 5 *Ibid.,* p. 218.

6 Vincent A. Smith, *The Oxford History of India* (3rd ed.; London: Oxford University Press, 1958), p. 613.

authority and left to it jurisdiction only in the religious matters of the Sikhs. Again, in the period from the early 1920s to independence, the Unionist party and the Congress party, with their limited political bases, attempted to provide a non-religious basis for politics, even though the Unionist party tried to do this by emphasizing another cleavage in the population.

The Authoritarian Heritage

The political tradition of the Punjab has been an authoritarian one. Although such a political tradition is said to be the norm in pre-industrial societies,[7] it was heightened by factors peculiar to the Punjab. The many invasions, the fear of invasions, and intermittent conflict and warfare, bordering at times on anarchy, made rule by the strong and ruthless military leader the only possible political model in the Punjab. As one present-day political leader of the Punjab said in an interview: "We Punjabis act best only when we are in *jathas* (military or semi-military formations). This is more prominent in the Sikhs. When we have a leader, like the Germans, we follow him."

The establishment of British rule brought peace and political stability and more stable political institutions, primarily in the realm of administration. But British rule itself, especially in the first fifty to seventy years, was highly authoritarian, paternalistic and, at the district level, personal. Directly after the conquest of the province the British made the Punjab a "non-regulation" province in which British rule became *par excellence* that of men rather than of law, with officers possessing great discretionary authority. A very simple legal code was adopted to serve the needs of the province. As one British officer wrote, "there was no law in the Punjab in those days. Our instructions were to decide all cases by the light of common sense and our own sense of what was just and right."[8] Furthermore, in the Punjab administration "it was the first article of faith that the man who is most ready to use force at the beginning will use least in the end. It was the second that juniors must be given a free hand and backed up with unswerving loyalty."[9] The drastic action taken at Jallianwala Bagh after World War I was a more extreme example of the normal pattern of administrative behavior in the Punjab. The Punjab police also evolved into the most ruthless of its kind in India—and even today it bears the marks of its past.

[7] Everett E. Hagen, *On the Theory of Social Change: How Economic Growth Begins* (Homewood, Illinois: The Dorsey Press, Inc., 1962), pp. 71-74.

[8] Quoted in Philip Mason, *The Men Who Ruled India* (London: J. Cape, 1953-54), II, 48-49.

[9] *Ibid.*, p. 236.

The concentration of all executive and judicial powers in the officers of the administration came to be modified in the 1870s. The courts assumed greater importance, and still later directly or indirectly elected bodies became the forum for the expression of sentiments of loyalty and antagonism. However, the tradition of plenitude of power in the executive in the Punjab continued.

Political Participation

By the time India achieved independence in 1947, the Punjab had had only a short and limited participation in government and politics. Until after World War I there was little association of local opinion with the administration to moderate the authoritarian rule in the Punjab.[10] The very idea of association of public opinion with the administration was highly repugnant to "the Punjab school," and constitutional reforms implemented in the rest of India before World War I were diluted or thwarted in the Punjab.[11] What existed in the Punjab in the fifty years or so after the British annexation of the province was the politics of administration confined to the British officialdom. There was no competitive politics open to the population. In the early 1870s the Kuka sect among the Sikhs engaged in agitational activity against the British, but their movement was crushed with such exemplary severity that for the next thirty years or so no local group dared raise its voice against the British government.[12] At the same time, the government strenuously worked to isolate the province from the influence of the nationalist sentiment that was stirring itself in other parts of India. In this it was quite successful until after World War I.

The period of some seven years after World War I constitutes a watershed in terms of popular participation in politics. In April 1919 occurred the Jallianwala Bagh tragedy, and this was followed by the noncooperation movement of 1920-22, launched by the Congress party under the leadership of Gandhi. At this time, Hindus, Muslims, and Sikhs, forgetting their mutual quarrels, all joined in a popular agitation against the British government. This was the first, but also the last, time in which all three communities in the Punjab combined in a mass movement against the British government. In the same period, important new political groups emerged, such as the Akali Dal and the Unionist party,

10 See Azim Husain, *Fazl-i-Husain: A Political Biography* (Bombay: Longmans, Green and Co., 1946), pp. 75-76.

11 *Ibid.*

12 See the article by Fauja Singh, "Modern Punjab," in Ganda Singh (ed.), *Bhai Jodh Singh Abhinandan Granth: Punjab (1849-1960 A.D.)* (Patiala: Khalsa College, 1962).

and older political groups, such as the Congress party, widened their political base. Apart from the experience with mass politics and the emergence of new political alignments, this period also saw, under the Government of India Act of 1919, the sharing in a limited way in the governance of the province by popular representatives elected on the basis of a restricted franchise. Although the sphere of political participation and responsibility was further widened with the grant of provincial autonomy under the Government of India Act of 1935, when independence was achieved in 1947 the experience with electoral politics and sharing in political power had been limited and brief. Moreover, it was accompanied by the divisive institution of separate electorates.

Unlike many other provinces in India, the Congress party in the Punjab was outflanked in its attempts to integrate and mobilize the population in the nationalist movement. For a variety of reasons too complex to detail here, it was unsuccessful in establishing a mass base in the province and in gaining popular support cutting across religious ties. With the suspension of the non-cooperation movement in 1922, nationalism as a political force receded, by and large, into the background in the Punjab. Agitations in towns did continue and in the late 1920s there was a spurt of terrorist activity, but the rural population, constituting nearly 90 per cent of the total population, remained unaffected by these events. The civil disobedience movement launched by the Congress party in the 1930s failed to receive much support from the people in the Punjab.[13] As for the Quit India movement of 1942, it failed to engender great enthusiasm among the Punjab masses and, as one veteran Congressman sadly remarked, the Punjab "did not behave as bravely as some of the other Provinces did though it also suffered immensely."[14] At the same time, countless Congress leaders and workers made great sacrifices and spent many years in jail for the cause of nationalism.

After the non-cooperation movement of 1920-22, in contrast to other provinces in India, attention in the Punjab came to focus on the political aspects of administration and legislation rather than on revolutionary nationalism with the goal of ousting the British from India. The dominant feature of Punjab politics until the mid-forties remained one of cooperation with the British within the new pattern of government established under the constitutional reforms of 1919 and 1935. The dominant political party in the Punjab was the Unionist party.

[13] Duni Chand, *The Ulster of India, or An Analysis of the Punjab Problems* (Lahore: n.p., 1936), pp. 142-43.

[14] Duni Chand, *Congress Service Series: Events of 1937 to 1946* (Indore: Bhargava Fine Art Printing Works, 1946), p. 2.

Established in 1923, the Unionist party was organized around the interests of the landowning rural classes, cutting across religious ties, as against the urban classes. Although this party championed the rights of the peasant proprietor class and pressed for the advancement of the rural areas in general, it was by no means a mass party but rather a party of the landed gentry, "who dominated the political life of the districts."[15] The Unionist leadership was a conservative one, favoring the British government as against the Congress party. Although the Unionist party was able to form a party government for a short period in the 1920s and was a powerful influence on legislation throughout the period, its major success came with the elections of 1937, under the new scheme of provincial autonomy. In a House of 175 the Unionist party won 101 seats, and after its ministry started functioning, more members joined to increase its strength to 120. The Unionist party in the legislature included nearly all the Muslim members, some two-fifths of all the Hindu members and more than half of the Sikh members.[16] (In the general population, the Muslims were roughly 55 per cent, the Hindus 30 per cent, and the Sikhs 15 per cent.)

The same elections also demonstrated the weakness of the Congress party. Its initial strength in the elections was only about 20. Later it increased to 35 after some victories in by-elections and after members of the Akali Dal joined it. An urban communal party of the Hindus was able to capture some 15 seats though it later lost some of them to the Congress party in by-elections. The major strength of the Congress party at this time lay with the Hindu community in the urban areas, but obviously even this group was not fully aligned with it. The Congress had little support in the Muslim community, even though many Muslims were prominent in the party. As for the Sikh community, though the Congress party had some support here, the major political groups were the Akali Dal and those allied with the Unionist party.

During the period of World War II, however, there occurred a great change in political alignments in the Punjab. The Muslim League, with its new-found slogan of Pakistan, became immensely popular among the Muslim masses, and the Hindu and Sikh communities rallied to the Congress party and the Akali Dal. Political loyalties polarized along communal lines; the Muslims were now with the Muslim League and the non-Muslims with the Congress party and the Akali Dal. These changes were reflected in the first post-war elections in 1946. The Muslim League won 75 seats, while the Unionist party won only 20, including 13 by Mus-

[15] Husain, *op.cit.*, p. 318.

[16] *The Indian Annual Register*, 1938, II, 223-24.

lims.[17] The Congress party won 51 seats, including one Muslim seat and several Sikh seats; and the Akali Dal won 23 seats.

Thus, it was not until the 1946 elections that the Congress party emerged as a major political force in the Punjab. Even then it was ineffective as far as the Muslim population was concerned, and though it did draw a significant amount of support from the Sikh community, its major strength came from the Hindu community. But even in the case of the Hindu community, it is obvious that its roots were not of long standing by the time the partition of the Punjab took place in 1947.

British Development Policy

Although there is no denying the introduction by the British government of several measures of economic modernization, no breakthrough occurred in this sphere during British rule. At the end of nearly a hundred years of British rule, more than 85 per cent of the population was illiterate. If industrialization is the essence of modernization, nothing of the kind occurred in the Punjab. The economy of the province remained agriculture-based, much as it was before the British annexation. The reasons for this lay in the interest of the industrial colonial power not only to maintain the colony as a market for the manufactured goods of the colonial power and as a supplier of raw materials for the colonial industry, but also to keep the province, in view of its strategic location, secure against any radical disturbance of its social structure and to preserve its peasantry as a reservoir for army recruitment. Added to this was the general hostility toward the urban classes that characterized the administration during much of British rule in the Punjab. On the other hand, the British did provide the Punjab with one of the finest irrigation systems in the world and a good network of railroads, though some parts of the Punjab remained relatively neglected.

The Social and Economic Environment

The Punjab, like its predecessor province, is a landlocked state, but it is of even greater importance in the defense of India as it borders on two hostile countries.* It has a long border with Pakistan to the west and a very short one with China to the northeast. To the north of it lies the state of Kashmir, to the south the state of Rajasthan, to the east Uttar Pradesh and Delhi, and in the northeast the state of Himachal Pradesh.

[17] Gopal Das Khosla, *Stern Reckoning: A Survey of the Events Leading up to and Following the Partition of India* (New Delhi: Bhawnani and Sons [1949]), p. 94.

* All references to the Punjab hereafter, unless otherwise indicated, are to the state as in existence in mid-1966.

The Punjab of today consists of those non-Muslim majority districts of the former province of Punjab which came to India's share consequent to the partition, plus more than half a dozen of the former princely states. Though lying within the boundaries of the Punjab, the princely states were at first constituted into a separate state called PEPSU (Patiala and East Punjab States Union), which remained in existence from 1948 to 1956 when it was merged with the Punjab.

Even though the merger of PEPSU with the Punjab increased the territory of the state, the Punjab with over 47,000 square miles, divided into some 20 districts, is still one of the smaller states in India; only West Bengal, Kerala, and Nagaland are smaller. On the other hand, it is the tenth largest state in terms of population: with only 4.0 per cent of the territory of India, the state has 4.6 per cent of the country's population. With 430 persons per square mile, compared to India's 370, the Punjab is among the more densely populated states. Between 1951 and 1961, the population of the Punjab increased by 25.8 per cent, from 16.1 million in 1951 to 20.3 million in 1961.[18]

Economically, the Punjab is among the privileged states in India. It has a higher per capita income than the all-India average and is among the three states with the highest per capita income. This is especially noteworthy in view of the higher density of population and the absence of gross inequalities in income in the population. The state has a flourishing agricultural economy, backed by a good irrigation system, and supplies more than its own needs. In the years since independence, there has developed a substantial amount of small-scale industry. Unemployment or underemployment in the state is not as serious a problem as it is in some other states of India.[19] The major problems in agriculture are the increase in waterlogging and soil erosion. In the field of industry, the major problems are the absence of large-scale capital and mineral resources. In both industry and agriculture, the state's major asset is an energetic and vigorous population. In the ten years between 1951 and 1961, there has been some increase in literacy, from 15.2 per cent in 1951 to 24.2 per cent of the population (all ages) in 1961, but this only brought the Punjab up to the all-India average.

There are several internal cleavages in the social structure of the Punjab which are important for their implications for the state's politics. One of the more important of these is religion. The mass migration following

[18] See India (Republic), *Census of India: Paper No. 1 of 1962* (Delhi: Manager of Publications, 1962).

[19] National Council of Applied Economic Research, *Techno-Economic Survey of Punjab* (New Delhi, 1962), p. 120.

the partition made for a drastic change in the religious distribution of the population. The state now consists almost entirely of Hindus and Sikhs. In terms of the 1961 census, the Hindus formed 63.7 per cent of the population, the Sikhs 33.3 per cent, and the remaining religious groups only another 3.0 per cent. Differing claims of the two communities have been extremely important in the politics of the state.

For certain educational, administrative, and governmental purposes, the state is divided into the Punjabi-speaking region and the Hindi-speaking region. It is disputable whether this is actually a linguistic division or a political concession to the Sikh community. At any rate, the two regions represent separate concentrations of Hindus and Sikhs. On a rough estimate, the Sikhs form about 55 per cent and the Hindus 42 per cent of the total population of the Punjabi-speaking region, which in 1961 was about 11.5 million. The Sikhs claim Punjabi in Gurmukhi script as a language and have obtained official recognition for it as one of the two official languages of the state—as the language for district administration, and with some option, as the medium of instruction in the Punjabi-speaking region. The Hindus of this region declare Hindi in Devnagari script as their mother tongue and consider Punjabi as a mere dialect of Hindi and, in the Gurmukhi script, as the religious medium confined to the Sikh community. By and large, the rural areas are Sikh and the urban areas Hindu in the Punjabi-speaking region, though both communities are spread all over the region—rural and urban.

In the Hindi-speaking region, whose population in 1961 was 8.8 million, the Sikhs account for less than 10 per cent, the Hindus about 90 per cent. This region, however, is not a compact unit, but may be considered to consist of two sub-regions. There is the Hariana region, consisting of the state's southeastern districts which are largely dry plains, though the expansion of irrigation facilities is changing its agricultural prospects. This region remained neglected during the British period when the irrigation schemes were concentrated in central and western Punjab. The other sub-region consists of the mountainous districts in two separate parts, one of Simla district and the other of the districts of Kangra, Kulu, and Lahaul and Spiti. In the town of Simla are located the headquarters of the Himachal Pradesh government, and Simla district has the highest proportion (48.6 per cent) of urban population among the districts of the Punjab. The districts of Kangra and Lahaul and Spiti are unconnected with the rest of the Hindi-speaking region and are very sparsely populated because of the extreme cold and the mountainous terrain.

The Hindi-speaking region has been a rather backward tract economically in the Punjab, and its economic backwardness has been the basis of political grievances. The Punjabi-speaking region, on the other hand, is more advanced, lying in the more favored areas from the viewpoint of climate, fertility of soil, and irrigation. It has better means of transportation, a higher rate of literacy, better developed educational facilities and is the center of greater industrial activity.

Several kinds of divisions make for internal differentiation within each of the two major religious groups of Hindus and Sikhs—divisions between urban and rural, high caste and low caste (even though caste as a social phenomenon is weaker in the Punjab than in other parts of India), reformist and orthodox, refugee and non-refugee, old sects and new sects. The major cleavage in the Sikh community is that of caste,[20] which may quite often be superimposed on class. One aspect of this cleavage is the division between the high-caste landowning agriculturist classes, the most prominent and predominant among them being the Jats, and the high-caste urban classes, primarily the Khatris and Aroras, in trading, business, and the professions. The second aspect of this cleavage, and an even more important one, is the division among the Sikhs in the rural areas as between the high-caste landowning agriculturist classes on the one hand, and on the other the Sikh Harijans, the former untouchables, and other depressed groups, who in the main constitute the landless agricultural labor and tenant and menial classes.

Among the Hindus, there is the major division between those in Hariana and those in the Punjabi-speaking region. Some cultural differences combine with the dominant rural-urban patterns in this division. The settlement of Punjabi refugees in Hariana has tended to build new networks of ties between the two regions in addition to certain religious and denominational ties. Another major division among the Hindus is that between the Arya Samaj, a reformist group in Hinduism, and the Sanatan Dharam, representing the more orthodox group. According to the 1931 census, the Arya Samaj group constituted less than 6 per cent of the Hindu population in the Punjab, but the importance of the group has been far beyond its small numbers. Apart from making a commendable contribution in the educational field in the state, this group has been the most articulate among the Hindus in the political sphere, providing leaders in considerable numbers from its ranks. In general, it has been in the forefront of activity in behalf of the Hindu community, and this has often brought it into conflict with other religious communities. The Arya Samaj today, however, is itself ridden with factional splits based on

[20] The term "caste" in the Punjab refers to more than hereditary occupational groups. It includes also tribes organized around the principle of community of blood as well as other groups at various stages between tribe and caste.

rural-urban and regional differences as well as the older conflict between vegetarians and non-vegetarians and is therefore no longer as politically effective. Among the Hindus, the socially and politically important caste groups have been the Khatris, Aroras and Aggarwals in the urban areas, and the Jats and Rajputs in the rural areas. The major split among the Hindus in the rural areas is, as in the case of the Sikhs, between the high-caste landowning agriculturist classes and the Harijans and other depressed classes. In the case of both Sikhs and Hindus, there are several sub-divisions within the major caste groups here mentioned.

Another cleavage in the social structure of the state is that between and within the rural and urban areas. Although the Punjab has made remarkable progress in the economic field, by 1961 only 20.1 per cent of the population lived in urban areas as against 19.0 per cent in 1951. However, this is still a higher figure than the all-India average of 18.0 per cent in 1961, as against the 1951 figure of 17.4 per cent. The urban population is not equally distributed among the different districts; some of them have roughly 30 per cent of the population in urban areas. According to the 1961 census, there were 187 towns in the Punjab with over 5,000 population or a local administration. There were five cities with a population of over 100,000 people (Amritsar, Ludhiana, Jullundur City, Patiala and Ambala Cantonment), but they all had a population of less than one half million. There is no one dominant urban center with the commanding influence or power of a Calcutta or Bombay, nor is there the phenomenon of explosive urban politics associated with large human concentrations on the pattern of Calcutta. Chandigarh, the modern new city designed by Le Corbusier, serves as the new capital of the state. Amritsar, near the Pakistan border, is the religious center of the Sikh community. The one-time cultural center of the Punjabi Hindus—Lahore—is now in Pakistan.

In 1961 79.9 per cent of the population lived in rural areas as against 81.0 per cent in 1951. According to 1951 figures, the agricultural population made up a little over 66 per cent of the state's total population. The peasantry of the Punjab is considered to be one of the finest in India.[21] As before, it contributes heavily toward military recruitment. Following the Sino-Indian crisis of 1962, the Punjab was in the forefront in providing both army recruitment and financial contributions. The Punjab has often been described as the land of the peasant proprietor, but the description hides the total reality of the situation. Of the agricultural

[21] Malcolm Lyall Darling, *At Freedom's Door* (London: Oxford University Press [1949]), p. 65.

population in 1951, cultivators of owned land formed, to be sure, 61.5 per cent, but cultivators of lands belonging to others constituted 22.7 per cent and landless agricultural laborers another 12.5 per cent. Landlords and rent-receivers made up 3.3 per cent of the total.[22]

Of the state's total population in 1951, 17 per cent consisted of refugees from West Pakistan. In the transfer of population following the partition, the Punjabi-speaking region was the most affected. In terms of the quality of population, the state made a distinct gain.[23] In return for the largely landless Muslim peasantry and artisan classes, it received the skilled Sikh agriculturist classes from the canal colonies, with the Jats as the dominant group, and high-caste Sikhs and Hindus belonging to the professional and business classes.[24] The refugees from West Pakistan, though initially largely homeless and destitute, have done well since partition and are better off than they were in their former homes. Although refugees may constitute an important social group for analysis of the political process, there does not exist in the Punjab the pattern of bitter "refugee politics" prevalent in West Bengal.

THE POLITICAL PROCESS

In any consideration of the political process in the Punjab, it is important to remember that the Punjab is not an autonomous political unit but is part of a larger federal system. As a consequence, political developments in the state are not only of important interest to the center but also implicate the center in the politics of the state in certain areas of interest. This is especially so in the Punjab because of the state's strategic border position and its proximity to New Delhi. Insofar as the center is concerned, the Punjab commands the same importance today as the Northwest Frontier Province had for the center before partition. The fact that the only land route to Jammu and Kashmir lies through this state further enhances its military significance. Thus it is of vital concern to the center that there be political stability in the state.

Of special relevance to a consideration of the political process in the Punjab is another aspect of the federal system in India—the fact that the political institutions of the state and the political values that these institutions embody are the given conditions for the political process in the Punjab. The state's political process occurs within—or in reference to, positively or negatively—political institutions which are not of the

[22] Figures calculated from *Census of India 1951*, VIII, Part II-B, 2-13.

[23] See John Voekel, "Punjab Politics: A Demographic Analysis" (unpublished M.A. thesis, University of California, Berkeley, 1964).

[24] *Ibid.*

state's own construction. The political values embodied in these political institutions, though having their origin in many sources, represent the commitment of the all-India leadership of the Congress party. Basically, these political values are: (1) national unity; (2) the secular state; and (3) democracy.[25]

Although these political values of the Congress party constitute the operative dominant values in the Indian political system and in the Punjab, their legitimacy has not been without challenge. A brief consideration of the ideological viewpoints of the major political parties of the Punjab illustrates this point. Apart from the Congress party, there are three major political parties in the Punjab, all of which are diametrically opposed to one or more elements of the value system of the Congress party. The Akali Dal, professing to be the sole spokesman of the Sikh community, stands for the inextricable mixture of religion and politics, in repudiation of the ideal of the secular state. Its separatist claims also run counter to the goal of national unity. The Jan Sangh aims at Hindu supremacy, again in repudiation of the secular state and with disruptive consequences for national unity. The Communist party provides for a totalitarian political framework as against the democratic institutions to which the Congress party is committed. If to these is added a new entrant on the political scene which as yet has not given a good account of its strength in the Punjab—the Swatantra party—one finds opposition to another dominant political value of the Congress party, that is, planned economic development in which both the public and private sectors have an important role to play.

A consideration of the value systems of the different political parties provides at the same time a refutation of the common notion that the Congress party is a non-ideological party whereas the opposition parties are parties of ideology. The Congress party stands opposed to the dominant ideology of every major opposition party. It is not so much that the Congress party is without an ideology as that its ideological values are embodied in the political institutions of the country.

The differences in the basic ideological value systems of the various political parties in the Punjab find concrete expression in the political process through major issues involving the political framework in the Punjab. One issue that has dominated the politics of the state in the years after independence concerns the reorganization of the state's boundaries;

25 For a discussion of the development of these values, see O. P. Goyal and Paul Wallace, "The Congress Party—A Conceptual Study," *India Quarterly*, April-June 1964, pp. 180-201.

and it has been responsible for throwing the state into a crisis every few years.

States Reorganization in the Punjab

The most vociferous and vigorous case for the reorganization of the state has been made by the Akali Dal in the form of its demand for Punjabi Suba, or a Punjabi-speaking state. The exact territorial limits of Punjabi Suba have undergone many changes since the demand was originally articulated, but in recent years the Akali Dal had asked for the conversion of the Punjabi-speaking region into a Punjabi Suba. The demand for the Suba was presented as being based on language, but Akali leaders from time to time made explicit their aim of establishing a state in which Sikhs as a religious community would be able to hold political power.[26]

The Punjabi Suba demand had its origins in the period before independence when the Akali Dal demanded a Pakistan-like political arrangement for the Sikhs. Although the British government was sympathetic to such a demand, it was handicapped by the fact that the Sikhs were not in a majority in any significant part of the Punjab. With partition, a radical change occurred in the demographic situation in the Punjab when the resettlement of Sikh refugees in the Punjab made the area now referred to as the Punjabi-speaking region a Sikh-majority area. Immediately after partition, the Akali Dal first pressed for an arrangement which would give the Sikh community political control in a definite area of India and later, as the movement for linguistic reorganization of states all over India gathered force, it pushed for Punjabi Suba on the basis of language. But Akali leaders, depending on the audience, argued for both the Sikh religion and the Punjabi language as the underlying rationale for demanding Punjabi Suba.

Several factors, stated and unstated, figure in the Akali aspiration for political power in the hands of the Sikh community as such in the Punjab region of India. There are, of course, the historical memories of the Sikhs having been the rulers in this area before the annexation of the region by the British. There is the feeling that the Sikh religion can survive in the modern world only in a state where the Sikhs are politically dominant. Behind this is the fear that unorthodoxy in some sections in the form of clipping and shaving of the hair would result in the assimilation of the Sikhs into Hinduism. Still another factor has been the belief

[26] For documentation on this point and for a detailed analysis of the Akali demand for Punjabi Suba as well as Akali resources and political strategies, see Baldev Raj Nayar, *Minority Politics in the Punjab* (Princeton: Princeton University Press, 1966).

that the dynamics of the Sikh religion, with its emphasis on the inseparability of religion and politics, make the aspiration for a Sikh zone of political power inevitable.

Demands for states reorganization from regions other than the Punjabi-speaking region in the Punjab dovetailed with the Akali demand for Punjabi Suba, inasmuch as they would result in the separation from the Punjab of precisely those areas the Akali Dal would want excluded in order to form Punjabi Suba. One such demand was for the formation of a separate Hariana state by putting together the Hariana region and the western districts of Uttar Pradesh on the plea that they were culturally akin and that the Punjabi-speaking region was exploiting the Hariana region economically and politically. If this were not feasible, Hariana leaders asked for the separation at least of Hariana region from the Punjab and its establishment as a separate state. After 1956, when some political concessions were made to the two regions in the Punjab, this demand seemed to lose momentum; one factor in the lessening of enthusiasm for Hariana state was the fear on the part of Hariana leaders that, since the Congress leadership was unwilling to split Uttar Pradesh, the removal of Hariana region from the Punjab would only result, since it was small in area, in the splintering of its various districts among the different adjoining states. Another demand for states reorganization came from the hill districts of Kangra, Kulu, and Lahaul and Spiti for merger with the hill state of Himachal Pradesh, on the basis that the state government in the Punjab, dominated by the people of the plains, had neglected the development of the area, and that a merger with Himachal Pradesh would be to their advantage in terms of development.

These various demands, however, were not without opposition. The Hindus of the Punjabi-speaking region and Hindu refugees in the Hindi-speaking region strongly opposed any plan to divide the Punjab into different states and even into any regions. In the forefront of opposition to the splitting of the Punjab were the Jan Sangh and the Arya Samaj. The Hindus argued that the demand for Punjabi Suba was an attempt to establish Sikh hegemony and a Sikh theocracy in the Punjab. For them, there was no linguistic basis for the demand as people all over the region spoke the same generic language with its various dialects. The Hindus of the Punjabi-speaking region considered the demand for Hariana state as one inspired by the Akali Dal. In order to undercut the linguistic basis of the demand for Punjabi Suba, they denied that Punjabi was their language, and proclaimed Hindi as their mother tongue, thus intensifying the resentment between the two major religious communities of the Punjab.

In their opposition to Punjabi Suba, the Hindus of the Punjabi-speaking region and Hindu refugees in the Hindi-speaking region were joined by the Harijans, both Hindu and Sikh and in both the Punjabi-speaking and Hindi-speaking regions. The underlying reason for their opposition was the fear that the Harijans would be placed in an even weaker position in relation to the high-caste landowning classes who would be dominant in each of the separate states. For its part, the nationalist leadership was against the establishment of a Punjabi Suba not only because it felt that a large segment of the population to be included in the Suba was opposed to it, but also because it was considered to be a threat to both national unity and the secular state, since the basic motive force behind the demand was religion. On the other hand, the Communist party supported the demand, but criticized the communal orientation given to it by the Akali Dal, and asked that the demarcation of the boundaries be made on a linguistic basis.

The demands for Punjabi Suba and Hariana state were carefully considered by the States Reorganization Commission. In its report in 1955, the Commission pointed out that there was no linguistic basis for the demand, for "the Punjabi and Hindi languages as spoken in the Punjab are akin to each other and are both well-understood by all sections of the people of the State."[27] It also expressed its belief that to constitute Punjabi Suba would perhaps mean the imposition of the will of a substantial minority on the majority that was opposed to it.[28] It feared that the establishment of Punjabi Suba would worsen communal conflict in the state rather than solve it. In its recommendations, the Commission proposed the merger of Punjab, PEPSU, and the Hindu-majority state of Himachal Pradesh. Nonetheless, the Akali Dal, which had just concluded a massive agitation against the government, was violently opposed to the recommendations of the Commission. Eventually, in a political settlement, known as the "regional formula," reached between the Akali Dal and the government of India, the Punjab and PEPSU were merged in 1956 into a single state known as the Punjab, but Himachal Pradesh was retained as a separate state. The Punjab was declared a bilingual state with both Punjabi and Hindi as its official languages but, as a concession to the Akali Dal and the Hariana area, two committees of the state legislature were established consisting respectively of the members from the Hindi-speaking region and the Punjabi-speaking region. These committees were given certain legislative powers dealing with economic development.

Subsequent to the political settlement in the form of the "regional

[27] India (Republic), *Report of the States Reorganization Commission* (Delhi: Manager of Publications, 1955), p. 141.

[28] *Ibid.*, p. 146.

formula," Akali leaders and members joined the Congress party, and it seemed the issue of states reorganization in the Punjab had finally been resolved. But soon the Akali Dal under the leadership of Master Tara Singh, who had dominated the organization since 1930, once again revived the demand for Punjabi Suba, alleging its non-formation to be based on discrimination against the Sikhs. In 1960 a militant agitation was launched by the Akali Dal in which thousands of volunteers packed the jails. As this failed to coerce the government, Sant Fateh Singh, a top lieutenant of Tara Singh, went on a fast-unto-death, but gave it up on the urging of his leader. Negotiations between the Akali Dal and the government that followed the giving up of the fast ended in failure. Then in August 1961 Tara Singh himself undertook a fast-unto-death, but the government under Nehru refused to be moved on the issue of Punjabi Suba. Finally he ended his forty-eight-day fast when the government agreed to set up a commission to investigate any charges of discrimination against the Sikhs. However, this commission found that there was no basis for any charge of discrimination.

Meanwhile, the failure to coerce the government led to mutual recriminations among Akali leaders and divisions within the Akali Dal. The Akali organization even lost some electoral support in the third general elections. The divisions within the Akali Dal now deepened, and finally in 1962 Sant Fateh Singh set up a rival Akali Dal to that of Master Tara Singh's. In the succeeding years, Sant Fateh Singh was successful in building a new coalition among the Akalis, and defeated the Tara Singh group in the gurdwara (Sikh temple) elections in early 1965. He now pressed with great vigor the Punjabi Suba demand, but he and his lieutenants increasingly emphasized that they, in contradistinction to Master Tara Singh and his followers, were interested in a linguistic state as an integral part of the Indian Union. On the other hand, Master Tara Singh and his group, increasingly isolated, demanded ambiguously a "self-determined status" for the Sikhs. At the same time, Hariana leaders now pressed with equal vigor their demand for a Hariana state, and soon leaders from the hill districts demanded merger of their area into Himachal Pradesh.

Faced with these demands, Prime Minister Shastri, who held talks with Sant Fateh Singh, took the stand that the government was ready to do anything for the advancement of the Punjabi language and look into any Sikh grievances, but felt that the issue of Punjabi Suba had been thoroughly examined before and that there was no basis for its establishment. Then in August 1965 Sant Fateh Singh issued an ultimatum to the government to accept the Suba demand within twenty-five days; otherwise he would go on a fast-unto-death effective September 10 for fifteen days and, in case he survived the fast, he would then resort to self-immolation by burning himself in the fashion of Buddhists in South Viet Nam.[29] From among the opponents to Punjabi Suba came threats of counter-fasts if the government conceded the demand. Sikh leaders in the Congress party were themselves divided over the issue. Some fifteen Congress Sikh MLAs (members of the Legislative Assembly) met to urge the government to accept the Punjabi Suba demand,[30] while other Sikh MLAs dissociated themselves from this stand.[31] A few held the method of self-immolation to be against the principles of the Sikh religion, and criticized the Sant for using the Golden Temple in Amritsar as a privileged sanctuary for political ends.

Meanwhile, the conflict with Pakistan took a violent form in August 1965 and, as it intensified in early September, Akali leaders asked Sant Fateh Singh to give up the idea of his projected fast in view of the emergency facing the nation. Union Home Minister Nanda also announced that "the whole question could be examined afresh."[32] The Sant finally withdrew his threat of self-immolation, and called upon the Punjabis, and the Sikhs in particular, to rise in the defense of the country. It was during the time of the war with Pakistan that the government seems to have come to the decision that, whatever its earlier position, the issue of states reorganization in the Punjab needed to be examined anew. Precisely what considerations went into this decision are not known, but it is well to note some of the changes that had occurred over the years in the political situation amid which the new decision took place.

First of all, there was the genuinely loyal commitment of the Sikh community, as of all other Punjabis, whether in the armed forces or not, to the defense of the country in a region directly involved in war operations. Furthermore, those areas that the Akali Dal wished excluded from the Punjab in order to form Punjabi Suba were now equally anxious to separate, and consequently opposition to Punjabi Suba could not have as sound a basis as before. Again, there was the power of the idea—in this case, linguistic reorganization—whose time had come; with linguistic reorganization as a plausible slogan, the Akali Dal could effectively rally those elements in the Sikh population that would otherwise not be so enthusiastic to oppose the government. Very importantly, the leadership of Master Tara Singh—the one most identified with the communal aspect of the Punjabi Suba demand—had been discredited among the Akali sections of the Sikh community. To be sure, the demand for Punjabi

[29] *The Tribune*, August 17, 1965.

[30] *Ibid.*, September 1, 1965.

[31] *Ibid.*, September 3, 1965.

[32] Quoted in *ibid.*, September 24, 1965.

Suba had its origin in communal aspirations; even Sant Fateh Singh—whose group had defeated the Tara Singh group in the gurdwara elections—headed an organization solely confined to members of the Sikh community, and he himself was securely lodged within a Sikh temple, yet he and his lieutenants consistently proclaimed, at least publicly, that they were against the idea of a communal state, but merely wanted linguistic reorganization, regardless of the religious composition of the new state. At the same time, the two Congress leaders who had personally come to symbolize stern opposition to Punjabi Suba—Nehru and Partap Singh Kairon—were no longer on the political scene. And then the withdrawal of the Sant from the path of self-immolation during the war with Pakistan finally provided the government with the occasion when it could change policy without the embarrassment of seeming to act under pressure of Akali threats.

At any rate, immediately after the cease fire with Pakistan, Home Minister Nanda announced the establishment of a three-member cabinet committee which would, with the advice of a consultative committee—drawn from among members of Parliament and headed by Lok Sabha speaker Hukam Singh—seek a solution to states reorganization in the Punjab.[33] There was criticism of the consultative committee of MPs not only because it attempted to assume an independent role, but also because its chairman had been associated with the Akali Dal and the Punjabi Suba demand earlier. A massive number of memoranda were submitted to the consultative committee, later supplemented by oral evidence. Several proposals were made to the committee, chief among them: (1) the formation of Punjabi Suba and Hariana state, and merger of the hill districts in Himachal Pradesh; (2) the Punjab to be a unilingual state, with Punjabi as its official language along with guarantees for Hindi in the Hindi region; (3) detachment of a few of the southeastern districts from the Punjab and the rest being declared a unilingual state with Punjabi as the official language; and (4) merger of Himachal Pradesh in the Punjab, and the establishment of three regions—Punjabi, Hindi and hill—with substantial autonomy. However, nothing but the establishment of Punjabi Suba was acceptable to the Akali Dal. The Congress government and party in the Punjab, though divided, officially stood for the retention of the status quo. The Jan Sangh continued to oppose any plan that would result in the division of the Punjab. Meanwhile, the Congress high command also started giving consideration to the Punjabi Suba

[33] *Ibid.*

issue[34] and appointed a three-member committee of its own—consisting of Kamaraj, Dhebar, and Nanda—to help in the solution of the problem.

The consultative committee consisting of MPs was expected to submit its report by mid-March 1966, but by the end of February Sant Fateh Singh began to express dissatisfaction at the slow pace with which the work of the committees was proceeding and threatened to revive his plan of self-immolation unless a decision favoring the establishment of Punjabi Suba was made. Then on March 9, 1966, the Congress Working Committee passed a resolution recommending that "out of the existing State of Punjab, a State with Punjabi as the State Language be formed."[35] This decision was met with militant opposition from the expected quarters in the Punjab, and there was some resort to violence, but the opposition soon subsided and the opponents of Punjabi Suba gradually reconciled themselves to the decision. Later, the consultative committee of MPs submitted its report recommending that the Punjabi-speaking region be constituted into a unilingual Punjabi state, that the hill areas be merged with Himachal Pradesh, and that the Hariana region be formed into a Hariana state.[36] On March 22 Home Minister Nanda announced in the Lok Sabha that the government had accepted in principle the reorganization of the state on a linguistic basis,[37] and on April 18 he stated that the government proposed to create by October 1, 1966 two states—Punjab and Hariana—out of the existing state of the Punjab, while the hill areas contiguous to Himachal Pradesh would be merged in that state. Later, a three-man commission was appointed for the demarcation of the boundaries, and asked to report by the end of May 1966. The commission was told to demarcate on the basis of, among other things, the language principle, taking into account the 1961 census. This aroused criticism among the Akali leadership because of its fear that certain choice areas, like the hill station Dalhousie, the Una tahsil with the Bhakra-Nangal complex, and the modern capital of Chandigarh, would not come to Punjabi Suba as a result of the application of the 1961 census, because of its belief that Hindus of these areas had declared their language to be Hindi. The Akali Dal wanted the government to apply census data of any census between 1891 and 1931, ignoring the vast changes that may have taken place since then. On the other hand, the Hariana leadership, until then in a sort of alliance with the Akali Dal, declared that only the application of the 1961 census in the demarcation

34 *Ibid.*, February 14, 1966.

35 *Hindu Weekly Review*, March 14, 1966.

36 *Ibid.*, March 21, 1966.

37 *Ibid.*, April 25, 1966.

of boundaries would be acceptable.[38] Meanwhile, Master Tara Singh, faced with a possible complete loss of his own leadership in the Sikh community, demanded, in line with his earlier thinking, that Punjabi Suba should be vested with the right of secession from the Indian Union.[39] The decision to form Punjabi Suba in all but name is an accomplished fact, but disputes and campaigns about boundary alignments and adjustments are likely to continue in the future.

Other Issues in Punjab Politics

There have been several other important issues in Punjab politics but not of the order of importance of the question of states reorganization. One of these pertains to the countless charges of government discrimination against various religious groups and regions of the state. Hindus and Sikhs, the hill districts and Hariana, all express grievances against the government about discriminatory treatment in recruitment to the civil services, in political representation, and in financial allocations. In 1961, the government established a commission to inquire into any charges of discrimination against the Sikh community, but the Akali Dal refused to provide evidence. Other groups have insisted upon such an inquiry commission to look into their charges.

Another important issue is the question of language study. Hindus in the Punjab have expressed opposition to the compulsory study of Punjabi in schools in the state. On the other hand, the Sikhs strongly oppose any plan that does away with the compulsory study of Punjabi. The Hindus in the Punjabi-speaking region also oppose the present policy which makes Punjabi the only official language for district administration in that region. It is quite likely that the Hindus in the reorganized Punjab may press for the recognition of Hindi as a second official language apart from Punjabi or for the recognition of Devnagari as an additional script in which Punjabi may be written.

The subject of corruption among politicians and in the administrative services has been a serious issue in Punjab politics. The issue has been present in political discussions since partition, but was argued with special force during the tenure of Partap Singh Kairon as chief minister from 1956 to 1964 and was directed against him personally and his lieutenants. He was charged with favoritism and corruption at all levels of the administration. It was said that he favored his relatives and political supporters and victimized his political opponents. Eventually, the opposition parties and several dissident members of the Congress party en-

[38] *Ibid.*, May 9, 1966.

[39] See editorial, *ibid.*, May 23, 1966.

gaged in a noisy campaign, forcing the government of India to establish a commission of inquiry, known as the Das Commission, to investigate these charges. The commission found Kairon guilty of having indulged in conduct that was "unbecoming and reprehensible," having used his influence and powers to further his family's interests, and having "connived at the doings of his sons and relatives."[40] After Kairon's resignation, the new ministry launched a program of what has been called "de-Kaironization"—removing and transferring officials who were implicated in the Kairon "affair."

An issue which is going to assume increasing importance in the future is related to the demands of Harijans for greater attention to their needs, especially in relation to distribution of land among their landless laborers. The Harijans are among the new classes that are being increasingly mobilized in the political process. The feeling among the Harijan leaders, cutting across party lines, has been that the political leadership of the ruling party—as also of the Akali Dal and the Communist party—has been in the hands of the landowning classes and consequently has been slow in enacting land reforms legislation and active in frustrating its implementation. The Harijans feel that, without redistribution of land, all the privileges given to them in the fields of government, politics, and education are useless. The future may see intensified agitational activity on the part of Harijans, regardless of party affiliations, to secure their demands.

The rural-urban conflict, though finding expression in political discussion and strategy, does not present itself in the same strident form as it did before partition. The tension between the rural and urban classes is however there. The urban classes feel that the political leadership of the governing party is dominated by the rural classes who have sought increasingly to squeeze the urban classes. On the other hand, the rural classes feel that the urban classes, being more advanced, are able to take greater advantage of the expanding government services. In contrast to the pre-partition period, the rural-urban conflict is not expressed through separate major political groups, but rather at times takes the form of influencing the factional struggles within existing political parties. At the time of the first general elections, the Zamindara League emerged as a successor to the Unionist party, but its demise as the result of its merger in the Congress party in 1956 brought an end to the organization of political parties on a rural basis. In any case, the rural bloc has been the predominant group in the Congress party, the Akali Dal, and the Com-

[40] *The Tribune*, June 22, 1964.

munist party. The Jan Sangh, although not confined to the urban areas, does not command much strength in the rural areas.

Another issue in Punjab politics concerns the resistance of groups benefiting from economic development to share some of these benefits in the form of increased taxation. A betterment levy imposed by the government on those benefiting from certain types of public works provoked a militant and vigorous agitation against the government in 1959.

Party Politics in the Punjab

The party system in the Punjab may be characterized, as in the case of the larger political system in India, as a system of one-party dominance. Although such a characterization may be justified in that the same political party has been the governing party since the achievement of independence in 1947, the dominance of the Congress party in the Vidhan Sabha (lower house of the Punjab) has not consistently approached the level of dominance of the Congress party in the Lok Sabha. In the 1962 general elections the Congress party won more than 72 per cent of the seats in the Lok Sabha, but in the Punjab it secured only a little more than 58 per cent of the seats in the Vidhan Sabha. However, in terms of vote percentage and the fragmentation of the opposition, the Punjab reflects the situation at the national level.

The Congress Party

The year 1947 saw a change in the position of the Congress party in the Punjab. From an opposition group agitating for independence, it became the governing party in the state. Although an integral part of the all-India nationalist movement, the Congress party in the Punjab did not develop into a mass party or a mass movement. It was not successful in mobilizing political support in equal measure from all the communities, and it was not until the end of World War II that it was able to secure the support of an overwhelming part of the Hindu community. Since independence, however, the Congress party has managed to stay in power in the state by winning a majority of seats in three general elections. If electoral statistics are an index of popular strength, the Congress party in the years since independence has increased its support in the population.

In 1952 it had secured only 34.8 per cent of the vote polled. In 1957 it increased its share of the popular vote polled to 47.5 per cent, primarily as a result of the merger into it in 1956 of the Akali Dal in the Punjabi-speaking region and of the Zamindara League in the Hindi-speaking region. In 1962, even though the Akali Dal was once again the major political opponent in the Punjabi-speaking region and several important Congress leaders had defected from the party in the Hindi-speaking region, the Congress party was still able to secure 43.7 per cent of the vote polled. At the same time, although the popular vote for the Congress party declined in 1962 by only 3.8 percentage points, the party suffered a severe loss in the number of seats won. From 120 seats won in a House of 154 in 1957, the figure dropped down to 90 seats in 1962. This was largely a result of the increased cooperation among several of the opposition parties, primarily in the Punjabi-speaking region, in providing a joint opposition to the Congress party in the elections. On the other hand, one may note the "lodestone" feature of the Congress party—that is, its ability after the elections to attract to the party non-Congress members, especially from the ranks of "independents." Sometimes such members are really Congressmen who choose to run as independents when they cannot get Congress tickets for the elections. Through accepting these members, the Congress party is able to increase its majority and sometimes survive considerable defections of its own members.

On a regional basis, from the viewpoint of the popular vote the Congress party showed greater strength in the 1962 elections in the Punjabi-speaking region than in the Hindi-speaking region. Compared to the

TABLE 9.1

RESULTS OF THREE GENERAL ELECTIONS IN THE PUNJAB[a]

	1952		*1957*		*1962*	
Political Group	*% of vote*	*no. of seats*	*% of vote*	*no. of seats*	*% of vote*	*no. of seats*
Congress party	34.8	122[b]	47.5	120[b]	43.7	90
Akali Dal	14.7	33	—	—	11.9	19
Communist party	5.3	6	13.6	6	7.1	9
Jan Sangh	5.0	2	8.6	9	9.7	8
Republican party (SCF)	2.3	1	5.4	5	2.2	—
Swatantra party	—	—	—	—	3.9	3
Praja Socialist party	4.1	1	1.2	1	0.9	—
Independents	25.3	—	23.7	13	17.1	18
Others	8.5	21[b]	—	—	3.5	7
Totals	100.0	186	100.0	154	100.0	154
% voting (based on valid votes)	56.3		58.0		62.7	

[a] For the 1952 elections, the figures for Punjab and PEPSU have been combined in this table.

[b] Including one member elected unopposed.

1957 elections, the Congress party vote declined far more in the Hindi-speaking region than in the Punjabi-speaking region. However, the Congress party managed in 1962 to win a larger percentage of seats in the Hindi-speaking region than in the Punjabi-speaking region. This seems to be a result of the lack of any organized and coherent opposition in the Hindi-speaking region.

The Congress party seems to draw its electoral support from all sections of the population, but the extent of this support varies from region to region and from district to district. Thus, in the 1962 elections it was able to win six out of ten rural Sikh-majority constituencies in Amritsar district, but only two out of six such constituencies in Ludhiana district. Similarly, it won both urban Hindu-majority constituencies in Jullundur district, but lost two out of the three urban constituencies in Amritsar district. Again, in the Hindu-majority Hariana region, the Congress party was able to win 7 out of 14 seats in the Karnal district, but only 3 out of 10 in Hissar district. The specific electoral outcome in a particular district or constituency is related among other things to the nature of factional divisions within the state or local Congress party and to the relative strength of the Akali Dal or Jan Sangh.

Several factors seem to work in favor of the Congress party in its attempt to gain electoral support. As a secular, broad-based political party, standing for the protection of all religious and minority groups and ready to accommodate them within its fold, the Congress party is able to receive the votes of all those groups which fear domination by an opposing group. Thus, in a Sikh-majority constituency, it is likely to get the votes of Hindus and Harijans who would not like to see an Akali or Communist Sikh candidate elected.[41] On the other hand, in a Hindu-majority constituency in the Punjabi-speaking region, the Congress party is likely to get the votes of Sikhs and Harijans who would not like to see a Jan Sangh candidate elected. Thus, the Congress party may turn out to be the beneficiary of a situation in which groups do not like the Congress party so much as distrust the other political parties and the groups they represent. In such a situation, the electoral support for the Congress party may not reflect any attachment to the party or to the political system it seeks to uphold. Some would even say that the Congress party is really most unpopular in the Punjab. But even if only as a second preference, it manages to roll up the largest plurality of popular votes.

[41] See Baldev Raj Nayar, "Religion and Caste in the Punjab: Sidhwan Bet Constituency," in Myron Weiner and Rajni Kothari (eds.), *Indian Voting Behaviour: Studies of the 1962 General Elections* (Calcutta: Firma K. L. Mukhopadhyay, 1965), pp. 123-40.

One cannot explain the Congress party electoral strength, however, merely by reference to the alleged fear of each other on the part of different groups, for the Congress party secures victories in many constituencies in which a single religious group is in an overwhelming majority. Especially noteworthy in this connection is the victory of its Muslim candidate, Khan Abdul Ghaffar Khan, in the completely non-Muslim constituency of Ambala City in each one of the last three general elections.

Also of aid to the Congress party in its efforts to mobilize support is the prestige of being the government party and particularly the ability to utilize government patronage and government welfare activities in securing support. But patronage does not automatically make for political support, and the Congress party has given a poor electoral performance in some of the best-nursed constituencies, for example that of the then Chief Minister, Partap Singh Kairon, in 1962.

Although the Congress party has been the dominant political party in the Punjab, it has not been a monolithic and disciplined party, but has instead been characterized by multi-factionalism. Within the basic political framework of the Congress party there may be at any one time small or large ideological groups ranging from the left to the right, communal groups of Hindus and Sikhs, regional groups standing for the interests of different regions, caste groups such as Jats and Harijans; most important, there are the personal factions, cutting across ties of ideology, religion, caste, class, and region. There may be several of these factions—every minister in the government may have a faction of his own, so may an important individual. But most of these smaller factions may be aggregated into two, three or four larger factions under the leadership of some important political leaders. In this factional system, loyalties are not always constant. The factional leader may try to attract to himself whole opposing factions or members thereof and also to absorb more completely the smaller factions within his own faction.

The conflict between various factions in the Congress party at the state level may be generalized throughout the party and be present in both its wings—the ministerial wing and the organizational wing—and the two wings may themselves be in conflict if different factions are dominant within each. One political scientist characterizes the conflict between the two wings as constituting the real two-party system in India.[42] Although this has been true to a certain extent at various periods in the history of the Congress party in the Punjab, at other times both wings have been under the control of a single dominant faction.

[42] See Rajni Kothari, "Party System," *Economic Weekly*, June 3, 1961.

The presence of these factions and the struggles among them for achieving a dominant position within the party have several important consequences for the political process. Although the Congress party has continued in office indefinitely without the opportunity for another party to form an alternative government, the various factions within the party have kept it sensitive to changes in public opinion and public pressure.[43] As various political sentiments in the state are represented in the party to a greater or lesser degree, fluctuations in public opinion and changes in the configuration of political forces in the state have repercussions inside the party and may generate changes in political policy and style. Factions within the Congress party, and even important individuals, influence the political process at this time through the exercise of subtle pressure, public criticism, threats of bolting the party, conniving or openly siding with the opposition parties, and actually seceding from the party. Those that secede may return after some political concessions have been made by the party, but if in the process relations have been deeply embittered, they may choose to stay out, providing in the future a constant irritant for the Congress party. In this fashion, even though continuously in office, the Congress party is kept responsive to changes and pressures in the political environment.[44]

Apart from performing this function in the political process, the conflict among the factions also provides the Congress party at the center (hereafter referred to as the Congress high command even though the term has reference to a specific institution) with great leverage to intervene in and influence the affairs of the party in the Punjab. The high command has served as the mediator and arbiter between the factions, and at times the decision-maker for the party in the Punjab. Even when there has been a dominant faction in the party, the smaller factions have been vocal and persistent enough to involve the high command in the affairs of the state party. At times, the fortunes of the factions in the state have been influenced by the relative position of factions in the Congress high command to which they were linked. A closer look at the history of the Congress party in the Punjab since independence provides us with a better understanding of the factional process. Four major periods can be distinguished in this history.

[43] For an analysis of this point on an all-India basis, see Rajni Kothari, "The Congress 'System' in India," *Asian Survey*, IV, No. 12 (December 1964), 1161-73.

[44] One author holds this to be another form of democracy, in which the opposition does not have the opportunity to form an alternative government but the governing party is responsive to shifts in public opinion; see Amitai Etzioni, "Alternative Ways to Democracy: The Example of Israel," *Political Science Quarterly*, LXXIV, No. 2 (June 1959), 196-214.

1. From 1947 to 1951. In this period, the Congress party was torn by the conflict between two almost equal groups, with members often switching loyalties. In addition, there was serious tension between the ministerial and organization wings of the party. The conflict between the various groups not only made for ministerial instability, but also made possible and necessary frequent intervention by the Congress high command, and further provided a non-Congress political party the opportunity to influence the fortunes of each group and, in turn, obtain political concessions toward its objectives.

As the partition took place, Dr. Gopi Chand Bhargava took over the administration of east Punjab, along with Swaran Singh, a leader from the Akali Dal. Later, Congress MLAs of the Punjab legislature, whose constituencies were in that part of the Punjab which came to India's share, met and elected Bhargava to the position of the leader of the Congress legislature party and thus to the position of chief minister (then called premier). Bhargava then expanded his ministry, and brought in Ishar Singh Majhail as a minister. Majhail and Swaran Singh represented one of the two major groups in the Akali Dal—the Majhail-Nagoke group, which was considered pro-Congress, and the Giani Kartar Singh group, which though traditionally opposed to the Congress party favored Bhargava.

Soon, however, it was obvious that the Congress party was divided between two groups—the Bhargava group and the Satya Pal group. These two groups had their origins in the period before partition. In certain electoral contests in the 1920s, conflict developed between Lala Lajpat Rai, a prominent Congress leader of national stature, and Dr. Satya Pal, who supported two other important Congress leaders, Lala Duni Chand of Ambala and Dewan Chaman Lal. After Lajpat Rai's death, Bhargava succeeded to the leadership of his group.[45] Though Bhargava was born in a town in the Hindi-speaking region, he had settled in Lahore after finishing his medical education and was identified with the urban classes.

Up to about 1938 the Satya Pal group was in power in the Congress party, but then with the assistance of the Akalis, who had joined the Congress party, and of the Congress high command, the Bhargava group came into power in the party organization and continued in that position until after independence. Among the important Akalis that had come into the Congress party and into the Bhargava group at this time were Partap Singh Kairon and Gurmukh Singh Musafir. They chose to re-

[45] Pandit Nanak Chand, "The New East Punjab Cabinet," *The Tribune*, April 22, 1949.

main with the Congress party even after serious differences developed between the party and the Akali Dal.

In the 1946 elections the Bhargava group was unable to obtain a majority in the Congress legislature party in the Punjab. Since the differences between Bhargava and Chaman Lal, the two protagonists for the leadership of the legislature party, were unbridgeable, Bhim Sen Sachar, an urban Hindu leader, was elected as leader of the party.[46] Sachar seemed neutral enough for the position and was also perhaps favored by Maulana Azad personally. Even though Sachar had been a member of the Bhargava group, relations between him and Bhargava began to worsen. After his election, Sachar briefly served as a minister in the Unionist-Congress-Akali coalition ministry.

After the partition, Sachar's constituency fell in the Pakistan area, as did those of many other Hindu and Sikh MLAs, and Bhargava was elected unanimously the leader at the direction, it is believed, of Sardar Patel. It was common knowledge in political circles in the Punjab that Patel had always favored the Bhargava group, while Nehru and Azad preferred the Satya Pal group.

After the Bhargava ministry had been functioning for some time, differences between the ministerial and organizational wings of the party came to the fore. The party organization severely criticized the ministry for being under the direction of the Akalis, for giving the Akalis all the key positions in the administration, and for not consulting the party organization. Meanwhile, all those MLAs from west Punjab who had migrated to the Punjab were allowed to be included in the assembly. This brought Bhim Sen Sachar again in the Assembly, and he soon became the leader of the Satya Pal group, which later became known as the Sachar group.

Opposition to Bhargava now increased, and it became obvious in certain elections to the Constituent Assembly that he did not command majority support in the Congress legislature party. There was uncertainty now whether he would be re-elected leader of the party at a forthcoming meeting. At this time, the Akali Dal, whose two groups had already been working in alliance with Bhargava, instructed the Akali party in the Punjab legislature to disband itself and join the Congress party, thus assuring the election of Bhargava to the leadership of the party since the party was about evenly divided between the Bhargava and Sachar groups. With the joining of the Akali Dal and of some other members, the Punjab Legislative Assembly became totally a Congress

[46] *The Statesman*, January 16, 1956.

assembly of nearly 80 members. Subsequently, in 1948, Bhargava was elected to the leadership again, but he made changes in the ministry in accordance with the wishes of Giani Kartar Singh, who himself was now included in the ministry.

The Bhargava ministry, however, continued to be subjected to criticism by the party organization and members of the opposing factions. But in response to the wishes of the Congress high command, Bhargava was in March 1949 re-elected leader unanimously. This did not prevent conflict from developing among the various groups over shares in the ministry and the particular persons to be taken in the ministry. The Giani Kartar Singh group, until now in alliance with Bhargava, decided to support the Sachar group as did some other dissidents led by Shri Ram Sharma.[47] Three weeks after having been elected leader unanimously, Bhargava was faced with a no-confidence motion, but before it was moved he resigned. Bhim Sen Sachar was then elected leader of the Congress assembly party.[48]

Sachar, however, was not a favorite of the dominant faction of the Congress high command led by Sardar Patel, and he immediately encountered difficulties in the tasks ahead. To begin with, he was instructed to form a "composite" ministry, including three members of the Bhargava group utterly opposed to him. Since the latter owed their positions to the high command, they felt little need to give Sachar any cooperation. Sachar, however, had the support of Nehru. As chief minister, Sachar launched a campaign against black-marketing and corruption in the administration and among political leaders. Several members of the Bhargava group seemed directly implicated by Sachar's inquiries into corruption, and they turned their efforts now to overthrow him, openly campaigning against his leadership. They organized "signature campaigns," with memoranda to the Congress high command making allegations against Sachar.

On the basis of these allegations the Congress high command ordered Sachar, while Prime Minister Nehru was out of the country on his trip to the United States, to seek a vote of confidence on extremely short notice, giving him no opportunity to reply to the allegations or to reconstitute his ministry before such a vote. Meanwhile, the Akalis were bargaining with both Sachar and Bhargava and obtained a settlement of the language question favorable to the Akali Dal by promising continued support to one and a switch-over to the other. Eventually, they threw their support behind Bhargava. Sachar then resigned, and in October 1949 Bhargava

[47] *The Tribune*, April 8, 1949.
[48] *Ibid.*, April 7, 1949.

once again became chief minister of the Punjab. Sachar had been in office only about six months.

Bhargava did not have smooth sailing in his office. He was under constant pressure, primarily from Giani Kartar Singh, to reshuffle his ministry to accommodate Akali interests, and the ministry underwent several changes. Many Congress leaders were extremely critical of Bhargava for allegedly being under the dictates of the Akali group. Their major point of attack was that the ministry was not really representative of Congressmen, since it included Akalis and really rested on the artificial majority of the Bhargava group created by Akalis now posing as Congressmen. At the same time, the gulf between the ministerial wing and the organizational wing was as wide as ever. Partap Singh Kairon, who had been excluded from the Bhargava ministry at the insistence of Giani Kartar Singh, now became president of the Congress party organization in the Punjab. Though earlier a member of the Bhargava group, he was now thoroughly opposed to Bhargava. In this opposition he was joined by two other important members of the Bhargava group—Gurmukh Singh Musafir, several times president of the Punjab Congress, and Lala Jagat Narain, a Hindu Congress leader.

The Kairon group now joined hands with the Sachar group to bring forward a motion of no-confidence against Bhargava. However, this motion was defeated in a narrow vote, with the solid support of the two Akali factions behind Bhargava. Realizing the narrow vote in the legislature party and the fact that the Bhargava group did not have any strength in the party organization, the Congress high command asked Bhargava to reorganize his ministry. It instructed him to submit a list of ten members, elected on the basis of proportional representation from the Congress legislature party so as to give representation to the various groups, from which the high command would then select six members for a new ministry. The Bhargava group first rejected this suggestion,[49] but then accepted it and a list was submitted. The high command, in turn, gave him its list of suggested ministers, but since this did not include the names of Giani Kartar Singh and Isher Singh Majhail,[50] on whose support Bhargava was so dependent, Bhargava refused to accept the high command's directive.[51] Meanwhile, elections to the Congress Election Board in the Punjab showed the complete weakness of Bhargava in the party organization; all eight seats on the board went to the Sachar-Kairon group. Kairon therefore insisted on a ministry which would be

[49] *Ibid.*, May 13, 1951.
[50] *Ibid.*, May 23, 1951.
[51] *The Statesman*, May 24, 1951.

representative of the Congress and the people of the state.[52] At the same time, Nehru was infuriated at Bhargava's defiance of the high command. Finally, Bhargava was instructed to resign, and President's Rule was imposed in the state in June 1951, much to the relief of the general public.[53] Bhargava publicly complained that he had become the first victim of the attempt by the high command, after the death of Sardar Patel, to oust such people as were considered to have been loyal to Patel. Bhargava later contested the 1952 elections in opposition to the Congress party, but lost even his security deposits in both constituencies from which he ran. Several years later he returned to the Congress party and was made a minister in the government.

2. *From 1952 to 1956.* In this period, initially a dominant faction emerged in the Congress party under a duumvirate leadership. Later, both as a result of internal rivalry and external political pressures, this faction disintegrated into two, one of which finally emerged as the leading faction with the support of the Congress high command. During the whole period, the high command was constantly involved in the affairs of the party in the Punjab. Its final decision between the split factions was also influenced to a great extent by the activities of an opposition political party.

As President's Rule had been imposed in the state in 1951, the organizational wing of the Congress party became all important in the 1951-52 elections. Kairon was at the time the president of the Punjab Congress party. From this point began his rise to political power in the Punjab. His chief lieutenant in the party at the time was Lala Jagat Narain, a remarkable campaigner and organization man. Narain, a member of the Arya Samaj, was identified with the urban classes. The results of the first general elections were a surprise to the Congress party itself. Though it received only 37 per cent of the votes, it won 96 seats out of 126 seats in the Punjab Vidhan Sabha (PEPSU at this time was a separate state). The Congress had won a majority of both Hindu-majority and Sikh-majority constituencies. After the elections, the number of Congress MLAs increased to 100 as others joined the party.

In the Congress legislature party, the group led by Kairon and Narain was the largest, with perhaps a majority, while the other groups were small, most of them with no more than ten members each.[54] The newly

52 *The Tribune*, June 1, 1951.

53 *Hindusthan Standard*, June 25, 1951.

54 *The Tribune*, March 16, 1952. This newspaper gives the breakdown of the various groups as follows: Kairon-Narain, about 50; Sachar 11; Udham Singh Nagoke 6; Ranjit Singh 7; Satya Pal 5; Ram Kishan 5; Shri Ram Sharma 6; Khan Abdul Ghaffar Khan 3; "fluid element" 6.

elected Congress MLAs announced that they would leave the choice of the leader of the Congress legislature party to Prime Minister Nehru.[55] Even though the Kairon-Narain group was the leading group, with Kairon as its top leader, the Congress high command chose to recommend Bhim Sen Sachar, who did not have a base in the party organization but was known to be a man of integrity. Sachar was then elected unanimously by the legislature party. The reasons for the high command's choice are believed to be several: that Maulana Azad personally liked Sachar, that the civil service officers were opposed to Kairon for he had given a statement some time earlier that 90 per cent of the government officers were corrupt, and that Punjab ought to have a Hindu chief minister and PEPSU a Sikh chief minister.

Sachar included both Kairon and Narain in his ministry, and it seems that the real men of power behind the scenes were the latter two. Sachar had some difficulty in carrying the whole cabinet with him. He clashed with several members of the party and alienated important individuals—Shri Ram Sharma, Abdul Ghani Dar, and Kedar Nath Sehgal. In this controversy, the high command sided with Sachar. However, the opposing leaders toured the state, spreading propaganda against the ministry. Finally, they were expelled from the party for their anti-Congress activities, but Sharma complained that the Congress high command, with Maulana Azad in charge of Punjab affairs, was acting in a partisan manner. Sharma and his colleagues formed in 1954 a new political party, the Gandhi Janata party, but returned to the Congress party in 1956.

However, the coalition of Kairon and Narain soon began to fall apart. There was a clash of ambitions between the two as both apparently believed that since Sachar did not have a political base in the ministerial or organizational wings, he could not continue indefinitely. The differences between the two came into the open in early 1955 when Narain resigned from the party executive in protest against its formation without the persons that he wanted included.[56] He obviously detected an attempt to undermine his position in the party organization. He later withdrew his resignation, but the gulf between Kairon and Narain widened. In addition to the conflict of political ambitions were certain policy differences, primarily at this time the question of nationalization of motor transport in the state. Narain favored nationalization whereas Kairon, who drew considerable backing, financial and otherwise, from this Sikh-controlled industry, was against it. As the differences between

[55] *Ibid.*, February 26, 1952.
[56] *Hind Samachar*, November 13, 1956.

the two leaders became wider, some opposition leaders brought charges of corruption and maladministration against Narain. This tactic, it was believed, had been engineered by the Kairon group, and perhaps Kairon personally, in order to destroy Narain politically. However, the charges were found to be frivolous,[57] and the Congress high command exonerated Narain. The incident, however, made for increased bitterness.

The Kairon group now turned against Sachar for having supported Narain in the matter of the charges that had been made against him. The attacks by the Kairon group on both Sachar and Narain brought the latter two closer together. The Kairon group also started a signature campaign against Narain, protesting to the high command that Narain was a communalist.[58] They then turned their attention to ousting Sachar from the position of chief minister.

Meanwhile, Sachar was confronted with a political situation which rendered him open to attack. The Akali Dal launched a massive agitation in 1955 over the issue of shouting slogans for Punjabi Suba. Since such slogans inevitably invited counter-slogans, increased communal tension, and raised the possibility of communal riots, the Punjab government imposed a ban on the shouting of slogans. In the agitation against the ban, some 12,000 Akali volunteers courted arrest. While some Congress Sikh leaders criticized the Akali Dal for the agitation, others asked the government to conciliate the moderate sections of the Akali Dal. Finally, when Sachar withdrew the ban, the Akalis interpreted this as a sign of weakness, but so did many Congress leaders. The Kairon group now moved to exploit this situation.

The Congress party organization under Kairon's control officially disapproved of Sachar's action in removing the ban. Memoranda were submitted to the Congress high command asking for Sachar's removal from leadership as he had proven a failure in dealing with the Akali Dal. Most of the signatures on such memoranda were those of Hindu leaders from Hariana, who had now joined with Kairon. Deputations called on the high command, and in these activities Ch. Devi Lal and Professor Sher Singh, prominent leaders of Hariana, played a leading role, asking for Sachar's removal. The real target in all this, however, was Jagat Narain, who was now allied with Sachar.[59]

To the conflict of ambitions were added differences over the report of the States Reorganization Commission concerning the Punjab. The Punjab ministry under Sachar had recommended to the high command that Punjab, PEPSU, and Himachal Pradesh should be immediately

[57] *Times of India*, April 28, 1955.

[58] *Ibid.*, July 5, 1955.

[59] *The Statesman*, August 4, 1955.

merged. Kairon had first supported this proposal, but later finding that the high command seemed decided not to merge Himachal Pradesh with the Punjab, equivocated over the issue and finally favored exclusion of Himachal Pradesh. Gurmukh Singh Musafir, an ally of Kairon, told the high command as president of the Punjab Congress that the party was in favor of the exclusion of Himachal Pradesh. At this, prominent members of the Sachar-Narain group organized a convention, and declared that they wanted the Commission's report implemented in full insofar as the Punjab was concerned and further that the views conveyed by Musafir did not represent the feelings of the party. For this they were threatened with disciplinary action by the Punjab Congress executive, which was now dominated by the Kairon group.[60] Several attempts by the high command to bring about a reconciliation between Sachar and Kairon ended in failure. Kairon heckled Congress supporters of the Commission's report in debates in the Vidhan Sabha, and Prabodh Chandra, the right arm of Sachar, resigned from the government in protest against the indignity shown him by Kairon.

Finally, with the Congress legislature party split into rival blocs, Sachar went to the high command with the request that he be allowed to drop Kairon from the ministry. This the high command would not agree to. Then Sachar resigned, and Kairon was elected leader and became chief minister in early 1956. The high command had apparently felt that in view of the massive Akali agitation, a Sikh chief minister was called for to satisfy the Sikh community, and also that a strong leader like Kairon would be able to control future agitations in the state. With Kairon's assumption of the chief ministership, both the ministerial wing and the organizational wing came under the leadership of the same man. It also marked a change from an urban-oriented leadership to a rural-oriented one. Ch. Devi Lal at this time welcomed Kairon's elevation as signaling success for the rural people.[61] Sachar was later appointed as a governor of one of the states.

In 1956 the government of India reached a political settlement with the Akali Dal in the form of "regional formula." As part of the settlement, PEPSU was merged with the Punjab in November 1956, and PEPSU MLAs became members of the Punjab legislature. Having obtained the regional formula, the Akali Dal now decided to disband itself as a political organization and Akali MLAs joined the Congress legislature party. Earlier, several other non-Congress groups, such as the

[60] *Hindusthan Standard*, December 11, 1955, and *Hindustan Times*, December 12, 1955.

[61] *The Tribune*, July 20, 1956.

Gandhi Janata party and the Zamindara League, had also joined the Congress party, giving it an overwhelming majority in the legislature. After the merger of PEPSU in the Punjab, the Punjab ministry was reconstituted, and as usual, the high command's approval was obtained for the list of new ministers.

Although the Congress party was able temporarily to accommodate the Akali problem (even though it would now have to contend with Akali factions within the party), it faced vigorous and bitter criticism and opposition from Hindu parties in the state as well as from several Hindu leaders in the Congress party. Hindu organizations also launched an agitation against the regional formula, and Hindu groups now clashed several times with the police. Several Congress leaders issued press statements condemning police brutality and government policies responsible for it, and urged an impartial inquiry into incidents of police brutality. The Punjab Congress president, Musafir, threatened disciplinary action against some of these leaders for issuing statements damaging to Congress prestige. Jagat Narain, too, protested through newspaper editorials and public statements against the regional formula and the government actions against the agitation. The Congress president then charged him with violating party discipline and engaging in communal propaganda. Narain answered by reminding him that Kairon and Musafir had themselves engaged in precisely similar activities in the past. He also declared that the Kairon group was merely using the issue of regional formula to destroy all those who had formerly opposed Kairon, and further accused it of exploiting rural-urban differences for the sake of political power.[62] Some fourteen Congressmen, including Narain, then submitted their resignations from the party. Finally, as disciplinary action against Narain, he was debarred from elective positions in the party. In the 1957 elections to the Vidhan Sabha, Narain defeated the Congress candidate but failed to win in the 1962 elections. Later, however, he was elected to the Rajya Sabha. Throughout, he remained an inveterate and bitter critic of Kairon and his government.

3. From 1956 to 1964. In this period a dominant faction existed which controlled both the organizational wing and the ministerial wing of the Congress party and was headed by a strong and determined leader who had the backing of the Congress high command. As a consequence, not only was there ministerial stability over a considerable period of time, but agitations against the government ended in failure. The smaller dissident factions were unable to challenge the control of the dominant fac-

[62] *Hindusthan Standard,* August 6, 1956.

tion but managed frequently to involve the Congress high command in Punjab affairs. Some of them carried on an open campaign against the group in power, and several Congressmen actually seceded from the party in protest. Eventually, the dominant faction lost its pre-eminent position following the resignation of its leader who was found guilty by an inquiry commission of certain charges brought against him.

The Congress party went into the 1957 elections with several of the opposition parties—most important the Akali Dal and the Zamindara League—no longer in existence, but rather now an integral part of it. With Partap Singh Kairon at the helm, the Congress party won 120 seats out of 154 in the Vidhan Sabha. Although the Congress party won the overwhelming majority of constituencies in the Hindi-speaking region and in the Sikh-majority constituencies in the Punjabi-speaking region, it met with several serious defeats in the Hindu-majority urban constituencies in the Punjabi-speaking region. This was the result of Hindu dissatisfaction with the "regional formula" and the merger of the Akali Dal in the Congress party—the latter raising the prospect of domination of the Congress by former Akalis.

Among the newly elected MLAs, Kairon headed the leading faction. There were several other important factions, with Giani Kartar Singh heading a group of about twenty former Akalis, and Gian Singh Rarewala another half-dozen former Akalis. Prabodh Chandra had succeeded to the leadership of the Sachar group. Kairon was unanimously elected leader of the Congress legislature party at a meeting held under the chairmanship of Shriman Narayan, general secretary of the central Congress party.[63] In consultation with the Congress high command, Kairon then constructed his ministry, but there was immediate criticism of the new ministry. One sore point was that while veteran and experienced Congressmen had been excluded, one-time staunch enemies of the Congress party and supporters of the British government—the Akalis and the Unionists—had been included in the ministry. Prabodh Chandra personally protested to the Congress high command on the inclusion of these new elements.[64] Hindu opinion was critical of the fact that while powerful Akalis had been taken into the ministry, the Hindu ministers were unrepresentative, most of them being from the upper House, and ineffective. Congress leaders from Hariana complained about the lack of adequate representation for their region.[65] Many of the dissatisfied groups pressed for their demands in the debates of the Vidhan Sabha.

63 *The Tribune*, April 3, 1957.
64 *Ibid.*, May 18, 1957.
65 *Ibid.*, May 22, 1957.

Meanwhile, the Arya Samaj and the Hindi Raksha Samiti ("Hindi protection committee") started the "Save Hindi" agitation in protest against compulsion in the study of languages in the Punjab and demanded that the choice of medium of instruction in schools be left to children's parents. In this agitation, they received the tacit and open support of many Hindu Congressmen from both the Punjabi-speaking and Hindi-speaking regions. The government under Kairon was able to control the agitation as a problem of law and order. In addition, it made a political move to pacify Hindu opinion. Gopi Chand Bhargava, who had been in political eclipse for six years since the imposition of President's Rule in 1951, was now included in the ministry in the belief that "the Government will be able to inspire confidence among Hindus, particularly those from urban areas."[66] Some other ministerial changes were also made toward the same end.

Factional disputes, however, continued within the Congress party. The former Akalis in the Congress party also joined in the activities of the dissident factions against Kairon. Apparently, they had come to realize that they could not maneuver for their objectives as long as Kairon headed the ministry as they had been able to between 1948 and 1951 with the Congress party divided between the Bhargava and Sachar groups. Kairon's handling of the Hindi agitation had also underlined the lesson that no agitation for Akali objectives was likely to succeed with Kairon at the head of the state government. Some of Kairon's former supporters also joined in the efforts to remove him from the chief ministership. For its part, the Congress high command sent emissaries to the Punjab asking Congressmen to end their feuds. Union Home Minister Pant reminded them that similar factional quarrels had once led to the imposition of President's Rule in the state[67] and urged them to maintain internal unity.[68] U. N. Dhebar, president of the central Congress party, also visited the Punjab to investigate party matters. The high command was opposed to any change in leadership in the Punjab,[69] but deputations continued to visit New Delhi urging the removal of Kairon on grounds of corruption and despotic rule, and for assisting communalism, furthering rural-urban differences, demoralizing the administration, acting in a partisan way in party affairs, and victimizing political rivals and opponents.

The high command conducted an inquiry into the various charges made against Kairon but exonerated him on the whole, though acknowl-

66 *Times of India*, September 29, 1957.

67 *Hindustan Times*, March 3, 1958.

68 *The Tribune*, March 4, 1958.

69 *Hindustan Times*, March 5, 1958.

edging some charges of maladministration and favoritism. Prime Minister Nehru is believed to have played an important role in the final favorable verdict. At the same time, the high command asked Kairon to seek a vote of confidence from the Congress legislature party. Before the actual vote, Nehru spoke in "forthright and forceful language"[70] at a press conference, dismissing any charges of corruption against Kairon personally and "whittling down to a nullity whatever adverse remarks the Congress Parliamentary Board had thought fit to make" concerning him.[71] With the high command's wishes thus known, many members who were hitherto opposed to Kairon now rallied around him, and he survived the vote of no-confidence. However, some members of his own ministry, including Giani Kartar Singh and Gopi Chand Bhargava, voted against him. Some of the resentment of Congress dissidents was now directed against Nehru for shielding Kairon.

Despite their defeat in the no-confidence vote, Congress dissidents continued to express publicly their opposition to and criticism of Kairon and his government. While the Congress legislature party established a committee to scrutinize their speeches for disciplinary action,[72] the dissidents set up a committee to formulate a new "charge sheet" against Kairon.[73] As part of their public campaign against Kairon, 122 Congress dissidents, including 4 members of Parliament and 18 MLAs, met in a convention in 1959 under the chairmanship of Giani Zail Singh. They established a 15-man committee, with Giani Gurmukh Singh Musafir (a former staunch supporter of Kairon) as its chief adviser, to meet with important members of the Congress high command and ask for an immediate dismissal of the Kairon ministry.[74] This committee also asked for the establishment of an *ad hoc* committee to conduct party elections and requested an observer from the high command to supervise these elections since no fair elections could be expected with the Kairon faction in control of the party.[75] After a court gave a judgment critical of the Kairon government's conduct in a murder case, the dissidents stepped up their campaign with even greater vigor. Charges and counter-charges between the Kairon faction and the dissident factions were even voiced on the floor of the state legislature.

Meanwhile, the Akali Dal revived itself as a political organization in opposition to the Congress party and asked former Akalis who had

70 *The Tribune*, editorial, June 8, 1958.

71 *Ibid.*

72 *Hindustan Times*, March 13, 1959.

73 *Hindusthan Standard*, April 8, 1959.

74 *Times of India*, September 26, 1959.

75 *The Tribune*, October 5, 1959.

been elected on the Congress ticket to quit the Congress now and form a separate Akali group in the Vidhan Sabha. About eight Akali MLAs did so, but the large majority continued to remain with the Congress party. At the same time, the Akali Dal began a militant campaign against the government for the achievement of Punjabi Suba. The political scene in the Punjab during much of 1960 and 1961 was dominated first by Akali threats of a massive agitation and then by the actual agitation itself capped by two unsuccessful fasts-unto-death by two top leaders of the Akali Dal. The government stood firm, and the Akali agitation ended in October 1961, without the Akali Dal accomplishing any of its objectives. After this, preparations started among the political parties for the elections to be held in February 1962, and the factional struggle in the Congress party manifested itself in the distribution of party tickets.

In mid-October 1961 the nine-man Punjab Congress Election Committee met to decide the allocation of party tickets for the 22 Lok Sabha seats and the 154 Vidhan Sabha seats. Immediately, it found itself divided between a Kairon faction of four and a dissident faction of three led by Ch. Devi Lal, with the chairman Darbara Singh, also president of the Punjab Congress, and another member seemingly neutral. Devi Lal had been a close confidant of Kairon, but differences between the two leaders had grown since 1959, and Devi Lal was now providing leadership to the various dissident factions. Darbara Singh was considered to be close to Kairon, though some believed that there was an unstated clash of ambitions between the two leaders.

Since there was no harmony in the committee and it could not come to any unanimous decisions, a way out was found by delegating the task of preparing the nomination list to a three-man board consisting of Darbara Singh plus two officials of the Congress high command. The high command officials had already toured over parts of the Punjab in order to assess the political and electoral situation and the applicants for election tickets. The dissidents agreed to the procedure of having this board prepare the list of nominations, apparently in the belief that there was a conflict of ambitions between Darbara Singh and Kairon and that consequently he and perhaps one of the two officials would lend them their moral support in preparing the list.[76]

When the board finalized the list of nominations, the dissident leaders immediately expressed complete dissatisfaction, complaining of inadequate representation for their groups, and they submitted rival lists to the high command. Devi Lal now charged Darbara Singh with com-

[76] *Hindustan Times*, November 29, 1961.

munal bias and partisanship. He claimed that an excessive number of seats had been given to Sikhs whereas the Hindus had been denied their share. He pointed out that on the basis of the population of the Punjabi-speaking region, 40 seats should go to Hindus and 49 to Sikhs, but that in the list submitted by the board the Hindus had been given only 25 seats.[77] He also charged that the board had sought to mislead the high command by giving tickets to the prominent dissident leaders, but not to their supporters, and that in fact the faction of Kairon and Darbara Singh had about 136 tickets out of the 154 recommended.

With the submission of the list to the high command, the scene of political activity shifted to New Delhi. Various group leaders brought bus-loads of their followers to New Delhi to put pressure on the high command. In the final selection, Devi Lal and his group were denied Congress tickets.[78] But Devi Lal running as an independent defeated his Congress opponent, as did some of his supporters. After the elections, he became the leader of a group in the Vidhan Sabha called the Progressives and Independents party. Some of the other dissident leaders who had been given Congress tickets complained during and after the election campaign that Kairon and his group had sought to undermine their election by secretly assisting their opponents.

In the 1962 general elections, even though the decline in its share of the vote polled was not too big, the Congress party was able to win only 90 out of 154 seats in the Vidhan Sabha. In view of the reduced majority in the Vidhan Sabha and the various problems facing the state, the high command urged the various groups in the Congress party in the Punjab to close their ranks. Although Kairon had been elected by an extremely narrow vote in his own constituency in the elections, he was now elected unanimously the leader of the Congress legislature party. After a series of consultations with the Congress high command, Kairon then formed a large ministry of over thirty, providing representation for several of the factions within the Congress party. One of the most vociferous dissident leaders, Prabodh Chandra, was made Speaker of the Vidhan Sabha.

After the elections, the opposition parties in a joint move started a "save democracy" campaign and once again demanded an end to the so-called despotic rule in the Punjab by removing Kairon from the position of chief minister. They even asked for the imposition of President's Rule in the state. Within the Congress party a tussle developed between Kairon and Darbara Singh and their respective groups. Attempts by the Congress high command to bring about a reconciliation between the two

[77] *The Tribune*, November 14, 1961.
[78] *Hindustan Times*, December 7, 1961.

leaders, who for long had been such close allies, did not succeed. There was a brief respite in the mutual recriminations within the Congress party and between it and the various opposition parties following the Sino-Indian border crisis of October 1962. However, as the year 1963 opened, political events in the Punjab assumed their familiar pattern with greater intensity.

After having held the office for four years, Darbara Singh resigned from the presidentship of the Punjab Congress in January 1963,[79] and Kairon was later able to get a loyal protégé of his elected president, thus assuring for himself firm control over the party organization as well as over the government. Several dissident leaders in the Congress party now formed a "ginger" group within the party with the objective of removing allegedly "opportunist" elements from the organization. Many important Congress leaders were members of this group. In mid-1963 they organized a fairly successful open convention at Ambala and, in a resolution, condemned the corruption, maladministration, and political victimization in the Punjab.[80] Although its activities received considerable popular attention, the "ginger" group was badly defeated in the elections to the Punjab Pradesh Congress Committee. The Kairon group emerged with a large lead over the Darbara Singh group in these elections. Having failed to secure a position within the party organization strong enough to allow them to challenge Kairon's leadership, the leaders of the "ginger" group continued to campaign for the removal of Kairon and submitted charge-sheets against him to the high command. When the Punjab Congress president asked for their explanations for indulging in anti-Kairon, anti-Congress, and anti-Nehru activities, sixteen legislators belonging to the "ginger" group resigned from the Congress party. The Congress in a counter-action expelled them from the organization. Interestingly, since the elections, about an equal number of non-Congress legislators had joined the Congress party. The leaders who left the Congress party now formed a separate political party known as the Prajatantra party, maintaining that their political principles were the same as those of the Congress party, but that the Congress party was not following them in practice. They charged the present leadership in the Punjab with having brought the Congress party to ridicule in the state and given it an "ugly and immoral image." They also alleged that the Congress legislature party was a constitutional façade for Kairon's dictatorial rule.[81] They further expressed resentment at Nehru and the high command for striving to protect Kairon.

[79] *The Tribune*, January 3, 1963.

[80] *Ibid.*, June 3, 1963.

[81] *Ibid.*, November 15, 1963.

The opposition parties also conducted a noisy campaign on similar grounds and attempted to persuade the Prime Minister and the President to establish an inquiry commission to investigate their charges against Kairon. In July 1963 they formed a United Front of non-Communist parties under the leadership of Ch. Devi Lal, a former lieutenant of Kairon, to work for these objectives.

Although the efforts of the various political groups had thus far failed to move the high command to establish a commission of inquiry, the judiciary forced the hand of the government. In giving judgment on a case before it, the Supreme Court passed certain strictures against Kairon. The matter then came up for discussion in Parliament where opposition leaders urged the establishment of an inquiry commission. Prime Minister Nehru was at first reluctant. Evidently, his first concern was political stability in this strategic border state. Whatever his shortcomings, Kairon had seemingly become indispensable. All the agitations launched against the government by the various opposition parties during his tenure had ended in failure. However, Nehru finally agreed to the setting up of an inquiry commission, and in November 1963 S. R. Das, a former Chief Justice of India, was appointed to conduct the inquiry. For their part, the opposition parties and individuals readied themselves to present their evidence and affidavits.

While the work of the inquiry commission was in progress, conflict within the Congress party proceeded apace. Prabodh Chandra resigned in March 1963 from the speakership of the Vidhan Sabha, alleging that Kairon had made it impossible for him to continue in that office by heaping indignities on him through various devices, including the bringing forward of motions of no-confidence against him in the Congress legislature party. The Kairon group also started a "signature" campaign for the removal of Darbara Singh from the ministry. On the other hand, nearly 150 members of the Punjab Pradesh Congress Committee called on Nehru, telling him that Kairon had the support of the Punjab Congress.

With the death of Nehru in May 1964, Kairon lost one of his greatest supporters in the high command. When Kamaraj Nadar, president of the central Congress party, was assessing the opinions of various Congress chief ministers so as to arrive at some "consensus" in the choice of Nehru's successor, Kairon is reported to have supported the claims of Morarji Desai as against Lal Bahadur Shastri, who finally succeeded to the position of Prime Minister. Events now moved with great rapidity. After the report of the Das Commission had been submitted to the government of India, but before it was released, Kairon resigned from the position of chief minister of Punjab, and the search for a successor began.[82] The process of selection of a successor to Kairon once again reveals the nature of the influence of the Congress high command in Punjab Congress affairs.

When Kairon resigned, he urged the members of the Congress legislature party to insist on their democratic right of selecting their leader.[83] This body was packed with his supporters who would have assured that only a protégé of his or someone acceptable to him would be elected. His supporters also let it be known that they would elect their leader in a straight vote and would have nothing to do with any high command efforts to arrive at a "consensus."[84] The high command first delayed any precipitate election on the part of the Congress legislature party. Meanwhile, the government released the report of the Das Commission, and its damaging conclusions about Kairon served to demoralize his supporters. Some of them now said that whatever the high command decided would find "unqualified support" among Punjab Congressmen,[85] and Kamaraj declared that the high command's decision would be binding on the Punjab Congress legislature party.[86] Some members of the Kairon group now changed sides, and Darbara Singh claimed that he had a majority with him. Various leaders and deputations on their behalf called on the high command in New Delhi to press their claims. Several names had been suggested, but the Kairon group and its opponents were so bitterly opposed to each other that they could not agree on any name. The high command then delegated Swaran Singh, later to become Foreign Minister, to go to the Punjab and hold consultations with Congress leaders in an attempt to find an acceptable name. The Congress high command then recommended Ram Kishan, a veteran Congressman, and he was elected unanimously by the Congress legislature party. Meanwhile, with Kairon's resignation, the Prajatantra party was disbanded and its members returned to the Congress fold.

4. From 1964 to 1966. In the fourth period from 1964 to 1966 the ministerial wing and the organizational wing were opposed to each other, but neither was powerful enough to oust the other. Moreover, both were internally divided and without a strong leadership. Real power in the Punjab seemed to rest with the Congress high command, which tolerated the state of animated conflict among the different factions but refused to allow any leadership changes.

[82] *Ibid.*, June 15, 1964.

[83] *Ibid.*

[84] *Ibid.*

[85] *Ibid.*, June 23, 1964.

[86] *Ibid.*, June 17, 1964.

After his election to the leadership of the Punjab Congress legislature party in 1964, Ram Kishan formed his ministry in consultation with the Congress high command. The party organization, however, continued to be under the control of the Kairon group. As it recovered from the impact of the sudden ouster from power of Kairon and his lieutenants, the party organization under the leadership of Bhagwat Dayal Sharma subjected the ministry, through public platform and official resolutions, to bitter criticism. On the other hand, Ram Kishan and his supporters urged the Congress high command to reorganize the Congress party in the Punjab at all levels. Soon Kairon joined the chorus of criticism directed against the government. However, Kairon's activity came to a tragic end in February 1965 with his murder just outside Delhi, a murder which was more the result of personal enmity than political conspiracy.

Not only was there conflict between the organizational wing and the ministerial wing, but the ministerial wing was a house divided within itself, with the primary challenge to Ram Kishan's leadership coming from Darbara Singh. Signature campaigns were launched to oust Ram Kishan. Kamaraj counseled moderation on all sides, the Congress high command insisted on no change in leadership until the next general elections, and Home Minister Nanda visited Chandigarh to bring about a reconciliation among the different groups.

If internal problems were not enough for the Congress party, the Punjabi Suba issue came once again to the fore in 1965 and 1966, creating serious indiscipline within the party, with leaders and members taking opposing positions in public. Amidst all this, the Congress high command bestrode the Punjab as the dominant political figure. One observer alleged that the Punjab had become a colony of the high command, with Punjab leaders constantly in motion between Chandigarh and New Delhi, and considered it damaging to the self-respect of the people of the state that their leaders were so dependent on New Delhi.[87]

Opposition Political Parties

The major opposition parties in the Punjab are three—the Shiromani Akali Dal, the Bharatiya Jan Sangh, and the Communist party. An important aspect of the party system in the Punjab is the presence of a strong political party confined only to the state—the Akali Dal. The Jan Sangh and the Communist party in the Punjab are, like the Congress

[87] Mehr Chand Mahajan, in *The Tribune*, March 7, 1966.

party, state branches of national parties. A few other national parties are represented in the Punjab, but have little electoral support. In the 1962 general elections, the Swatantra party, the Republican party, and the Praja Socialist party were able to secure only 3.9, 2.2, and 0.9 per cent of the total vote polled in the Punjab. There are some additional local parties, such as the Hariana Front and Haryana Lok Samiti in the Hindi-speaking region, but they represent the following of one political leader or another without any sustained political organization. From time to time new parties arise, especially at election time, and after a brief appearance, vanish.

Shiromani Akali Dal. The Akali Dal is not only confined to the Punjab but is open only to members of the Sikh community. Since the Sikh community is concentrated in the Punjabi-speaking region, the Akali Dal commands little support outside that region. In the 1962 general elections the Akali Dal won no seats in the Hindi-speaking region and secured only 0.4 per cent of the vote polled in that region. The Akali Dal claims to be the sole representative body of the Sikhs and stands for the protection of the Sikh religion and the furtherance of the interests of the Sikh community.[88] In terms of specific objectives, its most immediate and important objective in post-independence India has been that of Punjabi Suba.

In the 1962 general elections, the Akali Dal secured 19 seats with 11.9 per cent of the vote polled in the Punjab as a whole, as against 33 seats and 14.7 per cent (combined figures for PEPSU and Punjab) of the vote in 1952. Over the years, there has thus been a decline in the electoral strength of the Akali Dal. As it had merged with the Congress party at the time of the 1957 elections, it did not contest those elections as a separate party. In the Punjabi-speaking region in the 1962 elections, the Akali Dal obtained 20 per cent of the total vote polled. This suggests that the Akali Dal secured no more than 40 per cent of the Sikh vote (assuming that the Sikhs constitute about 55 per cent of the region's population) despite the organization's claim to be the sole representative body of the Sikh community. However, the political importance of the Akali Dal extends far beyond its electoral strength. Its activities in the years since independence have overshadowed to a great extent other political developments in the Punjab, primarily as a result of its ability to marshal thousands of Sikh volunteers into militant agitations. Its strength in the Sikh community lies in its historic posture as the protec-

[88] For an extended analysis of the Akali Dal and its leadership, see Nayar, *Minority Politics in the Punjab*.

tor of that community and in its control over a centralized network of Sikh shrines with their extensive patronage and financial resources exceeding six million rupees annually.

Like the Congress party, the Akali Dal too has been divided into factions, often bitterly and openly opposed to each other. Since 1930, however, Master Tara Singh, a convert from Hinduism, had managed to dominate the Akali organization. In 1962, following an unsuccessful fast-unto-death, his leadership was seriously challenged, and his former lieutenant, Sant Fateh Singh, established a rival Akali Dal. The rivalry between the two groups led to bitter denunciation of each other. In 1965 the Akali Dal led by Fateh Singh defeated the Tara Singh group in the gurdwara elections, and destroyed Tara Singh's claim to be the spokesman of the Sikh community. Fateh Singh's subsequent success in pressuring the government to concede Punjabi Suba served to enhance his own leadership.

Communist Party. In terms of both its membership and its leadership, the Communist party in the Punjab is largely a Sikh party. In contrast to the situation in West Bengal, the party's strength lies in the rural areas, primarily in the Punjabi-speaking region. As for its class base, it derives support not from the landless tenants and laborers (largely Harijan) but from the small-scale landowning agriculturists, largely Jat Sikh. The party has difficulty in appealing simultaneously to both these groups in the rural areas and has tried to solve it by establishing two separate peasant organizations, the Dehati Mazdoor Sabha and the Kisan Sabha, to work among the two groups.

The Communist party in the Punjab has been a supporter of the demand of Punjabi Suba, even though it has defined its boundaries differently. This support of Punjabi Suba has often created tension between its Hindu and its Sikh members. In the 1962 general elections the Communist party entered into an unofficial alliance with the Akali Dal against the Congress party, and this became the basis later of an inner-party dispute. Like the Congress party and the Akali Dal, the Communist party has been split into factions. The party in the Punjab had been under the dominance of the "leftist" group under the leadership of Harkishen Singh Surjeet. After the Sino-Indian crisis of 1962, taking advantage of the fact that the "leftist" leaders were in jail, the "rightist" group captured the party organization. The "leftists" then established a rival party.

In the 1962 elections the Communist party secured 7.1 per cent of the vote polled in the Punjab and won 9 seats to the Vidhan Sabha. In the 1957 elections the party had secured 6 seats, but with 13.6 per cent of the vote polled. The large vote in 1957 was largely due to its ability, in the absence of the Akali Dal and the Zamindara League, to capitalize on the anti-government vote in the rural areas. In the Punjabi-speaking region in the 1962 elections, it secured 10.0 per cent of the vote polled in contrast to only 2.9 per cent in the Hindi-speaking region. All nine of the candidates elected to the Vidhan Sabha in the 1962 elections were from the Punjabi-speaking region, and all were from Sikh families—seven Jat Sikhs and two Scheduled Castes. In the 1957 elections, however, the party had won 2 seats in the Hindi-speaking region as against 4 in the Punjabi-speaking region.

Jan Sangh. The Jan Sangh stands in the same relation to the Hindu community as does the Akali Dal to the Sikh community. Both are communal parties. The support of the Jan Sangh lies with the urban Hindu middle class, especially among the refugees, though it has increasingly been making inroads into the rural areas. The basic strength of the Jan Sangh is its band of dedicated and disciplined workers who are members of the semi-military cultural Hindu organization, RSS (Rashtriya Swayam Sewak Sangh). In fact, the Jan Sangh is often characterized as the political arm of the RSS, and its active membership and leadership come from that organization. One major feature that distinguishes the Jan Sangh from the other opposition parties, and in fact from all other political parties, is the absence of overt factionalism in the party. It is a well-knit group with authoritarian inner party procedures.

The Jan Sangh has been opposed to the Akali Dal and its objective of Punjabi Suba. Further, it favored the merger of Himachal Pradesh with the Punjab, and the party's branch in the region until recently was known as the Punjab and Himachal Pradesh Jan Sangh. The party also opposed the regional formula as well as the compulsory study of Punjabi. It is a protagonist of Hindi. The Jan Sangh advocates the abolition of state legislatures and the formation of a unitary state in India. Despite its staunch opposition to the Akali Dal, it is not above making alliances with it for electoral and other limited political purposes.

Founded as late as 1951, the Jan Sangh has shown a consistent increase in its electoral strength over the three general elections. In the 1962 elections it won 8 seats with 9.7 per cent of the vote polled in the Punjab as against 9 seats with 8.6 per cent of the vote in 1957 and 2 seats with 5.0 per cent of the vote in 1952. The Jan Sangh is distinguished from the other two major opposition parties in that its support, confined to the Hindu community, is more uniformly spread over the whole state. In the 1962 elections it secured 4 seats with 7.6 per cent of the vote in the Punjabi-speaking region and 4 seats with 12.7 per cent of the vote in the Hindi-speaking region. However, it is the Punjabi-speaking region that constitutes the center of its major political activities because of the presence there of the Akali Dal, and it is from that region that most of its prominent leadership comes.

Opposition Techniques and Tactics

Apart from participation in the electoral and parliamentary processes and utilizing the constitutional freedoms to influence public opinion, the opposition parties place a heavy reliance on extra-constitutional methods. Every opposition political party has engaged in a major agitation in which thousands of volunteers have disobeyed the law deliberately to court arrest. In the Punjab agitations are not merely techniques of political action but a way of life, and the state has often been called the land of agitations. Even the constitutional activities of the opposition parties are characterized by a high note of militancy and symbolic violence.

One feature that distinguishes the Akali Dal from the other opposition parties is the large-scale use of the tactic of boring from within in relation to the Congress party. Its membership and leadership has at times joined the Congress party to influence its policy by acting as a well-knit faction from within, and also to share directly in the political governance of the state. Although the opposition parties are badly divided from each other from the viewpoint of ideology and their communal composition, they may at times form united fronts for limited purposes, such as for the ouster of Kairon and opposition to measures of taxation.

Political Leadership

What kind of political leaders are recruited into politics? What is the background of these leaders? What are the changing patterns of political recruitment? These are all important questions in relation to the political process of the state, but all require considerable research. Here an attempt will be made at only a brief analysis of the social background of the membership of the Punjab Vidhan Sabha as a whole for the session from 1957 to 1962. This analysis is based on data provided in a Who's Who published by the Punjab government.[89]

In the 1957-62 Vidhan Sabha there was very little representation for women. About 94 per cent of the MLAs were men. The Vidhan Sabha consisted, by and large, of married persons: of the 98 members for whom information is available, about 93 per cent were married. On the basis of

[89] Punjab Vidhan Sabha, *Who's Who 1960* (Chandigarh: Controller of Printing and Stationery, 1960).

information for 144 members of the Sabha, the average year of birth of the MLAs was 1913.

The 1957-62 Vidhan Sabha was largely a rural body. Of the 107 MLAs on whom information is available, about 76 per cent were born in villages. About 85 per cent of the MLAs represented rural constituencies, while 8 per cent represented urban constituencies, and another 7 per cent "mixed" constituencies.[90]

About 56 per cent of the 1957-62 MLAs were Hindus, 41 per cent Sikhs, 2 per cent Muslims, and 1 per cent Ad-Dharmis. As for caste, among the 115 members for whom information is available, the Jats constituted the largest group with 37 per cent of the membership, followed by the Scheduled Castes or Harijans with 28 per cent. About 9 per cent of the MLAs were Brahmans. Concerning the business and trading castes, the Khatris were 5 per cent, the Aggarwals 4 per cent, and the Aroras 2 per cent.

Information on education is available for all but 6 members of the Vidhan Sabha. Only 4 per cent had received no formal education. About 17 per cent had studied below the high school level, 26 per cent had completed high school, 11 per cent had finished intermediate college, 31 per cent had received the B.A. degree and 6 per cent the M.A. degree. About 22 per cent of the MLAs had earned a law degree. Over 90 per cent of the members of the Vidhan Sabha had received their education in the Punjab, while some 19 per cent had additionally, or solely, studied abroad.

In terms of occupation, information is available for 141 members. Of these, the largest group was that of the agriculturists with 39 per cent, followed by political workers with 25 per cent. About 23 per cent were lawyers, 11 per cent businessmen, 6 per cent social workers, and 16 per cent in other professions.[91]

GOVERNMENTAL PERFORMANCE

The political and administrative load on the government of the Punjab has been immense ever since the inception of the state. At its very birth, the state was engulfed by mass rioting and murder and by mass migration. Under these pressures the administrative machinery of the

90 Constituencies with more than 66 per cent of the population living in villages have been considered as rural; constituencies with more than 66 per cent of the population living in urban areas have been considered as urban; the rest have been considered "mixed."

91 For an analysis of leadership at the panchayat and samiti levels, see Indian Institute of Public Opinion, *Monthly Public Opinion Surveys*, VI, Nos. 8-9 (May-June 1961) and VII, Nos. 7-8 (April-May 1962).

state broke down. Between two and a half and three million refugees from West Pakistan came to the state, creating the vast problem of immediate relief and then of resettlement. Several more million refugees passed through the state to other parts of India.

In the political arena, the state has lived from one crisis to another. Every few years, there has been some massive agitation, not only threatening public law and order but bringing the whole political and economic life of the state to a standstill and diverting the energies of the administration away from normal business. Every major opposition group has been involved in such agitational activity. In 1957 certain Hindu organizations, including the Jan Sangh and the Arya Samaj, launched an agitation in favor of Hindi and the removal of any compulsion in the teaching of languages in the state; some 8,000 to 10,000 persons were arrested. In 1959 the Communist party carried out a major agitation in protest against the imposition of a betterment levy, and about 9,000 persons were arrested. The most massive agitations, however, have been the work of the Akali Dal. In 1955 it launched an agitation against the ban on the shouting of slogans concerning states reorganization; in this agitation, some 12,000 Akali volunteers courted arrest. In 1960-61 the Akali Dal carried out another agitation for the achievement of Punjabi Suba, and some 26,000 volunteers were arrested (the Akali Dal places the figure at 57,000).[92] In addition, at this time, two top leaders of the Akali Dal went on fasts-unto-death, but later gave them up. In 1965 and 1966 Sant Fateh Singh of the Akali Dal threatened to fast for fifteen days and then burn himself to death if Punjabi Suba were not conceded.

It is in the context of these various threats to public law and order, indeed to the very existence of the government, that complaints about sternness on the part of the Punjab government, especially during the tenure of Partap Singh Kairon as chief minister, ought to be evaluated. Of course, it has often been suggested that Kairon himself instigated these crises as it enhanced the myth of his indispensability in the state. It may be true that Kairon aggravated at times a politically delicate situation, but agitations and threats of agitations were endemic in the Punjab long before Kairon ever assumed any position of real power in the administration. His distinction lay in his ability to control these agitations. His achievement is all the more remarkable in view of his concomitant problem of maintaining control of a faction-ridden Congress party.

The government's relations with the opposition have not been confined merely to containing the threat to public law and order. In the period since independence, the government has adopted several meas-

[92] *The Tribune*, February 23, 1961.

ures, especially in relation to the Akali Dal, to conciliate and accommodate the opposition. Twice it established inquiry commissions to investigate charges brought against the government by the opposition. It extended several important political concessions to the Akali Dal—the "services formula," the "parity formula," the "Sachar formula," and the "regional formula." Over and above these concessions, the Congress party allowed the Akali Dal twice to become a part of the Congress party and share positions in cabinet, government, and party. In fact, the Akali Dal was able to obtain several of the political concessions by working within the Congress party.

Apart from tackling the problems involved in refugee relief and rehabilitation and in frequent agitations against the government, the administrative apparatus in the Punjab has had to contend with problems connected with the integration of princely states. In 1956 the territories of PEPSU were merged into the state of Punjab, increasing the state's population by more than one-third. The merger brought "a whole series of problems, such as the unification of the legal and the taxation systems, apart from the problem of the absorption, at all levels, of the officials in these areas."[93] Furthermore, there has been a dramatic change, both quantitative and qualitative, in the functions of government since 1947. No longer is the function of government merely to maintain law and order; it is to act positively in the economic and social fields. A whole series of plans and programs have been implemented, largely on the initiative or recommendation of the center. Among these are land reforms legislation, economic development programs, community development services, and panchayati raj. Although such programs add greatly to the resources of the government in securing political support, they have also meant an increase in the complexity and burden of the load on the administrative apparatus of the state. A whole host of agencies has been created for the programming, execution, and evaluation of the new activities.

The headquarters of the administrative apparatus of the state are located at Chandigarh and consist of about forty departments[94] under the political control of a Council of Ministers which is responsible to the state legislature. Normally, the Council of Ministers consists of about ten members, and each minister is in charge of several departments. On the civil service side, one or more departments are headed by a Secretary

[93] E. N. Mangat Rai, *Civil Administration in the Punjab: An Analysis of a State Government in India* (Occasional Papers in International Affairs, Number 7), Cambridge: Center for International Affairs, Harvard University, 1963, p. 3.

[94] *Ibid.*, p. 12.

who is a permanent civil servant. There are some 20 Secretaries, assisted by a staff of about 2,000.[95]

Below "the Secretariat," the state is divided into three divisions, each headed by a commissioner. These administrative units are further divided into districts, of which there are some 20 in the Punjab. Each district is headed by a district officer called the deputy commissioner. The district further consists of *tahsils* headed by a *tahsildar*; there are some 3 to 5 tahsils to a district. The linchpin of this territorial division of the administration is the district, which is "the basic regional unit of administration,"[96] and the deputy commissioner, who "has overriding coordinating powers and functions in respect of all departments dealing with district work in his area."[97] The primary function of the deputy commissioner before independence, with both the executive and judicial arms united in him, was the maintenance of law and order. But now to this have been added all the development functions undertaken by the government. More recently, the Punjab government has acted to separate completely the judiciary from the executive.

About 175 officers from the centrally recruited IAS form the elite corps in the state's administration, backed up by a second line of some 450 officers recruited through the state's own public service commission.[98] The state depends on this superior staff for the efficient execution of the various projects in the economic and social fields and also the police functions of the state. On the ability and morale of this staff depends the performance of the government.

Given the political problems of the state and the rapid expansion in the functions of government, it would seem that the state's administrative system has performed reasonably well in the economic as well as in the non-economic spheres. Nonetheless, there are frequent complaints and charges that the morale of the administrative staff has gone down, that the services are demoralized, and that the political masters of the state are responsible for this state of affairs.[99] However, the matter of morale in the services is not a simple one: there are several components to it.

First, the tremendous increase in state activities has been accompanied by a plethora of coordinating agencies and coordinating procedures, "cutting across the decision-making processes in the departments."[100] The "orgy of coordination"[101] involves constant checking and counter-

95 *Ibid.*, p. 11.

96 *Ibid.*, p. 12.

97 *Ibid.*

98 *Ibid.*, pp. 18-19.

99 See Hardwari Lal, "District Administration—Then and Now," *The Tribune*, May 18 and 19, 1964, and "Govt. versus Administration," *ibid.*, September 23, 1964.

100 Rai, *op.cit.*, p. 29.

101 *Ibid.*, p. 28.

checking with a variety of departments and accounting agencies and results in a situation where "responsibility is diffuse, and difficult to pinpoint, or to drive home to a particular individual, or sometimes even to a particular department."[102] An individual officer then tends to feel that "there is too much beyond his control." As a result, there is loss of self-confidence and self-assurance and little incentive for initiative.[103] Decision-making is pushed to higher and higher levels, with the middle and lower levels feeling deprived of any role in the administration while the public feels unnecessarily delayed and harassed in its business. In this instance, the loss of morale in the services is due to certain administrative procedures which are not organic to the administration and can certainly be changed. An administrative reforms commission has been appointed by the Punjab government to suggest improvements.

Second, there is the matter of the existence of "vigilance" agencies of the government to check corruption in the administration, which seems to have "a bad effect on morale. A false accusation, sufficiently supported by ostensibly credible data, may bring an honest officer under suspicion, and even enquiry. He will no doubt be cleared, in the last resort, when all the evidence and counterevidence has been sifted; the processes involved, however, meanwhile may have caused him considerable harassment and created an atmosphere where effective work is difficult."[104] As long as checking corruption in the administration is a major goal of the government, there can be no avoidance of this factor of vigilance in morale except such procedures as may penalize the making of frivolous charges. Third, certain personnel procedures, such as recruitment by public service commissions instead of by individual departments or promotion on the basis of seniority instead of merit, are held to be factors in loss of morale. But perhaps the alternative procedures suggested may lead to even more complaints.

Finally, there is the question of the relationship of the politicians to the administrators. This has two aspects which need to be distinguished. One is the change since independence in the political framework which places the political leaders of the majority party at the head of government, answerable to the people through their representatives in the legislature, and the reduction of the civil servants to the position of givers of advice to the ministers and executors of decisions made by the ministers within the framework of the constitution. This is a drastic change from the pre-independence era when effective power rested in the hands of civil servants who executed what they conceived

[102] *Ibid.*, p. 39.
[103] *Ibid.*, p. 40.
[104] *Ibid.*, p. 37.

to be the public interest. Even when the supreme position of the civil servants in the administration was modified by the Government of India Act of 1935, the politicians were nonetheless still more or less on probation under the tutelage of the "guardians," who held the politicians in contempt. But now the civil servants have to contend with the demands of the people as articulated and aggregated through their political leaders. This is not merely a matter of executing decisions reached at the top, but involves a change at all levels of the administration. There are, for example,

> the influence and pressures exercised by individual party members and social workers, in their particular districts and constituencies. The MLA (member of the legislative assembly), and to an extent the MLC (member of the legislative council) are persons to be reckoned with. They are naturally rallying points for the redress of grievances, and the fulfillment of demands, expressed not only through committees and forums, from the state headquarters downward, but more frequently in individual requests and group pressures at the local level. These include matters of policy, but in the main are matters of individual or group interest such as the investigation of a police case, the settlement of a land dispute, the demand for an arms license, complaints of favoritism and corruption, and the like. Party members tend to have contacts all along the line, from the lowest official to the Chief Minister himself.[105]

The elimination of that freedom to act without reference to politics and the political will, and the consequent diminution in the authority and prestige of the civil service, results no doubt in the loss of morale to a certain extent, but the occasion calls more for an adjustment on the part of the civil service to the changed times. At the same time, it is necessary to realize that conflict between politicians and administrators is a generic one, not confined to the Punjab or India. "All political systems," Lucian Pye points out, "generate tension between the ethos of those who administer public programs and the ethos of those who deal in choices and values. In transitional societies that tension tends to be peculiarly acute."[106] However, there must be limits to such conflict for it has been "a chief cause of disillusionment with democratic institutions"[107] in transitional societies.

Of a different species is the contention that politicians in the Punjab

[105] *Ibid.*, p. 55.

[106] Lucian W. Pye, *Politics, Personality, and Nation Building: Burma's Search for Identity* (New Haven and London: Yale University Press, 1962), pp. 97-98.

[107] *Ibid.*

have invaded the sphere of administration for partisan and personal purposes. The person most accused of bringing about such a situation in the Punjab is Partap Singh Kairon, who was chief minister from 1956 to 1964, though similar charges were made by Sachar against Bhargava before 1951. Kairon allegedly assigned in strategic places in the administration such men as were personally loyal to him. His own political machine exercised undue influence over administrative decisions in the districts, and the administrative personnel seem to have dreaded both him and his personal agents. Kairon resigned eventually when an inquiry commission found him guilty of having used his public office to advance the interests of his family and relatives. To the extent that there was nepotism, favoritism, and political corruption, it certainly needs to be condemned, especially in view of its grave implications for public attitudes not only toward particular politicians but also toward all politicians and politics in general. In any case, it brought for Kairon its own retribution. But for it, he could have retired as a political hero and an elder statesman in the Punjab, with a unique place in the state's history because of his contribution, for whatever motives, to the cause of secular nationalism.

Apart from the question of corruption, however, much of what happened in the Punjab in terms of the intervention of politics in administration, at Kairon's instance, can be said to be justified by the nature of the turbulent politics of the state and the factional divisions within the Congress party. Where the opposition has constantly hurled challenges to the very existence of government and has not hesitated to bring the state to the brink of disorder, the use of patronage and the stationing of loyal men in strategic places, plus a certain sternness in administration, are legitimate instruments for the government. In other words, Kairon's methods were, in part, more or less dictated by the political compulsions of the situation in the Punjab—they were part of the requirements of effective rulership in the state. As for the civil service, though perhaps the pendulum swung a little too far, the Kairon era was a necessary corrective to the pre-independence tradition of monopoly of authority in the civil service—a tradition which reached its zenith in the Punjab.

In the economic field, the Punjab has given a commendable performance. The state's economy had been badly hit by the partition, with the state receiving 47 per cent of the population of the parent province but only 34 per cent of the territory and 20 per cent of the irrigated area.[108] The agriculturally productive areas and much of the industrial po-

[108] *Techno-Economic Survey of Punjab*, p. 105.

tential of the former province went to Pakistan. Also, the exchange of populations initially had a serious adverse impact on the state's economy. However, since independence the Punjab has made notable economic progress, and significantly, it has done so in both the agricultural and industrial spheres. One economist hypothesizes on the basis of incomplete data that "over the period 1952-53 to 1958-59 domestic product of Punjab advanced, at 1952-53 constant prices, by three-fifths at an annual rate of 10 per cent. Over the same period the national product of the country as a whole is known to have gone up by 24 per cent at an annual rate of 4 per cent."[109] In terms of per capita income, it would mean that, since the Punjab had a comparatively higher average than most other states in India to begin with, economic growth since the beginning of the First Five Year Plan has given the state an even more advantageous position. Some have referred to the state's economic performance as "the Punjab Leap Forward."[110] Table 9.2 provides the statistics on economic development over the first two Five Year Plans. It is obvious that production of foodgrains, sugar cane, and cotton doubled or more than doubled over a period of ten years. Similarly, great strides have been made in the generation of electricity and the production of sugar, cement, paper, bicycles and sewing machines. The advance in the industrial sphere has been mainly in the area of small-scale industry, and much of it is confined to the Punjabi-speaking region.[111] The economic progress in the state is due not only to the efforts of the population itself but also to the provision of economic and social overheads by the government. One indicator of such overheads is the increased availability of electric power. In terms of per capita consumption of electricity, the Punjab ranked third among the Indian states in 1961-62.[112]

Comparisons are often made between India and China in terms of whether democracy or totalitarianism is more suited for purposes of economic development. Perhaps it is unfair to make economic growth rates the only test for choice between democracy and totalitarianism. However, even granting such a basis for comparison, it is necessary not merely to make inter-nation comparisons but also to examine the performance of intra-nation units. If one looks within India, the case of the Punjab stands out as a living refutation of the notion that economic

109 S. B. Rangnekar, "The Emerging Perspective," in Punjab University, *The Growth of Punjab Economy* (Chandigarh: Department of Economics, 1960), pp. I-2, I-3.

110 J. Krishnamurty, "Some Regional Contrasts," *Seminar*, May 1964, p. 32.

111 Private communication from Mr. Stephen L. Keller, Department of Economics and Social Science, Massachusetts Institute of Technology, Cambridge, Mass.

112 Krishnamurty, *op.cit.*, p. 32.

TABLE 9.2

THE PUNJAB: DEVELOPMENT OVER TWO FIVE-YEAR PLANS, 1951–61

Item	*Unit*	*1951*	*1961*
1. Irrigated area	Acres	6,400,000	7,700,000
2. Production of food grains	Tons	3,379,000	6,177,000
3. Sugar cane	Tons	440,000	988,000
4. Oilseeds	Tons	140,000	200,000
5. Cotton	Bales	310,000	788,000
6. Area consolidated	Acres	Nominal	14,747,000
7. Cooperatives	Number	15,505	32,169
	Members	600,000	2,000,000
	Working capital in rupees	140,000,000	750,000,000
8. Electricity	Installed capacity (KW)	84,000	324,000
	Units generated	207,000,000	981,000,000
	Consumers	103,342	500,000
	Towns and villages electrified	97	3,016
9. Sugar production	Tons	10,000	102,000
10. Cement	Tons	350,000	637,000
11. Paper	Tons	13,000	25,000
12. Textiles	Yards	38,000,000	67,000,000
13. Sports goods	Rupees	5,500,000	10,400,000
14. Hosiery goods	Rupees	45,000,000	47,500,000
15. Brassware	Rupees	30,000,000	73,900,000
16. Iron and steel re-rolling	Tons	—	120,000
17. Cycles	Number	25,000	408,000
Cycle parts	Rupees	10,000,000	82,000,000
18. Sewing machines	Number	—	61,000
Sewing machine parts	Rupees	4,500,000	15,400,000
19. Children in schools	Number	544,000	2,500,000
20. Literate persons	Number	1,786,000	4,895,000
21. Engineering colleges	Student intake per annum	40[a]	490
22. Medical colleges	Student intake per annum	50[a]	280
23. Agricultural colleges	Student intake per annum	50[a]	250

[a] Figures are for 1947.

SOURCE: E. N. Mangat Rai, *Civil Administration in the Punjab: An Analysis of a State Government in India* (Occasional Papers in International Affairs, No. 7, Cambridge: Center for International Affairs, Harvard University, 1963), p. 52.

growth is possible only within a totalitarian framework.[113] Such an examination is called for especially when the intra-nation units in the Indian case are larger than scores of nations in the world. The Punjab is among the smaller states in India, but it has a larger population than any country in sub-Saharan Africa except Nigeria,[114] any country in the

[113] *Ibid.*

[114] Gabriel A. Almond and James S. Coleman, *The Politics of the Developing Areas* (Princeton: Princeton University Press, 1960), p. 250.

Near East except the UAR, Turkey, and Iran,[115] and any country in Latin America except Brazil and Mexico.[116]

Some other parts of India do not show the kind of economic growth that has taken place in the Punjab. This may only demonstrate that economic growth perhaps has nothing to do with the absence or presence of democracy, which should be desired or rejected on other grounds. No full-scale study has been done on the sociological and cultural factors in the economic growth of the Punjab, but perhaps the explanation lies in the border position of the region and the implications it has for innovative attitudes in the population, the weakness of caste as a social phenomenon, the lack of orthodoxy in religion, the heavy military recruitment from the area resulting in increased technical skills in the population and increased capital, the social mobility and the monetization of the rural economy, and the fermentation in the population as a result of the refugee movement. One anthropologist compares the movement of refugees in the Punjab to the medieval urban immigrants in Europe and writes that "the status of 'refugee' appears to have opened up a new avenue for occupational and social mobility among peoples of diverse social backgrounds; the term 'refugee' became synonymous with a new class of 'free men.' "[117]

In the matter of structural changes in the rural sector, the Punjab has made rapid strides in the consolidation of landholdings, which explains to some extent the progress in agricultural productivity.[118] The state's record is less enviable so far as land reforms are concerned, but its total performance in the agricultural sector raises issues of fundamental importance. Under pressure from the center, legislation was enacted, but too late to prevent landlords from taking the necessary precautionary measures.[119] In practice, the legislation has been frustrated at the administrative level. In a note commenting on a study by Wolfe Ladejinsky of five districts in different states of India, one of the editors of the *Economic Weekly* pointed out that "only in Uttar Pradesh has the land reform legislation been found to be well thought-out and comprehensive. In Madras and Andhra, legislation continues to be of a temporary, stop-gap nature, and comprehensive legislation has yet to be enacted," whereas in the case of the Punjab the legislation is "extremely defective

[115] *Ibid.*, pp. 372-73. [116] *Ibid.*, p. 457.

[117] Leighton W. Hazlehurst, "Social Structure, Credit and Market Networks Among Commercial Communities of the Punjab" (Berkeley: University of California, mimeographed, 1963).

[118] Rai, *op.cit.*, p. 53.

[119] See Daniel Thorner, *The Agrarian Prospect in India* (Delhi: University Press, 1956), pp. 44-45.

and needs complete overhauling."[120] The editor then went on to advocate urgent land reforms. If he had urged land reforms merely for welfare reasons it would be quite understandable, but he based his argument on the "inadequate performance of the agricultural sector."[121] If the comparative performance of Uttar Pradesh and the Punjab in agriculture were really made the basis for recommending land reforms, the actual record would run counter to any such advocacy. This is not to argue against land reforms, but merely to point out that perhaps the real causes making for growth, and lack of it, in the agricultural sector are not so obvious.

To sum up the total record of the Punjab in the period since independence, one may say that while there is much to be desired and still much more to be done, a good deal has been accomplished both in terms of assuring political stability in the state and providing for a commendable rate of growth in the economic sphere.

CONCLUSION

The political problems of the Punjab in relation to nation-building and the development of a political culture appropriate to democracy are not likely to disappear in the near future. They have deep historical roots, and there are no short-cut dramatic solutions for achieving what took centuries to develop in certain countries of the West that serve as the model for the leadership in India. On the other hand, despite the reduction in social diversity as a result of the states reorganization in 1966, the social configuration in the Punjab would still seem to favor, under a democratic set-up, dominance in the political system of a broad-based political coalition, cutting across parochial ties and built around moderate policies, rather than the domination of one social group over another. This is so not only because the different groups are so large and antagonistic to each other as to reject any domination by an opposing group, but also because none is without such internal divisions as to make it difficult for it to act as a monolithic unit. Thus, a broad-based coalition as the ruling group seems to be rooted in the social configuration of the state. At the same time, the state will have to learn to live with conflict. Fortunately, while there has been a great deal of militancy in the politics of the state there has been little violence. By and large, the state has been quite successful in containing conflict.

As for the Congress party, to the extent that it is a secular, broad-based political party, the Punjab situation would seem to favor the continuance in power of that party, but it does not make it a certainty. Any

[120] *Economic Weekly*, XVI, No. 35 (August 29, 1964), 1428.
[121] *Ibid.*, pp. 1428-29.

party that remains in power, as long as the Congress party has, accumulates enough resentment in the population to call for a change. However, there is nothing to unite the opposition parties in a common coalition. In order to replace the Congress party they have to become like the Congress party; given their present ideological positions, this they cannot do. Even if the Congress party should fail to receive a majority of seats in the legislature at the time of any future elections, it may in all likelihood be able to form a government either by the accession to it of members of other parties or in coalition with some small moderate and non-communal groups. Should the Congress party fail to form a government, the experience of the present opposition groups in government would most probably only result in a clamor for the return of the Congress party to power. On the other hand, the Congress party may not have to face the eventuality of being thrown out of power if it can, through adequate policies, hold the support it receives from the Harijans and the moderate sections of the Hindu and Sikh communities. In the absence of a strong leader with a dominant faction both in the ministerial and organizational wings, however, the factional divisions within the Congress party may make for ministerial instability or political immobilism.

Much may depend, however, on what happens to and at the center, for in large measure the political stability and the existence of democracy in the Punjab are related to the fact that it is part of a larger political unit. It is hard to imagine, given the social and political situation in the state, that the Punjab as a separate and sovereign unit would have ever been able to maintain political stability and democracy in the same measure.

In the economic sphere, the pace of economic growth will have to be pushed, for substantial as has been the growth in the Punjab, the level of aspirations and expectations has risen even more. The population expects the government to undertake many economic and welfare programs, though that expectation is not matched by a willingness to make sacrifices by way of increased taxation. Fortunately, there are many forces of economic change lodged outside the government. Given some state investment at strategic points and some assistance in securing supplies of industrial raw materials not available in the state, there seems to be enough dynamism among the people of the state to assure an adequate rate of growth in the economic sphere.

POSTSCRIPT

Since the preceding study was completed, events have moved with great rapidity to change the political map of the Punjab in more ways than one.

At the end of May 1966, the three-member Punjab Boundary Commission submitted its recommendations on the proposed boundaries for the states of Punjab, Haryana, and Himachal Pradesh. Except for Chandigarh and the surrounding area, the Commission's recommendations were unanimous and, by and large, corresponded to the existing division between the Hindi-speaking and Punjabi-speaking regions. The Commission recommended the merger of the hill tracts in Himachal Pradesh and the remaining territory to be demarcated along the existing regional boundary to constitute the Punjab and Haryana. With one member dissenting, the Commission further recommended that Chandigarh and the surrounding Kharar Tehsil should belong to Haryana.

The government of India accepted the recommendations of the Commission except on the question of Chandigarh where, noting the deep resentment in the Sikh community, it decided to make Chandigarh and the surrounding area a Union territory but available as a joint capital for the Punjab and Haryana. Some observers suspected that this decision, contrary to the majority recommendation of the Boundary Commission, was an interim measure to soften opposition preparatory to a final merger of the area in the Punjab. In the legislation proposing the creation of the new states of the Punjab and Haryana, provision was also made for several interim joint links—such as a common governor, high court, and electricity board—between the two states.

Meanwhile, in order to prepare for the creation of the two states, Chief Minister Ram Kishan was asked to submit the resignation of his ministry in the Punjab, and in July 1966 President's Rule was imposed on the state. Finally, the new states of the Punjab and Haryana came into being on November 1, 1966. On the basis of the 1961 census, Punjab would have a population of 11.1 million to Haryana's 7.5 million. For the first time in history, the Punjab now had a Sikh majority, with the Sikhs constituting 55 per cent of the population and the Hindus the remaining 45 per cent. However, for some the formation of the new Punjab served only to restrict the area of opportunity for the Sikhs, whereas the creation of Haryana and the merger of the hill areas in Himachal Pradesh widened the same for the Hindus of those areas.

With the creation of the two states, President's Rule came to an end, and popular government was restored. In the Punjab, Gurmukh Singh Musafir, after resigning his seat from the Lok Sabha, became the new Chief Minister. Musafir had been a member of the central legislature since 1947 and had served as president of the Punjab Congress for most of the decade between 1948 and 1958. He had little political base now in the Punjab, but was favored by the central Congress leadership where, since the ouster of Kairon in 1964, the counsels of Defense Minister Swaran Singh weighed significantly. In the state of Haryana, Bhagwat Dayal Sharma, who had been President of the Punjab Congress for several years, was installed as the Chief Minister.

Any expectation that the new states could now settle down and attend to their economic and social problems was short-lived. In early November 1966, Sant Fateh Singh issued an ultimatum to the government to concede three demands, asking for (1) immediate severance of the common links between the Punjab and Haryana, such as the governor and high court, (2) the return to the Punjab of what he considered Punjabi-speaking areas, especially the city of Chandigarh, and (3) sole control with the new Punjab government over the Bhakra-Nangal multi-purpose project. On December 17, he commenced a fast unto death and threatened that unless his demands were conceded he and seven other associates would commit self-immolation within ten days. The central government refused to make concessions under such threats. While remaining firm, however, it indicated its willingness to honor any agreement reached between the two states of Punjab and Haryana on the various points at dispute. The Sant and his associates were equally adamant, and things became very tense as the deadline for self-immolation approached. However, after dramatic last-minute negotiations, the fast was ended and the threats of self-immolation were given up. Since the common links between the two states had already been agreed to be severed by the two Chief Ministers, the two major points at issue related to claims and counter-claims over territory, with Chandigarh as the real bone of contention, and control over the Bhakra-Nangal project. It was now agreed that the issue relating to Chandigarh and Bhakra-Nangal would be submitted to the Prime Minister for arbitration and that her decision would be binding on all parties concerned, while other territorial claims would be investigated by a committee of experts.

As this matter was temporarily set aside, the two states turned their attention to the campaign for the general elections in February 1967. Indeed, it was speculated that the fasts and threats of self-immolation were part of an election strategy to mobilize support for the Akali Dal, especially since Punjabi Suba had already been achieved. Efforts were also made to bring unity between the Sant group and the Master group of the Akali Dal, which were operating as two parties. Although these were not successful, the Sant group was able to make an electoral alliance with several other opposition parties, including the two Communist groups and the Republican party. The Master group of the Akali Dal continued to demand a Sikh state, though with the qualification that it could be within the Indian Union.

The Congress party was faced with an uphill task for the elections took place here, as in the rest of India, in the midst of a grave economic crisis with rising prices and food shortages. Moreover, without a forceful state leader such as Kairon or a national political hero such as Nehru, divisions within the Congress party were an even more serious liability than in the past. The nomination of candidates by the Congress party also led to a great deal of criticism; Hindu Congressmen were bitter that while the Hindus constituted 45 per cent of Punjab's population they had been given less than 22 per cent of the party nominations for the Vidhan Sabha. They suspected that Chief Minister Musafir and Defense Minister Swaran Singh were attempting, through this distribution of party nominations, to give an impression of the Punjab as a homeland of the Sikhs. On the other hand, the Chief Minister justified the allocation of nominations as necessary from the viewpoint of electoral success.

As in most other states in India, the election results were a blow to the Congress party in the Punjab. It lost both in terms of seats, securing less than a majority, and in votes polled. In the new Vidhan Sabha of 104 members, it won 48 seats, with 37.4 per cent of the votes (see Table 9.3). It was believed that a majority of the Congress MLAs were allied with Defense Minister Swaran Singh, who reportedly emerged as an even more powerful force in Punjab politics. Among the important seats lost was that of Chief Minister Musafir. The Akali Dal maintained its position as the second largest party in the legislature, but significantly improved its standing in terms of seats as well as votes. However, the group led by Master Tara Singh was badly defeated; only two of its sixty-two candidates for the Vidhan Sabha could manage to win whereas none was elected to the Lok Sabha. The Jan Sangh turned in a better performance than in 1962, winning eight seats. On the other hand, the Communists failed to hold their earlier strength. Among the independents elected were some important leaders like the Maharaja of Patiala and Rajinder Singh "Sparrow," a hero of the India-Pakistan War of 1965. It is significant that the Congress party did not put up a candidate against the Maharaja of Patiala; it was believed that this was to ease his leading a future coalition of the Congress and the Akali Dal in case the Congress failed to win a majority. The Congress gave a better account of itself in the elections to the Lok Sabha, winning nine out of thirteen seats, while the Akali Dal won three. The Jan Sangh for the first time also won a seat in the Lok Sabha from this region.

TABLE 9.3

1967 ELECTION RESULTS FOR PUNJAB AND HARYANA

	Punjab		Haryana	
	Seats	Votes (tentative percentage)	Seats	Votes (tentative percentage)
Congress party	48	37.4	48	41.4
Akali Dal (Sant Group)	24	20.5	–	–
Akali Dal (Master Group)	2	4.5	–	–
Jan Sangh	9	9.4	12	14.5
Communist party	5	4.8	–	1.0
Communist party (Marxist)	3	3.3	–	0.4
Republican party	3	2.2	2	2.9
Swatantra	–	0.5	3	3.2
PSP	–	0.5	–	0.2
SSP	1	0.7	–	3.5
Independents	9	16.2	16	32.9
Totals	104	100.0	81	100.0
Voting participation	71 per cent		73 per cent	
Electorate	6.3 million		4.4 million	

SOURCE: *The Tribune*, February 26 and 27, 1967

In Haryana, the Congress party, in view of its perennial divisions and caste factionalism, surprised many by winning an absolute majority with forty-eight out of eighty-one seats. The Jan Sangh emerged as the second largest organized party, winning twelve seats. In fact, the independents constituted the second largest contingent in the Vidhan Sabha with sixteen seats, a factor that assumed critical importance later. At the parliamentary level, the Congress party won seven out of nine seats, the remaining two going to the Jan Sangh. However, Swami Rameshwaranand (Jan Sangh) and Mani Ram Bagri (SSP), who had previously created considerable turbulence in the Lok Sabha, were both defeated.

As for the parliamentary constituency of the centrally administered city of Chandigarh, the Jan Sangh candidate, who had run on a platform of continuation of the status quo for the city or its merger in Haryana, won the seat with 23,989 votes. The Akali candidate, who had asked for the city's merger in the Punjab, secured only 10,528 votes, while the Congress candidate, who had refused to make the city an election issue, obtained another 11,323 votes. This decision of the city's population is likely to present a difficult choice for Mrs. Gandhi in her arbitration over the city's future.

What happened in the Punjab subsequent to the elections provides an instructive illustration of the powerful influence of political structure over the political process. The Congress party tried to gather support from independents in order to form a government, but it was out-maneuvered by the opposition parties. Suggestions for the Congress party to bring in the Maharaja of Patiala as a possible Chief Minister, who would mobilize the support of some independents to give the party a majority in the legislature, aroused opposition and threats of withdrawal from within the party. In the meantime, the Akali Dal and the Jan Sangh, normally bitterly hostile to each other, agreed to form a united front together with other opposition parties. Significantly, at a meeting of top leaders of the Akali Dal and Jan Sangh on March 1, 1967, when the move to form a united front of opposition parties was initiated, a resolution was passed which stated, in part: "Whereas we stand for amity and goodwill among all sections of Punjabis, irrespective of caste or creed, and promise to take steps to strengthen the new State of Punjab economically and politically, we resolve to oppose all separatist trends and moves aimed at weakening the unity and integrity of the country." In early March 1967, a united front ministry was formed with Justice Gurnam Singh of the Akali Dal as Chief Minister. If such a united front shows stability and cohesion, then it would essentially constitute a reincarnation of the Congress party as a coalition of many groups. It would seem that the social diversity in the state is compelling the opposition to take a form after the Congress, even though it is organized in the legislature after the elections. The united front government, however, has only a slight majority, which makes for an uncertain future for the state in terms of political stability. But, in the matter of attracting new supporters from the Congress party, it seems to have learned its lesson well from the Congress past.

In Haryana, Bhagwat Dayal Sharma was unanimously re-elected leader of the Congress legislature party and was sworn in as Chief Minister. However, his tenure was short-lived, for within less than a month about a dozen Congress legislators crossed the floor and joined with the opposition to establish a new ministry. This event provided dramatic evidence of the fragile nature of cohesion of the Congress party. Students of Indian politics have explained the party's past cohesion by factors such as the consensus within the party over major issues, the existence of adjudicative machinery and mechanisms for resolution of inner-party conflicts, and, most importantly, the patronage at the disposal of the Congress party. It seems, however, that in such consideration of internal factors of the Congress party, a most important factor external to the party—that of popular electoral support—has not been given adequate weight. In fact, it was precisely the popular support for the Congress party in the past that made possible the successful operation of the mechanisms of conflict resolution as well as of patronage. But now, with lack of popular support in many states, power and patronage can be had outside the Congress party. It is no longer true that outside the Congress there is political wilderness, or that outside the Congress party there is no political salvation. With the erosion of popular support for the Congress party, or rather with the definite unpopularity of the Congress, salvation indeed lies outside the party now. There are definite rewards, rather than penalties, in leaving the party. The point of this analysis is that if restoration of party cohesion is an objective of the Congress party, it is not likely to be achieved through organizational gimmicks, but rather through the forging and implementation of policies that command popular support.

REFERENCES

Chand, Duni. *The Ulster of India, or An Analysis of the Punjab Problems.* Lahore: n.p., 1936.

Darling, Malcolm Lyall. *At Freedom's Door.* London: Oxford University Press, 1949.

———. *The Punjab Peasant in Prosperity and Debt.* London: Oxford University Press, 1925.

Husain, Azim. *Fazl-i-Husain: A Political Biography.* Bombay: Longmans, Green and Co., Ltd., 1946.

Moon, Penderel. *Divide and Quit.* Berkeley: University of California Press, 1962.

Nayar, Baldev Raj. *Minority Politics in the Punjab.* Princeton: Princeton University Press, 1966.

Prior, L. F. Loveday. *Punjab Prelude.* London: John Murray, 1952.

Rai, E. N. Mangat. *Civil Administration in the Punjab: An Analysis of a State Government in India* (Occasional Papers in International Affairs, No. 7). Cambridge: Center for International Affairs, Harvard University, 1963.

Singh, Khushwant. *The Sikhs.* London: George Allen and Unwin Ltd., 1953.

Tandon, Prakash. *Punjabi Century 1857-1947.* London: Chatto & Windus, 1961.

Trevaskis, Hugh Kennedy. *The Land of the Five Rivers.* London: Oxford University Press, 1928.

———. *The Punjab of Today.* 2 vols. Lahore: The "Civil and Military Gazette" Press, 1931 and 1932.

List of Contributors

PAUL BRASS, born in Boston, Massachusetts in 1936, is Assistant Professor of Political Science at the University of Washington. He holds a B.A. from Harvard College and an M.A. and Ph.D. from the University of Chicago. He did his field research in India in 1961-63 under a grant from the Ford Foundation Foreign Area Training Program. He was a Lecturer in Political Science at Bryn Mawr College in 1964-65. He is the author of *Factional Politics in an Indian State: The Congress Party in Uttar Pradesh.*

MARCUS F. FRANDA, born in Nassawaupee Township, Wisconsin, in 1937, is Assistant Professor of Political Science at Colgate University. He received his B.A. with Honors from Beloit College and his M.A. and Ph.D. from the University of Chicago. He has published articles in *The Economic Weekly* (Bombay), *Pacific Affairs,* and *Asian Survey.* He is the translator of a Bengali novel, *Mahanagar* ("The Great City"), and has recently completed a study of federal-state relations in India.

HUGH GRAY is a Member of the British Parliament for Yarmouth, Norfolk (Labour Party) and a Lecturer in Sociology at the School of Oriental and African Studies and the Institute of Commonwealth Studies. He holds a B.Sc. and Ph.D. from the London School of Economics. He did his field research in Telengana, Andhra, in 1961-1962 for his doctoral thesis on *Power and Politics in Hyderabad.* He is the author of a number of articles on the politics of Andhra.

RAM JOSHI, born in Padghe, Maharashtra, in 1924, is principal of the South Indian Education Society's College of Arts and Sciences in Bombay and head of its Department of Politics. He took his Master's degree from the University of Bombay in Economics and Politics. His articles have appeared in *Asian Survey, The Journal of the Developing Areas, The Radical Humanist,* and *Quest.* He is the author of *Essays in Indian Federalism* and several monographs on Indian politics, including *Liberalism in Prospect, Retrospect,* and *The Indian Party System.* In 1966 he was appointed Fulbright lecturer to the universities of Texas and Denver.

BALDEV RAJ NAYAR, born in Gujrat (Punjab) in 1931, is Associate Professor of Political Science at McGill University in Montreal, Canada. He completed his B.A. and M.A. at the Punjab University and his M.A. and Ph.D. at the University of Chicago. He was an Assistant Professor of Political Science at California State College at Hayward in 1963-64. He is the author of *Minority Politics in the Punjab*.

Balraj Puri, born in Jammu in 1928, is a journalist and politician and an expert on Kashmir. As a student at the Punjab University College in New Delhi, from which he received an M.A. in Economics in 1949, he participated in the "Quit India" movement and was responsible for starting two Urdu weeklies from Jammu, *Kashmir Sansar* and *Desh Sewak*. He was editor of *Sach* and, from 1959 to 1961, of *Kashmir Affairs*. He has been actively involved in the Praja Socialist party, which he has served in various official and advisory capacities, and is the author of *Communism in Kashmir, Cooperative Farming —A Critique, Recreation and Social Education,* and *Jammu—A Clue to the Kashmir Problem*. He makes his home in Delhi.

Lawrence L. Shrader, born in Columbia, Missouri, in 1925, is Assistant Professor of Political Science at Mills College. He received his Ph.D. from the University of California at Berkeley, where he was a research assistant with the *Indian Press Digest* and a teaching associate. He was a Fulbright Fellow in India from 1961 to 1962, studying political leadership in Rajasthan and Maharashtra. In collaboration with Ram Joshi he has published a study of Zilla Parishad elections in one district of Maharashtra in *Asian Survey*.

Wayne Wilcox, born in Pendleton, Indiana, in 1932, is Associate Professor of Government and Research Member of the Institute of War and Peace Studies at Columbia University. He did his undergraduate work at Purdue University and took his M.A. and Ph.D. at Columbia University. At the conclusion of service in the U.S. Navy he received a Ford Foundation Foreign Area Fellowship for study in South Asia. He is the author of *Pakistan: The Consolidation of a Nation,* and *India, Pakistan and the Rise of China*. He is also a consultant to The RAND Corporation and to the Department of State.

Myron Weiner, born in Brooklyn, New York, in 1931, is Professor of Political Science at the Massachusetts Institute of Technology and Senior Research Associate at its Center for International Studies. He holds a B.A. degree from City College, New York, and an M.A. and Ph.D. from Princeton University. He has done extensive field work in India since 1953 and is the author of *Party Politics in India, Politics of Scarcity, Political Change in South Asia,* and *Party Building in a New Nation: The Indian National Congress*. He is also editor of *Modernization: The Dynamics of Growth,* co-editor of *Voting Behaviour in India,* and co-author of *Politics of the Developing Areas.* He has taught at Princeton University and at the University of Chicago and is presently a member of the Editorial Board of the American Political Science Association, the Committee on Comparative Politics of the Social Science Research Council, and the Board of Directors of the Association for Asian Studies. He is also a consultant to the Department of State.

Index

References to maps, tables, and figures appear in italics.